THE ORIGINS OF MUSIC

THE ORIGINS OF MUSIC

edited by Nils L. Wallin, Björn Merker, and Steven Brown

A Bradford Book
The MIT Press
Cambridge, Massachusetts
London, England

Second printing, 2001

This book was set in Times Roman by Best-set Typesetter Ltd., Hong Kong and was printed
and bound in the United States of America.

Library of Congress Cataloging-in-Publication Data

The origins of music : edited by Nils L. Wallin, Björn Merker, and Steven Brown.
　　p.　cm.
Consists of papers given at a workshop on the origins of music held in Fiesole, Italy, May
1997, the first of a series called Florentine Workshops in Biomusicology.
"A Bradford Book."
Includes bibliographical references and index.
Partial Contents: Vocal communication in animals—Music, language, and human evolu-
tion—Theories of music origin—Universals in music.
ISBN 0-262-23206-5 (hc : alk. paper)
　1. Music, Origin of—Congresses. 2. Human evolution. 3. Musicology. I. Wallin, Nils
Lennart. II. Merker, Björn. III. Brown, Steven, 1963 Mar. 26–
ML3800.074　1999
781′.1—dc21
　　　　　　　　　　　　　　　　　　　　　　　　　　　　　　98-54088
　　　　　　　　　　　　　　　　　　　　　　　　　　　　　　CIP
　　　　　　　　　　　　　　　　　　　　　　　　　　　　　　MN

Contents

Preface

The present volume is based on a workshop entitled "The Origins of Music" arranged by the Institute for Biomusicology in the Etruscan town of Fiesole outside Florence in late May 1997. As the workshop was the first international gathering held under the auspices of the Institute since its founding in 1995, a few words are in order concerning the Institute's background.

In 1982 one of us (NLW) published his dissertation *Den musikaliska hjärnan* ("The Musical Brain") in Swedish, which was followed in 1991 by the book *Biomusicology: Neurophysiological, Neuropsychological and Evolutionary Perspectives on the Origins and Purposes of Music*. Both works gave expression to long-standing curiosity on the part of a musicologist regarding what light modern neuroscience might shed on questions such as the origins, evolutionary development, and purposes of music, questions that he felt were incompletely dealt with by his discipline. Ever since his student days, this musicologist had been on a quest for a musicological paradigm to complement traditional approaches. He now hoped to find in modern biology what he had not found in Hume's empiricism, in the logical empiricism of the Vienna and Chicago schools, or in the phenomenological trends that flourished in the 1940s and 1950s. Time was on his side.

Since the Second World War, and more particularly in recent decades, the neurosciences and behavioral biology have made significant strides in areas relevant to the foundations of musicology. Thus there is now hope of gaining an understanding of the processes of musical cognition as well as biological factors that, together with cultural determinants, shaped mankind's musical behavior and the rich global repertoire of musical structures it has produced. In 1994 a symposium inspired by the book *Biomusicology* was held in Milan, sponsored by the Royal Swedish Academy of Sciences, the Institute for Futures Studies, and Pharmacia AB. Under the title "Man, Mind, and Music" the symposium brought together neuroscientists, mathematicians, systems theorists, musicologists, ethnomusicologists, a composer, and a conductor for fruitful discussions. One result of this was the creation of the Foundation for Biomusicology and Acoustic Ethology, with its executive organ the Institute for Biomusicology, in March 1995. The Institute is located in the town of Östersund, situated close to the geographic midpoint of Scandinavia.

As part of its efforts to stimulate biomusicological research, the Institute sketched a series of international workshops to be held in Florence, Italy, a place where in the late sixteenth century the scholastically oriented music theory of the Middle Ages started to give way to more empirically oriented musicology, represented among others by Vincenzo Galilei, the father of Galileo Galilei. These Florentine Workshops in

Biomusicology were to deal with the origins (phylogeny) of music, with its ontogeny, and with the interaction of biology and culture in music, respectively. The planning of the first of these, on "The Origins of Music," on which the present volume is based, was undertaken by us in collaboration with François-Bernard Mâche of the *Ecole des hautes études* in Paris. It was carried through with support of the European Community (EC), the Swedish Institute, the Swedish National Concert Institute, and the Regione Toscana.

We have the pleasure of thanking all contributors, including those who were not with us in person in Florence, for their great interest in and commitment to the topics and issues of the workshop, questions that for the greater part of this century have been discussed only rarely, and never before in a framework of joint discussions among representatives of most of the disciplines that reasonably can be expected to have something to contribute to the elucidation of the evolutionary history and biological roots of music.

The editors' introduction documents the Institute's current perspective on systematic and methodological questions connected with the origins of music, and how this perspective has developed since *Biomusicology* was published. This introductory chapter is in some ways a latter-day sequel to one part of the systematic and historically important survey of the whole field of musicology (*Musikwissenschaft*) presented by Guido Adler in 1885, the part, namely, which he called *Musikforschung* ("music research").

We thank Judy Olsson, of the Institute staff, for technical assistance. Our warm thanks, finally, to the MIT Press and to Amy Brand and Katherine A. Almeida of its editorial staff for their interest and efforts in making these studies available to an international audience.

Nils L. Wallin
Björn Merker
Steven Brown

Contributors

Simha Arom
CNRS
Laboratoire de Langues et
Civilisations à Tradition Orale
Paris, France

Derek Bickerton
Department of Linguistics
University of Hawaii
Honolulu, Hawaii

Steven Brown
Department of Clinical
Neuroscience
Karolinska Institute
Huddinge, Sweden

Ellen Dissanayake
Seattle, Washington

Dean Falk
State University of New York
Albany, New York

David W. Frayer
Department of Anthropology
University of Kansas
Lawrence, Kansas

Walter Freeman
Division of Neurobiology
University of California
Berkeley, California

Thomas Geissmann
Institute of Zoology
Tieraerzliche Hochschule
Hannover
Hannover, Germany

Marc D. Hauser
Departments of Psychology and
Anthropology
Harvard University
Cambridge, Massachusetts

Michel Imberty
Department of Psychology
Université de Paris X
Nanterre, France

Harry Jerison
Department of Psychiatry and
Biobehavioral Sciences
University of California, Los
Angeles
Los Angeles, California

Drago Kunej
Institute of Ethnomusicology
Scientific Research Centre of the
Slovene Academy of Sciences and
Arts
Ljubljana, Slovenia

François-Bernard Mâche
Ecole des Hautes Etudes
Paris, France

Peter Marler
Center for Animal Behavior
University of California
Davis, California

Björn Merker
Institute for Biomusicology
Mid Sweden University
Östersund, Sweden

Geoffrey Miller
Center for Economic Learning
and Social Evolution
University College London
London, England

Jean Molino
Ecublens, Switzerland

Bruno Nettl
University of Illinois at Urbana-
Champaign
Urbana, Illinois

Chris Nicolay
Department of Anthropology
Kent State University
Kent, Ohio

Bruce Richman
Cleveland Heights, Ohio

Katharine Payne
Bioacoustic Research Program
Cornell Laboratory of
Ornithology
Ithaca, New York

Peter J. B. Slater
School of Environemental and
Evolutionary Biology
University of St. Andrews
Fife, UK

Peter Todd
Max Planck Institute for Human
Development
Center for Adaptive Behavior
and Cognition
Berlin, Germany

Sandra Trehub
Department of Psychology
University of Toronto at
Mississauga
Mississauga, Ontario, Canada

Ivan Turk
Institute of Archaeology
Scientific Research Centre of the
Slovene Academy of Sciences and
Arts
Ljubljana, Slovenia

Maria Ujhelyi
Institute of Behavioral Sciences
Semmelweis University of
Medicine
Budapest, Hungary

Nils Wallin
Institute for Biomusicology
Mid Sweden University
Östersund, Sweden

Carol Whaling
Animal Communication
Laboratory
University of California
Davis, California

As neither the enjoyment nor the capacity of producing musical notes are faculties of the least direct use to man in reference to his ordinary habits of life, they must be ranked amongst the most mysterious with which he is endowed. They are present, though in a very rude and as it appears almost latent condition, in men of all races, even the most savage. . . . Whether or not the half-human progenitors of man possessed, like the before-mentioned gibbon, the capacity of producing, and no doubt of appreciating, musical notes, we have every reason to believe that man possessed these faculties at a very remote period, for singing and music are extremely ancient arts.

—Charles Darwin, *The Descent of Man, and Selection in Relation to Sex* (1871)

Mythology is wrong. Music is not the merciful gift of benevolent gods or heroes. Wrong is the banal desire to see all slow, imperceptible germination emerge ready-made from the head of a single inventor; music is not the clever exploit of some ingenious man. And wrong, so far, are the many theories presented on a more or less scientific basis—the theories that man has imitated the warbling of birds, that he wanted to please the opposite sex, that his singing derived from drawn-out signaling shouts, that he arrived at music via some coordinated, rhythmical teamwork, and other speculative hypotheses. Were they true, some of the most primitive survivors of early mankind would have preserved a warbling style of song, or love songs, or signal-like melodies, or rhythmical teamwork with rhythmical worksongs. Which they hardly have. To call living primitives to the witness stand will at first sight bewilder those who are not familiar with modern methods of settling questions of origin. They probably would prefer the more substantial, indeed irrefutable, proofs of prehistorians, who excavate the tombs and dwelling places of races bygone. But not even the earliest civilizations that have left their traces in the depths of the earth are old enough to betray the secret of the origins of music.

—Curt Sachs, *Our Musical Heritage* (1948)

I THE BEGINNING

1 An Introduction to Evolutionary Musicology

Steven Brown, Björn Merker, and Nils L. Wallin   *editors of This volume*

Abstract
In this introduction to the new field of evolutionary musicology, we see that the study of music origins provides a fresh and exciting approach to the understanding of human evolution, a topic that so far has been dominated by a focus on language evolution. The language-centered view of humanity has to be expanded to include music, first, because the evolution of language is highly intertwined with the evolution of music, and, second, because music provides a specific and direct means of exploring the evolution of human social structure, group function, and cultural behavior. Music making is the quintessential human cultural activity, and music is an ubiquitous element in all cultures large and small. The study of music evolution promises to shed light on such important issues as evolution of the hominid vocal tract; the structure of acoustic-communication signals; human group structure; division of labor at the group level; the capacity for designing and using tools; symbolic gesturing; localization and lateralization of brain function; melody and rhythm in speech; the phrase-structure of language; parent-infant communication; emotional and behavioral manipulation through sound; interpersonal bonding and synchronization mechanisms; self-expression and catharsis; creativity and aesthetic expression; the human affinity for the spiritual and the mystical; and finally, of course, the universal human attachment to music itself.

Music Origins and Human Origins

What is music and what are its evolutionary origins? What is music for and why does every human culture have it? What are the universal features of music and musical behavior across cultures?

Such questions were the among the principal areas of investigation of the members of the Berlin school of comparative musicology of the first half of the twentieth century, as represented by such great figures as Carl Stumpf, Robert Lach, Erich von Hornbostel, Otto Abraham, Curt Sachs, and Marius Schneider.[1] After the 1940s, however, the evolutionary approach to music fell into obscurity and even disrepute. How this came to pass entails a long and very political history, one that has as much to do with rejection of racialist notions present in much European scholarship in the social sciences before the Second World War as with the rise of the cultural-anthropological approach to musicology in America during the postwar period.[2] Both influences were antievolutionary in spirit and led to a rejection of biological and universalist thinking in musicology and musical anthropology. Musicology did not seem to need an official decree, like the famous ban on discussions of language origin by the *Société de Linguistique de Paris* in 1866, to make the topic of music origins unfashionable among musicologists. It appeared to happen all by itself. And with that, musicology seemed to relinquish its role as a contributor to the study human origins as well as any commitment to developing a general theory of music.

The current volume represents a long-overdue renaissance of the topic of music origins. If its essays suggest nothing else, it is that music and musical behavior can no longer be ignored in a consideration of human evolution. Music offers important insight into the study of human origins and human history in at least three principal areas. First, it is a universal and multifunctional cultural behavior, and no account of human evolution is complete without an understanding of how music and dance rituals evolved. Even the most cursory glance at life in traditional cultures is sufficient to demonstrate that music and dance are essential components of most social behaviors, everything from hunting and herding to story telling and playing; from washing and eating to praying and meditating; and from courting and marrying to healing and burying. Therefore the study of music origins is central to the evolutionary study of human cultural behavior generally.

Second, to the extent that language evolution is now viewed as being a central issue in the study of human evolution, parallel consideration of music will assume a role of emerging importance in the investigation of this issue as it becomes increasingly apparent that music and language share many underlying features. Therefore, the study of language evolution has much to gain from a joint consideration of music. This includes such important issues as evolution of the human vocal tract, the hominid brain expansion, human brain asymmetry, lateralization of cognitive function, the evolution of syntax, evolution of symbolic gesturing, and the many parallel neural and cognitive mechanisms that appear to underlie music and language processing.

Third, music has much to contribute to a study of human migration patterns and the history of cultural contacts. In the same way that genes and languages have been used successfully as markers for human migrations (Cavalli-Sforza, Menozzi, and Piazza 1994), so too music has great potential to serve as a hitherto untapped source of information for the study of human evolution. This is because musics have the capacity to blend and therefore to retain stable traces of cultural contact in a way that languages do only inefficiently; languages tend to undergo total replacement rather than blending after cultural contact, and thus tend to lose remnants of cultural interaction. In summary, these three issues, the universality and multifunctionality of music, the intimate relationship between music evolution and language evolution, and the potential of music to shed light on patterns of cultural interaction, are important applications of evolutionary musicology to the study of human origins and human culture.

The new field of "biomusicology" (Wallin 1991) places the analysis of music origins and its application to the study of human origins at its very foundation. As shown in figure 1.1, biomusicology comprises three main branches. *Evolutionary musicology* deals with the evolutionary origins of music, both in terms of a comparative approach to vocal communication in animals and in terms of an evolutionary psychological approach to the emergence of music in the hominid line. *Neuromusicology* deals with the nature and evolution of the neural and cognitive mechanisms involved in musical production and perception, as well as with ontogenetic development of musical capacity and musical behavior from the fetal stage through to old age. *Comparative musicology* deals with the diverse functional roles and uses of music in all human cultures, including the contexts and contents of musical rituals, the advantages and costs of music making, and the comparative features of musical systems, forms, and performance styles throughout the world. This field not only resuscitates the long-neglected concept of musical universals but takes full advantage of current developments in Darwinian anthropology (Durham 1991), evolutionary psychology (Barkow, Cosmides, and Tooby 1992), and gene-culture coevolutionary theory (Lumsden and Wilson 1981; Feldman and

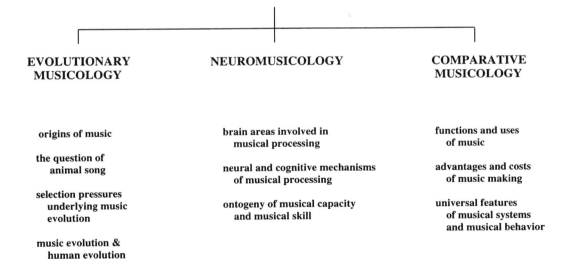

BIOMUSICOLOGY

EVOLUTIONARY MUSICOLOGY	NEUROMUSICOLOGY	COMPARATIVE MUSICOLOGY
origins of music	brain areas involved in musical processing	functions and uses of music
the question of animal song	neural and cognitive mechanisms of musical processing	advantages and costs of music making
selection pressures underlying music evolution	ontogeny of musical capacity and musical skill	universal features of musical systems and musical behavior
music evolution & human evolution		

Figure 1.1
The science of biomusicology. The term "biomusicology" was coined by Wallin (1991). It comprises three principal branches, as described in the text: *evolutionary musicology*, *neuromusicology*, and *comparative musicology*. The synthetic questions that evolutionary musicology (the subject of this volume) addresses incorporate all three branches, as elaborated in the rest of the chapter. Not shown in the figure is a series of more practical concerns that fall under the purview of *applied biomusicology* (see text).

Laland 1996) in analyzing musical behavior from the standpoint of both natural selection forces and cultural selection forces.

To complete this picture of biomusicology, it is important to point out that each of these three major branches has practical aspects that contribute to what could be referred to as *applied biomusicology*, which attempts to provide biological insight into such things as the therapeutic uses of music in medical and psychological treatment; widespread use of music in the audiovisual media such as film and television; the ubiquitous presence of music in public places and its role in influencing mass behavior; and the potential use of music to function as a general enhancer of learning.

The theme of the current volume falls within the evolutionary musicology branch of biomusicology. The remainder of this chapter is devoted to providing an overview of the major issues and methods of evolutionary musicology. To those who are coming across these ideas for the first time (which, we suspect, is most readers), our overall message is quite simple: it is time to take music seriously as an essential and abundant source of information about human nature, human evolution, and human cultural history.

Major Issues in Evolutionary Musicology

This section presents some of the major topics in evolutionary musicology. It serves as an overview of these topics, allowing ensuing chapters to provide detailed theoretical perspectives on them.

The Question of Animal Song

The question what is music? is one that has no agreed-upon answer. For every structural feature that can be claimed as being a defining feature of music, one can always find (or dream up) a musical style that lacks this property. John Cage's composition *4'33"*, composed in 1952, is probably only the most extreme and postmodern example of this. (For those who do not know this piece, it consists of four minutes and thirty-three seconds of uninterrupted silence, to be performed by "any instrument or combination of instruments.") Because of these problems in defining music in purely structural terms, ethnomusicologists have usually preferred to focus on functional contexts and roles: music as an organized cultural activity. However, this easily leads to the conclusion that music is simply whatever people consider it to be. Clearly, such a definition is too open-ended and culture-specific to be useful, which is why a consideration of musical universals (discussed below) is going to assume a role of increasing importance in biomusicology. Musical universals place the focus on what music *tends to be like* in order to be considered music, even if not every example has all the features of the majority of musics (properties such as sound in the case of *4'33"*!).

Modernist classical music aside, the important biological question of how music evolved remains. Biomusicology is a discipline defined in part by its commitment to exploring the relevance of modern biological knowledge about the evolution and functions of animal behavior to the question of the origins of human music and dance, and this includes the rich treasure of theory and observation provided by behavioral biology on topics such as animal vocalization, communication, emotive expression, and display. Just as the lack of a clear definition has not prevented musicologists from advancing our understanding of music, so too lack of a categorical means of sorting animal "songs" from animal "calls" has not prevented biologists from learning much about the more structurally complex forms of animal vocal displays—whether called song or not— that might in fact be relevant to our attempts to understand the beginnings and foundations of music in the course of anthropogenesis. Since singing behavior emerged independently, and in a variety of forms, on several occasions in the animal kingdom (see Marler, Slater, Jerison, and Geissmann, this volume), the question arises as to whether any of these instances of animal song is capable of shedding light on the genesis of singing and music in our own species. There is no a priori way of excluding the possibility, for example, that our distant forebears might have been singing hominids before they became talking humans, and if so, that hypothetical fact would surely have some bearing on the way we approach the question of the origins of music.

To come to a better understanding of such issues will require addressing many important questions. Does song have common functional roles? Do common selection pressures and selection mechanisms explain the repeated occurrence of song? What is the relationship between the singing style and habitat of the singing animal? What is the relationship between the singing arrangement and social structure of the species? Where singing serves more than one function for a species, how do the different vocal styles or vocal forms correlate with their presumed roles? Do common generative and perceptual principles underlie the various forms of song? What kinds of neural changes and specializations mediate the emergence of singing behavior in singing species? To what extent does song acquisition depend on learning, and what is the social arrangement for this learning when it is necessary? Where social learning is involved, do song forms evolve culturally? Many of these questions are addressed in part II entitled "Vocal Communication in Animals."

Music Evolution versus Language Evolution

Not only does music have an ambivalent relationship with animal song, but it has an equally ambivalent relationship with human language. Thus, the question what is music? has not only phylogenetic significance in terms of the question of animal song, but also evolutionary-psychological significance in terms of the evolutionary relationship between the two major vocal-communication systems that emerged in the human line. Whereas the debate about the status of animal song will probably always come down to a philosophical consideration of how music and song should be defined, the language-music relationship represents a much more tractable question at many levels of analysis. We predict that this will become one of the central issues in the areas of music psychology, intonational phonology, and biomusicology in years to come, which is why a large part of this volume is devoted either directly or indirectly to the topic.

Many parallels exist between music and language at the structural level (discussed extensively by Brown, this volume). The major question for the purposes of this book deals with the evolutionary basis of the connection. There are at least three possible interactive theories for the evolution of music and speech: that music evolved from speech, that speech evolved from music, or that both evolved from a common ancestor. As Erich von Hornbostel wrote in 1905: "The close correlation between language, music, and dance has already occupied the attention of earlier theoreticians. Spencer (1857) considered singing to be emotionally intensified speaking; for Darwin (1871), it was the inherited and mellowed remnant of the courting periods of our animal ancestors, from which language derived at a later stage; Richard Wagner (1852) believed that language and music issued from a common source, that of speech-music" (p. 270).[3] Unfortunately, despite the age of this issue, it is still too early to predict its resolution. However, we suggest that a consideration of music will be central to any study of speech and language evolution in the future.

In addition, at least five other points have a bearing on this question. First, changes to the human vocal tract thought to underlie the evolution of speech (see Frayer and Nicolay, this volume) are just as relevant to the evolution of human singing. In fact the distinction between speaking and singing is best thought of as a difference in degree rather than a difference in kind. This is demonstrated nicely by intermediate cases, such as heightened speech, *sprechstimme*, *recitativo*, and poetic discourse, that blur the distinction between speaking and singing. At a more fundamental level, tone languages, which comprise more than half of the 5,000 languages spoken in the world today (Fromkin 1978), bring together music's use of level tones and pitch contours with language's role in generating semantic meaning. Thus, it is not unreasonable to think that evolutionary changes in the human vocal tract were adaptations for singing rather than for speaking, or perhaps even adaptations for joint musical and linguistic vocalization processes in the form of tone languages.

Second, the human brain, and most especially the human cerebral cortex, has undergone tremendous expansion in size compared with previous hominid stages, and at least some of this expansion is proposed to be driven by the evolution of human linguistic capacity (Deacon 1992; see Jerison, Falk, Bickerton, and Merker, this volume). However, there is an alternative candidate for a structurally complex, syntactically rich, acoustically varied, socially meaningful human function that might have driven this brain expansion, namely, music. Therefore, the relationship between the cerebral localizations of music and language is essential for understanding the evolutionary relationship between these two important human functions.

In this regard, it is interesting to point out that three arrangements for localization of music and language in the brain have been reported (reviewed by Falk, this volume): that music and language share cerebral representation; that they have overlapping representations in the same hemisphere; and that they have corresponding (i.e., homologous) localizations in the opposite hemispheres. As Falk points out, this issue is further complicated by the discovery that lateralization effects for music and language differ between the sexes, with greater degrees of lateralization in the brains of men. However, to the extent that linguistic function is seen as driving at least some evolutionary brain expansion and that lateralization of function is seen as being an important concern in human brain evolution, then the shared, overlapping, and/or corresponding localizations of music and language in the cerebral hemispheres of this expanded human brain would seem to provide an important test case for evolutionary theories of both brain expansion and brain asymmetry. What are the important similarities and differences between music and language and how are they manifested in the respective localizations and lateralizations of these functions in the human brain?

Third, structural accounts of language evolution usually present a dichotomy between gestural theories and vocal theories of language origin, where such theories are either seen as mutually exclusive accounts of language evolution or as sequential accounts in which vocalizing is viewed as a replacement for gesturing (Corballis 1991; Armstrong, Stokoe, and Wilcox 1995; Beaken 1996; Rizzolatti and Arbib 1998). In this regard, a parallel consideration of music has much to offer toward understanding this question, as musical expression tends to be inextricably linked to movement and gesture in the context of most group rituals. In musical rituals, gesture and vocalizing function as coordinated, mutually reinforcing processes at both the individual and group levels, rather than serving as sequential or alternative manifestations of communicative intentions (see Dissanayake, this volume). Extension of these ideas might offer important insight into the origins of language-based communication. And in fact it seems quite plausible to assume that gesturing and vocalizing occurred in parallel during language evolution just as they most certainly did during music evolution (see Molino, this volume).

Fourth, functional accounts of language evolution make reference not only to individual-level representational and communicative capacities but to driving forces related to group function and social interaction capacities (see Ujhelyi and Richman, this volume). Most current theories make explicit reference to the idea that language evolution has some privileged status with relation to the evolution of human group structure and its underlying social relationships (Dunbar 1996). This is certainly no less true of music, and again we see that the situation is even clearer for music than it is for language. In fact, the relationship between social structure and musical form/expression has been much better studied in ethnomusicology than has the relationship between social structure and linguistic form/expression in sociolinguistics (e.g., Lomax 1968). Thus, to the extent that the evolution of linguistic structure (i.e., syntax) is thought to depend on certain behavioral arrangements between people, as reflected in the nature of human group structure, much important information about this can be gleaned by considering how similar processes operated to mold important structural features of music, such as pitch blending and isometric rhythms. The issue of music evolution raises as many essential questions about the evolution of human social structure as does the issue of language evolution.

Finally, although songs do not fossilize, and no musical notation systems exists before the Sumerian system of 3,500 years ago, large numbers of musical artifacts have been discovered throughout the world. In 1995, what is perhaps the oldest one so far—a fragment of a putative bone flute—was found at a Mousterian site in Slovenia and determined to be about 44,000 years old (see Kunej and Turk, this volume). It is probably safe to assume that musical instruments are at least as old as anatomically modern humans if not much older. They reflect the human capacity to make socially useful artifacts, no less interesting than the capacity to make weapons or hunting implements, and no less revealing than the capacity to paint images on the walls of caves.

So with regard to communicative vocalizing, vocal anatomy, brain mechanisms controlling vocalizing and symbolic gesturing, lateralization of brain function, the hominid brain expansion, tool production, tool use, social structure, group rituals, evolution of syntax, and the like, analysis of music origins provides many avenues for addressing critical questions related to the origins of language and the evolution of human social behavior.

Selection Mechanisms for Music

This discussion of the evolution of culture raises several important questions about the evolution of music. What is music for? under what conditions did it evolve? what types of selection pressures led to the evolution of human musical capacity? It seems quite clear that no known human culture lacks music and that all human beings are capable of creating and responding to music. Furthermore, neurological studies demonstrate the brain's specificity for music (Peretz 1993; Peretz and Morais 1993), again suggesting that musical capacity represents a specific biological competence rather a generalized cultural function. Yet, music is a highly multifunctional adaptation; it serves a large diversity of functional roles in all cultures. The logical question then becomes whether we can ascertain anything about the selection pressures that led to the evolution of this function by analyzing music's many roles in contemporary human cultures.

Many functional accounts for the origins of music have been proposed, and include everything from its uses in promoting domestication of animals and coordinating human social activity, to its roles in sexual display and parental care. If anything, such a diversity of roles would seem to discourage any simple determination of its underlying selection pressures. However, a number of evolutionary hypotheses are presented in this book. They fall into a few categories. First, several authors hold that music evolved by sexual selection, in other words that it evolved as a courtship device in the service of mate selection, a proposal closely connected to theories of singing in nonhuman animals, as many examples of animal song are thought to play a role in either intrasexual or intersexual selection (Darwin 1871; Andersson 1994). Such concepts can be found in the chapters by Slater, Payne, Merker, Miller, and Todd. Second, several authors link music's adaptive role to its ability to promote coordination, cohesion, and cooperation at the level of the social group. Such ideas can be found in the chapters by Geissmann, Ujhelyi, Brown, Richman, Dissanayake, and Freeman (see also Brown in press). Third, Dissanayake (this volume) proposes a parental care hypothesis in which music evolved to increase individual fitness by means of increasing offspring survival through improved parent-offspring communication. Finally, a number of contributors discuss the origins of music in terms of homology with language rather than in terms of adaptive consequences per se. For example, Ujhelyi, Molino, Jerison, Falk, and Brown propose that the emergences of music and language are in some way linked during human evolution.

These notions are likely to harbor different predictions about the nature of musical form and performance style, and might actually explain complementary features of music. In this connection it is important to emphasize that present-day uses of music need not bear one-to-one correspondence to its uses at its origins, and furthermore, that several speciation events intervene between the present day and the time when our distant forebears parted company with chimpanzees on their evolutionary journey. That is, music's multifunctional nature may reflect the action of many selection pressures, and there is thus every reason to entertain a spectrum of selectionist hypotheses at this early stage in the exploration of the origins of music.

The Evolution of Meter

One of the most distinct features of music, with reference to both animal song systems and human speech, is its use of isometric rhythms. The human ability to keep time should be distinguished from the ability of most animals (including humans) to move in a metric, alternating fashion. What is special about humans is not only their capacity to move rhythmically but their ability to *entrain* their movements to an external timekeeper, such as a beating drum. This is a key feature of both music and dance, and evolutionary accounts of music must explain the emergence of this ability of humans to synchronize their movements in a rhythmic fashion to that of conspecifics or other external timekeepers. Neurological studies reveal that this ability is dissociable from the capacity to produce and perceive the tonal features of music (Peretz 1990; Peretz and Kolinsky 1993). So a "modular" view of musical capacity (see Imberty, this volume) would suggest that metric timekeeping is a distinct feature of the human brain, one that most likely evolved in the context of groupwide music and dance rituals. This topic is discussed further by Merker and Molino (see also Brown in press).

Absolute Pitch

Absolute pitch is described as "the ability attach to labels to isolated auditory stimuli on the basis of pitch alone" (Ward and Burns 1982), and is demonstrated by a person's ability either to recognize or produce specific tones without need of a pitch reference (as is required in the case of relative pitch among trained Western musicians). It is curious, given the general human capacity for categorical perception of sensory stimuli (such as in the case of speech sounds and color categories), that so few people have absolute pitch. What seems to be beyond dispute at this point is that absolute pitch acquisition depends obligatorily on musical exposure and training during what is thought to be a critical period in cognitive development, somewhere between the ages of 3 and 6 (reviewed in Takeuchi and Hulse 1993). One explanation for why so few people have absolute pitch is that it is a genetic trait, and several pedigree analyses of families containing members having this ability concluded that it is an autosomal dominant genetic trait (Profita and Bidder 1988; Baharloo et al. 1998). Suffice to say that the search for the absolute pitch gene is now under way.

This suggestion of a genetic basis for absolute pitch should not be accepted uncritically, however, as it raises a large number of as-yet-unaddressed evolutionary issues, including the significance and role of absolute pitch-processing capacities in nonhuman species (D'Amato 1988; Hulse, Takeuchi, and Braatan 1993) and in human nonmusicians (Halpern, 1989; Levitin 1994), as well as the importance of cultural exposure to music on the expression of absolute pitch at the *population* level. Absolute pitch might be nothing more than a general human capacity whose expression is strongly biased by the level and type of exposure to music that people experience in a given culture.

Musical Universals

We conclude this section of major topics in evolutionary musicology with a discussion of musical universals. Since Chomsky, linguistics has been preoccupied with the study of universals, both grammatical and phonological. In the case of ethnomusicology, universals have been a subject of great skepticism, as they are seen as smacking too much of biological determinism, and therefore of denying the importance of historical forces and cultural traditions in explaining the properties of musical systems and musical behavior. However, the contemporary biocultural view of social behavior (e.g., Boyd and Richerson 1985; Durham 1991) calls for a balance between genetic constraints on the one hand, and historical contingencies on the other. The idea of musical universals does nothing if not place all of humankind on equal ground, acting as a biological safeguard against ethnocentric notions of musical superiority. In this balancing act between biological constraints and historical forces, the notion of musical universals merely provides a focus on the *unity* that underlies the great diversity present in the world's musical systems, and attributes this unity to neural constraints underlying musical processing (see Trehub and Imberty, this volume, for discussions of innateness in musical processing).

Regarding the common viewpoint in musicology that maintains that the search for musical universals is a fruitless endeavor not (merely) because the enterprise is marred by biological determinism but because there are no universals to be found,[4] it is critical to emphasize Bruno Nettl's important point (this volume) that universals need not apply to *all* music. Certainly a feature that is found in three out of four musical styles in the world is of great interest to anyone studying the evolution of music. As a preview to a universal theory, let us just mention that octaves are perceived as equivalent in almost all cultures, that virtually all scales of the world consist of seven or fewer pitches (per octave), that most of the world's rhythmic patterns are based on divisive patterns of twos and threes, and that emotional excitement in music is universally expressed through loud, fast, accelerating, and high-registered sound patterns. There is clearly fertile ground for a discussion of structural and expressive universals in music (see Arom, Mâche, and Nettl, this volume; Brown, submitted). It is simply wrong to say that a demonstration of musical universals denies anything of the uniqueness or richness of any culture's particular forms of musical expression. If anything, it protects this uniqueness against ethnocentric claims that some cultures' musics are "more evolved" than those of other cultures, claims frequently heard even in contemporary times.

Methods in Evolutionary Musicology

The evolutionary musicological issues discussed thus far are amenable to scientific analysis by a host of empirical techniques, as well as by formal modeling and computer simulation (an example being provided by Todd, this volume). For theory building to be fruitful, it must ultimately be based on empirical evidence, and in this section we focus on the principal methods that are available to evolutionary musicology.

The Comparative Method and Analysis of Animal Song

Whether or not animal song is viewed as a type of music, it is important to analyze the behavioral-ecological and generative factors that unite it with human music as common adaptations. This includes three major areas of study: acoustic analysis of song, neurobiological analysis of song production and perception, and behavioral-ecological analysis of singing behavior and its associated displays. The first applies the standard methods developed for the acoustic analysis of musical and speech sounds to the realm of animal vocalizations, such as frequency analysis, spectral analysis, and a number of modern computer-based methods for discriminant and correlational analysis. Powerful as these methods are as aids in acoustical characterization and statistical classification of sounds, much remains to be done to bridge the gap between the working tools of the biologist and the powerful notational system developed in the Western musical tradition, which is the chief working formalism of the musicologist. We believe that bridging this methodological gap will allow a number of problems in evolutionary musicology to be addressed with new precision and to be illuminated by new sources of comparative data (e.g., Szöke and Filip 1977).

The second area, the neurobiology of song, was developed as a natural extension of the pioneering acoustic and developmental studies of birdsong by Thorpe in the 1950s (see Thorpe 1961). A highly successful paradigmatic combination of experimental methods and questions allowed investigators such as Konishi (1965), Nottebohm (1967), and Marler (1970) not only to refine knowledge of the mechanisms of birdsong but to elucidate their neural substrates (Nottebohm 1989; Konishi 1994). This involves a description of the song-specific nuclei and neural pathways underlying song production and song perception in singing species, as well as consideration of the ontogenetic mechanisms and sex differences that underlie the development of these song pathways, especially in the case of sexually dimorphic species, which includes most singing species other than humans. Unfortunately, the impressive advances made in the study of the structure, development, and mechanisms of birdsong have not been duplicated in any other singing species, and from the standpoint of evolutionary musicology it is urgent to extend the paradigmatic power of avian studies to the analysis of other singing species.

The third area includes analysis of the behavioral contexts during which singing occurs, as well as the presumed functions and meanings of animal song and its associated display behaviors. A major goal of this research is to establish the link between song function and structure, in other words, to relate communicative meaning to acoustic sound patterns. Catchpole and Slater (1995) and Hauser (1996) provide promising approaches to the question of meaning in animal communication systems (see also Marler, Slater, Whaling, Geissmann, Hauser, Ujhelyi, and Payne, this volume), and it is hoped that such approaches will be exploited in future work on the behavioral ecology of animal song.

Physical Anthropology and Musical Archeology

The study of both fossils and artifacts will contribute to an understanding of music evolution in a manner that has already greatly benefited the study of language evolution. New findings in the reconstruction of hominid vocal anatomy and brain anatomy will contribute to an understanding of not only the evolution of speech but to parallel understanding of the evolution of singing (see Frayer and Nicolay, this volume). In addition to these inferences based on the vocal and cognitive capacities of our hominid ancestors, a crucial aspect of the reconstruction of musical history lies in the study of musical artifacts themselves. Musical

archeology is a relatively young discipline that promises to supply important new information about the origins of music. It is represented in this
volume by Kunej and Turk's analysis of what may be the oldest musical
instrument discovered to date. They demonstrate both the difficulties and
the promise of this approach to the evolution of music. But in addition,
excavation and study of a rich and diverse assortment of stone, bronze,
ivory, and clay musical artifacts from all parts of the world are helping
to fill the historical gap between the Paleolithic horizon[5] and modern-
day music making (e.g., Hickman and Hughes 1988; and the series of
volumes put out by the Study Group on Musical Archaeology of the
International Council for Traditional Music).

Music-Language Comparative Analysis

One important area for future research in biomusicology will be the
interface between music and language and the evolutionary roots of this
relationship. This work will come as much from the study of phonology
and sign language as from the study of music and dance. Intonational
phonology is now developing mature theories for the analysis of intonation in all languages. This includes autosegmental theory for the analysis of tone (Goldsmith 1990, 1995; Ladd 1996) and metrical phonology
for the analysis of rhythmic patterns in speech (reviewed in Kiparsky and
Youmans 1990). Such studies will benefit as well from the cognitive psychological approach, which will help elucidate the cognitive mechanisms
of both acoustic and expressive processing in music and speech.
Although most of this research will focus on contemporary linguistic and
musical function, it will unquestionably provide insight into and fuel
speculations about the intertwined evolutionary origins of music and
language.

Human Brain Imaging

Undeniably one of the most important sources of new information for
the field of biomusicology will be the ever-expanding array of studies
using both structural and functional brain-imaging techniques in humans.
Such techniques have already demonstrated their potential to elucidate
brain areas mediating both the production and perception of music,
including tonal, rhythmic, and emotive aspects of music processing
(reviewed in Sergent 1993; Peretz and Morais 1993; Hodges 1996).

Such studies will provide great insight into the localization and the
lateralization of these functions, as well as touch on such important
issues as ontogenetic development, sex differences (Hough et al. 1994),
musical performance (Sergent et al. 1992), the effects of musical training on brain structure (Schlaug et al. 1995a; Elbert et al. 1995; Pantev
et al. 1998), neural correlates of skills such as absolute pitch (Schlaug

et al. 1995b; Zatorre et al. 1998) and musical score reading (Nakada et al. 1998), the effects of disease and aging on brain structure and function, and so on.

As mentioned, a key evolutionary question deals with the neurobiology of metric timekeeping, and it is predicted that the analysis of brain areas underlying meter will be a central area of interest for both music and speech (Penhune, Zatorre, and Evans 1998). Also, the relationship between the localizations of musical function and language function in the brain will be a central concern in mapping studies. This will touch especially on the domains of intonational phonology and metrical phonology, where the greatest potential for overlap between music and language seems apparent (Jackendoff 1990; Pierrehumbert 1991).

Comparative Musicology

Finally, a great beneficiary of the evolutionary approach to music will be musicology itself, especially ethnomusicology. Darwinian anthropology and evolutionary psychology will provide many new evolutionary models of music, several of which are presented in this volume, that will be testable in comparative musicological studies. We believe that musicology has much to gain from these new models, and should not shy away from evolutionary approaches to culture. Testing such models will require a highly cross-cultural approach to the five following major aspects of musical events:

1. Selection of who the *musicians* of a given culture are: their age and sex; do all people participate in musical events or are musicians and nonmusicians segregated? are the singers and instrumentalists of a given culture the same people? if segregation exists in any of these areas, how are the roles determined? what is the status of musicians in a culture? etc.

2. The *contexts and contents* of musical rituals: when, where, and how musical events occur; the organization of ceremonies involving music; song texts and other supporting narratives; myths and symbolisms; coordination of music with dance, poetry, theater, storytelling, trance, mime, etc.

3. The *social arrangement of musical performance*: solo versus group performance arrangement; gender or age specificity of particular musical forms; responsorial versus antiphonal choral singing arrangement; degree of soloist domination in instrumental performance; etc.

4. *Musical reflectors of this social arrangement* (Lomax 1968): use of monophonic versus heterophonic versus polyphonic versus homophonic multipart arrangements; use of measured versus unmeasured rhythmic patterns; the predominant vocal style of a culture; etc.

5. The *mode of transmission* of musical knowledge from generation to generation: how musical repertoires of a culture are organized; the nature of musical pedagogy; use of a musical notation system; tolerance versus intolerance to change; use of guided improvisation in pedagogy and performance; etc.

Analysis of these five broad factors does not depend so much on new methods in ethnomusicology as on a new commitment to a comparative approach to musical behavior, performance style, and meaning. But in addition to this, comparative musicology must seriously return to the issues of musical universals and classification to understand not only the deep evolutionary roots of music but how contemporary musical systems undergo change and stasis from historical and geographic perspectives. In fact, this applies as much to the behavioral and semiotic levels of music as to its acoustic level. This need will become all the greater as the degree of intercultural influence and overlap increases in the third millennium.

Music Evolution: Biological versus Cultural

It is unfortunate that the term "music evolution" (like the term "language evolution") has such an ambiguous meaning, as it refers both to biological evolution of a capacity and to cultural evolution of that capacity's output. In other words, the term refers both to the biological emergence of music through evolution of the capacity to make it (an evolutionary psychological consideration) as well as to the historical changes in musical systems and styles that occur over time and place (a comparative musicological consideration). This distinction highlights differences in the nature and dynamics of biological and cultural evolution. This section looks at music evolution from the standpoint of cultural evolution and tries to tie it in with the biological evolution of musical capacity during hominid evolution (see also Molino, this volume).

One way to think about this issue is from the perspective of Darwinian theories of culture (Durham 1990, 1991, 1992), which are "particulate" theories that view cultural objects as *replicators*; in other words, as objects capable of being reproduced and transmitted to future generations. According to such theories, the basic unit of cultural replication is the "meme" (Dawkins 1982; Durham 1991). A meme can refer to any kind of cultural object, for example, a musical instrument, song text, musical style, musical myth, or scale type, so long as it is capable of being replicated and transmitted culturally. Because a given meme in a culture usually has many related forms (e.g., several different designs for the same instrument; several different performance styles of a given musical genre; different scale types or rhythms for a given musical style, etc.), Darwinian theories of culture posit that differential replication of memes is dependent on the process of *cultural selection* (a process analogous to but different from natural selection), whereby certain forms of a meme are transmitted to future generations while others become extinct. Let there be no confusion: cultural objects are not biological species, and cultural selection (according to cultural consequences) is not natural selection (according to reproductive consequences). However, the Darwinian mechanics of replication, variation, and selection can be thought of as operating in both spheres in a formally analogous fashion, thus making these theories both parsimonious and attractive.

The final topics to be addressed in this chapter are musical classification and the reconstruction of musical history. To what extent is it possible to talk about monophyly in world musics in the same manner that this notion is seriously debated in the field of linguistics? It is important to point out that any discussion of the evolution of musical styles throughout the world depends strongly on a theory of musical classification, and that this topic has been all but taboo in musicology, a situation we hope will be rectified in the coming years. The concept of musical classification has unfortunately suffered the same fate as many other evolutionary ideas in musicology, as it has been seen as depriving cultures of the individuality and specialness of their musical styles. This kind of thinking, despite its good intentions, will only perpetuate the state of isolation that musicology has faced for many decades with regard to the question of human origins. Clearly, some kind of balance must be found between the need of ethnomusicologists to preserve the image that the music of a given culture is individual and special, and the important need of evolutionary musicologists to use music as a tool to study human evolution. There is no question that classification is an artificial activity, one that downplays individual differences for the sake of large-scale coherence. As such, it has the potential to offend the sensibilities of people through its tendency to lump together musical styles that transcend ethnic and political barriers. However, classification should not be viewed as an academic exercise for its own sake, or as a device for suppressing and denigrating cultures, but as an important tool for understanding the deep roots of musical styles and thus human cultural behavior in general. No evolutionary approach to music can avoid the topic of classification in some form. Nor should it.

Let us consider briefly the only serious hypothesis put forth to explain the evolution of contemporary global musical styles. It is based on a concept proposed by Alan Lomax (1980) in a paper that summarized the results of his "cantometrics" approach to musical classification in the 1960s. This hypothesis is almost certainly wrong in detail, but gives serious food for thought about the origins of musical styles. It begins with a comparative look at musical performance style in 233 world cultures. Based on an analysis of a diverse set of structural and performance properties for 4,000 songs, Lomax was able to classify the performance styles of the 233 cultures into 10 basic families. Next, he discovered that two of these ten model styles stood out for their highly contrastive nature. One is thought to have emerged in eastern Siberia and the other in sub-Saharan Africa. The former is characterized by "male dominated solos or rough unison choralizing, by free or irregular rhythms, and by a steadily increasing information load in various parameters—in glottal, then other ornaments, in long phrases and complex melodic forms, in increasingly explicit texts and in complexly organized orchestral accompaniment." The latter, by contrast, is "feminized, polyvoiced, regular in rhythm, repetitious, melodically brief, cohesive, well-integrated, with rhythmically oriented orchestras" (Lomax 1980:39–40).

Lomax's major hypothesis is that the phylogenetic tree of musical style had two evolutionary roots, one in eastern Asia and the other in sub-Saharan Africa, and that *all contemporary musical styles emerged as either offshoots or blends of them.* This idea certainly has great intuitive appeal, yet contrary to it are the results of Eric Minch and Steven Brown (unpublished data) showing that unrooted phylogenetic trees generated from Lomax's own cantometric data set of musical performance style do *not* place the Siberian style (and its offshoots) and the African style at opposite ends of the tree, as predicted by Lomax. Thus, this "biphyletic" hypothesis is almost certainly incorrect in detail. However, given the fact that it is the first and only one of its kind in the published literature, it will certainly function as a useful null hypothesis against which future models will be tested.

The cultural evolutionary issues discussed in this chapter, including musical universals, classification, replicators, and the musical map of the world, are critical concerns that contemporary ethnomusicology has either ignored or simply rejected. In our opinion, ethnomusicology has not met its calling. It is time for an evolutionary-based musicology to revive these forgotten issues if there is to be any hope of using the outstandingly rich database we have about music and musical behavior to enlighten music's own biological origins. "Mythology is wrong. Music is not the merciful gift of benevolent gods or heroes," wrote Curt Sachs in 1948. However, musicologists for the better part of the twentieth century operated under the illusion that music was simply a merciful gift, one whose origin was never questioned. It is time now to start asking questions about the origins of music, and in doing so, to address fundamental questions about the origins of our species.

The Future of Evolutionary Musicology

It is hoped that this brief introduction to the major issues and methods of evolutionary musicology sets the stage for the many essays that are to follow. Evolutionary musicology has great potential to contribute to the study of so many questions of interest to contemporary scholars. We realize that a research career in the field requires a technical training in both music and biology, and that few people up till now have either acquired the necessary double background or (like musical physicians) have taken the time to apply their two areas of training to the synthetic questions that biomusicology addresses. It is our hope that this situation will change in coming years, and that the next generation of students will realize the great rewards that await them in making the extra effort to develop training both in the arts and in the experimental sciences such as biology.

The future of evolutionary musicology is beginning now. In the same way that the current chapter is the beginning of this book, so too this book is the beginning of a new field devoted to the analysis of music evolution, both its biological and its cultural forms. We conclude this introduction by saying that just as music brings us in touch with the very deepest levels of our emotions, so too the study of music evolution has the potential to bring us in touch with the very deepest aspects of our humanity, our origins, our reasons for being.

Let the discussions begin.

Notes

1. See Nettl and Bohlman (1991) for an excellent discussion of the history of the Berlin school, especially the essays by Blum, Christensen, Ringer, and Schneider.

2. It is unfortunate that so few of the works of the Berlin school have been translated into English. It is very important that musicology come to terms with its own history and see it in proper perspective. There is no question that much scholarship in comparative musicology was permeated by racialist notions about the superiority of European tonal music, and that much faulty reasoning was used in creating "unilinear" evolutionary arguments about the origins of musical systems. This was no less true of much theorizing in sociology or anthropology at the time. Yet, this comment must be balanced by the realization that the comparative musicologists succeeded in bringing recordings and analyses of non-European musics to the European public for the first time, thus educating Western people about these musics in a way that no scholarly anthropological text could have done. Racialism should not be confused with racism, and it must be emphasized that despite their use of dated terms such as "primitive cultures" and "primitive music," the comparative musicologists wrote about the musics of non-Western cultures with nothing less than respect. It is a credit to the members of the Berlin school that they were attempting to develop a general theory of music, one that applied to all human beings and all musics. The spirit of this universalist approach to music and musical behavior unquestionably permeates this entire volume. In sum, we believe that it is high time that the Berlin school of comparative musicology be viewed beyond the racialism that was so predominant in all areas of

scholarship at the time, and be seen for the truly seminal contribution it has made to musicology, and especially to the type of universalist thinking that evolutionary musicology is once again trying to revive.

3. Unfortunately, we have not been able to track down this 1852 reference to Wagner.

4. Consider the following quotation by George List (1971): "... the only universal aspect of music seems to be that most people make it. And that is about the only universal involved. I could provide pages of examples of the non-universality of music. This is hardly worth the trouble. Every ethnomusicologist could do the same. ... since we are unlikely to ever find the universals."

5. For an excellent French-language review of the musical archeology of the Upper Paleolithic, see Dauvois (1994).

References

Andersson, M. (1994). *Sexual Selection*. Princeton: Princeton University Press.

Armstrong, D. F., Stokoe, W. C., and Wilcox, S. E. (1995). *Gesture and the Nature of Language*. Cambridge, UK: Cambridge University Press.

Baharloo, S., Johnston, P. A., Service, S. K., Gitschier, J., and Freimer, N. B. (1998). Absolute pitch: An approach for identification of genetic and nongenetic components. *American Journal of Human Genetics* 62:224–231.

Barkow, J. H., Cosmides, L., and Tooby, J. (1992). *The Adapted Mind: Evolutionary Psychology and the Generation of Culture*. Oxford: Oxford University Press.

Beaken, M. (1996). *The Making of Language*. Edinburgh: Edinburgh University Press.

Boyd, R. and Richerson, P. J. (1985). *Culture and the Evolutionary Process*. Chicago: University of Chicago Press.

Brown, S. (in press). Evolutionary models of music: From sexual selection to group selection. In F. Tonneau and N. S. Thompson (Eds.) *Perspectives in Ethology*, XIII. New York: Plenum.

Brown, S. (submitted). Toward a universal musicology.

Catchpole, C. K. and Slater, P. J. B. (1995). *Bird Song: Biological Themes and Variations*. Cambridge, UK: Cambridge University Press.

Cavalli-Sforza, L. L., Menozzi, P., and Piazza, A. (1994). *The History and Geography of Human Genes*. Princeton, NJ: Princeton University Press.

Corballis, M. C. (1991). *The Lopsided Ape: Evolution of the Generative Mind*. Oxford: Oxford University Press.

D'Amato, M. R. (1988). A search for tonal pattern perception in cebus monkeys: Why monkeys can't hum a tune. *Music Perception* 5:453–480.

Darwin, C. (1871). *The Descent of Man, and Selection in Relation to Sex*. London: Murray.

Dauvois, M. (1994). Les témoins paléolithiques du son et de la musique. In *La Pluridisciplinarité en Archéologie Musicale*, Vol. 1 (pp. 151–206). Paris: Centre Français d'Archéologie Musicale PRO LYRA.

Dawkins, R. (1982). *The Extended Phenotype: The Gene as Unit of Selection*. San Francisco: Freeman.

Deacon, T. (1992). The neural circuitry underlying primate calls and human language. In J. Wind, B. Chiarelli, B. Bichakjian, A. Nocentini, and A. Jonker (Eds.) *Language Origins: A Multidisciplinary Approach* (pp. 121–162). Dordrecht: Kluwer.

Dunbar, R. (1996). *Grooming, Gossip and the Evolution of Language*. London: Faber and Faber.

Durham, W. H. (1990). Advances in evolutionary culture theory. *Annual Review of Anthropology* 19:187–210.

Durham, W. H. (1991). *Coevolution: Genes, Culture and Human Diversity*. Stanford, CA: Stanford University Press.

Durham, W. H. (1992). Applications of evolutionary culture theory. *Annual Review of Anthropology* 21:331–355.

Elbert, T., Pantev, C., Wienbruch, C., Rockstroh, B., and Taub, E. (1995). Increased cortical representation of the fingers of the left hand in string players. *Science* 270:305–307.

Feldman, M. W. and Laland, K. N. (1996). Gene-culture coevolutionary theory. *Trends in Ecology and Evolution* 11:453–457.

Fromkin, V. (Ed.) (1978). *Tone: A Linguistic Survey*. New York: Academic Press.

Goldsmith, J. A. (1990). *Autosegmental & Metrical Phonology*. Oxford: Blackwell.

Goldsmith, J. A. (Ed.) (1995). *The Handbook of Phonological Theory*. Cambridge, MA: Blackwell.

Halpern, A. R. (1989). Memory for the absolute pitch of familiar songs. *Memory and Cognition* 17:572–581.

Hauser, M. D. (1996). *The Evolution of Communication*. Cambridge: MIT Press.

Hickman, E. and Hughs, D. W. (Eds.) (1988). *The Archaeology of Early Music Cultures*. Bonn: Verlag für Systematische Musikwissenschaft GmbH.

Hodges, D. A. (1996). Neuromusical research: A review of the literature. In D. A. Hodges (Ed.) *Handbook of Music Psychology*, 2nd ed. (pp. 197–284). San Antonio, TX: IMR Press.

Hornbostel, E. M. (1905/1975). Die probleme der vergleichenden Musikwissenschaft. Reprinted with English translation as "The problems of comparative musicology." In K. P. Wachsmann, D. Christensen and H.-P. Reinecke (Eds.) *Hornbostel Opera Omnia* (pp. 249–270). The Hague: Nijhoff.

Hough, M. S., Daniel, H. J., Snow, M. A., O'Brian, K. F., and Hume, W. G. (1994). Gender differences in laterality patterns for speaking and singing. *Neuropsychologia* 32:1067–1078.

Hulse, S. H., Takeuchi, A. H., and Braaten, R. F. (1993). Perceptual invariances in the comparative psychology of music. *Music Perception* 10:151–184.

Jackendoff, R. (1990). A comparison of rhythmic structures in music and language. In P. Kiparsky and G. Youmans (Eds.) *Phonetics and Phonology*, vol. 1, *Rhythm and Meter* (pp. 15–44). New York: Academic Press.

Kiparsky, P. and Youmans, G. (Eds.) (1990). *Phonetics and Phonology*, vol. 1, *Rhythm and Meter*. New York: Academic Press.

Konishi, M. (1965). The role of auditory feedback in the control of vocalization in the white-crowned sparrow. *Zeitschrift für Tierpsychologie* 22:770–783.

Konishi, M. (1994). An outline of recent advances in birdsong neurobiology. *Brain, Behavior and Evolution* 44: 279–285.

Ladd, D. R. (1996). *Intonational Phonology*. Cambridge, UK: Cambridge University Press.

Levitin, D. J. (1994). Absolute memory for musical pitch: Evidence from the production of learned melodies. *Perception and Psychophysics* 56:414–423.

List, G. (1971). On the non-universality of musical perspectives. *Ethnomusicology* 15: 399–402.

Lomax, A. (1968). *Folk Song Style and Culture*. New Brunswick, NJ: Transaction Books.

Lomax, A. (1980). Factors of musical style. In S. Diamond (Ed.) *Theory & Practice: Essays Presented to Gene Weltfish* (pp. 29–58). The Hague: Mouton.

Lumsden, C. J. and Wilson, E. O. (1981). *Genes, Mind and Culture*. Cambridge: Harvard University Press.

Marler, P. (1970). A comparative approach to vocal learning: Song development in white crowned sparrows. *Journal of Comparative and Physiological Psychology Monographs* 71:1–25.

Nakada, T., Fujii, Y., Suzuki, K., and Kwee, I. L. (1998). "Musical brain" revealed by high-field (3 Tesla) functional MRI. *NeuroReport* 9:3853–3856.

Nettl, B. and Bohlman, P. V. (Eds.) (1991). *Comparative Musicology and the Anthropology of Music*. Chicago: University of Chicago Press.

Nottebohm, F. (1967). The role of sensory feedback in the development of avian vocalizations. *Proceedings of the Fourteenth International Ornithological Congress, Oxford, 1966* (pp. 265–280).

Nottebohm, F. (1989). From bird song to neurogenesis. *Scientific American* 260:74–79.

Pantev, C., Oostenveld, R., Engelien, A., Ross, B., Roberts, L. E., and Hoke. M. (1998). Increased cortical representation in musicians. *Nature* 392:811–814.

Penhune, V. B., Zatorre, R. J., and Evans, A. C. (1998). Cerebellar contributions to motor timing: A PET study of auditory and visual rhythm reproduction. *Journal of Cognitive Neuroscience* 10:752–765.

Peretz, I. (1990). Processing of local and global musical information in unilateral brain-damaged patients. *Brain* 113:1185–1205.

Peretz, I. (1993). Auditory agnosia: A functional analysis. In S. McAdams and E. Bigand (Eds.) *Thinking in Sound: The Cognitive Psychology of Human Audition* (pp. 199–230). Oxford: Oxford University Press.

Peretz, I. and Kolinsky, R. (1993). Boundaries of separability between melody and rhythm in music discrimination: A neuropsychological perspective. *Quarterly Journal of Experimental Psychology* 46A:301–325.

Peretz, I. and Morais, J. (1993). Specificity for music. In F. Boller and J. Grafman (Eds.) *Handbook of Neuropsychology*, vol. 8 (pp. 373–390). New York: Elsevier.

Pierrehumbert, J. (1991). Music and the phonological principle: Remarks from the phonetician's bench. In J. Sundberg, L. Nord, and R. Carlson (Eds.) *Music, Language, Speech and Brain* (pp. 132–145). Houndmills, UK: Macmillan.

Profita, J. and Bidder, T. G. (1988). Perfect pitch. *American Journal of Medical Genetics* 29:763–771.

Rizzolatti, G. and Arbib, M. (1998). Language within our grasp. *Trends in Neuroscience* 21:188–194.

Sachs, C. (1948). *Our Musical Heritage*. New York: Prentice-Hall.

Schlaug, G., Jancke, L., Huang, Y., Staiger, J. F., and Steinmetz, H. (1995a). Increased corpus callosum size in musicians. *Neuropsychologia* 33:1047–1055.

Schlaug, G., Jancke, L., Huang, Y., and Steinmetz, H. (1995b). In vivo evidence of structural brain asymmetry in musicians. *Science* 267:699–701.

Sergent, J. (1993). Mapping the musician brain. *Human Brain Mapping* 1:20–38.

Sergent, J., Zuck, S., Tenial, S., and MacDonall, B. (1992). Distributed neural network underlying musical sight reading and keyboard performance. *Science* 257:106–109.

Spencer, H. (1857). The origin and function of music. *Fraser's Magazine* 56:396–408.

Szöke, P. and Filip, M. (1977). The study of intonation structure of bird vocalizations: An inadequate application of sound spectrography. *Opuscula Zoologica* XIV/12.

Takeuchi, A. H. and Hulse, S. H. (1993). Absolute pitch. *Psychological Bulletin* 113:345–361.

Thorpe, W. H. (1961). *Bird-Song: The Biology of Vocal Communication and Expression in Birds*. Cambridge, UK: Cambridge University Press.

Ward, W. A. D. and Burns, E. M. (1982). Absolute pitch. In D. Deutsch (Ed.) *The Psychology of Music* (pp. 431–451). New York: Academic Press.

Wallin, N. L. (1991). *Biomusicology: Neurophysiological, Neuropsychological and Evolutionary Perspectives on the Origins and Purposes of Music*. Stuyvesant, NY: Pendragon Press.

Zatorre, R. J., Perry, D. W., Beckett, C. A., Westbury, C. F., and Evans, C. A. (1998). Functional anatomy of musical processing in listeners with absolute pitch and relative pitch. *Proceedings of the National Academy of Sciences* 95:3172–3177.

II VOCAL COMMUNICATION IN ANIMALS

Prolegomena to a Biomusicology

Simha Arom

The very idea that there is a continuum of living creatures that encompasses music elicits in me two types of questions, one concerning the kinds of criteria we use in defining that thing we call music, the other concerning the learning and transmission of musical knowledge. I have had occasion to comment briefly on the question of learning in my published work on traditional African music (see especially Arom 1990, 1991) and so I focus here on the first question, which relates most closely to my expertise.

How can we decide if there is or is not a type of continuity between *zoo*musicolgy (Mâche 1992) and what one would have to call *anthropo*-musicology, which would be the scientific discipline, supposing we could create it, that would deal with the suite of human musical properties as they are manifested in the ensemble of known musics? Is it possible to determine a minimal set of criteria for defining music, and can we identify these criteria in some form or another in the songs of animals?

Concerning the kind of music produced by human beings, one could make a list of criteria, a type of inventory of universals specific to music. The first of these criteria is *intentionality*. A given music—in fact, all music—implies an act of intentional construction, in other words, an act of creation that actualizes an intention. There is purpose and finality to it, shared between the creators of the music and members of their culture, through which they confirm their common identity. This is demonstrated especially in ritual behaviors, most notably in analogical symbolic rituals (e.g., using the stylized imitation of the sound of rainfall to induce the coming of rain). But human beings also possess the capacity to "decontextualize" these constructions by performing such chants independent of all such contexts, "for free" in a manner of speaking. Music possesses a self-referential system that ignores the signifier-signified contrast. It has an immemorial relationship with language, and most especially with poetry.

All human music is set into motion by a formal process, itself the result of convention. In so far as this formal process is operative, music is detached from the sound environment in which it is produced, giving it a delimited time frame all its own, a kind of rupture with all that precedes and all that follows. The substance contained in this time frame is internally articulated in terms of proportions, in other words, *temporal ratios*. This, together with the existence of measured music—music subject to an isochronous temporal pulse—constitutes a quasi-universal. Measured musics are often associated with collective activities, thus contributing to the social life of the group, first and foremost to dance. In the same way that we do not know of any human society that lacks music, we do not know of a single society that does not express itself through dance. In Africa, nonmeasured music—music one cannot dance to—is not usually considered music at all, but is classified as a lamentation ("tears") or a type of signaling device. This formalization of time is supported by the idea of *periodicity*: a great majority of musics, from those of archaic cultures to those of Western societies, take advantage of invariant periodicities. The time within them is "closed." Very often these musics appeal to the principle of *symmetry*. This is the case for even the most archaic ones that depend on alternation between a soloist and a chorus or between two choruses based on symmetric distribution of the musical material. This symmetry and these parallelisms seem to bear witness to a search for balance. Might they be universals?

Next, for the construction of melodies, each society selects from the sound continuum a set of contrastive pitches. These pitches form a system, a *musical scale*. Such a scale, itself an abstract model but also the basis for the elaboration of all melodies, is the analog for what in a language would be its phonological system. It serves as a matrix for the organization of pitches, and by doing so determines a set of constant relationships among these pitches. Is the pentatonic scale, based on the cycle of fifths and found throughout the world, a universal? Do musical scales, as cognitive models, have a biological foundation?

As soon as a musical event requires two or more individuals, even a simple chant executed in unison, it demands a mode of coordination. A fortiori, in multipart music an *ordered* and *simultaneous interaction* exists between the participants, with a distribution of roles.

Humans have the capacity to classify their songs with respect to function or context into categories or *repertoires*. This gives symbolic meaning to any acoustic production and furthermore to any coherent ensemble of these productions.

Such are traits of human music. What distinguishes human music from what is supposed to be the music of the animals is that, first and foremost, there is necessarily an association between at least two of the criteria. Can one observe such an association in the animal world? Certain animals possess vocal repertoires considered as distinct entities. Can one say that these vocalizations are founded on structural musical principles: scale, melody, metric organization, meter, rhythm, etc.?

In conclusion, it seems to me that if a biomusicology is possible, it must be able to integrate, in one way or another, certain of the criteria enumerated above, by combining them *by at least two*.

Note

Translated from the French by Steven Brown.

References

Arom, S. (1990). La "mémoire collective" dans les musiques traditionnelles d'Afrique Centrale. *Revue de Musicologie* 76:149–162.

Arom, S. (1991). *African Polyphony and Polyrhythm: Musical Structure and Methodology*. Cambridge, UK: Cambridge University Press.

Mâche, F. -B. (1992). *Music, Myth and Nature: Or the Dolphins of Arion*. Chur, Switzerland: Harwood Academic Publishers.

3 Origins of Music and Speech: Insights from Animals

Peter Marler

Abstract
This review of recent work on vocal communication in animals, especially birds and primates, focuses on three basic questions that are relevant to the relationship among animal signaling, language, and music. One is the meaning of animal signals, many, probably most, of which are affective and rooted in the emotional state of the signaler. But careful study has shown that some alarm and food calls function symbolically. The second question is whether there is anything equivalent to a sentence in naturally occurring animal communication. The answer appears to be negative. The distinction is between lexical syntax or lexicoding, which provides criteria for defining a true sentence, and phonological coding or phonocoding. Phonocoding concerns the ability to create new sound patterns by recombination simply to generate signal diversity. The potential for lexicoding arises only when recombined signal elements are endowed with meaning. Lexicoding appears to be distinctively human, but phonocoding is widespread in certain groups, especially songbirds and whales, some of whose vocalizations are learned. It is less common in nonhuman primates, whose vocalizations are innate. A comparison between chimpanzees and gibbons, on the one hand, and songbirds on the other, reveals that birds with learned songs have much larger vocal repertoires, depending on extensive exploitation of phonocoding in their development. In response to the third question, whether animals make music, I suggest that the ability to engage freely in phonological rearrangement of sound elements to create new sequences is a necessary precursor not only of language but also of the ability to create music. Given that animal songs that are learned and that depend on phonocoding for signal diversity are, like human music, primarily nonsymbolic and affective, their study may be a source of insights into the animal origins of human music.

When animals communicate, every available sense is likely to be exploited, but speculations about relationships to language and music must focus primarily on communication by ear. In contemplating what we know about auditory communication in animals, we begin with some serious handicaps. Our understanding of the principles of vocal communication in animals is still very limited. With human speech and music, the situation is obviously very different. We are born and bred as users of both. As a consequence, we have an unsurpassed view from within, and our insights are authentic to a degree that we can never attain with communication systems of other species, especially with research still in its infancy. Our present state of relative ignorance about animal communication sometimes forces us to simplify and to focus not on their highest, often idiosyncratic achievements, that are among the most intriguing, but rather on the fundamental underlying principles.

In the interests of science, I have adopted this reductionistic spirit, and pose three basic questions, drawing illustrations from the animals that I know best, birds and monkeys. The first question is what do animal sounds mean? are they just displays of emotion, or is there more? do some animal calls serve as symbols? Second, I will grapple with just one aspect of the central linguistic theme of syntax. Adopting once more a reductionistic approach, I ask, do animals speak in sentences? Third, I offer some elementary speculations about a possible animal antecedent to that other distinctively human achievement, making music. Do animals create music?

What Do Animal Sounds Mean?

Some fifteen years or so ago, the thinking of zoologists about the semantics of calls of animals, especially the vocalizations of monkeys and apes, underwent something of a revolution. Not long ago, speculations about how best to interpret animal calls were all based on what Donald Griffin (1992) aptly described as the "groans of pain" (GOP) concept of animal communication. This approach assumes that vocalizations of monkeys and other animals are displays of emotion or affect, much like our own facial expressions. Only humans are thought to have progressed beyond this condition and to have achieved symbolic signaling. Premack (1975) stated the prevailing view clearly and succinctly: "Man has both affective and symbolic communication. All other species, except when tutored by man, have only the affective form." Symbolic signals are taken to be those that have identifiable referents that the signal can be said to connote in an abstract, noniconic fashion. For an animal communication system to qualify as symbolic, information about one or more referents has to be both encoded noniconically by signalers and decoded in equivalent form by receivers.

Note that this is not a discussion about whether animal signals are meaningful or meaningless. Both affective and symbolic animal signals are meaningful and are often rich in information content; both serve important and diverse functions, some communicative to other individuals, some with repercussions for the physiological and mental states of the signaler. At issue here is not the presence of meaning but the *kind* of meaning that affective and symbolic signals convey. This is a complex subject with many dimensions. Some view the contrasts as differences in degree rather than kind. In some circumstances signals traditionally thought of as affective, such as human facial expressions, can assume a symbolic function. Complex signals may contain within them intimately blended components in which the balance between affective and symbolic content can vary dramatically from one to another. Speech is an obvious case. Anonymous computerized speech, lacking individual identity, gender, and emotion, is a sadly impoverished vehicle for social communication. We must not fall into the trap of assuming that signal systems that are not languagelike are necessarily impoverished as vehicles for social communication.

Emotion-based calls are widespread in animals and may represent the most typical condition; but some vocalizations do not fit neatly into the GOP mold. The revisionist process began in earnest with descriptive studies and later with experiments conducted in the field in Africa, on the remarkably rich repertoire of alarm calls of the vervet monkey, *Cercopithecus aethiops*, first described by Struhsaker (1967). A further step was taken by playing taperecordings of alarm calls to free-ranging vervets in the absence of any predators, in their natural habitat on the edge of the rainforest (Seyfarth, Cheney, and Marler 1980a, b). The monkeys often venture out on to the savannah where they are exposed to many predators, hence presumably the enrichment of their alarm call repertoire. Different predators demand different escape strategies, and distinct alarm calls aid responding monkeys in deciding which strategy to adopt. Some vervet alarm calls are generalized signs of anxiety and fall squarely in the GOP mold; companions respond with varying degrees of vigilance and anxiety. Others are much more specific, so much so that it is not unreasonable to begin thinking of them as labels or names for particular predator classes.

Some calls were identified in the literature as leopard calls, snake calls, and eagle calls. This usage was rendered all the more reasonable with the results of the playback experiments showing that the calls elicited natural reactions that were already known from Struhsaker's work to be specific and appropriate to particular predators. Responses differed in ways that made good ecological sense, given the hunting strategies of the predators. For example, in response to eagle calls, monkeys searched the sky and ran into bushes. In response to leopard calls they leaped up into the canopy of the nearest fever tree where a leopard could not reach them. When a snake call was played, they reared up on their hind legs and scanned the underbrush around them. In other words, there was every indication that the calls served as symbols for the different classes of predators (Cheney and Seyfarth 1990).

Since these vervet studies, many other demonstrations of animal alarm and food calls (table 3.1) displayed what is defined as "functional reference" (Marler, Evans, and Hauser 1992; Evans and Marler 1995; Marler and Evans 1996). The underlying concept is that functionally referential calls seem to stand for the class of objects or referents that they represent in the minds of others. In other words, they function as abstract, non-iconic symbols. However, the role of the many dimensions of mindfulness still remains unclear (Hauser 1996). Without benefit of introspection, and

Table 3.1
Some calls of birds and mammals that function symbolically

Animal	Type of Call	Investigator
Red jungle fowl	Alarm, food	Collias 1987
Chickens	Alarm, food	Gyger et al. 1987
		Evans et al. 1993
		Evans and Marler 1994
Lapwings (3 sp)	Alarm	Walters 1990
Chimpanzees	Food	Hauser et al. 1993
Rhesus macaques	Food	Hauser and Marler 1993a,b
Toque macaques	Food	Dittus 1984
Vervet monkeys	Alarm	Seyfarth et al. 1980a
Ring-tailed lemurs	Alarm	Macedonia 1990
Malaysian tree squirrels (3 sp)	Alarm	Tamura and Yong 1993
Alpine marmots	Alarm	Boero 1992

lacking appropriate experiments, we do not know whether these transformations involve conscious thought and cognition, with an intent to change the mental state of others (Cheney and Seyfarth 1992, 1996), or whether they are innate, reflexive, and relatively mindless, and thus quite unlanguage-like. The term "functional reference" was coined to make it possible to discuss the issue of reference while remaining agnostic about the nature of the underlying mental and neural processes.

Food calls of birds and mammals also appear to function referentially, conveying to others not only that food has been found, but also occasionally giving some inkling, understood by others, as to its quality and quantity (Dittus 1984; Marler, Dufty, and Pickert 1986; Elowson, Tannenbaum, and Snowden 1991; Benz, Leger, and French 1992; Benz 1993; Hauser and Marler 1993a, b; Hauser et al. 1993; Evans and Marler 1994; reviewed in Hauser 1996). Evidence from birds even suggests deceptive use of food calls to attract others when in fact no food is present (Gyger and Marler 1988).

It is thus clear that some animal calls do not conform to the GOP theory. But although some vocalizations do function symbolically, several issues remain equivocal. We have only limited information on the role of experience in the development of this type of communication. Learning does seem to play some role. Eagle calls by adult vervets are quite specific, but infants give eagle calls to almost anything moving above in free space at a certain rate, even a falling leaf; however, they do not give eagle calls to a snake or a leopard (figure 3.1). Field data gathered by Seyfarth and Cheney (1980) suggest that the relationship between referents and call types sharpens with experience, as though only experienced monkeys develop specific predator-related concepts, perhaps hinting at a role for cognition. However, there are also indications of

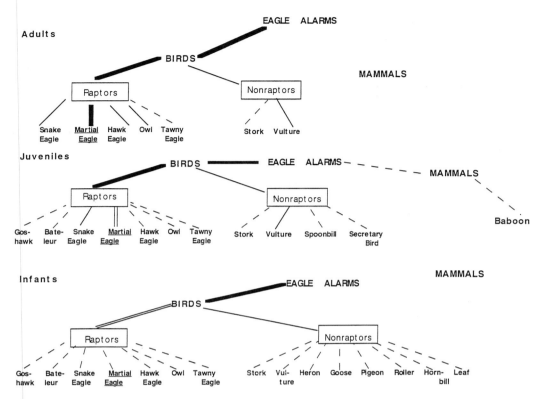

Figure 3.1
A diagrammatic representation of field observations from Africa of stimuli that elicit production of the eagle alarm call by adult, juvenile, and infant vervet monkeys. The width of the bars represents the number of observations. The martial eagle, which preys on infant vervets, is the major stimulus in adults, but in infants is only one of many. (Data from Seyfarth, Cheney, and Marler 1980.)

innate underpinnings to this behavior. The monkeys behave as though they are innately able to divide up the world of predators into several broad, ill-defined classes when they first encounter them, leaving it to individual experience and social example to bring each general referent class of aerial predators, ground predators, and snakes into sharper focus. Note that actual call structure is only minimally dependent on experience, a point that will be returned to.

We also have to equivocate on another aspect of call meaning, because we cannot distinguish between the alternatives of a label or a prescription (the labeling of an object), whether a predator or food, on the one hand, and a prescription for the actions relating to that object, on the other (Marler 1961; Hauser 1996). But despite these gaps in our understanding, it is nevertheless clear that the linkages between call and referent are more specific than we usually associate with emotional displays. So some animal calls are indeed symbolically meaningful, even though those that are entirely emotionally based probably predominate.

Do Animals Speak in Sentences?

A primary source of the power of speech is its two-level temporal structure, what Charles Hockett (1960) called the duality of patterning. The three most basic requirements of all for speechlike behavior are, first, one must be able to arrange words into different sentences, second, a lexicon of words must be available from which sentences are assembled, and third, one needs a way to construct these words. One efficient way to generate large numbers of words is to have a small repertoire of distinct articulatory gestures or phonemes and sequence them in many different ways, as we do in speech. The phoneme repertoire can average up to forty or so in the speech patterns of a given language, drawn from a universal pool of sixty or so. The two key points I want to emphasize now are that these phonemes and arbitrary sequences of them are meaningless in themselves, and they can be sequenced in many, many different ways. Only when meanings are attached to them are they transformed from nonsense into words. When words are properly sequenced, the result is a sentence. So words and sentences are the essence of spoken language.

Several different levels of syntactical organization apply in constructing a sentence, and we need terms for them if we are to make comparisons between animal communication and language (figure 3.2). The higher level, with semantically meaningful words and sentences, is appro-

Phonological Syntax

Recombinations of sound components (e.g. phonemes) in different sequences (e.g. words), where the components themselves are not meaningful. I call this "phonocoding."

Lexical Syntax

Recombinations of component sequences (e.g. words in the lexicon) into different strings (sentences). Here there is meaning at two levels, the word and the sentence. The meaning of the string is a product of the assembled meanings of its components. I call this "lexicoding."

Figure 3.2
Definitions of phonocoding (phonological syntax) and lexicoding (lexical syntax).

priately called lexical syntax or lexicoding. The lower level, with meaningless sounds combined into sequences, may be termed phonological
syntax or phonocoding. Meaningful sentences require lexical syntax.
Phonological syntax concerns the rules for sequencing, not the generation of meanings. Does evidence exist that either of these steps toward
language has been taken by animals?

We can begin with the sentence and work down in reductionistic
fashion. Some animal sounds do posses symbolic meanings, but although
in some cases animals string symbolically meaningful calls together in
the course of their natural vocal behavior, I know of no case in which a
string qualifies as a sentence. Aside from marginal cases (e.g., Mitani and
Marler 1988), we do not seem to have any recorded natural example of
an animal unambiguously satisfying the crucial criteria for lexical syntax.
No naturally communicating animal is known to sequence symbolically
meaningful calls to make a sentence that has a new, emergent meaning
derived from the combined meanings of its assembled parts.

So much for lexical syntax. How about words and phonemes, or their
equivalent? Symbolically meaningful animal signals such as alarm and
food calls of monkeys and birds all seem to come as indivisible packages.
It is true that their meanings are not completely fixed and immutable,
and can be modulated by giving calls singly or repeatedly, quickly or
slowly, loudly or softly (Marler 1992). But their basic indivisibility suggests no obvious analogue to phonological syntax in their construction.
However, if we widen the search to embrace not only animal vocalizations with symbolic meanings, but also those of a more classical, affective kind, impoverished in referential content, but rich in emotional
content, we find something very different. Here are many cases of phonological syntax (Ujhelyi 1996). In particular, scrutiny of the literature on
the structure of learned birdsongs reveals case after case of birds that
employ phonocoding to create individual song repertoires numbered in
the hundreds. These repertoires are generated by reusing again and
again, in many different sequences, a basic set of minimal acoustic units,
the bird's equivalent of phonemes and syllables. I will limit myself to two
examples, one with a very small individual song repertoire, the swamp
sparrow, the other, the winter wren, with a larger one.

The common song of the swamp sparrow is a simple case. Each male
has two or three songs, each consisting of a two-second string of repeated
syllables, uttered in the spring and summer, many times each day (Marler
and Pickert 1984). The natural songs of this species have many syllable
types. Each syllable, repeated in identical fashion to form the song, is
made up of two to six different notes in many different combinations.
The notes themselves are meaningless, but assembled into distinctive
clusters, they form the basic building blocks of swamp sparrow song.

Particular selections and sequences are passed as learned traditions from generation to generation. Constituent notes are all drawn from a simple specieswide repertoire of six note types, each with a range of within-type variants (figure 3.3). With the right combination drawn from this specieswide note-type set, one can describe any natural swamp sparrow song, just as one can describe the speech patterns of any language with the right combination of phonemes and syllables drawn from the universal set to which all humans have potential access. But whereas different words have different symbolic meanings, different swamp sparrow songs all carry the same basic message, modulated only by whatever nuances are conveyed by individual differences, local dialects, variations in loudness, and completeness of the song pattern.

The swamp sparrow is a simple case. For others, such as the familiar call of the chickadee (Hailman and Ficken 1987; Hailman, Ficken, and

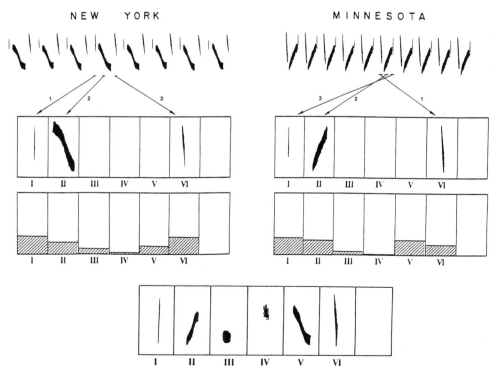

Figure 3.3
Sound spectrograms of songs of the swamp sparrow. Songs are composed of six basic sound categories (bottom), each with some degree of within-category variation. Rules for assembling note types into song syllables vary locally, as shown in the samples for New York and Minnesota birds (top). Note types, which recur in similar proportions in different populations (middle boxes), can be combined into many different patterns, with up to six notes per syllable. This is a clear case of phonocoding. (From Marler and Pickert 1984.)

Ficken 1985), the individual bird itself recombines the same basic set of call components in many different ways, thus increasing repertoire size. As another illustration of this strategy for enlarging repertoires, consider the song of the winter wren (Kroodsma 1980; Kroodsma and Momose 1991). Every male has his own distinctive learned repertoire of five to ten song types, each up to ten seconds in duration, composed of many different notes. Each song type is distinct from all others in a male's repertoire and from songs of any other male. Close inspection reveals, however, that at the level of their microstructure, shared features are present both within and between repertoires (figure 3.4). Each song in the repertoire contains phrases drawn from a large pool that recur again and again, but in each song type they are arranged in a different sequence. Evidently what happens when a young male learns to sing is that he acquires a set of songs from the adults he hears and breaks them down into phrases or segments. He then creates variety and enlarges his repertoire by rearranging these phrases or segments in different patterns.

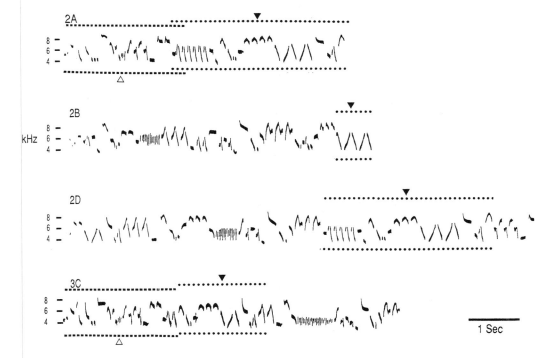

Figure 3.4
Sound spectrograms of songs of the winter wren, three from the repertoire of one male (2A, B, and D) and one from a neighbor (3C). Two sections are marked with dots and arrows to illustrate sharing of large segments between songs, clearly the result of recombining sections of learned songs during development. (From Kroodsma and Momose 1991.)

The mistle thrush of Europe engages in similar behavior (Marler 1959), and learned birdsongs provide many other examples.

Some of the most complex songs of all are found in birds that, as they acquire and develop their repertoire, take this process to extreme. Mockingbirds and their relatives create hundreds of distinctive sequences using phrases that are both invented and acquired not only from their own species, but from other species as well, all recast into mockingbird form and tempo (Boughey and Thompson 1976; Baylis 1982). The record is held by a male brown thrasher, a relative of the mockingbird, with an individual repertoire of over 1,000 distinct songs (Kroodsma and Parker 1977).

At some primitive level, the accomplishments of these songsters are reminiscent of our own speech behavior. The more accomplished songbirds create huge vocal repertoires, making extensive use of the same basic process of syntactical recombination or phonocoding that we use to create words. But of course there is a crucial contrast with language. Song sequences are not meaningfully distinct, in the referential sense; they are rich in affective content, but lacking in symbolic content.

Each of the thousands of winter wren songs that exist means basically the same thing. Each serves as a kind of badge or emblem, a sign that denotes identity, population membership, and social status. The diversity may impress the listener with the performer's virtuosity, and in some species certainly enhances his reproductive prospects (Catchpole and Slater 1995), as is argued for human music (Miller, this volume). Such functions are important enough from a communicative point of view, and there may be others. Many wood warblers have two distinct classes of songs, one associated more with sex and the other more with male-to-male interactions and aggression, as though there is a contrast in the quality or nature of the underlying emotional state (Kroodsma 1988). But as far as I know, no one has suggested that they are in any way symbolically distinct.

Songs have none of the semantic content that some alarm and food calls possess. The variety introduced by the generation of repertoires serves not to enrich meaning but to create sensory diversity. We could think of repertoires as providing aesthetic enjoyment or as alleviating boredom in singer and listener. But in these learned birdsongs, phonocoding does not augment the knowledge conveyed, in the symbolic sense, as is so obviously the case in our own speech behavior. On the other hand, symbolic functions are less at issue in music, and something like phonological syntax is also involved in musical composition. Could it be that more parallels with music than with language are to be found in the communicative behavior of animals?

Do Animals Make Music?

If it is at all true that phonocoding in animals has some relationship, however remote, to the creation of human music, where in the animal kingdom should the search begin? The potential for the unusually rich exploitation of phonological syntax that generates the wonderfully diverse sound patterns of birdsong seems to depend in turn on their learnability. Phonocoding does occur in innate songs of both birds and mammals (Craig 1943; Robinson 1979, 1984), but never on the elaborate scale that we find in some learned birdsongs. The only other case in which something remotely similar is to be found in animals is in the learned songs of the humpback whale (Payne, Tyack, and Payne 1983; Payne and Payne 1985). Note that the only animal taxa for which we know for sure that vocal learning shapes the development of naturally occurring vocal behavior are birds and cetaceans. With the possible exception of bats (Boughman 1998), other animals, including nonhuman primates, have vocal repertoires that are innate. We can infer that the ability to learn new vocalizations, evident in no primate other than humans (Snowdon and Elowson 1992), greatly facilitated the emergence and rich exploitation of phonocoding, employed subsequently as a basic step in the evolution of speech behavior. On this basis I would argue that human music may have predated the emergence of language (see chapter 1 and Merker, this volume). What gave the human brain the capacity for language was more than the ability to learn and produce new sounds in an infinite number of combinations. Much more remarkable was the completely novel ability of our immediate ancestors to attach new meanings to these sounds and recombine them into a multitude of meaningful sentences, something that no other organism has achieved. So if what birds and whales can tell us about the evolution of language is so limited, it is not unreasonable to wonder if they have more to say about the origins of music.

The fact that many animal calls are fundamentally affective and non-symbolic augurs well for the prospect of some kind of commonality between those sounds and music. Both are immensely rich in emotional meaning, but generally speaking, neither animal song nor, except in very special cases, human music is usually viewed as meaningful in the strict, referential, symbolic sense. So rather than referential alarm and food calls of animals, we would be more likely to gravitate to animal songs if we were looking for roots for human music. As we have seen, some are complex enough to offer intriguing possibilities. I focus here on one basic theme, namely, creativity, which I take to be a fundamental requirement for the origins of music. Adopting once more a reductionistic stance, I concentrate on one ingredient of the creative aspect of music, essential for composers, performers, and other makers of music, and for those who delight in listening to music performed by others: the ability to create acoustic novelty.

I will begin by considering sounds of two higher primates. Both chimpanzees and gibbons are close relatives of humans, and vocalizations of both are considered as protomusical (Wallin 1991). I will make no effort to review their entire repertoires, which are well documented (Goodall 1986; Mitani 1994; Marler and Tenaza 1977; Geissmann 1993). Instead I will focus on those sounds that most obviously qualify as songs. Figure 3.5 illustrates a typical example of the chimpanzee vocalization called pant-hooting, recorded from an adult male in Africa. This is a loud, rhythmical hooting, typically about ten seconds in duration, beginning softly and working up to an almost screamlike climax (Goodall 1986; Marler and Hobbett 1975). As recorded from different individuals and from the same individual in different circumstances, variation is substantial, but typically consists of four parts: introduction, build-up, climax, and let-down. One pant-hoot includes anything from fifteen to thirty distinct sounds, characterized as hoots, screams, and whimpers, some on produced on inhalation, some on exhalation.

Pant-hooting is the longest and most complex of all chimpanzee vocalizations. Rather like birdsong, it is used as an affective, nonsymbolic display in many different situations, especially during intergroup encounters, when excited, after prey capture, to assert dominance, and, often in chorus, to keep in touch in the forest (Goodall 1986). The key point here is that, despite variations, each individual chimp always pant-hoots in

CHIMPANZEE PANT-HOOT

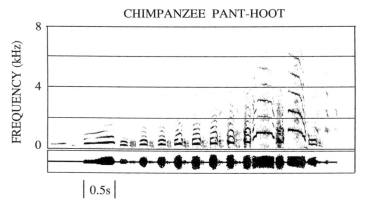

Figure 3.5
A sound spectrogram of a single pant-hooting sequence of an adult male chimpanzee recorded at the Gombe National Park, Tanzania. Sound is produced on both inhalation and exhalation. The bottom trace shows the amplitude envelope.

basically the same way, but differently from others. It is easy for experienced human observers to identify each animal's pant-hoot as a kind of signature. Variation is considerable and probably meaningful, but it is always based on a single modal form. As far as I know, no one in the field who has studied the behavior of chimpanzees, in the wild or in captivity, ever hinted at the possibility that an individual chimpanzee has a repertoire of several consistently distinct patterns of pant-hooting.

Consider the song of the Kloss gibbon in Indonesia (see Geissmann, this volume). Again, this is an emotive, nonsymbolic signal used in different forms by both sexes for locating each other in the forest and for maintaining territories (Tenaza 1976; Geissmann 1993). As with chimpanzee pant-hooting, a lot of variation exists, but each individual has its own distinctive, modal song pattern (figure 3.6). As far as I know, there is no recorded case from any of the ten species of gibbons of an individual repertoire of more than one basic song type, although several gibbons perform interesting male-female duets (Lamprecht 1970; Geissmann 1993). A final point will be relevant later. In both chimpanzees and gibbons the basic patterning of these complex calls appears to be innate, and develops normally in social isolation and, as Geissmann (1993) showed in gibbons, in intermediate or mixed form in hybrids.

These elaborate and highly individualistic sequences of patterned sounds, although clearly candidates for consideration as animal songs, are quite constrained from an acoustic point of view. Each individual has one fundamental modal pattern, stable over long periods of time, around which all of its variants are grouped. There is no individual "repertoire" of songs or pant-hoots, if we take that term to imply a set of acoustically

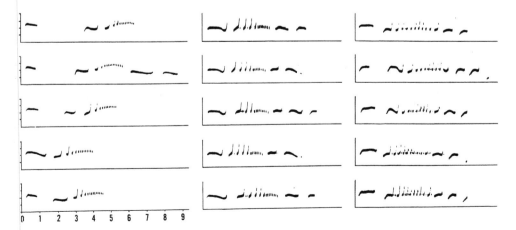

Figure 3.6
Samples of songs of three female Kloss gibbons show that, although there is variation, each tends to conform to a single, individually distinctive pattern. (From Tenaza 1976.)

distinct, more or less discretely different songs. It is true that the individual distinctiveness of each animal's pant-hoots and songs may be taken as a hint that a degree of inventiveness, or at least of indeterminacy, enters into the development of these calls, but their innateness and rather strict species-specificity suggest a limited degree of developmental plasticity (Geissmann 1993). In other words, the indications of creativity in their development are minimal.

For comparison, I return to the learned song of the winter wren (figure 3.7). This is a much more complex pattern, more elaborate than anything that an ape ever produced. As we have seen, each male winter wren has a repertoire of distinct song types. These are assembled during development as a collage of learned phrases and notes, in a number of different, set sequences, to create the repertoire of multiple song types (Kroodsma 1980; Kroodsma and Momose 1991).

How does this compare with the songs of gibbons and the pant-hooting of chimpanzees? From a functional viewpoint they have certain aspects in common. They are all affective, nonreferential displays, given in a state of high arousal, and used especially for achieving and modulating social contact and spacing. They are all highly individualistic, within limitations imposed by phonocoding rules that prevail in each species. But how do birds and apes rank with regard to creativity? In this respect, the two are as different as chalk and cheese. Ape song repertoires are limited to one pattern per animal, supplemented by a range of

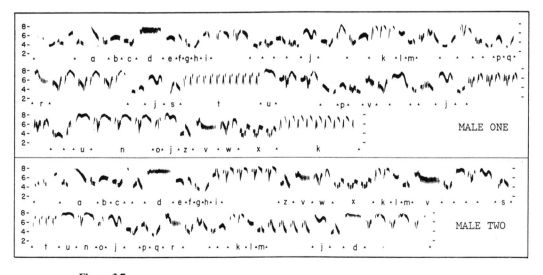

Figure 3.7
Songs of two neighboring winter wrens, marked with an alphabetical code to illustrate sharing of sound components between individuals. The song of male one is about seven seconds in duration. This is another clear case of phonocoding. (From Kroodsma 1980.)

variations grouped around that pattern. The accomplishments of a winter wren are of an altogether different magnitude. Each male has a repertoire of maybe ten song types and the winter wren is only a beginner as wrens go; other wren species have repertoires numbered in the hundreds (Kroodsma and Verner 1978). So this is the first bird-ape contrast. Some songbirds with learned songs have individual repertoires that are huge; repertoires of monkeys and apes are strictly limited.

If we examine the way in which large birdsong repertoires develop, we find an ontogenetic principle operating that is either feeble or simply lacking in nonhuman primates. Vocalizations of monkeys and apes are innate. Songbirds, with their learned songs, have a developmental strategy with all the hallmarks of a truly creative process. As far as I know, phonocoding with this degree of richness has never been recorded in any animal with innate vocalizations. In a classic manifestation of phonological syntax, wrens and other songbirds display a remarkable ability to rearrange learned phrases, seemingly doing so almost endlessly in some species. Many different sequences are created, generating, in effect, a kind of animal music. The sequences are not random but orderly, organized by definable rules and structured in such a way as to yield many stable, repeatable, distinctive patterns, the precise number varying from species to species and bird to bird. Together with whale songs, also learned (Payne, Tyack, and Payne 1983; Payne, this volume), these birdsongs are an obvious place to look for insights into what underlying aesthetic principles, if any, are shared between animal and human music.

I draw two modest conclusions from this overview of animal communication, language and music. From a reductionistic point of view, a convenient basis for animal-human comparisons is provided by the realization that the potential for phonocoding is a critical requisite for the emergence not only of speech and language but also of music. I suggest that we can already see a version of such a process in operation, albeit in primordial form, in some learned songs of animals, especially songbirds. An obvious next step would be to analyze phonocoding rules that birds use when they sing. Is it possible that they conform to our own compositional rules? A minimalist definition of music, at least of the Western, tonal variety, might be couched in terms of notes with specific pitches, intervals, and distinctive timbres combined into phrases that are repeated with additions and deletions, assembled into series with a particular meter and rhythm, and so constituting a song or melody. One approach to the human-animal comparison would be to see whether any animal sounds conform to similar taxonomic criteria, all of which are potentially studiable in animals. Do the rules vary among species in relation to repertoire size? Are correlations seen among lifestyle, temperament, and song tempo in different bird species? It is my conviction that the vocal behavior of birds will prove to be as profitable to study as that of our much closer relatives, monkeys and apes, as we explore them for insights into the origins of music.

References

Baylis, J. R. (1982). Avian vocal mimicry: Its function and evolution. In D. E. Kroodsma and E. I. Miller (Eds.) *Acoustic Communication in Birds* (pp. 51–83). New York: Academic Press.

Benz, J. J. (1993). Food-elicited vocalizations in golden lion tamarins: Design features for representational communication. *Animal Behaviour* 45:443–455.

Benz, J. J., Leger, D. W., and French, J. A. (1992). The relation between food preference and food-elicited vocalizations in golden lion tamarins (*Leontopithecus rasalia*). *Journal of Comparative Psychology* 106:142–149.

Boero, D. L. (1992). Alarm calling in Alpine marmot (*Marmota marmota L.*): Evidence for semantic communication. *Ethology, Ecology and Evolution* 4:125–138.

Boughey, M. J. and Thompson, N. S. (1976). Species specificity and individual variation in the songs of the brown trasher (*Toxostoma rufum*) and catbird (*Dumetella carolinensis*). *Behaviour* 57:64–90.

Boughman, J. W. (1998). Vocal learning by greater spear-nosed bats. *Proceedings of the Royal Society of London, Series B. Biological Sciences* 265:227–233.

Catchpole, C. K. and Slater, P. J. B. (1995). *Bird Song: Themes and Variations*. Cambridge, UK: Cambridge University Press.

Cheney, D. L. and Seyfarth, R. M. (1990). *How Monkeys See the World: Inside the Mind of Another Species*. Chicago: Chicago University Press.

Cheney, D. L. and Seyfarth, R. M. (1992). Meaning, reference, and intentionality in the natural vocalizations of monkeys. In T. Nishida, W. C. McGrew, P. Marler, M. Pickford, and F. de Waal (Eds.) *Topics in Primatology*, Vol. 1, *Human Origins* (pp. 315–330). Tokyo: Tokyo University Press.

Cheney, D. L. and Seyfarth, R. M. (1996). Function and intention in the calls of non-human primates. *Proceedings of the British Academy* 88:59–76.

Collias, N. E. (1987). The vocal repertoire of the red junglefowl: A spectrographic classification and the code of communication. *Condor* 89:510–524.

Craig, W. (1943). The song of the wood pewee, *Myiochanes virens* Linnaeus: A study of bird music. *New York State Music Bulletin* 334:1–186.

Dittus, W. (1984). Toque macaque food calls: Semantic communication concerning food distribution in the environment. *Animal Behaviour* 32:470–477.

Elowson, A. M., Tannenbaum, P. L., and Snowdon, C. T. (1991). Food-associated calls correlate with food preferences in cotton-top tamarins. *Animal Behaviour* 42:931–937.

Evans, C. S., Evans, L., and Marler, P. (1993). On the meaning of alarm calls: Functional reference in an avian vocal system. *Animal Behaviour* 46:23–38.

Evans, C. S. and Marler, P. (1994). Food-calling and audience effects in male chickens, *Gallus gallus*: Their relationships to food availability, courtship and social facilitation. *Animal Behaviour* 47:1159–1170.

Evans, C. S. and Marler, P. (1995). Language and animal communication: Parallels and contrasts. In H. Roitblatt (Ed.) *Comparative Approaches to Cognitive Science* (pp. 341–382). Cambridge: MIT Press.

Geissmann, T. (1993). *Evolution of Communication in Gibbons (Hylobatidae)*. Doctoral dissertation, University of Zurich, Switzerland.

Goodall, J. (1986). *The Chimpanzees of Gombe: Patterns of Behavior*. Cambridge: Belknap Press of Harvard University Press.

Griffin, D. R. (1992). *Animal Minds*. Chicago: Chicago University Press.

Gyger, M. and Marler, P. (1988). Food calling in the domestic fowl (*Gallus gallus*): The role of external referents and deception. *Animal Behaviour* 36:358–365.

Gyger, M., Marler, P., and Pickert, R. (1987). Semantics of an avian alarm call system: The male domestic fowl: *Gallus domesticus. Behaviour* 102:15–40.

Hailman, J. P. and Ficken, M. S. (1987). Combinatorial animal communication with computable syntax: Chick-a-dee calling qualifies as "language" by structural linguistics. *Animal Behaviour* 34:1988–1901.

Hailman, J. P., Ficken, M. S., and Ficken, R. W. (1985). The "chick-a-dee" calls of *Parus atricapillus*: A recombinant system of animal communication compared with written English. *Semiotica* 56:191–224.

Hauser, M. D. (1996). *The Evolution of Communication*. Cambridge: MIT Press.

Hauser, M. D. and Marler, P. (1993a). Food-associated calls in rhesus macaques (*Macaca mulatta*). I. Socioecological factors influencing call production. *Behavioral Ecology* 4:194–205.

Hauser, M. D. and Marler, P. (1993b). Food-associated calls in rhesus macaques (*Macaca mulatta*). II. Costs and benefits of call production and suppression. *Behavioral Ecology* 4:206–212.

Hauser, M. D., Teixidor, P., Field, L., and Flaherty, R. (1993). Food-elicited calls in chimpanzees: Effects of food quantity and divisibility? *Animal Behaviour* 45:817–819.

Hockett, C. F. (1960). Logical considerations in the study of animal communication. In W. E. Lanyon and W. N. Tavolga (Eds.) *Animal Sounds and Communication* (pp. 392–430). Washington, DC: American Institute of Biological Sciences.

Kroodsma, D. E. (1980). Winter wren singing behavior: A pinnacle of song complexity. *Condor* 82:357–365.

Kroodsma, D. E. (1988). Song types and their use: Developmental flexibility of the male Blue-winged Warbler. *Ethology* 79:235–247.

Kroodsma, D. E. and Momose, H. (1991). Songs of the Japanese population of the winter wren (*Troglodytes troglodytes*). *Condor* 93:424–432.

Kroodsma, D. E. and Parker, L. D. (1977). Vocal virtuosity in the brown thrasher. *Auk* 94:783–785.

Kroodsma, D. E. and Verner, J. (1978). Complex singing behaviors among *Cistothorus* wrens. *Auk* 94:703–716.

Lamprecht, J. (1970). Duettgesang beim Siamang, *Symphalangus syndactylus* (Hominoidea, Hylobatinae). *Zeitschrift für Tierpsychologie* 27:186–204.

Macedonia, J. M. (1991). What is communicated in the antipredator calls of lemurs? Evidence from playback experiments with ring-tailed and ruffed lemurs. *Ethology* 86:177–190.

Marler, P. (1959). Developments in the study of animal communication. In P. R. Bell (Ed.) *Darwin's Biological Work* (pp. 150–206 and 329–335). Cambridge, UK: Cambridge University Press.

Marler, P. (1961). The logical analysis of animal communication. *Journal of Theoretical Biology* 1:295–317.

Marler, P. (1992). Functions of arousal and emotion in primate communication: A semiotic approach. In T. Nishida, W. C. McGrew, P. Marler, M. Pickford, and F. B. M. de Waal (Eds.) *Topics in Primatology,* Vol. 1, *Human Origins* (pp. 235–248). Tokyo: University of Tokyo Press.

Marler, P., Dufty, A., and Pickert, R. (1986). Vocal communication in the domestic chicken. I. Does a sender communicate information about the quality of a food referent to a receiver? *Animal Behaviour* 34:188–193.

Marler, P., Evans, C. S., and Hauser, M. D. (1992). Animal signals. Reference, motivation or both? In H. Papoušek, U. Jürgens, and M. Papoušek (Eds.) *Nonverbal Vocal Communication: Comparative and Developmental Approaches* (pp. 66–86). Cambridge, UK: Cambridge University Press.

Marler, P. and Evans, C. S. (1996). Bird calls: Just emotional displays or something more? *Ibis* 138:26–331.

Marler, P. and Hobbett, L. (1975). Individuality in a long range vocalization of wild chimpanzees. *Zeitschrift für Tierpsychologie* 38:97–109.

Marler, P. and Pickert, R. (1984). Species-universal microstructure in the learned song of the swamp sparrow (*Melospiza georgiana*). *Animal Behaviour* 32:673–689.

Marler, P. and Tenaza, R. (1977). Communication in apes with special reference to vocalizations. In T. A. Sebeok (Ed.) *How Animals Communicate* (pp. 965–1033). Bloomington: Indiana University Press.

Mitani, J. C. (1994). Ethological studies of chimpanzee vocal behavior. In R. W. Wrangham, W. C. McGrew, F. B. M. de Waal, and P. G. Heltne (Eds.) *Chimpanzee Cultures*. Cambridge: Harvard University Press.

Mitani, J. C. and Marler, P. (1988). A phonological analysis of male gibbon singing behavior. *Behaviour* 109:20–45.

Payne, K. and Payne, R. (1985). Large scale changes over 19 years in songs of humpback whales in Bermuda. *Zeitschrift für Tierpsychologie* 68:89–114.

Payne, K., Tyack, P., and Payne, R. (1983). Progressive changes in the songs of humpback whales (*Megaptera novaeangliae*): A detailed analysis of two seasons in Hawaii. In R. Payne (Ed.) *Communication and Behavior of Whales* (pp. 9–57). Boulder, CO: Westview Press.

Premack, D. (1975). On the origins of language. In M. S. Gazzaniga and C. B. Blakemore (Eds.) *Handbook of Psychobiology* (pp. 591–605). New York: Academic Press.

Robinson, J. G. (1979). An analysis of the organization of vocal communication in the titi monkey *Callicebus moloch*. *Zeitschrift für Tierpsychologie* 49:381–405.

Robinson, J. G. (1984). Syntactic structures in the vocalizations of wedge-capped capuchin monkey, *Cebus nigrivittatus*. *Behaviour* 90:46–79.

Seyfarth, R. M. and Cheney, D. L. (1980). The ontogeny of vervet monkey alarm-calling behavior: A preliminary report. *Zeitschrift für Tierpsychologie* 54:37–56.

Seyfarth, R. M., Cheney, D. L., and Marler, P. (1980a). Monkey responses to three different alarm calls: Evidence of predator classification and semantic communication. *Science* 210:801–803.

Seyfarth, R. M., Cheney, D. L., and Marler, P. (1980b). Vervet monkey alarm calls: Semantic communication in a free-ranging primate. *Animal Behaviour* 28:1070–1094.

Snowdon, C. T. and Elowson, A. M. (1992). Ontogeny of primate vocal communication. In T. Nishida, F. B. M. de Waal, W. McGrew, P. Marler, and M. Pickford (Eds.) *Topics in Primatology*, Vol. 1, *Human Origins* (pp. 279–290). Tokyo: Tokyo University Press.

Struhsaker, T. T. (1967). Auditory communication among vervet monkeys (*Cercopithecus aethiops*). In S. A. Altmann (Ed.) *Social Communication Among Primates* (pp. 281–324). Chicago: Chicago University Press.

Tamura, N. and Young, H.-S. (1993). Vocalizations in response to predators in three species of Malaysian Callosciurus (*Sciuridae*). *Journal of Mammalogy* 74:703–714.

Tenaza, R. R. (1976). Songs and related behavior of Kloss' gibbons (*Hylobataes klossii*) in Siberut Island, Indonesia. *Zeitschrift für Tierpsychologie* 40:37–52.

Ujhelyi, M. (1996). Is there any intermediate stage between animal communication and language? *Journal of Theoretical Biology* 180:71–76.

Wallin, N. L. (1991). *Biomusicology: Neurophysiological, Neuropsychological and Evolutionary Perspectives on the Origins and Purposes of Music*. Stuyvesant, NY: Pendragon.

Walters, J. R. (1990). Anti-predator behavior of lapwings: Field evidence of discriminative abilities. *Wilson Bulletin* 102:49–70.

Peter J. B. Slater

Abstract
Song in birds is largely a male preserve, although females may sing also, especially in the tropics where some species exhibit complex duets. Song has two main functions: repelling rivals and attracting mates. Species with the most complex songs, in which individuals may have hundreds or even thousands of different phrases, appear to be those in which sexual selection leads females to choose mates with more elaborate songs. Even where repertoires are large, they tend, once learned, to be fixed, and little evidence exists for improvisation. Mimicry probably evolved as an alternative means to generate variety in song. Any similarity between birdsong and human music is by analogy, as vocal learning evolved quite separately in the two cases. As there are around 4,000 species of songbirds with a rich variety of vocal patterning, the occurrence of some with features also found in our music does not necessarily imply a deep similarity between the phenomena.

Birds are among the most vocal of animals and, given the rhythmicity, tonality, and variety of the sounds they produce, it is not surprising that many of these sounds have come to be labeled songs. Is this just by analogy with our own music, or can some real and useful parallels be drawn? In this chapter I start by reviewing how and why birds sing. I discuss examples of song repertoires in rather more detail, as the wonderful variety of some of these is perhaps what gives the closest link with music. In addition, I devote some attention to choruses and duets, as these phenomena are especially striking in this context. Finally, I make a few comments on the comparison between birdsong and music and whether it has anything useful to tell us.

The How and Why of Birdsong

Perhaps the first question to ask is why animals, like birds or humans, should use sound to transmit messages. Animals communicating with each other from a distance can use several different senses, but smell, sight, and sound are the most usual. Each sense has its advantages and disadvantages (Alcock 1989). Whereas many animals, including birds, display to each other with visual signals, such signals are mainly of use in short-range and private communication. They are of little use at night, or when objects intervene between signaler and receiver. Olfactory signals are excellent when persistence is required and, as with animals marking their territories, even operate when the signaler has moved on. Like sounds they can be detected at long range and spread round obstacles. But their very persistence raises a disadvantage in that it is difficult to change quickly from one message to another: they are thus not well adapted for the rapid transmission of complex sequences of information. By contrast, sound combines a number of features that make it ideal for many forms of communication. It travels fast by day and by night, it goes around obstacles, it can be detected at long range, and it can encode complex and changing messages. Given these features, it is not surprising that it is the medium adopted in our own language and music as well as in the song of birds.

Birds produce sounds in a different way from ourselves. Whereas we have a larynx high in the throat, the syrinx that birds use is much lower, at the point where ducts from the two lungs (bronchi) join to form the trachea. Most birds produce quite simple sounds, and their syrinx is similarly uncomplicated.

Most complex singers belong to a group known as the songbirds (order Passeriformes, suborder Oscines), which comprises nearly half the known bird species. In keeping with the sounds they produce, a defining feature of this group is that their syrinx is operated by five or more pairs of muscles, unlike the three or fewer in most other bird groups. The syrinx has two membranes, one on either side, and the sound produced depends on tension in them. Because there are two membranes, each with its own set of muscles, birds can produce two separate and harmonically unrelated sounds at the same time. Lips on each side of the syrinx can be opened or closed independently, and this also means that one side can produce a sound while the other is silent (Suthers, Goller, and Hartley 1994). A further complication is that resonances within the vocal tract, for long ignored, are now realized to influence the sound produced (Nowicki and Marler 1988). The exact workings of the syrinx are still a matter of controversy (see, for example, Goller and Larsen 1997), but there is no doubt that it is a superb musical instrument.

Birds make a variety of different sounds, the simpler of which are referred to as call notes. The word "song" tends to be applied only to longer and more complex vocalizations. Most of these are produced only by males and only in the breeding season, but this is not a hard and fast rule. Female European robins (*Erithacus rubecula*) sing in the winter (Lack 1946), and in the tropics the females of many species sing (Morton 1996). The male house sparrow (*Passer domesticus*) has no song in the sense of a long and complex sequence of sounds, but the "cheep cheep" he calls out from the rooftop may well serve the same function. Some songs are certainly very simple. Nevertheless, most of them are easily distinguished as the longest and most complex sounds of a species, and these are commonly produced only by males in the breeding season.

The fact that song is, in many species, a preserve of breeding males provides a clue as to its function. Considerable evidence shows that its role is in part to attract and stimulate females and in part to repel rival males from the territory of a singing bird (see Catchpole and Slater 1995 for a more extensive review). A number of lines of evidence point to its part in rival repulsion. At the start of the breeding season many male songbirds fight each other for territories. Neighbors also often have duels with song across territorial boundaries and, if the birds involved have repertoires of different song phrases, each tends to match the song of the other as they sing. A male red-winged blackbird (*Agelaius pheoniceus*) that cannot sing suffers more intrusions onto his territory by others than one that can (Smith 1979). If a male great tit (*Parus major*) is removed from his territory, it will be less rapidly invaded if recordings of the song of his species are played from loudspeakers (Krebs 1977). Experiments such as these provide the best evidence for song having a role as a "keep out" signal.

What of song's part in attracting females? Many male birds stop singing once they are mated (e.g., sedge warbler, *Acrocephalus schoenobaenus*; Catchpole 1973), and song increases enormously if a male loses his partner for any reason (e.g., great tit; Krebs, Avery, and Cowrie 1981). In several species, song attracts females (e.g., in European flycatchers, *Ficedula* sp; Eriksson and Wallin 1986), and in canaries (*Serinus canaria*) it increases nest-building behavior and boosts the growth of eggs in the ovaries (Kroodsma 1976). Female birds that are ready to mate show a particular display to the male, referred to as soliciting, during which they adopt a horizontal posture, spread their wings, and flutter their tail up and down. Perhaps no surprise, females do not normally show this display when song is played from a loudspeaker. However, those of a number of species do so if made highly receptive by treatment with the female sex hormone estrogen (Baker et al. 1987).

In some cases males have only a simple song that labels them as belonging to their species, and this seems to be adequate both to keep rivals out and to attract a mate. However, in other cases females are known to be most attracted by males with large repertoires, such as the sedge warbler (Catchpole 1980) and starling (*Sturnus vulgaris*; Eens, Pinxten, and Verheyen 1991a). If, for whatever reason, females prefer males with larger song repertoires, males with the most elaborate songs will be most successful or rapid in attracting a mate and therefore likely to have greater breeding success. This process of sexual selection is thought to be a prime reason why animals have large repertoires of different sounds. Here we have a distinct difference from language, because the message of each sound is the same: "I am a male sedge warbler in breeding condition." But the male that can say it in the most varied way is more attractive to females, and thus most likely to be successful in leaving his genes to the next generation. In such birds, unlike those with small repertoires, it is much less common for the same song to be repeated several times in a row, as the main message is variety itself (Slater 1981).

A crucial feature that songbirds have in common with humans is that learning plays an important role in their vocal development. In this they differ from their closest relatives, suboscines in the case of songbirds and primates in our own case, so that it is clear that vocal learning evolved quite separately in the two cases. Indeed it also appears to have evolved at least twice elsewhere among birds (parrots, hummingbirds) and three times among mammals (seals, whales and dolphins, bats; Janik and Slater 1997). Although vocal learning is a key feature in the evolution of sound communication, and of complex repertoires in particular, I will not discuss it further here. It is reviewed extensively elsewhere (Catchpole and Slater 1995; Slater 1989; Whaling, this volume).

Repertoires and Their Use

Repertoires have a wide range of sizes even among close relatives. Thrushes, for example, range from the European redwing (*Turdus iliacus*), which only has a single type, to the song thrush (*T. philomelos*) with its repertoire of over 200 (Ince and Slater 1985). Here we are talking about distinct songs, with little if any sharing of elements between them. However, some birds build up what sounds like a formidable repertoire from just a few elements assorted in all sorts of different ways. Catchpole (1976) suggested that a male sedge warbler, in the course of his life, may never repeat exactly the same sequence of elements twice. This is because the song is long, and the few dozen elements follow each other in highly varied orders. At one level (that of the song) his repertoire size is enormous, but at another (that of the element) it is not very large at all.

Of course, if a bird does not often sing the same song type twice it may be either because it has a huge repertoire of types or because it is improvising so that its repertoire is continuously changing. The latter may occur in some species, as suggested for the Sardinian warbler (*Sylvia melanocephala*; Luschi 1993), but it is certainly rare. In some other species, songs change more slowly from one part of the season to another or from one year to the next (e.g., thrush nightingale; Sorjonen 1987). When they appear to generate new songs much more rapidly than this, so that the same one is seldom repeated, it may be because a limited repertoire of elements is reassorted between songs. Jumbled and rambling though many birdsongs may seem to be, examination of sonograms reveals that they are in reality usually far from that; exactly the same elements or song phrases occur again and again, albeit perhaps in very different orders.

When a repertoire is large, it may be quite difficult to measure by looking through the bird's output and searching for repetitions (Kroodsma 1982). The brown thrasher (*Toxostoma rufum*) from North America is the best example here, and it is the current record holder for song repertoire size. As each bird has over 1,000 song types, arriving at its repertoire size is no easy matter, but Kroodsma and Parker (1977) solved the problem in an ingenious way by taking every hundredth song in a sample of 4,654, and looking to see if it recurred anywhere else in the whole sample. There were 45 different song types among the 46 examined, and they accounted for 116 of the songs in the whole sample. In other words they were repeated an average of 2.6 times each. The repertoire of the bird could therefore be estimated as 4,654/2.6 = 1,805.

To illustrate the diversity of singing birds, we will now consider six case histories, two birds with small repertoires and four with large ones.

Small Repertoires

Chaffinch

The way in which chaffinches (*Fringilla coelebs*) use their songs was studied particularly by Hinde (1958) and Slater (1983). Most chaffinches have two or three song types, although some have only one and others may have up to six. Each song type is fixed in form and consists of exactly the same sequence of syllable types every time it is produced, although syllables in the trill part of the song may be repeated a varied number of times. Two songs within the repertoire of a single bird can be quite similar, although with practice they can usually be distinguished by ear.

The chaffinch is typical of a species with a small repertoire that sings with what is called eventual variety. A male with more than one song type will sing a whole series of one type before switching to another. If he has three or four types, he will usually sing a sequence of each in turn before returning to the first again, although not necessarily always in the same order. It is also quite common for one song to be a much larger part of a bird's output than another. Indeed, a song type may be so rare that it puts in only an occasional appearance.

Whereas all these features may not be true of other species, it is certainly common for birds with small repertoires to sing with eventual, rather than immediate, variety, such as the great tit (Krebs 1976) and western meadowlark (*Sturnella neglecta*; Falls and Krebs 1975). Such redundancy is likely to function to ensure that each song gets through to the hearer and is fully received and understood. Singing in this pattern is likely to have evolved primarily in the context of male-male encounters, where song matching is a common phenomenon.

Grace's Warbler

Grace's warbler (*Dendroica graciae*), in the southwestern United States, also has a small repertoire of song types, but uses them in a different way from the chaffinch (Staicer 1989). One or two songs in a bird's repertoire are type A and are sung in long strings of the same type. They tend to be simple and stereotyped and are often shared between neighbors. This sort of singing behavior predominates before pairing and is thought to function primarily in interactions between the sexes. Type B songs are not sung in long sequences of the same type, but alternate with each other. They also tend to be more complex, are likely to be specific to a particular bird, and are mostly sung late in the season. Staicer suggests that this sort of singing is mainly in male-male interactions. The main difference between types A and B is more in singing behavior than in the songs themselves: one bird may use a song in type A singing that another uses in type B.

Similar singing behavior was described for the yellow warbler (*Dendroica petechia*; Spector 1991) and American redstart (*Setophaga ruticilla*; Lemon et al. 1985). In the latter, one song type, which Lemon et al. called its repeat song, is sung in long bouts (AAAAA), and the others, its serial songs, are sung with immediate variety (BCDECBCE). They too suggest that repeat singing functions between the sexes, whereas serial singing is used as a signal between males, albeit without the redundancy usually found in this context.

The notion that different song types, or forms of singing behavior, function in different ways has been proposed for a number of other species. Many American warblers have two types of songs that occur in rather different circumstances. The so-called accented song has a distinctive stress on its last element and is produced largely in the presence of females, whereas the unaccented song occurs mostly in male-male encounters. Cases such as these, where song types differ in meaning, are, however, comparatively rare. In most species, all types convey the same message and are exactly equivalent to one another, as is the case in the chaffinch.

Large Repertoires

Nightingale

The song of the European nightingale (*Luscinia megarhynchos*) was studied extensively by Todt and Hultsch (1996). Each song type that a bird has occurs in identical form whenever it is sung, except that a particular element may be repeated a variable number of times. However, the nightingale has a large repertoire that may include over 200 song types. These fall into small groups, or packages, that tend to be sung close together (Hultsch and Todt 1989). Thus a bird may start off ABCDEF and perhaps half an hour later it might sing BEDF. There is always immediate variety: the same song is not repeated twice. The order within a package is not necessarily identical, however, nor is the sequence as the bird moves from one package to another. Every song is not sung each time the bird cycles through its repertoire. Thus, in the example above, song types A and C are omitted the second time round and will not occur again until the next time that package crops up. In a bird with 200 types it may be common for songs to show a recurrence interval of around 100 types, about half the songs being omitted during each passage through the repertoire.

The songs of the nightingale may appear to be rather fixed in sequence, falling into groups and the same ones often occurring close to each other, but they are in fact highly varied. Once a song has been sung it is seldom repeated for some time. If impressing potential mates is what it is all about, a female nightingale would need a very good memory to recall having heard a particular phrase before!

Sedge Warbler

The sedge warbler is a good example of a species in which elements can be reassorted to make many different song types. Here successive songs consist of different combinations of elements and elements are recombined continuously, so that there is no fixed repertoire of types. Songs produced in flight are even more complicated, but Catchpole (1976) limited himself to describing the features of those sung by perched males.

Each bird has a repertoire of about fifty different element types. A song is typically around one minute in length and consists of over 300 elements. It starts with a long section in which short series of two elements alternate with each other. There is then a sudden switch to a louder, more rapid, and complex central section in which five to ten new elements are introduced in quick succession. In the last part of the song the patterning is similar to that at the start, except that the two elements are selected from among those that occurred in the central section. These same two elements are typically those that are employed at the start of the next song.

Because it is long and has this varied patterning, the song of the sedge warbler is extremely complex. Although it involves a relatively small number of elements, "the probability of a song type ever being exactly repeated seems remote" (Catchpole 1976). The sedge warbler thus achieves variety in a different way than the nightingale: it has a limited number of elements that it reassorts in particular ways to achieve an apparently endless repertoire.

Starling

Starlings are well known for their long and complex songs, and for the mimicry of other species that occurs within them. But, what at first may seem to be a random outpouring is in fact highly organized (Eens, Pinxten, and Verheyen 1989, 1991b). A bout of singing lasts an average of twenty-five seconds and consists of a sequence of phrases or song types with very short intervals (mostly less than 0.1 second) between them. Each phrase tends to be repeated several times before the bird moves on to the next. Repertoire size varies: among twenty-seven males it ranged from twenty-one to sixty-seven song types (Eens, Pinxten, and Verheyen 1991b).

The order of song types within a bout of singing is relatively fixed. Types fall into four broad categories, which also tend to occur at particular points in the sequence:

1. The bout normally starts with a number of whistles, each male having a repertoire of seven to twelve (Hausberger and Guyomarc'h 1981).

2. The second section consists of a series of variable and complex phrases including cases of mimicry; each male has fifteen to twenty different imitations in his repertoire (Hindmarsh 1984).

3. The third part of the bout consists of rattle song types. These phrases include a rapid succession of clicks sounding like a rattle, and each male has a repertoire of two to fourteen of them.

4. Most song bouts that are not interrupted earlier end with some loud, high-frequency song types; a male may have up to six of these.

Again, as with the nightingale, starling song may seem endlessly varied to the ear, but closer analysis reveals that each male has a limited repertoire of types and that these are ordered according to quite well-specified rules.

Marsh Warbler

Most birds learn only the song of their own species. The fact that they are reared by, and normally imprint upon and develop social relations with, members of that species is one reason for this. But some species, of which the starling is one, usually include imitations within their song. Given the rarity of improvisation among birds, the best guess is that this is a way in which males can enhance the variety, and hence the attractiveness, of their songs.

One of the most remarkable cases of mimicry, which forms a good case study, is that of the European marsh warbler (*Acrocephalus palustris*) studied by Dowsett-Lemaire (1979). This species breeds in Europe and migrates to East Africa. Young birds are thought to learn their song entirely in the first few months of life. They cannot base it on other members of their own species, as adult males cease to sing before their chicks hatch. Instead, Dowsett-Lemaire estimated that each young male copies the sounds of many other species, on average seventy-seven, including those that they hear in Africa as well as in Europe. Many of the incorporated sounds are call notes, and the major limitation to what is copied seems to be whether the syrinx of a small bird such as a marsh warbler can cope with the sound. The absence of deep sounds is not surprising. The song may well be built up entirely by mimicry but this is uncertain: in such a widely traveled species, some sounds included of unknown origin may well be derived from other species that have not been identified.

Mimicry thus enables a male marsh warbler to build up a wonderfully elaborate song before it hears any members of its own species singing. It might be imagined that this would lead to some confusion as far as species identity is concerned. However, apart from the fact that many of the birds imitated do not nest in Europe, the patterning of the song also has a distinctive marsh warbler stamp on it.

Choruses and Duets

Communal singing is especially prevalent among humans, with groups of people often singing or chanting in synchrony with one another (see Merker, Richman, Nettl, and Mâche, this volume). Similar phenomena in birds may therefore give some insight into the origins and functions of human music; however, such similarities as exist are not particularly close. Some birds, such as the Australian magpie (*Gymnorhina tibicen*; Brown, Farabaugh, and Veltman 1988) sing in choruses, but the sounds of different birds within the chorus have no clear and organized relations. The same is true of the dawn chorus, in which individuals of many different species join together to produce a tremendous burst of sound (Staicer, Spector, and Horn 1996). There is no doubt that these choruses are partly due to the fact that animals stimulate each other into sound production, but the sounds are not clearly synchronized with each other. Tightly coordinated, simultaneous singing of the same song, so frequent in human music, is not a phenomenon that appears to occur elsewhere in nature.

Duetting is a different matter: here two birds contribute to a song, often in a tightly coordinated fashion. Some duets have phenomenal precision of timing. Indeed, whereas bouts may overlap, the sounds themselves may not do so, the birds fitting their sounds together so precisely that it is hard to believe that more than one individual is involved. This form of duetting, in which male and female use different notes and sing alternately, is known as antiphonal singing (Hooker and Hooker 1969) and has been documented in a wide variety of species from African shrikes (Thorpe 1972) to Australian whipbirds (Watson 1969).

Duetting is most common in the tropics, and this probably relates to the fact that birds there frequently hold year-round territories (Farabaugh 1982). This in turn is associated with birds that form long-term monogamous pair bonds. One other association often claimed is that between duetting and sexual monomorphism, and although Farabaugh (1982) failed to find this, she said that that could be because her definition of duetting was a rather undemanding one. It is certainly striking that many species with tight antiphonal duets that have been studied are monomorphic.

Duetting may have a role in maintaining the long-term pair bond and in keeping contact between members of a pair, especially in the dense and noisy environment of a species-rich tropical forest (Hooker and Hooker 1969). However, evidence on these matters is equivocal (Todt and Hultsch 1982; Wickler 1976). Wickler (1976) maintains that, in addition to possible roles within the pair, duetting is primarily a signal used in cooperative territory guarding.

The idea that duetting pairs are jointly defending their territories raises the question of why this evolved in certain species but not in others in which only the male sings. The answer must lie in detailed field studies of the species concerned, and few of these have been conducted to date. One study on bay wrens (*Thyothorus nigricapillus*) in Panama suggests an intriguing answer (Levin 1996a, b). In many duets, one bird sings an initial section that is followed by a reply from the other. It has often been assumed that the duet is initiated by the male, with the reply being the contribution of the female. However Levin showed that this is not so in bay wrens. Although these birds are monomorphic, she examined them using a technique called laparotomy and found that the individuals leading the duets were female. She suggests that duetting in these birds may have originated because, for some reason, females are the more territorial sex. They therefore sing just like female European robins in winter to defend their territories and attract prospective mates. However, bay wrens are monogamous, and once a female has attracted a male, he deters others by adding a coda to her song. She thus keeps females out of their territory while he puts off other males.

This idea for different roles of the sexes in duetting species is an ingenious one and may also apply to other species. Despite the fact that the phenomenon has been extensively documented, few studies in the field went beyond the stage of observation and description, and the subject of duetting calls for more experimental work. As yet, any possible link between this aspect of birdsong and coordinated singing in humans would be decidedly tenuous!

Birdsong and Music

Might our understanding of birdsong help to shed light on the origins of human music? The first point is that any similarity is more likely to be by analogy than homology because humans shared a musical ancestor with other singing animals. Our closest living relatives, the great apes, communicate more by gesture and by facial expression than by sound. They do have loud vocal displays, such as the pant-hoot of chimpanzees (*Pan troglodytes*), but these are far from elaborate or musical. Further-more, little evidence exists that any monkey or nonhuman ape learns sounds that it produces from other individuals (Janik and Slater 1997). Humans obviously do so, and this is also the way in which whales and songbirds, the most notable singers elsewhere in the animal kingdom, obtain their sounds. Indeed, learning seems essential to build up large repertoires. For some reason, therefore, elaborate singing behavior arose quite separately in different animal groups, and in our case this was in the relatively recent past, since the common ancestor that we shared with chimpanzees died about two million years ago.

Straight comparison may not be justified, but does analogy with birds help to suggest why singing and other musical attributes in humans may have arisen? With any complex or varied display, sexual selection is a prime suspect, and the fact that in many cultures singing (and in our own culture, composition) is predominantly a feature of young males (see Miller, this volume) confirms that suspicion. However, why singing behavior should have been favored in early humans in particular rather than in other species remains a matter of speculation. The singing of humans also has some features, such as the simultaneous chanting of the same tune by groups of individuals (see Nettl and Merker, this volume), that have not been described among animals.

Do birds produce music? This is not an easy question to answer, partly because no definition of music seems to be universally agreed upon. Many animal sounds are rhythmic, such as the trill of a stridulating grasshopper. Others are pure and tonal, such as whistles common in bird-songs. Energy efficiency alone might predict these features. A regular rhythm is shown by a mechanism operating at its resonant frequency, and this is where energy cost is least. Concentrating all the energy in a narrow frequency band to produce fairly pure sounds is also economi-cal as the sounds carry further. But rhythmical and tonal sounds may have arisen in the animal kingdom for other good reasons. For most animal signals, and especially those concerned with attracting mates and repelling rivals, it is essential that the signal incorporate species identity. Some areas of the world, notably tropical rainforest, may contain literally hundreds of different bird species in a small area. To stand out against both this cacophony of sound and other environmental noises, and to be distinctive, may impose features such as tone and rhythm as each species homes in on its own broadcasting bandwidth. Complex patterns of songs and species differences in the rules that underlie them may also have their origins in the need for distinctiveness.

But is this musicality? It is not difficult to find examples in animal song of complex features that we would also attribute to music. In addition to choruses and duets, some birds sing in near perfect scales (e.g., musician wren, *Cyphorhinus aradus*) and other features of our own music can also be illustrated with examples from the animal kingdom (see Payne and Mâche, this volume). But caution is required here. Considering only songbirds (oscine passerines), there are close to 4,000 species in the world, and all of them are thought to learn their songs. The variety in the form and patterning of these songs is impressive, and it is likely that many possible patterns remain unexplored given this huge array of species. It would thus not be surprising if almost any characteristic found in human music were discovered in one or a few of them. But such similarities are likely to be coincidental, and certainly due to convergence rather than because features of music arose in a common ancestor. Nevertheless, although animals may not share music in the strict sense with us, there is no doubt that some of them do have complex and beautiful vocal displays. Understanding the reasons why they evolved may help to shed light on why only we among the primates have gone along a similar pathway.

One final point is worth making. It is suggested from time to time that the songs of some birds that seem to us especially beautiful may be more so than is strictly necessary for their biological function (Thorpe 1961; Boswall 1983). Could this indicate some primitive aesthetic sense, and that the bird is taking pleasure in song for its own sake? Candidates would be songs of the song thrush in Europe, the superb lyrebird (*Menura novaehollandiae*; Robinson and Curtis 1996) in Australia, and the mockingbird (*Mimus polyglottos*; Wildenthal 1965) in North America, all of which have large, varied, and beautiful repertoires. The difficulty with such ideas is how to test them. Sexual selection is an open-ended process that will lead to larger and larger song repertoires until other constraints, such as storage space in the brain, set limits. Where it is responsible, it is unlikely that song could be more elaborate than it demanded. On the other hand, there is nothing incompatible between this and either aesthetics or the enjoyment of song; indeed, sexual selection is likely to have been the basis for its evolution in humans. But this is where the testability problem comes in. We personally feel enjoyment in hearing or performing music, and we know that other humans do too, as we can ask them about it and discuss their feelings with them. When it comes to animals, however, we have no access to their inner feelings, so that the question can only be a matter of speculation (Slater in press).

Acknowledgments

This chapter is based in part on ideas about song repertoires and about the relationship between animal sounds and music that I developed elsewhere (e.g., chapter 8 in Catchpole and Slater 1995; Slater in press). However, it also gained enormously from the novel interdisciplinary perspective provided by the first Florentine Workshop in Biomusicology. I am very grateful to the Institute of Biomusicology for arranging this, and to Nils Wallin and Björn Merker in particular for inviting me to it.

References

Alcock, J. (1989). *Animal Behaviour: An Evolutionary Approach.* Sunderland, MA: Sinauer.

Baker, M. C., Bjerke, T. K., Lampe, H. U., and Espmark, Y. O. (1987). Sexual response of female yellowhammers to differences in regional song dialects and repertoire sizes. *Animal Behaviour* 35:395–401.

Boswall, J. (1983). The language of birds. *Proceedings of the Royal Institution* 55:249–303.

Brown, E. D., Farabaugh, S. M., and Veltman, C. J. (1988). Song sharing in a group-living songbird, the Australian magpie, *Gymnorhina tibicen.* I: Vocal sharing within and among social groups. *Behaviour* 104:1–28.

Catchpole, C. K. (1973). The functions of advertising song in the sedge warbler (*Acrocephalus schoenobaenus*) and reed warbler (*A. scirpaceus*). *Behaviour* 46:300–320.

Catchpole, C. K. (1976). Temporal and sequential organisation of song in the sedge warbler (*Acrocephalus schoenobaenus*). *Behaviour* 59:226–246.

Catchpole, C. K. (1980). Sexual selection and the evolution of complex songs among warblers of the genus *Acrocephalus. Behaviour* 74:149–166.

Catchpole, C. K. and Slater, P. J. B. (1995). *Bird Song: Biological Themes and Variations.* Cambridge, UK: Cambridge University Press.

Dowsett-Lemaire, F. (1979). The imitative range of the song of the marsh warbler *Acrocephalus palustris,* with special reference to imitations of African birds. *Ibis* 121:453–468.

Eens, M., Pinxten, R., and Verheyen, R. F. (1989). Temporal and sequential organisation of song bouts in the starling. *Ardea* 77:75–86.

Eens, M., Pinxten, R., and Verheyen, R. F. (1991a). Male song as a cue for mate choice in the European starling. *Behaviour* 116:210–238.

Eens, M., Pinxten, R., and Verheyen, R. F. (1991b). Organisation of song in the European starling: Species specificity and individual differences. *Belgian Journal of Zoology* 121:257–278.

Eriksson, D. and Wallin, L. (1986). Male bird song attracts females: A field experiment. *Behavioral Ecology and Sociobiology* 19:297–299.

Falls, J. B. and Krebs, J. R. (1975). Sequence of songs in repertoires of western meadowlarks (*Sturnella neglecta*). *Canadian Journal of Zoology* 53:1165–1178.

Farabaugh, S. M. (1982). The ecological and social significance of duetting. In D. E. Kroodsma and E. H. Miller (Eds.) *Acoustic Communication in Birds* (pp. 85–124). New York: Academic Press.

Goller, F. and Larsen, O. N. (1997). *In situ* biomechanics of the syrinx and sound generation in pigeons. *Journal of Experimental Biology* 200:2165–2176.

Hausberger, M. and Guyomarc'h, J.-C. (1981). Contribution à l'étude des vocalisations territoriales sifflées chez l'étourneau sansonnet *Sturnus vulgaris* en Bretagne. *Biology of Behaviour* 6:79–98.

Hinde, R. A. (1958). Alternative motor patterns in chaffinch song. *Animal Behaviour* 6:211–218.

Hindmarsh, A. M. (1984). Vocal mimicry in starlings. *Behaviour* 90:302–324.

Hooker, T. and Hooker, B. I. (1969). Duetting. In R. A. Hinde (Ed.) *Bird Vocalizations* (pp. 185–205). Cambridge, UK: Cambridge University Press.

Hultsch, H. and Todt, D. (1989). Memorization and reproduction of songs in nightingales: Evidence for package formation. *Journal of Comparative Physiology Series A* 165:197–203.

Ince, S. A. and Slater, P. J. B. (1985). Versatility and continuity in the songs of thrushes *Turdus* spp. *Ibis* 127:355–364.

Janik, V. M. and Slater, P. J. B. (1997). Vocal learning in mammals. *Advances in the Study of Behavior* 26:59–99.

Krebs, J. R. (1976). Habituation and song repertoires in the great tit. *Behavioral Ecology and Sociobiology* 1:215–227.

Krebs, J. R. (1977). Song and territory in the great tit *Parus major*. In B. Stonehouse and C. Perrins (Eds.) *Evolutionary Ecology* (pp. 47–62). London: Macmillan.

Krebs, J. R., Avery, M., and Cowie, R. J. (1981). Effect of removal of mate on the singing behaviour of great tits. *Animal Behaviour* 29:635–637.

Kroodsma, D. E. (1976). Reproductive development in a female songbird: Differential stimulation by quality of male song. *Science* 192:574–575.

Kroodsma, D. E. (1982). Song repertoires: Problems in their definition and use. In D. E. Kroodsma and E. H. Miller (Eds.) *Acoustic Communication in Birds* (pp. 125–146). New York: Academic Press.

Kroodsma, D. E. and Parker, L. D. (1977). Vocal virtuosity in the brown thrasher. *Auk* 94:783–785.

Lack, D. (1946). *The Life of the Robin*. London: Witherby.

Lemon, R. E., Cotter, R., MacNally, R. C., and Monette, S. (1985). Song repertoires and song sharing by American redstarts. *Condor* 87:457–470.

Levin, R. N. (1996a). Song behaviour and reproductive strategies in a duetting wren, *Thryothorus nigricapillus*. I: Playback experiments. *Animal Behaviour* 52:1107–1117.

Levin, R. N. (1996b). Song behaviour and reproductive strategies in a duetting wren, *Thryothorus nigricapillus*. I: Removal experiments. *Animal Behaviour* 52:1093–1106.

Luschi, P. (1993). Improvisation of new notes during singing by male Sardinian warblers. *Bioacoustics* 4:235–244.

Morton, E. S. (1996). A comparison of vocal behavior among tropical and temperate passerine birds. In D. E. Kroodsma and E. H. Miller (Eds.) *Ecology and Evolution of Acoustic Communication in Birds* (pp. 258–268). Ithaca, NU, and London: Comstock.

Nowicki, S. and Marler, P. (1988). How do birds sing? *Music Perception* 5:391–426.

Robinson, F. N. and Curtis, H. S. (1996). The vocal displays of lyrebirds Menuridae. *Emu* 96:258–275.

Slater, P. J. B. (1981). Chaffinch song repertoires: Observations, experiments and a discussion of their significance. *Zeitschrift für Tierpsychologie* 56:1–24.

Slater, P. J. B. (1983). Sequences of song in chaffinches. *Animal Behaviour* 31:272–281.

Slater, P. J. B. (1989). Bird song learning: Causes and consequences. *Ethology, Ecology and Evolution* 1:19–46.

Slater, P. J. B. (In press). Animal music. In S. Sadie (Ed.) *The New Grove Dictionary of Music and Musicians*. London: Macmillan.

Smith, D. G. (1979). Male singing ability and territory integrity in red-winged blackbirds (*Agelaius phoeniceus*). *Behaviour* 68:193–206.

Sorjonen, J. (1987). Temporal and spatial differences in traditions and repertoires in the song of the thrush nightingale (*Luscinia luscinia*). *Behaviour* 102:196–212.

Spector, D. A. (1991). The singing behavior of yellow warblers. *Behaviour* 117:29–52.

Staicer, C. A. (1989). Characteristics, use, and significance of two singing behaviors in Grace's warbler. *Auk* 106:49–63.

Staicer, C. A., Spector, D. A., and Horn, A. G. (1996). The dawn chorus and other diel patterns in acoustic signalling. In D. E. Kroodsma and E. H. Miller (Eds.) *Ecology and Evolution of Acoustic Communication in Birds* (pp. 426–453). Ithaca, NU, and London: Comstock.

Suthers, R. A., Goller, F., and Hartley, R. S. (1994). Motor dynamics of sound production in mimic thrushes. *Journal of Neurobiology* 25:917–936.

Thorpe, W. H. (1961). *Bird Song*. Cambridge, UK: Cambridge University Press.

Thorpe, W. H. (1972). Duetting and antiphonal song in birds: Its extent and significance. *Behaviour Supplement* 18:1–197.

Todt, D. and Hultsch, H. (1982). Impairment of vocal signal exchange in the monogamous duet-singer *Cossypha heuglini* (Turdidae): Effects on pair bond maintenance. *Zeitschrift für Tierpsychologie* 60:265–274.

Todt, D. and Hultsch, H. (1996). Acquisition and performance of song repertoires: Ways of coping with diversity and versatility. In D. E. Kroodsma and E. H. Miller (Eds.) *Ecology and Evolution of Acoustic Communication in Birds* (pp. 79–96). Ithaca, NU: Comstock.

Watson, M. (1969). Significance of antiphonal song in the eastern whipbird *Psophodes olivaceus*. *Behaviour* 35:157–178.

Wickler, W. (1976). Duetting songs in birds: Biological significance of stationary and non-stationary processes. *Journal of Theoretical Biology* 61:493–497.

Wildenthal, J. L. (1965). Structure in primary song of the mockingbird (*Mimus polyglottos*). *Auk* 82:161–189.

What's Behind a Song? The Neural Basis of Song Learning in Birds

Carol Whaling

Abstract

Songbirds must learn to sing. Vocal learning involves several different processes, including selection of an appropriate song to serve as a model, memorization of the model, and retrieval of the model to direct development of adult song. To learn to sing, many species must hear song during a sensitive period early in development. Birds deprived of this experience sing abnormal songs that are not improved by exposure to song later in life. Selection of a song to serve as a model for learning is guided by instinct. When young birds raised in captivity are played tape recordings of their own species' songs as well as those of other species, they choose to learn the ones of their own species, demonstrating innate ability to recognize these songs.

Studies of the neuroanatomy of songbirds have uncovered neural circuits involved in song learning, production, and perception. I review aspects of the development and the organization of these brain regions in relationship to song learning to address the neural basis of sensitive periods and learning preferences. The knowledge we have gleaned from these studies may provide a new perspective from which to approach studies of human music acquisition.

Calls and songs of birds are an almost inescapable part of our surroundings, and reveal how essential vocalizations are in the life of birds. Simple vocalizations, referred to as calls, often function to maintain contact among a flock, or alert others to danger or to a potential food source. Songs, longer and more complex than calls, are used to identify individuals, establish and defend territory boundaries, attract mates, and even stimulate the reproductive tract and reproductive behavior of one's mate.

Learning plays an important role in the development of song. All species of songbirds that have been studied to date must learn to sing (Kroodsma and Baylis 1982). Since songbirds make up almost half of the existing 9,000 avian species, song learning is presumably widespread. It also is in other branches of the avian family tree including parrots and their relatives (Todt 1975; Farabaugh, Brown, and Dooling 1992) and hummingbirds (Baptista and Schuchmann 1990). Birds with simple vocalizations, however, such as chickens and doves, do not have to learn their calls (Konishi 1963; Nottebohm and Nottebohm 1971).

To test whether learning is required for normal song production, birds are raised in captivity without an opportunity to hear other members of their species. Chickens raised in such acoustic isolation still sound like chickens, whereas songbirds sing abnormal, simple songs, called isolate songs (Marler 1970; Marler and Sherman 1985; figure 5.1). This dependence on learning by many avian species is surprising considering that even our closest relatives, monkeys and apes, do not have to learn

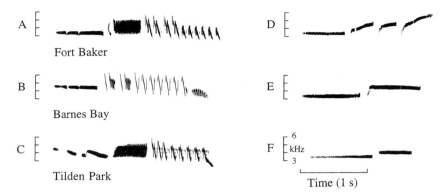

A   Fort Baker

B   Barnes Bay

C   Tilden Park

D

E

F   6 kHz 3

Time (1 s)

Figure 5.1
Sound spectrograms of normal and isolate white-crowned sparrow songs. A–C are normal songs of three males singing different white-crowned sparrow dialects (noted under each spectrogram). D–F are isolate songs of three males raised in captivity and prevented from hearing white-crowned sparrow song during the sensitive period for song learning.

vocalizations characteristic of their species. In this regard songbirds share a niche with humans, whales, and dolphins.

The role of learning in song production has made songbirds important subjects in research on both the neurobiology of learning (Konishi 1994; Nottebohm 1991) and the process of vocal learning (Kroodsma 1996; Marler 1987) with an eye toward parallels with language acquisition in humans. It is my hope that by reviewing knowledge of birdsong learning, we may have another angle from which to approach our inquiry into the way that people acquire knowledge of music. An important idea to emerge from the study of birdsong is that this process is shaped by preferences and constraints. I will organize my discussion around two such constraints: song learning is often restricted to one period during development or to one time of year; and the learning preference influences selection of an appropriate model to imitate. In other words, a what and when are imposed on song learning, the details of which vary across avian species.

Avian song learning occurs in two stages: first, songs must be memorized and, second, they must be practiced. In some species these two events overlap (zebra finches, *Taeniopygia guttata*; Immelmann 1969), but in others memorization can precede practice by several months, providing an impressive example of long-term memory storage (swamp sparrows, *Melospiza georgiana*; Marler and Peters 1982). The young bird's initial efforts to reproduce the memorized song are usually not successful. These early songs may have faltering pitch, irregular tempo, and notes that are out of order or poorly reproduced. However, sonograms of songs recorded over several weeks or months reveal that during this practice period the bird fine-tunes his efforts until he produces an accurate copy of the memorized template. This process requires hearing oneself sing; birds are unable to reproduce memorized songs if they are deafened after memorization but before the practice period (Konishi 1965).

Sensitive Periods for Song Learning

In many species, referred to as closed-ended learners, song memorization occurs during a restricted period of development, often within the first few months after hatching. This sensitive period has been demonstrated in the laboratory by presenting young birds with a series of taperecorded songs drawn from the dialects of their own species. By replacing each song with a new variant after a limited period of time (on the order of ten days or two weeks), it is possible, with time and patience, to determine the age at which memorization occurred by matching the bird's adult song to the library of songs presented (Marler and Peters 1987; Nelson, Marler, and Palleroni 1995). In other species, referred to as open-ended learners, song learning reoccurs each year. For example, the repertoires of starlings (*Sturnus vulgaris*; Eens, Pinxten, and Verheyen 1992) and canaries (*Serinus canaria*; Nottebohm and Nottebohm 1978) increase or change from year to year.

Variation across species with respect to when songs are learned raises several interesting questions: what determines the length of the sensitive period for song learning? why do some species learn songs during a short period in development whereas others continue to expand their repertoires in adulthood? do changes take place in the brains of closed-ended learners to prevent further learning?

The length of the sensitive period appears to be regulated by both external and internal factors. Young birds deprived of an opportunity to hear song will memorize at a later age than those that were tutored as fledglings, indicating delayed closure of the sensitive period (Kroodsma and Pickert 1980; Slater, Jones, and TenCate 1993). However, closure cannot be delayed indefinitely. Birds prevented from hearing the songs of their own species throughout this period will produce abnormal songs, as shown in figure 5.1. Once the bird begins to practice an abnormal song, subsequent tutoring will not improve it, indicating that irreversible changes have occurred in the brain.

The Neurobiology of Sensitive Periods

If a bird is able to learn to sing at one age but not another, we must conclude that some change occurs in the brain between these two time points. It should be possible, if we knew where to look, to find neural changes that correspond to the duration of the sensitive period. Songbirds have a specialized network of neurons in their brains dedicated to song learning and production (Nottebohm, Stokes, and Leonard 1976). The cell bodies of these neurons are organized into a series of clusters referred to as *song control nuclei*. The axons of these neurons project to adjacent song control nuclei to form synaptic connections. Lesion studies, electrophysiological recordings, and histological studies reveal that these nuclei form two circuits, an anterior forebrain pathway involved in song learning, and a posterior motor pathway involved in song production (reviewed by Brenowitz and Kroodsma 1996).

Nuclei of the anterior forebrain pathway undergo several changes during the period of song learning. Studies of zebra finches and canaries reveal that new neurons are added to the nucleus referred to as the higher vocal center (HVC), suggesting that these new neurons may encode new memories acquired by listening to the songs of others (Sohrabji, Nordeen, and Nordeen 1993; Kirn et al. 1994). This observation suggests that learning ceases when neurogenesis is complete (Nottebohm 1981). In other areas of the anterior forebrain pathway, connections between nuclei appear to decrease during song learning by reducing the number of synapses (Herrmann and Arnold 1991), decreasing the number of receptors for chemicals used to communicate across the synapse (NMDA receptors; Aamodt et al. 1992), or decreasing the number of dendritic spines where synapses are formed (Wallhausser-Franke, Nisdorf-Bergweiler, and DeVoogd 1995). These observations indicate a different mechanism from the one mentioned above; namely, learning involves simplifying connectivity between neurons (Changeux and Danchin 1976). This model suggests that unused synapses are eliminated during song learning, thus paring down the initial network of connections. Further learning would not be possible once synapse selection was complete. A similar model was proposed for imprinting in chickens (Wallhausser and Scheich 1987).

Before we can begin to understand the neural basis of song learning and regulation of the sensitive period, we must distinguish changes in the brain that are a consequence of maturation from those that are functionally related to learning, regardless of age. The critical question is whether the neural changes described above would be observed if birds were prevented from learning to sing. This experiment was done in two ways. One method compared the neural development of deafened and hearing birds of the same age (Aamodt, Nordeen, and Nordeen 1995; Burek, Nordeen, and Nordeen 1991). The other compared the brains of tutored birds that had begun practicing song with those of song-deprived birds of the same age that had not begun to sing (Wallhausser-Franke,

Nisdorf-Bergweiler, and DeVoogd 1995). Both studies uncovered few differences in the brains of control and experimental groups, indicating that most neural changes are likely to be developmental rather than a cause or consequence of song learning. However, one effect that did persist between tutored and untutored zebra finches was the number of dendritic spines in a region of the anterior forebrain loop (LMAN; Wallhauser-Franke, Nisdorf-Bergweiler, and DeVoogd 1995). The number of dendritic spines was significantly smaller in birds that had learned to sing, supporting the idea proposed by Changeux and Danchin (1976) that learning may involve pruning unused connections between neurons.

Innate Preferences Guide Song Learning

The second learning constraint is the predisposition to learn songs of one's own species (Thorpe 1958; Marler 1970; Marler and Peters 1977). With the exception of mimics such as starlings and mockingbirds (*Mimus polyglottos*), most birds, when given a choice, prefer to learn the songs of their own species. Vocal learning was studied in the laboratory with sparrows collected as nestlings before they had an opportunity to learn songs. The birds learned readily from taperecordings during the sensitive period that extends from one to four months of age. Work with sparrows and other species uncovered an interesting paradox: young birds must hear the songs of their own species in order to learn them, but when faced with a potentially confusing array of songs, they are able to select the ones of their own species to serve as learning templates.

Young birds raised by their parents in the wild presumably hear a range of sounds, including songs of other species that inhabit the same geographic range. One might assume that they decide which sounds to memorize by observing their parents (most likely their fathers) singing. However, laboratory experiments with tutor tapes in which social cues are not available produce the same outcome. Another possibility is that the size and structure of the vocal tract limits the type of sounds that can be produced, predisposing the bird to learn the correct song. Clearly some anatomical restrictions come into play in the sense that it would be impossible for a hummingbird to produce the call of a crow. However, birds can be induced to learn the songs of other species if they are prevented from hearing the ones of their own, establishing that anatomy of the vocal tract does not dictate learning preferences (Marler 1991). In conclusion, laboratory studies that remove social cues and provide learnable songs, including those of other species, reveal a learning bias that is guided by instinct.

This innate contribution to vocal learning raises some interesting questions: by what criteria does the naive bird select a song to memorize? does a specific note or phrase act as a flag, allowing the bird to recognize the song? or do tonal or temporal qualities of the whole song provide the necessary cues? what is the neural basis for this type of guided learning? One can imagine circuits in the brain that act as feature detectors and, when stimulated in an appropriate combination, cause the song to be selected as a model for vocal learning.

Working with Jill Soha in Peter Marler's laboratory at the University of California, Davis, and in collaboration with Allison Doupe at the University of California, San Francisco, we approached innate song recognition using two complementary techniques to study both brain and behavior of fledgling white-crowned sparrows (*Zonotrichia leucophyrus*). The behavioral test is simple to perform (Nelson and Marler 1993). Fledgling sparrows are housed alone in soundproof boxes that are outfitted with a speaker and a microphone. Once an hour they hear ten repetitions of a taperecording of normal white-crowned sparrow song, the song of another species (song sparrow, *Melospiza melodia* or savannah sparrow, *Passerculus sandwichensis*), or a white-crowned sparrow song that has been experimentally altered. When fledglings hear normal white-crowned sparrow song, they give a series of begging calls that, under natural conditions, help their parents locate them for feeding. The songs of other species usually elicit no vocal response. Thus, by counting the number of begging calls given in response to our altered white-crowned sparrow songs, we can learn whether the fledglings perceive them to be acceptable renditions of white-crown song or to be of a foreign species.

We used this behavior test to compare responses to normal white-crowned sparrow song with responses to isolate white-crowned sparrow song, the simple song produced by white-crowns that have not heard other white-crowns sing. The isolate song consisted of a series of whistles and lacked the trills and buzzes typical of normal song. The isolate song was as effective as the normal song in eliciting begging calls from fledglings. One hypothesis to explain the efficacy of isolate song is that the whistle, universal to all white-crown dialects, acts as a marker for recognition. We tested this hypothesis using songs artificially constructed by repeating a single white-crowned sparrow phrase such as a whistle, buzz, or trill, while maintaining normal song duration and tempo. If the whistle acts as the critical flag for identifying the white-crowned song, we predicted that it would elicit as strong a response as the normal song, and the trill or buzz would be comparatively weaker.

All of the repeated phrase songs, including buzz and trill songs, proved to be as effective as the normal song in eliciting calls from the fledglings.

This indicates that all of the phrase types we tested, not just whistles, can be recognized by naive fledglings, even though the phrases are divorced from normal syntax (Whaling et al. 1997). Although avian vocal signals are greatly simplified compared with human language, these results parallel findings of studies of language recognition in human infants. Human infants can recognize the phonemes of all human languages, providing them with the capacity to learn any language. They are even able to discriminate phonemes not used in their local language, although this sensitivity disappears once they begin to speak (Eimas, Miller, and Jusczyk 1987; Kuhl 1995).

It is possible that, rather than relying on note structure, young birds use tonal or temporal qualities to identify songs of their own species. We have begun to test songs that are altered in pitch. White-crowned sparrow fledglings tested in the laboratory did not treat those songs differently from unaltered songs until the pitch was shifted more than six standard deviations away from the dialect mean (Whaling, unpublished observations). Adult sparrows of other species can distinguish shifts in pitch that are two or three standard deviations from the mean (Nelson 1989), suggesting that the fledglings may be more forgiving of pitch manipulations than adult birds.

The Neurobiology of Learning Preferences

Armed with this information on the abilities of inexperienced fledglings to recognize song, Allison Doupe and her colleagues undertook an examination of the neural basis of innate discrimination by examining the neurons in and around the song control nucleus HVC. HVC contains both motor neurons for song production and auditory neurons for song perception. These auditory neurons fire when the adult bird hears a taperecording of himself singing (Margoliash 1986), a response that is acquired as the result of learning to sing (Volman 1993). Furthermore, auditory neurons were found in an area near HVC that are more responsive to the songs of one's own species than to foreign songs, as revealed by patterns of gene activation (Mello, Vicario, and Clayton 1992). We wondered whether fledglings would also have neurons that respond most to the songs of their own species, even though they had not yet heard those songs, much less learned to sing them. Would these brain areas contain neurons whose properties could explain how young birds recognize and choose to learn the songs of their own species?

Extracellular recordings were made from neurons in HVC and the surrounding neostriatum by lowering a recording electrode into the brain of an anesthetized bird and searching for neurons that were activated when sounds were played. As in the behavioral tests, these fledglings were housed in acoustic isolation so that they had no opportunity to learn songs. Test stimuli included those used in behavioral tests, as well as broad band noise bursts and pure tones of varying durations.

Similar to the behavioral results, neurons in and around HVC responded strongly to normal and isolate white-crowned sparrow song, and individual phrases such as whistles, buzzes, and trills taken from white-crown songs. In contrast to the behavioral results, however, neurons also responded to similar phrases contained in foreign songs. Such neurons might serve as phrase detectors, and could underlie strong behavioral responses to artificial songs composed of only one repeated white-crowned sparrow phrase type.

When results from the behavior test and electrophysiological recordings are compared, it appears that fledglings discriminated white-crowned sparrow song from foreign song more reliably than did the population of neurons that were sampled. There are a couple of possible reasons for the difference between these results. The behavioral response to taped stimuli is the final product of many neuronal inputs and processing steps. Thus, one possibility is that we recorded from an area close to the beginning of the auditory pathway that detects simple acoustic features of song. These auditory neurons may then project to areas of the brain responding to more complex song features, eventually giving rise to species-selective neurons. Alternatively, it is possible that no single neuron will exhibit species selectivity. Instead, the response of many neurons in unison may provide a recognition signal to the bird that the song is to be learned, for example, the synchronous firing of ensembles of whistle-, buzz-, or trill-responsive neurons. Although some foreign songs contain these phrase types, they are not composed entirely of them, as are white-crowned sparrow songs, and thus would not produce as strong a signal.

To summarize, young birds recognize and choose to learn the songs of their own species, even when raised in the laboratory in acoustic isolation. In our studies, such white-crowned sparrow fledglings were able to recognize songs composed of single white-crown phrases, indicating that recognition of song is not dependent on normal phrase order or song complexity. This ability may allow youngsters to identify and memorize the songs of any white-crowned sparrow that they encounter, whether or not all phrase types are present. Electrophysiological studies with fledglings uncovered auditory neurons that were responsive to phrase type, although these neurons were not yet selective for white-crowned sparrow song. However, in adult birds the response properties of auditory neurons in these brain regions are more selective, responding strongly to the songs of one's own species, but strongest of all to the song of the individual being tested. Presumably the process of vocal learning alters the tuning of these neurons to render them selective for the bird's own song.

Learning about Music

Does the information that we have gained through studies of birdsong learning provide a useful perspective for studies of music in human society? In the questions that follow, I use the concept "learning about music" to refer to the process by which an individual acquires an internalized copy of the scale used by his or her culture and expectations regarding how those notes are used. I do not focus on acquisition of skills such as memorizing a melody, developing proficiency on a musical instrument, or understanding music theory. Rather, I think about the unconscious assimilation of a musical system that allows one to break up a continuous spectrum of sound frequencies into a meaningful series of notes.

Studies of avian song learning have revealed that instinct guides the process of learning. How this relates to humans is unclear but raises some tantalizing questions. Are human children similarly predisposed to structure the acquisition of music according to species-specific universals? For example, do surveys of the ways in which different musical systems divide an octave uncover any universals with respect to preferred note intervals? Is the special emphasis we place on octave intervals, even going so far as using the same name for tones of doubled frequency, evidence of a human perceptual bias that serves to simplify and order a potentially overwhelming range of sounds? Would children as readily learn a musical system that does not contain an interval that is twice the fundamental frequency?

As we have seen, birds enter the world prepared to learn a song that must be supplied by their environment. They are not eager to learn just any song though; an innate program focuses their attention on the correct song for their species. Similarly, human infants are able to recognize speech sounds, even those not included in their native language. As humans engage in the process of learning about music, what are the pieces that must be supplied to us from our environment? Perhaps we are programmed to organize sounds we encounter into a musical system using our own blend of constraints and preferences (Zentner and Kagan 1996). Jackendoff (1994) suggests there may be a universal musical grammar based in part on the preexisting organization of auditory perception.

Another question suggested from avian studies is whether a sensitive period exists for learning about music. Can we learn the scales, intervals, and predictable patterns of a new musical system equally well at any age? Can we develop complete fluency in nonnative music later in life and derive from it the same meaning and emotions reported by native musicians?

Studies suggest that responses of auditory neurons in the song control nuclei of birds are altered as a consequence of song learning. Perhaps regions of our brain involved in perceiving or producing music are similarly altered as we acquire musical knowledge, making it more difficult to participate in a different musical system. It would be interesting to compare the abilities of adults and children to learn intervals and scales that are different from those of their native music. Equally interesting would be to determine whether difficulties reproducing unfamiliar intervals are the result of a deficiency in perceiving the interval or in producing it.

Undeniably vast differences in cognition exist between humans and avian species, making the value of literal comparison of vocal behavior questionable at best. However, all species must solve the challenge of coordinating their behavior with other members of their species, which requires sending as well as decoding signals. In gaining an understanding of song learning in birds, we have an opportunity to learn how other species have responded to these common challenges and may find ourselves returning to studies of our own species with a new perspective.

Acknowledgments

I thank Nils Wallin, Steven Brown, and Björn Merker for organizing an invaluable, cross-disciplinary discussion of musicology, and Chris Bauer, Peter Marler, Jill Soha, and Anne Whaling for commenting on this manuscript.

References

Aamodt, S. M., Kozlawski, M. R., Nordeen, E. J., and Nordeen, K. W. (1992). Distribution and developmental change in [^{3}H]MK-801 binding within zebra finch song nuclei. *Journal of Neurobiology* 23:997–1005.

Aamodt, S. M., Nordeen, E. J., and Nordeen, K. W. (1995). Early isolation from conspecific song does not affect the normal developmental decline of N-methyl-D-aspartate receptor binding in an avian song nucleus. *Journal of Neurobiology* 27:76–84.

Baptista, L. F. and Schuchmann, K. (1990). Song learning in the anna hummingbird (*Calypte anna*). *Ethology* 84:15–26.

Brenowitz, E. A. and Kroodsma, D. E. (1996). The neuroethology of birdsong. In D. E. Kroodsma and E. H. Miller (Eds.) *Ecology and Evolution of Acoustic Communication in Birds* (pp. 285–304). Ithacan, NY: Cornell University Press.

Burek, M. J., Nordeen, K. W., and Nordeen, E. J. (1991). Neuron loss and addition in developing zebra finch song nuclei are independent of auditory experience during song learning. *Journal of Neurobiology* 22:215–223.

Changeux, J.-P. and Danchin, A. (1976). Selective stabilization of developing synapses as a mechanism for the specification of neuronal networks. *Nature* 264:705–712.

Eens, M., Pinxten, R., and Verheyen, R. F. (1992). Song learning in captive European starlings, *Sturnus vulgaris. Animal Behaviour* 44:1131–1143.

Eimas, P. D., Miller, J. L., and Jusczyk, P. W. (1987). On infant speech perception and language acquisition. In S. Harnard (Ed.) *Categorical Perception* (pp. 161–195). New York: Cambridge University Press.

Farabaugh, S. M., Brown, E. D., and Dooling, R. J. (1992). Analysis of warble song of the budgerigar *Melopsittacus undulatus. Bioacoustics* 4:111–130.

Herrmann, K. and Arnold, A. P. (1991). The development of afferent projections to the robust archistriatal nucleus in male zebra finches: A quantitative electron microscopic study. *Journal of Neuroscience* 11:2063–2074.

Immelmann, K. (1969). Song development in the zebra finch and other estrilidid finches. In R. A. Hinde (Ed.) *Bird Vocalizations* (pp. 61–74). Cambridge, UK: Cambridge University Press.

Jackendoff, R. (1994). *Patterns in the Mind*. New York: Basic Books.

Kirn, J., O'Loughlin, B., Kasparian, S., and Nottebohm, F. (1994). Cell death and neuronal recruitment in the high vocal center of adult male canaries are temporally related to changes in song. *Proceedings of the National Academy of Science USA* 91:7844–7848.

Konishi, M. (1963). The role of auditory feedback in the vocal behavior of the domestic fowl. *Zeitschrift für Tierpsychologie* 20:349–367.

Konishi, M. (1965). The role of auditory feedback in the control of vocalizations in the white-crowned sparrow. *Zeitschrift für Tierpsychologie* 22:770–783.

Konishi, M. (1994). An outline of recent advances in birdsong neurobiology. *Brain, Behavior and Evolution* 44:279–285.

Kroodsma, D. E. (1996). Ecology of passerine song development. In D. E. Kroodsma and E. H. Miller (Eds.) *Ecology and Evolution of Acoustic Communication in Birds* (pp. 3–19). Ithacan, NY: Cornell University Press.

Kroodsma, D. E. and Baylis, J. R. (1982). A world survey of evidence for vocal learning in birds. In D. E. Kroodsma and E. H. Miller (Eds.) *Acoustic Communication in Birds* (pp. 311–337). New York: Academic Press.

Kroodsma, D. E. and Pickert, R. (1980). Environmentally dependent sensitive periods for avian vocal learning. *Nature* 288:477–479.

Kuhl, P. K. (1995). Learning and representation in speech and language. *Current Opinion in Neurobiology* 4:812–822.

Margoliash, D. (1986). Preference for autogenous song by auditory neurons in a song system nucleus of the white-crowned sparrow. *Journal of Neuroscience* 69:1643–1661.

Marler, P. (1970). A comparative approach to vocal learning: Song development in white-crowned sparrows. *Journal of Comparative and Physiological Psychology* 71:1–25.

Marler, P. (1987). Sensitive periods and the role of specific and general sensory stimulation in birdsong learning. In J. P. Rauschecker and P. Marler (Eds.) *Imprinting and Cortical Plasticity* (pp. 99–135). New York: Wiley.

Marler, P. (1991). Song-learning behavior: The interface with neuroethology. *Trends in Neuroscience* 14:199–206.

Marler, P. and Peters, S. (1977). Selective vocal learning in a sparrow. *Science* 198:519–521.

Marler, P. and Peters, S. (1982). Long-term storage of learned birdsongs prior to production. *Animal Behaviour* 30:479–482.

Marler, P. and Peters, S. (1987). A sensitive period for song acquisition in the song sparrow, *Melospiza melodia*: A case of age-limited learning. *Ethology* 76:89–100.

Marler, P. and Sherman, V. (1985). Innate differences in singing behaviour of sparrows reared in isolation from adult conspecific song. *Animal Behaviour* 33:57–71.

Mello, C. V., Vicario, D. S., and Clayton, D. F. (1992). Song presentation induces gene expression in the songbird's forebrain. *Proceedings of the National Academy of Science USA* 89:6818–6822.

Nelson, D. A. (1989). Song frequency as a cue for recognition of species and individuals in the field sparrow (*Spizella pusilla*). *Journal of Comparative Psychology* 103:171–176.

Nelson, D. A. and Marler, P. (1993). Innate recognition of song in white-crowned sparrows: A role in selective vocal learning? *Animal Behaviour* 46:806–808.

Nelson, D. A., Marler, P., and Palleroni, A. (1995). A comparative approach to vocal learning: Intraspecific variation in the learning process. *Animal Behaviour* 50:83–97.

Nottebohm, F. (1981). A brain for all seasons: Cyclical anatomical changes in song control nuclei of the canary brain. *Science* 214:1368–1370.

Nottebohm, F. (1991). Reassessing the mechanisms and origins of vocal learning in birds. *Trends in Neuroscience* 14:206–211.

Nottebohm, F. and Nottebohm, M. E. (1971). Vocalizations and breeding behaviour of surgically deafened ring doves. *Animal Behaviour* 19:313–327.

Nottebohm, F. and Nottebohm, M. E. (1978). Relationship between song repertoire and age in the canary *Serinus canaria*. *Zeitschrift für Tierpsychologie* 46:298–305.

Nottebohm, F., Stokes, R., and Leonard, C. (1976). Central control of song in the canary. *Journal of Comparative Neurology* 165:457–486.

Slater, P. J. B., Jones, A., and TenCate, C. (1993). Can lack of experience delay the end of the sensitive period for song learning? *Netherlands Journal of Zoology* 43:80–90.

Sohrabji, F., Nordeen, E. J., and Nordeen, K. W. (1993). Characterization of neurons born and incorporated into a vocal control nucleus during avian song learning. *Brain Research* 620:335–338.

Thorpe, W. H. (1958). The learning of song patterns by birds, with special reference to the song of the chaffinch, *Fringilla coelebs*. *Ibis* 100:533–570.

Todt, D. (1975). Social learning of vocal patterns and modes of their application in grey parrots (*Psittacus erithacus*). *Zeitschrift für Tierpsychologie* 39:178–188.

Volman, S. F. (1993). Development of neural selectivity for birdsong during vocal learning. *Journal of Neuroscience* 13:4737–4747.

Wallhausser, E. and Scheich, H. (1987). Auditory imprinting leads to differential 2 deoxyglucose uptake and dendritic spine loss in the chick rostral forebrain. *Developmental Brain Research* 31:29–44.

Wallhausser-Franke, E., Nisdorf-Bergweiller, B. E., and DeVoogd, T. J. (1995). Song isolation is associated with maintaining high spine frequencies on zebra finch IMAN neurons. *Neurobiology of Learning and Memory* 64:25–35.

Whaling, C. S., Solis, M. M., Doupe, A. J., Soha, J. A., and Marler, P. (1997). Acoustic and neural bases for innate recognition of song. *Proceedings of the National Academy of Science USA* 94:12694–12698.

Zentner, M. R. and Kagan, J. (1996). Perception of music by infants. *Nature* 383:29.

6 The Sound and the Fury: Primate Vocalizations as Reflections of Emotion and Thought

Marc D. Hauser

Abstract

In this chapter I review work on the mechanisms underlying primate vocal communication, focusing in particular on my field studies of rhesus monkeys. By understanding the neurocognitive substrates of animal vocal signals we will be in a stronger position to evaluate the roots of our musical sense. Primate vocalizations use different acoustic parameters to convey information about their emotional states as well as about objects and events in their environment. Nonhuman primates have the capacity to produce vocalizations that evidence some of the rudimentary properties of our system of reference. Furthermore, some of these vocalizations play a role in a system of conventions, crucially related to the maintenance of social relationships within a group. A certain amount is currently known about hemispheric asymmetries underlying the production and perception of species-typical vocal signals. Contrary to earlier claims, nonhuman primates show significant asymmetries, paralleling some findings in humans. Specifically, the left hemisphere plays a dominant role in the perception of conspecific vocalizations, and during production of functionally referential signals.

I can remember the first time I heard Elizabeth Schwarzkopf singing Wagner. Not only was I moved emotionally, but I was astounded by the clarity with which her words resonated, carried by one of Wagner's many memorable themes. But an equally memorable acoustic moment happened just a few minutes later. When I stepped outside the opera house, a newborn was looking up at its mother, cooing and gurgling, composing its own music; and next to the mother and child sat an obedient dog that occasionally let out a contented moan. Other melodies, other voices. Music certainly can be the voice of the heart, and it can also be the messenger of meaning for human adults, human infants, and all animals.

In thinking about the melodic utterances of animals, we can ask several comparative questions that may help us understand the origins of our own species' musical capacity—our musical sense. To avoid confusion, however, we must be careful to distinguish questions of underlying mechanism (e.g., developmental change, neurophysiological substrates) from those of evolutionary function (i.e., adaptive significance) and history (i.e., phylogeny). Thus, we might ask, when birds, whales, gibbons, and humans sing, are the same neural and hormonal systems recruited? This is a mechanistic question, one centered on proximate causation. Another question, focusing on a different set of causal issues, is, when birds, whales, gibbons and humans sing, does their performance influence reproductive fitness? does it contribute to the propagation of genes into subsequent generations? This is a question about ultimate causation. By understanding both kinds of problems, we will be in a better position to evaluate the design features and evolutionary history of musical systems.

This chapter focuses on problems of mechanism. I briefly discuss some traditional views of animal vocal communication, and then show by examples that many of these ideas must either be modified or rejected. The empirical work is divided into two sections. The first explores how the acoustic space of a nonhuman primate's vocal repertoire can be captured by quantifying both affective and referential components of the signal. The second draws on our understanding of call meaning and function to assess whether brain asymmetries underlie acoustic perception and vocal production. All of the empirical work centers on one species, the rhesus macaque (*Macaca mulatta*). I will, however, refer to other species where relevant.

Cries of the Heart and Mind

By the late 1970s, studies of trained apes and dolphins revealed that the conceptual tools required to produce a referential system of communication were present in these animals, and could be expressed by means of an artificial language (Premack 1986; Gardner, Gardner, and Van Canfort 1989; Savage-Rumbaugh et al. 1993; Herman, Pack, and Palmer 1993). In contrast, there was no evidence that natural vocalizations produced by these animals were referential. The general consensus, dating back to Aristotle, Descartes, Darwin, and other luminaries, thus remained: animal vocalizations reflect changes in the signaler's affective state, emotions, and motivations. In 1980, however, a crucial experiment (Seyfarth, Cheney, and Marler 1980) forced this view to undergo a significant facelift. The first insight emerged from Struhsaker's (1967) observation that vervet monkeys produce acoustically distinctive alarm calls in response to three predatory classes: big cats (leopards, cheetah), birds of prey (martial and crowned eagles), and snakes (pythons, mambas). On hearing such calls or seeing the predator, individuals reacted with equally distinctive escape responses. Tight pairing between call type and response suggested that such calls might function as labels for a predatory type. Using taperecorded alarm calls, playback experiments were conducted. If the calls provide sufficient information about the predator encountered, playbacks should be sufficient to elicit behaviorally appropriate responses. They were. In essence, when vervet monkeys hear an alarm call, they are not only struck by a salient emotional event (i.e., they experience fear), but they are provided with information that enables them to make a highly adaptive response. If a leopard is about, the best place to be is high up on the thin branches of an acacia tree. If an eagle is near, the best place is under a bush; eagles can scoop vervets out of trees. Finally, if a snake is in the vicinity, the response is to stand bipedally and scan the ground nearby.

Each of the vervets' escape responses is fine-tuned to the hunting skills of the predator. Natural selection favors an acoustic division of labor: different calls for different predators. A general-purpose alarm call would fail because there is no general-purpose escape response. Similarly, a system requiring vervets to find out what the caller was alarmed about would fail because approaching by ground would leave one vulnerable to each predator type, whereas approaching by tree would leave one vulnerable to eagles and tree mambas, and leopards in the lower branches of the tree.

Building on these initial results, Cheney and Seyfarth (1990) provided an increasingly sophisticated description of the function and meaning of vervet monkey vocalizations. It is clear that some of these vocalizations are functionally referential (Marler, Evans, and Hauser 1992; Marler, this volume) in the sense that they appear to map onto salient objects and events in the environment. Similar kinds of claims for referentiality have been made for other primate species (e.g., ring-tailed lemur, diana monkey, pigtailed macaque, rhesus macaque, toque macaque), and one bird, the domestic chicken (Dittus 1984; Gouzoules, Gouzoules, and Marler 1984; Macedonia 1991; Evans, Evans, and Marler 1994; Zuberbuhler, Noe, and Seyfarth 1997; reviewed in Hauser 1996). What is lacking from these analyses is a more careful dissection of the acoustic features associated with the caller's affective state and those associated with the object or event referred to. To address this gap, I turn to my own research on rhesus monkeys and in particular, their food-associated calls.

Natural Observations of Food-Associated Calls in Rhesus: Dissecting Content

For almost sixty years research has been conducted on a population of semifree-ranging rhesus monkeys living on the island of Cayo Santiago, Puerto Rico. As a result, we know a great deal about this population's demography, social behavior, mating system, and communicative signals. In particular, when rhesus find food, they give one or more of five acoustically distinctive vocalizations: warble, harmonic arch, chirp, coo, and grunt. Although the monkeys are provisioned with chow, they forage throughout the day on naturally available food items such as leaves, fruit, flowers, grass, soil, and insects, many of which elicit calling. Beginning in 1988, I started a long-term study designed to reveal the sources of acoustic variation in this restricted calling context. Research concentrated on the following questions:

1. How does motivational state affect the production of food-associated calls?

2. Does each call type refer to something like the kind of food or its relative quality?

3. When rhesus hear such calls, how do they classify them? Are natural categories constructed on the basis of the caller's affective state, type of food discovered, or some combination of factors?

Based on a large sample of adult males and females, we first looked at changes in call production as a function of food consumption and time of day—a proxy for hunger level. Chow was placed into the dispensers early in the morning and was finished by midday. Thus, rhesus did little foraging from about 4:00 P.M. to 8:00 A.M. the next day. We therefore assumed that they would be most hungry in the early morning and maximally satiated in the late afternoon.

In general, males produced food-associated calls less frequently than females. If these calls function to recruit kin, this sex difference makes sense. As in most mammalian societies, male rhesus monkeys leave their natal groups on reaching sexual maturity, whereas females stay. Consequently, groups consist of closely related females and distantly related males. Other factors may also contribute to this pattern, such as sex differences in arousal levels, social relationships with nonkin, and so forth; at present it is not possible to determine which of these potential factors is most important. In addition to a sex difference, we found that the rate of food call production was highest in early morning before chow was put out and declined rapidly thereafter. In particular, the rate peaked before the peak in food consumption and dropped more rapidly than did food consumption. This pattern suggests that call rate is positively correlated with hunger level.

To explore further the relationship between hunger level and vocal production, we looked at call rate and an individual's latency to arrive and feed at a chow dispenser. While chow was placed into a dispenser, one or more groups sat around the corral waiting to feed. During this time, a number of animals called, apparently in anticipation of feeding. Figure 6.1 plots the rate of food calling against latency to arrive and feed (time elapsed from the placement of chow in the dispenser to feeding); although all food call types are pooled here, most of them were coos. The data set includes one to four focal samples each from twenty adult males and females. Results indicate that as latency to feed increased, call rate decreased; that is, individuals who called at high rates fed first. This pattern is not accounted for by systematic individual differences. Individual patterns of calling varied on a daily basis, as revealed by subject 480 (figure 6.1). On one day, this low-ranking female called at a high rate and fed first, and on a second day, called at a low rate and fed relatively late. Thus, and in parallel with the first set of analyses, call rate appears to provide some information about the caller's hunger level and motivation to feed.

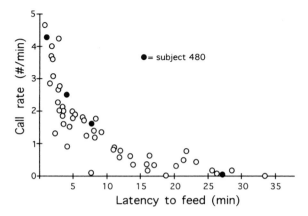

Figure 6.1
The relationship between rate (number of calls/minute) of food-associated calls by rhesus monkeys and latency (minutes) to arrive and feed at the chow dispensers.

Although our understanding of the acoustic correlates of affective state in humans is largely restricted to studies of trained actors, research carried out in more natural settings reveals that systematic changes in call morphology arise in response to changes in emotional state (Scherer 1986; Scherer and Kappas 1988). To contribute to the comparative literature, we have begun to look at more subtle changes in the acoustic structure of rhesus calls (in contrast to call rate) at the time of feeding.

Figure 6.2 illustrates two common situations. Early in the morning, the rhesus began moving toward the feeding corrals. When personnel arrived, individuals began cooing, apparently in anticipation of the chow. It is my impression that these coos were produced with minimal vocal effort. They tended to be relatively low in amplitude and the fundamental frequency contour is flat. When personnel moved toward the feeding corrals and began putting the chow into dispensers, the coo's morphology was transformed. In particular, individuals appeared to put greater effort into the call. Based on spectrographic analyses, this change in production mode appears to cause increased vocal turbulence or noise. In the upper panel of figure 6.2, the first coo was produced while sitting outside the dispenser. There was virtually no noise between the harmonics. In the second coo, noise disrupted the harmonic structure for a brief period of time. By the final coo, the harmonic structure was almost completely disrupted. Such acoustic changes are clearly perceptible to the human ear and thus, presumably, to the rhesus ear as well.

In the second panel of figure 6.2, an adult male saw some coconut at a distance and approached. The first three calls, given before and during the approach to coconut, were coos. As the male grabbed and then ate

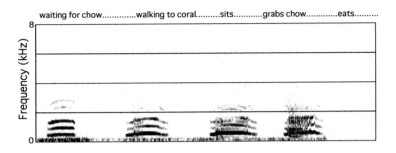

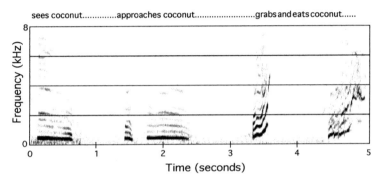

Figure 6.2
Upper panel shows changes in acoustic morphology of the rhesus coo vocalization as a function of proximity to chow. The y axis plots frequency in kilohertz, the x axis plots time in seconds. The lower panel plots changes in call structure and type as functions of movement toward coconut.

the coconut, he gave two harmonic arches. In contrast to the first panel, this sequence represented a change in call type as well as some within-call type changes in structure. Our current hypothesis, based on such cases, is that rhesus monkeys experience changes in emotional state as they approach and then eat food. Such changes may also lead to changes in more coarse-grained morphology as they shift from one call type to another.

Natural observations also revealed systematic differences in the contexts eliciting each call type. In particular, warbles, harmonic arches, and chirps were produced only by individuals finding high-quality, rare food items, coconut being one of these. Grunts and coos sometimes accompanied other call types, but were primarily given in response to finding and eating lower-quality, common items such as chow. Time of day (as a proxy for hunger level) had no effect on the type of call produced. Only food type did. These results suggest that the characteristic spectral and temporal morphology of the call maps onto something like food type or quality. In this sense, rhesus food-associated calls appear to be functionally referential.

With these observations in hand, we turned to field experiments. Production experiments were designed to provide a more rigorous test of our hypotheses concerning the acoustic correlates of affective and referential information. Perception experiments were designed to assess how rhesus classify food-associated calls.

Field Experiments: Further Dissection of Affective and Referential Components

When a rhesus monkey finds food, what determines whether or not it produces a food-associated call, and if it does, at what rate and which kind? We combed the island for lone individuals (targeted "discoverers") visually isolated from all other group members. Once located, we set up our experiments. Some individuals were tested before chow was placed in the dispensers (early morning, hungry group) and others late in the afternoon (satiated group). Our target discoverers were adult males and females, from social groups or peripheral to them (only males), and of high and low dominance ranks. Some discoverers were presented with fifteen pieces of coconut (high-quality rare food) and others with fifteen pieces of chow (low-quality common food).

Only 50% of subjects called on discovering the food cache. Of those who did, females called more often than males, and call rate was highest early in the morning and in response to coconut; dominance rank was not significantly correlated with any aspect of calling behavior. Further paralleling the natural observations, only coos and grunts were given to chow, whereas warbles, harmonic arches, and chirps were given to the coconut. Peripheral males (individuals who had yet to join a social group) never called. Together, these results support our earlier conclusions: call rate covaries with hunger level and acoustical structure covaries with food type or quality.

Interesting functional consequences arose for those who called as opposed to those who remained silent. For discoverers who were members of a social group, those who remained silent and were caught at the food source received significantly higher rates of aggression from other group members than those who called; among females, those who called obtained more food than those who were silent. The story has two further twists. First, discoverers who failed to call and were never detected obtained more food than any other discoverer. Second, although peripheral males never called on discovery, they were never attacked when caught at the food source. These results raise two intriguing ideas with respect to vocal communication and the emergence and maintenance of a convention. One, given the targeted aggression toward discoverers who failed to call, it is possible that this rhesus population evolved a calling convention: members of a social group are expected to call when food is discovered. In the absence of calling, the convention is violated, and thus others respond with aggression. Whether this kind of targeted aggression functions as a form of punishment remains to be investigated in greater detail. Two, because peripheral males were never recipients of targeted aggression, it is possible that this form of attack is reserved for social group members for whom the possibility of future interactions is high; peripheral males that one interacts with may or may not join the group. Since aggression is costly for attacker and attackee, there may be strong selection against attacking those with whom one is unlikely to interact in the future. Again, much more work is needed before we can properly evaluate these ideas.

Given our understanding of the contexts and apparent functions of food-associated calls, we set up a playback experiment to determine how they are classified (Hauser, in press). We borrowed a technique from developmental psychologists interested in understanding the processes underlying speech processing in prelinguistic infants. Specifically, a habituation-discrimination procedure was used to determine whether the primary factor guiding classification of rhesus food calls is its acoustic morphology or referent. This procedure had been run in the field with vervet monkey intergroup and alarm calls (Cheney and Seyfarth 1990), and thus we had some confidence that it would work with rhesus monkeys as well. Our experiments focused on three calls: warble, harmonic arch, and grunt. All three are acoustically different; however, warbles and harmonic arches are produced in the same general context and thus may mean something quite different from grunts.

To set the stage, consider the following situation. You are at a restaurant and someone eating a dish of mashed potatoes repeatedly says, "Yum, potatoes." You turn and look after the first utterance, but then stop responding. At some point, the customer says, "Yum, caviar" as the second course arrives. You would certainly perk up and look back toward the diner. In this case, did you look because you detected a mere acoustic change or because you noticed a salient semantic change? My guess is that the semantic change is largely responsible for your renewed interest. If the diner continued to repeat "yum, caviar" for a while and then switched to "yum, salmon eggs," my guess is that you would not respond. Although there is clearly a perceivable acoustic change, there is no accompanying semantic change.

This hypothetical example is analogous to the situation confronted by rhesus monkeys on Cayo Santiago. If a discoverer repeats the warble over and over and then switches to a harmonic arch, will a listener's interest be revived or not? If a discoverer repeats the harmonic arch and switches to a grunt, will the listener's interest be revived? If interest is revived, is this due to an acoustic or semantic difference?

Figure 6.3 provides a schematic illustration of the experimental design. Test subjects participated in either a within-referent session (habituate to warble and test with harmonic arch, or the reverse) or a between-referent session (habituate to warble or harmonic arch and test with grunt, or the reverse); the identity of the caller was held constant throughout a session. Different exemplars of one call type were played until the subject failed to look in the direction of the speaker on two consecutive trials. Having habituated, we played back one exemplar from a different call type category. If the subject responded (interest revived, subject orients), we ended the session. If the subject failed to respond (transferred habituation), we ran a posttest trial using an exemplar from a different call type category. The reason for the posttest trial was to

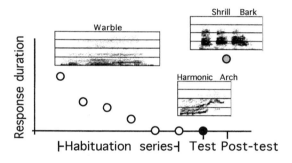

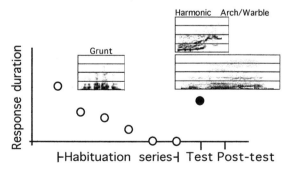

Figure 6.3
Experimental design for habituation-discrimination playback with rhesus monkey food-associated calls. In the upper panel, a hypothetical within-referent condition is shown, with habituation to warbles and then test with harmonic arch. The posttest trial involves a single playback of a shrill bark. The lower panel shows a hypothetical between-referent condition, with habituation to grunts and test with a harmonic arch or warble.

assess whether the subject had habituated to the playback situation in general or to the particular call type. For example, if an individual fails to respond on the test trial, it could be for one of two reasons: it has perceptually clustered the habituation and test stimuli into one category (i.e., they are the same) or it has habituated to all sounds coming from this test area. Response to the posttest suggests that the first explanation is correct: habituation and test stimuli are processed as a single, perceptually meaningful category.

Figure 6.4 shows results from within- and between-referent sessions. For within-referent sessions (left panel), subjects showed a stronger response to the harmonic arch than to the warble on the first trial. Due to the experimental design, however, all subjects entered the test phase after failing to respond on two consecutive trials. In the test trial, subjects failed to respond even though they consistently responded in the posttest trial. This suggests that warbles and harmonic arches are clustered into one category, even though they are acoustically different. Turning to between-referent sessions, subjects consistently responded in the test trial, but response magnitude was contingent on the stimuli presented during the habituation series. Specifically, when subjects were habituated to grunts, they showed a strong and highly significant response to either the warble or harmonic arch. In contrast, when they were habituated to the warble or harmonic arch, their response to the grunt was weak. Putting it in anthropomorphic terms, grunts are to potatoes as warbles and harmonic arches are to caviar and salmon eggs. If you have been eating potatoes for a while, a switch to caviar represents a welcome change. In contrast, if you share my gustatory biases, a switch from caviar to potatoes is far less exciting. Similarly, it appears rhesus are far more interested in a switch from chow to coconut than to the reverse. What remains a puzzle is why they have what appear to be three acoustically distinctive calls for the same food category. Are they like synonyms: food, chow, grub, eats? Or, are they emotional turns? When the caviar first arrives, you might shout, "Caviar" with gusto. Once you have had a few spoonfuls, you might say "caviar" in a more moderate fashion. It is still caviar, however.

These results, together with those obtained from other species, suggest one conservative interpretation and one radical one. We have sufficient data to argue that in certain animals the acoustic morphology of the repertoire consists of some featural components that map onto the caller's affective state and other components that map onto objects and events in the external environment. Although we are in a somewhat primitive state with respect to identifying the precise emotion or referent, we are equipped with a set of powerful tools for investigating the problem more deeply. The more radical idea is this: although animal

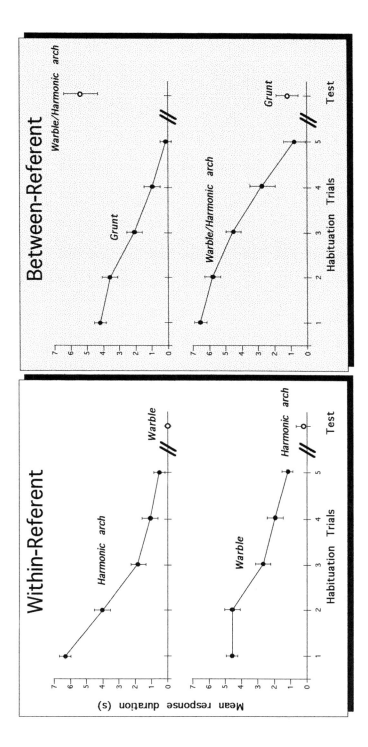

Figure 6.4
Results of habituation-discrimination experiments plot changes in mean response duration (i.e., amount of time looking to the speaker; seconds) to each trial, including habituation and test trials. Standard deviations are shown.

vocalizations may not approach the referential power of our own words, either in terms of the kinds of objects and events that can be referred to (imagined objects, future states) or the mental states that accompany their production (beliefs, intentions), they may represent a sufficiently advanced system to warrant classification as a precursor. This position makes the assumption that part of our language faculty was constructed out of an evolutionarily antecedent system.

Some, such as Deacon (1997), consider this position fallacious because language is not an end point. It is, however, a species-specific communication system driven by a species-specific brain. Therefore, in the same way that we can look for precursors to a humanlike eye or heart, we can look for precursors to a humanlike language. To date, most consider the evidence for language precursors to be pathetic (see Bickerton 1990, this volume). I would like to propose that before we lay such issues to rest we tighten up our notion of precursor and refine our understanding of animal referents and the thoughts that underlie them. Whether or not the vocalizations of primates capture the status of linguistic precursors requires a more precise articulation of both the conceptual tools underlying them in humans and the kinds of selection pressures that would have been necessary to evolve such a system during primate history.

Calls of the Lopsided Brain

Several neuroscientists (Corballis 1991; Hellige 1993; Hiscock and Kinsbourne 1995) maintain that although nonhuman animals show evidence of neuroanatomical asymmetries, and even some evidence of behavioral asymmetries, only humans have extensive differentiation of cognitive function between the hemispheres, with evidence of asymmetry at the population level. Specifically, most humans have left hemisphere dominance for language processing and right hemisphere dominance for spatial reasoning, emotional perception, and expression (see reviews in Bradshaw and Rogers 1993; Hellige 1993; Davidson and Hugdahl 1995). As research in this area has developed since the late 1980s, however, it is clear that the original claims regarding hemispheric dominance were far too general, that dichotomies for right and left hemisphere dominance covered up important overlap in function (Efron 1990; chapters in Davidson and Hugdahl 1995). For example, although the left hemisphere is dominant with regard to semantics and formal combinatorial properties of language (syntax), the right hemisphere appears dominant for processing paralinguistic features of language such as melody and changes in pitch (Ross et al. 1988; but see Peretz and Babai 1992). Thus, the right hemisphere is certainly not silent during language processing, and in some cases of damage to the left hemisphere, evidence indicates that the right hemisphere can take on a number of significant linguistic functions. Similarly, studies show that musicians with perfect pitch evidence left hemisphere dominance during music perception.

Recent electroencephalographic data suggest that the right hemisphere may play a dominant role in negative-withdrawal emotion whereas the left hemisphere appears dominant for positive-approach emotion (Davidson 1992, 1995; see Lee et al. 1990 for the reverse pattern of emotional valence and hemisphere bias using epileptic patients receiving intracarotid administration of sodium amobarbital). Thus, for example, when people are given explicit instructions to move their face into a Duchenne smile—what Ekman and colleagues (1988, 1990) consider to be the only true or honest smile—they have far greater left hemisphere activation than right (Ekman, Davidson, and Friesen 1990). In contrast, Gazzaniga and Smiley (1991) provided important information on split-brain patients who have much greater asymmetries in smiling on the left side of the face than on the right.

If we are to understand how and why hemispheric specialization evolved, it is important to look more closely at the neural specializations of our closest living relatives, monkeys and apes. This movement has begun thanks in part to MacNeilage, Studdert-Kennedy, and Lindblom (1987) who critically examined the evidence for hand preferences in nonhuman primates. This work (see also updated review by MacNeilage 1991) demonstrated that individuals in several nonhuman primate species preferentially use one hand more than the other in both unimanual and bimanual tasks (Ward and Hopkins 1993). For most monkeys, the left hand appears dominant, whereas some studies of apes reveal right hand dominance. Data on handedness, coupled with work on asymmetries in nonhuman primate neuroanatomy (Falk 1987; Heilbroner and Holloway 1988; Perrett et al. 1988; Falk et al. 1990; Cheverud et al. 1991) and cognitive function (Hopkins, Washburn, and Rumbaugh 1990; Hamilton and Vermeire 1991; Hopkins, Morris, and Savage-Rumbaugh 1991; Vauclair, Fagot, and Hopkins 1993), are important in that they provide insights into the phylogenetic precursors of human hemispheric specialization (for recent synthetic discussions of this point, see Bradshaw and Rogers 1993; Hauser 1996).

Call Perception

One of the earliest attempts to assess hemispheric biases in acoustic perception in primates took advantage of a detailed field study and psychophysical techniques. The empirical foundation for this research was Green's (1975) in-depth analysis of wild Japanese macaque vocalizations, in particular, their coo. This call type is acoustically variable, with much of the variation resulting from modulations in fundamental frequency contour. For example, coos with one frequency contour pattern were given during group progressions, whereas coos with a different contour were given by estrous females. Experiments by Petersen et al. (1978) showed that Japanese macaques, but not closely related species, responded faster in a discrimination task when the call was played into the right ear (left hemisphere) than when it was played into the left ear (right hemisphere). Follow-up studies (Heffner and Heffner 1984, 1990) indicated that lesioning the left temporal lobe, but not the right, caused subjects to lose the ability to discriminate coos on the basis of their characteristic frequency contours; although this deficit was observed early on, subjects with left hemisphere lesions recovered quite rapidly. In general, these results have been taken as support for the view that, as well as humans, monkeys also show a left hemisphere bias for processing species-typical vocal signals.

The interpretation offered for Japanese macaque data has two potential problems. First, only one call type was used. Thus we do not yet understand whether the perceptual bias extends to other calls within the repertoire. Second, the claim that Japanese macaques show a pattern of hemispheric bias that is comparable with that shown for humans processing language hinges on the assumption that coos are languagelike, that they convey, at some level, semantic information. And yet, studies of this call type in both Japanese macaques (Owren et al. 1992, 1993) and the closely related rhesus macaque (Hauser 1991, section 2) suggest that the information conveyed is likely to be entirely emotive (currently no evidence exists that the call conveys even functionally referential information, *sensu* Marler, Evans, and Hauser 1992).

To address some of these concerns, a field study of rhesus macaques was conducted (Hauser and Andersson 1994). Playback experiments were carried out with a large number of adults and infants (age <12 mo), using most call types from the repertoire. A speaker was placed 180 degrees behind an individual, and a single exemplar of a call type was played. The logic underlying the design was that if subjects preferentially turned their right ear toward the speaker, they would bias the intensity of input to the left hemisphere; if they turned the left ear, they would bias input to the right hemisphere. Note that both ears receive acoustic input, but interaural time and intensity differences are present due to the orienting bias. For all conspecific calls played, adults consistently showed right ear bias despite an overall lefthand motor preference for reaching and manipulating objects in this population (Hauser et al. 1991), with no correlation between handedness and orienting bias in a subset of subjects. In contrast, no ear bias was observed in infants for any call types. Moreover, when the alarm call of a local bird (ruddy turnstone) was played, adults preferentially turned the left ear, whereas infants failed to show bias; the turnstone's call is familiar to rhesus, but is a signal that is clearly not from a conspecific. Together, these results provide additional support for the idea that macaques have right ear bias for perceiving conspecific signals, implying left hemisphere dominance for processing conspecific calls.

To determine which acoustic features of a signal influence the preferential head-turning response and thus the suggested hemispheric bias underlying perception in rhesus (Hauser and Andersson 1994), a second experiment was carried out (Hauser, Agnetta and Perez, in press). Digital signal-editing tools (Beeman 1996) were used to modify the structure of naturally produced calls. The idea, in a nutshell, is this. Call types within the repertoire are characterized by a suite of parametric features, including both temporal and spectral ones. We hypothesized that when particular features of a signal are manipulated beyond the range of natural variation, such signals will no longer be perceived as conspecific calls; call types within the repertoire will differ in terms of their characteristic defining features and consequently, no single manipulation is likely to be meaningful across all call types, except at extremes. Given the observation that rhesus respond to playbacks of one avian species' alarm call by preferentially turning their left ear to listen (Hauser and Andersson 1994), we predicted that playbacks of calls shifted outside the species-typical range would also elicit left ear bias; such manipulations may lead to no response bias if the acoustic signal caused significant activation in both hemispheres as a result different causal factors. Calls that have been manipulated, but remain within the species-typical range, would continue to elicit right ear bias, that is, continue to be classified as conspecific calls.

The focus of this experiment (Hauser, Agnetta, and Perez, in press) was the salience of temporal parameters in call classification. All three call types presented are characterized by pulses of energy separated by silence. For each call type, we started with a naturally recorded call consisting of three pulses, together with pulse and interpulse intervals that fell close to the population mean. We then shrunk as well as stretched interpulse intervals to create four additional stimuli. Calls with reduced interpulse intervals were reduced to the minimum observed in the population or were completely eliminated. Calls with stretched interpulse intervals were increased to the maximum in the population or twice the maximum.

Figure 6.5 shows representative spectrograms of the three call types used in this experiment: grunt, shrill bark, and copulation scream (Hauser 1993b; Hauser and Marler 1993a; Bercovitch, Hauser, and Jones 1995). Three factors guided our decision to use these particular call types.

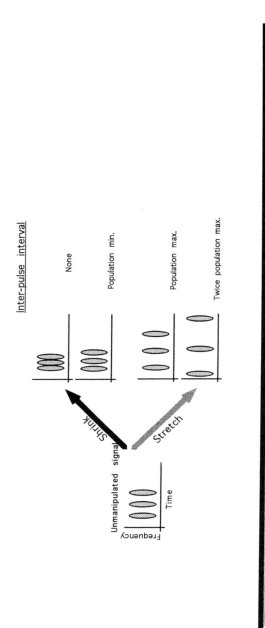

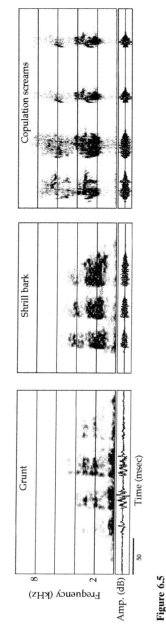

Figure 6.5
Schematic illustration of the experimental design for playbacks on orienting biases to rhesus monkey vocalizations. The upper panel shows temporal manipulations imposed and the lower panel shows spectrograms and time-amplitude waveforms of the three call types used. Frequency is measured in kilohertz, time in milliseconds, and amplitude in decibels.

First, each one is produced in a context that can be clearly identified. Thus, grunts are produced during affiliative interactions involving food or a conspecific (Hauser and Marler 1993a, section 2). Shrill barks are given exclusively in the context of alarm, and for rhesus monkeys on Cayo Santiago, represent their only alarm vocalization (Hauser and Marler 1993a; Bercovitch, Hauser, and Jones 1995). Copulation screams are given only by adult males during copulation and in no other context (Hauser 1993b). Second, quantitative acoustic analyses were already available from published results (Hauser and Marler 1993a) and unpublished data. Thus, before starting our experiments, we had a good understanding of the range of acoustic variation both at the population level and in terms of specific features of the call. Third, in manipulating the structure of a call away from its species-typical morphology, it is important to avoid changing its structure into that of a different call from within the repertoire. Thus, for example, adding a broad, frequency-modulated component to the terminal portion of the end of a coo turns the signal into a harmonic arch (see figure 6.2). For grunts, shrill barks, and copulation screams, manipulating interpulse interval does not transform them into different call types from within the repertoire.

Having manipulated one parameter of the call, we conducted playback experiments using the design of our previous experiments (Hauser and Andersson 1994). Specifically, calls were broadcast from a speaker located 180 degrees behind the subject and head orientation was scored. Figure 6.6 shows results from playbacks of each call type. For all three types, playbacks of unmanipulated exemplars, and exemplars with interpulse intervals reduced to the population minimum, subjects showed a highly significant right ear bias. For grunts and shrill barks, eliminating interpulse interval eliminated orienting bias, with some individuals turning to the right, some to the left, and some not responding at all; for copulation screams, however, right ear bias was preserved. When interpulse interval was stretched to the maximum in the population, the tendency was for subjects to orient with the left ear leading for both grunts and shrill barks, but this pattern was not statistically significant; for copulation calls, right ear bias was preserved. Finally, when interpulse interval was stretched to twice the maximum, subjects showed a statistically significant left ear bias for the grunt and shrill bark, but a right ear bias was preserved for the copulation scream.

For grunts and shrill barks, manipulating interpulse interval beyond the species-typical range of variation (at least for this population) caused a shift from right ear bias to either no bias (eliminating interpulse interval) or to a significant left ear bias (two times the maximum interpulse interval). This pattern of change was not observed in playbacks of copulation screams.

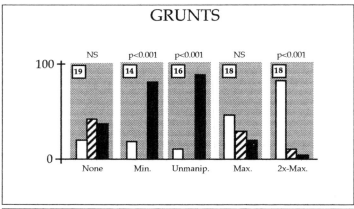

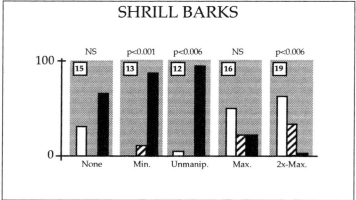

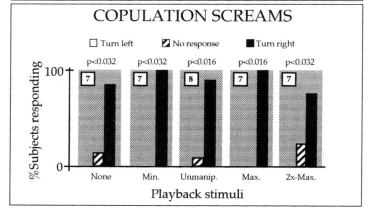

Figure 6.6
Results of playback experiments on orienting asymmetries. Each panel shows data on unmanipulated calls as well as on calls whose temporal structure has been altered by stretching or shrinking the interpulse interval. Numbers inside the white boxes refer to sample sizes per condition.

Why did manipulations of the interpulse interval have a detectable effect on responses to grunts and shrill barks, but no effect on responses to copulation screams? Closer inspection of the natural variation in acoustic morphology provides a clue. Whereas grunts and shrill barks are produced with no fewer than two pulses, copulation screams can be produced with a single pulse. Thus, although the number of pulses and interpulse interval in a copulation scream may be relevant to male quality (Hauser 1993b), such temporal features do not appear to be important in terms of classifying the call as a rhesus copulation scream.

In summary, we appear to have identified at least one feature that defines a rhesus monkey call, and showed that altering this feature causes a shift in the direction of acoustic orientation. We interpret this orienting bias as evidence that the left hemisphere is dominant with respect to processing conspecific calls. This interpretation must be considered in greater detail because there are possible noncortical mechanisms (biases at the periphery) and at the cortical level, alternative pathways for guiding the orienting bias (auditory, visual, cross-modal).

Call Production

Neurophysiological studies of squirrel monkeys and several macaque species revealed homologues to Broca's and Wernicke's areas (reviewed in Jürgens 1990; Deacon 1992, 1997). When the homologue to Broca's area was lesioned in these species, however, no detectable differences in the acoustic morphology of the vocal repertoire were observed (reviewed in Larson, Ortega, and DeRosier 1988; Hauser 1996). These results led to the conclusion that in nonhuman primates, the locus of control for production of species-typical vocalizations is the limbic system. A problem with this interpretation is that both studies obtained relatively crude measurements of preoperative and postoperative effects on call structure (Kirzinger and Jürgens 1982). Specifically, spectrographic differences in call structure were assessed qualitatively, rather than quantitatively using detailed acoustic analyses. Given that damage to Broca's and Wernicke's areas can lead to quite subtle linguistic effects in humans, it is possible that comparably subtle effects would emerge among nonhuman primates as well. Moreover, the potential effects of these experimental lesions were measured only over a short period of time; production and perception deficits may not reveal themselves immediately after injury. In sum, the importance of higher cortical structures in nonhuman primate vocal production remains ambiguous.

Studies of cortical physiology aside, considerable interest has been shown in the possibility that the fundamental units of human language (phonemes, words) evolved from a homologous nonhuman primate ancestor. For example, MacNeilage (1994) suggested that syllables evolved from primate lip smacks and other mandibular cyclicities associated with vocal production. Thus far, however, no study has explored whether nonhuman primates exhibit asymmetries during vocal articulation.

In humans, Graves and colleagues (Graves, Goodglass, and Landis 1982; Graves and Landis 1985; Graves and Potter 1988; Graves and Landis 1990; Graves, Strauss, and Wada 1990) demonstrated that during speech production, the right side of the mouth opens wider than the left. Moreover, in aphasics with damage to the left hemisphere, bias for the right side of the mouth is observed for spontaneous speech, repetition, and word list generation, whereas bias for the left side of the mouth is observed for serial speech (counting to ten) and singing (familiar rhymes). This difference suggests that when an automatic motor sequence is enlisted for vocal production, the right hemisphere is dominant. In contrast, even aphasics show left hemisphere dominance for nonautomatic vocal articulations, specifically those involving speech articulation. Studies such as these in humans are now critically needed for nonhuman primates. Given our increasing knowledge of primate vocal communication, including its function, acoustic architecture, and mechanisms underlying its production (Jürgens 1990; Cheney and Seyfarth 1990; Snowdon 1990; Hauser, Evans, and Marler 1993; Hauser 1993b, Hauser and Schön Ybarra 1994), we are in an excellent position to examine hemispheric biases underlying the production of species-typical vocalizations.

In parallel with our analyses of facial expressions (Hauser 1993a), assessment of articulatory gestures was derived from two measures. First, for each vocalization (acoustics and visual articulation captured on video), we scored whether or not one side of the mouth opened or shut before the other—a timing measure. An articulation was scored as asymmetric if one side of the mouth started or ended the articulation at least one frame earlier than the other side. Second, we scored, frame by frame, which side of the mouth was open wider at the start of articulation as well as the midpoint of the call. Specifically, a frame was digitized and the mouth divided down the middle, and the number of pixels on the right and left sides were derived. For both the timing clips and the digitized frames, half of the exemplars were flipped in the horizontal plane so that observers were blind with regard to the subject's original orientation. The end product of this analysis was an overall assessment of articulatory asymmetry and its production time course. Below, I focus on results from the timing measure.

The first set of analyses focused on three call types: coos, screams, and grunts. Coos and grunts are produced by lip protrusion and an open mouth, whereas screams are produced by lip retraction. Results (figure

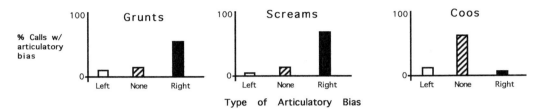

Figure 6.7
Asymmetries in timing of articulation for rhesus monkey grunts, screams, and coos. The photograph is of an individual producing a scream vocalization, with production bias on the right side of the face.

6.7) from three adult males and two adult females (five to nine call exemplars per individual) indicate that for both screams and grunts, there was bias for the significant right side of the face (p < .05–.01). In contrast, for coos, the articulation appeared highly symmetrical, with only a small proportion of exemplars showing bias for left or right side. Although the samples were small, these results are promising, especially when contrasted with the kinematics of facial expressions (Hauser 1993a). Specifically, fear grimaces and screams are both produced by retracting the lips. When they are produced, bias is for the left side of the face, whereas it is for the right side for screams. If screams were merely expressions of affective state (fear), we would expect bias for the left side of the face (right hemisphere), as shown for fear grimaces. Given that screams show right side bias, we suggest that the dominant message is semantic. If correct, this would provide neurobiological support for the behavioral observations of Gouzoules and colleagues (1984) indicating that the rhesus monkey's scream system consists of functionally referential signals that map onto variation in the details of the social interaction (e.g., aggressive interactions with kin or nonkin).

Conclusion

Production and perception of human music depend on particular neurocognitive mechanisms. Some of these mechanisms are innately specified, such as our capacity to perceive differences among melodies, to hum a tune, and to extract emotion from a musical composition. Such mechanisms also guide and constrain subsequent experiences, as we learn to play an instrument or sing, each of us with different degrees of skill and expertise. Most forms of musical performance require conventions, formalized symbolic notation, or coordinated action, often led by one individual (e.g., a conductor leading the orchestra, a mother singing with her child). Our curiosity and creative impulses, however, give us a capacity to break conventions, sometimes resulting in success and sometimes in failure.

In this chapter I discussed some of the mechanisms underlying primate vocal communication. Based on our research with rhesus monkeys and other species, it appears that several components of our own musical capacity have been in place for a long time. Some of them may have evolved independently several times, suggesting convergent evolution. In the case of primates, however, it seems likely that similarities with humans represent homology, characteristics shared by a common ancestor. Specifically, I propose that humans and nonhuman primates share three critical mechanisms, with some admittedly important differences in their form and function. First, some nonhuman primate vocalizations encode information about affective state and external referents. Listeners are sensitive to such information and use it to classify salient objects and events. Second, for some vocalizations, use is guided by a convention of sorts. Violators of the convention may incur significant costs if they are caught by group members. Third, hemispheric biases underlie the production and perception of vocalizations.

It would be misleading to conclude from the data presented that, because of these underlying mechanisms, nonhuman primates have the capacity to produce music. Many primate vocalizations are certainly musical in that they sound, to the human ear, like a melody, one that could readily be incorporated into a formal composition. But in the same way that a piano and a sheet of music require a piano player, the neurocognitive substrates of a monkey or an ape must similarly be commandeered by a musician. The problem is to figure out what kind of mechanism evolved to take advantage of the existing substrate for music performance, perception, and appreciation. The end product of this evolutionary fusion of mechanisms was the emergence of a species with a musical sense.

Acknowledgments

Funding for this research was provided by an NSF-Young Investigator Award, NSF-Physical Anthropology, National Geographic Society,

Wenner-Gren Foundation, Leakey Foundation, and Harvard University. I thank the staff on Cayo Santiago and, in particular, the scientists in charge of the CPRC: Drs. M. Kessler, J. Berard, and F. Bercovitch.

References

Beeman, K. (1996). *SIGNAL User's Guide*. Belmont, MA: Engineering Design.

Bercovitch, F., Hauser, M. D., and Jones, J. (1995). The endocrine stress response and alarm vocalizations in rhesus macaques. *Animal Behaviour* 49:1703–1706.

Bickerton, D. (1990). *Language & Species*. Chicago: University of Chicago Press.

Bradshaw, J. L. and Rogers, L. (1993). *The Evolution of Lateral Asymmetries: Language, Tool Use, and Intellect*. San Diego: Academic Press.

Cheney, D. L. and Seyfarth, R. M. (1990). *How Monkeys See the World: Inside the Mind of Another Species*. Chicago: University of Chicago Press.

Cheverud, J., Falk, D., Hildebolt, C., Moore, A. J., Helmkamp, R. C., and Vannier, M. (1991). Heritability and association of cortical petalias in rhesus macaques (*Macaca mulatta*). *Brain Behavior and Evolution* 35:368–372.

Corballis, M. (1991). *The Lopsided Ape*. Oxford: Oxford University Press.

Davidson, R. J. (1992). Emotion and affective style: Hemispheric substrates. *Psychological Science* 3:39–43.

Davidson, R. J. (1995). Cerebral asymmetry, emotion, and affective style. In R. J. Davidson and K. Hugdahl (Eds.) *Brain Asymmetry* (pp. 361–389). Cambridge: MIT Press.

Davidson, R. J. and Hugdahl, K. (Eds.) (1995). *Brain Asymmetry*. Cambridge: MIT Press.

Deacon, T. W. (1992). The neural circuitry underlying primate calls and human language. In J. Wind, B. Chiarelli, B. Bichakjian, A. Nocentini, and A. Jonker (Eds.) *Language Origins: A Multidisciplinary Approach* (pp. 131–172). Dordrecht: Kluwer.

Deacon, T. W. (1997). *The Symbolic Species*. New York: Norton.

Dittus, W. P. G. (1984). Toque macaque food calls: Semantic communication concerning food distribution in the environment. *Animal Behaviour* 32:470–477.

Efron, R. (1990). *The Decline and Fall of Hemispheric Specialization*. Hillsdale, NJ: Lawrence Erlbaum Associates.

Ekman, P., Davidson, R. J., and Friesen, W. V. (1990). Emotional expression and brain physiology. II. The Duchenne smile. *Journal of Personality and Social Psychology* 58:342–353.

Ekman, P., Friesen, W. V., and O'Sullivan, M. (1988). Smiles while lying. *Journal of Personality and Social Psychology* 54:414–420.

Evans, C. S., Evans, L., and Marler, P. (1994). On the meaning of alarm calls: Functional reference in an avian vocal system. *Animal Behaviour* 45:23–38.

Falk, D. (1987). Brain lateralization in primates and its evolution in hominids. *Yearbook of Physical Anthropology* 30:107–125.

Falk, D., Hildeblolt, C., Cheverud, J., Vannier, M., Helmkamp, R. C., and Konigsberg, L. (1990). Cortical asymmetries in frontal lobes of rhesus monkeys (*Macaca mulatta*). *Brain Research* 512:40–45.

Gardner, R. A., Gardner, B. T., and Van Cantfort, E. (1989). *Teaching Sign Language to Chimpanzees*. Albany: State University of New York Press.

Gazzaniga, M. and Smiley, C. S. (1991). Hemispheric mechanisms controlling voluntary and spontaneous facial expressions. *Journal of Cognitive Neuroscience* 2:239–245.

Gouzoules, S., Gouzoules, H., and Marler, P. (1984). Rhesus monkey (*Macaca mulatta*) screams: Representational signalling in the recruitment of agonistic aid. *Animal Behaviour* 32:182–193.

Graves, R., Goodglass, H., and Landis, T. (1982). Mouth asymmetry during spontaneous speech. *Neuropsychologia* 20:371–381.

Graves, R. and Landis, T. (1985). Hemispheric control of speech expression in aphasia: A mouth asymmetry study. *Archives of Neurology* 42:249–251.

Graves, R. and Landis, T. (1990). Asymmetry in mouth opening during different speech tasks. *International Journal of Psychiatry* 25:179–189.

Graves, R., Strauss, E. H., and Wada, J. (1990). Mouth asymmetry during speech of epileptic patients who have undergone carotid amytal testing. *Neuropsychologia* 28:1117–1121.

Graves, R. E. and Potter, S. M. (1988). Speaking from two sides of the mouth. *Visible Language* 22:129–137.

Green, S. (1975). Variation of vocal pattern with social situation in the Japanese monkey (*Macaca fuscata*): A field study. In L. A. Rosenblum (Ed.) *Primate Behavior*, Vol. 4 (pp. 1–102). New York: Academic Press.

Hamilton, C. R. and Vermeire, B. A. (1991). Functional lateralization in monkeys. In F. L. Kitterle (Ed.) *Cerebral Laterality: Theory and Research* (pp. 19–34). Hillsdale, NJ: Lawrence Erlbaum Associates.

Hauser, M. D. (1991). Sources of acoustic variation in rhesus macaque vocalizations. *Ethology* 89:29–46.

Hauser, M. D. (1993a). Right hemisphere dominance for production of facial expression in a monkey. *Science* 261:475–477.

Hauser, M. D. (1993b). Rhesus monkey (*Macaca mulatta*) copulation calls: Honest signals for female choice? *Proceedings of the Royal Society, London* 254:93–96.

Hauser, M. D. (1996). *The Evolution of Communication*. Cambridge: MIT Press.

Hauser, M. D. (1998). Functional referents and acoustic similarity: Field playback experiments with rhesus monkeys. *Animal Behaviour* 55:1647–1658.

Hauser, M. D., Agnetta, B., and Perez, C. (In press). Orienting asymmetries in rhesus monkeys: The effect of time-domain changes on acoustic perception. *Animal Behaviour*.

Hauser, M. D. and Andersson, K. (1994). Left hemisphere dominance for processing vocalizations in adult, but not infant rhesus monkeys: Field experiments. *Proceedings of the National Academy of Sciences USA* 91:3946–3948.

Hauser, M. D., Evans, C. S., and Marler, P. (1993). The role of articulation in the production of rhesus monkey (*Macaca mulatta*) vocalizations. *Animal Behaviour* 45:423–433.

Hauser, M. D. and Marler, P. (1993a). Food-associated calls in rhesus macaques (*Macaca mulatta*). Socioecological factors influencing call production. *Behavioral Ecology* 4:194–205.

Hauser, M. D., Perry, S., Manson, J., Ball, H., Williams, M., Pearson, E., and Berard, J. (1991). It's all in the hands of the beholder: New data on handedness in a free-ranging population of rhesus macaques. *Behavioral and Brain Sciences* 14:342–344.

Hauser, M. D. and Schön Ybarra, M. (1994). The role of lip configuration in monkey vocalizations: Experiments using xylocaine as a nerve block. *Brain and Language* 46:232–244.

Heffner, H. E. and Heffner, R. S. (1984). Temporal lobe lesions and perception of species-specific vocalizations by macaques. *Science* 226:75–76.

Heffner, H. E. and Heffner, R. S. (1990). Role of primate auditory cortex in hearing. In M. A. Berkley and W. C. Stebbins (Eds.) *Comparative Perception*, Vol. 2, *Complex Signals* (pp. 136–159). New York: Wiley.

Heilbroner, P. L. and Holloway, R. L. (1988). Anatomical brain asymmetries in New World and Old World monkeys: Stages of temporal lobe development in primate evolution. *American Journal of Physical Anthropology* 76:39–48.

Hellige, J. B. (1993). *Hemispheric Asymmetry: What's Right and What's Left*. Cambridge: Harvard University Press.

Herman, L. M., Pack, A. A., and Palmer, M.-S. (1993). Representational and conceptual skills of dolphins. In H. L. Roitblat, L. M. Herman, and P. E. Nachtigall (Eds.) *Language and Communication: Comparative Perspectives*. (pp. 403–442). Hillsdale, NJ: Erlbaum.

Hiscock, M. and Kinsbourne, M. (1995). Phylogeny and ontogeny of cerebral lateralization. In R. J. Davidson and K. Hugdahl (Eds.) *Brain Asymmetry* (pp. 535–578). Cambridge: MIT Press.

Hopkins, W. D., Washburn, D. A., and Rumbaugh, D. (1990). Processing of form stimuli presented unilaterally in humans, chimpanzees (*Pan troglodytes*) and monkeys (*Macaca mulatta*). *Behavioral Neuroscience* 104:577–582.

Hopkins, W. D., Morris, R. D., and Savage-Rumbaugh, E. S. (1991). Evidence for asymmetrical hemispheric priming using known and unknown warning stimuli in two language-trained chimpanzees (*Pan troglodytes*). *Journal of Experimental Psychology: General* 120:46–56.

Jürgens, U. (1990). Vocal communication in primates. In R. P. Kesner and D. S. Olton (Eds.) *Neurobiology of Comparative Cognition* (pp. 51–76). Hillsdale, NJ: Erlbaum.

Kirzinger, A. and Jürgens, U. (1982). Cortical lesion effects and vocalization in the squirrel monkey. *Brain Research* 358:150–162.

Larson, C. R., Ortega, J. D., and DeRosier, E. A. (1988). Studies on the relation of the midbrain periaqueductal gray, the larynx and vocalization in the awake monkey. In J. D. Newman (Ed.) *The Physiological Control of Mammalian Vocalizations* (pp. 43–65). Englewood Cliffs, NJ: Plenum Press.

Lee, G. P., Loring, D. W., Meader, K. J., and Brooks, B. B. (1990). Hemispheric specialization for emotional expression: A reexamination of results from intracarotid administration of sodium amobarbital. *Brain and Cognition* 12:267–280.

Macedonia, J. (1991). What is communicated in the antipredator calls of lemurs: Evidence from playback experiments with ring-tailed and ruffed lemurs. *Ethology* 86:177–190.

MacNeilage, P. F. (1991). The "postural origins" theory of primate neurobiological asymmetries. In N. Krasnegor, D. Rumbaugh, M. Studdert-Kennedy, and R. Schiefelbusch (Eds.) *Biological Foundations of Language Development* (pp. 165–188). Hillsdale, NJ: Erlbaum.

MacNeilage, P. F. (1994). Prolegomena to a theory of the sound patterns of the first language. *Phonetica* 51:184–194.

MacNeilage, P. F., Studdert-Kennedy, M. G., and Lindblom, B. (1987). Primate handedness reconsidered. *Behavioral and Brain Sciences* 10:247–303.

Marler, P., Evans, C. S., and Hauser, M. D. (1992). Animal signals? Reference, motivation or both? In H. Papoušek, U. Jürgens, and M. Papoušek (Eds.) *Nonverbal Vocal Communication: Comparative and Developmental Approaches* (pp. 66–86). Cambridge, UK: Cambridge University Press.

Owren, M. J., Dieter, J. A., Seyfarth, R. M., and Cheney, D. L. (1992). "Food" calls produced by adult female rhesus (*Macaca mulatta*) and Japanese (*M. fuscata*) macaques, their normally-raised offspring, and offspring cross-fostered between species. *Behaviour* 120:218–231.

Owren, M. J., Dieter, J. A., Seyfarth, R. M., and Cheney, D. L. (1993). Vocalizations of rhesus (*Macaca mulatta*) and Japanese (*M. fuscata*) macaques cross-fostered between species show evidence of only limited modification. *Developmental Psychobiology* 26:389–406.

Peretz, I. and Babai, M. (1992). The role of contour and intervals in the recognition of melody parts: Evidence from cerebral asymmetries in musicians. *Neuropsychologia* 30:277–292.

Perrett, D. I., Mistlin, A. J., Chitty, A. J., Smith, P. A., Potter, D. D., Broennimann, R., and Haries, M. (1998). Specialized face processing and hemispheric asymmetry in man and monkey: Evidence from single unit and reaction time studies. *Behavioural Brain Research* 29:245–258.

Petersen, M. R., Beecher, M. D., Zoloth, S. R., Moody, D. B., and Stebbins, W. C. (1978). Neural lateralization of species-specific vocalizations by Japanese macaques. *Science* 202:324–326.

Premack, D. (1986). *Gavagai! or the Future History of the Animal Language Controversy.* Cambridge: MIT Press.

Ross, E. D., Edmondson, J. A., Seibert, G. B., and Homan, R. W. (1988). Acoustic analysis of affective prosody during right-sided wada test: A within-subjects verification of the right hemisphere's role in language. *Brain and Language* 33:128–145.

Savage-Rumbaugh, E. S., Murphy, J., Sevcik, R. A., Brakke, K. E., Williams, S. L., and Rumbaugh, D. M. (1993). Language comprehension in ape and child. *Monographs of the Society for Research in Child Development* 58:1–221.

Scherer, K. R. (1986). Vocal affect expression: A review and a model for future research. *Psychological Bulletin* 99:143–165.

Scherer, K. R. and Kappas, A. (1988). Primate vocal expression of affective state. In D. Todt, P. Goedeking, and D. Symmes (Eds.) *Primate Vocal Communication* (pp. 171–194). Berlin: Springer-Verlag.

Seyfarth, R. M., Cheney, D. L., and Marler, P. (1980). Monkey responses to three different alarm calls: Evidence of predator classification and semantic communication. *Science* 210:801–803.

Snowdon, C. T. (1990). Language capacities of nonhuman animals. *Yearbook of Physical Anthropology* 33:215–243.

Struhsaker, T. T. (1967). Auditory communication among vervet monkeys (*Cercopithecus aethiops*). In S. A. Altmann (Ed.) *Social Communication Among Primates* (pp. 281–324). Chicago: University of Chicago Press.

Vauclair, J., Fagot, J., and Hopkins, W. D. (1993). Rotation of mental images in baboons when the visual input is directed to the left cerebral hemisphere. *Psychological Science* 4:99–103.

Ward, J. P. and Hopkins, W. D. (1993). *Primate Laterality: Current Behavioral Evidence of Primate Asymmetries*. New York: Springer-Verlag.

Zuberbuhler, K., Noe, R., and Seyfarth, R. M. (1997). Diana monkey long-distance calls: Messages for conspecifics and predators. *Animal Behaviour* 53:589–604.

7 Gibbon Songs and Human Music from an Evolutionary Perspective

Thomas Geissmann

Abstract

Gibbons (*Hylobates* spp.) produce loud and long song bouts that are mostly exhibited by mated pairs. Typically, mates combine their partly sex-specific repertoire in relatively rigid, precisely timed, and complex vocal interactions to produce well-patterned duets. A cross-species comparison reveals that singing behavior evolved several times independently in the order of primates. Most likely, loud calls were the substrate from which singing evolved in each line. Structural and behavioral similarities suggest that, of all vocalizations produced by nonhuman primates, loud calls of Old World monkeys and apes are the most likely candidates for models of a precursor of human singing and, thus, human music.

odd for ABSTRACT

Sad the calls of the gibbons at the three gorges of Pa-tung;
After three calls in the night, tears wet the [traveler's] dress.
(Chinese song, 4th century, cited in Van Gulik 1967, p. 46).

NOT ABSTRACT?

Of the gibbons or lesser apes, Owen (1868) wrote: ". . . they alone, of brute Mammals, may be said to sing." Although a few other mammals are known to produce songlike vocalizations, gibbons are among the few whose calls elicit an emotional response from human listeners, as documented in the epigraph.

The interesting questions, when comparing gibbon and human singing, are: do similarities between gibbon and human singing help us to reconstruct the evolution of human music (especially singing)? and are these similarities pure coincidence, analogous features developed through convergent evolution under similar selective pressures, or the result of evolution from common ancestral characteristics? To my knowledge, these questions have never been seriously assessed.

Gibbons and Their Songs

What Are Gibbons?

The gibbons or lesser apes form a highly specialized and homogenous group of primates. Twelve gibbon species are currently recognized (Geissmann 1994, 1995) and are usually combined in the family Hylobatidae within the Hominoidea, the group of primates that includes apes and humans (figure 7.1).

Gibbons are arboreal apes living in the tropical rain forests of southeast Asia. Their specializations include, among others, a type of locomotion called brachiation. Thus they are able not only to walk on branches but to locomote swiftly and economically below branches, making them more efficient foragers in the thin-branch niche of trees than other

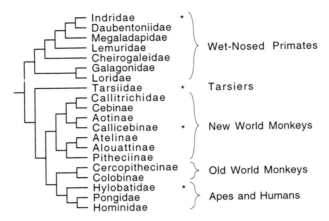

Figure 7.1
Phylogenetic tree of extant primate families and some subfamilies (phylogeny adapted from Purvis 1995; nomenclature after Groves 1993). Stars indicate singing and duet singing behavior, which is known of only four primate genera (*Indri, Tarsius, Callicebus, Hylobates*) representing four only distantly related species groups.

mammals of comparable body weight. Along with their locomotor specialization are a large number of correlated anatomical adaptations, among which the elongation of their arms and hands is most easily noticed (figure 7.2).

Gibbons have a monogamous social structure. Monogamy is quite unusual in mammals and has been suggested to be a social characteristic of only approximately 3% of species, in marked contrast to approximately 90% of bird species (Kleiman 1977). As in most other monogamous species, gibbon groups usually consist of one adult pair and one to three dependent offspring. These groups live in exclusive territories that they actively defend. The most interesting specialization in gibbons, especially with regard to the topic of this book, are their loud morning vocalizations, commonly known as songs.

What Are Gibbon Songs and Duets?

For the purposes of this chapter, a song is what fulfills the criteria set forth by Thorpe (1961:15): "What is usually understood by the term song is a series of notes, generally of more than one type, uttered in succession and so related as to form a recognizable sequence or pattern in time," or a succession of phrases with nonrandom succession probability (*Strophenfolgen mit nicht-zufälliger Folgewahrscheinlichkeit*, Tembrock 1977:33).

Gibbons produce loud and long song bouts. Depending on species and context, the bouts have an average duration of ten to thirty minutes, but I also recorded an uninterrupted song bout of a male *Hylobates lar* with

Figure 7.2
Singing male white-handed gibbon (*Hylobates lar*, Zoo Rapperswil).

a duration of eighty-six minutes. Songs are preferentially uttered in the early morning hours, with species-specific preferences for specific hours before, around, or after dawn.

The songs are stereotyped and species-specific (Marshall and Marshall 1976, 1978; Marler and Tenaza 1977; Haimoff 1984; Marshall and Sugardjito 1986; Geissmann 1993, 1995). Species can easily be identified by their songs (figure 7.3), and vocal characteristics have been used to assess systematic relationships among hylobatids and reconstruct their phylogeny (Haimoff et al. 1982, 1984; Creel and Preuschoft 1984; Marshall, Sugardjito, and Markaya 1984; Geissmann 1993).

Another specialization is the occurrence of duet singing in all gibbons with the exception of *H. klossii* and *H. moloch* (Geissmann 1993). Duets are mostly sung by mated pairs (figure 7.4). Typically, mates combine their repertoire in relatively rigid, more or less precisely timed vocal interactions to produce well-patterned duets.

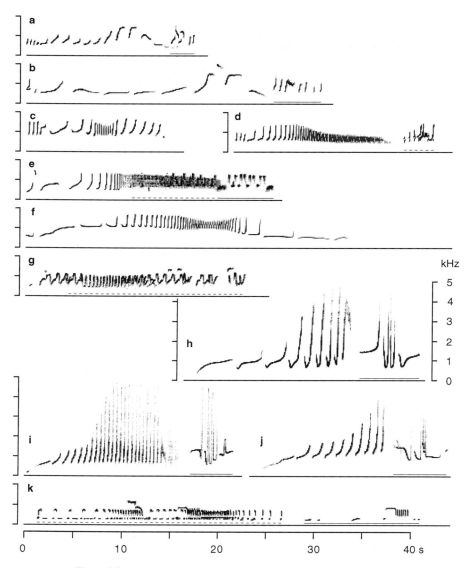

Figure 7.3
Sonagram of gibbon great call sequences. Sonagrams c and f are excerpts from female solo song bouts; all others show duets. Male solo contributions to duets are underlined with a solid line, synchronous male and female vocalizations are underlined with a dashed line.
a. *Hylobates agilis* (Asson Zoo); b. *H. lar* (Paignton Zoo); c. *H. moloch* (Munich Zoo), d. *H. muelleri* (Paignton Zoo); e. *H. pileatus* (Zürich Zoo); f. *H. klossii* (South Pagai, rec.: R.R. Tenaza); g. *H. hoolock* (Kunming Zoo); h. *H. concolor* (Xujiaba, Ailao Mountains); i. *H. leucogenys* (Paris, Ménagerie); j. *H. l. gabriellae* (Mulhouse Zoo); k. *H. syndactylus* (Metro Zoo, Miami).

Figure 7.4
A duetting pair of siamangs (*Hylobates syndactylus*, Munich Zoo).

Males of many gibbon species produce one or several distinct types of short phrases that often become gradually more complex (e.g., in the number of notes, number of distinct note types, degree of frequency modulation) as the song bout proceeds. At more or less regular intervals, females insert long, female-specific phrases that are commonly referred to as great calls. In most species, great calls consist of a particularly rhythmic series of long notes uttered with increasing tempo and/or increasing peak frequency. Males usually stop vocalizing at the beginning of each great call and provide a special reply phrase (coda) to the great call before resuming their more common short phrases. In addition, one or both partners often exhibit an acrobatic display at the climax of the great call, which may be accompanied by piloerection and branch shaking (figure 7.5). The combination of the female great call and male coda is termed a great call sequence, and it may be repeated many times during a single song bout.

Of course, this is a very simplified description of gibbon duetting. Most gibbon species produce sequences other than great call sequences during a song bout. In addition, females of most species contribute phrases other than great calls to the duets, but because great calls (and great call sequences) are so loud and stereotyped, most studies simply ignore the more variable portion of the female repertoire.

In the siamang (*H. syndactylus*) and possibly the hoolock (*H. hoolock*), duet interactions are considerably more complex—even within the great

Figure 7.5
Locomotor display of a male siamang (*Hylobates syndactylus*) during the duet song. Note piloerection (Munich Zoo).

call sequence—than a simple great call-coda combination and include several different phrases and repeated vocal interactions between male and female (Geissmann, in press). According to Marshall and Sugardjito (1986:155) "the [siamang] duet is probably the most complicated opus sung by a land vertebrate other than man."

Inheritance

In contrast to what might be expected in primates and to what we know about song development in many bird species, species-specific characteristics in gibbons are not learned, as demonstrated by studies on the vocal repertoire of a large number of various hybrid gibbons (Geissmann 1984, 1993). A hybrid raised by its parents in a zoo where no other gibbons are present receives only the male song of one parental species and only the female song of the other parental species as potential templates from which song learning would be possible.

For instance, a female hybrid between a male *H. lar* and a female *H. muelleri* never hears a great call other than that of *H. muelleri*. If great calls were learned, the hybrid should produce those of *H. muelleri*. If the parents are a male *H. muelleri* and a female *H. lar*, on the other hand, the hybrid will hear only great calls from *H. lar* and should end up producing those great calls. But neither of these options occurs (figure 7.6). Both types of hybrids produce the same, hybrid-specific types of great

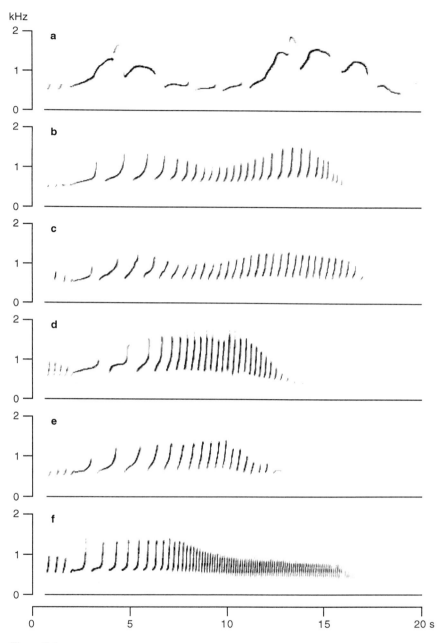

Figure 7.6
Sonagrams of female great calls of two gibbon species, *Hylobates lar* (a) and *H. muelleri* (f), and several unrelated, first-generation hybrids *H. muelleri* × *H. lar* (b–d) and *H. lar* × *H. muelleri* (e). a. *Hylobates lar* (Al Maglio Zoo); b. Micky (Duisburg Zoo); c. no name (private owner, Mazé); d. Tina (Ravensden Farm, Rushden), e. no name (Micke Grove Zoo, rec.: R.R. Tenaza); f. *H. muelleri* (Paignton Zoo).

calls that combine elements of both parental species, although each hybrid has heard great calls of only one of the two species, and each had a different species as a potential template. This and similar results with male and female hybrids among various gibbon species clearly indicate that gibbons do not learn their repertoire from their parents.

Functional Interpretations

Clearly, song serves more than one function in birds and gibbons. Marshall and Marshall (1976) proposed that different selection pressures act on male and female repertoires in gibbon duets. Possibly, different parts of the same individual's duet contribution may also differ in function (Goustard 1985).

Apparently, most songs are produced either without any recognizable external stimulus or in response to songs of neighboring groups. Only occasionally are they produced in response to alarming situations (I repeatedly observed Hainan crested gibbons directing great calls to me).

Functions most frequently suggested for duet songs include territorial advertisement and strengthening of pair bonds (Chivers 1976; Farabaugh 1982; Brockelman and Srikosamatara 1984; Mitani 1985a). The latter in particular is a matter of debate (Cowlishaw 1992) and "has not yet been demonstrated in any animal species that sings" (Haimoff 1983:iv). According to Brockelman (1984:286), "this function of duetting is poorly understood, for it is not clear how exactly duets would do this, or what kind of evidence would support the idea. In short, there is no explicit paradigm for analyzing such communicative behavior."

Wickler (1980) first suggested a plausible mechanism by which duet songs could affect the cohesiveness of the pair bond. If duetting has to be learned at the beginning of each pair formation, this would reduce the probability of partner desertion, since learning investment would have to be provided anew with every new partner. To support this pair-bonding hypothesis, the following three conditions must be met: duet amelioration after pair formation has to be a necessary precondition to copulation; duets have to be pair-specific; and pair-specificity must be based on a mate-specific duetting relationship of at least one mate. To test these predictions, changes in duet structure in two pairs of siamangs (*H. syndactylus*) during a forced partner exchange were examined (Geissmann, in preparation). The two newly formed pairs appear to be the first documented cases to fulfill the requirements underlying Wickler's (1980) hypothesis: the animals showed a stable song pattern with pair-specific traits. After the partner exchange, new pair-specific traits occurred, some of them apparently achieved through a directed effort of one or both individuals.

That study did not prove, however, that duetting in siamangs strengthens the pair bond, because evidence of a direct relationship between pair bond strength and quality of duetting is lacking. If duetting is related to pair bonding, one would expect to find a relationship between its intensity and indicators of pair bond strength. To test this, daily frequency and duration of duetting and three generally accepted indicators of pair bond strength (mutual grooming, behavioral synchronization, and interindividual distance between mates) were recorded in ten siamang groups observed in various zoos (Geissmann and Orgeldinger 1998, in preparation). This revealed that duetting activity was positively correlated with grooming activity and behavioral synchronization, and negatively correlated with interindividual distance between mates. These results suggest that production of coordinated duets by siamang pairs is indeed related to pair bonding.

As mentioned, considerable differences exist among gibbon species in the complexity of song structure and interaction rules, ranging from species that produce solo songs only (e.g., *H. klossii*), to those with a relatively simple duet structure (e.g., *H. leucogenys*), to the siamang with its highly complex vocal interactions. These differences indicate that song bouts also differ in their functions or in the importance of these functions, and interpretations in one species may not necessarily apply to all species. If the complex duet song of the siamang serves, among other functions, to strengthen the pair bond, this may not necessarily apply to gibbons of the *lar* group or the *concolor* group, whose simpler duet structure may not require practicing among newly mated animals. Strengthening of the pair bond may indeed be a highly specialized function of the siamang duet song. The loudness of this song suggests, however, that other functions are also involved. These are most probably related to pair territorial advertisement, bond advertisement, and possibly mate attraction (Geissmann, in preparation).

In birds, experimental evidence supports the notion that songs function as a courtship display in at least some species. In whales, only males appear to sing. Here, the song may function less as a courtship display, but rather play a role in male-male competition (K. Payne, personal communication). In all singing primates (*Indri, Tarsius, Callicebus, Hylobates*; see below), on the other hand, females contribute to singing often as much as males. Experimental data failed to support the hypothesis that gibbon songs may have a mate-attracting function (Mitani 1988). It has repeatedly been observed, on the other hand, that subadult males in wild *H. agilis, H. lar, H. klossii,* and *H. syndactylus* tend to sing more often, for longer durations, or earlier in the morning than mated males (Aldrich-Blake and Chivers 1973; Ellefson 1974; Tenaza 1976; Gittins 1978; Tilson 1981; Raemaekers and Raemaekers 1984;

Raemaekers, Raemaekers, and Haimhoff 1984; personal observation). In another siamang group in Sumatra, a subadult male was twice observed producing solo songs within the territory of his family group before his dispersal (Palombit 1992:319).

Phylogenetic Comparisons

Phylogeny of Singing in Primates

In contrast to birds, singing behavior is rare in mammals and, among primates, is known only for members of the four genera—*Indri, Tarsius, Callicebus,* and *Hylobates* (Robinson 1979, 1981; MacKinnon and MacKinnon 1980; Haimoff 1986; Niemitz et al. 1991; Geissmann 1993; Thalmann et al. 1993; Müller 1994, 1995; Nietsch and Kopp 1998). These singing primates comprise about twenty-six species (depending on the currently accepted taxonomy), amounting to about 11% of primate species or 6% of primate genera.

In all singing primates, males and females both sing, and in most singing primates, duet singing occurs. It is interesting to note that all primate species that are known to sing are also thought to have a monogamous social structure. In birds, too, duet songs mainly occur in monogamous species. This suggests that the evolution of singing behavior in primates and of duet singing behavior in general are somehow related to the evolution of monogamy.

Since the four species groups of primates that exhibit singing (and duet singing) behavior are not closely related, it is likely that singing (and duet singing) evoled four times independently within the order of primates.

Phylogeny of Singing in Gibbons

Long, loud, and complex song bouts have been described for all gibbon species. What did ancestral gibbons sound like? It is probably safe to assume that vocal characteristics shared by all modern gibbon species were also present in their last common ancestor. Just what are these common characteristics? Gibbon songs consist of phrases that are typically pure in tone and with energy concentrated in the fundamental frequency. Depending on species, the fundamental frequency of song vocalizations ranges between 0.2 and 5 kHz. During the song bout, male contributions exhibit some form of gradual development from initially simpler phrases to increasingly complex phrases. Females contribute a stereotyped great call phrase and exhibit a ritualized locomotor display at the climax of the great call. In many species, the male contributes a vocal coda to the female's great call and may also participate in the display.

A comparative phylogenetic analysis of gibbon songs, taking into consideration comparative characteristics of loud calls of other Old World monkeys and apes, came to the following conclusions concerning the evolution of gibbon songs (Geissmann 1993). The recent hylobatids represent a monophyletic group whose common ancestor produced duet songs, although not all recent species are known to duet. Duet songs of recent gibbon species are likely to have evolved according to the song-splitting theory (a term coined by Wickler and Seibt 1982). Accordingly, the duets probably evolved from a song that was common to both sexes and only later became separated into male-specific and female-specific parts. In addition, a process tentatively called duet splitting is suggested to have led secondarily from a duetting species to nonduetting species such as *H. klossii* and *H. moloch*, in that the contributions of the partners split into temporally segregated solo songs.

Great calls of all gibbon species are, indeed, a homologous song phrase. The acceleration of the rate of note emission during the great call (and possibly the subsequent slow-down in rhythm near the end of the call) are probably the ancestral condition. The ancestor of modern gibbons probably produced great calls with a relatively moderate acceleration similar to that of *H. moloch*. The use of biphasic notes (alternate production of exhalation and inhalation sounds) probably represents a primitive characteristic for both male and female vocalizations. Of interest, biphasic notes occur in the great calls of only few gibbon species (*H. agilis*, *H. lar*, *H. hoolock*), but are dominant in those of a hybrid between *H. muelleri* and *H. syndactylus*, although neither males nor females of the two parental species are known to produce these types of notes. Biphasic notes are dominant in the female great calls of *H. hoolock* and *H. syndactylus*, and they also occur rarely in *H. agilis*, *H. lar*, and *H. moloch*. These types of notes are also dominant in the male song of *H. hoolock*, *H. agilis*, and *H. pileatus*, and occur occasionally in *H. lar* and *H. moloch* as well (figure 7.7).

Comparison with Old World Monkeys and Great Apes

Great apes and humans are usually recognized as being the phylogenetic sister group to the gibbons. Among members of this group, some vocalizations can be discerned that at least in part resemble elements of the gibbon song (i.e., great call) in their presumed functions and to a lesser degree in structure. These vocalizations are thought to be used primarily in interindividual or intergroup spacing.

In orangutans (*Pongo pygmaeus*), long calls are given by males only, and are often accompanied by piloerection and branch-shaking displays. Calls last up to one minute in Sumatra and up to three minutes in Borneo. Their frequency is concentrated below .7 kHz in Sumatra and

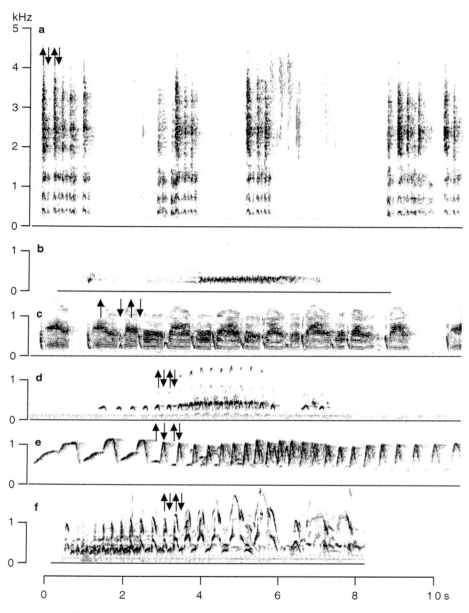

Figure 7.7

Occurrence of biphasic notes in loud calls (or excerpts of loud calls) of Old World monkeys (a–d) and apes (e, f). Alternating exhalation and inhalation notes are indicated by upward and downward arrows, respectively. In (b), no arrows are used, because exhalation and inhalation notes are produced very rapidly in this example. a. *Chlorocebus aethiops* (two individuals, South Africa; Roché 1994); b. *Lophocebus albigena* (adult male, Gabon, Bouchain, and Gautier 1995); c. *Colobus satanas* (Gabon; Roché 1994), d. *Trachypithecus johnii* (India; rec.: G. Hohmann); e. *Hylobates hoolock* (adult female and juvenile male, Kunming Zoo); f. *Pan troglodytes* (Gambia; Roché 1994).

below 1.3 kHz in Borneo. Long calls begin with a short series of low-frequency, low-intensity bubbling notes that build up to a long series of evenly spaced, high-intensity moans or roars, then tail off gradually in another series of bubbling notes. The number of notes is rarely more than twenty-five in Sumatra, but sometimes up to fifty in Borneo. Bubbling inhalation notes occur in the inhalatory pauses between roars (Rijksen 1978). Long calls are mostly produced during the night in Sumatra, but during the daytime in Borneo with a peak between 9:00 and 10:00 A.M. They are the only orangutan vocalization that can be heard over long distances and are hypothesized to mediate interindividual spacing among males (Brandes 1931; Hofer 1972; MacKinnon 1974; Rijksen 1978; Galdikas 1983; Mitani 1985b; Roché 1994).

In gorillas (*Gorilla gorilla*), hoot series are most frequently given by silverback males and may be terminated by chest beating, branch breaking, or runs through thick foliage. Hoot series last only a few seconds (Schaller 1963; Fossey 1972, 1983; Hess 1988; Roché 1994; Bouchain and Gautier 1995) with frequency concentrated between 1 and 1.8 kHz. They typically consist of two to twenty, but exceptionally up to eighty-four, hoots that may become slurred at the end, blending into a growling sound. Hoots are often presented in accelerated series, with individual sounds resembling a bubbling trill at the climax. Hoot series often begin softly and with low frequency, but intensity and frequency build up during a call. Inhalation notes were not reliably recognized in the recordings and sonagrams available during this study. Hoot series are fairly loud and "may travel for roughly a mile" (Fossey 1983). This call is hypothesized to be used primarily in long-range intergroup communication.

In common chimpanzees (*Pan troglodytes*), a distinctive loud call known as the pant-hoot is uttered by both sexes and all ages, but most often by males (Marler 1969; Marler and Hobbett 1975; Marler and Tenaza 1977; Goodall 1986; Mitani et al. 1992; Roché 1994). Pant-hoots last from two to twenty-three seconds and their fundamental frequency ranges from .2 to 1 kHz. Pant-hoots have four distinct phases. Calls may begin with a brief introduction consisting of a series of unmodulated tonal elements of low frequency. A progressively louder build-up follows, containing elements that are typically shorter than those in the introduction and produced on both inhalation and exhalation (figure 7.7f). Some further acceleration in rhythm may occur during this phase. The third phase, the climax, is characterized by one or several long, frequency-modulated elements resembling a scream in acoustic properties. This section is frequently present during pant-hooting of male chimpanzees and typically absent in females. Frequency reaches its peak in this phase. It is often accompanied by a vigorous charging display, which may include erection of hair, running along the ground, dragging or flailing branches, throwing rocks or other loose material, slapping the ground with hands, stomping with feet, hitting or stamping at a tree (drumming display), seizing branches and swaying them vigorously from side to side, or showing exaggerated leaps or brachiation in a tree (Goodall 1986). Pant-hoots conclude with a let-down portion, which includes unmodulated tonal elements of low frequency, similar to those of the build-up.

Pant-hooting is given in several contexts, including in response to other pant-hooting individuals, after rejoining other community members, in response to strange conspecifics, on arriving at a particularly rich food source, during agonistic displays, on capturing prey items, and during the night. It can be heard over long distances and its functions have been hypothesized to include long-range announcement of an individual's presence and sex, hence mediating interindividual spacing among some individuals and groups, and reunion of others. In bonobos (*P. paniscus*), apparently homologous vocalizations are known under the term hooting complex and occur in similar contexts as pant-hooting of common chimpanzees (de Waal 1988).

Characteristics of these great ape calls resembling at least some gibbon songs (especially female great calls) include loudness, a hypothetical function in long-distance interindividual or intergroup communication (all species), acceleration of note rhythm (common in chimpanzees and gorillas, apparently absent in orangutans), a final slow-down in rhythm (chimpanzees), higher intensity in the central section of the call (apparently in all species of great apes, but variable in orangutans), biphasic notes consisting of alternating exhalation and inhalation (absent in gorillas), higher frequency in the central section of the call, pure tone of notes (most prominent in chimpanzees), and frequent accompaniment with piloerection and a locomotor display that may include leg kicking, stomping, branch shaking, vegetation slapping or throwing, jumping, running, chest beating, or ground thumping.

Among members of Old World monkeys, too, certain vocalizations can be discerned that resemble some elements of the gibbon song (great call) in function and to some degree in structure. In many species these characteristics are restricted to loudness and a hypothetical function in long-distance interindividual or intergroup communication (Vogel 1973; Horwich 1976; Tilson and Tenaza 1976; Waser 1977, 1982; Oates and Trocco 1983; Herzog and Hohmann 1984; Hohmann and Herzog 1985; Gautier 1988). Other characteristics mentioned above are frequently absent. In many species (*Cercocebus* spp., *Lophocebus* spp., *Macaca silenus*, *Papio* spp., *Presbytis potenziani*, *P. thomasi*, *Simias concolor*, *Trachypithecus* spp.) the occurrence of biphasic notes consisting of alternating exhalation and inhalation has been reported. In some species

(*Cercocebus galeritus*, *Macaca silenus*, *Trachypithecus johnii*, *Semnop-ithecus entellus*) notes are remarkably pure in tone, and in some (*Cercocebus galeritus*, *Trachypithecus johnii*) they are produced with accelerating rhythm. In addition, these calls are often supplemented with a ritualized locomotor display (Vogel 1973; Horwich 1976; Tilson and Tenaza 1976; Tilson 1977; Byrne 1981; Waser 1982; Herzog and Hohmann 1984; Steenbeek and Assink 1998).

Among great apes, chimpanzee pant-hooting apparently shares most similarities with gibbon great calls. Among Old World monkeys, similar-ities with great calls are particularly prominent in the whooping display of the Nilgiri langur (*Trachypithecus johnii*) and some other Asian colobines. These similarities do not necessarily imply homology, but it is tempting to assume that loud calls with biphasic notes and an acceler-ated rate of note emission followed by a slowing down represent the ancestral condition of hominoids, and perhaps even of Old World monkeys.

Long, uninterrupted vocal bouts that correspond to the definition of songs are, however, not known for any of these species. The sequential nature of female solo song bouts and duet song bouts, as well as the gradual development of increasingly complex phrases observed in male solo song bouts, appear to be synapomorphic characteristics of gibbons not reported for other Old World monkeys and apes. It should also be noted that the loud calls of most Old World monkeys and great apes described above are mainly male-specific vocalizations or preferentially uttered by males, whereas their main structural similarities to gibbon songs are concentrated on great calls, which are essentially female-specific. The occurrence of female loud calls may to some degree be related to the monogamous mating system of gibbons. In addition, the gap between male and female loud calls is reduced to some extent by the observation that pant-hooting also occurs in female chimpanzees (see above), whereas male gibbons of the *concolor* group, and occasion-ally of other gibbon species, typically produce great call-like phrases before reaching adulthood (personal observation). Moreover, loud calls of male Mentawai langurs (*Presbytis potenziani*) directed toward adja-cent groups may be supplemented by a facultative coda of three to four loud, apparently pure tones produced by the female, hence forming a simple duet (Tilson and Tenaza 1976).

Most primate species produce specific, at least partly stereotyped loud calls in territorial or alarming contexts. It may be speculated that the alternate use of inhalation and exhalation notes may be ancestral to an even larger taxonomic group than just Old World monkeys and apes, maybe to all primates. Although available evidence is inconclusive, it should be noted that biphasic vocalizations are apparently used in loud calls by some New World monkeys (*Alouatta, Callicebus*) and wet-nosed primates (*Propithecus, Avahi*; personal observation).

A Link to Human Music?

Music may be one of the most ancient and universal forms of human communication. Song is one of the most prominent features in most forms of popular music, and the human voice has often be identified as the most ancestral instrument used in music (Ewens 1995).

As pointed out above, singing behavior appears to have developed several times in primate evolution. Both the context in which singing occurs in nonhuman primates and the structure of some song contributions show similarities to territorial calls or alarm calls in nonsinging species. This suggests that singing in primates evolved each time from loud calls used in a territorial or alarm context. It makes sense to assume that the same applies to the evolution of human singing behavior, and that loud calls of early hominids may have been the substrate from which human singing and, ultimately, music evolved.

Most forms of music are tied to emotionality and have a powerful effect on both the audience and the performer, compelling them to shake body parts to the rhythm, beat the rhythm by clapping or stomping, or locomote (dance) to the rhythm. Often, dancing appears to be inseparably linked with music (Ewens 1995). The almost universal, almost hypnotic effect of music on most humans suggests that this is an ancestral characteristic that may have a strong inherited component. In addition, this behavior bears an obvious similarity to ritualized locomotor displays (drumming, stomping, branch shaking) associated with loud calls of many Old World primates, providing additional support that music is derived from loud calls.

It is tempting to assume that early hominid singing shared many characteristics with loud calls of modern Old World monkeys and especially apes, such as loudness for long-distance communication, pure tonal quality of notes, stereotyped phrases, biphasic notes, accelerando in note rhythm and possibly a slow-down near the end of the phrase, a locomotor display, and a strong inherited component.

After the divergence between early humans and some forms of African apes from a common ancestor, several characteristics of human music evolved that are not found in loud calls of modern monkeys and apes. The most conspicuous of these are a steady rhythm (pulse, beat), reduction of inherited stereotypy in favor of increased importance of learning phrases and sequence rules, and the option to invent new signal patterns (improvisation) and new conventions (exact repetition of improvised units) spontaneously. Universals of human music are difficult to identify but probably include a steady, accentuated beat (see Arom, Nettl, and Mâche this volume). Although some primates are able to produce short, monosyllabic calls for several seconds at a relatively steady pulse (e.g., some galagos, Galagonidae; E. Zimmermann, personal communication) and mouse lemurs (Cheirogaleidae; personal observation), nonhuman primates, unlike humans, do not seem to be able to keep a steady pulse in their song vocalizations.

There is an interesting report on pulse-keeping behavior in a female white-handed gibbon (*H. lar*). This zoo animal was observed to follow the beats of a metronome with its short calls (Ziegler and Knobloch 1968) as long as the speed remained within the limits of 60 to 122 (the authors probably referred to beats per minute). Outside of these tolerance limits, the animal produced short notes at a rhythm of approximately 112. The gibbon's response was best at a metronome tempo of 60, and not when presented with its own normal speed of 112. The relevance of this observation is difficult to assess. The authors provided no sonagrams of the vocalizations, but the description may refer to a form of contact call rather than a song vocalization.

What fitness advantage is there to add a steady beat to a song vocalization? The beat may help larger social groups to participate in a song, to coordinate it. A well-coordinated song may be a more effective display than a cacophony of voices, and other social groups are less likely to attack or threaten well-coordinated groups. In addition, introduction of a steady beat may make it easier to assess a groups cohesiveness and therefore its strength based on group display.

The main message of this chapter is that loud calls in modern apes and music in modern humans are derived from a common ancestral form of loud call. If this interpretation is correct, early hominid music may also have served functions resembling those of ape loud calls. Loud calls are believed to serve a variety of functions, including territorial advertisement; intergroup intimidation and spacing; announcing the precise locality of specific individuals, food sources, or danger; and strengthening intragroup cohesion. The most widely distributed (albeit not universal) function, and probably the most likely function of early hominid music, is to display and possibly reinforce the unity of a social group toward other groups. In humans, this function is still evident today whenever groups of people, be they united by political, religious, age, or other factors, define themselves by their music. National hymns, military music, battle songs of fans and cheerleaders encouraging their favorite sports teams, or the strict musical preferences of youth gangs may serve as examples of this phenomenon, whose origin may go back to the very beginning of human evolution.

Acknowledgments

Some taperecordings used in the present study were kindly made available by Dr. G. Hohmann and Dr. R. R. Tenaza. I am grateful to Almut Hold and Thomas Schmid for reading and commenting on this manuscript.

References

Aldrich-Blake, F. P. G. and Chivers, D. J. (1973). On the genesis of a group of siamang. *American Journal of Physical Anthropology* 38:631–636.

Bouchain, C. and Gautier, J.-P. (1995). *Le Monde des Singes / Primate World*, vol. 2. Compact disk. Mens, France: Sitelle.

Brandes, R. (1931). Über den Kehlkopf des Orang-Utan in verschiedenen Altersstadien mit besonderer Berücksichtigung der Kehlsackfrage. *Morphologisches Jahrbuch* 69:1–61.

Brockelman, W. Y. (1984). Social behaviour of gibbons: Introduction. In H. Preuschoft, D. J., Chivers, W. Y., Brockelman, and N. Creel (Eds.) *The Lesser Apes: Evolutionary and Behavioural Biology* (pp. 285–290). Edinburgh: Edinburgh University Press.

Brockelman, W. Y. and Srikosamatara, S. (1984). Maintenance and evolution of social structure in gibbons. In H. Preuschoft, D. J. Chivers, W. Y. Brockelman, and N. Creel (Eds.) *The Lesser Apes: Evolutionary and Behavioural Biology* (pp. 298–323). Edinburgh: Edinburgh University Press.

Byrne, R. W. (1981). Uses of long-range calls during ranging by Guinea baboons. In A. B. Chiarelli and R. S. Corruccini (Eds.) *Primate Behavior and Sociobiology* (pp. 104–109). Berlin and New York: Springer-Verlag.

Chivers, D. J. (1976). Communication within and between family groups of siamang (*Symphalangus syndactylus*). *Behaviour* 57:116–135.

Cowlishaw, G. (1992). Song function in gibbons. *Behaviour* 121:131–153.

Creel, N. and Preuschoft, H. (1984). Systematics of the lesser apes: A quantitative taxonomic analysis of craniometric and other variables. In H. Preuschoft, D. J. Chivers, W. Y. Brockelman, and N. Creel (Eds.) *The Lesser Apes: Evolutionary and Behavioural Biology* (pp. 562–613). Edinburgh: Edinburgh University Press.

Ellefson, J. O. (1974). A natural history of white-handed gibbons in the Malayan peninsula. In D. M. Rumbaugh (Ed.) *Gibbon and Siamang*, vol. 3 (pp. 1–136). Basel and New York: Karger.

Ewens, G. (1995). *Die Klänge Afrikas: Zeitgenössische Musik von Kairo bis Kapstadt* (T. Brückner, Trans.). München: Marino Verlag. (Original work published 1991.)

Farabaugh, S. M. (1982). The ecological and social significance of duetting. In D. E. Kroodsma, E. H. Miller, and H. Ouellet (Eds.) *Acoustic Communication in Birds* (pp. 85–124). New York and London: Academic Press.

Fossey, D. (1972). Vocalizations of the mountain gorilla (*Gorilla gorilla beringei*). *Animal Behavior* 20:36–53.

Fossey, D. (1983). *Gorillas in the Mist*. Boston: Houghton Mifflin.

Galdikas, B. M. F. (1983). The orangutan long call and snag crashing at Tanjung Puting reserve. *Primates* 24:371–384.

Gautier, J.-P. (1988). Interspecific affinities among guenons as deduced from vocalizations. In A. Gautier-Hion, F. Bourlière, J.-P. Gautier, and J. Kingdon (Eds.) *A Primate Radiation: Evolutionary Biology of the African Guenons* (pp. 194–226). Cambridge, UK: Cambridge University Press.

Geissmann, T. (1984). Inheritance of song parameters in the gibbon song, analyzed in 2 hybrid gibbons (*Hylobates pileatus* x *H. lar*). *Folia Primatologica* 42:216–235.

Geissmann, T. (1993). *Evolution of Communication in Gibbons (Hylobatidae)*. Doctoral thesis, Anthropological Institute, Philosophy Faculty II, Zürich University.

Geissmann, T. (1994). Systematik der Gibbons. *Zeitschrift des Kölner Zoo* 37:65–77.

Geissmann, T. (1995). Gibbon systematics and species identification. *International Zoo News* 42:467–501.

Geissmann, T. (In press). Duet songs of the siamang, *Hylobates syndactylus*. I. Structure and organisation. *Primate Report*.

Geissmann, T. (In preparation). Duet songs of the siamang, *Hylobates syndactylus*. II. Testing the pair-bonding hypothesis during a partner exchange.

Geissmann, T. and Orgeldinger, M. (1998). Duet or divorce! [abstr]. *Folia Primatologica* 69:283.

Geissmann, T. and Orgeldinger, M. (In preparation). Duet or divorce: The relationship between duet singing and the pair bond.

Gittins, S. P. (1978). Hark! The beautiful song of the gibbon. *New Scientist* 80:832–834.

Goodall, J. (1986). *The Chimpanzees of Gombe. Patterns of Behavior*. Cambridge and London: Bellknap Press of Harvard University Press.

Goustard, M. (1985). Structure acoustique et fonctions des vocalisations territoriales, chez le Gibbon à mains blanches (*Hylobates lar*), observé dans son habitat naturel, en Thaïlande. *Annales des Sciences Naturelles, Zoologie, Paris, 13e série* 7:265–279.

Groves, C. P. (1993). Order primates. In D. E. Wilson and D. M. Reader (Eds.) *Mammal Species of the World: A Taxonomic and Geographic Reference*, 2nd. ed. (pp. 243–277). Washington, DC: Smithsonian Institution Press.

Haimoff, E. H. (1983). *Gibbon Songs: An Acoustical, Organizational, and Behavioural Analysis*. Doctoral dissertation, University of Cambridge.

Haimoff, E. H. (1984). Acoustic and organizational features of gibbon songs. In H. Preuschoft, D. J. Chivers, W. Y. Brockelman, and N. Creel (Eds.) *The Lesser Apes: Evolutionary and Behavioural Biology* (pp. 333–353). Edinburgh: Edinburgh University Press.

Haimoff, E. H. (1986). Convergence in the duetting of monogamous Old World primates. *Journal of Human Evolution* 15:51–59.

Haimoff, E. H., Chivers, D. J., Gittins, S. P., and Whitten, A. J. (1982). A phylogeny of gibbons based on morphological and behavioural characters. *Folia Primatologica* 39:213–237.

Haimoff, E. H., Gittins, S. P., Whitten, A. J., and Chivers, D. J. (1984). A phylogeny and classification of gibbons based on morphology and ethology. In H. Preuschoft, D. J. Chivers, W. Y. Brockelman, and N. Creel (Eds.) *The Lesser Apes: Evolutionary and Behavioural Biology* (pp. 614–632). Edinburgh: Edinburgh University Press.

Herzog, M. O. and Hohmann, G. M. (1984). Male loud calls in *Macaca silenus* and *Presbytis johnii*: A comparison. *Folia Primatologica* 43:189–197.

Hess, J. (1988). *Berggorillalaute: Akustische Erinnerungen an die Berggorillas der Familie 5* (audio cassette). Fuchsmattstr. 27, CH—4107. Ettingen: HM Produktion.

Hofer, H. (1972). Über den Gesang des Orang-Utan. *Zoologische Garten (N.F.)* 41:299–302.

Hohmann, G. M. and Herzog, M. O. (1985). Vocal communication in lion-tailed macaques (*Macaca silenus*). *Folia Primatologica* 45:148–178.

Horwich, R. H. (1976). The whooping display in Nilgiri langurs: An example of daily fluctuations superimposed on a general trend. *Primates* 17:419–431.

Kleiman, D. G. (1977). Monogamy in mammals. *Quarterly Review of Biology* 52:39–69.

MacKinnon, J. (1974). The behaviour and ecology of wild orang-utan (*Pongo pygmaeus*). *Animal Behavior* 22:3–74.

MacKinnon, J. and MacKinnon, K. (1980). The behavior of wild spectral tarsiers. *International Journal of Primatology* 1:361–379.

Marler, P. (1969). Vocalizations of wild chimpanzees: An introduction. In C. R. Carpenter (Ed.) *Proceedings of the Second International Congress of Primatology, Atlanta, GA 1968*, vol. 1: *Behavior* (pp. 94–100). Basel and New York: Karger.

Marler, P. and Hobbett, L. (1975). Individuality in a long-range vocalization of wild chimpanzees. *Zeitschrift für Tierpsychologie* 38:97–109.

Marler, P. and Tenaza, R. (1977). Signaling behavior of apes with special reference to vocalization. In T. A. Sebeok (Ed.) *How Animals Communicate* (pp. 965–1033). Bloomington and London: Indiana University Press.

Marshall, J. T. and Marshall, E. R. (1976). Gibbons and their territorial songs. *Science* 193:235–237.

Marshall, J. T. and Marshall, E. R. (1978). *The Gibbons* (phonograph disk). J.W. Hardy and C.K. Hardy (Eds.). Gainesville, FL: ARA-Records.

Marshall, J. T. and Sugardjito, J. (1986). Gibbon systematics. In D. R. Swindler and J. Erwin (Eds.) *Comparative Primate Biology*, vol. 1: *Systematics, Evolution, and Anatomy* (pp. 137–185). New York: Liss.

Marshall, J. T., Sugardjito, J., and Markaya, M. (1984). Gibbons of the lar group: Relationships based on voice. In H. Preuschoft, D. J. Chivers, W. Y. Brockelman, and N. Creel (Eds.) *The Lesser Apes: Evolutionary and Behavioural Biology* (pp. 533–541). Edinburgh: Edinburgh University Press.

Mitani, J. C. (1985a). Gibbon song duets and intergroup spacing. *Behaviour* 92:59–96.

Mitani, J. C. (1985b). Sexual selection and adult male orangutan long calls. *Animal Behavior* 33:272–283.

Mitani, J. C. (1988). Male gibbon (*Hylobates agilis*) singing behavior: Natural history, song variations and function. *Ethology* 79:177–194.

Mitani, J. C., Hasegawa, T., Gros-Louis, J., Marler, P., and Byrne, R. (1992). Dialects in wild chimpanzees? *American Journal of Primatology* 27:233–243.

Müller, A. (1994). *Duettieren beim Springaffen (Callicebus cupreus)*. Diploma thesis, Anthropological Institute, Zürich University.

Müller, A. (1995). Duetting in the titi monkey *Callicebus cupreus*. *Neotropical Primates* 3:18–19.

Niemitz, C., Nietsch, A., Warter, S., and Rumpler, Y. (1991). *Tarsius dianae*: A new primate species from central Sulawesi (Indonesia). *Folia Primatologica* 56:105–116.

Nietsch, A. and Kopp, M.-L. (1998). Role of vocalization in species differentiation of Sulawesi tarsiers. *Folia Primatologica* 69 (Supplement 1):371–378.

Oates, J. F. and Trocco, T. F. (1983). Taxonomy and phylogeny of black-and-white colobus monkeys: Inferences from an analysis of loud call variation. *Folia Primatologica* 40:83–113.

Owen, R. (1868). *On the Anatomy of Vertebrates*, vol. 3: *Mammals*. London: Longmans, Green.

Palombit, R. A. (1992). *Pair Bonds and Monogamy in Wild Siamang (*Hylobates syndactylus*) and White-Handed Gibbon (*Hylobates lar*) in Northern Sumatra*. Doctoral thesis, University of California, Davis.

Purvis, A. (1995). A composite estimate of primate phylogeny. *Philosophical Transactions of the Royal Society of London B* 348:405–421.

Raemaekers, J. J. and Raemaekers, P. M. (1984). Vocal interactions between two male gibbons, *Hylobates lar*. *Natural History Bulletin of the Siam Society* 32:95–106.

Raemaekers, J. J., Raemaekers, P. M., and Haimoff, E. H. (1984). Loud calls of the gibbon (*Hylobates lar*): Repertoire, organization and context. *Behaviour* 91:146–189.

Rijksen, H. D. (1978). *A Field Study on Sumatran Orang-Utans (*Pongo pygmaeus abelii Lesson 1827*): Ecology, Behaviour and Conservation*. Wageningen, The Netherlands: Veenman and Zonen.

Robinson, J. G. (1979). An analysis of the organization of vocal communication in the titi monkey, *Callicebus moloch*. *Zeitschrift für Tierpsychologie* 49:381–405.

Robinson, J. G. (1981). Vocal regulation of inter- and intragroup spacing during boundary encounters in the titi monkey, *Callicebus moloch*. *Primates* 22:161–172.

Roché, J. C. (1994). *Le Monde des Singes / Primate World*, vol. 1. Compact disk. Mens, France: Sitelle.

Schaller, G. B. (1963). *The Mountain Gorilla: Ecology and Behavior*. Chicago: University of Chicago Press.

Steenbeek, R. and Assink, P. (1998). Individual differences in long-distance calls of male wild Thomas langurs (*Presbytis thomasi*). *Folia Primatologica* 69:77–80.

Tembrock, G. (1977). *Tierstimmenforschung: Eine Einführung in die Bioakustik*. Wittenberg Lutherstadt: Ziemsen.

Tenaza, R. R. (1976). Songs, choruses and countersinging among Kloss' gibbons (*Hylobates klossi*) in Siberut island, Indonesia. *Zeitschrift für Tierpsychologie* 40:37–52.

Thalmann, U., Geissmann, T., Simona, A., and Mutschler, T. (1993). The indris of Anjanaharibe-Sud, northeastern Madagascar. *International Journal of Primatology* 14:357–381.

Thorpe, W. H. (1961). *Bird-Song: The Biology of Vocal Communication and Expression in Birds*. Cambridge monographs in experimental biology no. 12. Cambridge, UK: Cambridge University Press.

Tilson, R. L. (1977). Social organization of Simakobu monkeys (*Nasalis concolor*) in Siberut island, Indonesia. *Journal of Mammalogy* 5:202–212.

Tilson, R. L. (1981). Family formation strategies of Kloss's gibbons. *Folia Primatologica* 35:259–287.

Tilson, R. L. and Tenaza, R. R. (1976). Monogamy and duetting in an Old World monkey. *Nature* 263:320–321.

van Gulik, R. H. (1967). *The Gibbon in China: An Essay in Chinese Animal Lore*. Leiden: Brill.

Vogel, C. (1973). Acoustical communication among free-ranging common Indian langurs (*Presbytis entellus*) in two different habitats of north India. *American Journal of Anthropology* 38:469–480.

de Waal, F. B. M. (1988). The communicative repertoire of captive bonobos (*Pan paniscus*), compared to that of chimpanzees. *Behaviour* 106:183–251.

Waser, P. M. (1977). Individual recognition, intragroup cohesion and intergroup spacing: Evidence from sound playback to forest monkeys. *Behaviour* 60:28–74.

Waser, P. M. (1982). The evolution of male loud calls among mangabeys and baboons. In S. T. Snowdon, C. H. Brown, and M. R. Petersen (Eds.) *Primate Communication* (pp. 117–143). Cambridge, UK: Cambridge University Press.

Wickler, W. (1980). Vocal dueting and the pairbond. I: Coyness and partner commitment. A hypothesis. *Zeitschrift für Tierpsychologie* 52:201–209.

Wickler, W. and Seibt, U. (1982). Song splitting in the evolution of dueting. *Zeitschrift für Tierpsychologie* 59:127–140.

Ziegler, P. and Knobloch, J. (1968). *Vergleichende und experimentelle Untersuchungen zur Lautgebung der Hylobatini*. Staatsexamensarbeit, Zoologisches Institut, Mathematisch-Naturwissenschaftliche Fakultät, Humboldt-Universität, Berlin.

8 **Social Organization as a Factor in the Origins of Language and Music**

Maria Ujhelyi

Abstract
The social organization of primate species is a key factor in the evolution of vocal communication, and this is relevant to the emergence of music and language. The most elementary languagelike characteristics, both in structure and function, arise in the context of vocal territorial marking, which among present-day species has attained its most sophisticated form in the solo and duet singing of the lesser apes (gibbons). The social organization of the great apes, especially that of common chimpanzees and bonobos, makes it possible to preserve and maintain these characteristics while adding new, essential functions, namely, an increase in voluntary control and social transmission. However, specializations present in these species, which differ from those of humans ancestors, are obstacles to further elaboration of these capacities. Either typical speech sounds and true grammar, or the application of representational meaning to external objects, is as yet missing at this stage. This primatological perspective provides a heuristic framework for the reconstruction of a social setting in which these limitations would not have been operative and, consequently, might have permitted language to emerge as a qualitative novelty.

In this chapter I suggest that issues pertaining to the origins of music and of language are related by more than superficial parallelism. Since human language differs qualitatively from animal communication systems, any attempt to reconstruct its origin within the framework of biology must come to grips with the problem of qualitative change. Qualitative change, the emergence of new qualities, implies system-level organizational change. For the evolution of communication, the most important system level is sociality: evolution of the social system.[1] Since the social system, the network of social behaviors and interactions, supplies the framework and field for possible communicative interactions, evolutionary change there may result in drastic and discontinuous transitions at the level of communication and vocal signals. Thus, the connection between sociality and mental capacities, including communicative ones, becomes a central issue for understanding the primate order (Ujhelyi 1979). As early as the 1970s primatologists suggested that social contexts pose stronger challenges for primate intelligence than manual tasks (Humphrey 1976). Since then a number of field studies and laboratory investigations showed that monkeys and apes have more sophisticated problem-solving skills in dealing with social relations than in object manipulation (see Cheney and Seyfarth 1990). Sociality as a principal selection factor in the evolution of primate intelligence is thus gaining wider acceptance (Whiten and Byrne 1988).

Since communication itself (including language) is an aspect of social interactions, it may not be independent of social organization, and its evolution may not be independent of the evolution of social systems. If we suppose that language and music have a long evolutionary history rooted in primate communication, we are forced to seek those special forms of primate sociality that might support evolution of languagelike and musiclike capacities.

This approach might also look to great apes for the emergence of intermediate stages between lower-level animal communication and human language. Presumably the potential for reorganization existed at the level of the common ancestor of apes and humans and led to nonhuman-type specializations in great apes, whereas a radical reorganization ensued in the course of language evolution.

Language Competence of Chimpanzees

Language-teaching experiments demonstrate that both common chimpanzees and bonobos are able to acquire two fundamental language characteristics, at least to a certain extent. First, trained chimpanzees understand that arbitrary signs can replace and represent objects. Premack's chimpanzee Sarah was able to carry out classification without the actual presence of objects, using only plastic figures representing words. She chose, for example, a pink square and blue triangle as identical, since they both meant fruits (Premack 1985). So, chimpanzees can learn and use the names of a number of objects, attributes, and actions, and can be taught a considerable vocabulary of words (Savage-Rumbaugh 1979; Gardner and Gardner 1984; Premack 1985). These animals' comprehension of words is not limited to gestures or pictograms, but can include spoken utterances (Brakke and Savage-Rumbaugh 1995). That is, they can acquire the meanings of spoken words even though they cannot produce articulated sounds themselves. Second, chimpanzees and bonobos are also able to learn that two or more linguistic elements can be linked into sentencelike structures in such a way that the order of their arrangement influences their meaning (Premack 1985; Savage-Rumbaugh et al. 1993).

With the extension of field studies directed to natural vocalizations, it became clear that laboratory results were not artificial products, but that vocalizations of both species in the wild have characteristics that furnish preconditions for these types of performances. Both chimpanzees and bonobos emit a special form of vocalization, a long call, that is composed of smaller, acoustically distinguishable elements (Mitani et al. 1992; Clark and Wrangham 1993; Hohmann and Fruth 1994). Although the order of the four fundamental units is not changed, the animals insert individually selected elements of the species-specific vocal repertoire into different positions of the call (Arcadi 1996). In this way a large number of syntactically different call variants can be produced.

To discover the function of these variants, Mitani, Gros-Louis, and Macedonia (1996) compared two types of calls, pant-hoots and pant-grunts. The former, typically a long-distance call, shows greater interindividual variability than the latter, which usually is uttered within visual distance of a conspecific. Moreover, individually distinguishable call variants inform group members not only about the location of the caller but also about his social status, and perhaps about his individual identity (Clark and Wrangham 1994).

The function of long call variability is related to chimpanzee-bonobo organizational patterns. In everyday activities, chimpanzees associate in temporary parties that vary in size and composition. This is in contrast to macaques or other group-living common monkeys, where members of the whole group spend their time permanently together and travel together. Chimpanzee group members and even favored partners are often spatially separated (Mitani 1994). However, they have a strong need to be assured of the permanent possibility of meeting and cooperating. Long call vocalizations serve as an effective means of maintaining social relations in such circumstances. In other words, the social structure of both chimpanzees and bonobos can be seen as a framework favoring a type of vocalization composed of units making variants possible by changing the arrangements of the units, and serving for marking individual animals. However, the origins of vocalizations with such characteristics can be traced to another, perhaps more ancient, social organization.

The composite nature of the long calls of present-day chimpanzees and bonobos is not manifested strongly, and the source of their units is not clear. However, in the compound territorial songs of gibbons, some elements (notes) also occur independent of song, such as in response to territorial intrusions (Mitani and Marler 1989). The parallel use of vocal elements, functioning both as communicative signals and as building blocks for compound calls, is perhaps more definite in the simpler call of capuchin monkeys (Robinson 1984), which sheds light on the evolutionary origins of this peculiar vocalization.

The syntactically variable compound call seems to evolve under the constraint of labeling individual territories. Every territorial primate species uses the acoustic channel for marking territory. Since primary sounds are limited in number, the differences needed for marking territory individually can be achieved only by combining elementary sounds and varying their arrangement.

There are indications that the chimpanzee's long compound call may originate in a territorial marking function similar to that of present-day gibbon song. This possibility is supported in comparing gorilla and chimpanzee calls. Gorillas also have a long call, the hoot, that is connected with group movements. It may be a territorial call since it is emitted only when encountering another group (Fossey 1972; Mori 1983). Gorillas have also another call type, the wrah, with the function of cohesive calling. A similar sound sometimes appears in the final part of the chimpanzee pant-hoot. Thus a compound call might have existed in the common ancestor of gorillas, chimpanzees, and humans, the function of which was territorial. As species diverged, the call split into constituents that acquired different functions in the separated lines, as the original function itself ceased to exist.

As we have seen, territorial marking requires acoustically distinguishable signals. However, producing a compound call is not the only solution to this need. Other nonterritorial monkey species can also emit acoustically variable calls, for example, vervets (Owren 1990) and macaques (Hauser, Evans, and Marler 1993). These variants are produced by small articulatory differences in one basic call type. They are produced through facial gestures modified by mandibular positioning or lip configuration. That is, the ability to produce different facial expressions also enables these animals to produce call variants. But elaborate facial gestures evolved only in primate species living in large, complex, intricate groups where modifiable faces play an immediate communicative role. Territorial species, on the other hand, have another, simpler form of social organization, namely monogamy. Since monogamous sociality relies on a closed social unit with more limited social relations, it does not promote evolution of facial gestures characteristic of group-living species.

This limits the means available for producing call variants by articulatory means, and promotes production of variants through combining available calls. Consequently, the emergence of compound calls was promoted by the social structure of monogamous territoriality.

If the compound call of great apes derives from the territorial song of monogamous ancestors, its retention after the breakdown of both territoriality and monogamy presumably is related to its capacity to distinguish individuals. That is, survival of the compound call is closely connected with the special way of life of both chimpanzees and bonobos. Its specificity is based on the survival of an ancient vocalization capacity that changed and evolved in new social circumstances, thus resulting in an essential transformation of communication.

Whereas much lower-level animal vocalization is highly constrained in its characteristics, the chimpanzee long call clearly shows elements of voluntary control and social transmissibility. Chimpanzee males often give the long call together, during which they attempt to match the acoustic characteristics of each other's vocalizations. Moreover, single males alter the acoustic structure of their calls when chorusing with different partners (Mitani and Brandt 1994; Arcadi 1996). This matching tendency shows that call variants can be learned; more specifically, learned not only early in ontogeny, but socially acquired in adulthood. This is already a new level of communication.

Barriers to Language Competence in Great Apes

This new, intermediate stage of language evolution in all probability was present in the common ancestor of chimpanzees, bonobos, and humans. However, specializations having taken place in lineages of the former species did not make possible further languagelike evolution. Neither finer articulation nor grammar evolved in their vocal communication. Moreover, communicative meaning did not develop further.

Signals of animal communication essentially express an emotional state that can serve as motivation for the actions of others. However, in the context of vocal territorial marking, a new type of meaning started to evolve, namely, referential meaning. Most mammals mark territory with physical or chemical signs, leaving a more or less permanent trace. Such signs can be placed directly on the territory, and even in the absence of the defender they inform other animals. When primates announce their territory acoustically, the territory itself is not marked, but the presence and location of the defender are broadcast. Since different combinations of available vocal elements result in interindividual differences in call production, a special call pattern may identify the caller. Thus, the indirect character of this territorial marking made possible the preservation of this type of vocalization in great apes long after its original function was lost.

Marking of social status or even individual identity is already a type of reference. This suggests a different origin for referential communicative signals relevant to the origin of language than that implied by the often-cited varieties of predator alarm calls in vervet monkeys (Cheney and Seyfarth 1990). As markers of individual identity, basic referential vocalizations of great apes would be closer to the individual vocal gestures of the highly encephalized bottle-nosed dolphins (Tyack 1993) than to vervet alarm calls. Although vervet signals appear to refer to external objects, their reference to objects instead of suggested modes of escape remains to be proved.

An origin of reference in calls marking individual agents in social interactions would associate an important attribute of language with the general context of the evolution of intelligence in primates, namely, sociality. As mentioned, monkeys and apes show more sophisticated skill in social contexts than in solving problems with objects, and chimpanzees are able to use objects as referential tokens within the confines of language-teaching experiments. However, extrapolation of referential meaning from the social context to the object world seems not to be accomplished in the wild in any nonhuman primate. This limitation can be explained by the social relations of both common chimpanzees and bonobos. Common chimpanzee males associate closely with one another, travel together in temporary parties, and form alliances. Females are more likely to range alone with their dependent offspring, especially during nonestrous periods. Cooperation and communication are stronger and more sophisticated among males than either among females or between males and females. Pant-hoot chorusing also occurs only between males; females give this vocalization only rarely.

Although extensive cooperation exists between males, tool-using behavior seems to be a female characteristic. Females use tools more often than males, and, as Boesch and Boesch (1984) pointed out in the case of Ivory Coast chimpanzees, most complex tool making is the exclusive activity of females due to the strong male need to be together. Division of activities between the sexes prevents communicative and tool-using behaviors from being joined.

In contrast, bonobos tend to form more stable and larger mixed parties, in which females are as likely to be found as males (Furuichi and Ihobe 1994), due to famales' extended sexual receptivity. Cooperative actions between the sexes are frequent, and males even take part in infant care. Accordingly, communication between males and females in bonobos is more extensive than in common chimpanzees. Even the pant-hoot analogue, the high hoot, is performed as a male-female duet.

Although the handicap resulting from divergence between cooperation and tool making in the common chimpanzee is absent in bonobos, the latter do not use tools in their natural habitat. Kano (1992), during a ten-year study, observed only one case of using an object as a tool: a branch with leaves was used as an umbrella. Living conditions in the habitat of bonobos do not require, and consequently do not demand, use of tools to obtain food.

Since linkage between sophisticated communication and object manipulation is absent in both species, selective forces to imbue communicative signals with object-referential meaning are also absent. Object-referent communication consequently has not evolved in either species.

Perspectives

Although transfer of referential meaning is hindered in both species in the wild, it does take place to a certain extent in the laboratory in human surroundings. There, however, the species perform differently; that is, laboratory results may reflect a species difference in communicative skill not directly observable in the wild. Representatives of both species understand and apply differences in meaning arising from different word orders. The bonobo generalizes and, without further training, is able to respond properly to several hundred pairs of utterances (Savage-Rumbaugh et al. 1993:91–97), whereas the common chimpanzee trained by Premack did not appear to understand the general rule but had to learn each case.

In a recent experiment, two female infants from each species and of the same age were reared together in the same conditions. Compared for their skill at comprehending spoken language, the bonobo performed well above her chimpanzee peer (Brakke and Savage-Rumbaugh 1995).

These performance differences in the laboratory strongly support the view that the bonobo's superior language skill is a species characteristic. This superiority may also reflect species differences in social organization. Although both chimpanzees and bonobos are primarily promiscuous in mating, among bonobos, long-term consortships between particular males and particular females are common (Kano 1992). Whereas in chimpanzees, as in most primate species, the reproductive unit is essentially coextensive with the whole group, in bonobos, temporarily separated reproductive units exist inside the group. This structure results in a complex social network with sophisticated communication patterns.

Moreover, the stronger male-female bonding in bonobos, which is maintained by extended female sexual receptivity, may be linked to greater preservation of ancestral territorial song. This is indicated by duetting between males and females, characteristic of primate territorial song (Haimoff 1986), and by more variable vocal performances compared with chimpanzees. As noted by de Waal (1988), bonobos show a high degree of synchronization, with duetting reminiscent in this respect of gibbon duetting.

These alternative solutions within an essentially similar basic pattern give some insight into a third possibility, which would join a bonobo-like social system to a chimpanzee-like manipulative activity, supposedly in the ancestor of the human lineage. In such circumstances an opportunity arose to extend referential use of vocal elements across and beyond the social context, presumably through further development of the preexisting ability to recombine vocal elements into new patterns. This would open new channels for development of vocal and cognitive capacities relevant not only to the origins of language, but presumably to the origins of music as well.

Acknowledgments

I am deeply indebted to the Foundation for Biomusicology and Acoustic Ethology for giving me the opportunity to participate in the first Florentine Workshop in Biomusicology. I am also grateful to John Maynard Smith for his suggestions and to Björn Merker for his helpful comments on an earlier version of this chapter.

Note

1. From a systems-organizational point of view, the major transitions of evolution—the emergence of prokaryotic cells, composite or eukaryotic cells, multicellular organisms, and sociality—are manifested as the emergence of higher-level systems. These higher-level systems are also subject to evolution; that is, they evolve as systems from a lower aggregational state through the inner differentiation of their components toward a higher level of organization. This latter state can be achieved only if the system is dependent on processes mediated by system-specific structures. That is, they are processes of structures without independent existence outside the given system (e.g., ribosomes in cells, organs in animals, communicative signals in animal societies).

Although every system exists and works by the presence and operations of its constituents, networks of mutual interactions of constituents establish system characteristics that are irreducible to characteristics of the constituents, and this, of course, includes sociality. The result is that the system as a whole acquires a life of its own, as it were. The degree of this autonomy, that is, the extent to which the system level integrates the component level, is dependent on the evolutionary state of the system. However, the integrational process, like other evolutionary processes, does not embody a linear continuum. For example, evolution of sociality in insects or in avian-mammalian lineages are alternative solutions. In terms of higher levels of integrity, the final state of the evolution of sociality as a system among mammals is represented only by human sociality established by the existence of culture, the reified form of all human action and interaction. This is what gives the human social system its radical particularity.

Emergence of new qualities pertains not only to the system as a whole but to its components as well. The higher-level, comprehending, system provides special possibilities as well as limitations for the evolutionary pathways of its components. In this downward direction of determination, sociality plays a preeminent (but naturally not exclusive) role in the evolution of mental capacities of individuals.

References

Arcadi, A. C. (1996). Phrase structure of wild chimpanzee panthoots: Patterns of production and interpopulation variability. *American Journal of Primatology* 39:159–178.

Boesch, C. and Boesch, H. (1984). Possible causes of sex differences in the use of natural hammers by wild chimpanzees. *Journal of Human Evolution* 13:415–440.

Brakke, K. E. and Savage-Rumbaugh, S. (1995). The development of language skills in bonobo and chimpanzee. I. Comprehension. *Language and Communication* 15:121–148.

Cheney, D. L. and Seyfarth, R. M. (1990). *How Monkeys See the World: Inside the Mind of Another Species*. Chicago: University of Chicago Press.

Clark, A. P. and Wrangham, R. W. (1993). Acoustic analysis of wild chimpanzee pant hoots: Do Kibale Forest chimpanzees have an acoustically distinct food arrival pant hoot? *American Journal of Primatology* 31:99–109.

Fossey, D. (1972). Vocalizations of the mountain gorilla (*Gorilla gorilla beringei*). *Animal Behavior* 20:36–53.

Furuichi, T. and Ihobe, H. (1994). Variation in male relationships in bonobos and chimpanzees. *Behaviour* 130:211–228.

Gardner, R. A. and Gardner, B. T. (1984). A vocabulary test for chimpanzees. *Journal of Comparative Psychology* 98:381–404.

Haimoff, E. H. (1986). Convergence in the duetting of monogamous Old World primates. *Journal of Human Evolution* 15:51–59.

Hauser, M. D., Evans, C. S., and Marler, P. (1993). The role of articulation in the production of rhesus monkey, *Macaca mulatta*, vocalization. *Animal Behavior* 45:423–433.

Hohmann, G. and Fruth, B. (1994). Structure and use of distance calls in wild bonobos (*Pan paniscus*). *International Journal of Primatology* 15:767–782.

Humphrey, N. K. (1976). The social function of intellect. In P. P. G. Bateson and R. A. Hinde (Eds.) *Growing Points in Ethology* (pp. 303–317). Cambridge, UK: Cambridge University Press.

Kano, T. (1992). *The Last Ape: Pygmy Chimpanzee Behavior and Ecology*. Stanford, CA: Stanford University Press.

Mitani, J. C. (1994). Ethological studies of chimpanzee vocal behavior. In R. W. Wrangham, W. C. McGrew, F. B. M. de Waal, and P. G. Heltne (Eds.) *Chimpanzee Cultures* (pp. 195–210). Cambridge: Harvard University Press.

Mitani, J. C. and Brandt, K. L. (1994). Social factors influence the acoustic variability in the long-distance calls of male chimpanzee. *Ethology* 96:233–252.

Mitani, J. C., Gros-Louis, J., and Macedonia, J. M. (1996). Selection for acoustic individuality within the vocal repertoire of wild chimpanzees. *International Journal of Primatology* 17:569–583.

Mitani, J. C., Hasegawa, T., Gros-Louis, J., and Marler, P. (1992). Dialects in wild chimpanzees? *American Journal of Primatology* 27:233–243.

Mitani, J. C. and Marler, P. (1989). A phonological analysis of male gibbon singing behavior. *Behaviour* 106:20–45.

Mori, A. (1983). Comparison of the communicative vocalizations and behaviors of group ranging in eastern gorillas, chimpanzees and pygmy chimpanzees. *Primates* 24:486–500.

Owren, M. J. (1990). Acoustic classification of alarm calls by vervet monkeys (*Cercopithecus aethiops*) and humans. I. Natural calls. *Journal of Comparative Psychology* 104:20–28.

Premack, D. (1985). "Gavagai!" or the future history of the animal language controversy. *Cognition* 19:207–296.

Robinson, J. G. (1984). Syntactic structures in the vocalizations of wedge-capped, capuchin monkeys, *Cebus olivaceus*. *Behavior* 90:46–79.

Savage-Rumbaugh, E. S. (1979). Symbolic communication: Its origin and early development in the chimpanzee. *New Directions for Child Development* 3:1–15.

Savage-Rumbaugh, S. E., Murphy, J., Sevcik, R. A., Brakke, K. E., Williams, S. L., and Rumbaugh, D. M. (1993). *Language Comprehension in Ape and Child*. Chicago: University of Chicago Press.

Tyack, P. L. (1993). Animal language research needs a broader comparative and evolutionary framework. In H. L. Roitblat, L. M. Herman, and P. E. Nachtigall (Eds.) *Language and Communication: Comparative Perspectives* (pp. 115–152). Hillsdale, NJ: Erlbaum.

Ujhelyi, M. (1979). Connections between social structure and individual learning ability. *Tajekoztato* 3:49–69 (in Hungarian).

de Waal, F. B. M. (1988). The communicative repertoire of captive bonobos (*Pan paniscus*) compared to that of chimpanzees. *Behaviour* 106:183–251.

Whiten, A. and Byrne, R. W. (1988). The Machiavellian intelligence hypothesis. In R. W. Byrne and A. Whiten (Eds.) *Machiavellian Intelligence: Social Expertise and the Evolution of Intellect in Monkeys, Apes, and Humans* (pp. 1–9). Oxford: Clarendon Press.

9 The Progressively Changing Songs of Humpback Whales: A Window on the Creative Process in a Wild Animal

Katharine Payne

Abstract

Male humpback whales (*Megaptera novaeangeliae*) sing long, complex songs in tropical waters during the breeding season. At any one time all the whales in a population sing the same song, which differs significantly from songs of other populations. The song of each population evolves continuously, progressively, and so rapidly that nonreversing changes can be measured from month to month in a singing season. Such changes, which affect the songs at all levels, seem to arise through improvisation and imitation rather than through accident or as conveyors of information. The greatest amount of change appears when singing is most pervasive and the effort of each singer is most intense. A study of humpback songs over thirty-two years in two isolated whale populations provides information about the underlying rules of structure and kinds of changes whales are selecting. Several examples of change within two- and five-year periods are presented. Rhymelike structures occur in songs that contain much thematic material, perhaps serving as a mnemonic device in the context of a rapidly changing oral culture. We speculate that sexual selection is the driving evolutionary force behind song changing.

Some decades ago I was involved in an extensive study of the songs of humpback whales. My focus was on the long, complex, repeating patterns of sounds as phenomena in themselves. Yet as an amateur musician I kept wondering whether what I was hearing might be relevant to a consideration of the biological origins of human music. It was interesting to find "musical" similarities in the creative processes and products of two mammals whose lives are as different from one another as those of whales and humans. Many species that are genetically and behaviorally closer to humans or to whales than they are to one another do not sing at all, yet singing appears in these two species as a complex and flexible social behavior with significance to both singers and listeners.

Humpback whales are intermediate-sized baleen whales, 4 to 5 meters long at birth and reaching 17 meters in length in adulthood. Their Latin name, *Megaptera novaeangeliae* ("large-winged New Englanders"), refers to their long white pectoral fins (5 meters long in adulthood) and to the northern center of one of their migration routes. In fact most if not all major ocean basins contain humpback whales. They feed in high latitudes during the summer months and migrate to tropical or semitropical waters, where some breed and others, having gestated for eleven to twelve months, give birth. North Pacific humpback whales summer in Alaskan waters and winter in a number of tropical areas, including the Hawaiian and Reveillagigedo Islands. North Atlantic wintering grounds include Bermuda and several Caribbean banks.

During the roughly five months of their stay in the tropics, male humpback whales sing songs that function in maintaining floating territories and dominance hierarchies, aspects of male competition during the season of courtship (Tyack 1981; Darling 1983). It seems likely that the songs also attract females, but this remains a matter of speculation, for although human observers have spent thousands of hours in the vicinity of humpback whales, nobody has yet observed them mating. The whales' acoustic behavior is easier to document, as sound travels well under water, and under calm conditions a song is powerful enough to be audible over thousands of square kilometers in favorable conditions (Christopher Clark, personal communication). If one has a hydrophone and a taperecorder, one can spend a day in a boat from which the only view of whales is an occasional distant spout, and come home with excellent recordings of their acoustic displays.

Over the course of fifteen years I examined more than 600 whale songs with a number of colleagues, including Roger Payne, Peter Tyack, Linda Guinee, and Jan Heyman-Levine. We and others, particularly Frank Watlington, recorded the songs over thirty-two years from whales in North Atlantic and the North Pacific humpback populations. We summarized most aspects of our comparisons of the songs in three papers (Payne, Tyack, and Payne 1983; Payne and Payne 1985; Guinee and Payne 1988) that give further details supporting the material I summarize, and here that are also the source of all the illustrations.

Humpback whales' songs are long, highly structured sequences of sound that repeat hour after hour, often without a pause even when the singer surfaces to breathe. They vary in length, usually lasting between eight and sixteen minutes (range 5 to 35 minutes). Each song includes an extraordinary assortment of notes, or units. These vary in frequency between 30 and 4000 Hz, and in length between 0.15 and 8 seconds; in harmonic structure they range from pure tones to tone bursts, and they show much variety in contour. Figure 9.1 shows how these units are organized into repeating groups or phrases. All the phrases of one sort are grouped together and constitute a theme. A song contains ten or fewer themes that proceed in an invariant order and repeat, often without a pause. A series of songs uninterrupted by a pause of more than a minute is a cycle. The longest song cycle on record lasted 21 hours (Howard Winn, personal communication).

The most flexible aspect of humpback song structure has to do with the number of phrases in each theme. This varies even in the successive songs of a single whale. We refer to songs in which the same kind of material appears in the same sequence as "the same," even if they differ in length due to different amounts of phrase repetition.

It is not easy to record whale songs for study, because one rarely hears a whale singing alone. Usually we heard several or many voices simultaneously, overlapping randomly and sometimes producing the

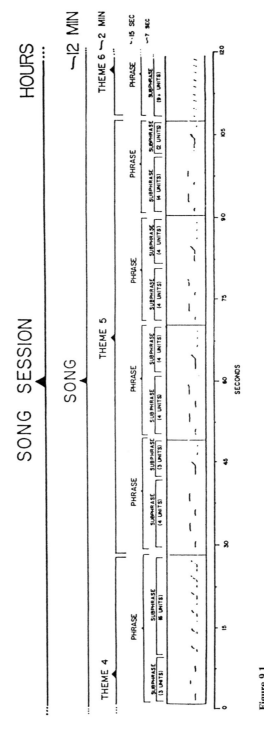

Figure 9.1
Diagram of hierarchical structure of all humpback whale songs, using a tracing of a spectrogram. Times given are rough indicators. Vertical lines are inserted between phrases. (From Payne, Tyack, and Payne 1983.)

cacophony that New Zealand whale listeners refer to as the barnyard
chorus. When we separated out the various voices in such a chorus we
discovered all the whales were repeating the same phrases and themes
in the same order, but not in synchrony with one another.[1]

When we expanded the study to include whales in more than one population, we discovered that the songs in different populations were
similar in structure but quite different in content. When we expanded it
to include more than one singing season, we discovered that in each population the songs were continuously and rapidly changing. Thus humpback whale songs were subject to two sources of change: geographical,
leading to between-population dialects, and temporal, leading to within-
population drift.

On the hunch that the processes involved in drift might reveal something about the innate sources of innovation—perhaps if I were bolder
I would use the word "composition"—I devote the rest of the chapter to
this phenomenon. Over the course of a few singing seasons, all elements
in the song of a humpback whale population change little by little, each
at its own rate. Basic units change in frequency, contour, duration, and
the ways they are organized to make phrases. Phrases change in the
numbers and types of units they contain and in their rhythmic patterning. Themes gradually occupy a larger or smaller percentage of the song
on average, for in spite of small-scale variability, there are also large-scale
trends in repetition. After some five or ten years, every theme is either
much changed as a result of many little changes, or it has become obsolete and dropped out of the song, or both. At the same time, new phrase
types have been introduced, imitated, and developed into new themes.
Usually new material arises organically in the form of transitional
phrases that merge the qualities of phrases in adjacent themes, but from
time to time new material seems to arise de novo.

Figure 9.2A and B shows a typical humpback whale song recorded
near the Hawaiian Island Maui in March 1977 and another recorded
from the same place in March 1978. The changes we measured in each
of several hundred songs from those seasons are characterized in these
examples. In the earlier year the song had nine themes, one of which was
often omitted; in the later year only seven themes were heard. Phrases
in the earlier song tended to be shorter than those in the later year, with
a different mechanism of phrase lengthening in different themes. Some
showed increases in the length of the units, whereas in others the number
of units increased.

Figure 9.3 shows the evolution of the phrase structure in one theme
in that song (theme 5) over five successive years. In the first subphrase
of each phrase we see the splitting of two units into four, the gradual
lengthening of these units, and their increased separation in pitch. In the

second subphrase we see an increasing number of grunts over time. As the result of these processes, the whole phrase grew progressively longer throughout the five years. Figure 9.4 presents these changes statistically and shows that they contributed to changes on a larger scale that were simultaneously subject to other changes. The trend for phrase lengthening continued progressively throughout both years, for instance, but phrase repetition decreased in the second year, with the result that the theme tended to be shorter early in the 1978 recording season than it had been in the last months of 1977.

Meanwhile, theme 6 was undergoing a different sort of change that proceeded rapidly enough to be measured on a monthly basis in the singing months of 1977. The replacement of "r's" (rising units with a sustained final tone) by "j's" (quick upward-sweeping units) is shown graphically in figure 9.5 and statistically in figure 9.6.

All the other themes were simultaneously changing as well, each in its own way. Changes in theme 7 were based on substitution of phrases rather than of units. We found four common and two uncommon alternate phrase types, which we classified by applying three criteria to the first subphrase (figure 9.7). There was steady progression of alternates (a change at the level of the theme) coupled with the dropping out of the theme (a change at the level of the song; figure 9.8).

Our analysis eventually included all the phrases from all the songs we collected from three decades in North Atlantic and Pacific humpback populations. The results suggest that the whales have an ever-expanding number of ways to modify the structure of their notes, phrases, and themes. Each theme continually changes in its own way and at its own ever-changing rate, apparently as the consequence of decisions (whether conscious or unconscious) that are shared by all the singers. At any given time all the singers seem to agree which themes are stable and which are changing. For those that are changing they agree as to which aspects are changing and which are not, and how and to what extent they are changing.

As biologists we ask, what accounts for and/or drives these rapid changes? A clue to the answer lies in the fact that during the six months on the feeding grounds, when there is very little singing, the song hardly changes: early songs on the breeding grounds are similar to those last heard in the previous season. It is in the middle of the season, when the number of singing whales is largest and the effort of each one is most intense, as reflected by the durations of song sessions, that songs change the most. Thus the changes appear to be not a consequence of between-season forgetting, but a natural, active part of singing—part of a display.

Do these changes contain information about some aspects of the environment that are significant to whales? Probably not, as their timing

Figure 9.2
Tracings of spectrograms of representative songs from March 1977 and 1978. We selected songs that contained all possible themes. In 1977, theme three was rare. Although the sample song shown here omitted it, it was included in the next song sung by that same whale. The star-in-circle symbol in the tracing indicates where theme three was placed when it was sung. The two phrases of theme three shown under the song were produced by the same whale in the song following the one fully traced here. The tracings omit all extraneous sounds (e.g., ocean noise such as ships, other whales, underwater echoes, etc.) as well as harmonics. Pulsive sounds, which on the spectrograms showed dense harmonics, are represented diagrammatically by closely spaced vertical lines, whose spacing does not necessarily reflect the repetition rate of the pulses. (From Payne, Tyack, and Payne 1983.)

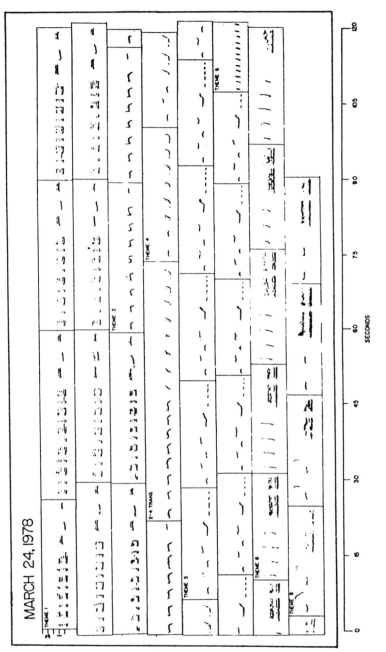

Figure 9.2 *Continued.*

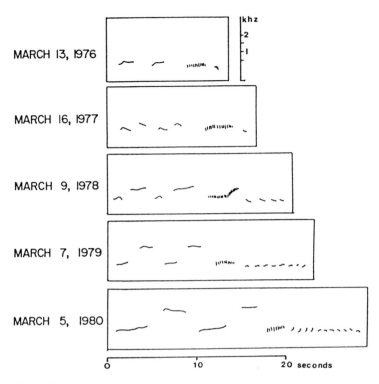

Figure 9.3
Sample phrases showing the evolution of theme five over five years. The units changed in frequency, duration, spacing, configuration, and numbers, and the phrases changed duration gradually. (From Payne, Tyack, and Payne 1983.)

(other than of the intensity of the singing itself) does not coincide with natural cycles that affect other aspects of whales' behavior, nor do they repeat. Like improvisation in human music, changes seem to be generated by an internal process, and as in music, the imitation that then occurs reveals listening and learning. Song changing in whales seems to be a clear example of cultural evolution in a nonhuman animal.

Our general understanding of biological forces that drive stylistic changes is that an individual who introduces an innovation gains some advantage from being different. However, an innovation may not be attractive if it is too different from the norm. Human psychology has a term describing the ideal degree of change that an innovation should have if it is to spread and set a new vogue: optimal mismatch. For a novelty to be introduced into a cultural trend, it must have a certain balance of conformity and originality.

With this in mind I found it puzzling that an examination of the songs of the few individual whales we had repeatedly recorded in different months and seasons did not reveal any stylistic leaders. At each interval

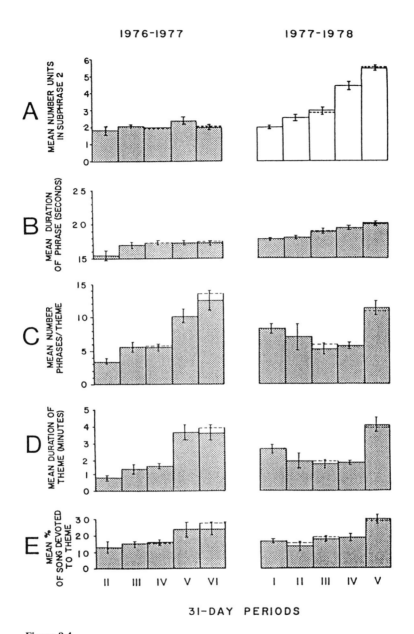

1976-1977   **1977-1978**

31-DAY PERIODS

Figure 9.4
Some changing parameters of theme five over two singing seasons. Each bar represents a thiry-one-day mean for the parameter being measured (see caption for Figure 9.6).
A: mean number of units per phrase in each song session.
B: mean phrase duration in each song session.
C: mean number of phrases per theme in each song session.
D: mean theme duration in each song session.
E: percentage of song occupied by theme five.
Dashed lines indicate means when a small number of very aberrant songs were included in the calculations. Vertical lines indicate standard errors. (From Payne, Tyack, and Payne 1983.)

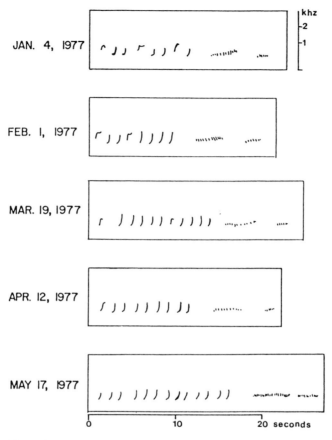

Figure 9.5
Tracings of single phrases of theme six in the months of a single singing season. The first part consists of two different units, rs, and js (see text) in various mixtures. Note that the rs are quickly replaced by js. (From Payne, Tyack, and Payne 1983.)

we found that each identified singer had changed his song about as much and in about the same ways as all the other singers in the population. Why change so fast and sophisticatedly if everyone else is changing at the same rate and in the same ways? In my opinion, lack of an answer suggests that the scale of our sampling system was inappropriate. Had we managed to collect many songs on a daily basis from more than a few known singers we might have found that leaders do in fact exist, and are imitated so rapidly that their moment of innovation did not show up in our analysis. Then we would have suspected a positive relationship between aspects of their innovation and their success in mating. Biologists have studied a variety of animals in which males indulge in displays that are not in themselves functional: these persist if females prefer to mate with the males who exhibit them.

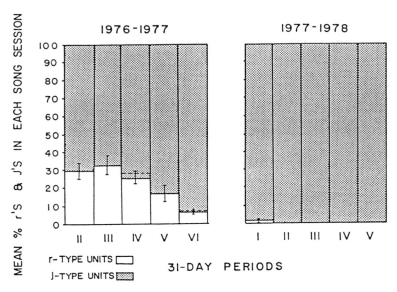

Figure 9.6
Percentage of r and j units per song session versus time. The time periods (labeled 2–6 and 1–5 in the two seasons 1976–1977 and 1977–1978) are both thirty-one days. Periods having the same number start and stop on the same dates of their calendar years. Notice that r units replace j units. Standard error is indicated by vertical lines. Dashed lines indicate means when aberrant songs are included in the calculations. (From Payne, Tyack, and Payne 1983.)

ALTERNATE FORMS OF THEME 7   SUBPHRASE I

	MINIMUM FREQUENCY	NUMBER OF UNITS IN EACH CLUSTER	RISE IN FREQUENCY WITHIN CLUSTER ?
7A	>900 Hz	N>4	NO
7B	<900 Hz	N>4	NO
7C	<900 Hz	2<N≤4	YES
7D	<900 Hz	N=2	YES
RARE INTERMEDIATE FORMS			
7BC	<900 Hz	2<N≤4	NO
7BC	<900 Hz	N>4	YES

Figure 9.7
Alternate forms of the first subphrase of theme seven, labeled A–D. They were all common at some point in the 1976–1977 season. Two rare alternate forms were intermediate between forms 7B and 7C. Tracings of spectrograms to the right of alternate phrases 7A–D are examples of each type. (From Payne, Tyack, and Payne 1983.)

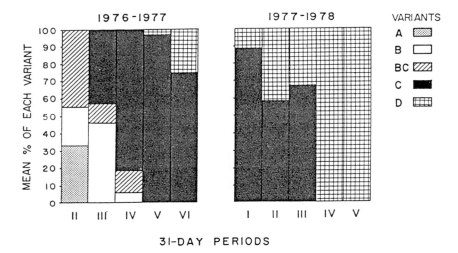

Figure 9.8
Percentage of occurrence of each alternate form of theme seven in each period of the 1976–1977 and 1977–1978 seasons. Only one song session in each of the two and one-half periods 1977–1978 contains theme seven because this theme was dying out. The percentages in those periods thus reflect the songs of just one whale. (From Payne, Tyack, and Payne 1983.)

I suggest that the innovation leading to song changing in whales may be driven by sexual selection. Geoffrey Miller (this volume) makes a powerful argument for this perspective as applied to human musicianship as well. Such a process does not necessarily imply conscious choice, yet it is evidence of mental versatility. The process of song change we documented in whales has much in common with a human phenomenon called linguistic drift. Edward Sapir (1921/1949:171–172), in his classic book *Language*, described drift without reference to purpose, as follows:

Language moves down time in a current of its own. It has a drift . . . Every word, every grammatical element, every locution, every sound and accent is a slowly changing configuration molded by the invisible and impersonal drift that is the life of the language. The evidence is overwhelming that this drift has a certain consistent direction. Its speed varies enormously according to circumstances that it is not always easy to define . . . The general drift of a language has its depths. At the surface the current is relatively fast. In certain features dialects drift apart rapidly. By that very fact these features betray themselves as less fundamental to the genius of the language than the more slowly modifiable features in which the dialects keep together long after they have grown to be mutually alien forms of speech. But this is not all. The momentum of the more fundamental, the pre-dialectic, drift is often such that languages long disconnected will pass through the same or strikingly similar phases . . .

Even though language is generally associated with conscious behavior, linguistic drift as Sapir described it is apparently not the result of conscious decisions. It has nothing to do with the meaning of words, phrases, or sentences being uttered.

Drift in whale song proceeds at a much faster rate than linguistic drift. Most changes originate as modifications of preexisting material, but within one decade a population's song may undergo so much change that one can no longer recognize its relation to the earlier version.

How do whales remember the current version of their song in the context of such a rapidly changing oral culture? Do they process material in memorable groups of units or chunks, as humans apparently do? (Miller 1956; Simon 1974). Linda Guinee and I noticed, while comparing whale songs from many years in two geographically isolated populations, that when songs were most complex they tended to contain several adjacent themes whose phrases had similar beginnings or endings (figure 9.9). Reminded of the fact that human rhyming sometimes acts as a mnemonic device, we speculated that rhymelike phrases might help whales remember the sequence of material in their rapidly changing song. To test this notion we collated the occurrence of rhymes in 548 songs (from seven years in the eastern North Pacific and twelve years in the western North Atlantic) with the number of themes these songs contained, a rough measure of complexity. We found a strong correlation, with the most complex songs containing the most rhyming (figure 9.10). In the same sample we found no relationship between rhyming and song duration, which may reflect repetition and not complexity. This pair of measurements strengthened our hunch that rhyming might play a role in whales' ability to keep up with current versions of their songs.

In the interest of clarity I have selected quite simple examples to illustrate the process of whale song evolution; songs of many periods showed greater variation in phrase and theme structure. In fact the further one looks, the more variation one finds. Eventually one discovers that the variation extends to the structure as well as the contents of the phrases and themes (Payne, Guinee, and Heyman-Levine, unpublished data). Like the songs themselves, the story of their evolution is ever developing.

Further studies of humpback whales' improvisational tendencies will be interesting as we continue to compare the vocal behavior of other animals with our own musical behavior. Most changes in human music reflect a blending of external and internal influences, making it difficult to isolate those that might be intrinsic to the process of singing itself. Song changing in whales appears to be less affected by outside influences, and to offer a cleaner window on the mental processes of these composers.

I can imagine many questions that human composers would like to ask whales. It would be nice to know, for instance, whether whales are aware

148   Katharine Payne

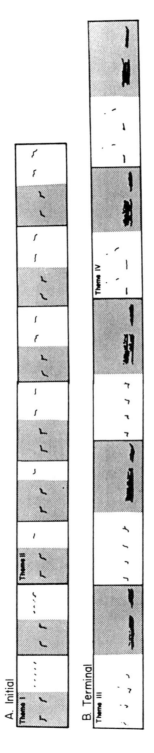

Figure 9.9
Tracings of spectrograms of rhymelike subphrases.
A: Phrases in two or more adjacent themes contain the same initial subphrase (Bermuda 1977).
B: Two or more adjacent themes contain the same terminal subphrase (Hawaii 1979). (From Guinee and Payne 1988.)

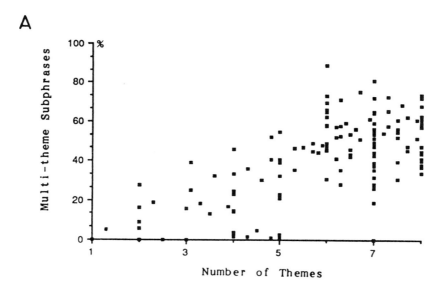

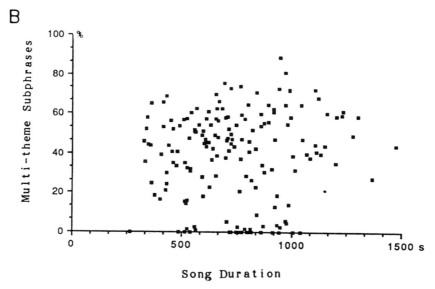

Figure 9.10
Scattergrams show single linear correlations for combined Atlantic and Pacific samples. Rhymelike subphrases are most likely to occur in songs having the greatest number of themes. Their presence is related to amount of different material, not simply to amount of material. To give roughly equal weight to the contribution of different whales, the mean value per song session (per whale), and not per song, is the unit of comparison. This was necessary since some song sessions contain many songs and others contain few. This explains the presence of intermediate values for number of themes (A).

of intentions as they compose and sing, and how they experience their own and other whales' songs. In deep water, when the sea is calm and singing whales are a certain distance away, all the sounds are resonant and followed by echoes—from the bottom of the sea, from the walls of underwater mountains, and from the undersurface of waves. Questions arise as to whether the acoustic properties have anything to do with their selection of singing places, whether they value an amplifying environment, and/or whether they make choices when singing and listening on the basis of the song's aesthetic quality as they perceive it. From the perspective of a person interested in music, these are important questions, but we may never be able to answer them fully.

Note

1. My impression that the overlapping of songs is random has not been systematically examined. It would be hard to examine because when more than one male is singing, the singers tend to be rather far apart. The time of arrival of a whale's utterance at the ears of each of his separated listeners will differ slightly, depending on their distance from him, making an intention toward unison or any particular kind of polyphony hard to detect. What I noticed during many months of listening was that when more than one whale was singing, their progress through the song was almost always asynchronous. It was unusual even to hear parts of the same theme being sung by two whales at the same time, and even rarer to hear two whales change from one theme to the next simultaneously.

References

Darling, J. D. (1983). Migrations, abundance, and behavior of "Hawaiian" humpback whales (*Megaptera novaeangeliae*). Doctoral dissertation, University of California, Santa Cruz.

Guinee, L. and Payne, K. (1988). Rhyme-like repetition in songs of humpback whales. *Ethology* 79:295–306.

Miller, G. A. (1956). The magical number seven, plus or minus two: Some limits on our capacity for processing information. *Psychological Review* 63:81–97.

Payne, K. and Payne, R. (1985). Large-scale changes over 19 years in songs of humpback whales in Bermuda. *Zeitschrift für Tierpsychologie* 68:89–114.

Payne, K., Tyack, P., and Payne, R. (1983). Progressive changes in the songs of humpback whales (*Megaptera novaeangeliae*): A detailed analysis of two seasons in Hawaii. In R. Payne (Ed.) *Communication and Behavior of Whales* (pp. 9–57). Boulder, CO: Westview Press.

Sapir, E. (1921/1949). *Language: An Introduction to the Study of Speech.* New York: Harcourt, Brace and World.

Simon, H. A. (1974). How big is a chunk? *Science* 173:585–597.

Tyack, P. (1981). Interactions between singing humpback whales and conspecifics nearby. *Behavioral Ecology and Sociobiology* 8:105–116.

III MUSIC, LANGUAGE, AND HUMAN EVOLUTION

Can Biomusicology Learn from Language Evolution Studies?

Derek Bickerton

very negative

Abstract
The study of the evolution of music may have something to learn from the study
of the evolution of language, although most of the lessons may be of a negative
kind. A variety of factors have impeded the study of language evolution: lack of
interest among linguists, the consequent predominance in the field of researchers
largely ignorant of linguistics, excessive concentration on selection pressures
rather than on the genetic variation that alone permits those pressures to yield
results, the mistaken belief that evolution requires dogmatic faith in gradualness,
and the belief that evolutionary continuity between humans and other creatures
entails direct linkage between human and antecedent nonhuman traits. The
extent to which biomusicologists can learn from these mistakes will depend in
part on the extent to which language and music truly resemble one another, and
the search for genuine universals of music that are not shared with other species
should play a significant part in such comparisons.

BiTTer

Interest in the origins of language goes back a good deal farther than
interest in the origins of music. The latter is not new, but did not really
begin until after the publication of Darwin's *On the Origin of Species*.
Interest in language origins, however, goes back at least as far as the
Pharaoh Psamtik (Psammetichus to the Greeks) who, 3,000 years ago,
isolated two neonates with a deaf shepherd in the hope that the language
they eventually acquired would represent the earliest form of human
language

Given this very considerable time depth, it would be nice to be able
to say that the topic was by now fairly well understood and that the
framework of theory and evidence constructed over the years should
prove of considerable assistance to those investigating the origins of
music. But, regrettably, this is not the case. On the contrary, the history
of the field consists of a series of false starts and blind alleys; if it has
anything to offer, biomusicology may be able to learn from language
origins studies some of the things that, if possible, it should try *not* to do.

One common problem that tends to loom large in negative evaluations is the absence of fossil evidence. Neither words nor notes fossilize,
and nor, save in vanishingly rare cases, do the brains that produce them.
This, at least in the case of language, led more than one commentator
to conclude that the origins of language can never be known. Even
the author of a work entitled *Biological Foundations of Language*
(Lenneberg 1967) concluded that it was impossible to find out how
those foundations came into existence, no matter how impressive the
evidence that such foundations did indeed exist. In 1866 the Linguistic
Society of Paris passed a resolution excluding from its meetings any
papers that dealt with language origins, and even in the last decade at

least one linguist (Lightfoot 1991) called for a reintroduction of the Paris ban.

In fact, that ban was not ill motivated when it was first put into action. The years immediately after publication of *On the Origin of Species* were filled with pseudoevolutionary speculations. Fixating on the appearance of the first words, steadfastly ignoring all that must have preceded and followed this, scholars produced a series of baseless proposals that survive today only as light relief in the introductory pages of some linguistic textbooks: the first words came from grunts of pain, from work chants, from imitations of the sounds of other species, from echoes that objects gave out, from gestures made by the tongue, and so on (the take-home message to students is, don't even bother thinking about how language began!). However, the situation has changed radically since the nineteenth century. Rapidly accumulating knowledge in a variety of convergent fields (ethology, paleoanthropology, neurology, evolutionary biology, and linguistics being among the most important) has radically reduced the problem space. These advances impose a series of rigorous constraints on possible theories of language origins. We may even be approaching a point at which only one among competing theories will be compatible with the entire range of constraints.

Unfortunately, most researchers show little awareness of the full range of knowledge that is now available. During the nineteenth century, human behavior was divided up by the disciplines of the day in much the same way as Africa was simultaneously being divided up by the colonial powers. No surprise, the boundaries of these disciplines were often determined as arbitrarily and as illogically as were the boundaries of colonial possessions. Consequently, many contemporary researchers, like many contemporary African states, remain trapped within their own history. They limit themselves to meeting those constraints on possible theories that are imposed by their own particular discipline, completely ignoring the often more rigorous constraints imposed by others.

These limitations loom largest when one of the ignored disciplines is linguistics. We have found out more about human language in the last thirty years than we did in the preceding three millennia. We can now be sure that all human languages share a number of nonobvious characteristics, and that these characteristics derive directly from human biology and are therefore as indisputably formed by evolution as our upright stance and opposable thumbs. Unfortunately, this certainty is still obscured by mainly terminological disputes between holders of rival but largely equivalent theories, and by arcane concepts and terminology ("subjacency," "empty categories," "the theta criterion," etc.) that remain totally opaque to the uninitiated. Linguists must be among the world's worst popularizers (although Pinker 1994 constitutes an exception that every nonlinguist should read), and the reluctance of other scholars to explore their territory, however regrettable, is all too easy to understand.

In addition to being poor popularizers, linguists are poor defenders of territory. In the 1970s and thereafter, they largely abandoned the debate over "animal language" projects such as those of Premack and Premack (1972) and Gardner and Gardner (1969). But long before that, and for long after the Paris ban, they abandoned language origins. Even today one can number on the fingers of one's hands the serious linguists who are genuinely interested in the topic. However, undefended territory does not remain vacant for long, and members of other disciplines (anthropologists, psychologists, biologists) hastened to colonize the area with deplorable consequences.

I call those consequences deplorable not because I am a linguist with a strong sense of territoriality but because, by ignoring all that we know about language, nonlinguists are doing the whole field a disservice. As I pointed out elsewhere (Bickerton 1996), if one is going to write about something evolving, it is helpful to know exactly what that something is. Features specific to human language (the most interesting of which are, as stated above, still unknown to most nonlinguists) form one of the most important constraints on evolutionary theories. Any valid theory of evolution should be able to explain not merely how language began but also why language is as it is and not otherwise. In other words, an evolutionary theory that fails to explain the universal properties of language is valueless.

Biomusicologists might derive benefit from two things. First, they can glean from linguists the folly of surrendering territory. They can convince musicologists in general of the legitimacy of evolutionary studies, and do their best to ensure that no one ignorant of music is allowed to pontificate on the topic. Second, they can determine the extent of similarity between language evolution and music evolution by determining whether human music, like human language, possesses nontrivial universal characteristics (see the Universals in Music section, this volume).

In music as in linguistics (Nettl, this volume), the search for universals and the search for origins have not always or necessarily gone together. Indeed, universals do not necessarily derive from evolutionary processes; they could, in principle, have arisen from historical accident or be due merely to the way the world is constituted.

Within linguistics two distinct approaches to the question of universals have long been established. The first is that of Greenberg (1963), which looks merely at surface similarities between languages and involves such things as the linear ordering of constituents; the second is that of Chomsky (1965), which seeks to analyze language at a deeper level and uncover highly abstract properties that all natural human languages must share, but which are not necessarily found among artificial languages or languagelike artifacts. For those whose major concern is evolutionary biology, a weakness of the former approach is suggested by the frequency with which that approach draws attention to what it calls implicational universals (generalizations of the type, "if language A has feature x, it will also have feature y") or partial or statistical universals, in which languages share a given feature with a frequency far greater than that of chance. Clearly in such cases there exists the possibility that the universals concerned could be merely contingent and in no way directly derive from the biological makeup of the species. Surely we would be on firmer ground if we confined ourselves to properties that are exceptionless and specific to natural language. Similarly, in biomusicology one should not expect to find universals lying conveniently on the surface ready for any untrained investigator to pick up. However, attempts to discover these universals, if properly conducted, should be crucial in determining whether music is a species-specific adaptation, like language, or something that may be shared, at least in part, by members of other species.

It should be borne in mind, too, that music may not be a natural kind (Molino, this volume) and may accordingly be decomposable into distinct modules. Chomsky (1980) suggested that language may be similarly decomposable into two components, conceptual and computational. This distinction was developed into the one between a meaningful but unstructured protolanguage, potentially sharable with other species, and a syntactic mechanism that imposed a complex hierarchical, parsable structure on this protolanguage to yield contemporary human language (Bickerton 1990, 1995). It is equally possible that music may turn out to contain elements specific to our species mingled with other elements that may be much more widely shared.

A further problem for an evolutionary study of human behavior concerns misplacing emphasis on one of the two basic ingredients that make up an evolutionary process. For any trait to emerge in the course of evolution, some kind of selective pressure must exist that is a set of circumstances that renders the trait adaptive in terms of increased progeny, and a degree of genetic variability must be present from which the trait can be selected. However, a number of recent studies have concentrated exclusively on possible candidates for the selective pressure that affected language, and ignored the variation that must have existed for the pressure to work. Thus a number of studies sought to attribute the emergence of language to the growing complexities of life in hominid groups, ignoring the fact that social life already achieved near-human complexity among many primate species (de Waal 1996) and that any additional hominid complexity was more likely a *result* of language (e.g., complexity introduced by possibilities of gossip, lying, tale-bearing, etc.) than the primary *cause* of it. More specifically, it was suggested that a hypothetical and unmotivated increase in hominid group size led to the emergence of language as a "grooming substitute" by which hominids could foster social cohesion by means more economical of time than mutual delousing (Dunbar 1996).

A widely respected popular introduction to modern evolutionary studies (Ridley 1993) endorsed the bizarre proposal that language evolved as a means by which, after the emergence of a sex-based division of labor, husbands could keep track of whether their wives remained faithful to them (the husband's mother could inform her son if his wife was cheating on him). Still more recent work proposed the birth of language from symbolic rituals required to establish primitive marriage, a factor allegedly inescapable in a species characterized by both reciprocal altruism and male provisioning of offspring (Deacon 1997), or, returning to a once popular Marxist analysis, from the requirements of communal problem solving in primitive forms of labor (Beaken 1996).

Given our present state of knowledge, no means exist, beyond very general considerations of plausibility, for testing any of these hypotheses. Indeed, the authors typically elaborated their own proposals with no discussion of, or even reference to, alternative proposals, a sure sign that, in this area, we are still at the level of "just-so stories." But a still more serious drawback to these approaches is that they divert attention from the other half of the evolutionary process.

For any of these alleged pressures to work, there must have been some kind of genetic variability in the hominid line that pressure could encourage, and this variability must have been in some domain that, directly or indirectly, was capable of affecting language. Clearly, certain types of this kind of variability must have existed. Candidate types would have included (but would not have been limited to) such things as variation in the ability to store lexical items in long-term memory and to retrieve them reliably. There can be no doubt that, once linguistic mode of communication became established, natural selection would have worked on such traits and given rise to autocatalytic effects. Improved vocal control would simplify the task of the hearer, who, even without auditory improvements, would be able to distinguish more sounds reliably and thus identify words more reliably. The ability to make and distinguish a greater range of speech sounds would make possible a wider variety of sound combinations, which, given a larger and more efficient memory for words, would give rise to a steadily increasing vocabulary.

Undoubtedly, these factors and processes would have combined to yield a much richer means of communication among hominids, however, they would not have affected certain aspects of language as we know it at all. All contemporary languages are characterized by an extremely robust syntactic structure. Although the syntax of a foreign language may appear on the surface to be dauntingly different from that of the learner's native tongue, research over the last few decades shows that these differences are relatively trivial, and that the deeper principles that underlie them are shared by all languages without exception (Chomsky 1981, 1988). It is wholly implausible that such abstract principles could have been invented consciously and deliberately, contrary to what was suggested by those who remain ignorant of those principles or who refuse, mainly on ideological grounds, to accept their existence (Beaken 1996). Since those principles seem to be specifically adapted for language and to have little in common with general principles of thought or other apparatuses that might be attributable to the human mind, it is no easy matter to determine where they came from. So the question is, where could the kind of variability have arisen on which pressure for an improved syntax could work?

Workers such as Pinker and Bloom (1990) simply assume variations in syntactic ability, without awareness of the problems this involves: just what did that variability consist of? how was it expressed in terms of behavioral differences? how could gradual improvements peak at a set of exceptionless principles? and so on. The fact that those principles can be expressed most successfully not as a set of positive admonitions but rather as a set of constraints on otherwise unlimited potentialities only exacerbates the problems. Although it might be possible to restate such principles in terms of a steady state that could have been achieved by small and gradual increments, no one has so far attempted to do so. But failing such an attempt, any claim that syntax developed gradually reduces to mere handwaving.

In the absence of such attempts, we can only assume that the original state of language was wholly without syntactic structure, and that some preexisting faculty was somehow appropriated to bring about an apparently catastrophic emergence of syntax. The protolanguage that preceded this emergence would then have had no rules or principles whatsoever. One could say, or not say, whatever combination of words one pleased. Whereas practice would have undoubtedly have yielded conventions that would have restricted and regularized speech outputs to some extent, the result would not have continued to labor under the difficulty that it lacked any units intermediate between the word and the complete utterance. Words you get as soon as you have the idea of creating symbols for concepts you already have, and utterances you get as soon as you add one word to another. But phrases and clauses, the intermediate units in terms of which all generalizations about syntax must be made, do not develop automatically in this way. They can develop only in the context of a hierarchical structure, which is created by adding one unit to another and then a third to the combination of the first two. We have no reason to suppose that in protolanguage any such operation took place.

In natural language, a variety of operations can be carried out that involve moving particular constituents around. For instance, instead of, "Mary baked a cake" you can say, "It was a cake that Mary baked," or "A cake was baked by Mary." These operations involve selecting just the right constituents—you can't say, "It was baked a cake that Mary"—and selecting the right constituents predicates hierarchical structure, since only items dominated by a single node (and usually by a particular type of node) can be treated in this way. Moreover, the results of such operations always change emphasis, and sometimes even meaning, in precisely predictable ways. In protolanguage, however, anything can be moved around quite freely, yet apparently without making a difference in meaning or emphasis, and certainly without making a predictable difference.

Now, the difference between flat structure (beads on a wire) and hierarchical structure is absolute, like the difference between life and death, or married and single, not graded. One cannot be partly married and a system cannot be partly hierarchical. Somehow a hierarchical system had to be imposed on protolanguage in a single operation, or else something else had to be imposed that automatically imposed hierarchical structure.

To discuss such issues in greater depth would take us too far from the topic of this chapter. Interested readers will find a full account in Calvin and Bickerton (in press). For now it is sufficient to note that biomusicology should not jump to the conclusion that the features of music necessarily evolved gradually and were selected for over a long period of time, the time during which music as we know it today was slowly developing. Some features may indeed have evolved in this way; others may not, and it is an empirical question which did and which did not.

This is a crucial point that can hardly be overemphasized. To date, gradualism seems not to play any significant role in studies of the evolution of music. However, this may merely reflect an early stage of inquiry, and may result from relative lack of exposure to evolutionary concerns, rather than from greater sophistication.

Certainly, indifference to evolutionists and their norms characterized studies of the evolution of language in the previous century. It may therefore be the case that, as biomusicology comes farther into the mainstream of evolutionary studies, it will be infected by the doctrinaire, quasi-religious gradualism so widespread in evolutionary circles.

A few words on the nature of gradualism may be in order, as it has had wholly negative effects on studies of language evolution. Support for gradualism derives from the fact that many, probably most, evolutionary processes are indeed gradual and incremental, and for very good reasons. Although radical mutations do occur in nature, they are almost always destructive—legs appear where wings ought to be, or vice versa—and it is easy to see why this should be so. If you have a complex organism whose sustainability depends on very fine adjustments among all the organs that compose it, any radical change, even if it brought a substantial advantage in one area, is all too likely to be paid for with devastating handicaps in other areas. For that matter, many minor alterations may prove dysfunctional, but there is less chance that a useful change will necessarily have to pay an excessive price in the disruption of unrelated functions. Such alterations may, if the advantage they convey is substantial enough, spread through a population and serve as the ground from which successive favorable changes may take off. If the changes are cumulative in effect, they may eventually yield organisms very different from, and better adapted than, those in which the long sequence of minor changes was initiated.

However, it is one thing to believe that gradual processes predominate in nature and quite another to hold that all evolutionary processes must be gradual. The issue is, after all, simply an empirical one: even if no nongradual changes were ever witnessed, one could never exclude the possibility that the next evolutionary process to be uncovered might be nongradual. But in fact, more than one nongradual type of change is already known. Sudden changes in the environment, such as droughts, floods, and iceages, especially if they radically modify the ecosystem, may release a cascade of associated changes that can radically modify a species in a space of time that is, by evolutionary standards, extremely short, mere thousands or a few tens of thousands of years. More striking still, one finds what have been called preadaptations or exaptations (Gould and Vrba 1982). These occur when a trait originally adapted for one purpose is switched to another. For example, the original insects were exclusively terrestrial, but some had fanlike structures that served as cooling mechanisms. These were selected for and become more and more efficient until they were large and long enough to lift the insects off the ground. Once insects could fly, and flight proved advantageous for avoiding ground predators, increasing foraging range, and so on, traits that would enhance flying capacity were obviously selected for. However, the original act of flying was not specifically selected for as it rested on a quite different capacity that *had* been selected for. Were this not the case, evolution would be impossible, and after four billion years single-celled creatures would still populate the earth.

If gradualism is an empirical issue, the same is certainly true of its off-spring, continuism. Continuism holds that evolutionary development must be a direct continuation of some trait found in an ancestral species. For example, continuists hold that language must have developed directly out of an early system of primate communication (Hockett and Ascher 1964) with some kind of warning calls developing into words (for the implausibility of such notions, see Bickerton 1990, chapter 1). But again, biomusicology may do well to keep an open mind on this score. Until I heard the stunning presentation by François-Bernard Mâche (this volume), I would probably have said, by analogy with language, that music was unlikely to be in any sense a continuation of nonhuman song or any other form of behavior. After I heard Mâche's recordings of a vast range of different traditions in human music, each one accompanied by an eerily similar effect produced by an avian, mammalian, or even amphibian species, I was not so sure. If anyone could produce such a performance with linguistic material, I would be tempted to convert to continuism overnight. But again, caution is in order, and one should ask to what extent music, especially music uninfluenced by the dominant culture, may exploit the repertoires of other species to achieve its effect.

What all this suggests is that one among many avenues of research open to biomusicology is a comparison of music and language (see Brown, this volume). At the very least, such a line of inquiry would greatly increase our understanding of the similarities and differences between the two. At best, it might yield insights into the evolution of both.

But mention of the relationship between music and language brings us to the final hurdle that students of any aspect of human evolution should face. The way the behavioral sciences are structured, discussed earlier in this chapter, encourages, even forces, students of the evolution of a human capacity to focus exclusively on that capacity instead of seeing its acquisition as part of a much larger and more complex process.

The rather ugly and cumbersome word for the whole process by which the human species developed is: "hominization." This is a process that includes acquisition of language, of music, of mathematics, of logic, of self-consciousness: all those traits that either have no equivalent in other species or that are developed to a degree unknown in other species. It would be bizarre to suppose that all of these capacities developed autonomously and independently, without constantly influencing one another. It would also be bizarre to suppose that each of these capacities had a separate and independent birth.

The time that has elapsed since the hominid line split from the rest of the primates is nowadays estimated as less than six million years (Campbell 1988). For any one of these unique or quasi-unique capacities to have sprung up in such a short (in evolutionary terms) period of time would be remarkable enough. That several unconnected capacities of this magnitude could have emerged in the same period is something entirely beyond belief. This clearly states the possibility that just one of these capacities was the original starting agent and that it, whether it was language, intelligence, or behavioral plasticity, triggered the rest. Of course that would not preclude the possibility that some capacities were rooted in the behaviors of antecedent species and were merely enhanced, rather than initiated, by the master capacity.

Disentangling the intricate knot of hominization will require skills drawn from every branch of human study, and musicologists have a significant role to play in that disentangling. All of us, however, should bear in mind the existence of the following paradox. Humans differ radically from all other animals but were produced, like all other animals, by processes of evolution. In the history of human thought, many attempted to escape this paradox by denying one or other of the propositions that compose it. Until this century, denial of the second part was the commonest response (and one maintained by fundamentalists of several religions). More recently, denial of the first part has gained in popularity, especially among students of evolution.

There's nothing special about humans, we are assured; we are in fact a unique species, but then so is every other species. It is assumed, counter to fact, that to insist on the first part of the paradox can only be the sign of some hidden theological agenda.

Unfortunately, the paradox cannot be resolved so simplistically. Both halves of it are true, and all researchers into human evolution should repeat both halves every morning before they start work. For we will not arrive at a true account of how we came to be human unless we succeed in resolving the paradox and in showing by what processes evolution could have produced people like ourselves.

References

Beaken, M. (1996). *The Making of Language*. Edinburgh: Edinburgh University Press.

Bickerton, D. (1990). *Language and Species*. Chicago: Chicago University Press.

Bickerton, D. (1995). *Language and Human Behavior*. Seattle: University of Washington Press.

Bickerton, D. (1996). Review of Robin Dunbar "Grooming, Gossip and the Evolution of Language." *Nature* 380:303.

Calvin, W. H. and Bickerton, D. (In press). *Lingua ex Machina*. Cambridge: MIT Press.

Campbell, B. (1988). *Humankind Emerging*. Glenview, IL; Scott, Foresman.

Chomsky, N. (1965). *Aspects of the Theory of Syntax*. Cambridge: MIT Press.

Chomsky, N. (1980). *Rules and Representatives*. Oxford: Blackwell.

Chomsky, N. (1981). *Essays on Government and Binding*. Dordrecht: Foris.

Chomsky, N. (1988). *Language and Problems of Knowledge*. Cambridge: MIT Press.

Deacon, T. W. (1997). *The Symbolic Species*. New York: Norton.

Dunbar, R. (1996). *Grooming, Gossip and the Evolution of Language*. London: Faber and Faber.

Gardner, R. A. and Gardner, B. T. (1969). Teaching sign language to chimpanzees. *Science* 156:664–672.

Greenberg, J. (1963). *Universals of Language*. The Hague: Mouton.

Gould, S. J. and Vrba, E. (1982). Exaptation: A missing term in evolutionary theory. *Paleobiology* 8:4–15.

Hockett, C. F. and Ascher, R. (1964). The human revolution. *Current Anthropology* 5:135–347.

Lenneberg, E. (1967). *Biological Foundations of Language*. Cambridge: MIT Press.

Lightfoot, D. (1991). Commentary on Newmeyer, *"Functional Explanation in Linguistics and the Origins of Grammar." Language and Communication* 11:67–69.

Pinker, S. (1994). *The Language Instinct*. New York: Morrow.

Pinker, S. and Bloom, P. (1990). Natural language and natural selection. *Behavioral and Brain Sciences* 13:707–784.

Premack, A. J. and Premack, D. (1972). Teaching language to an ape. *Scientific American* 227:92–99.

Ridley, M. (1993). *The Red Queen: Sex and the Evolution of Human Nature*. New York: Macmillan.

de Waal, F. (1996). *Good Natured: The Origins of Right and Wrong in Humans and Other Animals*. Cambridge: Harvard University Press.

11 Toward an Evolutionary Theory of Music and Language

Jean Molino

Abstract

To explain the genesis of music and language in evolutionary terms, an essential question has to be confronted: when and how did the transition occur from standard Darwinian evolution to a Larmackian form of evolution in which the inheritance of acquired characteristics, namely, cultural characteristics, became possible? The symbolic entities that make up cultures can be analyzed from the standpoint of an evolutionary semiotics or "memetics." Music and language are cultural artifacts that do not correspond to natural objects. If we reduce them to their constituent parameters (corresponding to autonomous modules), and take into account such activities as poetry, song, dance, and play, we notice that all these cultural products are based on a common set of modules: melody, rhythm, and affective semantics. The fundamental hypothesis is that all these activities have a common genesis, which leads me to make conjectures regarding the central importance of one or more rhythmic modules in the brain, and the essential role of imitation in these activities, leading to the hypothesized formation of mimetic culture based on mimetic representation, without language, but unified by rhythm. Given this common foundation, music and language would be seen as having diverged at some later time.

It is once again permitted for a linguist and a musicologist to be interested in the origins of music and language, even though the subject has seemed almost completely taboo for around a century. I am referring not only to the famous decision taken in 1866 by the *Société de Linguistique de Paris* to ban all discussions concerning the origins of language, but to a general atmosphere that has dominated the human sciences since the beginning of the century. One could draw as a symbol of this antievolutionary attitude the works of the anthropologist Franz Boas (1858–1942) which, with those of Ferdinand Saussure (1857–1913), set down principles of a synchronic and structuralist approach to the human sciences that was opposed to the historicist perspectives of the nineteenth century. This approach is still the predominant one among specialists in the social sciences, who continue to see evolutionary thinking as pure and simple ideological affirmation impregnated with the social Darwinism of the end of the nineteenth century. This was demonstrated no better than in the discussions provoked by sociobiology. I believe that it is now desirable and possible to move beyond these conflicts and to address calmly the problems posed by the origins and development of the human faculties. One additional reason for this is that the progress recently made in the study of cognitive capacities in nonhuman animal species forces us to set out on a new ground the question of continuity and discontinuity that unites and separates animals and humans.

Theoretical Problems: Lamarck and/or Darwin

Nobody should doubt that it is legitimate and necessary to place the study of animal behavior and intelligence in the context of Darwin's theory of evolution, this "dangerous idea" that still seems to evoke fear in so many people (Dennett 1995). But if we no longer have reason to doubt Darwin's idea, which is, according to its proper form, the notion of "descent with modification," the situation is much less certain with respect to mechanisms, to the tempo of evolution, as well as to the relationship between macroevolution and microevolution. (These remarks are almost certain to provoke irritation or scorn in many specialists of evolution: numerous divergences remain between them, even if, it must be added, these differences do not in any way threaten the stability of the edifice.) What is of greater interest to the specialist in the social sciences is that the notion of adaptation is often far from convincing, and this makes one think, according to the formula of Gould and Lewontin, of a type of "Panglossian paradigm": in this regard, it suffices to recognize the diversity and fragility of adaptive explanations to account for the behavior and capacities of animals and humans, and in particular for music and language.

But it is not here that the principal theoretical problem is presented to specialists in the social sciences when thinking about the evolution of human capacities and their origins. Let us place ourselves in the framework of what Richard Dawkins (1983) called "universal Darwinism." Darwinian principles of biological evolution are valid for all evolutionary processes, whatever their particularities may be; they occur in a more general and more abstract form that one could summarize in the following scheme:

Evolution = replication + variation + selection
        + isolation of populations.

One should recall in this regard that the very idea of extending Darwinism to cultural phenomena was presented by Darwin himself who, in a significant passage from *The Descent of Man, and Selection in Relation to Sex* (1874), suggested that the formation and transformation of languages was analogous to the evolution of living species: "The formation of different languages and of distinct species, and the proofs that both have been developed through a gradual process, are curiously parallel" (p. 106). But it is clear that one cannot simply transpose the mechanisms of biological evolution to the evolution of culture: that is the error that was committed by those who were too quick to use Darwinism in the service of their own ideological and political agendas.

Cultural evolution possesses characteristics that distinguish it from biological evolution.

Let us start off with a standard definition: cultures are "systems of symbolically encoded conceptual phenomena that are socially and historically transmitted within and between populations" (Durham 1991:8–9). This leads logically to the idea of a dual inheritance system: in the human species, a new system—culture—came to be added onto the genetic system characteristic of living things in general. This inheritance system is distinct from and partly independent of the genetic inheritance system, but is subject to the same law of perpetual transformation that is manifested in biological evolution: ". . . all human cultures are related by historical derivation" (Durham 1991:185). However, the system of cultural symbols differs from genetic systems in at least two major respects. First, biological evolution is Darwinian in that there is no transmission of acquired characteristics; on the other hand, cultural evolution seems quite Lamarckian, since information acquired at each generation can be transmitted in whole to the next generation.

Second, mutations, which introduce into the genotype variations that make evolution possible, occur by chance; cultural variation occurs, in part, in a random manner, but can also proceed in a *directed* manner. This corresponds to orthogenetic phenomena, excluded in biological evolution but central to this second hereditary system. Technology and science are striking examples of directed evolution, as if their development occurred by means of problems to which successively more satisfying solutions were given by trial and error. Phenomena of the same type are found in all of the many domains of culture.

If two systems of transmission and transformation of information exist in this way, musicologists, linguists, and more generally specialists in the human sciences have a privileged interest in the question of the relationship between these systems. Two approaches seem available. On the one hand, we could, together with evolutionary psychologists, search for mental modules that supposedly underlie the capacities that appeared during the course of human evolution as adaptations to environmental conditions (Barkow, Cosmides, and Tooby 1992). On the other hand, we could turn to the study of cultural transmission itself, which although dependent on the biological evolution of mental modules produced through environmental adaptation, deals with objects that are susceptible to the partly autonomous process of directed evolution. Thus, if one wants to apply the scheme of universal Darwinism to culture, the first step is to identify cultural units of replication, variation, and selection; in other words, units corresponding to genes in biological evolution. In his book *The Selfish Gene* (1976), Richard Dawkins proposed the name "meme" for this unit of information that passes from one brain to another during the process of cultural transmission. It is interesting to note that the example chosen by Dawkins to illustrate this notion is an air from the song "Auld Lang Syne." This brings us right back to the area of music: we know that protoforms of cultural transmission are present among animal species that proceed, at least partly, by learning, particularly in the case of vocalizations (see Whaling and Payne, this volume). This helps us see more clearly the questions that have to be addressed and the research avenues that are available. At what point does cultural evolution appear? How does it establish itself? What relationship does it have with genetic evolution? Or, if you wish, *when is Lamarck added onto Darwin*? The study of the origins of music, language, and related phenomena can help us find answers to these questions.

Music and Language Are Not Natural Kinds

When one is interested in the origins of music, numerous data are at one's disposal. On one hand is all information dealing with the behavior and acoustic productions of a diverse array of animal species, and on the other, all that we know about human music. This latter knowledge includes several distinct areas: analysis of the structure and elements of music, but also the ontogeny of musical behavior and its instantiation in the human nervous system. On first view, the natural point of departure would seem to be the structure of human music such as we conceive of it. But we immediately see the danger of this approach: if we define music according to structures of the European tradition, we commit a grave methodological error, because nothing guarantees that this conception has any kind of universal validity. By proceeding in this way, we suppose that music possesses some kind of stable essence, that it constitutes a *natural kind*. Logicians use this term to describe families of entities possessing properties bound by natural law: we know of natural kinds in the form of categories of minerals, plants, or animals, and we know that different human cultures classify natural realities that surround them in a completely analogous fashion. Is the same thing true for cultural artifacts?

It is significant to consider that anthropologists, who insist on the eminently variable nature of cultural phenomena, do not go to the point of placing into question the unity of human music. We really believe we know what music is, even though ethnomusicologists themselves have taught us that in many cultures no word exists that corresponds to what we know of as music, and that we are obliged to put under the vague term of "music" very different types of practices. It seems to be the case that, in a general manner, cultural artifacts do not constitute natural kinds: they never stop changing, and terms that designate them constitute only what Wittgenstein called "family resemblance predicates." Nothing guarantees that all the forms of human music contain a nucleus of common properties that would be invariant since the origination of music.

If music is not a unified and homogeneous reality, there is no reason to imagine that it emerged one day wholly made by evolution. The only legitimate approach (in the worst case an exercise in brain storming) is to recognize that there is no "music in and of itself," no musical essence, but only some distinct capacities that one day converged toward what we today call music. In addition, we have to place in perspective not only the mixed and heterogeneous nature of music itself but also the external relations that it maintains with what one could call the sister arts. I use this expression in a broad sense to refer not only to poetry and painting but also to the entire family of the performing arts—theater, mime, circus, dance—as well as to language. Contrary to common opinion, language is no more natural than music; it constitutes a heterogeneous reality. In a general manner, I believe that problems posed by the origins of music as well as by the origins of language can be resolved in a proper manner only by engaging in an exercise of systematic deconstruction of these notions. To take up once again the expression of François Jacob, evolution is a *bricolage*, and we have no reason to think that music and language, two capacities of which we are so proud, could have escaped this mode of production.

It is thus advisable to analyze music and language by reducing them to their constitutive elements, of which one could make the hypothesis that they correspond to independent modules, each of which has undergone a specific evolutionary trajectory. What are these features or constituents of music? In an elementary fashion, one could distinguish a temporal component consisting of meter and rhythm, and a melodic component consisting of contour, pitch, and interval. An essential argument in favor of the existence of distinct modules for each of these features is furnished by neuropsychology.

It must be pointed out first that the neuropsychology of music has shown a pronounced lag by comparison with the current state of knowledge of the neuropsychology of language. Even though aphasia and its different forms have been topics of great interest for well over a century—at least since the work of Broca and Wernicke—the study of the corresponding deficits in the domain of music, that is to say, the *amusias*, is still in its infancy. This seems significant to me: it shows that music, as it is viewed as an elevated art form, is difficult to submit to experimental scientific approaches. However, despite the insufficiency of our understanding, the study of pathological dissociations and double dissociations at the neurological level seems to lead to the hypothesis of specific modules for the temporal and melodic components of music, themselves composed of distinct submodules for, on the one hand, meter and rhythm, and on the other, contour, pitch, and intervals (Peretz 1993). To these diverse components, it seems necessary to add a semantic component.

We know of the great difficulty in specifying the nature of musical signification, vigorously challenged by the formalist tradition from Hanslick to Stravinsky and the latter's famous axiom, "I consider music, by its nature, incapable of *expressing* anything." I believe that to have a less artificial and less inexact idea of musical signification, one must abandon "great" music and instead turn to contemporary and primitive forms of dance music, from ritual to disco. The issue is not about representational semantics but about what I call *rhythmo-affective semantics*, which involves the body, its movements, and the fundamental emotions that are associated with them. This point seems to be essential: our conception of music, based on the production, perception, and theory of "great" European classical music, distances ourselves irremediably from the anthropological foundations of human music in general.

Let us now attempt the same exercise in the area of language, a field in which resistance is much greater, because it is difficult for us to think that language does not constitute, according to the formulas of Saussure, an organism in which everything is internally connected. Yet, language is not, any more than living organisms, a perfectly organized totality or a formal system: both are made from the pieces and fragments that evolution, bit by bit, adapted to the world, and coadapted among themselves. It is thus not certain that all of the components of language appeared at the same time (but see Bickerton, this volume, for a different viewpoint). The constitutive dimensions of language are well known, but I would like to emphasize especially those aspects that are most often underestimated.

We classically distinguish a phonetic-phonological level, a grammatical or morphosyntactic level, a lexicosemantic level, and a pragmatic level. Concerning the first level, an essential point is that this itself is composed of two sublevels: a segmental level of phonemes, and a suprasegmental level corresponding to the phenomena of accent, intonation, and duration. One sees here the appearance of a first point of meeting between language and music: the suprasegmental level of language depends on mechanisms close to those that are operative in the melodic component of music (see Brown, this volume). Moreover, language possesses, like music, a temporal and rhythmic component, essential for speech, and that appears, for example, in the fundamental unit of the syllable. A universal definition of the phoneme (if there is one and if we are on the right track) will have a rhythmic organization based on the emission of timed initiator powerbursts, each burst having a single peak (Lass 1984:250). It should be noted that these two aspects of language, the melodic and the rhythmic, are largely left by the wayside when trying to reconstruct protoforms of language.

If we move on to morphosyntax, we see that it clearly constitutes one of the specific characteristics of human language, which distinguishes it from other known forms of animal communication. We can describe morphosyntax from two points of view: formal and functional-semantic. From the formal point of view, it appears as a capacity to link and combine lower-level sequences. In this regard, it cannot be said that there is anything language-specific about this function since one finds analogous capacities in many other domains, from gesture to manual skills to the articulation of speech. The same cannot be said for the other aspect of morphosyntax, whose fundamental structure is the operation of predication. But here again, one should avoid getting stuck in strictly linguistic analyses. In fact, predication, that is, the association between a subject and a predicate, or, if you will, between a function and its arguments—as in the sentence "Peter hit Paul"—depends on prior capacities and operations (i.e., naming and categorization) preceded by pointing.

Pointing is particularly important. It leads us to distinguish two domains in language, which Karl Bühler (1965) called *Zeigfeld* and *Symbolfeld*: the *deictic* field, in which words directly refer to the speaker and the world and are dependent on context (e.g., indexical expressions such as "I," "here," "now," "this"); and the *symbolic* field, which proceeds through the intermediary of general concepts. The existence of the deictic field in language suggests a social origin for relations in the world: it is for their "socius" that humans designate and name objects. Moreover, the act of predication must not be interpreted as a logical or abstract operation, but instead as the *representation of a scene*. It is here that one can establish a link between language and the way in which problems of visual perception are conceptualized today: the major concern deals with understanding how the cerebral cortex represents an environmental scene. It is the same thing for language: it represents, that is, it "plays out," a scene, and we will soon see the importance of this process for the origins of language.

The lexicosemantic dimension of language has been largely ignored since the triumph of structural and generative linguistics and the emphasis that it placed on grammar. I would like to focus on one final component of language: affective semantics, something that I would relate to musical signification. Linguistic semantics is generally, and almost exclusively, conceived of in terms of a referential semantics couched in the form of abstract and emotionally neutral cognitive representations. Affectivity, when it is taken into account at all, intervenes only in the form of a response or an emotional discharge that is added onto some abstract cognitive state. However, this is an inversion of the importance and, without a doubt, the origins of these two components of semantics: affective semantics, which carries the mark of the ties that connect humans and our environment, is the foundation of cognitive semantics (and not vice versa). It is critical not to forget that the most important sentences in human language are not those that logicians and linguists have habitually analyzed of the type "the cat is on the mat," but of phrases "listen!" "stop!" "look out!" "I love you," aud so on. The emotive power of language is comparable with that of music and is dependent on similar mechanisms associated with the brain stem and limbic system (Edelman 1992).

Thus a certain number of components are common to music and language, among them the melodic component, which is found in the suprasegmental level of language; the rhythmic component, present in articulation, the syllable, and the organization of sentences; and affective semantics, whose nature is similar in the two cases. It must be added that syntax, as a combination and linking of sequences, is also present in music. The relationship between music and language seems greater yet if one takes into account what one could call, although incorrectly, hybrid forms, participating in the two processes. The most significant example of this is poetry, in which linguists and musicologists are almost never interested. Throughout the greater part of its history, that is, until the most recent period, poetry has been chanted, and a methodological error seems to the involved in seeing chant as a kind of mixture, as a hybrid form. Maybe, on the contrary, it gives us a clear idea of the first forms of something that was at the same time music and language, keeping in mind that music is first and foremost vocal. Similarly, a close relationship exists between music, language, and poetry, and the ensemble of performing arts—dance, pretend play, theater, festival, and ritual—in which song, rhythmic motion, imitation, and narrative are combined.

This leads me to a final comment concerning these diverse forms. We are accustomed to placing them within the framework of "communication," as this seems to be their common trait. I think that one should be dubious of this notion, first introduced in the 1940s by the creators of communication theory (Shannon and Weaver 1949) and taken up without much caution by specialists in almost all fields. The definition of communication as an abstract exchange of information belies the concrete reality that underlies interactions among living things. Alarm calls, territory markings, and sexual displays are not merely communications; they are, most especially, constructive and complex exchanges among members of a group. This is the same, a fortiori, for language as for music, both of which are above all social activities.

The Origins of Language and Music

Starting from this analysis of music, language, and related activities, I propose the following hypothesis: music, language, dance, chant, poetry, and pretend play all have a partly common origin. Among the neural modules responsible for this activity, it would be necessary to give a central place to one or more rhythmic modules, which come into play in behaviors such as throwing and constructing and using tools. The neurophysiologist William H. Calvin (1990) proposed that the preparation and organization of throwing movements is the source of a type of general syntax, the capacity to combine elementary sequences freely, a capacity that would come into play in language as much as in behavior. It is not certain if this (or these) module(s) have a unique origin, and we would prefer for our part to view them as operating as well, and perhaps rather than, in music and other collective activities as in technical operations such as throwing. The important thing is that they should have contributed in a decisive manner to the development of the following capacities: muscular and neural control of body movements, in particular the hand, and, in the case of the rhythmic organization of vocalizations, movements of the face and larynx, all of which are largely controlled at the level of the cerebral cortex. These modules would thus have major importance in the construction of speech rhythms and, in particular, syllable formation, the central point of phonetic articulation. In a general sense, this mastery of rhythm is the only imaginable route of access for the temporal organization of all activities: it is in this way that rhythmic modules are at the foundation of all types of syntactic constructions.

In our impending approach toward origins we must provide an essential place for another family of elementary behaviors, imitation. Specialists in child psychology have for a long time focused on the role of imitation in human ontogeny (e.g., Wallon 1942; Piaget 1945), and one could even characterize the human species by this capacity: it is for this reason that Meltzoff (1988) spoke of *Homo imitans*, which would take the place of the traditional *Homo faber*. We see here again a certain continuity between human and animal, since it seems that chimpanzees, for example, are capable of imitative behavior (Boesch 1993). But imitation is a rather vague term that covers a diversity of behaviors having different degrees of complexity. One could distinguish a first degree of complexity, mimicry, which arises from the domain of reflex; a second degree of complexity corresponds to simple imitation, which is more indirect and implies a certain form of learning. The third step corresponds to imitation-representation, delayed imitation in the absence of a model.

If one takes into account at the same time the connections among music, language, and related forms of expression, as well as the importance of rhythmic and imitation behaviors, one is led to hypothesize that a major step in the process of hominization was the creation of what we could call, along with Merlin Donald (1991), mimetic culture. Starting from the classic parallel between ontogeny and phylogeny, Henri Wallon proposed an age of imitation, ritual, and naissant representation before the age of language and bona fide representation (Wallon 1942:168–176). Any detailed reconstruction of this would obviously be, given the current state of our knowledge, without great interest. The main issue deals in wondering how humanity was able to pass to the age of true representation. This is the major difficulty all theories of the origins of language come up against.

Delayed imitation furnishes precisely such a route of passage in which there is no representation in the abstract sense of the word—no system of signs for carrying out representation in the form of an association between a signified and a signifier—yet beings, objects, and scenes are incarnated and played out in the very act of imitation. Mimetic culture would correspond to a step in the evolution of culture in which (and here we are obliged to give ourselves some leeway in imagining likely examples) a group of hominids would perform activities of collective imitation without language but accompanied by vocalizations and organized by rhythm: these would in fact be the first forms of the representation of scenes, that is, of narratives, leading to rite and to myth.

One could note in this regard that someone recently attempted to explain the syntactic and semantic structures of language in terms of prior narrative structure (Turner 1996). In this context, imitation would take place for the individual but above all for the collective, because imitation is not only imitation *of* something or someone but *for* someone. It is the same thing for representation. It is impossible to produce a representation of referents by signs from a pure state of nonrepresentation: the only intermediary stage possible is imitation-representation played out for other members of the group. Symbolic behaviors have a double character: when I play, imitate, or speak, the symbol that I use recalls its model but is not confused with it: it is the same yet it is not the same. This double character is first acted out before being spoken and thought. From this would emerge what one could call semiotic or symbolic function "which consists of being able to represent something (some 'signified' or other: an object, event, conceptual scheme, etc.) by means of a differentiated 'signifier' only serving this representation" (Piaget and

Inhelder 1984:41). Such would be the origin of language: the representation of scenes by elementary propositions of protolanguage would have been preceded and made possible by their played-out representation.

The consequences of these played-out and rhythmic imitations are of central importance for hominization. We have first the development of pointing and of exchanges that progressively construct the relations of intentionality among members of the group: imitation implies willingness to imitate and recognition of this intention. In parallel with this, control of the body in rhythmic games, which function at the same time for oneself and for others, leads, if not yet to a theory of mind, to a sense of consciousness of the self and of one's own body. Second, imitation, whatever the object is, leads to an analysis, first acted out, of movements necessary for the success of the imitation: to improve the accuracy of an imitation or of an act of throwing, the actor has to break down his motion into more elementary movements.

We previously underlined the importance of the combination of elementary sequences as the foundation for a general syntax: it must not be forgotten that combinatorial synthesis implies a movement parallel to analysis. What is true for gestures and movements is also true for music and language. How can we understand, in fact, the articulation of language in phonemes, word morphemes, and sentences as well as the articulation of music in degrees of the scale, motifs, and musical phrases? In both cases it is certainly necessary to conceive of, starting with unanalyzed global sequences similar to animal calls, a double process: a top-down analysis that decomposes the sequence into combinations of lower-level elements, and a bottom-up recombination of new sequences and, possibly, construction of higher-order sequences. Segmentation and recombination thus go hand in hand with motor control mechanisms that impose collective synchronization on activities.

All the elements of representation are thus combined, and at the same time the possibility of systematically transmitting a piece of information emerges: mimetic culture is one in which learning and teaching bring forth a new form of evolution that consists of transmission and transformation of new cultural units, memes. The cultural heritage is thus added onto biological inheritance.

Have I told fictions here? If so, I would at least have been faithful to the founding act of hominization: the telling of stories.

Note

Translated from the French by Steven Brown.

References

Barkow, J., Cosmides, L., and Tooby, J. (1992). *The Adapted Mind: Evolutionary Psychology and the Generation of Culture*. New York: Oxford University Press.

Boesch, C. (1993). Aspects of transmission of tool-use in wild chimpanzees. In K. R. Gibson and T. Ingold (Eds.) *Tools, Language and Cognition in Human Evolution* (pp. 171–183). Cambridge, UK: Cambridge University Press.

Bühler, K. (1965). *Sprachtheorie*. Stuttgart: Gustav Fischer.

Calvin, W. H. (1990). *The Ascent of Mind*. New York: Bantam.

Darwin, C. R. (1874). *The Descent of Man, and Selection in Relation to Sex*, 2nd ed. New York: Hurst.

Dawkins, R. (1976). *The Selfish Gene*. Oxford: Oxford University Press.

Dawkins, R. (1983). Universal Darwinism. In D. S. Bendall (Ed.) *Evolution: From Molecules to Man* (pp. 403–425). Cambridge, UK: Cambridge University Press.

Dennett, D. C. (1995). *Darwin's Dangerous Idea*. New York: Simon and Schuster.

Donald, M. (1991). *Origins of the Modern Mind*. Cambridge: Harvard University Press.

Durham, W. (1991). *Coevolution: Genes, Culture and Human Diversity*. Stanford, CA: Stanford University Press.

Edelman, G. M. (1992). *Bright Air, Brilliant Fire*. Harmondsworth: Penguin.

Lass, R. (1984). *Phonology*. Cambridge, UK: Cambridge University Press.

Meltzoff, A. N. (1988). *Homo imitans*. In T. R. Zentall and B. G. Galef (Eds.) *Social Learning: Psychological and Biological Perspectives* (pp. 319–342). Hillsdale, NJ: Erlbaum.

Peretz, I. (1993). Auditory agnosia: A functional analysis. In S. McAdams and E. Bigand (Eds.) *Thinking in Sound: The Cognitive Psychology of Human Audition* (pp. 199–230). Oxford: Clarendon Press.

Piaget, J. (1945). *La Formation du Symbole Chez l'Enfant*. Neuchâtel: Delachaux-Niestlé.

Piaget, J. and Inhelder, B. (1984). *La Psychologie de l'Enfant*. Paris: Presses Universitaires de France.

Shannon, C. E. and Weaver, W. (1949). *The Mathematical Theory of Communication*. Urbana: University of Illinois Press.

Turner, M. (1996). *The Literary Mind*. Oxford: Oxford University Press.

Wallon, H. (1942). *De l'Acte à la Pensée*. Paris: Flammarion.

Paleoneurology and the Biology of Music

Harry Jerison

Abstract

Paleoneurology, the study of fossil "brains," provides direct evidence about the 500-million-year history of the vertebrate brain. Analyzing changes in the external appearance of the brain as mirrored in casts molded by the cranial cavity, paleoneurology relates evolutionary changes in the brain to the evolution of behavior and of the capacity to perceive and know an external world. For any behavior, questions of evolutionary antecedents and relationships arise. The relevance of paleoneurology for our understanding of the evolution of human musical expression and experience lies in the relationship of these traits to gross features of brains. From present evidence, it may be especially important to seek connections with language rather than with nonlinguistic acoustic phenomena in other species, even when, to the human ear, the phenomena have an obviously musical dimension. We know that in mammals and birds, increases in the brain's capacity evolved to process information about the external world, a capacity related to the evolution of increased perceptual and cognitive capacity. The genetic blueprint for a brain to develop this intelligence-creating capacity is actually an epigenetic blueprint requiring a normal environment for the growth and development of the nervous system. In their fundamental biology, therefore, brain and intelligence result from a nature-nurture interaction. Different intelligences (in the plural) evolved in different species, depending on their neural specializations, and the human variety derives mainly from the evolution of language. It is this diversity of specializations that must be analyzed for an understanding of the evolution of human musicality, which is in many ways an adaptation within this specialized cognitive capacity.

Although my evolutionary work is with fossil brains, to show its relationship to the evolution of musical experience and expression I have to emphasize information about brain and behavior in living species. One must rely on such information for a proper perspective in all studies of fossils. Let me explain that perspective.

My primary research material is fossilized evidence of the brain in vertebrates, which is in the form of castings, endocasts, molded by the cranial cavity. Several hundred fossil endocasts are known, and they provide the most direct evidence of the brain's evolution (Jerison 1973). In living birds and mammals, they provide accurate pictures of the external surface of freshly dissected brains. This enables one to treat endocasts as if they were brains in which one can determine relationships between the external anatomy of the brain and its functions in controlling behavior and experience. To extend this to fossils, one relies on the classic uniformitarian hypothesis (Simpson 1970), which states that relationships true for living species were also true for fossils. With respect to external anatomy, endocasts from fossils are, therefore, truly fossil brains.

In analyzing fossil brains, I am necessarily limited to gross anatomy, and this in turn limits me to very general categories of behavior. These limitations are quite appropriate, however, for the relationship between brain and musical experience, because it is only at such general levels that one has good scientific information about the relationship.

Music is psychologically a human phenomenon. To identify the vocal behavior of other species as musical is, after all, a human activity. We humans recognize and categorize the songs of birds and whales and the calls of gibbons and howler monkeys as songs and calls. We create the vocabulary for describing these acoustic events, and it is we who group them as musical. Music thus begins as an activity of the human mind, and to learn more about its biological roots it is appropriate to examine adaptations in other species that are related to this mental activity.

Human musical experience is neurologically unique, a fact discovered a few decades ago with the finding that the brains of professional musicians were organized somewhat differently from those of nonmusicians. In both groups the neural correlates of the experience are lateralized, that is, represented to different extents in the two cerebral hemispheres. In professionals, focal neural activation by music occurs in the left "language" hemisphere of the neocortex, whereas in nonmusicians comparable foci are in the right hemisphere. To me, discoveries of this kind (reviewed by Falk, this volume), as well as the overall evidence on the localization of cognitive processes in the human brain, epitomize the peculiarly human nature of music as a cognitive activity, a way of knowing reality. Its lateralized localization in our brains is evidence of its cognitive dimension. Nothing like this degree of lateralization is known in the brain in other mammals with respect to any behavior. Comparable lateralization is known only in songbirds and is one of the reasons why birds are useful animal models for understanding the biology of music.

Lateralization of music in the human brain reinforces a natural inclination to distinguish between musical expression and musical experience. There is no real question that we share with other mammals the basic bodily structures used to vocalize and generate musical sounds and thus share with other species many aspects of our capacity for musical expression. We are evidently unique, however, in the way we know (i.e., "cognize") and understand sounds as musical. This is not really an unusual statement. All species are unique in some ways; that is what distinguishes them from one another. For humans, one way lies in the nature of our knowledge of the external world; that is, the nature of human cognitive capacity, or intelligence. That this includes the world of music is evidenced by the way our neocortex is lateralized when we experience music. Let me emphasize the point: the biological basis of our musical experience is related to the biology of human intelligence; that is, to our capacity to know the external world.

The evolution of unusual cognitive capacity is the special feature of the evolution of enlarged brains in birds and mammals. In mammals the enlargement is correlated with evolution of the cerebral neocortex of the forebrain, a structure that is seen only in mammals. The forebrain in birds does not have the layered structure that defines mammalian neocortex. It is called hyperstriatum because of its similarity in appearance to the basal ganglia (striatum) in mammals. From its connections to other brain structures, however, hyperstriatum appears to be functionally homologous to neocortex (Karten 1991), and it is of additional interest in light of discoveries of plasticity and lateralization of brain and behavior in the control of bird vocalization (Arnold 1980; Marler, this volume).

Evolutionary Distance

Throughout this volume a good deal of evidence is presented on musical expression in mammals and birds. Figure 12.1 is a phylogenetic tree (cf. Carroll 1988) that indicates the relationships among those animals as well as their evolutionary distance. Mammals and birds are very distant relatives, and even within the mammals, long periods of independent evolution separate groups from one another.

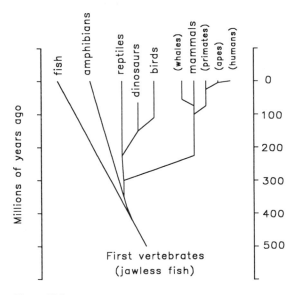

Figure 12.1
The phylogeny of vertebrates. Note especially the evolutionary distance between birds and mammals and among groups of mammals. Birds, cetaceans (e.g., whales), and primates are the groups emphasized in comparative studies of musicality.

The first birds probably evolved as small specialized dinosaurs with feathers, an event that occurred during the early to middle Mesozoic era more than 150 million years ago (mya). Mammals evolved at least 225 mya from therapsid (mammallike) reptiles, and separation of the dinosaur (*archosaurian*, or "ruling reptile") lineage from the therapsid lineage occurred during the Paleozoic era, at least 300 mya. This means that the suite of traits we share with birds has been stable during more than 300 million years of the history of animal life. During the same 300 million years other traits evolved that differentiate us from humming birds and ostriches. There was plenty of time for major divergences.

Within mammals, placentals appeared during the Cretaceous period of the Mesozoic era, about 100 mya. Primates may have diverged from other species of placental mammals during the late Cretaceous, about 70 mya. Some early Cenzoic fossil primates resembled living tarsiers and are grouped with them taxonomically. These are from the Lower Eocene epoch, and are about fifty-five million years old; other primatelike mammal fossils are about sixty million years old. And a few Cretaceous primatelike mammal teeth are at least seventy million years old. One can pick one's date for the divergence of primates from other mammals, but it happened a long time ago. An authoritative detailed discussion of primate evolution, including quantitative analysis of the evolution of the primate brain, is available in Martin (1990).

Gibbons, which call so impressively and musically, are related to primate lesser ape fossils from which the human and great ape lines diverged at least twenty mya, and we split from our great ape cousins about five mya according to the current consensus. Whales and other cetaceans diverged from other mammals early in the Cenozoic era, at least fifty-five mya. The morphological diversity represented by these groups illustrates the amount of evolutionary change that could occur over these long intervals.

These dates must be evaluated with respect to the common and specific traits that we recognize in various living animals, including humans. We know that many morphological traits, such as whether one has five fingers or a hoof, or a wing or an arm, diverged relatively rapidly from a basal condition. According to recently developed evidence (McKee, Tobias, and Clarke 1996), it was only about three mya that the primate foot with an opposable digit suitable for grasping and climbing evolved into the human foot specialized for walking and running. This, by the way, is evidence of the persistence of arboreal locomotion in some australopithecine hominids. Fully terrestrial habits evolved within the australopithecines and after hominids had separated from the great apes. The conclusion to emphasize is that evolution can be relatively rapid when environmental requirements drive it appropriately.

In the face of such evidence of rapid evolution and diversification of morphological traits, can we assume that behavioral traits could remain stable over very long periods of time? If we seek common mechanisms for behavior in humans and birds, can we assume that they survived despite the 300-million-year interval available for their divergent evolution? Such an assumption turns out to be at least not unreasonable, because the nervous system is one of the more conservative biological systems with respect to evolutionary change. Furthermore, the phenotypic condition is determined by significant environmental editing of the genotypic blueprint that governs the developing nervous system. Homologies in the control of behavior can exist even in the face of very extensive diversity of form and function of the whole organism. Let me explain with examples from the function of sensory systems.

Sensory cells of each type—retinal rods and cones in the case of vision (Polyak 1957) and cochlear hair cells, which are mechanoreceptors, in hearing (Stebbins 1983)—evolved from common roots in all mammals. Genetic blueprints, as it were, presumably set the main distinct features of each of these classes of cells, including the number to be produced in an individual animal. However, important differences exist among species.

These are quantifiable morphological traits, and it may help to look at some numbers. Surprising uniformity is seen among mammals in the size and number of hair cells in the cochlea of each ear, always a tiny organ usually with two or three turns in the spiral cochlea, about 35,000 hair cells, and the same number of bipolar neurons in the spiral ganglion, which lies beneath the cochlea. The visual system varies in the size of the eyeball, retina, and numbers of rods and cones. The vertebrate eye as a camera is an example of a great uniformity, but eyes are more variable in detailed structure in different species, reflecting the place of vision in the lives of the species. The number of rods relative to the number of cones varies enormously, with some nocturnal species having eyes consisting almost entirely of rods, and diurnal reptiles and birds having eyes consisting almost entirely of cones. The human eye is a fairly typical anthropoid primate eye, and its numbers, which are the same in rhesus monkeys, are impressive. I have seen no counts of the number of nerve cells in the neural retina, but it certainly numbers in the millions; about one million ganglion cells; that is, cell bodies of neurons make up the one million fibers in each optic nerve (cranial nerve II). One guesses that the retina has between five and ten million additional nerve cells. Each eye has about 100 million rods and about 7 million cones. To emphasize diversity, I should add that primate eyes are atypical among mammals in having many more cones and a fovea centralis for improved detail vision in the center of the visual field. The singularity of anthropoid primates is an aspect of their almost specific adaptation among mammals for diurnicity.

Sensory cells are homologous certainly for mammals and perhaps for all vertebrates. I refer specifically to rods and cones in vision and mechanoreceptors that are auditory hair cells. These sense cells function in essentially the same way at some levels of organization of behavior, whereas other levels reflect the diversification that has occurred. Diversity lies in the way that neural connections made by these cells are organized into systems involved in controlling vision and hearing. Yet the pathways between sensory cells in the retina and nerve cells in the retina and brain are fundamentally the same in all mammals until one reaches perhaps third- or fourth-order neurons in the synaptic pathway, when it reaches mammalian cerebral cortex. (Recall that cortex does not exist as a distinct structure in other vertebrates; neurons homologous to these in nonmammals can be identified as reaching forebrain structures such as the *Wulst* in birds [Butler and Hodos 1996]). I present these few details to suggest the complexity of the underlying system and do not pretend that it is a complete description.

The "instructions" that determine the pattern of connections at all levels are partly genetic and partly environmental. Genetic instructions set the number of nerve cells and "tell them" to grow by arborization, by sending out fibrils like branches of trees. Genetic instructions may also specify some environmental features, such as the nature of pathways along which cell growth can occur. Environmental instructions are in the actual formation of pathways, end points at which cells can make synaptic connections with other cells, and the amount of use to which cells are put, or extent to which they are stimulated by environmental events. Unused synapses may disappear, and unstimulated nerve cells may simply die. Cell death is an important phenomenon in the construction of the mature nervous system, a kind of editing of unnecessary connections. This is the kind of nature-nurture interaction that one may assume to be the basis of the evolution of musical expression and of some aspects of musical experience. Let us now consider some aspects of the organization of living brains in which that evolution occurred, the extent to which brains diversified, and the extent to which we can recognize uniformities in their organization.

Brain Organization: Uniformities

How much diversification of neurobehavioral traits can be expected to occur over the many millions of years available for their separate evolution? This is a general evolutionary issue for which no simple answer exists. Control of behavior (and experience) involves extensive neural circuitry in the brain, the function of which is becoming better understood, but we know relatively little about its evolution. The basic element, the neuron, is perhaps best understood, and like sensory cells, it must have been remarkably stable in function. Much of our knowledge of neuronal physiology comes from studies of single nerve cells in invertebrates, which have been separated from vertebrates for more than 500 million years. Fundamental aspects of a neuron's operation must have appeared before that separation and were evidently conserved in the face of other evolutionary developments.

Neural networks, which control complex behavior such as the conditioning of extending or contracting a body part, have been studied in sea slugs (invertebrate mollusks) in which only a few dozen nerve cells are involved. This provided important insights into the nature of learning (Kandel 1967; Byrne 1987), and such learning appears to follow common principles in sea slugs, locusts, pigeons, and rats. That their neural basis may be the same encourages one to expect homologous features in the development of neural control, even of complex behavior (Macphail 1993). Like the neuron, these fundamental adaptations of neural circuitry for the control of complex activity appeared early in the history of life, and unless they evolved independently in vertebrates and invertebrates, they must have been conserved during subsequent evolution. Therefore, important homologies may exist with respect to behavior and experience among rather distantly related species.

Important uniformities are observable at still higher levels of analysis. If one analyzes parts of the brain in mammals to determine how much their relative sizes were modified in different species, one reaches the surprising conclusion that some uniformities are impressive across species. For example, figure 12.2 shows the relationship between two substructures of the brain and the brain as a whole in seventy-six species of mammals (data from Stephan, Frahm, and Baron 1981).

The upper half of the figure shows the relationship between the size of the cerebellum and of the whole brain, and the lower half shows the relationship between the basal ganglia and the whole brain. The sizes of these two major structures involved in motor performance and in conditioning and learning are related in a very orderly way to the size of the whole brain. I have named a few species to indicate the diversity for which a single rule operates for the size of the brain and its parts. Notice that the homology is with respect to the rule, the equation, that relates the sizes of parts of the brain to the whole brain. It is easy to imagine relatively simple genetic instructions concerning growth of the brain and its parts that determine the rule and that have been conserved during all of mammalian evolution.

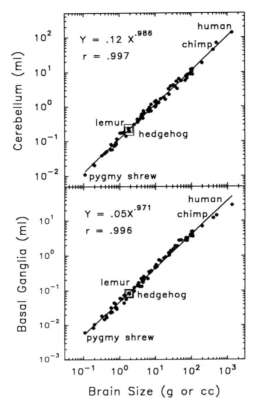

Figure 12.2
Volume of cerebellum and basal ganglia as a function of brain size in seventy-six species of mammals. Squares identify data points for the mouse lemur (*Microcebus murinus*) and desert hedgehog (*Hemiechinus auritus*); a few other species in the sample are also identified. (Data from Stephan, Frahm, and Baron 1981.)

To make a somewhat different point, I boxed the points giving data on the smallest known primate, the mouse lemur (*Microcebus murinus*), and a medium-size insectivore, the desert hedgehog (*Hemiechinus auritus*). Mammalian species do differ significantly in the sizes of their brains relative to body size, a difference in "encephalization" that I analyzed in great detail (Jerison 1991). Primates are the most encephalized order of living mammals and insectivores the least. I chose my specimens to show that the brain hangs together in more or less the same way, regardless of the evolutionary and genetic forces that resulted in its present size. In other words, whether a brain evolved to larger size because of selection for more information-processing capacity (encephalization) or because of the evolution of a larger body (allometric effect), its parts maintain approximately constant relationships with

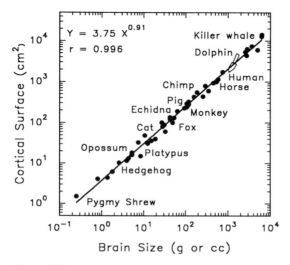

Figure 12.3
The relationship between cortical surface and gross brain size in fifty species of mammals. Each point represents a species. In addition, two labeled minimum convex polygons indicate within-species variability in twenty-three humans and thirteen dolphins (*Tursiops truncatus*). Several species are labeled to indicate the diversity of the sample. (From Jerison 1991, by permission.)

one another, following the rule of the equation of the best-fitting line that is drawn in the graph.

This does not mean that brains are alike in every way. Rather, it means in general that if evolutionary forces resulted in an enlarged brain, it is the brain as a whole that tends to become enlarged, and the sizes of its parts tend to be appropriate for the size of the whole. Neurologically, this makes good sense. The brain's parts work together. If one has an enlarged motor neocortex, other parts of the brain that tend to work with motor cortex must be appropriately enlarged, such as cerebellum and basal ganglia.

The most outstanding example of uniformity in brain structure relative to function is the relationship between the surface area of the cortex and gross brain size. This is illustrated in figure 12.3 for fifty species of mammals (more detailed citations for the data in the figure, which were collected in several different laboratories, are in Jerison 1991). The species are from the orders Monotremata, Marsupialia, Artiodactyla, Carnivora, Cetacea, Insectivora, Perissodactyla, Primates, and Xenarthra. As is evident, a single rule governs essentially all covariation of cortical surface area and gross brain size in living mammals. Data on twenty-three humans and thirteen dolphins that were available for this graphical analysis are enclosed in small convex polygons near the fitted line. The small sizes of these polygons show that individual differences within a species are relatively small compared with those between species.

The data of figure 12.3 are important because they indicate that gross brain size in living mammals is a good statistic, as it were, for estimating total information-processing capacity. This conclusion follows from uniformities in the way cortex is organized into columns of neurons, and from the way neurons are packed in the brain. The number of neurons under a given cortical surface area is remarkably uniform in mammalian brains that have been studied (Rockel, Hiorns, and Powell 1980). Since these features—the number of cortical columns and the number of neurons—are usually considered appropriate units for analyzing the capacity of a brain to handle information, the orderly relationship shown in figure 12.3 between surface area and brain size implies the same kind of relationship between brain size and information-processing capacity. From uniformitarianism we can extend the analysis to fossil brains.

This kind of evidence leads us to assume that at some levels of complexity the workings of animal brains are likely to be similar, even in distantly related species. Such uniformity of function enabled us to localize and map many brain functions and analyze them in great detail. The functions of auditory cortex, for example, were analyzed by studying this part of the brain carefully in house cats, and we know that it functions in a similar way in monkeys.

My doctoral dissertation was on this subject in monkeys (Jerison and Neff 1953), and I considered my negative result as something of a failure. I found that my macaques were affected by brain surgery in exactly the same way as cats in their ability to distinguish among patterns of pure tones. I had hoped for evidence of progression or a scale of nature that differentiated higher animals (monkeys) from lower animals (cats; cf. Hodos and Campbell 1969). Instead I found uniformity in behavior and brain function across species. The uniformity lay in a conditioned response to different patterns of pure tones (three-tone melodies): ablation of auditory neocortex resulted in unrelearnable loss of the habit in both species. A comparable habit to discriminate between single pure tones, however, although lost after surgery, could be relearned. I had run into a uniformity of behavior, or expression, at least between cats and monkeys. It is much more difficult to ask the same kind of question about the nature of the experience that is correlated with a behavior, or of the mental activity in which little or no overt behavior can be observed. We have no idea what was on each cat's or monkey's mind as it did its job. But it is reasonable to assume that the control mechanisms used by both animals in generating their performances were homologous and perhaps comparable with our own experience when we hear pure tones.

Brain Organization: Diversity

Although the uniformities are impressive, diversity among species with respect to their brains is even more compelling. It is not possible to convey its scope in this short chapter. The pages of major technical journals, such as *Brain, Behavior and Evolution, Journal of Comparative Neurology*, and *Zeitschrift für Hirnforschung* are filled with evidence. I recommend one text on the subject, Butler and Hodos (1996), that outlines the extent to which vertebrate brains are both similar to and different from one another. Readers with access by computer to the Internet may get an even better sense of diversity, at least in mammals, at http://www.neurophys.wisc.edu/brain/. Here one can see pictures of whole brains and of histological sections, accompanied by narratives relating brain to behavior in dozens of mammals, and thus have an easy introduction to the diversity of living species.

The relationship between uniformity and diversity is a kind of forest-and-trees problem. Uniformities enable one to view general features of the organization of brains, but when they are examined more closely, one is also impressed by the variety of specializations among species and of the parts of the brain. Furthermore, there are levels of organization. The size of the brain as a whole, at least in mammals, provides a measure of the total information-processing capacity that evolved in a species, as shown in figure 12.3. But the information must be broken down to be analyzed, and such analysis is performed hierarchically by specialized regions.

We are reasonably certain that some perceptual activity is indeed common to various species. Although we enjoy speculative excursions into the perceptual worlds, or *Umwelten*, of other species, emphasizing specific specializations (von Uexküll 1934; Jerison 1986), we have good reason to assume that in most vital features the world as experienced is stable among species; that is, their experienced worlds are similar. But we also see dramatic differences in the way distance-senses work and in the kind of information available to animals of different species about events at a distance.

Sensitivity to pure tones in mammals has been well understood for some time. Among cats and dogs, the upper limit of sensitivity extends about two octaves above the human upper limit to about 60 kHz, compared with a human maximum of about 20 kHz. Maximum sensitivity is also shifted upward by an octave from about 3 kHz in humans. Mice and rats, on the other hand, have their peak sensitivity shifted upward about two octaves to about 8 kHz and an upper limit of sensitivity to over 100 kHz. It is surprising that dolphins are comparable with rodents in this regard. We usually imagine the experience of other species of auditory events as primarily an extension of sensitivity rather than a fundamental difference in experience. We know, however, that the use of auditory information may be radically different in different species, usually eliciting stereotyped behavior patterns rather than the flexible information that we know from experience with language. The most unusual animal auditory activity is perhaps that of echolocation by microchiropteran bats, which appear to construct an analogue of our three-dimensional visual world from auditory data (Grinnell 1995). Although dolphins are also echolocators, there is no evidence of their using auditory information in this way. This has not inhibited my speculations about the dolphin's world as constructed from echoes (Jerison 1986). I suggested a dolphin multiple-ego psychology; too odd to say more here. Those who are intrigued will have to dig up the reference.

For me, the most evocative example of differences among species in perceptual worlds is distinction between the visual worlds of horses and rabbits and of anthropoid primates, including people. In addition to the fact that the primate world is colorful whereas that of horses and rabbits is probably one of gray pastels, our primate world is a proscenium stage on which events are played out in a narrowly but sharply focused central area with a peripheral background that extends only to our sides. Horses and rabbits live in the center of a domed sphere, with eyes in the back of their heads, as it were. Their visual field covers a full 360 degrees. Can you imagine their experience? There is no "behind one's back" for these animals. Their visual world cannot be as fine-grained as ours, since their largely rod vision cannot provide the detailed edge discrimination that we achieve with the pure cone fovea centralis. Nonprimate mammals do not have foveae, and their visual worlds are probably more nearly like those of the earliest mammals, which probably first evolved as nocturnal species of only slightly modified reptiles.

Major regions of the mammalian brain are specialized for receiving and analyzing visual information, other regions for auditory information, others for tactile information, and so forth. These are specialized in turn. Each hemisphere of the primate cerebral cortex has at least a dozen visual areas that are specialized in a variety of ways, for example, for responding differently to edges of objects, to their movement in different directions, to color, to size, and so forth (Zeki 1993). Comparable specialization for vision occurs in most mammalian brains, but are less elaborate in nocturnal species that rely less on vision for navigating their worlds. The same elaboration probably occurs for auditory information, although that domain is yet to be analyzed as elaborately as the visual system. In bats, which use auditory cues for navigation in ways comparable with the use of vision in primates, much of the cerebrum is specialized as auditory cortex. In the human brain, language areas have been identified, but these areas also contain specialized subareas. Evidence is good, for example, that when one learns a foreign language in adulthood, second-language information is focused in regions in the language areas quite distinct from those involved in establishing one's first language (Ojemann 1983; Calvin 1996).

We should recognize, however, that there is uniformity in this diversity. All specializations in mammalian behavior are reflected neurally as localized functions of the cerebral cortex. Careful analysis of sensory representation in the mammalian brain reveals that sensory and motor projection areas account for essentially all of the surface area of the brain. The extensive human language areas are unusual in this regard, being more purely association cortex to which there are no direct sensory or motor projections. However, if one thinks of language areas as processing centers for elaborated auditory information (secondary auditory cortex, as it were) with linkages to other sensory modalities and to motor areas for controlling the voice box, tongue, and lips, the same generalization for other mammals applies to humans. Essentially all of the surface of the cerebral cortex has been mapped as related to sensory and motor activities that enable animals to know their external worlds. Evolution of mammalian cerebral cortex is thus correlated with that of specifically mammalian features in cognitive and perceptual capacity. I discuss this issue as a view of the mind-brain problem in Jerison (1991). In summary, I conclude that knowing and perceiving are essentially the same thing described with different words when different aspects of essentially the same mental activity are studied. I view the brain's work in supporting this cognitive-perceptual activity as *creating* the experienced real world within which behavior occurs.

As I remarked at the beginning of this chapter, music is essentially a human category defining certain kinds of activities and experiences, and to appreciate its evolution we can examine the evolution of human capacities to categorize in this way. At the most general neurobiological level it is the evolution of the neocortex of the mammalian brain. Since birds have been important animal models for musicality, I will consider their brains, too. I wish now to summarize what we know from the fossil record about the evolution of the brain, in particular the neocortex, in mammals with a few words on the limited history of the evidence on birds.

Brain Evolution

All known vertebrate brains, both living and fossil, have clearly identifiable forebrain, midbrain, and hindbrain. As I do not have an illustration of a standard brain, I traced a fossil brain that could serve as a standard for mammals (figure 12.4). (Readers can see the original of the specimen for views of many mammalian brains at http://www.neurophys.wisc.edu/brain/paleoneurology.html). The species was a small ungulate, an "oreodont" that lived thirty-five mya in what is now the Big Bend area of the Rio Grande river in Texas. It is described in detail at the internet site and is also illustrated in other publications (Jerison 1990, 1991). The endocast shows many major structures of the brain, such as the olfactory bulbs, cerebral hemispheres, and cerebellum, as well as the marginal sulcus and longitudinal sulcus of the neocortex. One can use the position of the rhinal fissure, which is the boundary between six-layer neocortex and paleocortex, to analyze the evolution of neocortex. In the figure I have named a few neocortical convolutions using the same criteria as in living ungulates as presented in standard brain atlases.

The most important conclusion from such evidence may be to show that mammalian neocortex evolved to larger relative size during the past sixty million years (Jerison 1990). This verified the frequently stated hypothesis, based on comparisons among living species, that "neocorticalization" (an aspect of encephalization) occurred during mammalian evolution. From expected structure-function relationships, this implies

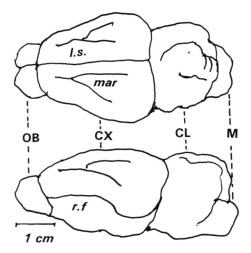

Bathygenys reevesi

Figure 12.4
Tracing from dorsal (top) and lateral (bottom) views of the fossil brain of *Bathygenys reevesi*, an upper Eocene oreodont (*Merycoidodontidae, Artiodactyla*). A view of the original in color is on the Internet at http://neurophys.wisc.edu/brain/paleoneurology.html. Olfactory bulbs (OB), cerebral cortex (CX), cerebellum (CL), and medulla (M) are labeled, as are several cortical sulci: the longitudinal sulcus (*l.s.*) separating the left from the right hemisphere, marginal sulcus (*mar*), and rhinal fissure (*r.f.*).

that perceptual-cognitive functions of neocortex evolved progressively in at least some lineages.

Complementing this information, we know from the analysis of brain size in many living species of mammals that diversification with respect to relative size included the evolution of species that remain at essentially the same level of encephalization as the earliest mammals of which we have records. Living Virginia opossums (*Didelphis marsupialis*) and living European hedgehogs (*Erinaceus europaeus*) are quite comparable with the earliest mammals in which brains are known in this regard. This is evidence, of course, that mammals do not live by brains alone, and that today in many niches an essentially minimal brain size is sufficient to control all necessary behavioral functions.

With respect to musicality, wherever we have evidence of mammalian vocal expression that we would describe as musical, we must consider that, from the perspective of the species, a variety of neural mechanisms may be involved in their generation and experience, and these may have little to do with music as a human dimension of experience.

The fossil record on the evolution of bird brains is limited. Information on the brain of the oldest known fossil bird, *Archaeopteryx lithographica* (Jerison 1973), adds little to our knowledge of the evolution of musicality in birds. With the exception of *Archaeopteryx*, fossil birds had brains that appear to have been very much like those of living species. Major structures in living birds known to be related to vocalization, although relatively large (Arnold 1980), are not manifested in the external appearance of the brain in a way that would be measurable on an endocast. The brain of *Archaeopteryx* differed from that of all living birds in lacking a *Wulst*, an expansion of dorsal forebrain that functions analogously to visual neocortex in mammals. In overall size, however, it was within the range of encephalization of living birds and more encephalized than brains of its relatives among the dinosaurs. (This evidence remains uncertain, since the brains of the closest dinosaur relatives of *Archaeopteryx* are not yet known as endocasts.)

One cannot discuss brain functions in birds in ways exactly comparable with those functions in mammals. One can make confident statements about neocortex in mammals with respect to a role in cognitive and perceptual activities, but neocortex is solely a mammalian structure. It may be that hyperstriatum in birds functions as an organ homologous to neocortex (Karten 1991), and evidence from studies of effects of brain damage is consistent with a view that, like mammalian neocortex, the bird's hyperstriatum has perceptual-cognitive functions (Macphail 1993; Divac 1994).

The place of birds as model animals for studies of musicality is determined by their use of elaborate songs for various behavioral controls, including establishing territories, courting, and communicating between parent and chick. The brain control of song, at least in passerine birds, is known to be lateralized to a degree greater than comparable in other systems in mammals, excepting only the control of language in the human. It is also the case, however, that peripheral auditory mechanisms for the reception of sound and the neuromuscular control of sound production are quite different in birds and mammals. Auditory sensitivity in birds is much less acute than in mammals, with an upper cutoff frequency of the order of 10 kHz, and sound sensitivity handled by an acoustic system much less elaborate than the chain of middle ear bones of mammals; the bird cochlea is also less elaborate than that in any mammal. One can therefore recognize systematic differences between birds and mammals in their handling of auditory information, and neural organization of their production and analysis of acoustic signals could be fundamentally different.

But birds remain acceptable models for the study of musicality and its evolution. Especially interesting is the plasticity of birdsong, in which the detailed song is demonstrably a product of nature and nurture. In some species of finches, for example, the adult song as used in courtship, and other displays are learned as a result of exposure to songs of conspecifics during critical periods of development. Furthermore, and even more unusual, some nerve growth apparently takes place seasonally in brain regions controlling song during the period when courtship and territorial vocal displays occur. The conclusion follows that the detailed circuitry controlling vocal behavior in birds is built up as a result of, and coordinated with, environmental events. One does not know details of either the construction or circuitry of the adult system, but this kind of process is also assumed to take place in the development of human neural control of speech and language. The process in humans differs most significantly from that in birds in that the number of neurons controlling human speech probably remains stable during development, and the neuronal growth that occurs is in arborization, increases in the number of dendrites and their synaptic connections. It should nevertheless be clear why birds are good models for such a process in view of the evident plasticity at a neural as well as behavioral level in birds and people.

We are still ignorant of how neural networks are put together in living brains, so much so that "neural networks" today typically refer to networks that exist only as computer programs, often for studies of artificial intelligence. In the face of this ignorance it is helpful to have animal models in which actual networks are constructed in real brains. It is likely that construction of such networks follows similar rules in all metazoans, and that the information could be applied cross-specifically much as information on conditioning in sea slugs has been applied to our understanding of neural mechanisms of learning in mammals.

Evolutionary evidence from fossil brains and from the diversity of structure of real brains in living species of birds and mammals is primarily a lesson about the importance of differences. This is also the lesson from the diversity of acoustic production systems in living species. The major uniformity that may exist with respect to musicality is in the construction of neural networks in real brains under environmental pressures. Construction of such networks by axodendritic growth of individual nerve cells and the establishment of synaptic connections among cells may follow very similar rules in very different species of birds and mammals. Plasticity is, therefore, a critical phenomenon for study in living species. Fossil evidence is helpful here primarily in suggesting lineages in which the amount of construction is greatest, that is, in which most encephalization has occurred. In birds this points to crows and parrots (cf. Pepperberg 1994). In mammals, in addition to our own species there are, of course, other anthropoid primates including apes, and despite difficulties in research with marine mammals, one might pay special attention to data on large-brained cetaceans, such as the bottlenose dolphin (*Tursiops truncatus*; Schusterman, Thomas, and Wood 1986). We are likely to learn most about the diversity of acoustic expression and some features of its evolution. With respect to musical experience, we are undoubtedly restricted to what we can learn from the human species. Of course, with the development of our ability to communicate with some large-brained species (Herman 1986; Savage-Rumbaugh et al. 1993), we may be able to "ask" them to describe their experiences, much as we have been able to learn about the chimpanzee's theory of mind (Premack and Woodruff 1978) with tools provided by clever experiments on animal "language."

Conclusion

There is not much question that we can develop a good understanding of the evolution of musical expression from our knowledge of the diversity of sound-generating devices in living species of birds and mammals, from the diversity of the neural control of the operation of those devices, and from the structure and function of the neural and sensory systems that are involved in the analysis of auditory signals.

Prospects for an evolutionary analysis of musical experience are much more limited. The most important of these is based on the fact that such experience is, to a significant extent, one in which cognitive-perceptual brain systems are involved. We have learned a good deal about the evolution of those systems, which is related to the evolution of encephalization: enlargement of the brain in birds and mammals relative to reptiles from which they evolved, and its further enlargement in the evolution of these classes of vertebrates. However, the enlargement called encephalization resulted from the increase in size in many different specialized neural systems and is an aggregate enlargement within which specialized increases are difficult to identify.

Falk's efforts (this volume) to analyze neural correlates of the evolution of a Broca's area in the frontal lobe of the hominid brain is the only one that is directly related to this problem. However, it is difficult to separate her evidence of increased gyrification and the appearance of a "third frontal convolution" in *Homo habilis* from the expected increments that would be correlated with increased brain size. The approach is correct, however, in recognizing that the evolution of musicality must be correlated with the evolution of cognitive capacities. Furthermore, there is little question that the evolution of human cognitive capacities and associated encephalization was primarily a correlate of the evolution of the capacity for language.

Let me review the problem of inferences from paleoneurology that comes from the fossil record of hominid brains. The earliest of these, of about three mya, were comparable with brains of living great apes in size and presumably in the complexity of their operation. (Size and complexity in brains are so intimately related that to distinguish them from one another may be impossible. As a first approximation, every neuron is connected to every other neuron in the mammalian brain, and because they are packaged efficiently, the number of neurons as well as the complexity of their interconnections are both estimated rather well by gross brain size.) The brains of great apes and australopithecines are very large, and we should not underestimate the cognitive capacities of our ancestors who lived with them. We are learning from behavioral studies of living great apes, including studies of their language capacities (Greenfield 1991), just how cognitively competent such animals can be. Whether or not their "language" is homologous to human language, and perhaps equivalent to an earlier stage of our linguistic evolution, remains an open question.

To extend these speculations to the problem of musical expression, I would contrast the acoustic dimension of human experience with its role in the animal world generally. The most striking result in the neurosciences on this issue is the discovery of the distinctive lateralization of brain activity in professional musicians in contrast to even knowledgeable amateurs, and its lateralization in both groups. The analogous lateralization of birdsong is a charming analogue to this human phenomenon, but it is obviously analogy rather than homology, to use classic evolutionary terms. Lateralization to this extent is not a trait shared by all birds and mammals. Among mammals, it is only human language that is so dramatically lateralized. Although we contrast emotional and cognitive aspects of human experience, I suggest that in fundamental ways, the evocative role of music in human experience is directly related to language as a specifically human adaptation.

References

Arnold, A. (1980). Sexual differences in the brain. *American Scientist* 68:165–173.

Butler, A. B. and Hodos, W. (1996). *Comparative Vertebrate Neuroanatomy*. New York: Wiley Liss.

Byrne, J. H. (1987). *Aplysia*: Associative modification of individual neurons. *Encyclopedia of Neuroscience* 1:65–67.

Calvin, W. H. (1996). *How Brains Think: Evolving Intelligence Then and Now*. New York: Basic Books.

Carroll, R. L. (1988). *Vertebrate Paleontology and Evolution*. New York: Freeman.

Divac, I. (1994). The prefrontal system: A smorgasbord. *Progress in Brain Research* 100:169–175.

Greenfield, P. (1991). Language, tools and brain: The ontogeny and phylogeny of hierarchically organized sequential behavior. *Behavioral and Brain Sciences* 14:531–595.

Grinnell, A. D. (1995). Hearing in bats: An overview. In R. R. Fay and A. M. Popper (Eds.) *Hearing by Bats* (p. 136). Heidelberg: Springer-Verlag.

Herman, L. M. (1986). Cognition and language competencies of bottlenosed dolphins. In R. J. Schusterman, J. A. Thomas, and F. G. Wood (Eds.) *Dolphin Cognition and Behavior: A Comparative Approach* (pp. 221–252). Hillsdale, NJ: Erlbaum.

Hodos, W. and Campbell, C. B. G. (1969). *Scala naturae*: Why there is no theory in comparative psychology. *Psychological Review* 76:337–350.

Jerison, H. J. (1973). *Evolution of the Brain and Intelligence*. New York: Academic Press.

Jerison, H. J. (1986). The perceptual worlds of dolphins. In R. J. Schusterman, J. Thomas, and F. G. Wood (Eds.) *Dolphin Cognition and Behavior: A Comparative Approach* (pp. 141–166). Hillsdale, NJ: Erlbaum.

Jerison, H. J. (1990). Fossil evidence on the evolution of the neocortex. In E. G. Jones and A. Peters (Eds.) *Cerebral Cortex*, Vol. 8A (pp. 285–309). New York: Plenum Press.

Jerison, H. J. (1991). *Brain Size and the Evolution of Mind: 59th James Arthur Lecture on the Evolution of the Human Brain*. New York: American Museum of Natural History.

Jerison, H. J. and Neff, W. D. (1953). Effect of cortical ablation in the monkey on discrimination of auditory patterns. *Federation Proceedings* 12:73–74.

Kandel, E. R. (1967). Cellular studies of learning. In G. C. Quarton, T. Melnechuk, and F. O. Schmitt (Eds.) *The Neurosciences* (pp. 666–689). New York: Rockefeller University Press.

Karten, H. J. (1991). Homology and evolutionary origins of the "neocortex." *Brain, Behavior and Evolution* 38:264–272.

Macphail, E. M. (1993). *The Neuroscience of Animal Intelligence: From the Seahare to the Seahorse*. New York: Columbia University Press.

Martin, R. D. (1990). *Primate Origins and Evolution: A Phylogenetic Reconstruction*. London: Chapman and Hall.

McKee, J. K., Tobias, P. V., and Clarke, R. J. (1996). Faunal evidence and Sterkfontein member 2 foot bones of early hominid. *Science* 271:1301.

Ojemann, G. (1983). Brain organization for language from the perspective of electrical stimulation mapping. *Behavioral and Brain Sciences* 6:189–230.

Pepperberg, I. M. (1994). Vocal learning in African grey parrots: Effects of social interaction. *Auk* 111:300–313.

Polyak, S. (1957). *The Vertebrate Visual System*. Chicago: University of Chicago Press.

Premack, D. and Woodruff, G. (1978). Does the chimpanzee have a theory of mind? *Behavioral and Brain Sciences* 4:515–526.

Rockel, A. J., Hiorns, R. W., and Powell, T. P. S. (1980). The basic uniformity in structure of the neocortex. *Brain* 103:221–244.

Savage-Rumbaugh, E. S., Murphy, J., Sevcik, R. A., Brakke, K. E., Williams, S. L., and Rumbaugh, D. M. (1993). Language comprehension in ape and child. *Monographs of the Society for Research in Child Development* 58:1254.

Schusterman, R. J., Thomas, J. A., and Wood, F. G. (Eds.) (1986). *Dolphin Cognition and Behavior: A Comparative Approach*. Hillsdale, NJ: Erlbaum.

Simpson, G. G. (1970). Uniformitarianism: An inquiry into principle, theory, and method in geohistory and biohistory. In M. K. Hecht and W. C. Steere (Eds.) *Essays in Evolution and Genetics in Honor of Theodosius Dobzhansky* (pp. 43–96). Amsterdam: North-Holland.

Stebbins, W. C. (1983). *The Acoustic Sense of Animals*. Cambridge: Harvard University Press.

Stephan, H., Frahm, H., and Baron, G. (1981). New and revised data on volumes of brain structures in insectivores and primates. *Folia Primatologica* 35:129.

von Uexküll, J. (1934). Streifzüge durch die Umwelten von Tieren und Menschen. Berlin and New York: Springer-Verlag. (Translated in C. H. Schiller, [Ed.] [1957]. *Instinctive Behavior: The Development of a Modern Concept* [p. 580]. New York: International Universities Press.)

Zeki, S. (1993). *A Vision of the Brain*. London: Blackwell.

Dean Falk

Abstract
Recent positron emission tomography and functional magnetic resonance imaging studies show that the cortical substrates for both language and music depend on widely distributed networks that in some cases overlap; use both sides of the brain, but are dominated by opposite hemispheres; and differ similarly in men and women. Because music and language are so neurologically intertwined, it is hypothesized that they evolved together as brain size increased during the past two million years in the genus *Homo*. Comparative behavioral and neurological data from a wide range of animals, together with information about brain evolution from the hominid fossil record, are incorporated into discussion of how, why, and when hominids evolved their musical and linguistic abilities.

Because no chimpanzee has ever spoken a sentence, post-Darwinian scientists have been fascinated with the human ability for speech and pondered its origins. Consequently, much is known about the neurological substrates for language, and a robust literature is available about its hypothetical evolution. What has been forgotten, however, is that no chimpanzee has ever played the violin. The neurological processing of music has just begun to be explored using available medical technology to image the brains of musicians as they perform. The first part of this paper provides information about the neurological substrates for language and music, and explores the relationship between the two. In the second part of this chapter, this neurological information is synthesized with paleoneurological data from the hominid fossil record, and incorporated into discussion about how, why and when elaborate auditory communications evolved in the human primate.

Neurological Substrates of Language and Music

Cortical Bases of Language

Recent applications of medical imaging technology using positron emission tomography (PET) and functional magnetic resonance imaging (fMRI) have made it possible to assess brain activity in human subjects as they perform specific cognitive tasks. Although many investigations have explored the specific neurological areas involved in language-related activities, few have focused on musical skills. Those that have, however, are very telling and even surprising, because they reveal that the neurological substrates for both endeavors overlap to a larger degree than one might have expected given the well-known fact of the left hemisphere's primary involvement with language and the right hemisphere's with music. In other words, despite their different dependence on the left and right hemispheres, language and music "time share" many neurological underpinnings.

Figure 13.1 illustrates a number of brain areas (44, 45, 22, 39, and 40 in Brodmann's numbering system) that are classically associated with specific language functions in the left hemispheres of humans. Arrows indicate areas of prefrontal cortex (Petersen et al. 1988; Martin et al. 1995) and neocerebellum (Petersen and Fiez 1993) that were only recently identified as participating in the semantic processing of language (e.g., naming the use for a particular object). The production of names

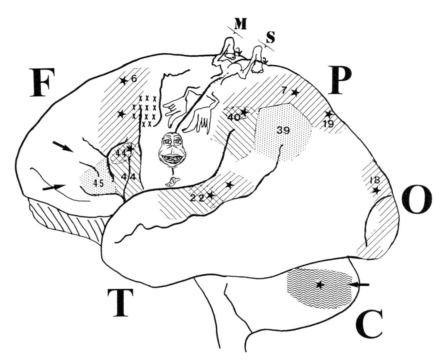

Figure 13.1
Left hemisphere of the human brain. Lobes are labeled at their edges: F, frontal; T, temporal; P, parietal; and O, occipital. C indicates the cerebellum. The homunculus is a simplification of the approximate organization of primary somatosensory (S) and primary motor (M) cortices. Representations of the tongue (illustrated) and larynx are located below the face regions. Numbers represent Brodmann's areas that provide foci for specific linguistic and musical processes. The Xs indicate an area that subserves writing; 44 and 45 form Broca's speech area, and 22 and 39 form Wernicke's area. Auditory areas 41 and 42 are not illustrated because they are buried deep within the sylvian fissure (above area 22), as is also the case for the planum temporale. Arrows indicate areas of prefrontal cortex and neocerebellum that recently were shown to participate in linguistic and musical processing. Stars represent areas activated on one or both sides as musicians sight-read, listened to, and played a Bach partita with their right hands (Sergent et al. 1992). It should be noted that processing of language and music entails activation of more widely distributed networks than indicated here, and that each uses both hemispheres to some extent. See text for discussion.

for different categories of objects (people, animals, tools) depends partly on different regions of the left temporal lobe that are below the classic language centers (Damasio et al. 1996), and a discrete region of the left precentral gyrus of the insula (buried within the Sylvian fissure and not visible in figure 13.1) is known to be specialized for motor planning of speech (Dronkers 1996). Thus, one can no longer speak of Broca's area (44 and 45 in figure 13.1) as the only, or even the primary, motor language (i.e., speech) association area, or of the cerebellum as involved purely in motor coordination. It is important to note, however, that figure 13.1 is simplified, and that various aspects of language are multifaceted, extremely complex, and distributed across all lobes of the brain, as well as both hemispheres (but mainly the left). Nevertheless, this illustration accurately identifies nodal areas that contribute to specific aspects of language in most people.

The map of the human figure (or homunculus) reflects the basic organization of the primary somatosensory cortex (S) in the parietal lobe, which is a mirror image of the primary motor cortex (M) of the frontal lobe. These two lobes-cortices are separated by the central sulcus that courses down the midline of the homunculus. Sensory components of language include hearing, reading, and comprehending words. Areas 41 and 42 (Heschl's convolutions), which are buried within the Sylvian fissure, are auditory cortices of the temporal lobe that receive initial inputs from all types of sounds in both hemispheres. Subsequently, the auditory association cortex that can be seen on the outside surface of the temporal lobes (area 22) further interprets these acoustic stimuli, with analysis of spoken words being undertaken largely by the left hemisphere. Damage to area 22 on the left side therefore results in word deafness, in which the individual's hearing is fine, but words are perceived as mere noises that have no meaning. These effects are severest if area 22 in both hemispheres is damaged. Another auditory association area long thought to be important for interpreting language sounds, the planum temporale, is directly behind areas 41 and 42 within the Sylvian fissure (again, not visible on the lateral surface of the temporal lobe). Area 39 (angular gyrus) in the left hemisphere is important in reading words, similar to area 22's role in hearing them. Thus a lesion in this area results in word blindness (alexia), in which a person can see well but cannot read (and therefore cannot write).

Together, areas 22 and 39 of the left hemisphere constitute Wernicke's area, damage to which results in classic receptive aphasia, or loss of auditory and visual comprehension of language. Area 39 is located in the parietal lobe, as is area 40 (supramarginal gyrus) directly in front of it. Both areas send and receive information from many other cortical regions; that is, they are association cortex. Area 40 is crucial for understanding the symbolism of language, so much so that a person with damage here may be mute.

Other areas that are located in the left frontal lobe are concerned with motor aspects of language—speech, writing, and signing associated with languages for the deaf. Thus, area 44 and the nearby part of 45 together form Broca's speech area. Complete destruction of this area results in a severe loss of articulate speech. However, the individual's muscles of speech are not paralyzed, because Broca's area is only one source of stimulation for the primary motor cortex (indicated by the face and tongue), which in turn influences the muscles in the head and neck that produce speech. Broca's area sends and receives information from many other parts of the cortex, and PET studies show that it also participates in motor activities that are not necessarily associated with speaking, such as tongue movements (Petersen et al. 1988). Furthermore, it has only recently been recognized that prefrontal cortex directly in front of Broca's area (indicated by arrows) has an important role in producing utterances that require some thought, unlike tasks such as simply naming an object. Just as Broca's area influences motor cortex that stimulates speech muscles, a region above it influences the shoulder, arm, and hand muscles (on the right side of the body) that are involved in writing (Xs). Thus, damage in this area results in agraphia, which, as noted, may also be caused by damage to area 39. The cerebellum is the great motor coordinator that sits beneath the occipital lobes. Its evolutionarily newest part, the neocerebellum, has connections with the frontal lobe and is active during thoughtful speech. This finding is not only recent (Petersen and Fiez 1993), but surprising, because the cerebellum was previously believed to have nothing to do with higher thought.

Many other parts of the brain, of course, participate in sophisticated cognition, including various aspects of language. Figure 13.1 is thus a gross simplification that merely illustrates nodal areas within highly complex cortical association pathways that contribute to the perception and production of language. It also should be stressed that, although most language processing takes place in the left hemisphere of most people, the right hemisphere comprehends a certain amount of language and participates in this activity to an extent, for instance, by understanding and providing intonations of utterances (tone of voice, or prosody).

Just as the major or dominant left hemisphere is well known for its language abilities, the minor right hemisphere is traditionally regarded as the musical part of the brain. Because recent advances in medical imaging technology make it possible to investigate the brains of subjects as they engage in various musical activities, the relationship between language and music is open to new exploration and, potentially, new surprises.

Neuroanatomical Substrates of Music

Although all normal people are competent in at least one language, not everybody is a proficient musician. Investigations pertaining to neurological processing of music are therefore complicated by the fact that some focus on musically trained subjects whereas others deliberately select subjects that are musically naive (i.e., "normal"). Despite the fact that differences between the groups can be illuminating, studies of musicians are particularly relevant for questions pertaining to the specific components of perceiving and producing music. For example, a PET study of ten professional pianists as they sight-read a little-known Bach partita on a keyboard with their right hands (Sergent et al. 1992) is particularly interesting in light of the above discussion about the neurological substrates of language. Listening to, reading, or playing the partita each recruited specific cortical areas.

Each of the ten musicians initially listened to and then played ascending and descending scales on the keyboard with their right hands (i.e., left hemispheres). Merely listening to scales activated area 42 in both hemispheres and area 22 on the left (indicated by stars in figure 13.1), a situation similar to that for subjects who listen to isolated words, and one that engages some of the same cortex (cross-hatched part of 22). When subjects played the scales themselves, the right cerebellum (star) that connects with the left frontal lobe became activated. As noted, the neocerebellum (especially on the right) is also engaged during thoughtful speech. Furthermore, an fMRI study (Khorram-Sefat, Dierks, and Hacker 1996) revealed that the neocerebellum is activated as individuals listen to music, an entirely nonmotor activity. In addition, playing scales stimulated portions of the left premotor cortex (stars in area 6) that, again, appear to overlap with language areas; that is, the left premotor cortex involved in writing with the right hand (Xs). Clearly, the perception and manual production of simple scales share some neurological substrates with the perception and manual production of simple words (Sergent et al. 1992).

Things get more interesting when it comes to the musical piece itself. When a musical score is simply read without listening or playing, the activated area of the brain is not 39 on the left as is the case when words are read, but rather part of visual area 19 (star) on the left (in addition to visual area 18 bilaterally), which is important for spatial processing, interpreting where rather than what a visual stimulus is. This makes sense because pianists read notes not as isolated items but in terms of their positions relative to one another (Sergent 1993). Listening to a score, as opposed to hearing scales, adds area 22 on the right side, affirming that listening to music involves differential activation of the right hemisphere, as is widely believed. Of interest, reading a score while listening to it adds another area to those that are stimulated by each activity alone, namely, the top part of the supramarginal gyrus (area 40) in both hemispheres (star and cross-hatching) that, on the left, is profoundly important for grasping the symbolism of language. Thus, Sergent et al. believe that the superior part of the supramarginal gyrus on both sides is important for mapping printed musical notation to its auditory representations, and they note that this area is adjacent to the inferior part of area 40 that, in the left hemisphere, is involved (along with area 39) in the same kind of mapping for words.

Finally, the main task investigated by Sergent et al. shows that sight-reading, playing, and listening to an unfamiliar piece is neurologically more demanding than one might expect from the sum of the neurological substrates of each activity. In addition to the areas outlined above, two areas are recruited that are not activated by any of these activities alone. One of these, the superior parietal lobule, or area 7 (star), is activated in both hemispheres. This area is important for realistic awareness of one's own body scheme, and also functions as sensory association cortex that unifies and interprets incoming sensory stimuli from the opposite side of the body into whole concepts. For example, a blindfolded pianist with a lesion in part of area 7 on the left would not be able to identify a piano key as such by touching it with his right hand, although he would know that it was cool, relatively small, and moved when pressed, but these sensations would not be synthesized into the concept of a piano key. Sergent et al. suggest that area 7 also mediates the transformation from sensory visual input (score reading) to motor output (skilled finger movements).

In addition to the left motor and premotor and right cerebellar activation that one expects from the simple playing experiment described above, another frontal lobe area is recruited in the left hemisphere in the reading-playing-listening task. This is the superior portion of area 44, the top part of Broca's speech area (star and cross-hatching) that is below the frontal lobe writing area (Xs). This finding makes perfect sense from a neurological perspective when one considers the organization of the primary motor cortex. Thus the lower portion of Broca's area borders and stimulates primary cortex for the laryngeal and oral organs of speech, the superior part of area 44 in the left hemisphere is closer to the right hand motor area, and the writing area above that borders hand representation and is relatively close to primary cortex for the arm and shoulder. In other words, the part of 44 that is recruited during the complicated sight-reading task apparently acts as a kind of Broca's area for the hand. As such, it would be interesting to learn if this region is specifically involved in production of American sign language that, like language, is left-hemisphere dominant and dissociated from nonlinguistic gesture (Hickok, Bellugi, and Klima 1996).

To summarize, the experiments of Sergent et al. (1992) are extremely important for three reasons. First, they document the existence of a distributed neural network that incorporates specialized nodal regions for processing sensory and motor aspects of music, as is the case for language. Second, in some cases, cortical areas that underlie musical activities have been shown to be next to, and partly overlap with, those engaged in similar language tasks. Finally, portions of certain areas are differentially activated in the left hemisphere during specific musical activities; for example, area 22 from listening to simple scales, part of area 19 with simple reading of a musical score, motor and premotor (area 6) cortices (plus right cerebellum) during simple playing of the keyboard with the right hand, and the top part of area 44 during the multifaceted sight-reading task. Thus, musicians, at least, rely a good deal on their left hemisphere when processing music.

These findings were confirmed and extended by other researchers. Chen et al. (1996) used fMRI to study four healthy subjects as they imagined a familiar piece of classical music. Again, area 42 became activated bilaterally and area 22 was more responsive on the right. Deeper brain structures that contribute to the auditory ascending pathway were also activated (medial geniculate nuclei, inferior colliculus, lateral lemniscus), causing the authors to conclude that imagining music and actually hearing it activate the same neurological substrates. They also noted that another deep structure, the putamen, which is activated on the left, may be involved with timing of the imagined music. (Of interest, the left putamen also lit up when bilingual volunteers spoke words in their second language, French, but not when they uttered words in their native English [Barinaga 1995].) Chen et al. also found that two limbic structures that participate in processing emotions including visceral reactions, the hypothalamus and amygdala, were activated differently in the right hemisphere. This study is important because it is one of the few that imaged deep brain structures during musical cognition.

If there is a surprise in the above recent findings, it is the extent to which musical activities engage the left hemisphere in a manner that parallels the processing of language. What, then, is the right hemisphere doing? For one thing, as noted, the right temporal association cortex (area 22) is recruited on first hearing a piece of music (Sergent et al. 1992; Zatorre, Evans, and Meyer 1994). In particular, the right hemisphere attends to melodic aspects of music. (Melody and rhythm appear to be neurologically dissociated [Peretz and Kolinsky 1993], with the left hemisphere apparently better at processing the latter.) The right hemisphere also provides and interprets the melodic nuances of speech, the tone of voice, that is important for conveying affective or emotional connotations of speech. It thus appears that melody has emotional content for both language and music; recall that limbic structures that process emotions were activated on the right as volunteers imagined music (Chen et al. 1996).

To be more specific, a PET study showed that simple judgments about musical pitch use a neural network that includes the right prefrontal cortex, whereas the more difficult task of judging remembered pitches recruits wider areas of the right (and to a lesser extent left) hemisphere, especially frontal and temporal cortices (Zatorre, Evans, and Meyer 1994). Prefrontal cortex is generally known to be important for keeping information in mind during goal-oriented tasks. Of interest, pitch discriminations during speech (Zatorre et al. 1992), as well as music, produce activation in the right prefrontal cortex. In general, the right hemisphere is also more sensitive to harmony (Tramo and Bharucha 1991), concordant with its proclivity for recognizing and producing harmonic ratios within complex tones (Preisler, Gallasch, and Schulter 1989). These authors (p. 139) suggest that the right hemisphere's apparent superiority at producing and recognizing simple ratios within steady-state auditory information might also hold for its processing of spatial information in other modalities, thus accounting for its greater aesthetic sensitivity (figure 13.2).

Music Meets Speech: Singing in the Brain

Given the widely held view that the left hemisphere is dominant for language and the right is superior for music, it seems obvious to ask about the neurological substrates for the one activity that clearly incorporates both endeavors, namely, singing with words. For some years singing without words (i.e., replacing words with "la, la, la") has been known to be disrupted much more by inhibition, or damage, to the right than to the left hemisphere (Gordon and Bogen 1974). In fact, the right hemisphere's ability to carry a tune is put to good use in melodic intonation therapy (Albert, Sparks, and Helm 1973), whereby patients with Broca's aphasia who cannot speak are taught to express their thoughts by embedding them in simple melodies. As patients improve, the melodic aspect is faded. In what may be the first experiment to investigate hemispheric dominance for singing both with and without words, Cadalbert et al. (1994) measured lip opening asymmetry in normal subjects during both tasks. Singing with words is associated with wider right-side lip opening than is the case for singing without words, indicating involve-

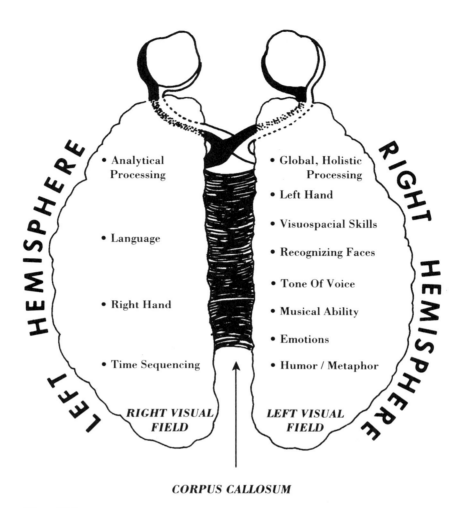

LEFT HEMISPHERE

RIGHT HEMISPHERE

- Analytical
  Processing

- Language

- Right Hand

- Time Sequencing

- Global, Holistic
      Processing

- Left Hand

- Visuospacial Skills

- Recognizing Faces

- Tone Of Voice

- Musical Ability

- Emotions

- Humor / Metaphor

*RIGHT VISUAL
FIELD*

*LEFT VISUAL
FIELD*

CORPUS CALLOSUM

Figure 13.2
Schematic of the left and right hemispheres of the human brain which summarizes abilities that are relatively lateralized in most people. See text for discussion.

ment of the left hemisphere when lyrics are part of the song, but greater dependence on the right hemisphere when they are not (Yamadori et al. 1977).

An fMRI study (Wildgruber et al. 1996) of ten volunteers as they silently sang a well-known melody using the syllable *la* in place of words confirmed that the right hemisphere is dominant for singing without words. However, landmarks were not available with which to identify the precise region in the right frontal lobe that was activated during singing. Because the same region was activated by nonspeech tongue movements, the investigators assumed that it must be part of the primary motor cortex. However, this assumption is not valid because Broca's area is known to be activated during nonspeech tongue movements (Petersen et al. 1988). A half-century ago (Nielsen 1948), singing was said to be bilaterally represented in the front part of area 45 (part of Broca's area on the left). Although the means are now available for better pinpointing the neurological foci that control singing, the crucial experiment remains to be done: subjects could be imaged using combined PET and MRI technology (the latter identifies exact anatomical regions that are activated) as they sing two different kinds of songs. The first would be a familiar song with words. Under the second condition, each subject would be asked to sing (by humming or by repeating one syllable) a familiar piece of music that, to avoid unconscious priming, is not associated with words (e.g., Beethoven's Fifth Symphony). Until such research is conducted, the precise foci associated with different kinds of singing in the brain will remain a mystery.

The Brains of Musicians

A number of gross anatomical differences were discovered that distinguish the brains of musicians from those of nonmusicians. One of the most interesting pertains to the planum temporale (PT), which is larger in the left than in the right hemisphere in most right-handed people, and has long been thought to be important for comprehending language. As it turns out, the PT of musicians with absolute pitch is significantly larger on the left relative to the right side than is the case for other musicians or nonmusicians (Schlaug et al. 1995b). Since musicians with absolute pitch do not differ from their matched controls in visual-spatial or verbal tests (Picone et al. 1997), it appears that they are more dependent on the left PT for processing musical stimuli than people who lack absolute pitch. This is in keeping with the well-known suggestion that musicians rely more on the left hemisphere to process certain aspects of music, such as melody, that are largely the domain of the right hemisphere in nonmusicians.

The anterior half of the midline area of the corpus callosum (the large fiber tract that connects the two hemispheres in figure 13.2) is significantly larger in musicians who began musical training before the age of 7 than in nonmusicians (Schlaug et al. 1995a). These authors interpreted their finding as indicative of increased communication between the right and left frontal lobes (e.g., premotor and supplementary motor hand representations). In another study (Amunts et al. 1996), the presumed motor hand cortex (as reflected in the depth of the central sulcus) was relatively enlarged in right-handed professional keyboard players compared with nonmusicians. As one would expect for right-handers, both musicians and nonmusicians have a significantly deeper left than right central sulcus.

However, the central sulcus on both sides is deeper in the musicians, especially those who began training at a young age, resulting in overall less asymmetry than appears in nonmusicians. String players who began training at an early age also differ from nonmusicians in the organization of their brains. Specifically, the sensory cortex in the right hemisphere is relatively enlarged in the region that represents the fingers of the left hand (Elbert et al. 1995). One must be cautious in interpreting these results, however. Although musicians apparently have greater primary cortical areas devoted to sensory and motor functions for hands, activation in these areas is less than in those of nonmusicians during the performance of simple repetitive finger tapping (Auer et al. 1996).

Brain waves associated with certain musical tasks also differ between musicians and nonmusicians. In one study (Besson, Faita, and Requin 1994), event-related potentials were recorded from electrodes over right and left parietal cortices in fifteen musicians and fifteen nonmusicians as they listened to musical phrases, some of which ended in incongruous notes. Subjects were asked to identify the last notes as either congruous or incongruous and, for the latter, to determine whether they were harmonically, melodically, or rhythmically incongruous. Wrong notes resulted in late positive components of event-related potentials that were larger and had shorter onsets for musicians versus nonmusicians, and for harmonic versus melodic incongruities. Both groups responded similarly to rhythmic incongruities. It was no surprise that the authors concluded that musicians are faster than others in detecting notes that depart from expectation. It is curious that musicians with absolute pitch lacked or had a greatly reduced brainwave, called a P300, in response to an auditory oddball task that required counting atypical tones that appear infrequently among other auditory stimuli (Klein, Coles, and Donchin 1984). Musicians without absolute pitch manifested a P300 during this task, leading the authors to speculate that it may be associated with maintenance or updating of working memory; whereas people with absolute pitch may "have access to permanently resident representations of the tones, so that they do not need, as the rest of us do, to fetch and compare representations for novel stimuli" (Klein, Coles, and Donchin 1984:1308).

Shannon (1984) wondered if the spatial arrangement of instruments in modern philharmonic orchestras, in which violins are on the left-hand side of the stage and celli are on the right, reflects aesthetic preferences of audiences. He therefore tested whether twenty musicians and twenty-four nonmusicians preferred to hear music in one left-right distribution of instruments versus another, using headphones and a lever that allowed subjects to reverse auditory input. There were no significant effects for nonmusicians, but musicians preferred leading (usually high-pitched) material to be heard by the left ear and accompanying low-pitched material to be heard by the right ear. Subjects expressed astonishment at how remarkable the effect of changing the lever was, and several commented that one left-right arrangement appeared highly differentiated, whereas the other seemed more blurred. These results were significant for men but not women musicians, which is consistent with other studies discussed below.

Men and Women Process Music Differently

The studies discussed above show that, like various aspects of language, components of musical processing are highly lateralized in the human brain. As a generalization, melody and chords appear to be processed holistically by the right hemisphere, whereas analyses involving brief sequences of discrete sounds, (e.g., rhythm) depend relatively more on the analytical left hemisphere. Singing, on the other hand, appears to engage the cortex bilaterally if words are involved, but depends differently on the right hemisphere if they are not. As we have seen, the degree to which these generalizations hold varies with the extent of musical training, and it is suggested that musicians are more analytical in processing certain aspects of music, for which they rely more than other people on their left hemisphere.

Another important factor is gender. Hundreds of behavioral and anatomical studies showed that men's brains are, on average, more lateralized than those of women (for reviews see Falk 1987, 1997; McGlone 1980). Furthermore, well-known differences between men and women on average performances of verbal, higher mathematical, social, and visuospatial skills are probably related at least in part to these differences in lateralization (McGlone 1980). What about gender and the neurological underpinnings of musical abilities? A study investigating which hemisphere benefits most from musical training revealed an interesting gender difference (Selby et al. 1982). Right-handed subjects were asked to judge whether two sequences of six tones were the same or different, and error scores were compared for each ear. As predicted, right ears of untrained subjects performed better than left ears. Musical training, however, benefited both ears of women, but only the left ear of men. Thus, musically trained men, but not women, seem to be right-hemisphere dominant for analyzing sequences of tones. These findings are concordant with generalizations that cognitive processing in women is less lateralized than that of men, and that men musicians prefer leading instruments of an orchestra to be delivered to their right hemisphere (Shannon 1984).

Another intriguing study that addresses gender differences in musical processing used a time-sharing interference paradigm in which changes in rate of finger tapping for each hand were measured during three conditions: repeating a simple spoken phrase, singing a rote song with words, and singing scales without words (Hough et al. 1994). The degree to which each condition caused departure from a baseline level of tapping for each hand is believed to indicate the approximate extent to which the opposite hemisphere (i.e., the one controlling the hand) was involved in each activity. As other studies concluded, speech and singing appeared to be mediated primarily by left and right hemispheres, respectively, and women were less lateralized than men for all three tasks. Of interest, men were especially lateralized for singing with words; finger tapping decreased noticeably for their right hands, indicating different involvement of the left hemisphere (LH) for this task. The authors concluded (Hough et al. 1994:1074):

> Thus, the laterality differences in females appear to be driven by both hemispheres whereas laterality differences in males are driven primarily by variation in the involvement of the LH. This finding is in accordance with previous suggestions that females are less lateralized or have more symmetrical representations than males.

Clearly, the human brain is an extremely complicated and variable organ. Nevertheless, studies using medical imaging technology help to clarify certain details about the neurological substrates for processing two interrelated endeavors that are specific to the human primate—language and music. As shown, musical processing varies not only with training but with gender. The latter finding is significant for understanding not only the origins of music but also for investigating human brain evolution in general.

Brain Evolution and the Origins of Music

Models of the kinds of behaviors that must have preceded humanlike music and language may be sought in other animals. For example, some birds (Slater, this volume), whales (Payne, this volume), and gibbons (Geissmann, this volume) sing without words, and at least some primates (e.g., vervet monkeys) have utterances that are part of "referential emotive vocalization systems" (Brown, this volume) that vary systematically with certain stimuli (e.g., alarm calls for specific predators). Because humans are evolutionarily closely related to gorillas and even more so to chimpanzees, the auditory communication systems of these African great apes are of particular interest to those pursuing the origins of music, language, and singing with words (see Geissmann and Ujhelyi, this volume). For example, male gorillas are likely to include a series of hoots in their physical displays and, according to Schaller (1963), two or more male gorillas sometimes vocalize together in a manner that perhaps foreshadows human singing without words (gorillian chants?):

One began hooting only to trail away to nothing before trying again. Then another joined in, and a third one. Their clear hu-hu rose and fell as each stopped and started independently. But when one reached a climax and beat his chest the others followed. Then they usually settled down for a few minutes before repeating the whole procedure. (p. 223)

Chimpanzees are generally more gregarious than gorillas, and this is reflected in their communication systems, which include rich repertoires of facial, postural, and tactile expressions, similar to human body language (e.g., chimpanzees and humans both greet conspecifics with hugs and kisses). The auditory-vocal domain is where chimpanzees and humans differ the most, although the former have a fairly elaborate system of graded calls based on modifications of grunts, hoots, barks, and screams (Marler, this volume) that express a variety of emotions ranging from puzzlement to the appreciation of food. Different populations of chimpanzees appear to have different accents, and adult males are usually the most vocal individuals among both gorillas and chimpanzees. For example, the long-distance pant-hoot is the most frequently used call by adult male chimpanzees (see Ujhelyi and Geissmann, this volume). These consist of a series of loud calls that are voiced on both inhalation and exhalation, rising and falling in pitch, often ending with a scream.

Because primatologists are able to identify individuals on hearing their pant-hoots, it is presumed that chimpanzees can too. In addition to revealing locations of individual animals, long-distance pant-hoots announce food sources or threaten individuals in other communities. Goodall (1986:134) noted that pant-hoot choruses may break out during the night, passing back and forth between parties that are sleeping within earshot. Besides such "singing," chimpanzees sometimes engage in drumming displays by pounding hands and feet on large trees. Drumming is, again, done primarily by males and is typically accompanied by pant-hoots (Goodall 1986:133). Although chimpanzees are naturally chatty, they actively suppress their vocalizations under some circumstances, such as when males go on patrols of territorial boundaries. In sum, chimpanzees engage in a rich variety of auditory communications. Their calls, however, are not strictly referential, unlike vervet alarm calls, and this fact more than any other reveals the limits of vocal communication in our nearest nonhuman primate cousin (Mitani 1996).

These comparative observations, together with evidence pertaining to the anatomy of the vocal tract (Frayer and Nicolay, this volume) and cerebral cortex (Falk 1992a, b) of fossil hominids, allow one to form reasonable speculations about auditory communication in our earliest hominid ancestors, the australopithecines. Minimally, they should have possessed a rich repertoire of calls employed in social contexts and used especially to express emotions. That is, rather than being referential as words are, their calls (entailing pitch changes) would have been generally emotive and affective. In addition, australopithecines probably did a certain amount of chorusing and drumming, similar to African great apes. It is possible that early hominids were also characterized by gender differences in their auditory communications, although no evidence pertaining to this is found in the fossil record to date. In short, modern linguistic and musical abilities probably evolved from beginnings such as these. But how, why, and when?

A hint at how humanlike auditory communication evolved may be glimpsed by examining neurological substrates for auditory-vocal communication in people and other animals. As documented, humans are, above all else, highly lateralized for processing language and music, respectively, to left and right hemispheres. Unlike any other animal, including nonhuman primates (McGrew and Marchant 1997), *Homo sapiens* is also highly lateralized for right-handedness, the neurological substrate of which is adjacent to Broca's speech area in the left hemisphere. What about other aspects of brain lateralization in animals? Contrary to previously held beliefs, other species are also neurologically lateralized for a variety of functions, including circling behaviors in rodents, production of songs in birds (left hemisphere dominant), and processing of socially meaningful vocalizations (left hemisphere dominant) as well as certain visual stimuli (dominance varies with task) in some monkeys (Glick 1985; Falk 1992a, b). Furthermore, it is the rule rather than the exception for these asymmetries to be sexually dimorphic with respect to side of dominance and/or frequency of occurrence (Glick 1985). From these data, we may surmise that complex human auditory communications evolved as hominid brains enlarged beyond the ape-size volumes characteristic of australopithecines (Falk 1992a, b), in conjunction with elaboration of basic cortical lateralization that was inherited from very early mammalian ancestors.

If one can discern a basic function for brain lateralization in animals, one might have a glimmer about why language and music eventually evolved in humans. In this context, it becomes important to explore Darwinian natural selection by assessing reproductive advantages that are gained by individuals or species as a result of lateralization. Within this framework, the gender differences in brain lateralization that characterize many species (Glick 1985) are tantalizing. For example, a study in the house mouse (Ehret 1987) offers an important clue about the possible evolutionary history of the neurological substrates that facilitate enhanced language skills in women relative to men (Falk 1997).

Specifically, ultrasonic calls emitted by young mice were recognized by their mothers' left hemisphere and evoked maternal caring (e.g., retrieving a lost pup to the nest). Clearly, there should be a strong selective advantage for these mothers, that is, more of their offspring will survive.

In a polygynous species of another small rodent, the meadow vole, males have enhanced visuospatial skills that apparently benefit them during mating season when they travel in search of mates (Gaulin and FitzGerald 1989). Similarly, male songbirds use lateralized singing to attract mates (Slater, this volume), thus increasing their reproductive fitness. These findings are suggestive in light of men's relatively greater lateralization for both singing and visuospatial skills, and women's relatively enhanced language and social skills. Limited as they are, these and other data (Falk 1997) suggest that mammalian brain lateralization may be rooted in different reproductive strategies for males (put energy toward finding mates) and females (devote efforts to raising offspring). It is not surprising, then, that aspects of language, music, singing, and visuospatial skills that evolved from a basic mammalian brain plan are lateralized differently in brains of men and women. It is even possible that neurological substrates for these activities are wired differently because the two sexes continued to depend on different reproductive strategies during the past five million years (Falk 1997) or even more recently (Miller, this volume).

Which brings us to the question of when language and music originated. The answer depends in part on how one defines the two endeavors. Returning to the African apes, one could almost argue that a chorus of rising and falling pant-hoots, or pant-hooting accompanied by drumming on trees, is tantamount to a kind of protosinging or protomusic. It is more difficult to view ape vocalizations as representative of protolanguage, however, because of the lack of referential calls (Mitani 1996). Clearly, apes are not capable of projecting chopped up bits of air from their mouths (phonemes) that can be recombined in an infinite number of meaningful utterances; their vocalizations manifest neither the semanticity nor the productivity of human language. These limitations presumably also applied to the earliest hominids. If one asks when humanlike as opposed to apelike music first appeared, the discussion regarding the neurological bases of music and language outlined above, as well as paleoneurological evidence from the hominid fossil record discussed below, have important implications for the answer.

Results from brain imaging studies may be interpreted as implying that music and language are part of one large, vastly complicated, distributed neurological system for processing sound in the largest-brained primate. Both systems use intonation and rhythm to convey emotions, that is, affective semantics (Molino, this volume). Both rely on partly overlapping auditory and parietal association cortices for reception and interpretation, and partly overlapping motor and premotor cortices for production. Each has a recently discovered input from the cerebellum. Music and language can both be produced by mouths or by tools, and each is processed somewhat differently by men and women. Each activity engages a frontal lobe-mediated ability to keep ideas in mind long enough to bring them to fruition, and recruits additional areas of temporal and parietal cortices for longer retention. Finally, humans are able both to speak and to hear music in their heads.

Fewer differences than similarities exist between the neurological processing of music and language. One can think of the two activities as simply being broadcast by different television or radio channels. For example, one may tune to the music channel (MTV on the author's television, mostly the right hemisphere in her brain) for sounds that communicate emotions in a holistic manner. Change to the Learning Channel (mostly the left hemisphere), and one is likely to receive a language lesson that involves analyzing sequences of referential sounds that communicate specific bits of meaning. One other remarkable difference distinguishes musical from linguistic processing: as a species, humans are generally better at listening to music than at composing it, which is left to specialists. Even many musicians seem content to perform other people's compositions. This is obviously not true for language, in which all normal people actively and continually compose and perform. Since people are universally more adept at language than at music, it is tempting to speculate that the former was a direct target of natural selection, whereas the latter went along for the ride (Finlay and Darlington 1995).

Be that as it may, because music and language are so neurologically intertwined, it is reasonable to speculate that they evolved together as brain size increased during the past two million years of evolution of the genus *Homo*. Therefore, if we can pinpoint the time by which language originated, we probably know when music did. The relevant paleoneurological data are these. By about two million years ago, brain size had increased somewhat in early *Homo* compared with the ape-size brains of australopithecines. This increase was accompanied by a rearrangement of the convolutions of the frontal lobes, resulting in a more human-like pattern in *Homo*. Specifically, the endocast of the left frontal lobe of specimen KNM-ER 1,470 (*Homo rudolfensis*) revealed sulci that are not seen in brains of apes or australopithecines, which delimit Broca's speech area in humans (Tobias 1981; Falk 1983). Shape also changed due to apparent expansion in prefrontal cortex (Falk 1983). Furthermore, analysis of contemporaneous stone tools suggests that knappers had become right-handed by that time (Toth 1985). However, the approximately 750-cm^3 brain of KNM-ER 1,470 was little more than half the size of the average human brain.

Together, these findings suggest that left-hemisphere-dominant, humanlike language may have *begun* to evolve by two million years ago. If so, right hemisphere-dominant music was probably also beginning to evolve. This is not the full story, however. As detailed above, findings from PET and fMRI experiments point to prefrontal cortex and the cerebellum as important foci for both semantic linguistic and musical tasks. Evidence shows that these two regions do not appear as fully developed in two middle Pleistocene endocasts from archaic *Homo sapiens* from Africa and Greece, although they have modern-size brains and are dated to only several hundred thousand years ago (Seidler et al. 1997). Although the jury is still out on the exact relationship of these fossils to living people, it appears that language and music areas may not have been fully humanlike in at least some hominids by that relatively recent time. Slow and progressive changes are documented for vocal communication in another highly intelligent mammal, the humpback whale (Payne, this volume), and the evolution of writing in humans also seems to have been prolonged (Falk 1992a). The fossil record has not yet revealed exactly when language or music became fully developed. At the moment, however, it is reasonable to hypothesize that they began evolving together (Finlay and Darlington 1995) by two million years ago, and that their subsequent evolution may have been long and progressive.

Acknowledgments

I am deeply grateful to Steven Brown, François-Bernard Mâche, Björn Merker, and Nils Wallin for planning the wonderful first Florentine Workshop in Biomusicology that inspired this volume. Julian Keenan and John Redmond are thanked for lively discussions and their help with acquiring library materials.

References

Albert, M. L., Sparks, R. W., and Helm, N. A. (1973). Melodic intonation therapy for aphasia. *Archives of Neurology* 29:130–131.

Amunts, K., Schlaug, G., Jaencke, L., Steinmetz, H., Schleicher, A., and Zilles, K. (1996). Hand motor skills covary with size of motor cortex: A macrostructural adaptation? *NeuroImage* 3:S365.

Auer, D., Jones, R., Rupprecht, R., and Kraft, E. (1996). Does motor skill influence the cortical activation pattern in musicians? An f-MRI study. *NeuroImage* 3:S374.

Barinaga, M. (1995). Brain researchers speak a common language. *Science* 270:1437–1438.

Besson, M., Faita, F., and Requin, J. (1994). Brain waves associated with musical incongruities differ for musicians and non-musicians. *Neuroscience Letters* 168:101–105.

Cadalbert, A., Landis, T., Regard, M., and Graves, R. E. (1994). Singing with and without words: Hemispheric asymmetries in motor control. *Journal of Clinical and Experimental Neuropsychology* 16:664–670.

Chen, W., Kato, T., Zhu, X.-H., Adriany, G., and Ugurbil, K. (1996). Functional mapping of human brain during music imagery processing. *NeuroImage* 3:S205.

Damasio, H., Grabowski, T. J., Tranel, D., Hichwa, R. C., and Damasio, A. R. (1996). A neural basis for lexical retrieval. *Nature* 380:499–505.

Dronkers, N. F. (1996). A new brain region for coordinating speech articulation. *Nature* 384:159–161.

Ehret, G. (1987). Left hemisphere advantage in the mouse brain for recognizing ultrasonic communication calls. *Nature* 325:249–251.

Elbert, T., Pantev, C., Wienbruch, C., Rockstroh, B., and Taub, E. (1995). Increased cortical representation of the fingers of the left hand in string players. *Science* 270:305–307.

Falk, D. (1983). Cerebral cortices of east African early hominids. *Science* 221:1072–1074.

Falk, D. (1987). Brain lateralization in primates and its evolution in hominids. *Yearbook of Physical Anthropology* 30:107–125.

Falk, D. (1992a). *Braindance*. New York: Henry Holt.

Falk, D. (1992b). *Evolution of the Brain and Cognition in Hominids: The 62nd James Arthur Lecture*. New York: American Museum of Natural History.

Falk, D. (1997). Brain evolution in females: An answer to Mr. Lovejoy. In L. D. Hager (Ed.) *Women in Human Evolution* (pp. 114–136). London: Routledge.

Finlay, B. L. and Darlington, R. B. (1995). Linked regularities in the development and evolution of mammalian brains. *Science* 268:1578–1584.

Gaulin, S. J. C. and FitzGerald, R. W. (1989). Sexual selection for spatial-learning ability. *Animal Behavior* 37:322–331.

Glick, S. (Ed.). (1985). *Cerebral Lateralization in Nonhuman Species*. New York: Academic Press.

Goodall, J. (1986). *The Chimpanzees of Gombe*. Cambridge: Belknap Press of the Harvard University Press.

Gordon, H. W. and Bogen, J. E. (1974). Hemispheric lateralization of singing after intracarotid sodium amylobarbitone. *Journal Neurology, Neurosurgery and Psychiatry* 37:727–738.

Hickok, G., Bellugi, U., and Klima, E. S. (1996). The neurobiology of sign language and its implications for the neural basis of language. *Nature* 381:699–702.

Hough, M. S., Daniel, H. J., Snow, M. A., O'Brien, K. F., and Hume, W. G. (1994). Gender differences in laterality patterns for speaking and singing. *Neuropsychologia* 32:1067–1078.

Khorram-Sefat, D., Dierks, T., and Hacker, H. (1996). Cerebellar activation during music listening. *NeuroImage* 3:S312.

Klein, M., Coles, M. G. H., and Donchin, E. (1984). People with absolute pitch process tones without producing a P300. *Science* 223:1306–1309.

Martin, D., Haxby, J. V., Lalonde, F. M., Wiggs, C. L., and Ungerleider, L. G. (1995). Discrete cortical regions associated with knowledge of color and knowledge of action. *Science* 270:102–105.

McGlone, J. (1980). Sex differences in human brain asymmetry: A critical survey. *Behavioral and Brain Sciences* 3:215–263.

McGrew, W. C. and Marchant, L. F. (1997). On the other hand: Current issues in and meta-analysis of the behavioral laterality of hand function in nonhuman primates. *Yearbook of Physical Anthropology* 40:201–232.

Mitani, J. (1996). Comparative studies of African ape vocal behavior. In W. C. McGrew, L. F. Marchant and T. Nishida (Eds.) *Great Ape Societies* (pp. 241–254). Cambridge, UK: Cambridge University Press.

Nielsen, J. M. (1948). The cortical motor pattern apraxias. *Research Publications Association for Research in Nervous and Mental Disease* 27:565–581.

Peretz, I. and Kolinsky, R. (1993). Boundaries of separability between melody and rhythm in music discrimination: A neuropsychological perspective. *Quarterly Journal of Experimental Psychiatry* 46A:301–325.

Petersen, S. E. and Fiez, J. A. (1993). The processing of single words studied with positron emission tomography. *Annual Review of Neuroscience* 16:509–530.

Petersen, S. E., Fox, P. T., Posner, M. I., Mintun, M., and Raichle, M. E. (1988). Positron emission tomographic studies of the cortical anatomy of single-word processing. *Nature* 331:585–589.

Picone, M., Goldberger, Z., Schlaug, G., Bly, B. M., Thangaraj, V., Edelman, R. R., and Warach, S. (1997). Neuroanatomical correlates of absolute pitch. *Cognitive Neuroscience Society Abstracts* 88.

Preisler, A., Gallasch, E., and Schulter, G. (1989). Hemispheric asymmetry and the processing of harmonies in music. *International Journal of Neuroscience*. 47:131–140.

Schaller, G. B. (1963). *The Mountain Gorilla*. Chicago: University of Chicago Press.

Schlaug, G., Jancke, L., Huang, Y., Staiger, J. F., and Steinmetz, H. (1995a). Increased corpus callosum size in musicians. *Neuropsychologia* 33:1047–1055.

Schlaug, G., Jancke, L., Huang, Y., and Steinmetz, H. (1995b). In vivo evidence of structural brain asymmetry in musicians. *Science* 267:699–701.

Seidler, H., Falk, D., Stringer, C., Wilfing, H., Muller, G., zur Nedden, D., Weber, G., Recheis, W., and Arsuaga, J.-L. (1997). A comparative study of stereolithographically modeled skulls of Petralona and Broken Hill: Implications for future studies of middle Pleistocene hominid evolution. *Journal of Human Evolution* 33:691–703.

Selby, B., Rosenfeld, J., Styles, E., and Westcott, J. (1982). Which hemisphere is trained? The need for a new strategy for interpreting hemispheric asymmetries in music perception. *Psychology of Music Special Issue* 101–103.

Sergent, J. (1993). Music, the brain and Ravel. *Trends in Neuroscience* 16:106–109.

Sergent, J., Zuck, E., Terriah, S., and MacDonald, B. (1992). Distributed neural network underlying musical sight-reading and keyboard performance. *Science* 257:106–109.

Shannon, B. (1984). Asymmetries in musical aesthetic judgments. *Cortex* 20:567–573.

Tobias, P. V. (1981). The emergence of man in Africa and beyond. *Philosophical Transactions of the Royal Society of London, Series B* 292:43–56.

Toth, N. (1985). Archaeological evidence for preferential right-handedness in the lower and middle Pleistocene, and its possible implications. *Journal of Human Evolution* 14:607–614.

Tramo, M. J. and Bharucha, J. J. (1991). Musical priming by the right hemisphere post-callosotomy. *Neuropsychologia* 29:313–325.

Wildgruber, D., Ackermann, H., Klose, U., Kardatzki, B., and Grodd, W. (1996). Functional lateralization of speech production at primary motor cortex: A fMRI study. *NeuroReport* 7:2791–2795.

Yamadori, A., Osumi, Y., Masuhara, S., and Okubo, M. (1977). Preservation of singing in Broca's aphasics. *Journal of Neurology, Neurosurgery and Psychiatry* 40:221–224.

Zatorre, R. J., Evans, A. C., and Meyer, E. (1994). Neural mechanisms underlying melodic perception and memory for pitch. *Journal of Neuroscience* 14:1908–1919.

Zatorre, R. J., Evans, A. C., Meyer, E, and Gjedde, A. (1992). Lateralization of phonetic and pitch discrimination in speech processing. *Science* 256:846–849.

Fossil Evidence for the Origin of Speech Sounds

David W. Frayer and Chris Nicolay

Abstract

Morphological evidence and skeletal markers related to speech sound production are reviewed. Based on the fossil record, markers for vocal tract anatomy indicate that the ability to produce the sounds of language and song appeared early in the human lineage.

The production of speech sounds, whether for language or song, involves the interaction of multiple anatomical regions (Wind 1992). Two major anatomical areas are the processing center for organizing and controlling utterances, and the sound-production unit that creates and modifies individual speech sounds. Other chapters in this volume address specific areas of the brain that are important for language and music production, so other than referring to these contributions and noting that brain expansion and reorganization of specific areas associated with language occur early in the hominid lineage, this chapter focuses on paleontological evidence for the production of speech. Actual physical evidence for speech-production units below the brain is sparse and in some cases controversially interpreted. This might not be predicted by those on the more theoretical side of language origins. For example, Hewes (1975) compiled more than 11,000 references relating to language origins, covering approximately 400 years. His bibliography began with Medieval citations and ended with those published in 1972. In the more than twenty-five years since Hewes' bibliography, we suspect another 11,000 publications related to language origins have appeared.

From the thousands of references on language origins, it is logical to assume a considerable fossil record relevant to questions about when, where, how, and why language arose. Yet, this is far from the case. Just considering the papers published since Hewes' bibliography, if one stacked copies of all the single publications about language origins, surely the pile would weigh orders of magnitude more than all the physical evidence for linguistic abilities in the human fossil record. Whereas it is probably true that a "fossil is worth a thousand words," the paltry amount of actual evidence for language origins as recorded in fossils should be a little sobering to those willing to offer opinions about the origin of linguistic ability.

A number of problems are associated with attempts to reconstruct the evolution of the speech-production apparatus. First and foremost relates to the aggravating fact that most of the critical anatomy is not preserved in the fossil record since the vocal tract is made up of soft tissue. Most speech sounds are produced when air from the lungs is forced through the larynx, and bursts of energy are modified initially by the vocal cords, then shaped and modified by the supralaryngeal vocal tract, tongue, nasal and oral chambers, and lips. These anatomical structures and chambers have long been analyzed in living humans (Negus 1929), so that we know exactly where and how various sounds (formants) are produced in the vocal tract (see Borden, Harris, and Raphael 1994). It becomes quite another matter to extend similar kinds of analyses to the fossil record when, at best, essential parts are estimated from contingent bony areas. In fact, no patent skeletal structure directly predicts laryngeal anatomy or the shape and size of the supralaryngeal vocal tract, tongue, or lips. Correlations exist, but these are essentially inferences that suggest anatomical structure, and not necessarily the specificity and effectiveness of linguistic functions leading to speech.

Other problems relate to the incompleteness of the fossil record, both in the uneven chronological representation of various hominid forms and the fragmentary nature of specimens that constitute the fossil record. These shortcomings are constantly being overcome by field work. For example, the hyoid bone that sits atop of the larynx was recently added to the inventory, but only western Eurasia and later aspects of the fossil record are represented. It is also important to recognize that anatomical regions used to infer speech ability (e.g., the external cranial base) are commonly missing in fossils or, if present, are often distorted or incomplete. The consequence is that in some cases a fragmentary, distorted area is estimated in the original fossil, and this estimated region is used to "estimate" further the shape of the supralaryngeal vocal tract. Such extrapolations are far removed from the bony anatomy of the fossil, let alone from the soft tissue that made up the vocal tract when the fossil was alive. They are also susceptible to fundamental errors in anatomical detail, since it is not always a straightforward matter to repiece or reconstruct a complicated area such as the external cranial base. Given all this, it should be apparent that it is not a simple matter to marshal the fossil record and review various anatomical regions to determine when speech, let alone language, arose. Further complicating the issue of origins is the fact that it is not even clear that modern human speech abilities arose only once, since a few markers thought to be associated with a modern vocal tract occur in fossils considered (without dispute among paleoanthropologists) to be offshoots from the main branch leading to modern *Homo sapiens*.

Even with a perfect fossil record and perfect correlation between bony anatomy and soft tissue sound-production units (neither of which exists), problems remain in determining when language arose. In our view, this is because language is primarily neurologically based and not simply predicted by the ability to produce the necessary sounds. It is important to remember that humans can conduct language without a larynx, without a tongue, with a greatly modified palate, without opening the mouth, without hearing, and even without uttering sound. From our perspective, brain anatomy, evidence for handedness, behavior patterns (e.g., art, burial of the dead), and archeological evidence for other complex activities (e.g., home bases) are fundamentally more important indicators of language ability than is the sound-generating apparatus (e.g., Gibson 1991, 1993; Schepartz 1993).

Consequently, whereas we review evolutionary changes in anatomical regions related to speech production, we make no claim to a time when language definitely appeared or music must have been part of the human repertoire. It is possible, however, to determine when anatomical components in the modern human speech apparatus appear to be in place, allowing language and song to be coordinated by the brain. Coupled with chapters in this book about brain areas involved with language and music (e.g., Jerison and Falk), readers may make up their own minds about what constitutes critical evidence for determining when language and song first appeared.

The Hyoid

The laryngeal portion of the vocal tract is made up primarily of cartilage, except for the hyoid bone, which caps the larynx and serves as the attachment for muscles involved in swallowing and tongue movements, and ligaments for anchoring the thyroid cartilage. In humans this horse-shoe-shaped bone is not directly involved in speech-sound production, but in apes and other primates it serves as the attachment for the laryngeal air sacs (Swindler and Wood 1973) that are important in some vocalizations. The human hyoid is distinct from that in other primates in that it is broader across the base, shorter from top to bottom, and broader across the greater horns (Swindler and Wood 1973). Although possibly of limited value in predicting linguistic ability, the only two hyoids known from the fossil record are completely modern in anatomy. If they were fundamentally different, it would be straightforward to argue that anatomical differences constituted important inadequacies in linguistic production. But the fact that they are similar is used by some to suggest that hyoid morphology is irrelevant to the question.

The most complete of these is the Kebara Neanderthal hyoid from a middle Paleolithic context (~50,000 years ago) in Israel. According to the description of the original (and our separate analysis), it

is not notably different, in either size or morphology, from that of modern human hyoids. The relations of the hyoid to the mandible and cervical vertebrae probably did not differ from the modern pattern. . . . These new data strongly suggest

that Middle Paleolithic people shared structural relationships with modern
humans in terms of their vocal tracts. They appear to be as "anatomically
capable" of speech as modern humans . . . (Arensburg et al. 1990)

Some contested this conclusion, maintaining that hyoids of pigs more
closely resemble humans than the Neanderthal hyoid from Kebara
(Laitman, Gannon, and Raidenberg 1989; Lieberman 1993, 1994; Stringer
and Gamble 1993). For example, Laitman stated, "using the exact same
measurements [of Kebara], I can show you that pigs' hyoids in many
ways are more similar to modern humans" (quoted in Gibbons 1992:34).
To some this may seem like an odd animal to draw comparisons with,
especially since pigs are considered offensive to both Arabs and Jews in
the Levant, but perhaps the animal was selected since a pig tooth was
found in the grave fill surrounding the Kebara Neanderthal. Since
pigs are incapable of the full range of human vocal sounds, it would be
of some consequence if their hyoid and that of humans more closely
resembled each other than either resembled the Kebara Neanderthal.
As shown in figure 14.1, the hyoids of living humans and pigs have little
morphological resemblance. We leave it to readers to determine if the
hyoid of the Kebara Neanderthal is more distinct from the human hyoid
than the pig hyoid from the human. Eventually, when hyoids of early
Homo or of australopithecines are found, it will be interesting to see if
they more closely resemble chimpanzee hyoids, but for now, available
evidence indicates that at least the Neanderthal hyoid was utterly
modern.

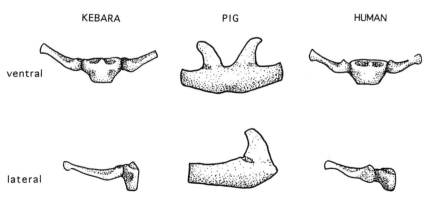

Figure 14.1
Ventral (anterior) and lateral (side) views of hyoids from Kebara (Neanderthal), a pig, and
a modern *Homo sapiens*. The pig hyoid has huge lesser horns projecting from either side
of the midline. These *cornua minus* are extremely small in hominids and not depicted in
the drawings of either the Kebara Neanderthal or the modern human. Unlike pigs, they
are seldom fused to the hyoid body.

External Cranial Base

Early work attempting to reconstruct linguistic abilities in fossils is represented by the now classic studies of Lieberman and Crelin (1971) and Lieberman, Crelin, and Klatt (1972). The authors focused on soft tissue modeling of the vocal tract for reconstructing vocal-linguistic ability. Their example was a reconstructed cast of the French Neanderthal from La Chapelle-aux-Saints. The original lacked most of its teeth, which were lost long before the individual died, and the restored specimen has a damaged, incomplete skull base. From the reconstructed cast the researchers rebuilt laryngeal structures, throat muscles, and air spaces of the vocal tract; sectioned their model; measured the reconstructed regions; and by computer simulation estimated the sound-production capability of the modeled regions. Based on this work, they held that Neanderthals had reduced linguistic capacity compared with more recent *Homo sapiens*, especially in their inability to produce specific vowels (/a/, /i/, /u/) and consonants (/k/ and /g/). More recent summaries by Crelin (1987) and Lieberman (1991) reviewed soft tissue reconstructions of other hominids using this same technique and continued to deny full linguistic ability to numerous fossils, especially Neanderthals.

The original reconstruction of the La Chapelle-aux-Saints Neanderthal and subsequent reconstitutions of soft tissue vocal tracts have not been without criticism. For the La Chapelle case these ranged from noting that the reconstructions did not take into account distortions and incompleteness in the original fossil (Carlisle and Segal 1974, 1978; Houghton 1993) to pointing out anatomical inaccuracies in the placement of certain structures and the resulting incapability of basic functions such as swallowing (Falk 1975; Du Brul 1977), to the impossibility of making certain parts of the reconstruction from casts (Burr 1976). In the last case, it is reasonable to wonder how nasal chambers could be modeled from a cast that does not mold the region. Some of these criticisms were verified when Heim (1989) completed a new reconstruction of the La Chapelle skull. He noted that the original reconstruction (done in the early 1900s) made the external cranial base too flat (apelike), and that when the actual anatomical configuration was done, details of cranial base angulation did not differ from those in living humans. Heim maintained there was no basis for stating that Neanderthals lacked a modern vocal apparatus, but his work has been ignored by those who base their conclusions on the old reconstruction or on the inaccurate cast made from it.

A less controversial technique was introduced by Laitman, Heimbuch, and Crelin (1979) who used a direct measurement technique for describing the skull base and estimating the shape of the supralaryngeal vocal tract. As posited by Laitman and colleagues in a series of papers and abstracts (1982, 1988, 1991, 1992), the primitive condition in living nonhuman mammals (including nonhuman primates) is represented by a flat, unflexed external cranial base. Based on the anatomy of the supralaryngeal region, this flattening is associated with a high-positioned larynx in living nonhuman taxa, which is correlated with a reduced capacity to produce the varied sounds of human speech (Laitman and Heimbuch 1982; Laitman, Heimbuch, and Crelin 1979). On the other hand, contemporary humans have arched (flexed) skull bases (figure 14.2) that in the living are correlated with a larynx positioned low in the throat. This arched morphology results in the modern adult condition of a large supralaryngeal resonating chamber capable of producing the full range of linguistic sounds (Lieberman 1975). Thus, although not directly measuring the supralaryngeal vocal tract, this technique estimates its likely shape and infers that the angulation of the external cranial base predicts larynx positions and speech sound capacity. Note, however, that at least one study (Gibson and Jessee 1994) failed to find a consistent association between features of the external cranial base and laryngeal position in a collection of modern Americans from Texas. These observations were tentatively confirmed by Lieberman et al. (1998) who, in a short

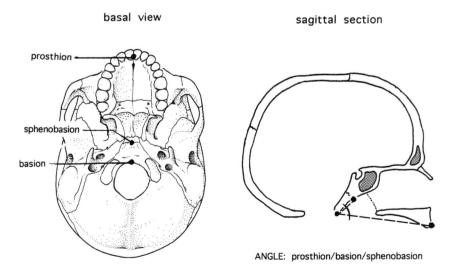

Figure 14.2
Views of a modern human skull shows the external cranial base, three points used in determining the angle of flexion, and the highly flexed external cranial base typical of linguistically competent humans.

abstract, reversed about twenty-five years of research on vocal tract positioning based on the contours of the cranial base. Since Lieberman has been an outspoken critic of anyone proposing different opinions from his about the significance of cranial base variations, these preliminary findings have extremely important implications for reconstruction of linguistic sound production in fossil hominids.

Here, given all the emphasis on cranial base morphology and vocal tract (upper respiratory) anatomy, we briefly review evidence about the shape of the cranial base in a series of fossil hominids. Our work is similar to Laitman's, but we streamlined his approach by eliminating a couple of measuring points, since both are often absent in crucial fossils. We calculate the angle made between two lines that are used to approximate the flexion of the cranial base (figure 14.2). One line is defined by a point on the anterior palate between the two central incisors (prosthion) and a point at the front of the foramen magnum (basion). The other line is defined by the same point (basion) and another on the midline of the basilar process (sphenobasion). The latter point roughly defines the highest point of the vocal tract. Data for this angle are presented in table 14.1 and show the substantial difference between the flat cranial base of chimpanzees, used here to illustrate the anatomical condition of a phylogenetically close relative known to lack the ability for the full range of human sounds, and the flexed condition in contemporary humans, as

Table 14.1
External cranial base angle in degrees (*prosthion/basion/sphenobasion*)

	Mean	Range
Recent modern humans (n = 100)	46.3	31.5–68.6
Homo sapiens ancestor?		
Skhul 5	48.4	
Neanderthals		
La Ferrassie 1	49.0	
Shanidar 1	42.2	
La Chapelle aux Saints	41.0	
Saccopastore I	39.0	
Teshik-Tash	38.5	
Gibraltar 1	38.0	
Early *Homo* from Africa		
East Turkana 3,733	43.5	
Olduvai hominid 24	38.0	
Australopithecines		
East Turkana 406	41.3	
Swartkrans 47	29.5	
Olduvai hominid 5	28.1	
Sterkfontein hominid 5	17.6	
West Turkana 17,000	8.3	
Chimpanzees (n = 50)	15.3	0.0–31.2

measured in humans from collections of the Cleveland Museum of Natural History who certainly had language.

From these data it is clear that modern humans differ markedly from modern chimps in mean values and in the range of variation for the external cranial base angle. It is also clear that many extinct hominid forms have an external cranial base angle that fits within the modern human range and lies totally beyond the chimpanzee range. For example, all the Neanderthals have external cranial base angles well above the chimp range and none are substantially different from Skhul 5, a specimen considered by many to be closer to living humans than any Neanderthal. Some expressed no doubts about the ability of Skhul 5 to produce the full range of human linguistic sounds (Lieberman 1975; Crelin 1987) based on soft tissue vocal tract reconstruction. If this is the case, it is difficult to deny similar linguistic capacities to Neanderthals who had virtually identical external cranial base angles.

Early *Homo* from Africa also have flexed cranial bases that fall above the chimpanzee range. Specimens ER 3733 from east Turkana and OH 24 from Olduvai Gorge both show considerable flexion, substantially greater than chimpanzees and fully within the modern human range. On the contrary, for the five australopithecines, the external cranial base is generally flatter than that of later hominids and within the chimp range. This is true for all but specimen ER 406 that is a hyperrobust australopithecine from east Turkana. This specimen, dated to about 1.6 million years ago, is identified as a member of a splinter group of hominids that went extinct without issue by about 1 million years ago (Wolpoff 1996). These hominids split from the one leading to *Homo* by about 2.5 million years ago based on fossil ancestors as represented by WT 17000, an early robust australopithecine from west Turkana (Walker et al. 1986). Without getting bogged down in taxonomic issues, it is important to recognize that if WT 17000 (or specimens like it) are broadly ancestral to ER 406 (or specimens like it), a trend for increased external cranial base flexion occurs in a line of hominids that no one considers to be in even the same genus as living humans let alone ancestral to them. But the same may be true for OH-24, who most consider belongs to *Homo habilis*, which also is probably an extinct side branch of the human line (Wolpoff 1996). Moreover, it likely derived from populations represented by forms like Sterkfontein 5, which have a flat, apelike external cranial base.

The implication of these patterns is that marked flexion of the external cranial base occurred in three separate hominid lines. If this flexion is related to a lowered larynx and increased supralaryngeal vocal tract, does this mean that speech capacity also evolved independently three separate times? It is an intriguing question and is made more provocative by the fact that these same three lines show trends for increased cranial capacity over time.

Hypoglossal Canal Size

Research by Kay, Cartmill, and Balow (1998) provides additional evidence for language capacity going back at least as far as Neanderthals. This work concerns the size of the hypoglossal canal, which is a bony chamber located on the base of the skull, just superior to the foramen magnum. It transmits the twelfth cranial nerve, which is responsible for innervation of the tongue. Dimensions of the canal were measured in chimpanzees, gorillas, and modern humans, and in a small sample of fossil hominids. Compared with modern humans, apes had significantly smaller canals (and by inference, smaller hypoglossal nerves) in absolute dimensions or relative to palate size. Australopithecines and earliest *Homo* from South Africa fell within or below the ape range in hypoglossal canal size, and a small sample of Neanderthals and other archaic hominids from Africa and the Levant were completely within the modern *Homo sapiens* range. In agreement with work reviewed here, this evidence is consistent with an early origin for linguistic capacity.

Respiratory System

The respiratory system of the earliest hominids does not resemble that of modern humans. Rather, both the source of the air stream (the lungs, as determined by the shape of the rib cage) and one of the potential exits (the nose, as measured by the bony nasal surfaces) of the earliest hominids strikingly resemble modern chimpanzees. For lungs, early australopithecines (as represented by *Australopithecus afarensis*) have a rib cage that continuously expands from the first to the last rib. This funnel-shaped or lampshade pattern (Jellema, Latimer, and Walker 1993) is typical of modern chimpanzees and deviates from all modern humans, which have a barrel-shaped thoracic cage shape (figure 14.3). The earliest appearance of the modern human rib cage pattern occurs at about 1.5 million years ago with the Nariokotome boy from west Turkana, Kenya. This specimen (WT-15000) has a rib cage described as "in almost all respects indistinguishable from those of modern humans" (Jellema, Latimer, and Walker 1993:324). Another study of the same specimen (MacLarnon 1993) corroborated the modernity of the vertebral column of WT-15000. However, vertebral arches (which enclose the spinal cord) have diameters smaller than expected, and this may indicate deficiencies in fine muscular control of intercostal (interrib) muscles. Based on this

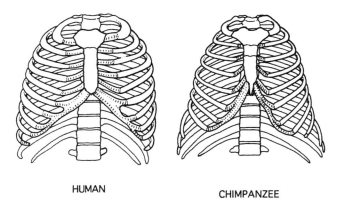

HUMAN   CHIMPANZEE

Figure 14.3
Thoracic cages typical of humans and chimpanzees. The rib cage in modern humans is
barrel-shaped and that in chimpanzees resembles a lampshade. The barrel-shaped rib cage
appears at least by 1.6 mya in early *Homo.* (Modified from Schultz 1969:66.)

observation MacLarnon (1993) and Walker (1993) contend that smaller
arches may indicate an underdeveloped muscular control of breathing
and consequent incapability of language at this period of human
evolution.

This conclusion contradicts other indications pointing to linguistic
ability in the same specimen, such as a large brain size with petalial and
other left-right brain asymmetries. Moreover, chimpanzees with small
neural arches have adequate intercostal muscle control to generate
sounds with complex pitch, intensity, and volume (Goodall 1986; Marler,
this volume). Other explanations are proposed for the small neural
arches in WT-15000. For example, Wolpoff (1996:403) reviewed unpublished work by Childress who postulated that the arch dimensions
relate to underdeveloped neural control of hand movements. Another
researcher theorized that the small size relates to reduced capacity to
"send and receive neural messages to his lower extremities" (Mackway-
Girardi 1997). It is hard to accept either of these speculations. The only
cervical vertebra preserved in WT-15000 is C7, and the neural canal on
this bone is not reduced (MacLarnon 1993:371). Since most of the
muscles involved in speech respiration are innervated by either cranial
or cervical nerves, there is no evidence that these were smaller, since the
vertebrae are not preserved. Similarly, arm and hand movements are
controlled by the brachial plexus, and no evidence exists for reduction
in these areas, since MacLarnon (1993) reported reduced neural arches
in only thoracic portions of the vertebral column. As for reduced bipedal
capacity, no evidence from any other area of the skeleton points to
lowered locomotor ability. Hunley (1998) confirmed the small size of the
thoracic canals, but when cranial capacity is considered, WT-15000

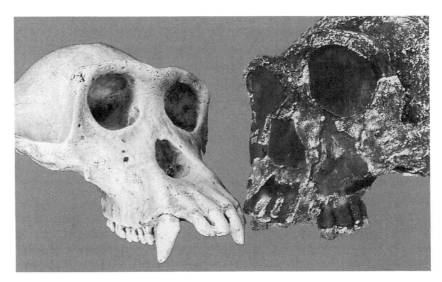

Figure 14.4
Views of nasal areas of a chimpanzee (left) and an early *Homo* (right). In the chimpanzee the nasal bones are depressed and level with the sides of the face. In the early *Homo* (cast of ER-3733) the nasal bones are arched and project away from the face, forming an external nose.

vertebral canals fall within the range of modern humans. Whereas some may debate interpretation of vertebral arch size, it is evident that the thoracic cage perfectly matches the modern human condition.

At the other end of the respiratory tract, a modern humanlike external nose also makes its appearance by about 1.5 million years ago. First described in detail by Franciscus and Trinkaus (1988), the bony architecture forming the structure of the human external nose is virtually identical in australopithecines and chimpanzees (and other apes), but is distinctly humanlike in fossils such as ER-3733 and others identified as *Homo erectus* or early *Homo sapiens* (figure 14.4). In apes and australopithecines, the nasal bones are flat (from side to side and top to bottom) and the upper nasal margins are even with or sunken below the transverse plane of the orbits. In living humans, the nasal bones are curved and arched forward, and the upper nasal area projects away from the face forming a true external nose. Franciscus and Trinkaus (1988:524–525) emphasized important increases in "effectiveness in humidification and temperature modification of inspired air" these anatomical modifications signal, but development of the external nose also has implications for speech sounds, since some consonants (e.g., /n/) are produced by nasal resonance. Apes apparently lack the ability to produce consonants (Savage-Rumbaugh and Lewin 1994), which may in part relate to their lack of an external nose. However, with the earliest appearance of members of our genus, the external nose typical of modern humans appears.

In short, substantial evidence supports the appearance of a modern respiratory system in the hominid line beginning about 1.5 million years ago. Chests were barrel-shaped and noses projecting, neither feature being typical of the earliest hominids (*Australopithecus*) or living apes. As shown in table 14.1, for the most part australopithecines had upper respiratory tracts as measured by the external cranial base angle that were also within the chimpanzee range, the exception being east Turkana 406. However, early *Homo* have more flexed external cranial bases and, at least for specimens such as east Turkana 3733 and WT-15000, external noses resembling people living today. None of this evidence establishes language, linguistic ability, or singing, but it does suggest that hominids for the first time had the anatomical bellows and nasal resonating chambers typical of language-competent humans.

Oral Chamber

The oral chamber is a crucial area for speech-sound production and one often glossed over in studies of the evolution of language. Duchin (1990) is a main exception. She contended that the dimensions of the oral cavity, defined by the hard palate and mandible in skeletal material, constitute an important component of the speech apparatus. Chimpanzees and humans differ in palate dimensions, as shown in figure 14.5. Chimps have relatively long, narrow maxillas, whereas human palates are shorter and broader. In her work with radiographs of humans and chimpanzees, Duchin documented the patterns shown in figure 14.5, demonstrating greater mandibular and hard palate lengths in chimpanzees. She correlated these skeletal differences to dissimilar muscular arrangements in chimpanzees and humans, and concluded that the shortened oral space in humans provides "an anatomical advantage . . . in that it reduces the travel-distance to and between the articulatory target positions [so that] . . . the human tongue has . . . a more accessible series of articulatory positions" (1990:695). Since tongue position and the oral cavity are crucial in the articulation of consonants (Borden, Harris, and Raphael 1994), palate dimensions are important indicators of speech and sound-production capability. Coupled with their lack of an external nose, chimpanzees' inability to produce consonants is related to their long, narrow palates.

Duchin's technique cannot be directly repeated in fossil material, since specimens are rarely so intact as to allow using her full complement of measurements of the oral chamber. Thus, like other cases discussed,

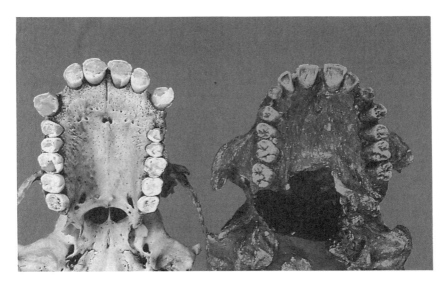

Figure 14.5
Palatal views of a chimpanzee (left) and early *Homo* (right, cast of WT-15,000, the Nariokotome boy). Typically, upper jaws of chimpanzees are more rectangular, whereas humans have more square palates.

dimensions of the oral chamber must be estimated and correlations made with intact anatomy. Here we use maximum palate length and internal palate breadth. These measurements are taken from standardized points on the hard palate and are fully comparable among various species. Chimpanzees are used to represent the primitive condition where modern speech sounds, especially consonants, are lacking. The human sample includes a large collection of European specimens ranging from modern *Homo sapiens* to fossils dating around 400,000 years before the present. We also included early *Homo* and *Australopithecus* specimens from Africa as examples of what must have been the hominid ancestral condition.

Figures 14.6 and 14.7 review the relative palate dimensions at the first and third molars. In both positions, average chimpanzee dimensions show that the length of the palate is about twice the breadth, whereas in humans the length is just slightly greater than the breadth. Chimpanzees and humans have means that are significantly different, and overall differences are so great that ranges do not overlap. As in Duchin's study, these plots show that apes have consistently longer, narrower palates than modern humans.

For the hominid fossil record, all Neanderthals fall totally within the human range, whereas most earlier fossils from Europe and Africa have much narrower, longer palates, often falling completely outside the

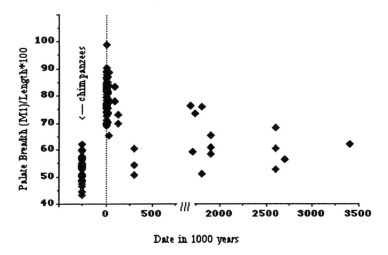

Figure 14.6
Palate proportions at M1 (palate breadth/maximum palate length) for humans and chimpanzees over the last 3.5 million years.

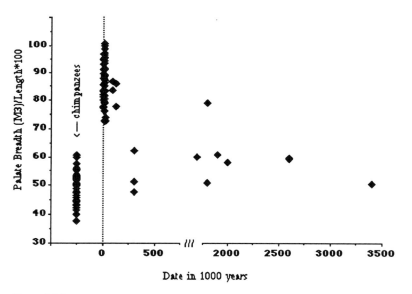

Figure 14.7
Palate proportions at M3 (palate breadth/maximum palate length) for humans and chimpanzees over the last 3.5 million years.

modern human range. In fact, most specimens older than roughly 250,000 years before the present do not differ from the chimpanzee. Put another way, beginning with Neanderthals, all humans show a relatively broad palate with a palate length reduced from the ancestral condition. Figures 14.6 and 14.7 also show that palatal proportions typical of modern humans are found in some early fossils. It is no surprise that these cases are all members of the early *Homo* sample, with australopithecines falling at the low end or outside the modern human range.

Discussion and Summary

Data and inferences from bony regions surrounding critical areas for the production of human speech sounds indicate that the potential for uttering formants typical of modern speech and song may be ancient adaptations in hominids. Judging from the limited fossil record that preserves relevant morphology, in early members of the genus *Homo* the external cranial base is flexed, which presumably indicates a lowered larynx with an expanded and probably bent supralaryngeal vocal tract. The lungs (as measured by rib cage shape in one specimen) and nasal chamber (based on morphology of several fossils) also attained a modern human shape in these early *Homo* populations. Similarly, at least in some specimens, the general proportions of the oral cavity were comparable with modern those of humans at about 1.5 million years ago.

Inferences about speech- and sound-production abilities are big steps (maybe leaps) from these bits of fossilized morphology. Yet, others used even fewer data to show that some members of *Homo* lacked the ability to produce a human range of linguistic sounds. Our statements here do not necessarily justify extrapolations to language ability or the capacity to produce music, but it is reasonable to deduce that the presence of some morphological details indicate the ability to produce specific sounds. From our view of the available physical data, evidence for the ability to produce speech sounds appears early in the fossil record. In fact, such ability may have happened in independent lines of hominids and may have emerged as part of an adaptation completely unrelated to linguistic ability, such as dietary adaptation. At least in *Homo* dated to around 1.5 million years ago, a set of morphological features emerged that are correlated to speech sound production in modern humans. It may be no coincidence that with the appearance of these early *Homo* fossils other evidence is preserved further hinting at linguistic competence. This includes brain expansion and evidence for hemispheric laterality (Falk, this volume; Holloway 1976, 1983, 1985), appearance of more sophisticated tool inventories, evidence for handedness in the production of implements or in scratches on anterior teeth (Toth 1985; Lalueza Fox and Frayer 1997), geographic expansion and exploitation of new habitats (Wolpoff 1996), and changes in dietary habits through a greater reliance on hunting (Wolpoff 1996). All these fit the inference that the early members of our genus probably were capable of language.

And what of singing and music? On the one hand, certain constraints for creating song are less than those involved in creating speech. As singing depends on an open vocal tract and thus vowels, it demands fewer articulatory constraints than speech. To the extent that the hyoid bone and external cranial base of early *Homo* fossils show modern configurations, then it is quite likely that these hominids were capable of forming the vowels necessary for singing. On the other hand, singing requires a much greater control of airflow than does speaking, in terms of the duration, amplitude, and pitch range of sound. The paleontological evidence reviewed in this chapter suggests that by 1.5 million years ago, both the respiratory and nasal systems of hominids assumed the form of anatomically modern humans. It thus seems likely that by this date, both the articulatory capacity to form vowels and the respiratory capacity to maintain high-volume airflow were present in our hominid ancestors, and therefore, most likely, the capacity to sing as well.

Acknowledgments

We thank the Cleveland Museum of Natural History for access to their skeletal collections, and Milford H. Wolpoff for some of the hominid fossil data.

References

Arensburg, B., Schepartz, L., Tillier, A. M., Vandermeersch, B., and Rak, Y. (1990). A reappraisal of the anatomical basis for speech in middle Pleistocene hominids. *American Journal of Physical Anthropology* 83:137–146.

Borden, G. J., Harris, K. S., and Raphael, L. J. (1994). *Speech Science Primer*. Baltimore: Williams & Wilkins.

Burr, D. B. (1976). Further evidence concerning speech in Neanderthal man. *Man* 11:104–110.

Carlisle, R. C. and Segal, M. I. (1974). Some problems in the interpretation of Neanderthal speech capabilities: A reply to Lieberman. *American Anthropologist* 76:319–322.

Carlisle, R. C. and Segal, M. I. (1978). Additional comments on problems in the interpretation of Neanderthal speech capabilities. *American Anthropologist* 80:367–372.

Crelin, E. S. (1987). *The Human Vocal Tract*. New York: Vantage Press.

Du Brul, E. L. (1977). Origins of the speech apparatus and its reconstruction in fossils. *Brain and Language* 4:365–381.

Duchin, L. E. (1990). The evolution of articulate speech: Comparative anatomy of the oral cavity in *Pan* and *Homo*. *Journal of Human Evolution* 19:687–697.

Falk, D. (1975). Comparative anatomy of the larynx in man and the chimpanzee: Implications for language in Neanderthal. *American Journal of Physical Anthropology* 43:123–132.

Franciscus, R. G. and Trinkaus, E. (1988). Nasal morphology and the emergence of *Homo erectus*. *American Journal of Physical Anthropology* 75:517–528.

Gibbons, A. (1992). Neandertal language debate: Tongues wag anew. *Science* 256:33–34.

Gibson, K. R. (1991). Tools, language, and intelligence. *Man* 26:602–619.

Gibson, K. R. (1993). Tool use, language, and social behaviour in relationship to information processing capacities. In K. R. Gibson and T. Ingold (Eds.) *Tools, Language and Cognition in Human Evolution* (pp. 251–269). Cambridge, UK: Cambridge University Press.

Gibson, K. R. and Jessee, S. A. (1994). Cranial base shape and laryngeal position: Implications for Neanderthal language debates. *American Journal of Physical Anthropology* [supplement 18]:93.

Goodall, J. (1986). *The Chimpanzees of Gombe*. Cambridge: Harvard University Press.

Heim, J. L. (1989). La nouvelle reconstitution du crâne Néandertalien de la Chapelle-aux-Saints méthode et résultats. *Bulletins et Mémoires de la Société d'Anthropologie de Paris* 1:95–118.

Hewes, G. (1975). *Language Origins: A Bibliography*. The Hague: Mouton.

Holloway, R. L. (1976). Paleoneurological evidence for language origins. *Annals of the New York Academy of Sciences* 280:330–348.

Holloway, R. L. (1983). Human paleontological evidence relevant to language behavior. *Human Neurobiology* 2:105–114.

Holloway, R. L. (1985). The poor brain of *Homo sapiens neanderthalensis*: See what you please. In E. Delson (Ed.) *Ancestors: The Hard Evidence* (pp. 319–324). New York: Aldine Press.

Houghton, P. (1993). Neanderthal supralaryngeal vocal tract. *American Journal of Physical Anthropology* 90:139–146.

Hunley, K. L. (1998). Vertebral canal size and function: A comparison of extant and fossil hominoids. *Journal of Human Evolution* 34:A10.

Jellema, L. M, Latimer, B., and Walker, A. (1993). The rib cage. In A. Walker and R. Leakey (Eds.) *The Nariokotome* Homo erectus *skeleton* (pp. 294–325). Cambridge: Harvard University Press.

Kay, R. F., Cartmill, M., and Balow, M. (1998). The hypoglossal canal and the origin of human vocal behavior. *Proceedings of the National Academy of Sciences* USA 95:5417–5419.

Laitman, J. T., Gannon, P. J., and Reidenberg, J. S. (1989). Charting changes in the hominid vocal tract. *American Journal of Physical Anthropology* 78:257–258.

Laitman, J. T. and Heimbuch, R. C. (1982). The basicranium of Plio-Pleistocene hominids as an indicator of their upper respiratory systems. *American Journal of Physical Anthropology* 59:323–344.

Laitman, J. T., Heimbuch, R. C., and Crelin, E. S. (1979). The basicranium of fossil hominids as an indicator of their upper respiratory systems. *American Journal of Physical Anthropology* 51:15–34.

Laitman, J. T. and Reidenberg, J. S. (1988). Advances in understanding the relationship between the skull base and larynx with comments on the origin of speech. *Human Evolution* 3:99–109.

Laitman, J. T., Reidenberg, J. S., Freidland, D. R., and Gannon, P. J. (1991). What sayeth thou Neanderthal? A look at the evolution of their vocal tract and speech. *American Journal of Physical Anthropology* [supplement 12]:109.

Laitman, J. T., Reidenberg, J. S., Freidland, D. R., and Gannon, P. J. (1992). The demise of the Neanderthals: The respiratory specialization hypothesis. *American Journal of Physical Anthropology* [supplement 14]:104.

Lalueza Fox, C. and Frayer, D. W. (1997). Non-dietary marks in the anterior dentition of the Krapina Neanderthals. *International Journal of Osteoarchaeology* 7:133–149.

Lieberman, D. E., McCarthy, R. C., Hiiemae K., Lieberman, P., and Palmer, J. B. (1998). New estimates of fossil hominid vocal tract dimensions. *Journal of Human Evolution* 34:A12–A13.

Lieberman, P. (1975). *On the Origins of Language: An Introduction to the Evolution of Speech*. New York: Macmillan.

Lieberman, P. (1991). *Uniquely Human*. Cambridge: Harvard University Press.

Lieberman, P. (1993). On the Kebara KMH 2 hyoid and Neanderthal speech. *Current Anthropology* 34:172–175.

Lieberman, P. (1994). Hyoid bone position and speech. *American Journal of Physical Anthropology* 94:275–278.

Lieberman, P. and Crelin, E. S. (1971). On the speech of Neanderthal man. *Linguistic Inquiry* 2:203–222.

Lieberman, P., Crelin, E. S., and Klatt, D. H. (1972). Phonetic ability and related anatomy of the newborn and adult human, Neanderthal man, and the chimpanzee. *American Anthropologist* 74:287–307.

Mackway-Girardi, A. (1997). Letter to the editor. *National Geographic* 192:xii.

MacLarnon, A. (1993). The vertebral canal. In A. Walker and R. Leakey (Eds.) *The Nariokotome* Homo erectus *Skeleton* (pp. 359–390). Cambridge: Harvard University Press.

Negus, V. E. (1929). *The Mechanism of the Larynx*. London: Heinemann.

Savage-Rumbaugh, S. and Lewin, R. (1994). *Kanzi: The Ape at the Brink of the Human Mind*. New York: Wiley.

Schepartz, L. A. (1993). Language and modern human origins. *Yearbook of Physical Anthropology* 36:91–126.

Stringer, C. and Gamble, C. (1993). *In Search of the Neanderthals*. London: Thames and Hudson.

Swindler, D. R. and Wood, C. D. (1973). *An Atlas of Primate Gross Anatomy*. Seattle: University of Washington Press.

Toth, N. (1985). Archaeological evidence for preferential right-handedness in the lower and middle Pleistocene, and its possible implications. *Journal of Human Evolution* 14:607–614.

Walker, A. (1993). Perspectives on the Nariokotome discovery. In A. Walker and R. Leakey (Eds.) *The Nariokotome* Homo erectus *Skeleton* (pp. 411–432). Cambridge: Harvard University Press.

Walker, A. C., Leakey, R. E., Harris, J. M., and Brown, F. H. (1986). 2.5-Myr *Australopithecus boisei* from west of Lake Turkana, Kenya. *Nature* 322:517–522.

Wind, J. (1992). Speech origin: A review. In J. Wind, B. Chiarelli, B. Bichakjian, A. Nocentini, and A. Jonker (Eds.) *Language Origin: A Multidisciplinary Approach* (pp. 21–37). Dordrecht: Kluwer.

Wolpoff, M. H. (1996). *Human Evolution*. New York: McGraw-Hill.

15 New Perspectives on the Beginnings of Music: Archeological and Musicological Analysis of a Middle Paleolithic Bone "Flute"

Drago Kunej and Ivan Turk

Abstract

A flutelike perforated thighbone of a young cave bear was found in 1995 in solid breccia of layer 8 at Divje babe I cave site in Slovenia. The find originates from a reliably dated middle Paleolithic level, and could thus be the oldest musical instrument so far known. What in fact does this find represent, and what does it mean for Paleolithic archeology? Two main hypotheses have been proposed: the find is a human artifact although it lacks preserved tool marks, and the bone was pierced by a carnivore in an abnormal way and shows clear traces of carnivore chewing. We performed tests on a set of careful reconstructions of the bone. These show that it is possible to produce a variety of sounds on such an object, lending support to the idea that it may have been used as a sound or signal aid, perhaps even as a musical instrument with specific expressive power. Of course, this interpretation raises a large number of additional questions, many of which can be answered at the present time.

There is no doubt that the beginnings of music extend back into the Paleolithic, many tens of thousands of years into the past. The question is how far back. In Europe, the first intentionally produced musical instrument is a bone flute from the start of the Upper Paleolithic, or Aurignacian[1] that was found in the cave of Geissenklösterle in Germany. The age of the find was assessed by the radiocarbon method at c. 36,000 years old (Hahn and Münzel 1995). In addition there are other relatively rare finds of bone flutes from later phases of the Upper Paleolithic, mainly the Gravettian and Magdalenian (Fages and Mourer-Chauviré 1983; Buisson 1990; Rottländer 1996). In terms of the number of finds, the French cave of Isturitz (Buisson 1990) certainly holds first place. Since the beginning of the Upper Paleolithic (c. 40,000 to 30,000 years ago) in Germany, as everywhere in Europe, was accompanied by a high degree of development of art (Hahn 1983), the Geissenklösterle find from the Aurignacian is not particularly surprising but rather to be expected. However, before the Upper Paleolithic, the situation was very different. Art from this period is practically unknown, although this does not mean that it did not exist (Marshack 1988; Stepanchuk 1993). Perhaps it remains archeologically unperceived, embodied in objects that have fallen prey to the ravages of time. This fate is likely to befall objects made of wood, and in the past, as now, flutes must have been made from hollow plant stems as well as from bone. It seems unlikely that our scattered finds provide a true reflection of the prevalence of flutes (and music) in the Paleolithic. All Paleolithic finds of bone flutes together can only be the tip of the iceberg. What is hidden from archeologists is the far larger mass of flutes made from plant stems, which are lost forever.

After this introduction, questions and riddles raised by the recent find of a flutelike fragment of the thigh bone of a young cave bear from the cave site of Divje babe I in Slovenia (figure 15.1) will perhaps be more understandable. The find is firmly dated to the middle Paleolithic, and may thus represent the oldest such find in the world (Turk, Dirjec, and Kavur 1995, 1997a; Turk 1997). Doubt about the correctness of the interpretation of the find as a flute has existed ever since its discovery (Turk, Dirjec, and Kavur 1995, 1997a, b), since the find is nearly 10,000 years older than the flute from Geissenklösterle and other bone products with clear signs of deliberate working (Mellars 1996). Thus, dissenting archeological viewpoints are to be expected (Albrecht et al. 1998; Chase and Nowell 1998; d'Errico et al. 1998; Holdermann and Serangeli 1998). However, the find deserves special attention, since other weak archeological signals from its time suggest that we may have to rethink our views on the origin of Paleolithic art and technology. Unfortunately, these signals have been altered by time and numerous other external

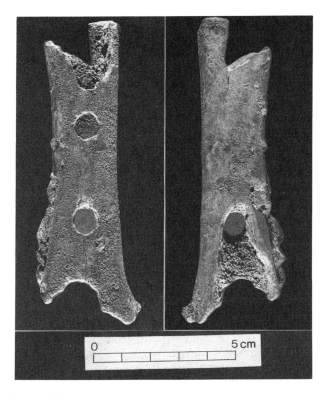

Figure 15.1
Presumed bone flute from Divje babe I site immediately after its discovery. Posterior (left) and anterior (right) views. (Photo: M. Zaplatil.)

factors, adding to difficulties in classifying them in relation to their importance. One of these signals may be the "flute" from Divje babe I.

The Archeological Setting

The Divje babe I site is located at 230 m above the valley of the river Idrijca, which has an altitude of 220 m above sea level at the cave. The Idrijca cuts through the picturesque Idrijsko and Cerkljansko hills (heights to 1,622 m) with their associated high plateaus, and opens into one of the most beautiful rivers in Europe, the Soca, which flows into the Adriatic Sea. Geographically, this is the medium range of mountains of western Slovenia, where today Alpine and sub-Mediterranean influences are mixed because of the proximity of the Alps (Julian Alps, heights to 2,864 m) and the Adriatic Sea. In the last Glacial, sub-Mediterranean influences were less pronounced since most of the northern part of the Adriatic Sea was land (Bortolami et al. 1997).

The cave of Divje babe I is among the key Paleolithic sites in the southeastern Alpine region (Turk 1997). Other well-known sites in the vicinity include Krapina (Gorjanović-Kramberger 1913; Malez 1970), Vindija (Malez 1978; Karavanić 1995), and Šandalja (Malez 1974; Miracle 1995) in Croatia. The first two are famous for skeletal and other remains of Neanderthals (Wolpoff et al. 1981; Smith 1982; Radovčić et al. 1988). In terms of culture and past environment, Divje babe I is linked to fairly distant northern Italian sites from around Verona, which belong to an exceptionally rich Paleolithic province (Leonardi and Broglio 1962; Broglio 1984; Palma di Cesnola 1996).

The site of Divje babe I was excavated in 1978 and 1980–1986 by Mitja Brodar from the Institute of Archaeology, Ljubljana, and after him, from 1989–1995 and in 1996, by Ivan Turk and Janez Dirjec from the same Institute (Turk 1997). The excavations established an exceptionally thick cave infilling consisting of twenty-six main layers. The total thickness of all layers is a good 12 m. Bedrock has not been reached. The main constituents, for the most part unconsolidated sediment, are autochthonous gravel and silt. The main allochthonous constituent, in addition to carbonate and phosphate precipitates, is a mass of fossil remains of cave bear. Because of admixtures of organic origin contributed by cave bear, powerful diagenetic processes have occurred in most layers. Many years of research provided some good chronostratigraphic anchorage points for the existing stratigraphic sequence, as follows, from top down:

1. Flowstone (calcite flows and stalagmites) on the present surface of the cave. They were deposited in the Holocene, in the last 10,000 years, discordantly with underlying sediments from the Upper Pleistocene.

2. Aurignacian finds, among them a bone point with split base in layers 2 or 3 under the flowstone crust. The age of layer 2 was assessed by the radiocarbon method at c. 35,000 years (Nelson 1997), which corresponds well with the radiocarbon age of Aurignacian sites on the southern side of the Alps (Broglio 1996–1997) and in Europe in general (Allsworth-Jones 1986; Broglio 1996–1997).

3. Global cryoturbation of the complex of layers 2 to 5 is linked with the cold peak of the last Glacial (Pleniglacial II) before c. 20,000 years, or with its anaphase. Soil in the region of the cave and in the cave itself up to 20 m inside the entrance was then deeply frozen, because of which gelifluction occurred.

4. Deeply cemented upper part of layer 8 in compact breccia. This event can reliably be linked to the pronounced interstadial in the Inter-pleniglacial of the last Glacial. The cementing has been radiocarbon dated to an interval from c. 43,000 to c. 45,000 years (Nelson 1997). It is therefore older than the Hengello interstadial, during which transition from middle to Upper Paleolithic began in eastern and central Europe (Allsworth-Jones 1986). This fact is important, since the flute from Divje babe I was found in this breccia.

5. Local cryoturbation of layer 16 and the upper part of layer 17 is linked with the glacial peak at c. 65,000 years (Pleniglacial I), when the soil in the area of the cave entrance was permanently frozen. The local event is temporally fixed by dating of the lower part of layer 17 by uranium series at c. 83,000 years (Ku 1997) and preliminarily by electron spin resonance (esr) from c. 77,000 to c. 96,000 years (Lau et al. 1997:table 4), and layer 13 by the radiocarbon method to an average 47,000 years (Nelson 1997).[2]

6. Results of pollen and charcoal analyses show that frigoriphilic vege-tation predominated in the upper layers up to and including the upper part of layer 17, and only in the deeper layers mezophilic vegetation (Šercelj and Culiberg 1991). Charcoal in all layers belongs predominantly to conifers with the exception of some layers immediately below the surface, in which charcoal broadleaf species greatly predominate (Culiberg and Šercelj 1997). From layer 18 downward, sediments are locally and, in layer 20, globally cemented into loosely bound breccia. Layer 20 also contains pieces of flowstone. Altogether it indicates an explicitly warm phase (interstadial) in the context of the early Glacial, which is also confirmed by the following dating of layer 20: one with the aid of uranium series to c. 80,000 years (Ku 1997) and two radiocarbon datings at more than 53,000 or 54,000 years (Nelson 1997).[3]

The find of the suspected flute originates from the cemented part of layer 8. So its stratigraphic location and age, both relative and absolute, are completely reliable and are not debated in professional circles. Layer 8 contains remains of hearths and modest Paleolithic finds that, in view of all the circumstances, can reliably be ascribed to the final phase of the middle Paleolithic (50,000 to 35,000 years). One of the hearths was in the direct vicinity of the find. Its absolute age has not been determined. In this phase, the people, probably Neanderthals, visited the cave only occasionally for a short time, but did not permanently occupy it.[4] This also applies to other layers, in which two peaks of visits are recorded. The first is older than layer 8 and is focused on layer 13. The second is younger than layer 8 and is focused on layer 4. In a total of 8 middle Paleolithic levels from various layers, 18 hearths, 570 stones, and, in addition to the suspected flute, 3 bone artifacts have been recorded. While in the cave, Paleolithic visitors did not carry out activities that can be identified by formal archeological methods. They did not make tools and did not process their prey in general. However, they had many fires and used stone tools in the cave intensively, for what activities exactly we do not know. Beside hearths, they probably crushed skulls and marrow bones of cave bear that had died naturally. Among tools, a great many are suitable for making holes. Some are damaged in such a way as to suggest their use for chipping bone, but they do not show the specific damage that occurs if used for that purpose.

Having established the rough time frame for the site as a whole and for the suspected flute, we can approach the problems surrounding the find from archeological and musicological points of view, allowing us to come to grips with the questions this find raises.

The object is reminiscent of a flute in terms of its shape and the regular string of artificial holes in the wall of the posterior side of the thigh bone. It is the left thigh bone (femur) of a one to two-year-old cave bear. Measurements of the preserved central tubular part of the bone, or diaphysis, are as follows: length 113.6 mm; width at the narrowest part 23.5 and 17.0 mm, because of the approximately oval shape of the transverse cross section; width of the marrow cavity at the narrowest part around 13.0 and 10.0 mm; and maximum diameters of complete holes 9.7 and 9.0 mm. The distance between the centers of the two complete holes is 35 mm (see Turk, Dirjec, and Kavur 1997b). The original length of the diaphysis plus the two ends (or epiphyses and metaphyses) would have been approximately 210 mm at this ontogenetic stage of an individual cave bear. So the posterior side of the bone has no space for any more holes than is indicated by the two additional possible remains of holes (cf. B. Fink in Anonymous [1997], whose reconstruction of the find as a flute is thus inappropriate). A putative fifth hole is only partly preserved below one of the complete holes, on the convex anterior side of the diaphysis. Here, the wall of the diaphysis is fractured in the shape of the letter V. The fracture extends from the end of the diaphysis to the suspected fifth hole. On the opposite, missing end of the bone, a projecting end with a straight edge is preserved. The morphology of the edges of the complete holes differ from that of the partial edge of the suspected hole on the anterior side and one of the suspected holes on the posterior side. The surface and almost all edges, including the edge of the two complete holes, have been greatly damaged mechanically and chemically by time. Clear traces of possible factors that may have given the bone the deliberate or coincidental shape of a flute have thus been erased.

Interpreting the Find: Problems and Issues

Who Made the Holes: Carnivores or Humans?

Approximately 600 femurs belonging to young cave bears one to four years of age have been found at the site to date. Almost all are more or less fragmented, and only some 10 pieces are approximately the same size as the bone with holes. Only one was artificially pierced in the center on both sides (Turk, Dirjec, and Kavur 1997b:figure 11.15). All other bones are without holes. Almost all 600 examples lack both articulating ends (epiphyses). The diaphysis has been preserved more or less whole. This part is without spongy tissue in young bears, which is present only in the region of the two epiphyses and metaphyses. The two epiphyses and metaphyses in most young femurs were probably removed by carnivores, which can be confirmed by traces and occasional impressions of teeth on individual examples (Turk and Dirjec 1997:figures 9.1 and 9.2; Turk, Dirjec, and Kavur 1997b:figure 11.19). A similar fate may also have befallen the suspected bone flute. It can be claimed with great probability that, in view of the way in which it is damaged, at least one of its ends was gnawed by a carnivore, although there are no clear traces of teeth (Turk, Dirjec, and Kavur 1997b; Chase and Nowell 1998).[5] However, it cannot be reliably ascertained when the bone was chewed— before or after the holes were made, or even at the same time (Chase and Nowell 1998). In any case, it was not damaged during excavation, although it was located deep in breccia.

Even if carnivore activity were established with regard to this bone (Turk, Dirjec, and Kavur 1997b; Albrecht et al. 1998; Chase and Nowell 1998; d'Errico et al. 1998), this still does not mean that only beasts formed the bone in the way that it was found. We are familiar with examples in which indisputable bone artifacts, such as Upper Paleolithic bone points, were greatly chewed by beasts after people ceased to use them (Turk and Stele 1997:figure 57; López Bayón et al. 1997:photo 1). A recently found Upper Paleolithic bone flute with drilled holes from the open-air loess site of Grubgraben in Austria also has both ends fragmented, at least one in a similar manner to our find (Einwögerer and Käfer 1998:abb. 2). Most other Paleolithic examples of flutes have also been preserved more or less fragmented. It is necessary to stress that in all cited examples the damage is of Pleistocene age. It is not possible to distinguish what damaged an object from what produced it when faced with deciding among various possibilities in specific cases.

The main question raised by archeologists is who pierced the bone on the flatter posterior side? The question is answered only through experimentation or through new similar finds of the same or greater age. Three answers are possible: the bone was pierced by some beast with teeth, by a human with a stone tool, or perhaps a combination of the two. If the holes were made by a beast, we know why it was done. If they were made by a human we are faced with another question. Why? To make a flute, or for some other purpose? Before writing this chapter, Turk undertook extensive experiments with bronze casts of the jawbones of wolves and hyenas and imitation tools from chert, with which he pierced analogous bones of recent brown bear and used them as comparative material for the original. He also reproduced specific damage to the tools that were created by chipping the holes. The results, presented at an international symposium held in Slovenia in May 1998, are briefly summarized here.

Since the site was above all a carnivore den, as were most sites from this time in Europe (Gamble 1986; Stiner 1995), we should consider some of the animals that fed on bones and bone marrow, primarily wolves and hyenas. The former are relatively richly represented in the site fauna, but of hyenas there is no trace, neither directly among faunal remains nor indirectly among the mass of bone fragments that were characteristic of the activity of hyenas in caves during the last Glacial in general (d'Errico and Villa 1997), and still less in the layer in which the pierced bone was found. The main candidate for piercing the bone is therefore wolf (*Canis lupus*), which is frequently found in Slovene Paleolithic sites before the peak of the last Glacial, before around 20,000 years ago. Even at that time it probably often stayed in the vicinity of humans and fed on their leftovers, or both used the same sources of food in cave dens, where cave bears perished.

Bearing in mind constraints of the laws of physics (i.e., biomechanics) and normal chewing behavior, both carnivores could pierce the bone almost exclusively with their carnassials (upper fourth premolar and lower first molar in the wolf) and precarnassials (upper and lower third premolar in the hyena) in the course of chewing. These teeth are pointed and, in addition to canines, the strongest teeth in the jaw, and like other molars are particularly adapted to compressive strength. Since carnivores always chew a bone from the end, most such holes are created in the region of the epiphyses and metaphyses (Brodar 1985:table 3; Turk and Dirjec 1997) where elastic and viscoelastic trabecular bone is covered with thin cortical shell or compact bone. This becomes thicker and thicker with increasing distance from the articular cartilage. Undoubtedly all puncture depressions are of carnivore origin (Turk, Dirjec, and Kavur 1997b:figure 11.16), whereas the origin of completely pierced holes without opposite bite marks, similar to ours, is uncertain. Everyone agrees that holes in the central part of the diaphysis, where cortical shell is thickest and where there is no trabecular bone, are unusual for activities carried out by carnivores. Such a disposition of holes could be achieved only if the animal were to grasp the bone first from one end and then from the other, and with at least two powerful bites (for other details connected with holes made in bones by carnivores, see Turk, Dirjec, and Kavur 1997; for an explanation of the creation of the holes in our bone by teeth, see Albrecht et al. 1998, Chase and Nowell 1998, and d'Errico et al. 1998).

The holes in the flute are too big for a wolf, and their shape matches the shape of wolf's carnassials not at all and the precarnassials of hyenas only slightly. Precarnassial and carnassial teeth do not produce circular holes but oval and rhomboid ones. Almost-circular holes are characteristic only of canines (figure 15.2c, d), where the bite force is half or less that of precarnassials and carnassials and the teeth behind them. Besides, canines are not functionally adapted to chewing, which requires maximum compressive and minimum shear strength, and are normally not used for this purpose (but see Albrecht et al. 1998; d'Errico et al. 1998). Holes in the flute could only match the shape of canines of hyenas and large carnivores such as bears (brown and cave bear) and lions. Except for hyenas, these animals are not interested in bones, although they are present in cave fauna and must be considered.

A force of 1300 to 1900 Newtons is necessary to pierce thick cortical bone (3 to 4 mm) with a pointed tooth in the middle part of the diaphysis of juvenile specimens.[6] It is questionable whether most medium-sized carnivores (e.g., wolves, perhaps hyenas) are capable of doing this with their canines, which in any case would be abnormal chewing behavior (Le Brech et al. 1997; Lindner et al. 1995). Besides, compact bone regularly splits longitudinally when a tooth penetrates this deep, as was the case with the holes in the suspected flute. The ultimate goal of every bone-eating carnivore is to split a bone into two pieces to get at the marrow. The question is why this goal was not achieved after so many attempts, when most of the necessary energy had been invested in piercing the cortical shell and widening the holes.

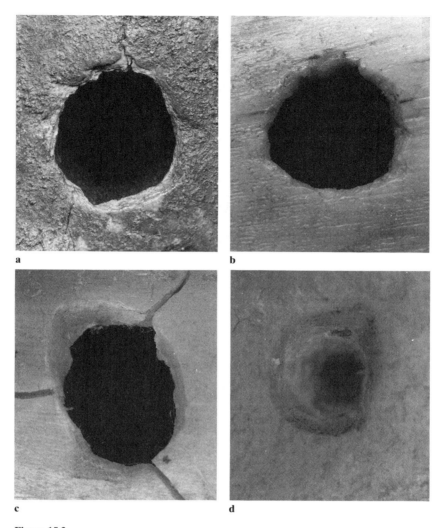

Figure 15.2
One of the holes (a) in the presumed flute from Divje babe I site, and experimentally chipped and punctured holes produced with a stone tool (b) or with a wolf's (c) or hyena's canine tooth (d) in the fresh femur of a young brown bear. (Photo: T. Lauko and I. Turk.)

The apparent hole, the only one on the anterior side of the diaphysis, is found below one of the complete holes and could therefore have been made by an opposing tooth (see Albrecht et al. 1998; Chase and Nowell 1998; d'Errico et al. 1998). The two holes, evidently different in morphology and size, are slightly displaced one below the other, which roughly corresponds to the position of upper and lower precarnassials, carnassials, and canines in carnivores. Since, in biting position, upper precarnassials and carnassials cover the lower ones from the side, and the lower canine is behind the upper, the remains of the hole on the anterior side, in relation to its displacement from the hole on the posterior side, could only have been made by the upper precarnassial or carnassials or canines. We can immediately exclude precarnassial and carnassial teeth because of the inappropriate position of the two holes in relation to the position of these teeth in the open jaw. So only canines enter into consideration. In piercing with two canines, with all possible bites, the disposition of the distal hole and opposing notch will be as on the flute. This is also the only feature that proves a carnivore origin of at least one hole and one notch on the flute. The paraxial direction of canine occlusion in carnivores could also explain the remaining hole and notch without opposing tooth marks, but does not explain different results of similar bites on the flute.

Since the anterior side of the bone is convex, punching it takes considerably greater strength than it would on the flat, posterior side, all other things being equal. So canines would at once pierce and break the central part of the diaphysis on the posterior side more easily than on the anterior side. However, this happened on the anterior side, that is, under the point of the upper canine; on the other side, only a hole was created that is even closer to the edge than the opposing hole would have been had this not been broken. On the basis of physical laws and experimental work, this is an entirely unexpected result. No such damage or any macroscopic trace is seen of the point of the opposing tooth or of other opposing teeth in suitable places beside the complete and half-holes on the other end of bone. Opposing and neighboring teeth should have made an impression with such a powerful bite force as is required for the tooth to pierce the thick, compact bone of the diaphysis.

In piercing compact bone with canines, the lower canine has much more opportunity to make a hole than the upper one. The reason lies in the geometry of the bone shell and in the explicit paraxial occlusion of canine teeth, which have the effect of splitting the force produced by the lower jaw into two components, axial and transverse (we owe this explanation to Dr. Pavel Cevc, Institute "Jožef Štefan," Ljubljana). The transverse component precludes the upper canine from penetrating the arched anterior surface of the bone. In this case it would be very difficult for a carnivore that pierced the bone several times with abnormal chewing behavior to place the same tooth (i.e., lower canine) each time exactly in line with a previous hole. All holes and notches on the posterior side are disposed in a straight line.

In summary, if the bone was modified exclusively by carnivores, which is an attractive and simple answer to our archeological problem (Albrecht et al. 1998; Chase and Nowell, 1998; d'Errico et al. 1998), it is necessary to recognize that numerous details do not conform with such a solution: for example, completeness of the diaphysis, lack of impressions from opposing and neighboring teeth, the regular string of holes, and the location, morphology, size, and shape of the holes. It is therefore necessary to examine many issues connected with the possibility that humans modified the bone, and that it may represent the oldest musical instrument known.

In the event that the holes were made by people, their manufacture can be directly linked with stone tools found at the site that would have been suitable for the specific task of piercing bone. The procedure can even be repeated experimentally, and this we actually did (but see Albrecht et al. 1998, who arrived at mostly negative results). Our results were as follows.

The irregular shape of the holes and occasionally disposed "corners" can be more suitably connected with the punching or chipping the holes with a pointed and/or tongued stone tool than with activities of a carnivore and subsequent enlargement of the small holes thus made by uneven weathering of the rims of the holes (see Chase and Nowell 1998). We must stress that the technique with which the holes could have been produced is essentially different from those (drilling, scraping, pressure flaking) with which holes were made in generally recognized Upper Paleolithic flutes and other perforated objects (see McComb 1989; Buisson and Dartiguepeyrou 1996; Albrecht et al. 1998; Hein and Hahn 1998).

Whereas more recent examples of flutes have bored holes, which is immediately evident from clear traces of drilling and indirectly from characteristic damage to drilling tools (borers), the holes in our example could only have been chipped (Bastiani and Turk 1997). This can be established directly from possible microscopic traces of chipping, and indirectly from specific damage to chipping tools. These tools, according to original typological nomenclature, are characterized as points, convergent scrapers, borers, denticulates, and so on (Bordes 1988). On socalled borers, which are older than the Upper Paleolithic, no damage would indicate a function in conformity with the name of the tool. The technique of boring is evidently more recent than the technique of chipping, although we can increase the effectiveness of chipping by rotating the tool (which does not mean drilling), making the hole more round than angular. We must stress that the technique of chipping is not recognized in the Upper Paleolithic and is so far completely unknown. An almost circular or oval hole is obtained only with a boring tool, that is, hand boring. Tools suitable for chipping holes have a number of irregular sharp edges on the sides, whereas the teeth of carnivores do not. Because of this, the outline of holes that have been chipped with stone tools are not completely circular and have at least one or more corners.

This was confirmed experimentally, in which chipped holes did not have distinct traces of tools and were indistinguishable in general and in detail from the holes on the flute as well as from holes experimentally punctured by artificial canine teeth. In chipping holes, specific damage, including breakage, occurred on the ventral side of pointed or tongued tools, similar to damage to numerous similar tools from the site (figure 15.3). A stone tool also more or less furrows the edge of a hole. Traces of such furrows (depressions) are present on the edges of both complete holes, and are difficult to explain if we opt for the hypothesis that the holes were made by a carnivore with teeth and subsequently enlarged by weathering (see Chase and Nowell 1998).

A bone with holes that is reminiscent of a flute is a very rare find. In all cases, they were made either accidentally by carnivores or by people who lived in the middle Paleolithic.

The probability that an undetermined carnivore pierced a bone several times and gave it the coincidental form of a flute without fragmenting it into pieces is very small. If this probability were greater, it is likely that there would have been more such finds, since there were at least as many beasts of prey in the middle Paleolithic as people. In addi-

a   b

c   d

Figure 15.3
Specific damage to the tip of the experimental tool (a, b) and similar damage to the tips of Mousterian tools (c, d) from Divje babe I site. (Photo: I. Lapajne.)

tion, such carnivores in cave dens were at least as active on bones, if not more so, than people in cave dwellings or shelters.

How likely it is that the holes in the bone were made by people is hard to estimate. However, for several reasons this find may, for the moment, be the only object of its kind. First, most Paleolithic sites throughout the world contain almost exclusively durable stone tools and waste created in their manufacture. Very few or none contain the less-durable or non-durable products for which, among other things, these tools were intended. Second, considerable time passes from the "invention" of some product to its general distribution and use; in the Paleolithic, in certain cases this lasted some tens of thousands of years. Third, archeology has very little chance of discovering the origin of anything (e.g., instrumental music) if such beginnings are restricted to a fraction of the huge space and time dimension, which it masters poorly anyway. Fourth, great danger exists that we overlook or mistakenly evaluate weak archeological signals because we do not want to reject generally accepted methodologies and seek new ones, and because we do not want to accept results of unproved methodologies.

It is quite clear that the enormous mass of Paleolithic stone tools were intended not only for hunting and collecting food, but also for manufacturing other accessories that served various purposes. The few very old spears from yew wood that were preserved are sufficient evidence of this (Oakley et al. 1977; Thieme and Veil 1985; McNabb 1989; Thieme 1996). In two hearths in Divje babe I, and only in Slovenia, we also found charcoal from yew in addition to more common charcoal. Yew wood probably did not serve as normal fuel, but is more likely to have been burned trimmings that were created during the production of unknown products, perhaps spears (Culiberg and Šercelj 1997). Most other products, including flutes, could also have been of wood. The wood of the elder is very suitable for flutes because of its large pith cavity. In the Epigravettian layer of the site at Jama v Lozi in western Slovenia, among the charcoal was found an 8-mm-long piece of elderwood charcoal with the pith cavity preserved (Šercelj and Culiberg 1985:60). This is the only example of such charcoal in Paleolithic sites in Slovenia.[7] Like yew, elderwood is an unusual fuel. It cannot be excluded that in this case, too, it is the remains of wood as a raw material and not as fuel. Why would someone go to the effort of making something from bone and similar raw materials if it could be made from wood? Bone, although more durable, is more difficult to work with and the desired result would, at least initially, be an exceptional occurrence!

Gradually, these exceptions would become more frequent in a specific cultural center and natural environment. Only then would archeology suddenly note and recognize an object that had been in use for a long time before this but had not been preserved because of nondurability of the material. The transition from a nondurable to a more durable material or the reverse could also occur so rapidly that it creates a false impression of the sudden flowering of something that gradually developed over an extended period or the decline of something that in reality persisted. With this we have arrived at the complex question of continuity and discontinuity which is raised so strongly in part of Europe between the middle and Upper Paleolithic by the (questionable) link between the different intellectual capacities of two human subspecies: Neanderthal and modern human.

Concerning unusual, mostly single, holes in bones (for a critical review, see Albrecht et al. 1998), Brodar (1985) established that they were present in large numbers in Slovenia at the beginning of the Upper Paleolithic and then completely disappeared. Some are almost identical to the holes in the Divje babe I bone (Turk, Dirjec, and Kavur 1997b: figure 11.12). The sudden appearance and disappearance of problematic holes in bones and their concentration to Aurignacian sites and scarcity in Mousterian sites (Holdermann and Serangeli 1998) may not be due to mass occurrence of cave bears as indicated by their remains in the Interpleniglacial, sudden extinction of carnivores, or sudden change in their behavior, but something else. From the European perspective in general and the Italian in particular (Leonardi 1988), it is notable that Slovenia in the late phase of the Upper Paleolithic (Gravettian and especially Epigravettian) was extremely poor in bone products and art.

If we assume that not all the holes were made by carnivores, we have no explanation in the literature of the purpose of individual unusual holes which sometimes appear on bones together with impressions of carnivore teeth and other characteristic carnivore damage. The following is possible. Paleolithic hunters were predators just like carnivores with whom they came in contact daily. They therefore identified with them. They saw that carnivores left traces on bones that long remained visible. Holes punctured by teeth made a great impression and they started to copy them by adding their own chipped holes, which meant simply, I, too, was here. Later, by adding holes and experimenting on other materials, a flute was created (Dauvois 1994:14).

In summary, if we bear in mind an explanation that is based on exceptional possibilities and positive results of every variety of experiment of archeological and biomechanical character, it is highly probable that the pierced bone from Divje babe I site is the product of human hands from the invention phase of some technological and cultural process; this is a great deal more probable than that it was heavily chewed. This raises the new question of what the product actually was. It is surprisingly similar to formally recognized Paleolithic bone flutes, so it seems appropriate to reconstruct the damaged object and experimentally verify its acoustic properties. We rely for this on our own knowledge of music in general and of instrumental music in particular. Our knowledge undoubtedly exceeds that of the people who made the object and perhaps used it as a flute, so any kind of reconstruction must be made very carefully.

Reconstruction and Musical Testing of the Suspected Bone Flute

The following hypothetical reconstruction of the object as a flute is possible: the hollow bone was cut straight and broken at the proximal end to create a fairly sharp cut edge. The distal end could have been untouched and closed. This end was later gnawed by some carnivore, or could have already been chewed when the presumed flute was made. Before cementing the flute in the breccia, both ends were additionally broken, each to the remains of a hole. In the flat, posterior side, two holes had been chipped. Perhaps a third hole was here; however, it was not made in the same way as the first two or contemporaneously with them. On the same side is a further irregular semicircular notch that may represent a mouthpiece or possibly the remains of a fourth hole. The morphology of the edges of the notch corresponds to the morphology of the rims of both complete holes. However, it is highly probable that a carnivore actually made the notch (Chase and Nowell 1998; d'Errico et al. 1998), and that it is not the remains of a hole or an artificial mouthpiece. The anterior side of the bone may have had a fifth hole. This "thumb hole" was made in the same way and at approximately the same time as the suspected third hole.

If we make a very free reconstruction, we get a flute with three finger holes and one thumb hole, a straight mouthpiece, and a closed or open end (figure 15.4a). The open end could serve as a second naturally formed mouthpiece. If we make a more conservative reconstruction, we get a flute with two finger holes, a straight mouthpiece, and a closed or open end (figure 15.4b). In this case, too, the open end could serve as a second naturally formed mouthpiece.

With the help of physical reconstructions based on these considerations, we analyzed the acoustic properties of the flute. We used a number of reconstructions since the original, despite its good condition and only partial damage, is inappropriate for such experiments, which might leave traces on it. The reconstructions were made from various materials and, as far as possible, corresponded to the original (figure 15.5). Several were made from the femurs of young bears, but only two are described here. The first was made from a fossilized bone of a cave bear of approximately the same age as the original find (figure 15.5a). Fossilized bone is not the most suitable material for acoustic experiments because, due to moisture

250 Drago Kunej and Ivan Turk

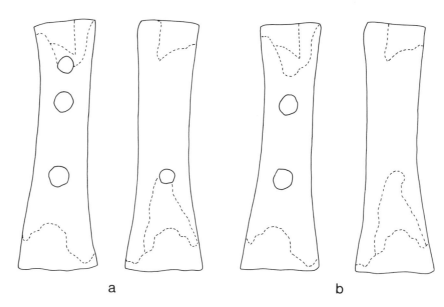

Figure 15.4
Archeological reconstructions of the pierced thigh bone as a flute. (a) A three-hole flute, and (b) a two-hole flute. The left part of each panel shows the posterior surface of the flute, and the right part the anterior surface.

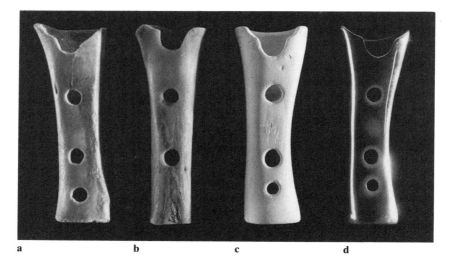

Figure 15.5
Photograph of four reconstructions of the suspected bone flute from (a) fossil bone of an extinct cave bear, (b) fresh bone of a contemporary brown bear, (c) plaster, and (d) metal.

and warmth from blowing, longitudinal cracks tended to appear on it and thus affect the acoustic properties. However, it best corresponded to the original in terms of natural shape, measurements, and other properties. The second flute was made from the fresh femur of a contemporary young brown bear (figure 15.5b). Experiments with it attempted to document the acoustic properties of fresh bone and how well such bones had to be cleaned and "processed" in order to sound. The shape of the bone matched the original fairly well, although its measurements were slightly different, since the analogous bone of a modern brown bear is longer and thinner (less robust) than that of Paleolithic cave bear.

We were best able to approximate the original measurements with reconstructions from plaster and metal (figures 15.5c and d). We modeled the flute, made a mold, and cast some specimens from plaster and metal. With these we were able to test the effect of the cut edge, the length of the bone, the size and position of individual holes, variation of individual pitch, and the like.

The basic acoustic question with any instrument is how it produces sound. Experiments with reconstructions of the flute attempted to answer this question. Determining the instrument's possible tuning and tonal range was initially of secondary importance. It has even been questioned whether such finds lend themselves to these kinds of determinations. In the literature, too, it is often noted (e.g., Horusitzky 1995) that holes in suspected flutes were probably made according to specific patterns and perhaps visual criteria, and that the role of changing pitch could be of secondary importance.

Similarities of the find to contemporary, mainly folk instruments (wind instruments) and numerous similar archeological finds that were interpreted as flutes led us to the idea that the bone with holes may represent an aerophone instrument, i.e., a wind instrument. In such an instrument, a standing wave in the column of air is stimulated in the cavity of the pipe. Depending on the way in which this occurs, aerophones can be divided into trumpets, reed pipes, and edge instruments (flutes) according to the classification of Hornbostel and Sachs (1914).

From acoustic and ethnomusicological points of view, the find most closely corresponds to an edge instrument (flute). It is characteristic of a trumpet that waves in the air column are stimulated by vibration (oscillation) of the musician's lips, which rest against the open part of the pipe (mouthpiece), which can also be specially shaped or adapted. Trumpets normally have fairly long pipes in which individual overtones can be formed. With shorter pipes, the sound is for the most part unclear and weak, similar to that of a modern mouthpiece for a brass instrument. The bone flute, tested as a trumpet, sounded unclear and weak. The role of holes in such a method of playing becomes questionable since they have barely any effect in changing the sound. We thus conclude that this find probably does not belong among trumpetlike instruments.

With reed pipes, a single or double reed made from bamboo or wood vibrates and stimulates a standing wave of air in the tube. Such musical instruments have a specially shaped mouthpiece for inserting or setting the reed, which is for the most part demanding to produce. Even greater skill is necessary for making or preparing the reed. The bone flute has no trace of any such mouthpiece or embouchure for a reed, nor in the archaeological literature can we find explanations or assumptions of Paleolithic finds of wind instruments of this type. We did not test our find as a reed pipe, since it seemed to us very unlikely that the find belonged to the family of reed instruments.

Cutting the narrow jet (lamella) of air that is directed at the cut edge (mouthpiece) of the instrument stimulates sound waves in the pipe. Eddies of air are created around the cut edge that vibrate the air in the tube and stimulate standing waves in the flute. To create a tone, the cut edge must be the right distance from the source of the jet of air, and the speed of the jet of air (strength of blowing) and sharpness and shape of the cut edge must be right. Frequencies of tones produced on the cut edge correspond to the flute's own harmonics. So a selection of a flute's harmonics can thus be achieved by varying the distance of the cut edge from the source of the jet of air and by various strengths of blowing. If the cut edge is not at an appropriate distance and of the right shape, or if it is not sharp enough for a specific flute, waves, and thus sound, cannot be stimulated, regardless of changes in froce and method of blowing.

With thin walls, the edge of the pipe provides a sufficiently sharp cut edge to stimulate sound. Such a method is familiar in end-blown flutes, for example panpipes, simple clef whistles, and rim-blown flutes (e.g., Balkan *kaval*). The manufacture of such instruments can be very simple, since the mouthpiece does not have to be specially shaped, but it is perhaps more difficult to play, since it must be properly placed against the lips, with a jet of air formed and directed at the cut edge to stimulate sound.

Acoustic experiments with reconstructions of the bone flute demonstrated that the wall of bone (compact bone) can in itself be a sharp enough cut edge, and it is unnecessary to process it further. This is particularly true at the point of transition from the diaphysis to the epiphysis, or metaphysis (at both proximal and distal ends), where the compact bone is thinner and more suitable for a cut edge (figures 15.6 and 15.7).[8]

Production of such a flute can be fairly simple. The bone is cut or broken at the metaphysis and the other end is left closed with the unremoved epiphysis. We thus obtain an instrument we can play as a clef whistle (pan pipe). If we remove both epiphyses, the lower end of the

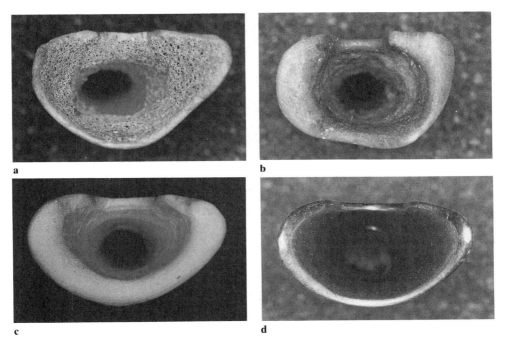

Figure 15.6
Photograph of the distal part of the bone in reconstructions of the bone flute from (a) fossil bone of an extinct cave bear, (b) fresh bone of a modern brown bear, (c) plaster, and (d) metal.

instrument can be closed with the hand or fingers, and thus at least two different tones can be produced. The upper and lower ends are determined in relation to the method of blowing into it: the upper end is the part that features the cut edge, the part we blow into. In the anatomic sense, the terms proximal and distal are used. We can say from experiments that it is easier to stimulate sound in the manner of panpipes with a closed pipe than an open one. (A closed flute is understood as having a closed lower end and an open flute as having the lower end open). With holes in the pipe, one can theoretically produce even more different tones, although playing such a flute (playing on a clef) is fairly difficult and demanding and, at least judging from our experiments, does not give greater sound possibilities (the function of the holes may thus become questionable).

We obtained completely different results if we rested the bone against the mouth lengthwise and slightly obliquely, and blew on the edge as with a rim-blown flute (figure 15.8). The sound was clear and pure, and with the aid of the holes and closing the lower end of the instrument, we could obtain tones of various pitch and even succeeded in overblowing to produce overtones. We could blow on the proximal or distal part, and

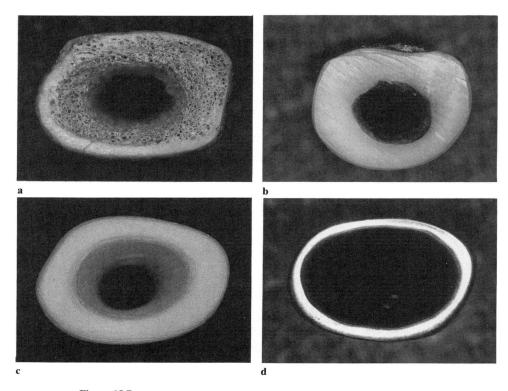

Figure 15.7
Photograph of the proximal part of the bone in reconstructed bone flutes from (a) fossil bone of an extinct cave bear, (b) fresh bone of a modern brown bear, (c) plaster, and (d) metal.

the thickness of the bone could be fairly large (4 mm). With a thinner cut edge (e.g., bone wall around 2 mm thick), blowing was easier to perform and the range of tone was significantly greater than with thicker cut edges, with which it was possible to produce only some lower tones. We could produce sound in such a way in all the reconstructions, at both proximal and distal ends. Blowing on the distal part of the bone, however, it was necessary to close the semicircular notch with plasticine or a finger. A sharp cut edge (thickness 1 to 2 mm) can be created fairly quickly and simply by removing the spongiosa at the metaphysis. A musical instrument of a number of ranges and tonal possibilities is thus obtained. If the spongiosa is not completely removed, the range of tone is reduced, and producing sound from the flute is more difficult.

If one of the (partial) holes at the edge is used as a simple mouthpiece with a cut edge (compare with figure 15.9a), we get a very widespread type of folk instrument, a notched flute (e.g., the South American *Kena* or Japanese *shakuhachi*). Specifically, the shallow notch at the wider distal end lends itself to this by the very shape and the manner of the

Figure 15.8
Producing sound in the bone flute as a rim-blown flute.

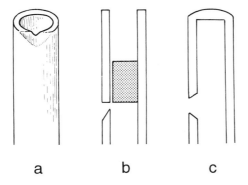

a   b   c

Figure 15.9
Common mouthpieces of flutes: (a) notched flute, (b) duct (block) flute, and (c) transverse flute.

break. The fanlike distal widening at the metaphysis forms a kind of natural mouthpiece and thus facilitates the embouchure. Such a manner of stimulating sound in a flute is also mentioned several times with other related archeological finds (Galin 1988), including an Upper Paleolithic find from Pas du Miroir in France (Marshack 1990) where a mouthpiece is clearly visible on a beautifully made and preserved flute. Some authors reject the possibility of such a manner of playing because, in their opinion, the femur of a young cave bear is too wide at the metaphysis for it to be possible to close most of the bone with the lips and at the same time direct air at the cut edge (Horusitzky 1955). This is the main reason for instruments similar to this one being classified among transverse flutes.

We demonstrated that it is possible to make sound on a bone flute in such a manner. We succeeded in doing this with all of the reconstructions. The flute could be held against the lips in various ways (for a more exact description, see Kunej 1997). The bone wall by the distal shallow notch, with a thickness of around 2 to 3 mm, had a sharp enough cut edge to enable a fine and pure sound, a fairly large tonal range, and the ability to produce overblowing. Even badly cleaned spongiosa on the fossil bone did not greatly hinder a fair range of tones; it was only more difficult to achieve higher tones and prevent overblowing. With the reconstruction from fresh bone, badly removed spongiosa had significantly less influence, since it is more homogeneous and even fatty and was not explicitly porous as is fossil bone. Thus it was simpler to produce sound and to achieve higher tones and overblowing with the reconstruction from fresh bone than with fossil bone.

This manner of stimulating sound seemed at first more suitable from acoustic and ethnomusicological standpoints, and was therefore the most thoroughly tested. The basic pitch and overblowing to produce overtones could be executed on the open or closed flute, and with the closed flute occasionally even to the second overtone (i.e., third harmonic).

Many modern flutes belong to the family of block or duct flutes. In principle, our find could also have been adapted into such an instrument if a short block (fipple) had been set in the bone to shape the jet of air and direct it at the cut edge (figure 15.9b). A block can also be provided by unremoved spongy bone in which a narrow incision is made (horizontal hole) that directs the jet of air at the cut edge. Production of such mouthpieces seems more demanding, and our find has no trace of such a mouthpiece or way of blowing, so a flute of this type was not acoustically tested.

Archeologists have classified a large number of bones with holes as transverse flutes, a possibility suggested in our instrument by the one hole that at least theoretically enables stimulation of sound. The cut edge is provided by the sharp edge of the hollowed-out hole on which we blow, and the instrument is thus held crosswise to the mouth (figure 15.9c). It can often be found in the professional literature that such a method of blowing on an instrument is more recent than lengthwise production of sound (e.g., Andreis 1958; Horusitzky 1955 after Sachs 1929).

We could also stimulate sound with reconstructions in the manner of transverse flutes. This was especially possible where the bone wall was thin, in which any kind of hole easily sufficed as a sharp cut edge. With thicker walls, it was necessary to make the hole more carefully in order to create a sharp, rectangular edge. We were able to achieve individual tones only with such a method of blowing, some fairly indistinct and difficult to produce. Overblowing to produce overtones was not possible.

The basic tone of a flute depends on its length and is fairly simple to calculate for cylindrical pipes, or at least pipes of the same mensure (internal cross section and shape, internal profile) throughout their length (e.g., Adlešič 1964; Kunej 1997). The basic frequency of flutes in which the mensure changes (conically, exponentially, etc.) is a great deal more difficult to calculate mathematically. The basic pitch, despite the same physical measurements (length, cross section at the ends), can differ considerably because of different internal profiles. The internal profile also greatly affects the sound spectrum (timbre, higher harmonic oscillations) and the practical possibility of producing sound at all. So with too wide or too narrow an internal profile, sound cannot be produced at all.

The interior (medullary cavity) of the femur of a young bear is not a regular cylindrical shape. At the proximal end, and even more at the distal end, the bone widens in a fan shape, which greatly influences the internal cross section of cortical bone. Determining the basic frequencies of a flute with such an internal profile from the physical measurements of the bone is extremely difficult. An additional difficulty in our find was caused by the fact that the exact length of the suspected flute is unknown, since the bone was damaged at the ends. However, we concluded that it could not have been much longer than as it was found, since bone itself does not allow this.[9] Therefore, we used the same length of bone as the original, except that we suitably terminated the damaged ends.

Changes in embouchure and strength of blowing represent a problem in determining the basic frequency of the flute. They can cause major differences in the basic pitch—by a whole tone or more—in the same flute and with the same method of blowing. Figure 15.10 shows the limits of intonation of the basic tone, which was fairly simple to produce for a particular reconstruction and method of blowing. The basic tone lay

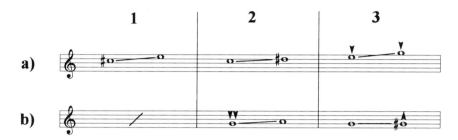

Figure 15.10
Comparison of the basic tones of notched flute reconstructions of the bone flute from (1) fossil bone, (2) fresh bone, and (3) metal. A range of basic tones is shown for each flute because of changes to the embouchure and strength of blowing. *Legend for signs used in figures 15.10–15.16*: The first note system (a) represents open flutes in which the first line shows obtained tones without overblowing, and the second line (where applicable), possible overblowing. The second note system (b) shows closed flutes in the same way. The third system (c) describes the obtained tones by tonal sequence. Empty notes represent boundary values of a specific tone due to changes in the embouchure and strength of blowing, and filled notes represent our estimate of tones that appeared most often with specific combinations of holes. An arrow above a note marks the direction of deviation of the marked intonation by around twenty cents, and a double arrow by around forty cents. Filled arrows (triangles) replace notes of a high penetrating whistle, which were difficult to measure and notate. The effect of partial closing and stopping of the lower end of the instrument is marked with a vertical line under the basic note. The light fields represent combinations, which we obtained with the two holes completely preserved on the original.

somewhere between the cited limits and is difficult to determine clearly, since it also depends on the temperature and playability of the instrument, which, judging from the experiments, could change intonation by around half a tone. Not least, the experience and practice of the experimenter are also important.

We obtained interesting results from testing and comparing almost identical plaster and metal reconstructions (casts). Five flutes were made of plaster from the same mold. Their distal and proximal ends were processed by hand and kept as uniform as possible. The deviation of basic intonation of individual flutes was surprising, assessed at more than a whole tone. Exact measurement was difficult to perform because of the change in pitch due to the embouchure and strength of blowing. With cast metal flutes, which had no hand molding, no such deviation occurred—they were almost indistinguishable. The deviation can be explained by the different internal profiles of flutes from plaster and different positions against the mouth of the experimenter. Thus even small deviations can create considerable changes in the basic tone of similar instruments.

Even greater deviation among flutes of the same length and played in the same way can be noticed in comparing various reconstructions having similar mouthpieces (figures 15.6 and 15.7). Limits of the range

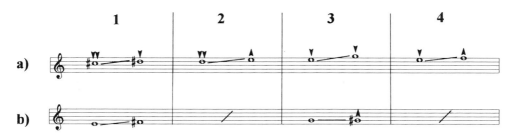

Figure 15.11
Comparison of the basic tones of a metal reconstruction of the bone flute played in different ways: (1) as a rim-blown flute blown at the distal end, (2) as a rim-blown flute blown at the proximal end, (3) as a notched flute, and (4) as a transverse flute blown at hole two and with the proximal part closed.

of basic intonation of individual flutes can be seen in figure 15.10, and the largest deviation achieves an interval of almost a perfect fifth. Here, too, the internal shape and size of the mouthpiece (manner and shape of distal widening of the bone at the metaphysis and how thoroughly the spongiosa is removed) are clearly very important.

A new difficulty in determining basic pitch was seen in the various possible ways of blowing into the flute (e.g., notched, rim-blown, transverse), since basic tones produced in the different ways varied greatly. As an example, figure 15.11 shows the basic tones of the metal flute played in four different ways. It follows from this that we can only guess at the more exact basic frequency of the flute.

Even greater difficulties appeared when we attempted to determine the selection of sounds (possible musical scale) that could be drawn from a flute, since a change in pitch can be achieved in a number of ways: changing the embouchure and strength of blowing, partly or completely closing the lower end of the instrument, overblowing, and lengthening and shortening of the length of the instrument. We successfully used all these methods in our experiments, and they appreciably affected the pitch. Embouchure and strength of blowing had an influence on changing the basic tone and had similar effects on other possible tones (figures 15.12, 15.13, and 15.14).

Partly closing the lower part of the flute theoretically enables a continuous change of pitch between closed and open instruments. With our reconstructions, we succeeded in executing small, continuous changes of tone, and the instruments quickly transformed from closed to open type (or vice versa). Such closure could also be achieved by placing the fingers at the lower end of the instrument (stopping the hole). In such a way, the tone could be precisely changed continuously downward by more than a perfect fourth. The length of the instrument could be extended in a simple way only with the hand, but this did not have much effect in

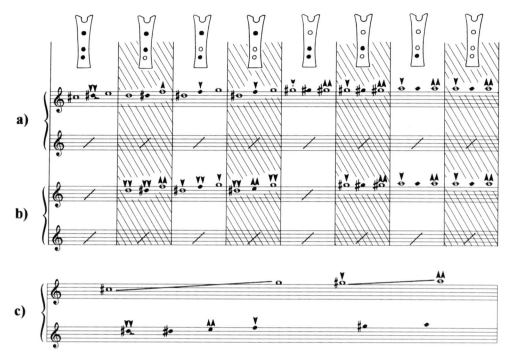

Figure 15.12
Obtained tones from fossil reconstruction of the bone flute with various combinations of open and closed holes. The flute was blown as a notched flute.

changing the sound. However, it could be combined successfully with partial or complete closure of the end of the flute.

The most common method of changing the sound with wind instruments is apparent shortening of their length with the aid of holes. One can achieve fairly pure and exact changes of pitch (jumps) with holes. In general, it is true that the appearance of holes represents a somewhat higher level of development of wind instruments, since it increases their expressive power.

The bone find has at least two indisputable holes. We made two or three holes on the various reconstructions and tested their effect on changing the sound (we have not yet tested the effect of the possible thumb hole). The number and probability of individual holes are not satisfactorily clarified from an archeological point of view, so we can assume only two holes with certainty.

Figures 15.12, 15.13, and 15.14 show the measured tones we obtained with various combinations of closing and opening the holes of individual reconstructions. For each combination, empty notes mark the limit values of the continuous range of tone we obtained with the same grip

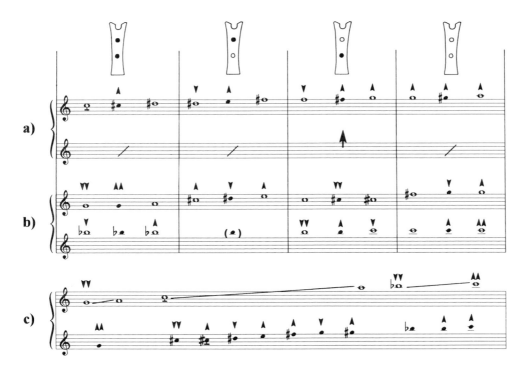

Figure 15.13
Tones obtained from a reconstruction of the bone flute from fresh bear bone with various combinations of closed and open holes. The flute was played as a notched flute.

and various embouchures and strengths of blowing. With the full notes in the center, we indicated our assessment of the tone that sounds most often and most readily with a specific combination. Deviation from the cited (assessed) tone could be considerable in individual cases, but lies somewhere within the marked range. (A table of tones of the flute from plaster is not given since results were fairly similar to those with metal flutes.)

All the flutes in figures 15.12, 15.13, and 15.14 were treated as notched flutes. They have the same length, very similar shape, and almost the same mouthpiece (see figure 15.6). A comparison and analysis of the results in the different tables is very interesting. We were above all surprised that we could produce a fairly wide range of tones with all reconstructions. So, within specific ranges of frequency, we could produce individual popular tunes (and thus scales). This fact does not make the task of seeking possible original scales any easier; in fact it blurs it and makes it much more difficult (see B. Fink in Anonymous 1997). If we attempt an uncritical generalization of the results and take into consideration only individual assessments of the most frequent tones with each

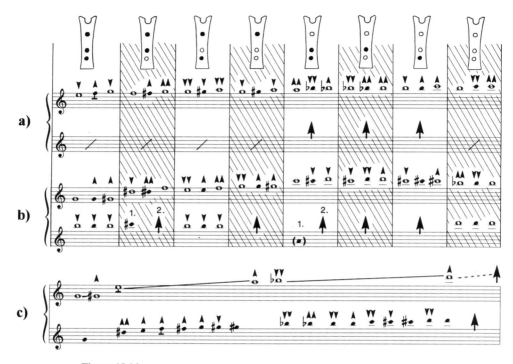

Figure 15.14
Tones obtained from a metal reconstruction of the bone flute with various combinations
of closed and open holes. The flute was played as a notched flute.

combination, we obtain fairly varied and apparently disorganized results.
The search for possible scales of the flute was not our basic purpose,
however, so we did not enter into it in detail.

The difficulties increase further if we compare figures 15.14 (notched
flute) and 15.15 (rim-blown flute). Figure 15.15 shows possible tones
from the same flute (metal reconstruction) produced by blowing the
distal end of the bone as a rim-blown flute. The effect of the holes on
changing pitch is somewhat altered. This is understandable, since the
effective length of the flute changed because of stimulating the instrument at different places, and thus also the relative positions of the holes.
This is even more clearly noticeable by blowing the metal flute as a rim-
blown flute at the proximal end (figure 15.16). In contrast, it can be established that the influence of holes in the central part (both entirely
preserved holes) does not essentially change with substitution of the
proximal and distal parts for blowing into the flute, since the holes are
made in the bone fairly symmetrically. So we can play on such an instrument from either end and obtain almost the same result.

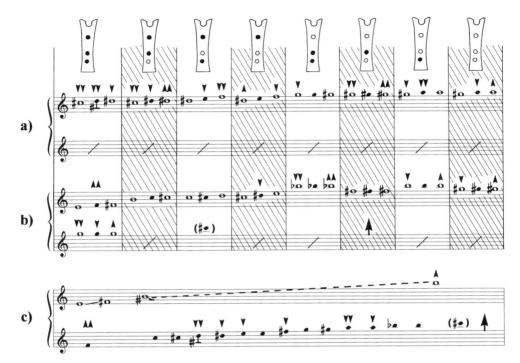

Figure 15.15
Tones obtained from a metal reconstruction of the bone flute with various combinations of closed and open holes. The flute is played at the distal end of the bone as a rim-blown flute.

Finally, the size of individual holes has a great influence on changing pitch. Holes of smaller diameter have less of an effect and larger-diameter holes have more. But this finding in principle does not apply to the same extent to all holes in the flute. The closer the hole is to the cut edge, the more the pitch changes with changes in diameter. We also tested and demonstrated this on our reconstructions. By way of illustration let us mention just one comparison of two extreme holes. In playing the plaster reconstruction as a notched flute, we changed the size of the hole nearest to the cut edge (hole no. 1) and the most distant hole (hole no. 3). The same change in the diameter of the hole from 4 to 6 mm affected pitch differently in the two holes. With hole number 3, the intonation was raised by around 30 cents, but with hole number 1, it was raised by more than 80 cents.

From what has been said, it can be concluded that seeking the possible tonal sequence of the suspected bone flute may for the moment be questionable and even senseless, especially since we do not know the exact length of the instrument, the number of holes in it, or the way of

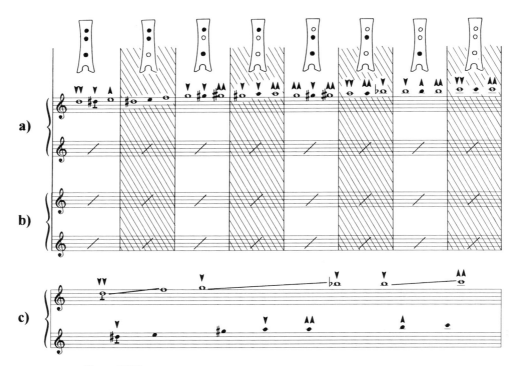

Figure 15.16
Tones obtained from a metal reconstruction of the bone flute with various combinations of closed and open holes. The flute is played at the proximal part of the bone as a rim-blown flute.

playing it, all of which decisively influence its tonal possibilities. Even if we were to know all this (as we assumed with our reconstructions), the pitch is so changed by the method of producing sound, changes to the embouchure, and strength of blowing that we can obtain an almost continuous tonal spectrum in a wide range of frequencies and produce tones of almost arbitrary pitch. If we attempt to reconstruct the sound possibilities of an instrument merely from external measurements of the only archeological find of this type from this period, and on this basis further define the aesthetic standards of the population that used it, we can easily reach mistaken conclusions and results.[10]

This chapter attempted to clarify at least partially the meaning and acoustic properties of the archeological find of a bone with holes and show its possible ethnomusicological significance. The find can be explained as a sound or signal aid, perhaps even as a musical instrument with specific expressive power. Of course, it opens a large number of additional questions and it is not possible for the moment to answer all of them. Perhaps future finds of the same age will assist in answering these questions.

Notes

1. We will limit ourselves in the rest of the text to the European Paleolithic, which, because of a long tradition of archeological research, is relatively well known.

2. Preliminary dating by electron spin resonance gave a range for layer 13 from c. 34,000 to c. 88,000 years (Lau et al. 1997:table 4). New datings are being prepared.

3. Preliminary electron spin resonance dating of layer 20 showed that the layer is only from c. 38,000 to c. 49,000 years old (Lau et al. 1997:table 4), which is undoubtedly too young.

4. No find of a skeleton of a completely modern human in Europe is older than 35,000 years (Allsworth-Jones 1986:217; Heiss 1994).

5. Carnivores usually made such damage (notches) on the thinner, anterior side of bone, as seen in numerous examples from the site. We must stress that the unusual location of the notch on the flatter posterior side bone is appropriate for the mouthpiece of the flute.

6. Strength was measured at the Laboratory of Non-linear Mechanics, Faculty of Mechanical Engineering in Ljubljana using steel points, bronze casts of wolf and hyena dentition, and fresh thigh bones of brown bear. In widening the experimental holes to the size of those on the suspected flute, exerting the same force as for piercing, all juvenile bones cracked. We thank Professors J. Grum and F. Kosel for their help.

7. Elder appears only among pollen in one case at the Divje babe I site, which proves its presence in the period of the Middle Paleolithic in Slovenia (Šercelj and Culiberg 1991).

8. Sound can also be produced with only partly or poorly removed spongiosa of both fresh and fossil bones.

9. If we envisage an open flute, it is necessary to remove both epiphyses. It is most suitable and simplest to remove the epiphysis at the transition to the diaphysis, where bone widens and its wall is thinner, since trabecular bone can be fairly easily removed there to obtain the necessary hollow pipe. In the case of a closed flute, only one epiphysis need be removed. However, despite considerable external changes, the cavity of the pipe in the bone is not increased (perhaps even shortened), since at the metaphysis, spongiosa fills the cavity. This also appeared in the reconstructions.

10. Even today with many folk instruments, players do not exploit all the theoretical and practical sound possibilities of instruments, but restrict themselves to a relatively narrow tonal range that is entirely sufficient for them (see Strajnar 1988). Thus the tonal possibilities of an instrument in and of themselves can in no way determine its method of use.

References

Adlešič, M. (1964). *Svet zvoka in Glasbe*. Ljubljana: Mladinska knjiga.

Albrecht, G., Holdermann, C.-S., Kerig, T., Lechterbeck, J., and Serangeli, J. (1998). "Flöten" aus Bärenknochen: Die frühesten Musikinstrumente? *Archäologisches Korrespondenzblatt* 28:1–19.

Allsworth-Jones, P. (1986). *The Szeletian and the Transition from Middle to Upper Palaeolithic in Central Europe*. Oxford: Clarendon Press.

Andreis, J. (Ed.) (1958). *Muzička Enciklopedija*. Zagreb: Leksikografski zavod FNRJ.

Anonymous (1997). Early music. *Science* 276:205.

Bastiani, G. and Turk, I. (1997). Results from the experimental manufacture of bone flute with stone tools. In I. Turk (Ed.) *Mousterian "Bone Flute" and Other Finds from Divje babe I Cave Site in Slovenia* (pp. 176–178). Ljubljana: Založba ZRC.

Bordes, F. (1988). *Typologie du Paléolithique Ancien et Moyen*. Paris: Presses du CNRS.

Bortolami, G. C., Fontes, J. C., Markgraf, V., and Saliege, J. F. (1977). Land, sea and climate in the northern Adriatic region during the late Pleistocene and Holocene. *Palaeogeography, Palaeoclimatology, Palaeoecology* 21:139–156.

Brodar, M. (1985). Fossile Knochendurchlochungen. Luknje v fosilnih kosteh. In S. Grafe-nauer, M. Pleničar, and K. Drobne (Eds.) *Ivan Rakovec volume. Zbornik Ivana Rakovca. Razprave IV. Razreda SAZU*, 26 (pp. 29–48). Ljubljana: Slovenska Akademija Znanosti in Umetnosti.

Broglio, A. (Ed.) (1984). Paleolitico e Mesolitico. In A. Aspes (Ed.) *Il Veneto nell'antichita: Preistoria e Protostoria*, vol. 1 (pp. 37–56). Verona: Banca Popolare di Verona.

Broglio, A. (1996–1997). L'estinzione dell'uomo di Neandertal e la comparsa dell'uomo moderno in Europa. Le evidenze della Grotta di Fumane nei Monti Lessini. *Atti dell'Isti-tuto Veneto di Scienze, Lettere ed Arti: Classe di Scienze Fisiche, Matematiche e Naturali* 155:1–55.

Buisson, D. (1990). Les flutes paléolithiques d'Isturitz (Pyrénées-Atlantiques). *Bulletin de la Société Préhistorique Française* 87:420–433.

Buisson, D. and Dartiguepeyrou, S. (1996). Fabriquer une flute au Paléolithique supérieur: Récit d'une expérimentation. *Antiquités Nationales* 28:145–148.

Chase, P. G. and Nowell, A. (1998). Taphonomy of a suggested middle Paleolithic bone flute from Slovenia. *Current Anthropology* 39:549–553.

Culiberg, M. and Šercelj, A. (1997). Palaeobotanic research of the Divje babe I cave. In I. Turk (Ed.) *Mousterian "Bone Flute" and Other Finds from Divje babe I Cave Site in Slove-nia* (pp. 73–83). Ljubljana: Založba ZRC.

Dauvois, M. (1994). Les témoins sonores paléolithiques extérieur and souterrain. In M. Otte (Ed.) *"Sons originels." Préhistoire de la Musique*, E.R.A.U.L. 61 (pp. 11–32). Liège: Université de Liège.

d'Errico, F. and Villa, P. (1997). Holes and grooves: The contribution of microscopy and taphonomy to the problem of art origins. *Journal of Human Evolution* 33:1–33.

d'Errico, F., Villa, P., Pinto Llona, A. C., and Ruiz Idarraga, R. (1998). A middle Palaeolithic origin of music? Using cave-bear bone accumulations to assess the Divje babe I bone "flute." *Antiquity* 72:65–79.

Einwögerer, T. and Käfer, B. (1998). Eine Jungpaläolithische Knochenflöte aus der Station Grubgraben bei Kammern, Niederösterreich. Mit einem Beitrag von Florian A. Fladerer. *Archäologisches Korrespondenzblatt* 28:21–30.

Fages, G. and Mourer-Chauviré, C. (1983). La flute en os d'oiseau de la grotte sépulcrale de Veyreau (Aveyron) et inventaire des flutes préhistoriques d' Europe. In F. Poplin (Ed.) *La Faune et l'Homme Préhistorique: Dix Etudes en Hommage à Jean Bouchud* (pp. 95–103). Paris: C.N.R.S. and Service des Fouilles et Antiquités.

Galin, K. (1988). Archaeological findings of musical instruments in Yugoslavia. In Zorica Rajković (Ed.) *Narodna Umjetnost*, special issue 2 (pp. 123–148). Zagreb: Institute of Folklore Research.

Gamble, C. (1986). *The Palaeolithic Settlement of Europe*. Cambridge, UK: Cambridge University Press.

Gorjanović-Kramberger, D. (1913). Život i kultura diluvijalnoga čovjeka iz Krapine u Hrvatskoj. (Hominis diluvialis e Krapina in Croatia vita et cultura.) In: Dijela Jugoslavenske akademije znanosti i umjetnosti, 23. Zagreb: Knjižara Jugoslavenske akademije (Đuro Trpinac).

Hahn, J. (1983). Eiszeitliche Jäger zwischen 35,000 und 15,000 Jahren vor heute. In H. Müller-Beck (Ed.) *Urgeschichte in Baden-Württemberg* (pp. 273–330). Stuttgart: Theiss.

Hahn, J. and Münzel, S. (1995). Knochenflöten aus dem Aurignacien des Geissenklösterle bei Blaubeuren, Alb-Donau-Kreis. *Fundberichte aus Baden-Württemberg* 20:1–12.

Hein, W. and Hahn, J. (1998). Experimentelle Nachbildung von Knochenflöten aus dem Aurignacien der Geissenklösterle-Höhle. In M. Fansa (Ed.) *Experimentelle Archäologie Bilanz 1997, Symposium in Bad Buchau Federsee Museum Oktober 1996* (pp. 65–73). Oldenburg: Isensee.

Heiss, S. J. (1994). Homo erectus, Neandertaler und Cromagnon. Kulturgeschichtliche Untersuchungen zu Theorien der Entwicklung des modernen Menschen. In H. Ziegert (Ed.) *Arbeiten zur Urgeschichte des Menschen*, vol. 17. Frankfurt am Main: Lang.

Holdermann, C.-S. and Serangeli, J. (1998). Flöten an Höhlenbärenknochen: Spekulatio-nen oder Beweise? *Mitteilungsblatt der Gesellschaft für Urgeschichte* 6:7–19.

von Hornbostel, E. M. and Sachs, C. (1914). Systematik der Musikinstrumente. *Zeitschrift für Ethnologie* 46:553–590.

Horusitzky, Z. (1955). Eine Knochenflöte aus der Höhle von Istállósko. *Acta Archeologica* 5:33–140.

Karavanić, I. (1995). Upper Paleolithic occupation levels and late-occurring Neanderthal at Vindija cave (Croatia) in the context of central Europe and the Balkans. *Journal of Anthropological Research* 51:9–35.

Ku, T.-L. (1997). Uranium series dating of bone samples from Divje babe I cave. In I. Turk (Ed.) *Mousterian "Bone Flute" and Other Finds from Divje babe I Cave Site in Slovenia* (pp. 64–65). Ljubljana: Založba ZRC.

Kunej, D. (1997). Acoustic findings on the basis of reconstructions of a presumed bone flute. In I. Turk (Ed.) *Mousterian "Bone Flute" and Other Finds from Divje babe I Cave Site in Slovenia* (pp. 185–197). Ljubljana: Založba ZRC.

Lau, B., Blackwell, B. A. B., Schwarcz, H. P., Turk, I., and Blickstein, J. I. (1997). Dating a flautist? Using ESR (electron spin resonance) in the Mousterian cave deposits at Divje babe I, Slovenia. *Geoarchaeology* 12:507–536.

Le Brech, C., Hamel, L., Le Nihouannen, J. C., and Daculsi, G. (1997). Epidemiological study of canine teeth fractures in military dogs. *Journal of Veterinary Dentistry* 14:51–55.

Leonardi, P. (1988). Art paléolithique mobilier et pariétal en Italie. *L'Anthropologie* 92:139–202.

Leonardi, P. and Broglio, A. (1962). Le paléolithiques de la Vénétie. *Annali dell'Universita di Ferrara (N.s.)* Supplement 1:3–118.

Lindner, D. L., Manfra Marretta, S., Pijanowski, G. J., Johnson, A. L., and Smith, C. W. (1995). Measurement of bite force in dogs: A pilot study. *Journal of Veterinary Dentistry* 12:49–52.

López Bayón, I., Straus, L. G., Léotard, J.-M., Lacroix, P., and Teheux, E. (1997). L'industrie osseuse du magdalenien du Bois Laiterie. In M. Otte and L. G. Straus (Eds.) *La grotte du Bois Laiterie. E.R.A.U.L.*, 80 (pp. 257–277). Liège: Université de Liège.

Malez, M. (Ed.) (1970). *Krapina 1899–1969.* Zagreb: Mladost.

Malez, M. (1974). Noviji rezultati istraživanja paleolitika u Velikoj pećini, Veternici i Šandalji (with German summary). *Arheološki Radovi i Rasprave Jugoslavenske Akademije Znanosti i Umjetnosti* 7:7–44.

Malez, M. (1978). Novija istraživanja paleolitika u Hrvatskom zagorju (with German summary). In Z. Rapanic (Ed.) *Arheološka Istraživanja u Sjeverozapadnoj Hrvatskoj: Izdanja Hrvatskog Arheološkog Društva* (pp. 6–69). Zagreb: Hrvatsko arheološko društvo.

Marshack, A. (1988). The Neanderthals and the human capacity for symbolic thought: Cognitive and problem solving aspects of Mousterian symbol. In M. Otte (Ed.) *L'Homme de Neandertal, 5: La Pensée* 32 (pp. 57–92). Liège: Université de Liège.

Marshack, A. (1990). Early hominid symbol and evolution of the human capacity. In P. Mellars (Ed.) *The Emergence of Modern Humans: An Archaeological Perspective* (pp. 457–498). Edinburgh: Edinburgh University Press.

McComb, P. (1989). *Upper Palaeolithic Osseous Artifacts from Britain and Belgium: An Inventory and Technological Description.* Oxford: B.A.R.

McNabb, J. (1989). Sticks and stones: A possible experimental solution to the question of how the Clacton spear point was made. *Proceedings of the Prehistoric Society* 55:251–271.

Mellars, P. (1996). *The Neanderthal Legacy: An Archaeological Perspective from Western Europe.* Princeton, NJ: Princeton University Press.

Miracle, P. T. (1995). *Broad-Spectrum Adaptations Re-examined: Hunter-Gatherer Responses to Late Glacial Environmental Changes in the Eastern Adriatic.* Doctoral Dissertation, University of Michigan.

Nelson, D. E. (1997). Radiocarbon dating of bone and charcoal from Divje babe I cave. In I. Turk (Ed.) *Mousterian "Bone Flute" and Other Finds from Divje babe I Cave Site in Slovenia* (pp. 51–64). Ljubljana: Založba ZRC.

Oakley, K. P., Andrews, P., Keeley, L. H., and Desmond Clark, J. (1977). A reappraisal of the Clacton spearpoint. *Proceedings of the Prehistoric Society* 43:13–30.

Palma di Cesnola, A. (1996). *Le Paléolithique Inférieur et Moyen en Italie: Préhistoire d'Europe 1.* Grenoble: Jérome Millon.

Radovčić, J., Smith, F. H., Trinkaus, E., and Wolpoff, M. H. (1988). *The Krapina Hominids: An Illustrated Catalog of Skeletal Collection.* Zagreb: Mladost and Croatian Natural History Museum.

Rottländer, R. C. A. (1996). Frühe Flöten und die Ausbildung der Musikalischen Hörgewohnheiten des Paläolithischen Menschen. In J. Campen, J. Hanh and M. Uerpmann (Eds.) *Spuren der Jagd: Die Jagd nach Spuren. Festschrift für Hansjürgen Müller-Beck* (pp. 35–40). Tübingen: Mo Vince.

Sachs, C. (1929). *Geist und Werden der Musikinstrumente.* Berlin: D. Reimer.

Sadie, S. (Ed.). (1984). *The New Grove Dictionary of Musical Instruments*, 1. London: Macmillan.

Šercelj, A. and Culiberg, M. (1985). Rastlinski ostanki v paleolitskih postajah v Sloveniji (with German summary). *Poročilo o Raziskovanju Paleolita, Neolita in Eneolita v Sloveniji* 13:53–66.

Šercelj, A. and Culiberg, M. (1991). Palinološke in antrakotomske raziskave sedimentov iz paleolitske postaje Divje babe I (with English summary). *Razprave 4. Razreda SAZU* 32:129–152.

Smith, F. H. (1982). Upper Pleistocene hominid evolution in south central Europe: A review of the evidence and analysis of trends. *Current Anthropology* 23:667–703.

Stepanchuk, V. N. (1993). Prolom II: A middle Palaeolithic cave site in the eastern Crimea with non-utilitarian bone artefacts. *Proceedings of the Prehistoric Society* 59:17–37.

Stiner, M. C. (1995). *Honor Among Thieves.* Princeton, NJ: Princeton University Press.

Strajnar, J. (1988). Citira. Instrumentalna glasba v Reziji. La musica strumentale in Val di Resia. Udine: Pizzicato, and Trst: Založništvo tržaškega tiska.

Thieme, H. (1996). Altpaläolithische Werfspeere aus Schöningen, Niedersachsen. Ein Vorbericht. *Archäologisches Korrespondenzblatt* 26:377–393.

Thieme, H. and Veil, S. (1985). Neue Untersuchungen zum eemzeitlichen Elefanten-Jagdplatz Lehringen, Ldkr. Verden. Mit Beiträgen von W. Meyer, J. Möller and H. Plisson. *Die Kunde N.F.* 36:11–58.

Turk, I. (Ed.) (1997). *Mousterian "Bone Flute" and Other Finds from Divje babe I Cave Site in Slovenia.* Ljubljana: Založba ZRC.

Turk, I. and Dirjec, J. (1997). Taphonomy of limb bones of cave bear. In I. Turk (Ed.) *Mousterian "Bone Flute" and Other Finds from Divje babe I Cave Site in Slovenia* (pp. 115–118). Ljubljana, Založba ZRC.

Turk, I., Dirjec, J., and Kavur, B. (1995). Ali so v Sloveniji našli najstarejše glasbilo v Evropi? (with English summary). *Razprave IV. Razreda SAZU* 36:287–293.

Turk, I., Dirjec, J., and Kavur, B. (1997a). A-t-on trouvé en Slovénie le plus vieil instrument de musique d'Europe? *Anthropologie* 101:531–540.

Turk, I., Dirjec, J., and Kavur, B. (1997b). Description and explanation of the origin of the suspected bone flute. Experimantal manufacture of the bone flute with stone tools. In I. Turk (Ed.) *Mousterian "Bone Flute" and Other Finds from Divje babe I Cave Site in Slovenia* (pp. 157–178). Ljubljana: Založba ZRC.

Turk, I. and Stele, F. (1997). *At the Dawn of Time. Divje babe I: Potocka Zijalka.* Ljubljana: Znanstvenoraziskovalni center Slovenske akademije znanosti in umetnosti.

Wolpoff, M. H., Smith, F. H., Malez, M., Radovčić, J., and Rukavina, D. (1981). Upper Pleistocene human remains from Vindija cave, Croatia, Yugoslavia. *American Journal of Physical Anthropology* 54:499–545.

IV THEORIES OF MUSIC ORIGIN

16   The "Musilanguage" Model of Music Evolution

Steven Brown

Abstract

Analysis of the phrase structure and phonological properties of musical and linguistic utterances suggests that music and language evolved from a common ancestor, something I refer to as the "musilanguage" stage. In this view, the many structural features shared between music and language are the result of their emergence from a joint evolutionary precursor rather than from fortuitous parallelism or from one function begetting the other. Music and language are seen as reciprocal specializations of a dual-natured referential emotive communicative precursor, whereby music emphasizes sound as emotive meaning and language emphasizes sound as referential meaning. The musilanguage stage must have at least three properties for it to qualify as both a precursor and scaffold for the evolution of music and language: lexical tone, combinatorial phrase formation, and expressive phrasing mechanisms.

Beyond Music-Language Metaphors

Theories of music origin come in two basic varieties: structural models and functional models. Structural models look to the acoustic properties of music as outgrowths of homologous precursor functions, whereas functional models look to the adaptive roles of music as determinants of its structural design features. This chapter presents a structural model of music evolution. Functional models are presented elsewhere (Brown in press).

Before discussing music from an evolutionary perspective, it is important to note that two different modes of perceiving, producing, and responding to musical sound patterns exist, one involving emotive meaning and the other involving referential meaning. These I call, respectively, the acoustic and vehicle modes. The acoustic mode refers to the immediate, on-line, emotive aspect of sound perception and production. It deals with the emotive interpretation of musical sound patterns through two processes that I call "sound emotion" and "sentic modulation." It is an inextricably acoustic mode of operation. The vehicle mode refers to the off-line, referential form of sound perception and production. It is a representational mode of music operation that results from the influence of human linguistic capacity on music cognition.[1] The vehicle mode includes the contexts of musical performance and contents of musical works, where both of these involve complex systems of cultural meaning (see footnote 2 for details).

This distinction between the acoustic and vehicle modes addresses an important issue in contemporary musicology: the conflict between absolutists, who view music as pure sound-emotion, and referentialists, who view it as pure sound-reference (discussed in Feld and Fox 1994). Seeing music in terms of the acoustic mode-vehicle mode duality permits reconciliation of the two viewpoints by suggesting that two different modes of perceiving, producing and responding to musical sound patterns exist, one involving emotive meaning and one referential meaning. These two modes act in parallel and are alternative interpretations of the same acoustic stimulus.

The very notion of a vehicle mode for music (or of referentialism) leads immediately to the question of the extent to which music functions like a language. Serious consideration of this question dates back at least to the eighteenth century if not earlier (Thomas 1995). No doubt the question hinges on the criteria by which one calls a given system a language, and this has led many thinkers to clarify notions of musical syntax and semantics (Bernstein 1976; Sloboda 1985; Clarke 1989; Aiello 1994; Swain 1995, 1996). The reciprocal question deals with the extent to which speech exploits musical properties for the purposes of linguistic communication in the form of speech melody and rhythm. But, whereas the metaphors go both ways, from language to music and back again, it is important to realize that these accounts are only ever seen as metaphors. Concepts such as musical language (Swain 1997) and speech melody are never taken beyond the domain of metaphor into the domain of mechanism. That is why, to me, this metaphor making misses the point that music and language have strong underlying biological similarities in addition to equally strong differences. Converging evidence from several lines of investigation reveals that the similarities between music and language are not just the stuff of metaphors but a reflection of something much deeper.

Given the extensive practice of metaphor making in linguistics and musicology, how can we best think about the similarities that exist between music and language? (I discuss only the acoustic route of language communication, and thus speech. A discussion of gesture, which is relevant to the evolution of both language and dance, will be presented at a future time.) Perhaps the best place to start is at the point of greatest distinction: grammar. The grammar metaphor is quite pervasive in musicology. The notion that musical phrase structures (can) have a hierarchical organization similar to that of linguistic sentences, an idea presented elegantly by Lerdahl and Jackendoff (1983), must be viewed as pure parallelism. In other words, the hierarchical organization of pitches and pulses in a Bach chorale is only loosely related to the hierarchical organization of words in a sentence exactly because the constituent elements, and thus the phrases themselves, are so completely different. However, to the extent that the generativity analogy works at all in music, it is only because of important underlying features (which Lerdahl and Jackendoff themselves make mention of in their closing pages) that provide a biological justification for this potential for hierarchical organization in music. What this means is that music and language must converge at some deep level to have hierarchical organization flower from two such different grammatical systems.

What is this point of convergence? The answer, briefly, is combinatorial syntax and intonational phrasing. First, in both language and music, the phrase is the basic unit of structure and function. It is what makes speaking and singing different from grunting and screaming. In both, a limited repertoire of discrete units is chosen out of an infinite number of possible acoustic elements, such that phrases are generated through combinatorial arrangements of these unitary elements. Thus, the use of discrete building blocks and the generation of higher-order structures through combinatorial rules is a major point of similarity between music and language. But it is not the whole story, as both make extensive use of expressive phrasing. Phrasing refers to modulation of the basic acoustic properties of combinatorially organized phrases for the purposes of conveying emphasis, emotional state, and emotive meaning. It can occur at two levels, local and global. Local modulation selectively affects individual elements of the phrase in the context of the whole phrase, whereas global modulation affects the whole phrase in a rather equivalent manner. From this standpoint, both speech phrases and musical phrases are melodorhythmic structures in which melody and rhythm are derived from three sources: acoustic properties of the fundamental units (pitch sets, intensity values and duration values in music; phonemes and phonological feet in speech); sequential arrangement of such units in a given phrase (combinatorial rules in both domains); and expressive phrasing mechanisms that modulate the basic acoustic properties of the phrase for expressive emphasis and intention (phrasing rules in both domains).

These properties of combinatorial syntax and intonational phrasing set the stage for the overall structural features of music and language. Perhaps the most important realization about their cognitive organization is that both systems function on two separate levels, and that these levels emerge out of the common set of principles described above (figure 16.1). One plane is the phonological level and the other is the meaning level. The first one is acoustic and is based on the principles of discreteness, combinatoriality, and phrasing. It is governed by a type of phonological syntax (see Marler, this volume) dealing with the selection and organization of sound units for the purposes of communication. The meaning level is where these acoustic elements are interpreted for higher-order signification in a context-dependent and cultural fashion. It is here that we see the greatest divergence between music and language, as the elements of the phonological level feed into very different systems of meaning. In language, phonological units are interpreted as lexical words, and are fed into a system of propositional syntax, which can be used to describe the properties of objects or express an ordered set of relationships between actors and those acted upon. It can express relationships about being, intention, causality, possession, relatedness, history, and so on. In music's acoustic mode, the units of the phonological level are interpreted as motivic, harmonic, rhythmic, and timbral elements, and are fed into a system of pitch-blending syntax that specifies a set of relationships between sound patterns and emotion. It deals with the issues of sound emotion, tension and relaxation, rhythmic pulse, and the like. Music's vehicle mode involves an interaction between these two syntax types, as described below.

Thus, both music and language consist of two related but dissociable tiers, each derived from a common set of principles dealing with phrases and phrasing. The end result of this analysis is the realization that phonological phrases and meaningful phrases are related but distinct entities. This fact is well known in linguistics, where the relationship between intonational phrases and syntactic phrases is at best probabilistic (Pierrehumbert 1991; Ladd 1996; Cruttenden 1997). It is no less true of music. However, the effect for language is much more striking from an evolutionary standpoint, as this liberation of language's meaning level from the acoustic modality (phonological level) allows language to develop into a system of amodal representation so important in theories of symbolic representation and off-line thinking (Bickerton 1995).

Five Possible Models

Space limitations prevent me from providing a general analysis of the phrase structure of music and language. My goal here will merely be to place this issue in an evolutionary perspective: How can we account for the similarities between music and language in evolutionary terms? Can we talk about mechanisms rather than metaphors? To this end, it will be important to distinguish two types of features that are shared between music and language: *shared ancestral* and *analogous* features, terms taken from the theory of cladistic classification in evolutionary biology. The first group have their roots in the common evolutionary origins of music and language. The second group arise due to the parallel but independent emergences of similar processes during the evolution of music and language. Aside from these shared ancestral and analogous features are the *distinct* features that are unique to either music or language.

To the extent that music and language share underlying phonological and syntactic properties, we can imagine five basic evolutionary possibilities by which this could have occurred (figure 16.2). First, these

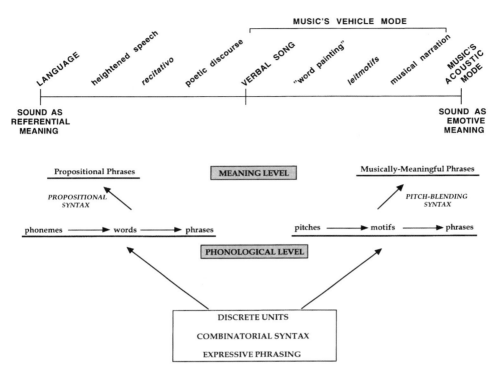

Figure 16.1
The two levels of functioning of music and language: phonological and meaning. Both levels are derived from the process of phrase formation involving discrete units, combinatorial syntax, and expressive phrasing. The phonological level is the acoustic level. It is governed by a type of phonological syntax in which discrete acoustic units (phonemes, pitches) are combined to form functional units (morpheme, motifs) that feed into the meaning level of each system. The meaning levels of language and music are governed by different types of syntax systems: propositional and blending, respectively. At their highest level of function, music and language differ more in emphasis than in kind, and this is represented by their placement at different ends of a spectrum. The poles of the spectrum represent the different interpretations of communicative sound patterns that each system exploits in creating meaningful formulas, where language emphasizes sound as referential meaning and music emphasizes sound as emotive meaning. A large number of functions occupy intermediate positions along this spectrum in that they incorporate both the referentiality of language and the sound-emotion function of music. Verbal song is the canonical intermediate function, which is why it occupies the central position. The functions of music's vehicle mode (see footnote 2 for details) lie toward the music side, whereas linguistic functions that incorporate sound-emotion or isometric rhythms lie toward the language side of the spectrum. ("Word painting" refers to the technique by which a composer creates an iconic relationship between music and words, such as the association of a descending melodic contour with the word "falling." This is use of music as symbolizer, as described in footnote 2).

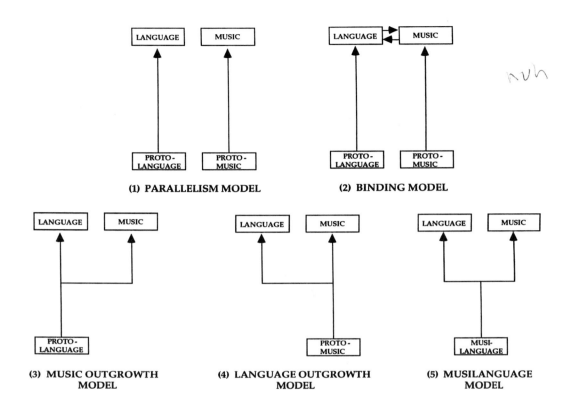

Figure 16.2
Five models for the evolution of the shared properties of music and language. In the parallelism model, language's evolution from a protolinguistic precursor and music's evolution from a protomusical precursor are thought to occur by completely independent processes. The binding model is quite similar except that it posits evolution of binding mechanisms that confer linguistic properties onto music and musical properties onto language (shown by the reciprocal horizontal arrows at the top of the figure). Neither of these two models invokes any notion of shared ancestral features. The next three models do. In the music outgrowth model, music is thought to evolve out of a linguistic precursor, whereas in the language outgrowth model language is thought to evolve out of a musical precursor. The musilanguage model is another outgrowth model in which shared properties of music and language are attributed to a common precursor, the musilanguage stage.

similarities could have come about completely fortuitously and arisen purely by parallel evolution. This parallelism model rejects any notion of shared ancestral features. Second, the similarities could have arisen from continuing interaction between discrete music and language modules, such that effective binding mechanisms evolved to confer musical properties onto language and linguistic properties onto music (binding model). Third, music could have evolved as an outgrowth of language (music outgrowth model). Fourth, language could have evolved as an outgrowth of music (language outgrowth model). Fifth, these similarities could have arisen due to the occurrence of an ancestral stage that was neither linguistic nor musical but that embodied the shared features of modern-day music and language, such that evolutionary divergence led to the formation of two distinct and specialized functions with retention of the shared features conferred onto them by the joint precursor (musilanguage model). Compared with the first two models, the last three invoke shared ancestral traits as being the basis for at least some similarities between music and language, but posit different evolutionary paths for their emergence.

I propose the musilanguage model for the origins of music and language. Why not adopt one of the other models? First, music and language have just too many important similarities for these to be chance occurrences alone. The parallelism model is the least parsimonious of the group evolutionarily. The binding model, which is implicitly the model of contemporary neurological studies (manifested by the credo "language: left hemisphere, music: right hemisphere"), rests on an overly dichotomous view of music and language, and is refuted by any type of neurological lesion that eliminates the musical properties of speech but spares those of music, or vice versa. Thus, studies showing that selective anesthesia of the right hemisphere of the brain disrupts the proper use of pitch during singing but leaves speech prosody intact (Borchgrevink 1991) indicate that binding models are too dichotomous. This is where outgrowth models present advantages. They assume that outgrowth of one function from the other permits not only the sharing of features due to common ancestry but redundant representation in the brain of similar functions by virtue of the divergence and differentiation events that led to outgrowth.

My reason for preferring the musilanguage model over either outgrowth model is that it greatly simplifies thinking about the origins of music and language. As it uses the common features of both as its starting point, the model avoids the endless semantic qualifications as to what constitutes an ancestral musical property versus what constitutes an ancestral linguistic property, exactly the kind of uncertainty that makes outgrowth models difficult to justify. The model forgoes this by saying that the common features of these two systems are neither musical nor linguistic but *musilinguistic*, and that these properties evolved first. In contrast, the distinct features of music and language, which are those that theorists can more or less agree upon, occurred evolutionarily later. They are specializations that evolved out of a common precursor and are thus (metaphorically) like the various digits that develop out of a common limb bud during ontogeny of the hand.

The model posits the existence of a musilanguage stage in the evolution of music and language (see figure 16.2). This stage must satisfy two important evolutionary criteria: first, it must provide for the common structural and expressive properties that are found in music and language (the shared ancestral features); and second, and quite important, it must provide an evolutionary scaffold on which music and language can evolve after a period a divergence and differentiation. In other words, the stage must be as much a precursor for the origins of language as it is for the origins of music, and should not have properties that are either too musical to permit evolution of language or too linguistic to permit evolution of music.

The Musilanguage Model

Much of what is described here was inspired by two basic ideas about music and language. The first one is the musilanguage idea, which contends that the two evolved as specializations from a common ancestral stage, such that their shared ancestral features evolved before their distinct, differentiated properties. The second idea is that despite the ultimate divergence between music and language during human evolution, these two functions differ more in emphasis than in kind, and are better represented as fitting along a spectrum instead of occupying two discrete, but partly overlapping, universes (see the top of figure 16.1). At one end of this spectrum we find the function of "sound reference" (semanticity, referentiality, lexical meaning) where arbitrary sound patterns are used to convey symbolic meaning. At the other end we find "sound emotion," where rather particular sound patterns (either culture-specific or species-specific) are used to convey emotional meaning.[3] According to this view, music and language differ mainly in their emphasis rather than in their fundamental nature, such that language emphasizes sound reference while downplaying its sound emotion aspect (although it certainly makes use of sound emotion), whereas music's acoustic mode emphasizes sound emotion while downplaying its referential aspect (although it certainly makes use of referentiality). Language and music are essentially reciprocal specializations of a dual-natured precursor that used both sound emotion and sound reference in creating communication sounds. However, along with this reciprocal specialization, various functions appear in the middle of the spectrum in figure 16.1 that bring these two specialized capacities together. From the music pole comes music's vehicle mode of action, in which language's referentiality and music's sound emotion function come together in a complex union of reenactment rituals, musical symbolism, musical narration, acoustic depiction, and the like. From the language pole comes a whole slew of features involved in heightened speech, *sprechstimme*, rapping, *recitativo*, poetic meter, and the abundant pragmatic uses of speech melody and rhythm to convey linguistic and paralinguistic meaning. Thus, the task of the musilanguage model is to describe a system containing both rudimentary referential and sound emotion properties such that it might be a reasonable precursor for the evolution of both music and language, and such that divergence from this precursor stage can be seen as an intensification of emphasis rather than the creation of new worlds.

The Musilanguage Stage

The present section attempts to characterize the necessary properties of the musilanguage stage, and later sections present a description of the origins of this stage as well as the divergence process that led to the formation of music and language. As will be seen shortly, development of these ideas was inspired quite a bit by phonological theory in linguistics, which has (surprisingly) played an even smaller a role in theories of language origin than it has in theories of music origin. The idea that speech and music are systems of expressively intoned sound is well accepted. But what is often ignored is the extent to which intonational concerns for melody, rhythm, and phrasing in speech strongly parallel those in music, not just in a metaphorical sense but in a mechanistic sense.

Several properties of the musilanguage stage contribute to the shared ancestral features of music and language. To facilitate discussion of a complex topic, a summary of the argument will guide the reader. I contend that at least three essential features of a musilanguage device are necessary for it to qualify as a precursor and scaffold for both language and music.

1. *Lexical tone*: use of pitch to convey semantic meaning. This involves creation of a tonal system based on level tones (discrete pitch levels).

2. *Combinatorial formation of small phrases*: generation of phrases by the combinatorial arrangement of unitary lexical-tonal elements. These phrases are melodorhythmic as well as semantic structures. One source of phrase melody is the sequential organization of the pitches contributed by the elemental units. A second one consists of global melodic formulas.

3. *Expressive phrasing principles*: use of local and global modulatory devices to add expressive emphasis and emotive meaning to simple phrases. Four general mechanisms of phrasing are envisioned that modify the acoustic features of the phrase to create basic intonational phrases.

Evolutionarily, this is seen as emerging through a two-step process in figure 16.3, proceeding from a primary stage of single lexical-tonal units

First Musilanguage Stage:

1) LEXICAL TONE
> Use of pitch to convey semantic meaning
> Discreteness of units: pitched vocalizations; level tones
> Broad semantic meaning

Second Musilanguage Stage:

2) COMBINATORIAL PHRASE FORMATION
> Simple combinations of lexical-tonal elements
> ¤ melodic and rhythmic units
> Two levels of meaning:
> ¤ local: relations between unitary lexical elements
> ¤ global: phrase-level (emotive) meanings

sum of local
pitch contours

global melodic
formulas

3) EXPRESSIVE PHRASING
> Four levels of phrasing:
> ¤ global/graded: global sentic modulation
> ¤ global/categorical: contour/meaning associations
> ¤ local/graded: local sentic modulation (prosody)
> ¤ local/categorical: prominence (accent/stress)

expressive
modulation

Figure 16.3
Summary of the properties of the musilanguage stage. The model highlights three important properties of the putative musilanguage precursor. Three general properties are
thought to provide an adequate description of the precursor of both music and language,
and emerge in the form of two distinct stages. The first musilanguage stage is a unitary
lexical-tonal system. This involves a system of discrete and pitched vocalizations that are
functionally referential in a very broad sense. The second musilanguage stage simultaneously introduces phrase formation and phrasing. Phrase formation is based on simple
combinatorial principles involving lexical-tonal elements introduced during the first
musilanguage stage. Four mechanisms of phrasing are also introduced that modulate the
acoustic properties of these combinatorially generated phrases, as described in the text.
Phrase melody is thought to receive three independent but related contributions: the sum
of lexical-tonal elements, global melodic contours, and expressive modulation.

(first musilanguage stage) to a later stage of phrase formation based
jointly on combinatorial syntax and expressive-phrasing principles
(second musilanguage stage). These three overall properties are thought
to make independent but related contributions to the global melody of
a musilinguistic phrase, as shown on the right side of figure 16.3.

Lexical Tone

This refers to the use of pitch in speech to convey semantic (lexical)
meaning. Languages that make extensive use of lexical tone as a
suprasegmental device are called tone or tonal languages. As they tend
to be viewed as oddities by linguists, theories of language origin tend to

ignore the fact that not merely a handful of exotic languages fall into this category, but that a majority of the world's languages are tonal (Fromkin 1978). The most parsimonious hypothesis is that language evolved as a tonal system from its inception, and that the evolutionary emergence of nontonal languages (intonation languages) occurred due to loss of lexical tone. In other words, this hypothesis states that tonality is the ancestral state of language. Intermediate cases exist, called pitch-accent languages, exemplified by Japanese, Swedish, and Serbo-Croatian, in which some limited use of contrastive tone is employed in the presence of intonation. Such limited uses of tone might represent either remnants of an earlier tonal stage, or, as is the case for Swedish and Norwegian, secondary acquisition of tonal properties from a nontonal precursor. As tone can be both acquired by and lost from languages, the goal here is not to describe the history of individual languages, but to describe the evolutionary history of language as a whole. I think that there are good evolutionary reasons for believing that tonality was the ancestral state of language, but this will have to be explored elsewhere.[4] The major point is that the notion of lexical tone implies that pitch can and does play an essential role in language, not just as a prosodic or paralinguistic device, but as a semantic device.

The single biggest complication in viewing lexical tone as a musilinguistic feature rather than a purely linguistic feature is the problem of level tones or pitch levels. Whereas all musical systems consist of sets of discrete pitches, intonation languages such as English appear on first view to make no such use of discrete pitch levels, but instead seem merely to be waves of sound punctuated by prosodic accents. It is here that my thinking is greatly indebted to autosegmental theories in phonology (Goldsmith 1976, 1990; Pierrehumbert 1980/1987; Ladd 1996). Historically, there has been a long-standing debate in phonology between a so-called levels perspective and a so-called configurations or contours perspective; that is, whether intonational events should be best thought of in terms of sequential movements between discrete pitch levels, or in terms of the pitch movements themselves irrespective of any notion of level tones. In the former view, pitch contours are merely transitions or interpolations between discrete pitch levels, whereas in the latter view they are the phonological events of interest. Many important phonological issues hinge on this levels-versus-configurations debate. Autosegmental theory was hailed as a resolution to this controversy (Ladd 1996). It supports the levels view by saying that phonological events should be modeled as sequential movements between discrete pitch levels, often only two levels, High and Low, and that all movements between them should be reduced to the status of transitions, rather than primary phonological events of importance (Goldsmith 1976). Thus, the notion of level tones is central to autosegmental theory, but, of importance, this applies as much to intonation languages as it does to tonal languages. Autosegmental theory confers onto level tones a status of general importance in all spoken language. In addition, it imposes an explicitly localist view on phonology, regarding all spoken utterances as series of steps from one level tone to the next. Two additional tonal features, downstep and boundary tones, are sufficient to confer onto utterances the overall wavelike properties that configurations supporters focus on (Pierrehumbert 1980/1987; Ladd 1996).

Autosegmental models have been applied to many languages, tonal and intonation alike (see Goldsmith 1995; Ladd 1996), and cognitive experiments have been highly supportive of the autosegmental interpretation. Ladd (1996) presents a general model of pitch-range effects from the autosegmental perspective that is of general relevance to the musilanguage model. Ladd contrasts two different ways of thinking about pitch in speech: an initializing approach in which phonological pitches are defined with reference to neighboring pitches (e.g., pitch Y is three semitones higher than proceeding pitch Z, and two semitones lower than preceding pitch X), and a normalizing approach in which such pitches are described in normalized terms with reference to their position on a scale describing a speaker's total pitch range (e.g., pitch Y is 80% of the speaker's highest pitch; alternatively, pitch X is 1.75-fold higher than the lowest frequency in the speaker's pitch range). Ladd supports the normalizing model, and it makes the most sense in terms of the current model.

Within the context of the autosegmental theory's focus on level targets, the normalizing approach to pitch predicts that scaling of these level targets should be systematic between speakers, and this is exactly what several studies showed (Thorsen 1980, 1981; Liberman and Pierrehumbert 1984; Ladd and Terken 1995). In other words, when multiple speakers are asked to read multiple sentences in a given language, and the absolute frequencies are normalized with respect to the speakers' pitch-range, an extremely high correlation (around .9) is found between target values of one speaker and those of another. The utterances are scaled. The scale may change as a function of pitch level (raising or lowering one's voice) but does not vary among speakers having different vocal ranges. The general implication of these findings for the musilanguage model are striking. They hold that speech, like music, is based on scales consisting of discrete pitch levels. The major difference between speech and music in this regard is that these scales change quite a bit during speech (e.g., when pitch level changes) and thus so do the level tones themselves. But this does not negate the basic observation that the scaling of pitch is used in speech, as predicted by the normalizing-autosegmental approach to pitch range.

Another important point that has bearing on the use of tone in speech is the observation of categorical perception of tone. House (1990) presented his experiments with Swedish speakers and reviewed the literature with regard to Chinese lexical tone, German categories of intonational meaning, and English pitch accent, and concluded that "results from perception experiments in four different languages support the concept of linguistic categories (both lexical and semantic) being perceived in terms of tonal levels during maximum spectral change after the CV [consonant-vowel] boundary and as tonal movement during relative spectral stability. The synchronization of tonal movement with vowel onset seems to be important for the perception of linguistically relevant tonal categories" (p. 81). Thus for both intonation languages and tone languages, cognitive experiments show that people tend to perceive level tones in a more or less categorical fashion, in support of autosegmental models of intonation and lexical tone.

What are the implications of these important findings for the musilanguage model? Three basic implications bear mentioning. First, the production and perception of *pitched* vocalizations is a necessary characteristic of such a system, in contrast to vocalizations based purely on portamentos (glides, slides, etc.). As most primate vocalizations systems rely heavily on unpitched grunts and pants (e.g., chimpanzee pant-hoots, vervet monkey alarm calls) or on high-contoured pitch glides (gibbon song), the musilanguage theory posits that a pitched vocalization system involving at least two pitch states would have had to evolve at some point in the hominid line. This theory does not demand evolution of new articulatory capacities to form novel types of segmental phonemes but simply the cognitive capacity to use level tones in a meaningful fashion. Nor does this argument have any bearing on the types of transitions that occur between level tones; they are just as likely to be pitch glides as pitch jumps. All that is important is that some notion of level tones be involved.

Second, the idea of lexical tone, as seen from the autosegmental perspective, suggests that level tones are just as important for intonation languages as they are for tone languages. Therefore, discrete pitch levels and pitch-scaling mechanisms are not merely features of tone languages and music but are important features of intonation languages as well. Speech, like music, is based on discrete pitch levels that themselves are scaled, although variably so. This is supported by experiments showing that normalizing approaches explain pitch-range effects better than do initializing approaches as well as by studies demonstrating the categorical perception of tone in both intonation languages and tone languages.

Third, any evolutionary expansion of this system to generate phrases will follow, at least to an important extent, localist rules whereby strings are assembled in a sequential, stepwise fashion (this is described in more detail below). The insight from autosegmental theory for the musilanguage model is that sequences of level tones can be the basis for semantic strings. The fact that intonation languages dissociate such strings of level tones from semantic strings emphasizes the earlier point that language's meaning level has no obligatory relationship to its phonological level or even to the acoustic modality. Intonation languages, like gesture languages, highlight the primary importance of creating semantic meaning from meaningless components, whatever these components may be. However, the evolutionary hypothesis here is that language began as a tonal system, and this seems to be borne out, at least in part, by the robust presence of lexical tone in the world's languages.

Finally, a natural question that emerges is, how can I argue that a system of lexical tone could be a precursor for music? Isn't music based on meaningless pitches rather than meaningful lexical units? This is a question that is central to the issue of musical semantics. First of all, I mentioned that divergence from the musilanguage stage would lead to differences in emphasis between music and language. So it is only natural to think that music would deemphasize its lexical tonal aspect during this divergence process. Yet at the same time, two other points have a bearing on this issue. The first is to emphasize that lexical words can have, and often do have, a very broad range of meanings, where semantic interpretation is highly dependent on the context of not only the sentence but the entire discourse arrangement. Thus, words have great semantic elasticity (Swain 1997), and this is seen in abundance during the development of speech in children, where lexical words start off having extremely broad meanings, and acquire precise meanings only as the lexicon and syntactic system expand during later stages of development. The second idea is that music has many devices available to it to give it semanticity. This was discussed above with reference to music's vehicle mode of action, especially in relation to the use of music for symbolization and narration (see note 2).

One example of this is the leitmotif in Western opera, where particular musical motifs become semantic tags for characters, objects, or concepts. Another example consists of drummed and whistled languages (Umiker 1974). There is no question that the semantic system of the musilanguage stage would have to have been very broad for lexical tone to qualify as a shared ancestral feature of music and language. However, ". . . a passage of music could have a semantic range that is essentially the same as that of any word in a language, only much broader in its scope; sharing the same kind of elasticity but of much greater degree than is typical in language" (Swain 1997:55). In sum, I believe that the notion of lexical tone, with its underlying level tones and semantically

out a precursor could have been holistic units of emotion/meaning

meaningful pitch movements, satisfies the criterion for being a joint feature of language and music, and a scaffold on which both systems could have developed. This first musilanguage stage would have been a system of unitary lexical-tonal elements which could have been combined to form phrases.

Combinatorial Phrase Formation

Given the establishment of a lexical tone-based vocalization system, we can envision the next evolutionary step in the musilanguage system's development whereby sequences of lexical-tonal units are strung together to make simple, unordered phrases having higher-order meanings. The semantic meaning of such phrases has both compound and global sources. The compound sources are derived from the relational juxtaposition of the individual semantic units being combined. A global level of meaning, due to the overall melodic contour of the phrase, is a second important semantic feature of a phrase-based system not possible in a single-unit system, such as the first musilanguage stage. These phrase-level melodies correspond to categorical formulas for conveying emotive and/or pragmatic meaning (see Richman, this volume). In the domain of speech, they include such discrete phonological formulas as question intonations and surprise intonations. Thus, phrase-based systems provide a dual advantage over single-unit systems in that they have two levels of meaning: compound—meaningful relations between the individual units, and global—categorical formulas characterizing the phrase as a whole. Such combinatorial phrases have not only a melodic structure but a rhythmic structure as well, and the rhythmic patterns of such phrases are derivable, at least in large part, from the temporal arrangement of elemental units.

I maintain that whereas the basic ingredients of hierarchical organization are present in such a system, this second musilanguage stage has neither a sense of ordering nor a strong sense of hierarchical grouping. The one exception to this, described below, is the notion of prominence. In general, hierarchical organization would have emerged in a modality-specific fashion after divergence from the musilanguage stage, leading to the creation of the specific grammars of language and music. Therefore, one important implication of this model is that *the general capacity for combinatoriality preceded the evolution of modality-specific syntaxes* As such, this model shares features with Bickerton's (1995) protolanguage model. The musilanguage stage should have had neither the propositional syntax of language nor the blending syntax of music, but should have merely been a system of combinatorial relations between basic elements in which an additional, global level of meaning was superimposed on the relational level of meaning. However, despite this absence of a complex syntax system, this second stage is a richer and more flexible communication system than a single-unit system in that it provides at least two levels of meaning from a single phrase. Thus, in one sense, phrases are simply the sum of their parts (localist features), but in another sense they are something more than the sum of their parts (globalist features).

The biggest complication of this model lies in trying to tie together combinatorial phrase formation with autosegmental ideas of level tones in speech. The case of music is far simpler. Virtually all of the world's musical systems are based on sets of discrete pitches, subsets of which are used to generate motifs and melodies. To what extent can we think of speech as being a melodic generative system in the same way? Pierrehumbert and Hirschberg (1990) proposed a localist, compositional approach to the production of phonological phrases that is based on the simple bitonal features of autosegmental models. However, such models have no explicit requirement that the High and Low level-tones correspond to anything like the discrete absolute-frequency (F_0) levels that go into formation of musical scales. Yet, my own argument is critically dependent on this. This was mentioned above in relation to lexical tone. I think that the resolution to the problem is to reconsider Ladd's (1996) normalizing approach to pitch features and say that whether people are actually aware of it or not, they tend to use pitch in a scaled fashion in producing speech utterances. In fact, I think the situation is no different in musical generative systems. People create melodies or songs using implicit cognitive rules based on the discreteness of pitch, which is dependent on the categorical perception of pitch (Lerdahl 1988). Phonological evidence suggests that people do something quite similar when speaking, thus supporting the basic combinatorial pitch arrangement in speech. So the general conclusion here is that speaking is not only pitched but scaled, and that people obey scaling principles in generating speech utterances. By this analysis, speech melody is no longer a metaphor, but a mechanistic parallel to musical melody, itself based on scaled pitches.

Expressive Phrasing

Cognitive musicology has placed such a premium on exploiting the grammar metaphor in music that it has all but ignored many important parallels that occur at the level of intonational phrasing. Generative theories of music have been rightly criticized for their failure to address these expressive properties, such as tempo, dynamics, rhythmic modulation, and the like. It is not sufficient for musical phrases to have hierarchical melodic and rhythmic structure; they must also function as intonational phrases for the expression of emotion and emphasis. But the most important point to emerge is that expressive phrasing is so general that it is wrong to dichotomize its forms in speech and music. Phonologists describing speech phrasing and musicologists describing musical phrasing often talk about exactly the same processes, but with two different sets of terms. Therefore it is important to subsume these phrasing mechanisms into a unified set of concepts and terms (figure 16.4) that are rooted in biological notions of common evolutionary ancestry.

Before talking about these mechanisms, I would like to introduce one concept that has general relevance to this topic: sentic modulation. The term "sentic" I borrow from Manfred Clynes (1977); however, I do not use it in exactly the same sense that Clynes did. I use it in a more limited sense, as expressed in Clynes' equivalence principle: "*A sentic state may be expressed by any of a number of different output modalities* ... gestures, tone of voice, facial expression, a dance step, musical phrase, etc." (p. 18, emphasis in original). My take on Clynes' equivalence principle is to say that the sentic system is a general modulatory system involved in conveying and perceiving the *intensity* of emotive expression along a continuous scale. It expresses intensity by means of three graded spectra: tempo modulation (slow-fast spectrum), amplitude modulation (soft-loud spectrum), and register selection (low-pitched-high-pitched spectrum). This system appears to be invariant across modalities of expression in humans, such as speech, music, and gesture, on which Clynes' equivalency is based. It also appears to function in a similar way in emotive behavior in nonhuman animals (Morton 1977, 1994),

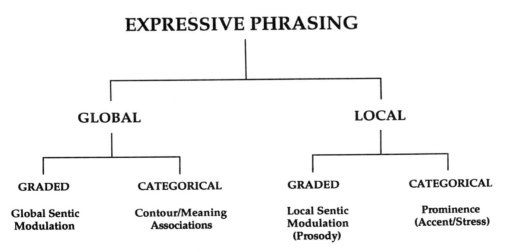

Figure 16.4
Four mechanisms of expressive phrasing are described along two dimensions, acting first either at the global level or the local level of the phrase, and second in either a graded manner (local and global sentic modulation) or in a more discrete, categorical manner (contour-meaning associations and prominence effects). See text for details.

suggesting that the sentic system might be one feature of musical processing that has homologues in vertebrate expressive behavior generally. The universality of this system for human emotional expression can be demonstrated by pointing out that in speech, gesture, and music, the same sentic profile occurs to express a given emotional intensity state, regardless of the modality of expression. For example, happy music and happy speech are both characterized by fast tempos, large-amplitude sounds, and high registers; sad music and sad speech are characterized by the opposite sentic spectrum. Looking at gesture instead of vocalization, one sees that happy movements are characterized by fast tempos, large amplitudes (broad gestures), and high positioning (the equivalent of high register), with sad gesturing showing exactly the opposite spectrum. In all cases, the level of sentic modulation reflects the intensity level of emotional expression, thus highlighting the gradient nature of the sentic system. Happy movements are fast, but ecstatic movements are ballistic; sad movements are slow, but depression is immobilizing. Again, much evidence suggests that sentic modulation is not merely cross-modal, but also cross-cultural and cross-species. Sentic factors are an excellent place to look for universal expressive features in music, speech, and gesture.

Four general mechanisms of expressive phrasing are used in speech and music. As seen in figure 16.4, they are divided along two dimensions, acting either at the local or global levels of the phrase, and acting in either a graded or categorical fashion with respect to the acoustic parameters being modulated.

Global Level

We can think about two phrasing mechanisms acting at the global level (figure 16.4, left side): global sentic modulation and contour-meaning associations. Global sentic modulation involves expressive devices that affect the intensity level of the whole phrase with regard to overall tempo, amplitude, and register. These effects occur along a continuous spectrum such that the level of sentic modulation correlates with the intensity of emotional expression. As mentioned, global sentic effects have the same emotional meaning in music and speech, and the sentic profile for a particular emotional state in music and speech is exactly the same.

The second factor of global expressive phrasing involves all categorical contour-meaning associations that relate phrase melody to particular meanings. Unlike global sentic modulation, contour-meaning associations work in categorical fashion, with each melody having a more or less specific meaning (see Richman, this volume). Things such as question intonations, surprise intonations, and call intonations are universal melodies that convey pragmatic features of discourse. Similarly, in Western music, "question phrases" (ascending contours) convey a feeling of tension and uncertainty, whereas "answer phrases" (descending contours) convey a feeling of resolution of that uncertainty. Interestingly, in both speech and music, ascending contours convey uncertainty and uneasiness, and descending contours certainty and stability, providing further evidence that these phrasing mechanisms arose from a joint precursor. As mentioned earlier, compositional approaches to speech intonation (Pierrehumbert and Hirschberg 1990) tend to reduce global phrase-level formulas to local-level sequential tone changes. Be that as it may, such formulas tend to operate in a global, categorical fashion.

Local Level

Two phrasing processes act at the local level (figure 16.4, right side): local sentic modulation (prosody) and prominence. Prosody encompasses our most basic idea about intonation, referring to the local risings and fallings, quickenings and slowings, and loudenings and softenings that are involved in expressively conveying our meanings in a pragmatic sense. To my mind, prosody is best represented as a series of sentic rules acting at the local level. These rules are in principle similar to those acting at the global level except that they act locally, involving small modulations in tempo (accelerando, ritardando), pitch (ascent, descent), volume (crescendo, diminuendo, sforzando), and length (ritenuto) at the level of the individual element or group of elements. As with global sentic modulation, local modulation occurs along a continuous intensity gradient, and this gradient effect is certainly one of the most important characteristics of speech intonation and musical phrasing. This level of phrasing is one feature that distinguishes one speaker from another or one musician from another.

The second local phrasing mechanism involves use of accent or stress as prominence devices to convey emphasis or focus in either speech or musical phrases. A phrase usually has a single point of emphasis, thus making prominence a categorical signal acting at the local level. There are several ways of effecting prominence: a rise in pitch, an increase in amplitude, an increase in duration, or some combination thereof. Local sentic modulation (prosody) and prominence interact in such a way that the part of the phrase that precedes the accent often demonstrates a continuous build-up, whereas the part that follows it shows a continuous fall-off. In both music and speech, prosody is used in the service of prominence by allowing phrases to be elaborated in a smooth rising-and-falling fashion, rather than in a punctuated manner.

These four phrasing mechanisms affect the ability of speakers and musicians to convey emphasis, emotional state, and emotional meaning.

Whether in speech or music, they modulate the same basic set of acoustic parameters, making interdependent contributions to the process of phrasing.

Summary

To summarize this section, I propose an evolutionary progression from a simple system involving a repertoire of unitary lexical-tonal elements (first musilanguage stage) to a less simple system based on combinatorial arrangements of these lexical-tonal (and rhythmic) elements (second musilanguage stage). The latter obtains its meaning not just from the juxtaposition of the unitary lexical elements but from the use of global phrase-level melodies. It is at the same time a phrasing system based on local and global forms of sentic modulation as well as on prominence effects. One offshoot of this analysis is that phrase melody has three important but distinct sources (figure 16.3): the sum of the local pitch contours from the lexical-tonal elements; phrase-level, meaningful melodies; and intonational modulation through expressive phrasing mechanisms. An important evolutionary point is that combinatorial syntax is seen to precede modality-specific grammars. This system is, to a first approximation, a reasonable precursor for the evolution of both music and language out of which both could have emerged while retaining the many important properties they share.

Before closing this section, it would be useful to return to the question of generativity and hierarchical organization. I stated at the beginning of the chapter that generativity is an analogous feature of language and music, not a shared ancestral feature. Music's and language's generativity are based on completely different syntactic principles whose only common denominators are discreteness and combinatoriality. At the same time, it is not difficult to imagine hierarchical organization evolving out of the musilanguage precursor stage, thereafter becoming exploited by modality-specific systems. All that is necessary is for some type of either grouping or segregation of elements (or both) to occur to differentiate different elements within the phrase. This could occur at the level of pitch (auditory streaming effects), rhythm (pulse relationships), amplitude (prominence effects), and so on. The point is that the musilanguage device, based on discreteness, combinatoriality, and intonation, provides all the necessary ingredients for hierarchical organization in what will eventually become two very different grammatical systems. So the actual forms of hierarchical organization in music and language are best thought of as resulting from parallelism rather than from common origins, again with the note that the shared ancestral features of the musilanguage stage provide fertile ground for evolution of hierarchical organization once the divergence process starts to take off. The only hierarchical function that seems to be a necessary part of the musilanguage stage is prominence. Acoustically, prominence can be effected by a diversity of mechanisms, including pitch, length, and strength.

Precursors

Given this analysis of the musilanguage stage as a joint precursor of music and language, two major questions remain: what are the origins of the musilanguage stage? and what is the process by which the divergence occurred to make music and language distinct, sometimes dichotomous, functions along the spectrum described in figure 16.1?

Regarding the first question, one hint comes from a very interesting and well-described class of primate vocalizations, which I call *referential emotive vocalizations*. A referential emotive vocalization (REV) is a type of call (not song) that serves as an on-line, emotive response to some object in the environment, but that also has the property of semantic specificity for the class of object being responded to. Thus, each call-type signifies a given object. From the standpoint of nearby conspecifics, REVs serve an important communicative function for the social group, as the meaning of each call is known to all members of the species, thereby encouraging appropriate behavioral responses. For the purposes of this discussion, the most salient feature of a REV is its dual acoustic nature: a given sound pattern has both emotive meaning and referential meaning, a property shared with the musilanguage stage that I proposed.

The best-described referential emotive system is the alarm call system of the East African vervet monkey, which has a repertoire of at least three acoustically distinguishable calls (Struhsaker 1967). In fact primates and birds have a large number of such functionally referential calling systems that have a similar level of semanticity to that of vervet alarm calls (see table 3.1 of Marler, this volume; Hauser, this volume; Marler, Evans, and Hauser 1992). Acoustically, vervet calls are short grunts that are specific for the predator eliciting the alarm. The best-characterized calls are the eagle, snake, and leopard calls. That vervet monkeys know the meaning of the calls is shown by audioplayback experiments in which the animals engage in appropriate escape behaviors to the different calls, running up into trees on hearing the leopard call, and looking to the sky or running into bushes on hearing the eagle call (Seyfarth, Cheney, and Marler 1980a, b). At the semantic level, REVs show the same type of broad semantic meaning that is suggested for the musilanguage device.

I propose that the precursor of the musilanguage stage was a type of REV. It is not important that this be an alarm call system per se, but merely a system with its characteristic dual acoustic nature and broad semantic meaning. The most important feature that would have been

This is possible
but I prefer the mother-infant woargdog,

required to move from a vervet-type REV to the first musilanguage stage would have been the meaningful use of discrete pitch levels, in contrast to the unpitched grunts of many primate calls. Although such a system has not been described, the vervet alarm call system holds out as an important model for how it might operate, providing clues as to how the musilanguage stage may have evolved.

Divergence

The second question was, by what process did the divergence from the musilanguage stage occur to make music and language distinct though related functions? How did language become "language" and music "music" starting from the hypothesized musilinguistic ancestor? This question relates most directly to the origins of language and music as they occur in their current forms. My goal is not to rehash the extensive series of functional theories that have been proposed to account for the origins of human language (reviewed in Wind et al. 1992; Lewin 1993; Beaken 1996), but to see how the current proposal of a joint musilanguage stage affects such theories. Let us look again at the functional spectrum presented in figure 16.1. As stated, music and language sit at opposite ends of a spectrum, with each one emphasizing a particular type of interpretation of communicative sound patterns. The two evolved as reciprocal elaborations of a dual-natured referential emotive system, again suggesting that they differ more in emphasis than in kind.

In thinking about the divergence process, it is useful once again to return to the distinction among shared ancestral, analogous, and distinct features of music and language. By definition, the first type of feature appeared before the divergence process and the second two after it. Divergence can therefore be characterized as the process by which the analogous and distinct features of music and language evolved. However, this probably came about two different ways. Analogous features most likely represent specializations emerging out of the shared ancestral features of the musilanguage stage. They are differentiation events. Distinct features, such as music's isometric rhythms and language's propositional syntax, are not. Instead they represent modality-specific (and human-specific) novelties of these two functions. Let us now consider these features.

Looking first to language, we see that this system not only develops an explosively large lexicon (some 100,000 words in adult humans), but a semantic system containing greatly specified meanings by comparison with a primate REV or the musilanguage system. At the level of grammar, language develops a kind of propositional syntax that specifies temporal and behavioral relationships between subjects and objects in a phrase. Because it makes reference to personal experience, this syntax system can be the basis for determinations of truth and falsity. Structurally, it involves not only simple hierarchical organization but recursiveness as well. Perhaps the point of greatest distinction from music is language's liberation from the acoustic modality altogether, leading to amodal conceptualization, off-line thinking, and human reason.

Looking to music, divergence from the musilanguage stage leads initially to the formation of its acoustic mode. The acoustic range and pitch repertoire become greatly expanded over anything seen in the musilanguage precursor or in spoken language, extending to more than eight octaves, each octave being divisible into at least a dozen differentiable pitches. At the level of grammar, music acquires a complex and hierarchical syntax system based on pitch patterning and multipart blending, leading to the creation of diverse motivic types, many forms of polyphony, and complex timbral blends. In addition to this pitch blending property, we see the emergence of many categorical formulas for expressing particular emotional states, leading to the various forms of sound emotion that are used in creating coherent and emotively meaningful musical phrases. Finally, at the rhythmic level, music acquires the distinct feature of isometric time keeping, so much a hallmark in Western culture. This metric-pulse function is based on a human-specific capacity to both keep time and to entrain oneself rhythmically to an external beat. This permits rhythmical hierarchies in both the horizontal and vertical dimensions of musical structure, including such things as heterometers and polyrhythms.

Evolutionary divergence results in significant differences between music and language at the highest levels. The last thing to explain is how these two systems came together to create yet newer functions. For this, it is important to distinguish between the shared properties and interactive functions. Shared properties of music and language are posited by the musilanguage model to be either shared ancestral or analogous functions. Interactive functions are areas in which music and language come together to create novel functions that strongly involve both systems. This was demonstrated on the spectrum presented in figure 16.1. It includes principally all those functions that I call the vehicle mode of music operation, not to mention the use of meter in poetry and the many exaggerated uses of intonation to convey information, attitude, and emotion. The major point is that interactive functions develop through a coevolutionary process that reflects the evolutions of both the linguistic and musical systems. For this reason, we expect interactive functions, such as verbal song, to evolve through a series of stages that reflect the evolution of the two systems contributing to these novel functions.

Summary

The full musilanguage model can now be presented. It posits that music and language evolved as two specializations from a common ancestor, such that a series shared ancestral features evolved before either analogous or distinct features. This model is distinguished from those holding that music evolved from a dedicated linguistic capacity (music outgrowth model) or that language developed from a dedicated musical capacity (language outgrowth model). It argues instead that shared ancestral features of music and language should be thought of as musilinguistic rather than either musical or linguistic. The model's principal contribution to the study of language evolution is to provide a new chronology for the development of language's structural features: language evolved out of a sophisticated referential emotive system; phonological syntax preceded propositional syntax; tone languages preceded intonation languages; speech could have evolved early, due to its exploitation of lexical tone instead of enlarged segmental inventories; lexical tone, combinatorial syntax, and expressive intonation were ancestral features of language that were shared with music; broad semantic meaning preceded precise semantic meaning; and language's acoustic modality preceded its representational state of amodality.

The model begins with a referential emotive system (figure 16.5) that in its most basic form provides for the dual acoustic nature of the musilanguage system: sound as emotive meaning and sound as referential meaning. This by itself establishes the functional spectrum that will later define music and language as two separate specializations. From this we see the development of the musilanguage stage, which is thought to have occurred in two steps. The first step was the use of level tones (discrete pitches) and pitch contours for referential communication. The second step was the development of meaningful phrases, generated through combinatorial rules for joining discrete elements into phrases, these phrases being subject to four levels of modulation: local sentic rules for expressive modulation; global sentic rules for the overall level (intensity) of expression; local categorical rules for prominence; and global categorical formulas for generating phrase-level contour-meaning associations. These devices make independent but related contributions to the overall acoustic properties of the phrase. Semantically, the musilanguage device is a sophisticated referential emotive communication system that generates meaning at two levels: first, from the relational juxtaposition of unitary elements (local level), and second, from overall contour-meaning associations (global level).

The next step in this evolution is the simultaneous occurrence of divergence and interaction, with continued retention of the shared ancestral

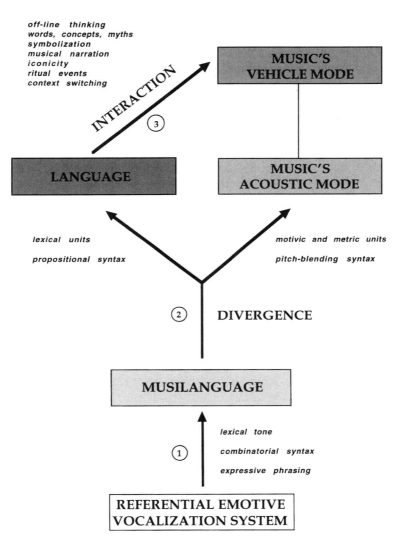

Figure 16.5
The full musilanguage model begins with a hominid referential emotive vocalization system, which provides for the dual acoustic nature of the musilanguage stage: sound as referential meaning and sound as emotive meaning. Next, the musilanguage stage is thought to evolve by a two-step process, beginning first with a unitary lexical-tonal system, followed by a phrase system involving both combinatorial syntax and expressive phrasing properties. This musilanguage stage provides for the shared ancestral features of music and language. The next step is divergence from the musilanguage stage, leading eventually to the mature linguistic system and music's acoustic mode. This occurs through reciprocal elaboration of either sound as referential meaning (language) or sound as emotive meaning (music's acoustic mode). This involves not only different fundamental units at the phonological level but different interpretations of these units at the meaning level. An important aspect of the divergence process is the formation of different syntax types: propositional syntax in the case of language, and blending syntax in the case of music. The final step is development of interactive properties by a coevolutionary process. This leads to, among other functions, music's vehicle mode of action, which involves such things as verbal song, iconic representation, and musical narration (see footnote 2 for details).

features. Divergence occurs due to the reciprocal elaboration of either sound as referential meaning or sound as emotive meaning, ultimately making language and music different in emphasis rather than in kind. This is accompanied by an important divergence of syntax types: language's propositional syntax is based on relationships between actors and those acted upon; music's blending syntax is based on pitch blending and pitch patterning leading to complex sound-emotion relationships. This establishes language's symbolic capacity for representation and communication and music's acoustic mode (with its sound-emotion system and broad semantics). Finally, simultaneous with the divergence process is the formation of interactive functions, exemplified by verbal song and all the other vehicle functions of music. In other words, divergence is accompanied by rebinding of music and language in the form of novel functions that evolve parallel to their separation. The emergence of these interactive functions reflects coevolution of the underlying linguistic and musical systems. Thus, we can imagine verbal song as evolving through a series of stages that parallel biological developments in both systems.

What of functional evolutionary concepts? I do not think anyone would deny that both music and language are highly multifunctional. However evolutionary models are adaptationist interpretations of how traits evolve, and tend to focus monolithically on a single adaptive function and a single selection mechanism for a given trait. So far, the monolithic approach to language has failed miserably, and I doubt that it will work for music either. But in addition, and more controversially, I sincerely doubt that functionalist concepts of music origins based exclusively on individual selection processes will, in the end, bear fruit. There is just too much about music making that reveals an essential role in group function to ignore the issue of multilevel selection (Sober and Wilson 1998). Nobody questions that music is done in groups, but Miller (this volume) seriously questions whether it is done *for* groups. Half a century of ethnomusicological research suggests that a principal function, if not *the* principal function, of music making is to promote group cooperation, coordination, and cohesion (Merriam 1964; Lomax 1968; Hood 1971). Music making has all the hallmarks of a group adaptation and functions as a device for promoting group identity, coordination, action, cognition, and emotional expression. Ethnomusicological research cannot simply be brushed aside in making adaptationist models. Contrary to strong sexual selection models, musical activity in tribal cultures involves active participation by the entire group, that is, both sexes and people of all ages. Such cultures make no distinction between musicians and nonmusicians. Where sex or age segregation is found at the level of performance style, it is usually a reflection of specialization at the level of the work group (Lomax 1968), and this is described by the universal ethnomusicological principal of functionality or context specificity in musical performance. Music making is done for the group, and the contexts of musical performance, the contents of musical works, and the performance ensembles of musical genres overwhelmingly reflect a role in group function. The straightforward evolutionary implication is that human musical capacity evolved because groups of musical hominids outsurvived groups of nonmusical hominids due to a host of factors related to group-level cooperation and coordination.

Finally, as a tie-in to our discussion of the musilanguage model and the divergence process leading to music's outgrowth from the musilanguage precursor, music has two distinct design features that reflect an intrinsic role in group cooperation. These two features account for a large part of what music is at the structural level: pitch blending and isometric rhythms. Whereas speech proceeds obligatorily by an alternation of parts, music is highly effective at promoting simultaneity of different parts through its intrinsic capacity for pitch blending; music's vertical dimension must be seen as a design feature for promoting cooperative group performance and interpersonal harmonization. In addition, musical meter is perhaps the quintessential device for group coordination, one which functions to promote interpersonal entrainment, cooperative movement, and teamwork. Pitch blending and metric rhythms are central to any evolutionary account of the melodic and rhythmic dimensions of music. *Theories of individual selection must explain how these essentially group-cooperative musical devices evolved in the service of within-group competition.* I doubt that such models will be able to account for them, and I suggest instead that multilevel selection models involving group selection (Sober and Wilson 1998) and/or cultural group selection (Boyd and Richerson 1990) offer great promise in elucidating the cooperative and group nature of music (Brown in press). Again, music making is not only about within-group cooperation, coordination, and cohesion, but it is principally about these things. How this may relate to the vocalization capacities, group structures, and social behaviors of our hominid ancestors is a matter of central importance for future research and theory in evolutionary musicology.

Acknowledgments

I thank several colleagues who have been generous with their advice and time: Gerhard Schlosser (University of Bremen) for reading the paper and for many stimulating discussions about the nature of homology; Tomas Riad (Stockholm University) not only for his insightful comments on an earlier draft of the paper but for generously spending many hours with me clarifying misconceptions about autosegmental theory and the nature of tone in spoken language; Ulrik Volgsten (Stockholm University) for his critical reading of the paper, and for invaluable discussions about musical semiotics; and Stephen Matthews (Hong Kong University) for many illuminating discussions through e-mail about tone languages. I dedicate this chapter to Mari Mar, Gerhard, and Cristian.

Notes

1. The dichotomy between the acoustic mode and the vehicle mode of music cognition has an important implication for the question of animal song discussed in chapter 1. As I see it, birdsong is not a form of music for exactly the same reason that linguists argue that it is not a form of language. What I call the vehicle mode consists of the representational, iconic, speech-related, and cultural aspects of music, and depends on the rich representational abilities of human beings (see Bickerton 1995). In contrast, when talking about animal song as an acoustic system (analogous to the acoustic mode of human music), it is simply impossible to create a line of demarcation between it and the family of human musics. The vehicle mode is this line of demarcation between music and all forms of non-human song.

2. The vehicle mode involves at least seven important functions of music: universal involvement of music in representational rituals; verbal song: songs with words or words with music; music as symbolizer: the use of musical works (or pitches, motifs, melodies, or rhythms therein) to represent cultural objects; music as symbol: extramusical associations of elements of the musical system; acoustic depiction of nonmusical sounds, such as animals, people, and environmental sounds; musical narration: music's use to color actions, events, and characters in the theatrical art forms, such as drama and film; and context switching: reuse of music from one context in another context, for example, classical music in television commercials.

3. The sound emotion system of music consists of at least four major processes: pitch-set effects: contrastive use of different pitch sets (i.e., scales or modes) to convey different emotional meanings; contour-meaning associations: contrastive use of different types of ascending and descending melodic patterns to convey different emotive meanings; blending effects: the emotive effect of sound blends, such as the blendings of pitches (homophony), melodic lines (polyphony), and rhythms (polyrhythms); and progression factors: phrase-level devices for building up coherent and organized musical phrases. In a hierarchical organization of these four components, progression factors sit at the highest level. They are fed into by contour-meaning associations (e.g., ascending and descending melodic lines) and blending effects (e.g., tonicization, cadential formulas, and coordinated motivic movements), which themselves are fed into by pitch-set effects, which contribute factors related to pitch contours, melodic contours, chords, polyphony, etc.

4. One stabilizing selection force that could have kept language tonal during the earlier stages of language evolution was the biological cost in creating anatomical changes to the vocal tract for permitting expansion of the segmental inventory. Evolution of human-specific features of the vocal tract is seen as being essential to the formation of consonants and thus consonant-vowel segments. The capacity to form consonants requires many complex changes in the articulatory mechanisms of the vocal tract, whereas production of several of the vowels can be accomplished even by chimpanzees (de Waal, 1988). Therefore, "it is not a great problem to suggest routes by which at least three distinctive vowels might find their way into the vocal activities of our [hominid] ancestors" (Beaken, 1996:111). The point is that whereas the evolution of new articulatory mechanisms, leading to new consonants, is a costly biological innovation, exploiting pitch contour with vowels is a relatively cheap and simple way of expanding the lexicon. This could have been a major stabilizing selection pressure keeping human language tonal during the earliest stages. One outcome of this reasoning is that intonation languages should have developed, in general, larger segmental inventories than tone languages, as expansion of the segmental inventory

is seen as the key step in reducing the necessity of lexical tone in spoken language. I am indebted to Dr. Stephen Matthews for pointing out to me this putative trade-off between lexical tone and segmental inventory size within languages. As this hypothesis demands the existence of lesser rather than greater sophistication of the vocal tract for speech to occur (fewer rather than more segments), it tends to support theories that call for the early emergence of speech in hominids (see Frayer and Nicolay, this volume).

P 2 1 7

References

Aiello, R. (1994). Music and language: Parallels and contrasts. In R. Aiello and J. Sloboda (Eds.) *Music Perceptions* (pp. 40–63). Oxford: Oxford University Press.

Beaken, M. (1996). *The Making of Language*. Edinburgh: Edinburgh University Press.

Bernstein, L. (1976). *The Unanswered Question: Six Talks at Harvard*. Cambridge: Harvard University Press.

Bickerton, D. (1995). *Language and Human Behavior*. Seattle: University of Washington Press.

Borchgrevink, H. M. (1991). Prosody, musical rhythm, tone pitch, and response initiation during amytal hemisphere anaesthesia. In J. Sundberg, L. Nord, and R. Carlson (Eds.) *Music, Language, Speech and Brain* (pp. 327–343). Houndmills, UK: Macmillan Press.

Boyd, R. and Richerson, P. J. (1990). Group selection among alternative evolutionarily stable strategies. *Journal of Theoretical Biology* 145:331–342.

Brown, S. (in press). Evolutionary models of music: From sexual selection to group selection. In F. Tonneau and N. S. Thompson (Eds.) *Perspectives in Ethology*, XIII. New York: Plenum.

Clarke, E. F. (1989). Issues in language and music. *Contemporary Music Review* 4:9–22.

Clynes, M. (1977). *Sentics: The Touch of Emotion*. London: Souvenir Press.

Cruttenden, A. (1997). *Intonation*, 2nd ed. Cambridge, UK: Cambridge University Press.

Feld S. and Fox, A. A. (1994). Music and language. *Annual Review of Anthropology* 23:25–53.

Fromkin, V. (Ed.) (1978). *Tone: A Linguistic Survey*. New York: Academic Press.

Goldsmith, J. A. (1976). *Autosegmental Phonology*. Bloomington: Indiana University Linguistics Club.

Goldsmith, J. A. (1990). *Autosegmental & Metrical Phonology*. Oxford: Blackwell.

Goldsmith, J. A. (Ed.) (1995). *The Handbook of Phonological Theory*. Cambridge: Blackwell.

Hood, M. (1971). *The Ethnomusicologist*. New York: McGraw-Hill.

House, D. (1990). *Tonal Perception in Speech*. Lund, Sweden: Lund University Press.

Ladd, D. R. (1996). *Intonational Phonology*. Cambridge, UK: Cambridge University Press.

Ladd, D. R. and Terken, J. (1995). Modeling intra- and inter-speaker pitch range variation. *International Congress of Phonetic Sciences 13* (Stockholm) 2:386–389.

Lerdahl, F. (1988). Cognitive constraints on compositional analysis. In J. Sloboda (Ed.) *Generative Processes in Music: The Psychology of Performance, Improvisation, and Composition* (pp. 231–259). Oxford: Oxford University Press.

Lerdahl, F. and Jackendoff, R. (1983). *A Generative Theory of Tonal Music*. Cambridge: MIT Press.

Lewin, R. (1993). *Human Evolution: An Illustrated Introduction*, 3rd ed. Boston: Blackwell.

Liberman, M. and Pierrehumbert, J. (1984). Intonational invariance under changes in pitch range and length. In M. Aronoff and R. Oerhle (Eds.) *Language Sound Structure* (pp. 157–233). Cambridge: MIT Press.

Lomax, A. (1968). *Folk Song Style and Culture*. New Brunswick, NJ: Transaction Books.

Marler, P., Evans, C. S., and Hauser, M. D. (1992). Animal signals: Motivational, referential, or both? In H. Papoušek, U. Jurgens, and M. Papoušek (Eds.) *Verbal and Vocal Communication: Comparative and Developmental Approaches* (pp. 66–86). Cambridge, UK: Cambridge University Press.

Merriam, A. P. (1964). *The Anthropology of Music*. Evanston, IL: Northwestern University Press.

Morton, E. S. (1977). On the occurrence and significance of motivation-structural rules in some bird and mammal sounds. *American Naturalist* 111:855–869.

Morton E. S. (1994). Sound symbolism and its role in non-human vertebrate communication. In L. Hinton, J. Nichols, and J. J. Ohala (Eds.) *Sound Symbolism* (pp. 348–365). Cambridge, UK: Cambridge University Press.

Pierrehumbert, J. (1980/1987). The phonology and phonetics of English intonation. Doctoral thesis, Massachusetts Institute of Technology. Published by Indiana University Linguistics Club (1987).

Pierrehumbert, J. (1991). Music and the phonological principle. Remarks from the phonetician's bench. In J. Sundberg, L. Nord, and R. Carlson (Eds.) *Music, Language, Speech and Brain* (pp. 132–145). Houndmills, UK: Macmillan.

Pierrehumbert, J. and Hirschberg, J. (1990). The meaning of intonational contours in the interpretation of discourse. In P. R. Cohen, J. Morgan, and M. E. Pollack (Eds.) *Intentions in Communication* (pp. 271–311). Cambridge: MIT Press.

Seyfarth, R. M., Cheney, D. L., and Marler, P. (1980a). Monkey responses to three different alarm calls: Evidence of predator classification and semantic communication. *Science* 210:801–803.

Seyfarth, R. M., Cheney, D. L., and Marler, P. (1980b). The assessment by vervet monkeys of their own and other species' alarm calls. *Animal Behavior* 40:754–764.

Sloboda, J. A. (1985). *The Musical Mind: The Cognitive Psychology of Music*. Oxford: Clarendon Press.

Sober, E. and Wilson, D. S. (1998). *Unto Others: The Evolution and Psychology of Unselfish Behavior*. Cambridge: Harvard University Press.

Struhsaker, T. T. (1967). Auditory communication among vervet monkeys (*Cercopithecus aethiops*). In S. A. Altmann (Ed.) *Social Communication Among Primates* (pp. 281–324). Cambridge, UK: Cambridge University Press.

Swain, J. P. (1995). The concept of musical syntax. *Musical Quarterly* 79:281–308.

Swain, J. P. (1996). The range of musical semantics. *Journal of Aesthetics and Art Criticism* 54:135–152.

Swain, J. P. (1997). *Musical Languages*. New York: Norton.

Thomas, D. A. (1995). *Music and the Origins of Language: Theories from the French Enlightenment*. Cambridge, UK: Cambridge University Press.

Thorsen, N. (1980). Intonation contours and stress group patterns in declarative sentences of varying length in ASC Danish. *Annual Report of the Institute of Phonetics, University of Copenhagen* 14:1–29.

Thorsen, N. (1981). Intonation contours and stress group patterns in declarative sentences of varying length: Supplementary data. *Annual Report of the Institute of Phonetics, University of Copenhagen* 15:13–47.

Umiker, D. J. (1974). Speech surrogates: Drum and whistle systems. In T. A. Sebeok (Ed.) *Current Trends in Linguistics* Vol. 12 (pp. 497–536). The Hague: Mouton

de Waal, F. (1988). The communicative repertoire of captive bonobos (*Pan paniscus*) compared to that of chimpanzees. *Behavior* 106:183–251.

Wind, J., Chiarelli, B., Bichakjian, B., and Nocentini, A. (Eds.) (1992). *Language Origin: A Multidisciplinary Approach*. Dordrecht: Kluwer.

17 How Music Fixed "Nonsense" into Significant Formulas: On Rhythm, Repetition, and Meaning

Great Paper
- new stuff
(To me)

Bruce Richman

Abstract

Given that the most basic function in any spoken language must be the ability of speakers to repeat utterances in the same way, exactly and precisely, and given that human language probably began with rich, diverse, long sequences from which meaningful utterances were selected (beginning with impoverished, short utterances begs the question about what natural selection had to work with—natural selection selects, but not from nothing!), a basic problem for language origins is how sequences became fixed for entire communities, so that everyone could repeat them exactly. Music making, in all human communities, is also based on the ability to repeat sequences exactly. I suggest that the original process of fixing sequences into recognizable, repeatable, and significant definite some-things by entire communities was accomplished by speech and music making in exactly the same way and by the same means. In other words, in the beginning, speech and music making were one and the same: they were collective, real-time repetitions of formulaic sequences.

As long as I have been studying gelada monkey "friendly" sounds (which has been on and off since 1969), they have struck me as being astoundingly like human conversation in their passion and complexity. They function as a kind of vocal grooming, allowing pairs of geladas to establish temporary, exclusive social bonds with each other. But that is also the main function of most of present-day human conversational speech (see Dunbar 1996). Also, the production units of friendly series sequences are similar in overall form and vocal detail to human vocal formulas (Richman 1996). People and gelada monkeys seem to have a remarkably similar relationship to their vocalizing: they both desperately need to establish continuing vocal relationships with a variety of conspecifics, and they both seem to spend huge amounts of emotional and vocal energy engaging in special kinds of friendly vocalizing to achieve these ends.

Also, for people and geladas, all their constant friendly vocalizing, which for both species is rich in vocal pattern variety, succeeds like social grooming in setting up minute-to-minute relationships despite (and because) of all the emotional and social conflicts they bring to each encounter. Extensive friendly vocalizing relaxes and dispels some of the tensions for participants in these conflict-filled encounters, and allows both people and geladas to continue the system of exclusive (almost jealous) relationships so crucial to their societies, despite the normal background of conflicts engendered by their intense group lives.

In both cases, friendly vocalizing is produced in units averaging a total length of about nine or ten syllables, produced at a rate of about five syllables per second, organized by differentiation of strong and weak beats with about three or four strong beats per unit, and all under an intonation contour (melodic contour) where the end of the unit is signaled by tonal changes. Finally, both human conversational formulas and gelada vocal units are produced with no hesitation phenomena and no internal pauses as one continuous gushing-forth of a whole unit of activity.

Both species use rhythm and melody to distinguish different kinds of utterance types. Geladas, for example, appear to signal the main difference between quick back-and-forth alternations and the long friendly series by rhythmic and melodic features. The long friendly series is always ended by sustained, stepwise rising tones that seem to indicate the completion of a series (see Richman 1976, 1987). In human speech, intonational features signal differences among questions, assertions, and commands.

The gelada productive unit for friendly vocalizing is quite variable in its internal details of length, tempo, rhythm, musical intervals, and syllable types, even though the overall rhythmic and intonational contours are generally similar for all units (Richman 1976). Such variability from unit to unit again makes these vocal units similar to human vocal formulas.

The source of the variability of internal details of units for geladas seems to be the presence of layer upon layer of different expressive features by means of which the animals express overlapping, conflict-filled motivations and emotions they bring to each friendly encounter (Richman 1996). These expressive features are carried by vocal articulatory gestures that are quite distinctive acoustically as well as visually. Such overlapping features lead to the presence in gelada units of a great variety of syllables with different consonant and vowellike features, as well as a great variety of rhythmic and melodic variation.

In one major respect, however, gelada vocal units offer a striking contrast to human vocal formulas: they are not formulaic at all; that is, a given sequence does not tend to be repeated as a vocal formula. In other words, we have no evidence that geladas are capable of repeating the same, exact succession of vocal features that would mark two vocal units as the same. At most, they can repeat or vocally match specific phrases, up to three syllables long, that they have just heard. This is in stark contrast to people, who in normal, everyday conversation frequently and effortlessly repeat exactly entire long formulas they have just heard (Tannen 1989). This contrast, I suggest, provides a significant clue to the nature and origin of human language.

The particular patterns of syllable types, rhythms, and melodies that we find in gelada sequences seem to reflect temporary, real-time changing motivations and interactions of the participants. No special formu-

Very nice
new to me ideas!

laic patterns seem to be attached to particular kinds of situations or to have particular meanings, as occur in human speech.

Human vocal utterances as they actually occur in everyday conversation have come into focus through a series of studies conducted by investigators committed to studying spoken conversation—real speech—as the true heart of language. Studies by Peters (1983), Tannen (1989), Chafe (1994), and Coates (1996), among others, generated new evidence about conversation, its formulaicness, its organization in time as an interactive activity, and its expressiveness, evidence that has not yet been assimilated into linguistics or into our general awareness about language. What this work shows is that the content of ordinary conversational speech is best described and understood as drawn from a collection of hundreds of thousands of open-slot formulas whose lengths amount to about a phrase or one or two clauses. People know, store, remember, have access to, and produce these formulas as holistic, independent, and highly idiosyncratic entities. On-line access to such a collection of open-slot formulas best explains how people are able to carry out the idiomatic fluency of conversational talking they do most of the time, at lightning speed (see Pawley and Syder 1983). Such formulas are exemplified by expressions such as, "I wouldn't do that, if I were you," with its open-slot variants, "I wouldn't say that, if I were you" and "I wouldn't go there, if I were you."

How might such a collection of repeatable formulas, such a repertory of holistic formulas, be built up? How, in fact, could it begin? How could it grow and accumulate? How could whole groups of speaker-participants work on and craft together sequences of sounds so that they became stuck-together, definite entities with meanings that everyone could agree upon, recognize, and use automatically? I suggest that the key is *regular expectancy* based on *repetition* and a *regular beat*; that is, on what are essentially *musical* dimensions.

Repetition and Rhythmic Expectancy in Formula Fixing

I will present an account of how people were first able to craft and stick together both spoken and musical formulas as definite somethings, and how they did it through using some of the same interactive devices that go on today in music making and almost as much in high-involvement, many-voiced, overlapping talking.

Present-day music making in all its varied cultural forms is basically and entirely built and organized around the principle of repetition (or repetition with variation) on all levels. All kinds of music constantly repeat, with variations, phrases, themes, motifs, riffs, rhythms, stanzas, movements, and so on, and this is a basic structuring element (see Meyer 1956; Bernstein 1976; Keil and Feld 1994). But this way of looking at it as structure is too static, and merely touches on music as a product, an already-made thing.

In music as a continuing process that people listen to or participate in, repetition is just one of three main redundancy devices. The other two are, first, music's high level of *formulaicness*, the storehouse of preexisting formulas, riffs, themes, motifs, and rhythms that people bring to music making (and vary and play around with), and second, the high sense of *expectancy* of exactly what is going to come next and fill the upcoming temporal slot, and this expectancy itself is produced by all this repetitiveness.

When we listen to or try to join some music, individual sequences become recognizable, become definite somethings, because we rely on these three redundancy factors. Either we recognize right off a melody or riff or rhythm as a familiar formula, or repetition over and over again of an unfamiliar pattern makes it familiar for a while, or the powerful expectancies created by the process of music let us have a pretty good sense of exactly what is going to come up next, and lo and behold, there it is! But our ancient ancestors, at the beginnings of music, familiar with only a few fixed formulas, must have depended hugely on the other two redundancy factors. They needed much constant repetition by everyone and a lot of expectancy of what was to follow to hear sequences as recognizable and hence repeatable.

The other crucial thing about music making is that it is inherently a group activity in which many voices and many people participate. This inherently social and group-participation aspect is clear from the role it plays in hunter-gatherer and other tribal societies today (Turnbull 1966; Seeger 1987; Feld 1994). Once a formula is fixed it can easily spread to the entire group, since involvement by all is essential to music making. I think that the repetition and expectancy created by music making is the best model we have of how early sound sequences first became fixed and then could spread to entire groups.

It is, however, not only music that gives us a clear model of how early people first fixed formulas. Today, spread widely throughout many diverse cultures, forms of talking exist that have a lot of the same expectancy and repetition features that are so prominent in making. Lively, high-involvement-style (Tannen 1989), many-voiced, overlapping, and collaborative (Marshall 1976; Feld 1994; Coates 1996) kinds of talking with huge amounts of repetition and a lively interactive rhythmic drive are typical of a lot of conversation in many different cultures today. Only with study of actual real-time conversations have the prominence and importance of this kind of talking become clear.

I have more to say about many-voiced kind of talking later, but for now, let me add that it, too, through the huge amounts of repetition and expectancies of what is to follow that it contains for all participants, is a good model of how early formulas were fixed. It is relatively easy to imagine the business of setting up group-interactive vocalizing, with much repetition and expectancy that would have been the best situation for the first fixing of formulas. It does not require anything beyond some basic kinds of behaviors that are quite common in many groups of animals and also in much human vocalizing.

First, all participants must try to repeat what they have just heard from others as best they can, as soon and as often as they can. The desire to repeat seems to be a basic, strong drive in all human beings, particularly infants and children. Listen to young children: my daughter constantly echoes a television dialog she likes, repeats bits of song lyrics, and replays to herself snippets of conversations from school. This is a fierce biological drive that ensures that human beings become and stay involved in speech and in interaction with others. This drive to repeat throws people into language and into vocal interactions with each other. It also ensures that their interactions will be in rhythmic synchrony with each other as their repetitions create an interactive rhythm. Such interactive rhythmic synchrony is crucial for people being able to predict and understand the communicative moves and movements of others. Finally, it ensures that people constantly show and demonstrate their agreement and acceptance of language terms by repeating them.

This is what we could imagine for the group vocal setting of the first fixing of formulas: a group of people or animals around a circle. (I am imagining a situation similar to what happens when present-day hunter-gatherers chat or sing through the night around a campfire, or go off into the forest loudly singing and talking among themselves.) In the ancient prelanguage period, everyone was compelled to express the current emotional or social conflicts they felt through somewhat random sequences of sounds. All participants tried to repeat some sequences that others just said, and they tried to keep on beat with the others. Attempts at repetition and mimicry overlapped, and this produced a dense vocal fabric with many cross-rhythms. Attempts at repetition, although constant and compelling, were not exact. A dissonance of melody and a dissonance of rhythm drew people in. People wanted to participate, to get in, and resolve those dissonances.

Constant, frequent repetition of the same few formulas by many voices makes it easy for people to remember these sequences as whole units. This is a kind of behavioral conditioning. It conditions people into remembering them as whole units, and enables them to recognize them whenever they came up and to repeat them with fidelity. The next step in making such sequences into meaningful formulas is to tie newly forged formulas into intensely felt, highly particular, multimodal scenes of real life.

How did this happen? Activities that a group of people were doing while they were vocalizing together, activities that were important or striking or richly emotional, came to be associated with particular sound sequences, so that each time the sound sequence came up again, highly specific memories would be evoked in participants. Whenever people sang or chanted a particular sound sequence they would remember the concrete particulars of the situation most strongly associated with it: ah, yes! we sing this during this particular ritual admitting new members to the group; or, we chant this during a long journey in the forest; or, when a clearing is finished for a new camp, this is what we chant; or these are the keenings we sing during ceremonies over dead members of our group.

Over the years and centuries more and more different chanted formulas came to be associated with more and more different aspects of group life, as human social life became more and more complex. Even though these chanted formulas became somewhat conventional and ritualized in form, and shortened by frequent use, and eventually, by becoming open-slot formulas, admitted the combining of different formulas and parts of formulas into each other, they were remembered and produced as holistic units whose processing was tied to limbic-emotional memory. This is the kind of memory that is specially developed in mammals (and even more developed in human evolution) that works as a gatekeeper in the brain so that creatures have to only deal with and process events that are especially salient and important and leave aside emotionally unimportant events. The limbic-emotional system works by comparing continuing events to emotionally important, remembered scenes that are stored as whole, multisensory scenes of real life remembered as concrete particulars. Such memory explains how we can remember hundreds of thousands of different, highly idiosyncratic formulas and use them so quickly and fluently.

At first, in childhood (or historically at the beginnings of language) we remember sequences as wholes tied to particular scenes. (This still is the case for me for some spoken formulas: "Ain't it the truth!" evokes a specific scene of the Cowardly Lion/Bert Lahr in the film *The Wizard of Oz*). But later in our language development and in language evolution our limbic system is able to generalize from the many thousands of occasions of use of such formulas so that we pick out a varied collection of highly schematic features, any family resemblance collection of which will trigger an instant comparison and tell us that this particular spoken formula is the appropriate one to use now. Consider a group of people around a circle, vocalizing back and forth in an overlapping, collaborative way. Not only was such overlapping, collaborative vocalizing crucial to fixing formulas, it also had an important social function in itself. Why do people stay with each other? What keeps them involved in relationships with each other? In a certain sense, one of the main ties that bind people to each other is just talking, just the talking and dialogue and vocalizing by itself. Samuel Beckett (1958) illustrated this mutual vocal dependence that we are all condemned to in his play *Endgame*, where the two main characters say this:

Clov: I'm leaving.

Hamm: No!

Clov: What is there to keep me here?

Hamm: The dialogue.

The cross-rhythms, dissonances of melody and rhythm, cross-purposes of power over others, and solidarity with them that are expressed in every dialogue and performance, the need to join in and exaggerate the differences while at the same time trying to resolve them, are among the "participatory discrepancies" (Keil 1994) that motivate people to keep on talking and keep on making music with each other no matter what. In egalitarian-cooperative societies, where most of human history was lived, to talk and make music with others in a high-involvement, overlapping, repeating style is precisely to be a full-fledged member of society. This style of relating is still quite important in our own more complex societies. The high-involvement style of vocalizing is not just a drag on freedom: it is also a sign of one's full citizenship and right of participation in society.

"Talking"

I am trying to recover what I call "talking"[1] as the biologically based form of human spoken vocalizing that drives people to engage in and participate in socially constructed language, but is separate from it and precedes it historically and logically. (In effect, talking is the foundation that makes socially constructed language possible. Notice that I say that language is a vast, socially constructed artifact, produced by discourse processes by thousands of people over many years. The biological part of human language that I call talking is what pushes people to engage in socially constructing language; it is not language itself. See Andrew Lock's work [1996, 1997] on how social discourse constructed human symbolic evolution.)

Talking is speech at its most expressive, most interactive, and most rhythmically repetitive. The best models for it are the kinds of fast, lively, collaborative, overlapping talk we find in Lorna Marshall's (1976) description of !Kung conversation, Erickson's (1981) description of Italian-American dinner table talk, Scollon's (1981) analysis of conversational ensemble, Tannen's (1989) accounts of high-involvement, rhythmically repetitive talking voices, Feld's (1994) account of Kaluli "lift-up-over-sounding" putting talk together, Coates' (1996) collaborative floor talking jam sessions of women friends, and Chafe's (1997) polyphonic topic development.

I am following the principle that richness and diversity of behavior at the beginning are the best things to look for if one wonders what really complicated behaviors such as human language developed from. We should not look for impoverishment at the beginning, as a general trend can be seen in the evolution of all sorts of things, whether in biological (Gould 1991) or cultural (Nietzsche 1887), that complexity always comes from previous, but different, complexity. Behavioral complexity is never created out of nothing.

Specifically, language always comes from previous language; all human utterances are repetitions, versions of previously spoken utterances. And the succession of repetitions with variations of previously spoken utterances goes back indefinitely into the distant past. Talkers who are maximally expressive, maximally interactive, with great repetition and rhythmic grooves, with the greatest richness and diversity of these forms, such as we see today in talkers referred to above, are the best candidates for a model of evolving and fixing and playing around with the thousands and thousands of formulas that eventually worked their way into socially constructed language. In contrast are talkers who are dumbly laconic, who do not say much, with little range of expressive forms, with little back-and-forth interaction, with little or no repetition of self or others, with no rhythmic repetition and thus no rhythmic grooves in which one expects certain forms to fill upcoming temporal slots, with no help from a huge variety of emotionally expressive intonation melodies and rhythmic riffs to individuate sequence formulas. Because these laconic talkers are monotonously nonexpressive of emotions, they are precisely the worst candidates we could imagine for developing the richness of spoken formulas we see in human language.

More generally, as far as human language discourses are concerned, all sorts of specialized forms of human discourse, such as complex speech acts, telling stories, speaking monologically in diatribes, or telling people what to do, and eventually written discourses—the whole diverse range of specialized forms of discourse people have developed over thousands of years of history—can be easily seen as narrow, specialized forms that developed as late offshoots of an originally rich and diverse form of multivoiced, expressive, collaborative, jam session talking. Being many-voiced and collaborative in the construction of utterances, using long sequences, being maximally emotionally expressive, and being rhythmically interactive describe a kind of talking that is surprisingly prevalent and powerful in many cultures and gives us a good model of the rich and diverse kind of vocalizing that existed at language's beginnings, a model that can most easily explain further developments in human language (but not the reverse).

There are good reasons for assuming that each feature of many-voiced talking represents primary, original features of human spoken vocalizations and not later developments. The long sequences that occur today can only have come from a history of people producing long sequences. People must have been quite adept at producing such sequences quite fluently from a very early time. The only alternative, the usual pointing-and-grunting-at-objects story that says that language began with isolated, monosyllabic, gruntlike separate "words," suffers from the problem of explaining how these separate, isolated units were ever forged into long, fluent sequences. In addition, rhythmic complexity must have come from previous rhythmic complexity. The incredibly intricate rhythmic forms of speech and speech interaction that occur when many voices converse must have come from a long history of intricate control and many-voiced interaction of rhythms.

For another thing, intense emotional expressivity must have been at the heart of spoken utterances from the beginning for two reasons. First, combining many different emotionally expressive vocal gestures during talking is the best model for how a sufficiently rich and diverse inventory of vocal raw materials was initially available for later use in socially constructed language. Second, unless sequences mattered intensely to people in an emotional way, they never would have become embedded so deeply into the human limbic system as to be stored there permanently. The limbic system originally evolved to deal with events that seriously mattered to creatures and their survival. That is what emotions were evolved to tell us. But if people originally spoke with little emotion, if the original functions of speech were as rational and unemotional as some think, no sequences would have penetrated and stayed in the limbic system. Only as gut responses and as limbic responses can we explain the original staying power of the first formulas.

The final reason for assuming that all these expressive, sequential, interactive features were in place at the earliest stages of the evolution of human language is that this allows us to see a remarkable continuity of vocal interactions with the complexity of choral and expressive vocal interactions of some nonhuman animals. Animals, as diverse as geladas

(Richman 1978, 1987), porpoises (Norris 1991), killer whales (Ford 1991), wolves, African hunting dogs, and Australian magpies try in their group vocal interactions to repeat (or at least mimic or vocally match as closely as they can) what others are saying, and repeat the beats and stay on beat with others. For these animals this also is part of a strong biological drive to remain attached and stay in behavioral synchrony with others. Joint production of utterances and vocal matching of melodic contours function as signals in a group context that all participants are in behavioral synchrony, that they are in solidarity with each other, and that they are attempting to resolve social and emotional conflicts. These are crucial social functions of vocal interaction, particularly for creatures like these and early humans as well, who were forced to live in large, changing groups in order to survive.

The intricate, precisely timed, vocal rhythmic synchrony, vocal matching, and collaboration in joint production of utterances that I assume was already in place in the earliest days of the evolution of human language is obviously a behavior that other, highly social animals are quite capable of producing. This is one among other examples of behavioral continuity that humans share with nonhuman animals when it comes to the vocal raw materials that were later worked into socially constructed language. It is important for us to see these animal continuities as powerful, particularly when we have the tendency to view human language as some sort of special creation.

Nonsense Formulas Used Today as Evidence for What the First Fixed Formulas Were Like

Human vocal practices seem to follow what I call the attic principle: like in an attic in an old house, nothing is ever really thrown away. Living remnants of ancient vocal practices are retained alongside the most up-to-date, seemingly more advanced ones. Among the most intriguing of these seemingly primitive vocal practices that have an active life today with the most abstract kinds of talk are nonsense vocable formulas used in all cultures. The best examples I know of which have been described and analyzed most closely are the "eeney-meeny-miney-mo" children's counting-out chant (Opie and Opie 1984; Rubin 1995), Havasupai nonsense chants (Hinton 1994), Seneca religious chants (Chafe 1994), and American and New Zealand cattle auctioneer chanting (Kuiper and Haggo 1984); there are many other examples in the world's cultures. These nonsense formulas can help us throw light on what the earliest fixed formulas in human history might have been like.

Nonsense vocable formulas have the following characteristics. They are highly memorable as whole units, and are tenaciously retained in exact copies even though they are spread widely in time over hundreds of years and spread widely in space over diverse languages and cultures.

Nonsense formulas have totally holistic meanings. The parts of the formula are, in effect, meaningless. If asked, people cannot say if the parts have any meaning at all. Meaning is attached to the entire, whole formula and reflects the social function of the whole formula. The meaning of a Havasupai snake venom-healing nonsense chant is its function in curing a wound; the meaning of eeney-meeny-miney-mo is its function in counting out potential players for a game. If contemporary nonsense formulas are good models for the first fixed formulas used in human talking, let me suggest briefly how it was possible for people to become aware of parts of formulas and use them in meaningful ways. Formulas that were used frequently sometimes were much shortened by overuse. This is a tendency in many spoken expressions: "God be with you" became shortened to "good-bye" and then "bye." "How are you doing?" became shortened to "howdy." Also, in formulas that were used frequently, sometimes a few noticeable or salient syllables, often the first or last two or three syllables of the entire sequence, came to stand for the whole formula. This ability of parts to stand for wholes is an important kind of figure of speech. Later, these parts were pushed into the open slots of entirely different formulas. Eventually, people became aware of and came to use parts of formulas in meaningful ways.

Present-day nonsense formulas are tied together more strongly by poetic parallelism features than most other spoken formulas. A huge amount of alliteration, rhyme, parallelism of rhythms and forms help them stick together and be memorable as whole units. Obviously, such poetic redundancy was quite crucial for the earliest fixed formulas. Of course, it is important to remember that many spoken formulas today, including most normal, meaningful clauses we speak, still show huge amounts of poetic parallelism and structuring; for example, "As good as it gets."

Some present-day nonsense formulas are laid out and structured in open-slot variation formats. That is, whole lines of the formulas are repeated, but at certain open slots variations occur. Exact repetition of lines of formulas with variations at certain open slots was probably an important early feature of fixed formulas. This was easily produced by having interacting participants in talking-chanting, repeat each sequence they had just heard as exactly as they could, but play around with variations or expansions at certain key points in the sequence. This is exactly what frequently happens when people speak collaboratively today. Someone says a clause, and other voices chime in with variations that change or expand it at certain points. For example:

A. I go out a lot.   X. I wanna go home.
B. I don't go out at all.   Y. I need to go home.
C. I go out and eat.   Z. I'd love to go home.

What this shows is that even the process of embedding something that is usually taken to be terribly abstract and presumably the product of individual cognition can be seen as the direct product of many-voiced, interactive performances. In these cases, embedding is not a mysterious mental process taking place in some hidden mind, but rather a performance acted out in real time.

How Sung Formulas Were Shanghaied into Dyadic Speech-Act Talk

Random, emotionally and interactionally driven sequences of syllables, rhythms, and melodies became fixed by constant, interactive repetition and by rhythmic expectancies into stuck-together, memorable, significant somethings. What was significant and meaningful about each formula was its connection to a situation and to the social actions of that situation. The meaning of a formula was, in the beginning, entirely holistic, a complex of the particular group of people involved, their actions, and the circumstances. Thus it was a complex social action. We vocalize in this kind of situation to accomplish these social ends; we (a group of young males, or older women, or children, or whatever) always ("this is what we do") chant this formula in situations of (grief, reconciliation, journeying, food gathering, before a hunt, during an initiation, in the morning, at night, etc.) in order to do such and such (overcome emotional tension, get others moving, agree on fair distribution, etc.).

Later, after much historical development, them or parts of them came to be used in more dyadic, speech-act kinds of discourse. Pairs of people used talk to question, request, affirm, demand, order, deny, or agree with each other, and they shanghaied formulas or their parts to be used in these dyadic speech acts. When formulas were imported from their original collective repetition contexts to more dyadic speech-act contexts, the entire holistic mix of original meanings became available as potential meaning components for the speech acts. Which of these meaning components was actually used varied depending on the speech act.

Thus, the raw materials for dyadic speech-act talk were already-fixed, already-stuck-together, already-meaningful (in a holistic way) formulas.

Note

1. I am indebted to John L. Locke (see 1995, 1996) for this notion of talking, but I have my own interpretation of it.

References

Beckett, S. (1958). *Endgame*. New York: Grove.

Bernstein, L. (1976). *The Unanswered Question: Six Talks at Harvard*. Cambridge: Harvard University Press.

Chafe, W. (1994). *Discourse, Consciousness, and Time*. Chicago: University of Chicago Press.

Chafe, W. (1997). Polyphonic topic development. In T. Givon (Ed.) *Conversation* (pp. 87–109). Amsterdam: Benjamins.

Coates, J. (1996). *Women's Talk*. Oxford: Blackwell.

Dunbar, R. (1996). *Grooming, Gossip and the Evolution of Language*. London: Faber and Faber.

Erickson, F. (1981). A conversation among Italian-Americans. In D. Tannen (Ed.) *Analyzing Discourse* (pp. 55–81). Washington, DC: Georgetown.

Feld, S. (1994). Lift-up-over-sounding. In C. Keil and S. Feld (Eds.) *Music Grooves* (pp. 109–156). Chicago: University of Chicago Press.

Ford, J. (1991). Family fugues. *Natural History* March: 68–76.

Gould, S. (1991). *Bully For Brontosaurus*. New York: Norton.

Hinton, L. (1994). *Flutes of Fire*. Berkeley: Heyday.

Keil, C. (1994). Participatory discrepancies. In C. Keil and S. Feld (Eds.) *Music Grooves* (pp. 96–108). Chicago: University of Chicago Press.

Keil, C. and Feld, S. (Eds.) (1994). *Music Grooves*. Chicago: University of Chicago Press.

Kuiper, K. and Haggo, D. (1984). Livestock auctions, oral poetry and ordinary language. *Language in Society* 13:205–234

Lock, A. (1996). *Handbook of Human Symbolic Evolution*. Oxford: Clarendon.

Lock, A. (1997). On the recent origin of symbolically-mediated language. In S. Lea and M. Corballis (Eds.) *The Evolution of the Human Mind* (pp. 42–78). Oxford: Oxford University Press.

Locke, J. L. (1995). More than words can say. *New Scientist* January: 30–41.

Locke, J. L. (1996). Why do infants begin to talk? Language as an unintended consequence. *Journal of Child Language* 23:251–268.

Marshall, L. (1976). *The !Kung of Nyae Nyae*. Cambridge: Harvard University Press.

Meyer, L. B. (1956). *Emotion and Meaning in Music*. Chicago: University of Chicago Press.

Nietzsche, F. (1887/1967). *The Genealogy of Morals* (W. Kaufmann, Trans.). New York: Vintage.

Norris, K. (1991). *Dolphin Days*. New York: Norton.

Opie, I. and Opie P. (1984). *Children's Games in School and Playground*. Oxford: Oxford University Press.

Pawley, A. and Syder F. (1983). Natural selection in syntax. *Journal of Pragmatics* 7:551–579.

Peters, A. (1983). *The Units of Language Acquisition*. Cambridge, UK: Cambridge University Press.

Richman, B. (1976). Some vocal distinctive features used by gelada monkeys. *Journal of the Acoustical Society of America* 60:718–724.

Richman, B. (1978). The synchronization of voices by gelada monkeys. *Primates* 19:569–589.

Richman, B. (1987). Rhythm and melody in gelada vocal exchanges. *Primates* 28:199–223.

Richman, B. (1996). Why humans can pronounce so many different sounds. Paper presented to the 12th annual Language Origins Society conference, Baltimore.

Rubin, D. C. (1995). *Memory in Oral Traditions: The Cognitive Psychology of Epic, Ballads, and Counting-Out Rhymes*. New York: Oxford University Press.

Seeger, A. (1987). *Why Suya Sing*. Cambridge, UK: Cambridge University Press.

Scollon, R. (1981). The rhythmic integration of ordinary talk. In D. Tannen (Ed.) *Analyzing Discourse* (pp. 45–71). Washington, D.C.: Georgetown.

Tannen, D. (Ed.) (1989). *Talking Voices*. Cambridge, UK: Cambridge University Press.

Turnbull, C. (1966). *Wayward Servants*. Garden City, NY: Natural History.

Debora?

Björn Merker

Abstract

Evenly paced time marking in measured music allows us to predict where the next beat is going to fall. This makes musical pulse a cardinal device for coordinating the behavior of several individuals in a joint, coherent, synchronized performance. Such behavioral synchrony to a regular beat on the part of many individuals is rare among higher animals and raises the question of its origination in anthropogenesis. The fit between one of the evolutionary models proposed to explain synchronous chorusing in insects and basic aspects of our earliest hominid ancestors' social structure suggests that synchronous chorusing may have played a fundamental and hitherto unsuspected role in the process of hominid divergence from our common ancestor with the chimpanzee. The possible elaboration of such an adaptation through female choice (acting both between and within groups of cooperatively chorusing males) and vocal learning (in both its receptive and productive modalities) is discussed with reference to hominoid behavior, the fossil record of hominid brain expansion, and its bearing on the relationship between the origins of language and of music.

A Musical Lacuna

Sometimes an unexploited dimension of potential variation in an art form or other behavioral domain can tell us of underlying constraints whose influence is so pervasive as to escape easy notice. A case in point from the world of music would seem to be the fact that among the many kinds of structural variations we meet with, we hardly ever encounter music employing discrete, that is, stepwise (from one beat to the next), and frequent tempo changes as a structural device for generating variety. Instead, tempo changes are almost invariably gradual, taking the form of accelerando or ritardando, or else they conform to the arithmetic of whole integer ratios; that is, they introduce changes such as doubling or halving the tempo, or tripling a halved tempo.

The constraint underlying this structural lacuna is of course the prepotency of a regular beat or pulse as an organizing principle in measured music. The structural device of an evenly paced timegiver appears to have such a hold over our sensibilities that music tends to come in two fundamental kinds. Either it is measured, that is, avails itself of a regularly paced timegiver, or it gives up reliance on time marking altogether, and is unmeasured (Arom 1991, and this volume). The half-way place between these two musical worlds that would be created by the device of discrete tempo changes, which necessarily violate the even spacing of the basic timegiver of the musical beat, is accordingly uninhabited, another way of stating our initial observation.

Within measured music the musical pulse is not an invariably fixed structural feature, but allows of different treatments of which there appear to be two principal varieties. In one, the even pace of the musical time marker is autonomous in the sense that deviations from it tend to be inadvertent or adventitious. In the other, the even spacing of the time-giver is not thus an ideal in its own right but is subject to manipulation as a means of expression through episodic stretching and compression (rubato and agogic accents). Since even in the case of such pulse subordination the stylistic effect is dependent on the presence of the regular pulse as a baseline from which deviations are made, it can be regarded as a special case of the more general pervasiveness of musical pulse in measured music. It is not possible within the confines of this chapter to discuss the voluminous literature on musical pulse and meter. Entry to this literature can be gained through Nielsen (1984), Kramer (1988), and Wallin (1991).

The musical pulse embedded in all measured music is what allows us to tap or clap to a piece of music. Fraisse (1982:154) pointed out a peculiarity in this behavior, namely, that whereas in most behaviors a response follows a stimulus, here the response is made to coincide with the stimulus (which can be as simple as the click of a metronome). The phenomenon is one of *entrainment*, and in this context the functional utility of an evenly paced timegiver is immediately apparent: it allows us to predict where the next beat is going to fall and thus synchronize our behavior with that of the pulse. Since many individuals, no less than single ones, can synchronize their behavior to a common timegiver, musical pulse is a cardinal device for coordinating the behavior of those individuals in a joint, coherent, synchronized performance, be they musicians among themselves or with dancers or soldiers (see McNeill 1995).

Synchronous Chorusing in Nature

Behavioral synchrony involving many individuals is not common in nature but is not altogether absent. Some species of fireflies synchronize their bioluminescent flashing in the tropical night (Buck 1988), a number of other insects synchronize their chirps in multimale chorusing (Otte 1977; Greenfield and Shaw 1983), synchronous calling is found among chorusing frogs (Wells 1977; Klump and Gerhardt 1992), and clusters of male fiddler crabs wave their claws in synchrony to attract females for mating (Backwell, Jennions, and Passmore 1998). Behavioral synchrony in these cases differs from behavioral coordination between individuals in, for example, the duets of gibbons and some birds by featuring rhythmic repetition of signals in conformity with a regular beat or pulse (Greenfield 1994). Such synchrony generally occurs in the context of multimale displays of sexual advertisement to attract females. Male cooperation in such displays raises the question of why a male should cooperate in attracting a female to a group with whom he might have to share her. Detailed studies of synchronous display have generated both formal treatments of mechanisms of entrainment (Sismondo 1990) and a number of models for the evolution of multimale synchrony (reviewed in Greenfield 1994).

For a number of chorusing species the assumption that synchrony represents male cooperation was overturned by good evidence that it is an epiphenomenal (nonadaptive) outcome of timing strategies employed in male competition to signal first (Greenfield and Roizen 1993; Backwell, Jennions, and Passmore 1998). Treatments of synchrony as an adaptation include its interpretation as an antipredator strategy to dilute predator attention to a male when his signaling attracts not only females but predators (Walker 1969; Otte 1977; Tuttle and Ryan 1982), and as a means of increasing peak signal output from a group of males competing with other groups of males to attract mobile females (Wells 1977; Buck and Buck 1978; Morris, Kerr, and Fullard 1978). This latter model is of particular interest in the present context, because its assumptions regarding the circumstances and function of male synchronous chorusing apply, in a most direct and robust manner, to the emergence of hominids from our common ancestor with the chimpanzees.

Synchronous Chorusing and Hominid Origins

The group sociality of our closest living relative among the apes, the chimpanzee, differs most markedly from that of, say, group-living common monkeys by featuring female exogamy. Females, rather than males, move from their natal group (Pusey 1979) to settle and to rear their young in a group where they may or may not have any kin and whose males jointly defend a group territory against similarly constituted groups of neighboring males (Wrangham 1975; Ghiglieri 1984, 1985; Pusey, Williams and Goodall 1997; see also Foley 1996). This pattern was suggested as a possible context for the evolution of male-male cooperation (Ghiglieri 1984; Rodman 1984). Under hunting and gathering (Ember 1978) and many other circumstances, humans share with chimpanzees the unusual social trait of female exogamy, and thus it presumably also characterized our earliest hominid ancestors. In the absence of strong reasons for assuming otherwise, we may picture the social behavior of our earliest hominid ancestors as based on groups of associated males with a reproductive interest in attracting migrating females away from other similar groups of males.

But this pattern conforms strikingly to one model for the evolution of synchronous male chorusing, the one, namely, according to which synchrony serves amplitude summation of signals within groups of co-operating males competing with other groups to attract females. It only remains to suggest that those early hominids who eventually gave rise to *Homo* engaged in such synchronous vocal signaling for mate attraction. Such behavior is most easily derived from the noisy bouts of coopera-tive calling (cooperative in the sense of benefiting absent individuals of both sexes within the territorial group) in which groups of chimpanzee males engage on discovering large fruiting trees (Wrangham 1975, 1979; Ghiglieri 1984). Synchronous calling in such circumstances would maxi-mize the summed amplitude of the multivoice display to extend its geographic reach beyond territorial boundaries.[1] It would represent an honest distance signal of group resources and male cooperativity, a signal that ought to be of interest to migrating females deciding which territo-rial group to join. That is, since group members falsely attracted to a calling bout are likely to retaliate, the number of calling bouts in a given territory over time reflects a combination of its actual abundance of fruit-ing trees and the cooperation of males inhabiting that territory.

Assuming synchronous calling bouts, the quality of the synchrony itself provides a further measure of male cooperation as well as vocal skill. These factors ensure that the distance signal is informative, which in turn introduces female choice on the part of migrating females as a sexual selection pressure on the calling behavior of territorial groups. For males in neighboring territories the same signal conveys a double message: it advertises desirable resources that might stimulate them to intrude on the territory and broadcasts a deterrent to encroachment through the evidence of cooperation it provides. Under such circumstances the ter-ritorial group whose calling synchrony extends the reach of its signal by decibel summation is likely to attract a greater number of migrating females than it would in the absence of the cooperative synchrony, thus increasing the potential mating opportunities of individual males in the group.

Synchronous calling of the kind postulated here, that is, true coopera-tive synchronous calling rather than synchrony as a default condition of competitive signaling, requires a motivational mechanism for mutual entrainment. We assume that such a mechanism was selected for in the course of hominid divergence from our common ancestor with the chimpanzee, and was retained to the present day in the form of our propensity to join in and entrain to a repetitive beat. This propensity is apparently lacking in the common chimpanzee, which seems unable to keep time even with training (Williams 1967), but may be present in bonobos. Such an ancestral adaptation for entrainment to a repetitive beat would supply, in other words, an ancient biological foundation for the musical pulse no human culture has failed to feature among its musical means of expression (Arom, this volume; Nettl, this volume). Indeed, if the present argument should turn out to have any merit, this adaptation for entrainment supplies an irreducible biological root of human music.

Genuine synchronous chorusing may exist, at least incipiently, among bonobos. A report by de Waal (1988:202–203) on captive bonobos describes a call variant apparently lacking a homolog in the vocal repertoire of common chimpanzees, namely, a loud and explosive sound called staccato hooting. According to de Waal "during choruses, staccato hooting of different individuals is almost perfectly synchronized so that one individual acts as the 'echo' of another, or emits calls at the same moments as another. The calls are given in a steady rhythm of about two per second." We note that both alternation and synchrony often occur in the same species of chorusing animals, and can result from a single timing mechanism (see Greenfield 1994:106). The issue of true synchrony is important in the present context because, of course, only simultaneous calling can serve amplitude summation. At least one field study of bonobo distance calls mentions only alternate and not simultaneous calling (Hohmann and Fruth 1994), but should simultaneous synchrony occur in wild bonobos and on further study be shown to conform to the regular beat of a pulse, humans would not be alone among higher animals in possessing pulse-born behavioral synchrony.

In contrast to the insect examples referred to above, the human capacity for entrainment is not tied to a fixed or narrow range of tempos, but extends more than an octave in either direction from approximately 100 beats per minute, a representative central tempo in an equally wide range of individual spontaneous tapping frequencies (see Fraisse 1982 for details). This, besides reinforcing the suggestion that adaptation must have motivational underpinnings, raises the issue of neural mechanisms capable of timing repetitive behaviors involved in synchronous chorusing over a wide range of tempos. It is to be noted that according to the above example the evolution of synchronous hominid chorusing took place *pari passu* with evolutionary changes in the control of locomotion linked to the fully upright mode of bipedalism (Leakey and Walker 1997). Motor and sensorimotor mechanisms for walking and running supply a convenient source of continuously graded (in tempo) and repetitive time-keeping signals on the simple assumption that our hominid ancestors paced and coordinated their calling bouts with the help of associated bodily movements derived from the repertoire of walking and running, but performed largely in place (with upright posture); that is, as a form of dancing display (for the correlation between walking rhythm and spontaneous tempo (see Fraisse 1982:154; see also Melvill-Jones and Watt 1971). This would be a natural extension, in the context of group synchrony, of locomotor and other physical displays associated with hominoid distance calls (Mori 1983; Geissmann, this volume). Needless to say, synchronous chorusing and dancing to a repetitive beat qualifies as music in the human sense, according to a wide range of construals of that elusive term.

Specifically, it fits the origin of our term "music" in the Greek *mousiké*, which included melody, dance, and poetry, whose common denominator is pulse-based rhythmicity. It is also in good agreement with the term *ngoma* of the Bantu language group, a term that subsumes drumming, singing, dancing and festivity under a single unitary concept. Similarly, the Blackfoot principal gloss for music, *saapup*, combines singing, dancing, and ceremony in a single concept (Nettl, this volume).

The net result of these conjectural developments would be the emergence among our hominid ancestors of a novel and unique social adaptation, namely, a behavioral forum featuring synchronous singing and dancing on the part of a higher animal. Just as chimpanzee pant-hooting displays at a newly discovered large fruiting tree attract mixed groups of males and females to the site of the commotion, we should picture these hypothetical hominid display bouts as key social gatherings with potential participation by all members of a given territorial group and attended by considerable excitement. Specifically, they would provide a convenient arena for the pursuit of individual mating tactics through efforts to attract the attention of members of the opposite sex in this setting of joint rhythmic singing and dancing. Sexual selection (see Kirkpatrick and Ryan 1991; also Miller, this volume; Todd, this volume) would, in other words, be capable of affecting the content of the display bout in a double, parallel fashion over evolutionary time: female choice would act between groups of chorusing males in connection with female migration as already described, and it would act between individual males within a group if, as assumed here, individual display behavior within the bout served as a means of mate attraction.[2] Should either or both of these pressures for elaboration of the content of the display bout have promoted the expansion of learning capacity in the relevant behavioral domains (vocal learning above all), far-reaching implications for our subsequent evolutionary trajectory follow.

Vocal Learning, Brain Expansion, and the Origin of Language

In mammals, expansion of cerebral capacity for a given functional purpose appears to proceed by global expansion of neocortical capacity as a whole, along with a more modest expansion of cerebellar cortical volume (Finlay and Darlington 1995). This means that any selected-for capacity increase will tend to generate adventitious or free cortical expansion in other areas without selection for those ancillary increases. Any given selection pressure for a cerebral capacity increase might therefore initiate a cascade of brain expansion with functional consequences far beyond the confines of the initiating adaptation, provided the energetic costs both for nutrient supply (Martin 1981; Armstrong 1983; Aiello and Wheeler 1995) and heat removal (Falk 1990) of such a development can be sustained. Synchronous hominid chorusing is well suited to trigger such development on the simple assumption that the vocal behavior it featured involved vocal learning (Marler and Mundinger 1971; Nottebohm 1975, 1976; Janik and Slater 1997; for evidence compatible with vocal learning in chimpanzees, see Boesch 1991:83).

Vocal learning may occur in chimpanzees, to judge by a report of instances in which individual chimpanzees take over the distinctive pant-hoot pattern of a fellow group member after the latter's disappearance or death (Boesch 1991:83). We note also the tendency of chorusing common chimpanzees, whose chorusing apparently consists of alternating, and not synchronous, calling (see Mitani and Brandt 1994; Hohmann and Fruth 1994) to match their vocal output to that of their calling partner (Mitani and Brandt 1994). The latter authors discuss a number of possible explanations for the genesis of the observed between-partner similarity in call characteristics, some of which involve that matching between auditory-receptive and vocal-productive functions that figure in vocal learning.

To begin with, a selection pressure is required to account for the considerable advance in brain size over great ape levels of *Homo* at its first appearance in the fossil record about 2 million years ago (Ruff, Trinkaus, and Holliday 1997; Falk, this volume). Vocal learning with its dual functional dependence on auditory-receptive and vocal-productive capacities (Marler 1990; Whaling, this volume) could supply the key to this increase by exerting a dual pressure for expansion of posterior as well as frontal cortical domains. Posteriorly its auditory-receptive requirements would most plausibly act to extend further the asymmetric enlargement of the planum temporale region already in evidence in chimpanzees (Gannon et al. 1998). Anteriorly, the functional requirements of vocal-productive capacity should promote elaboration, from a great ape starting point, of regions of the frontal lobe in which the endocast of KNM-ER 1470 (*Homo rudolfensis*) differs from the great apes (Tobias 1981; Falk 1983). Such changes are appropriate for growth of a cerebral substratum for increasingly elaborate vocal-musical behavior involving vocal learning, and offer no compelling reason to link them with referential functions of language (see also Petersen et al. 1988:587).

A possible exception to this lack of referential function for the postulated complex ancestral vocalizations might be their use as individually specific vocal signatures. Since they are assumed to have involved vocal learning, they might be analogous to the signature whistles of bottle-nose dolphins (Caldwell, Caldwell, and Tyack 1990; see also Janik and Slater 1997:79–82) and function as the equivalent of personal names in social situations. If so, they might at some point have become the prototype for generalized naming by distinctive, presumably elaborate, vocal phrase patterns in the formation of a semantic lexicon (see Ujhelyi as well as Richman, this volume, for discussions bearing on this issue). Any such development would benefit from the availability of a highly differentiated repertoire of unsemanticized, syntactically structured phrases of the kind that make up the learned vocal repertoires of some birds and humpback whales, and would presumably have to await the development of such repertoires.

Although unrelated to referential language, the conjectural developments sketched above nevertheless bear strongly on the issue of language origins. The possibility that our remote ancestors might have engaged in complexly structured but unsemanticized vocal behavior prevents us from attributing brain expansion, even in the posterior temporal-parietal region and frontal areas related to Broca's area, to human language or protolanguage unless we know that the carriers of those brains were in fact linguistic creatures. All we know for certain about the time of appearance of referential language in the evolution of *Homo* is that it forms an integral part of the cultural history of all current populations of *Homo sapiens sapiens*. One possibility is therefore that the use of complex human vocal behavior for referential purposes is a bona fide cultural *invention* on the part of fully modern humans within, say, the past 50,000 years or less. If so, this function, in contrast to preexisting auditory-vocal capacities of an advanced kind on which such an invention might have been based, would lack both an evolutionary history and cerebral mechanisms of its own, in the sense that these mechanisms would have evolved specifically for human language. Rather, it would be analogous in this regard to reading and writing. The cerebral distribution of different types of word memories provides indirect (if tenuous) support for such a view (Martin et al. 1995).

Working backward from this null hypothesis, one may attempt to assign increasing antiquity to the origin of language. Specific regions of prefrontal and neocerebellar cortices associated with language functions (and some of them with music as well) on the basis of imaging studies

(Petersen et al. 1988; Sergent et al. 1992; Petersen and Fiez 1993; Martin et al. 1995; Khorram-Sefat, Dierks, and Hacker 1996; summarized by Falk, this volume; see also Hassler 1950; Leiner, Leiner, and Dow 1991; Thach 1996) are not present in middle Pleistocene fossil endocasts of archaic *Homo sapiens* from Greece and Africa (Seidler et al. 1997). They may accordingly have evolved under a linguistic selection pressure that brought us above threshold for referential speech, unless, of course, they happen to represent the final twist of a spiral of sexual selection for sophisticated syntactic structuring of impressive vocal displays of a musical kind, and only later were partially taken over by language, as it were.[3]

To proceed backward beyond this point in attempts to link stages of brain evolution (see Ruff, Trinkaus, and Holliday 1997) with human language requires far more precise knowledge of the nature of language and its cerebral dependencies than we currently possess, particularly since we know far too little of the neurological requirements and dependencies of vocal learning in mammals, and more generally, of a vast domain of human behavior characterized by rules without meaning (Staal 1989), including nonverbal song, music, mantras, and ritual. Capacities underlying such behaviors are prime candidates for supplying preadaptations for human language; that is, behavioral capacities and biases based on perceptual, motivational, cognitive, and motor mechanisms evolved for other purposes (such as display) but so constituted as to supply essential foundations for human language.

In the foregoing I emphasized vocal productivity based on vocal learning in this role, because in contrast to language, it has arisen again and again in the world of nature, in a variety of taxonomic groups including mammals (see Janik and Slater 1997, and discussion of vocal learning in chimpanzees), and in a diversity of forms with different mechanisms and modes of development. These are epitomized in genuine cultural song traditions of humpback whales with their complex shared repertoires, individual innovation, and cumulative seasonal turnover in the repertoire of a given group of singers (Payne, this volume). Unless and until we can eliminate adaptations of this kind from consideration as factors in the evolution of hominids and *Homo*, the fossil record of human brain development cannot usefully be related to human language. For that it is necessary to know whether or not we were in fact singing and dancing hominids before we became talking humans, and if so whether and how long we might have been singing and dancing humans before we started to employ our cerebral equipment for referential language. It is even conceivable that without such an essentially musical preadaptation, the long step to language might have remained forever beyond our reach.

324   Björn Merker

Acknowledgments

I dedicate this chapter to Nils L. Wallin, without whose vision of a discipline joining biology to musicology it would never have been written. I am indebted to Maria Ujhelyi for calling my attention to the significance of female exogamy and to the possible existence of synchronous chorusing in bonobos, and to Nils Wallin, Simha Arom, and Steven Brown for stimulating discussions about the origins of music.

Notes

1. An individual chimpanzee pant-hoot used in fruit tree signaling carries at most 2 kilometers, whereas a chimpanzee group territory spans some 10 to 30 square kilometers (Ghiglieri 1984). It is, in other words, approximately 4.5 kilometers across. The "square law" relating sound level to distance gives us the rough estimate that four well-synchronized callers would have to be heard from any point on their territorial boundary irrespective of the location of their calling within the territory, and sixteen males would have to synchronize their calling to be heard from any point within any immediately neighboring territory, irrespective of the location they happened to be calling from within their own territory. With a chimpanzee total group size of around fifty individuals, these rough estimates do not exceed the bounds of biological plausibility.

2. It should be noted in this connection that there is no good reason to confine the effects of sexual selection to the vocal content of display behavior. Rather, it would presumably affect any traits or behaviors involved in mate choice. If, for example, females preferred males who were unusually steady on their feet as evidenced by the greater elegance or complexity of their dancing movements, sexual selection could have been a factor accelerating the perfection of the upright posture and bipedal locomotion.

3. Assume that, in parallel with the evolution of syntactically elaborate but unsemanticized synchronous chorusing from the hominoid distance call and its associated locomotor displays, our ancestral proximity vocalizations were also developing (perhaps as a side effect of brain expansion driven by vocal learning, as already explained, or through their own utility, possibly accentuated by developments such as a trend toward vocal grooming [Dunbar 1993]) by a differentiation of their capacity to convey a wide range of information concerning matters of rank, sex, age, class, emotional state (satisfaction, fear, aggression, affiliation, etc.), food source quality, predator classes, and other environmental contingencies (see Hauser, this volume). This is the domain of vocal semantics, encoded in the patterns of pitch, articulation, and dynamics of the primate voice. Against such a background, the radical novelty of human language might have been born in the appropriation, *by* the semantic capacity for conveying meaning socially through the voice in proximal communication, *of* the syntactic capacity for sequential patterning of vocal output evolved for musical display purposes, perhaps at a late date in our history as a species (see also Ujhelyi, this volume).

References

Aiello, L. C. and Wheeler, P. (1995). The expensive-tissue hypothesis: The brain and the digestive system in human and primate evolution. *Current Anthropology* 36:199–221.

Armstrong, E. (1983). Relative brain size and metabolism in mammals. *Science* 220:1302–1304.

Arom, S. (1991). *African Polyphony and Polyrhythm*. Cambridge, UK: Cambridge University Press.

Backwell, P., Jennions, M., and Passmore, N. (1998). Synchronized courtship in fiddler crabs. *Nature* 391:31–32.

Boesch, C. (1991). Symbolic communication in wild chimpanzees? *Human Evolution* 6:81–90.

Buck, J. (1988). Synchronous rhythmic flashing in fireflies. II. *Quarterly Review Biology* 63:265–289

Buck, J. and Buck, E. (1978). Toward a functional interpretation of synchronous flashing in fireflies. *American Nature* 112:471–492.

Caldwell, M. C., Caldwell, D. K., and Tyack, P. L. (1990). Review of the signature-whistle hypothesis for the Atlantic bottlenose dolphin. In S. Leatherwood and R. R. Reeves (Eds.) *The Bottlenose Dolphin* (pp. 199–234). New York: Academic Press.

Dunbar, R. I. M. (1993). Coevolution of neocortical size, group size and language in humans. *Behavioral and Brain Sciences* 16:681–735.

Ember, C. R. (1978). Myths about hunter-gatherers. *Ethnology* 17:439–448.

Falk, D. (1983). Cerebral cortices of east African hominids. *Science* 221:1072–1074.

Falk, D. (1990). Brain evolution in *Homo*: The "radiator" theory. *Behavioral and Brain Sciences* 13:333–381.

Finlay, B. L. and Darlington, R. B. (1995). Linked regularities in the development and evolution of mammalian brains. *Science* 268:1578–1584.

Foley, R. A. (1996). An evolutionary and chronological framework for human social behavior. *Proceedings of the British Academy* 88:95–117.

Fraisse, P. (1982). Rhythm and tempo. In D. Deutsch (Ed.) *The Psychology of Music* (pp. 149–180). New York: Academic Press.

Gannon, P. J., Holloway, R. L., Broadfield, D. C., and Braun, A. R. (1998). Asymmetry of chimpanzee planum temporale: Humanlike pattern of Wernicke's brain language area homolog. *Science* 279:220–222.

Ghiglieri, M. P. (1984). *The Chimpanzees of Kibale Forest*. New York: Columbia University Press.

Ghiglieri, M. P. (1985). The social ecology of chimpanzees. *Scientific American* 252:102–113.

Greenfield, M. D. (1994). Cooperation and conflict in the evolution of signal interactions. *Annual Review of Ecological Systems* 25:97–126.

Greenfield, M. and Roizen, I. (1993). Katydid synchronous chorusing is an evolutionarily stable outcome of female choice. *Nature* 364:618–620.

Greenfield, M. D. and Shaw, K. C. (1983). Adaptive significance of chorusing with special reference to the Orthoptera. In D. T. Gwynne and G. K. Morris (Eds.) *Orthopteran Mating Systems: Sexual Competition in a Diverse Group of Insects*. Boulder, CO: Westview Press.

Hassler, R. (1950). Über Kleinhirnprojektionen zum Mittelhirn und Thalamus beim Menschen. *Deutsche Zeitschrift für Nervenheilkunde* 163:629–671.

Hohmann, G. and Fruth, B. (1994). Structure and use of distance calls in wild bonobos (*Pan paniscus*). *International Journal of Primatology* 15:767–782.

Janik, V. M. and Slater, P. J. B. (1997). Vocal learning in mammals. *Advances in the Study of Behavior* 26:59–99.

Khorram-Sefat, D., Dierks, T., and Hacker, H. (1996). Cerebellar activation during music listening. *NeuroImage* 3:S312.

Kirkpatrick, M. and Ryan, M. J. (1991). The evolution of mating preferences and the paradox of the lek. *Nature* 350:33–38.

Klump, G. M. and Gerhardt, H. C. (1992). Mechanisms and function of call-timing in male-male interactions in frogs. In P. K. McGregor (Ed.) *Playback and Studies of Animal Communication* (pp. 153–174). New York: Plenum Press.

Kramer, J. D. (1988). *The Time of Music*. New York: Macmillan/Schirmer.

Leakey, M. and Walker, A. (1997). Early hominid fossils from Africa. *Scientific American* 276:60–65.

Leiner, H. C., Leiner, A. L., and Dow, R. S. (1991). The human cerebrocerebellar system: Its computing, cognitive and language skills. *Behavioral Brain Research* 44:113–128.

Marler, P. (1990). Song learning: the interface between behaviour and neuroethology. *Philosophical Transactions of the Royal Society of London B* 329:109–114.

Marler, P. and Mundinger, P. (1971). Vocal learning in birds. In H. Moltz (Ed.) *The Ontogeny of Vertebrate Behavior* (pp. 389–450). New York: Academic Press.

Martin, A., Haxby, J. V., Lalonde, F. M., Wiggs, C. L., and Ungerleider, L. G. (1995). Discrete cortical regions associated with knowledge of color and knowledge of action. *Science* 270:102–105.

Martin, R. D. (1981). Relative brain size and basal metabolic rate in terrestrial vertebrates. *Nature* 283:57–60.

McNeill, W. H. (1995). *Keeping Together in Time: Dance and Drill in Human History*. Cambridge: Harvard University Press.

Melvill-Jones, G. and Watt, D. G. D. (1971). Observations on the control of stepping and hopping movements in man. *Journal of Physiology* 219:709–727.

Mitani, J. C. and Brandt, K. L. (1994). Social factors influence the acoustic variability in the long-distance calls of male chimpanzees. *Ethology* 96:233–252.

Morris, G. K., Kerr, G. E., and Fullard, J. H. (1978). Phonotactic preferences of female meadow katydids (Orthoptera: Tettigoniidae: *Conocephalus nigropleurum*). *Canadian Journal of Zoology* 56:1479–1487.

Mori, A. (1983). Comparison of the communicative vocalizations and behaviors of group ranging in eastern gorillas, chimpanzees and pygmy chimpanzees. *Primates* 24:486–500.

Nielsen, F. V. (1984). *Oplevelse af Musikalisk Spaending*. Copenhagen: Akademisk Forlag.

Nottebohm, F. (1975). A zoologist's view of some language phenomena, with particular emphasis on vocal learning. In E. H. Lenneberg and E. Lenneberg (Eds.) *Foundations of Language Development* (pp. 61–103). New York: Academic Press.

Nottebohm, F. (1976). Discussion paper: Vocal tract and brain: A search for evolutionary bottlenecks. In S. R. Harnad, H. D. Steklis, and J. Lancaster (Eds.) Origins and evolution of language and speech. *Annals of the New York Academy of Sciences* 280:643–649.

Otte, D. (1977). Communication in Orthoptera. In T. A. Sebeok (Ed.) *How Animals Communicate* (pp. 334–361). Bloomington: Indiana University Press.

Petersen, S. E. and Fiez, J. A. (1993). The processing of single words studied with positron emission tomography. *Annual Review of Neuroscience* 16:509–530.

Petersen, S. E., Fox, T. P., Posner, M. I., Mintum, M., and Raichle, M. E. (1988). Positron emission tomographic studies of the cortical anatomy of single-word processing. *Nature* 331:585–589.

Pusey, A. (1979). Inter-community transfer of chimpanzees in Gombe National Park. In D. A. Hamburg and E. McCown (Eds.) *The Great Apes* (pp. 465–479). Menlo Park, CA: Benjamin/Cummings.

Pusey, A., Williams, J., and Goodall, J. (1997). The influence of dominance rank on the reproductive success of female chimpanzees. *Science* 277:828–831.

Rodman, P. S. (1984). Foraging and social systems of orangutangs and chimpanzees. In P. S. Rodman and J. G. H. Cant (Eds.) *Adaptations for Foraging in Nonhuman Primates* (pp. 134–160). New York: Columbia University Press.

Ruff, C. B., Trinkaus, E., and Holliday, T. W. (1997). Body mass and encephalization in Pleistocene *Homo*. *Nature* 387:173–176.

Seidler, H., Falk, D., Stringer, C., Wilfing, H., Muller, G. B., zur Nedden, D., Weber, G. W., Reicheis, W., and Arsuaga, J. L. (1997). A comparative study of stereolithographically modeled skulls of Petralona and Broken Hill: Implications for future studies of middle Pleistocene hominid evolution. *Journal of Human Evolution* 33:691–703.

Sergent, J., Zuck, E., Terriah, S., and MacDonald, B. (1992). Distributed neural network underlying musical sight-reading and keyboard performance. *Science* 157:106–109.

Sismondo, E. (1990). Synchronous, alternating, and phase-locked stridulation by a tropical katydid. *Science* 249:55–58.

Staal, F. (1989). *Rules Without Meaning. Ritual, Mantras and the Human Sciences*. New York: Lang.

Thach, W. T. (1996). On the specific role of the cerebellum in motor learning and cognition: Clues from PET activation and lesion studies in humans. *Behavioral and Brain Sciences* 19:411–431.

Tobias, P. V. (1981). The emergence of man in Africa and beyond. *Philosophical Transactions of the Royal Society of London B* 292:43–56.

Tuttle, M. D. and Ryan, M. J. (1982). The role of synchronized calling, ambient light, and ambient noise in anti-bat-predator behavior of a treefrog. *Behavioral Ecology and Sociobiology* 11:125–131.

de Waal, F. B. M. (1988). The communicative repertoire of captive bonobos (*Pan paniscus*) compared to that of chimpanzees. *Behavior* 106:183–251.

Walker, T. J. (1969). Acoustic synchrony: Two mechanisms in the snowy tree cricket. *Science* 166:891–894.

Wallin, N. L. (1991). *Biomusicology: Neurophysiological, Neuropsychological, and Evolutionary Perspectives on the Origins and Purposes of Music*. Stuyvesant: Pendragon.

Wells, K. D. (1977). The social behavior of anuran amphibians. *Animal Behaviour* 25: 666–693.

Williams, L. (1967). *The Dancing Chimpanzee: A Study of Primitive Music in Relation to the Vocalizing and Rhythmic Action of Apes*. New York: Norton.

Wrangham, R. W. (1975). *The Behavioural Ecology of Chimpanzees in Gombe National Park, Tanzania*. Doctoral dissertation, University of Cambridge.

Wrangham, R. W. (1979). On the evolution of ape social systems. *Social Sciences International* 18:335–368.

Geoffrey Miller

Abstract

Human music shows all the classic features of a complex biological adaptation. Adaptations must be explained either through natural selection for (individual) survival benefits or sexual selection for courtship and reproductive benefits. Darwin argued that both birdsong and human music evolved as sexually selected courtship displays. Whereas his explanation of birdsong is widely accepted, his courtship hypothesis for human music has been neglected. Darwin's courtship hypothesis can be updated in the light of contemporary evolutionary psychology, biological signaling theory, and sexual selection theory. Some features of music seem to function as costly and reliable indicators of the producer's fitness, and others may have evolved through Fisher's runaway process as purely aesthetic signals. Although human music is usually made in groups, like many other courtship displays, no group selection account is necessary. To distinguish better between survival and courtship functions of music, we do, however, need much more cross-cultural, quantitative data on music production as a function of age, sex, mating status, and audience composition. Given that almost all complex acoustic signals produced by other species are courtship displays, this hypothesis for human music is not only better supported by music's design features, but should be considered the evolutionary null hypothesis.

A Darwinian Approach to Music Evolution

. . . it appears probable that the progenitors of man, either the males or females or both sexes, before acquiring the power of expressing their mutual love in articulate language, endeavored to charm each other with musical notes and rhythm. (Darwin 1871:880)

In *The Descent of Man, and Selection in Relation to Sex*, Darwin (1871) devoted ten pages to birdsong and six to human music, viewing both as outcomes of an evolutionary process called sexual selection. Darwin's idea that most birdsong functions as a courtship display to attract sexual mates is fully supported by biological research (e.g., Catchpole and Slater 1995), but his idea that human music evolved to serve the same function has been strangely neglected. Although much has been written about the origins of human music (e.g., Rousseau 1761; Blacking 1987; Dissanayake 1988, 1992; Knight 1991; Storr 1992; Tiger 1992), very few theorists have taken a serious adaptationist approach to the question. Those who have, usually searched in vain for music's survival benefits for the individual or the group, overlooking Darwin's compelling theory that music's benefits were primarily reproductive and best explained by the same sexual selection processes that shaped birdsong. This chapter has the simple goal of reviving Darwin's original suggestions that human music must be studied as a biological adaptation, and that music was shaped by sexual selection to function mostly as a courtship display to attract partners. Fortunately, after a century of obscurity, Darwin's theory of sexual selection itself has undergone a renaissance in biology over the last two decades, so biology offers many new insights about courtship adaptations that are applied here to human music.

The historical analogy between the study of birdsong and the study of human music may prove instructive. Before Darwin, natural theologians such as William Paley considered birdsong to have no possible function for the animals themselves, but rather to signal the creator's benevolence to human worshippers through miracles of beauty. Birdsong was put in the category of the natural sublime, along with flowers, sunsets, and alpine peaks as phenomena with an aesthetic impact too deep to carry anything less than a transcendental message. The idea that birdsong would be of any use to birds was quite alien before about 1800. With the rise of natural history, writers such as Daines Barrington in 1773 and Gilbert White in 1825 (cited in Darwin 1871) argued that birdsong must have some function for the animals that use it, but must arise exclusively from male rivalry and territorial competition. They recognized that male birds sing much more than females, and mostly during the breeding season. But they insisted that song was a form of vocal intimidation between males rather than attraction between the sexes.

Darwin agreed that some songs function to intimidate, but maintained that female choice for male singing ability was the principal factor in the evolution of birdsong: "The true song, however, of most birds and various strange cries are chiefly uttered during the breeding-season, and serve as a charm, or merely as a call-note, to the other sex" (1871:705). Against the hypothesis that birdsong somehow aids survival, he cited observations that male birds occasionally drop dead from exhaustion while singing during the breeding season. His sexual selection theory was perfectly concordant with the idea that males sacrifice their very lives in the pursuit of mates, so that their attractive traits live on in their offspring.

The history of theorizing about the evolution of human music shows many of the same themes. Many commentators took Paley's creationist, transcendental position, claiming that music's aesthetic and emotional power exceed what would be required for any conceivable biological function. Claude Levi-Strauss (1970:18), for example, took a position typical of cultural anthropology in writing, "Since music is the only language with the contradictory attributes of being at once intelligible and untranslatable, the musical creator is a being comparable to the gods, and music itself the supreme mystery of the science of man." Where such commentators recognized any need for consistency with evolutionary principles, they usually explained music as a side effect of having a big brain, being conscious, or learning and culture. As we will see, none of these explanations is adequate if music can be shown to be a legitimate adaptation in its own right.

Other theorists adopted pre-Darwinian natural historians' rather narrow view of biological function as centered on competition for survival. This led to desperate searches for music's contribution to pragmatic survival problems in Pleistocene Africa, our ancestral environment. Here, quandaries arose. No one ever proposed a reasonable survival benefit to individuals taking the time and energy to produce music, which has no utility in finding food, avoiding predators, or overcoming parasites. But if one falls back on claiming survival benefits to the group through some musical mechanism of group bonding, one ends up in the embarrassing position of invoking group selection, which has never been necessary to explain any other trait in a mammalian species (see Williams 1966). If evolution did operate according to survival of the fittest, human music would be inexplicable.

Consider Jimi Hendrix, for example. This rock guitarist extraordinaire died at the age of 27 in 1970, overdosing on the drugs he used to fire his musical imagination. His music output, three studio albums and hundreds of live concerts, did him no survival favors. But he did have sexual liaisons with hundreds of groupies, maintained parallel long-term relationships with at least two women, and fathered at least three children in the United States, Germany, and Sweden. Under ancestral conditions before birth control, he would have fathered many more. Hendrix's genes for musical talent probably doubled their frequency in a single generation through the power of attracting opposite-sex admirers. As Darwin realized, music's aesthetic and emotional power, far from indicating a transcendental origin, points to a sexual selection origin where too much is never enough. Our ancestral hominid-Hendrixes could never say, "OK, our music's good enough, we can stop now," because they were competing with all the hominid-Eric Claptons, hominid-Jerry Garcias, and hominid-John Lennons. The aesthetic and emotional power of music is exactly what we would expect from sexual selection's arms race to impress minds like ours.

Darwin on Human Music

Although Darwin devoted only a few pages of *The Descent of Man* to the role of sexual selection in the evolution of human music (Darwin 1871:875–881), his insights remain so apposite that they are worth reviewing here. He seems to have considered music the single best example of mate choice having shaped a human behavioral trait. He first set the context by reminding the reader that sounds generally evolve for reproductive functions: "Although the sounds emitted by animals of all kinds serve many purposes, a strong case can be made out, that the vocal organs were primarily used and perfected in relation to the propagation of the species" (p. 875). He reviewed as examples the sounds of frogs, toads, tortoises alligators, birds, mice, and gibbons, which are produced only in the breeding season and usually only by males, but sometimes by both sexes. He then reviewed the anatomy of sound perception to suggest that the capacity to perceive musical notes could easily have begun as a side effect of the capacity to distinguish noises in general: "an ear capable of discriminating noises—and the high importance of this power to all animals is admitted by every one—must be sensitive to musical notes" (p. 877). The famous 1868 paper by Helmholtz on acoustic physiology was cited to explain why many animals would converge on using tones that belong to human musical scales. Darwin concluded with a strong critique of the natural theology position, proposing that if male birds sing to females, it must be because female birds are impressed by singing: "unless females were able to appreciate such sounds and were excited or charmed by them, the persevering efforts of the males, and the complex structures often possessed by them alone, would be useless; and this is impossible to believe" (p. 878).

Immediately after rejecting the possibility that animal sounds are useless, Darwin pondered the apparent frivolity of human music: "As neither the enjoyment nor the capacity of producing musical notes are faculties of the least use to man in reference to his daily habits of life, they must be ranked among the most mysterious with which he is endowed" (p. 878). He then cited the ubiquity of music across cultures, and even mentioned recently unearthed Paleolithic flutes made from reindeer bone to illustrate its antiquity. He mentioned how musical capacities may emerge spontaneously and reliably in human development: "We see that the musical faculties, which are not wholly deficient in any race, are capable of prompt and high development" (p. 878). He then illustrated how music arouses strong emotions, and how love is the most common lyrical theme in songs. Apart from his rather patronizing Victorian attitude toward non-European music, his strategy for arguing that human music is a biological adaptation and a product of sexual selection is almost identical to what a modern evolutionary psychologist would use. Darwin summarized: "All these facts with respect to music and impassioned speech become intelligible to a certain extent, if we may assume that musical tones and rhythm were used by our half-human ancestors, during the season of courtship" (p. 880). As the coup de grace, he preempted the objection that musicians do not mean anything sexual when they perform, by reminding us that a biological function requires no conscious awareness: "The impassioned orator, bard, or musician, when with his varied tones and cadences he excites the strongest emotions in his hearers, little suspects that he uses the same means by which his half-human ancestors long ago aroused each other's ardent passions, during their courtship and rivalry" (p. 881).

Darwin was not troubled by the fact that both men and women produce music. He admitted that the capacity and love for singing and music are not a sexual character in the sense of a sexually dimorphic trait (p. 875). In the 300 pages on sexual selection preceding his analysis of human music, he noted many sexually selected traits present in both sexes. His remarks on prehistoric marriage and on sexually selected physical traits present in both sexes suggest that he assumed both male and female mate choice among our ancestors.

What can we add to Darwin's hypothesis that human music arose through mate choice? We know more about music now, and we know more about mate choice, and we know more about mental adaptations. Although Darwin laid the foundations, a modern Darwinian approach to music can draw on the full power of evolutionary biology, evolutionary psychology, and evolutionary anthropology.

An Adaptationist Approach to Music

Before going too deeply into the relevance of sexual selection theory to music, it is important to step back and ask about the relevance of evolutionary theory in general. There are many ways of asking about the origins of music, but evolutionary biologists would focus on four key questions of increasing specificity (see Williams 1966; Tooby and Cosmides 1990, 1992). First, what is music for? Second, what adaptive functions are served by the specific behaviors of singing, chanting, humming, whistling, dancing, drumming, and instrument playing? Third, why did the fitness benefits of music making and music listening exceed the fitness costs? Fourth, consider music as a set of signals emitted to influence the behavior of other organisms (see Dawkins and Krebs 1978): who generates these signals, under what conditions, to what purpose? who receives these signals, with what sensitivity, resulting in what behavioral changes, benefiting whom?

All of these questions put music in the adaptationist arena where theories have to play by very strict rules. In this arena, it is not so important to worry about how to define music, exactly when it evolved, or what sequence of modifications occurred to transform nonmusical apes into musical humans. Most speculation about the origins of music identifies some ape or human behavior that shares certain features with music, such as the prosody seen in mother-infant ritualized verbal exchanges

(Dissanayake, this volume; Storr 1992), or adult speech (Pole 1924), and then supposes that identification of a plausible origin is sufficient to explain a complete adaptation. Evolution just does not work like that. Instead of speculating about precursors, the adaptationist approach puts music in a functional, cost-benefit framework and asks theories for just one thing: *show me the fitness*!

Fitness means survival or reproductive advantages of a trait that outweigh its biological costs. All traits, whether bodily or behavioral, have costs because they all require matter and energy that might be better spent on something else. Music production and dancing would have had particularly high costs for our ancestors: they are noisy so they could attract predators and hostile competitors, they require energetic body movements that are sometimes sustained for hours, they require long periods of practice to perform well, and they keep sleepy babies from getting their rest. Almost all traits that could evolve in a particular species do not evolve, because their fitness benefits do not exceed their fitness costs. Only a tiny minority do. To explain why music evolves in our lineage means explaining why it conferred net fitness benefits on our ancestors.

Of course, not all things that a species does require an adaptationist explanation of this sort. Only adaptations do. The first question for bio-musicologists must be: is human music a legitimate, complex, biological adaptation? If it is not, it might be explicable as a side effect of other evolutionary or cultural processes. But if it is, the rules change: complex adaptations can evolve only through natural selection or sexual selection (Williams 1966; Dawkins 1996). That's it. There are no other options, and any musicologist who is lucky enough to discover some other way of explaining adaptive complexity in nature can look forward to a Nobel prize in biology.

Both natural selection and sexual selection boil down to one principle: some genes replicate themselves better than others. Some do it by helping their bodies survive better, and some by helping themselves to reproduce better. Whereas individuals are the units of survival, genes are the units of selection and replication, and selection views individuals as transient vehicles for passing on their genes (Dawkins 1976, 1996). Between the level of genes and the level of individuals is the level of adaptations, which are units of biological function. Most complex adaptations grow through the interaction of many genes that were selected gradually over many generations. Because the chance combinations of genes necessary to produce a complex adaptation are astronomically unlikely in a single generation, cumulative selection over many generations is the only known mechanism for producing such adaptations (Dawkins 1996). This view of genes as the units of selection and adaptations as the unit of function is sometimes called adaptationism or neo-Darwinism or selfish gene theory, but it is the dominant, mainstream framework for modern biology, including animal behavior studies, physical anthropology, and evolutionary psychology. If we want ideas about the origins of music to be taken seriously by these communities, we have to play by their adaptationist rules, which have proved so successful for explaining so many other apparently baffling biological phenomena.

Music, like language (Pinker 1994), fulfills many classic criteria for being a complex biological adaptation in our species. It is found across cultures and in all epochs of recorded history. It unfolds according to a standard developmental schedule, resulting in high musical capacity in all normal human adults relative to the musical capacities of closely related species: almost everyone can learn a melody, carry a tune, and appreciate musical performances by others. Music seems to involve specialized memory capacity such that normal adults can almost instantly recognize and reproduce any of thousands of learned melodies. Musical capacities show strong cortical lateralization and are localized in standard, special-purpose cortical areas. Human music has clear analogs in the acoustic signals of other species (birdsong, gibbon song, whale song), suggesting convergent evolution. Music can provoke strong emotions, suggesting biological adaptations not only for production but also for reception.

With respect to these nine adaptationist criteria, music differs clearly from other human abilities such as proving mathematical theorems, writing legal contracts, or piloting helicopters, which depend on a tiny minority of individuals being able to acquire counterintuitive skills through years of difficult training. Some ethnomusicologists such as John Blacking (1976:7) also recognized that music is an adaptation: "There is so much music in the world that it is reasonable to suppose that music, like language and possibly religion, is a species-typical trait of man. Essential physiological and cognitive processes that generate musical composition and performance, may even be genetically inherited, and therefore present in almost every human being."

The adaptationist framework has been extended to cope with animal signaling systems (Dawkins and Krebs 1978; Krebs and Dawkins 1984; Hauser 1996), which would include human music. It seems strange at first for an animal to produce a costly signal that does not directly influence its environment. A signal that simply expressed feelings without having any fitness payoffs would never evolve. Even a signal that communicated information would never evolve unless an animal gained some indirect survival or reproductive benefit to that information having been sent to another animal. Altruistic information broadcasting has no place in nature: no species evolved to play the role of the BBC World Service. Because such indirect benefits of signaling are relatively rare, true animal communication is rare. The major exception is signaling between close relatives that share many of the same genes.

Most animal signal systems have been successfully analyzed as adaptations that manipulate the signal receiver's behavior to the signaler's benefit. Signals are usually selfish. If we take an adaptationist approach to music, and if music is not just directed at kin, we must analyze it as a biological signal that manipulates receivers to the benefit of signalers. Many such manipulative signals are sent between species: bee orchids attract male bees by looking and smelling like female bees (Darwin 1862); warning coloration keeps unpalatable insects from being eaten by their predators (Wallace 1889). A few manipulative signals, such as music, are sent primarily within a species from one conspecific to another. Such conspecific signals tend to fall into a very small number of categories (Hauser 1996), such as threats exchanged between competitors, warning calls exchanged between kin to signal the proximity of a dangerous predator, contact calls exchanged between group members to keep the group together during movement, dominance and submission signals, and courtship displays. Of these, courtship displays are almost always much the most complex, most varied, more prolonged, most energetically expensive, and most interesting to human observers. By these criteria, if alien biologists were asked for their best guess about the evolutionary function of human music as a conspecific signal, they would almost certainly answer that it is a sexually selected courtship display like almost all other complex, varied, interesting sounds produced by other terrestrial animals.

Music as a courtship adaptation does not mean that it stems from a Freudian sublimated sex drive. Sexually selected adaptations do not have to feel very sexy to their users. A trait shaped by sexual selection does not have to include a little copy of its function inside in the form of a conscious or subconscious sexual motivation (see Tooby and Cosmides 1990, 1992). The male human beard, although almost certainly an outcome of sexual selection through female mate choice, is not a jungle of hidden, illicit motives. It simply grows and displays that its possessor is a sexually mature male, without having any idea why it does that. Even psychological adaptations like music production may work similarly, firing off at the appropriate age and under the right social circumstances, without their possessor having any idea why he or she suddenly feels inspired to learn the guitar and play it where people congregate.

Identifying an adaptation and its function does not require telling the phylogenetic story of how it first arose at a particular time and place in prehistory, and how it underwent structural transformation through a series of intermediate stages. Even for morphological adaptations, biologists often have no idea when the adaptations that they study first arose or exactly how they reached their current form. For most psychological adaptations that leave no fossil record, it is not even possible to reconstruct phylogeny in this sense. Nor is it necessary. Adaptationist analysis does not worry very much about origins, precursors, or stages of evolutionary development; it worries much more about current design features of a biological trait, its fitness costs and benefits, and its manifest biological function. This is good news for theories of music evolution. It is just not very important whether music evolved 200,000 years ago or 2 million years ago, or whether language evolved as a precursor to music. The adaptationist's job is to look at the adaptation as it is now, to document its features and distribution within and across species, and to test hypotheses concerning its biological function against this evidence.

In sum, music is a complex adaptation, and it has costs but no identifiable survival benefits. Therefore, it is most likely to have evolved due to its reproductive benefits. Because such clear functional analogs exist among human music and birdsong, gibbon song, and whale song, which all seem to have been shaped by Darwin's process of sexual selection through mate choice, music seems most likely an outcome of mate choice. Its principal biological function, then, is sexual courtship.

Design Features of Music as a Sexually Selected Adaptation

Before opening the toolbox of sexual selection theory any wider, we should pause, summarize, and sharpen the preceding arguments. Music, like art, language, and ideology, shows the hallmarks of being a complex behavioral adaptation. It is easy and fun for humans to learn but very hard for artificial intelligence programs, suggesting that its production is objectively very complex and difficult, although seemingly effortless. It is universal across cultures and across history. It is universal across normal individuals, although with some genetic heritability in aptitude. It develops spontaneously according to a standard life history pattern, without formal instruction or conscious awareness of its underlying principles (except for professional musicians). But music also has special features as products of sexual selection. It is spontaneously practiced and produced despite energetic costs and lack of survival utility. Over the short term, it is used conspicuously in courtship, and its production tends to decline after mating (as Miles Davis famously observed, male musicians, like athletes, avoid having sex before important concerts because they need the sexual "edge" to play well). Over the life span, public music production rockets upward after puberty, reaches its peak in young adulthood during the period of most intense courtship, and declines gradually with age and parenting demands. Musical tastes lead to strong assortative mating. Finally, music is functionally analogous to sexually selected acoustic displays in other species.

Sexual Selection Theory: The Basics

Darwin (1871) identified two different kinds of sexual selection: aggressive rivalry and mate choice. Rivalry, especially between males, tends to produce weapons, such as sharp teeth, large horns, and strong muscles. Mate choice, especially by females, tends to produce ornaments, such as colorful tails, innovative sounds, and musky smells. Although Darwin provided overwhelming evidence for the importance of female mate choice in producing male ornaments, biologists after him focused almost exclusively on male rivalry, rejecting the possibility of female choice (Cronin 1991). For a century, sexual selection was seen as a process where active, competitive males struggled for "possession" of passive females by acquiring territories and status, and repelling rivals. Ornaments were usually interpreted as species-recognition signals for helping animals avoid mating with the wrong species. Only in the last couple of decades did the picture change, with astounding vindication of Darwin's mate choice idea in hundreds of experimental and theoretical studies (Ridley 1993; Andersson 1994). Research on sexual selection through mate choice is currently one of the most active areas of behavioral science, with papers saturating major animal behavior journals. The sophistication and complexity of mate choice theory have grown enormously in recent years. But for our purposes, we need to understand only two key ideas: mate choice for indicators, and mate choice for aesthetic displays.

Music as a Set of Sexually Selected Indicators

The idea of indicators is that sexual selection shapes animals to advertise reproductively important things like age, health, fertility, status, and general fitness (see Andersson 1994). For example, the peacock's tail may function as an indicator, because unhealthy, weak, peacocks cannot grow very large tails, and even if they could, they could not escape from predators that easily notice large tails. The result is that the size of a peacock's tail statistically correlates with the bird's age, health, and heritable fitness. Peahens thus have a strong incentive for paying attention to tail size, because by mating with a large-tailed peacock, they are getting good genes that will give their offspring survival and reproductive advantages. Whereas some indicators reveal good genes, others reveal good resources, good parenting skills, or good fertility.

Indicators are usually subject to the "handicap principle" (Zahavi 1975, 1997) that they must have high costs in order to be reliable. Cheap, easy-to-grow, easy-to-maintain indicators could be faked too easily by unhealthy, unfit individuals, so they would lose their informative value. Technically, the key feature is that an indicator must have a higher relative cost to an unfit animal than it does to a highly fit animal (Grafen 1990). For example, male elephant seals typically get to breed only by becoming the single most dominant male on a beach full of hundreds of females, which requires constantly fighting off all the other males with hardly any sleep or food for weeks on end. Being dominant might cost a male many thousands of calories a day in food energy previously stored as fat. Thin males might have the strength to become dominant for short periods, but each day may burn off 10% of their fat reserves. They cannot long bear the calorie cost of chasing off all their rivals, and they usually starve to death early in the breeding season. They are replaced by fatter males for whom the same calorie cost represents perhaps only 2% of fat reserves per day, and for whom the relative, marginal cost of dominance is lower. Thus, dominance in male elephant seals is a reliable indicator of fat reserves, and hence of male foraging ability. Thus, traits that are most informative as indicators are those that are easy to mess up, and that are highly sensitive to disruption by poor nutrition, injury, parasites, pathogens, genetic inbreeding, or developmental disorders. This leads to the apparent paradox that animals advertise their fitness with displays that, being most costly, most reduce their fitness.

Many traits function as reliable indicators in various animals (Andersson 1994). Body size indicates age and nutritional state. Body symmetry indicates resistance to developmental insults such as disease and injury. Bright colors indicate ability to escape from predators and resistance to parasites that dull those colors. Even more numerous are behavioral indicators. Loudness of songs indicates energy level in tungara frogs. Length of roaring displays indicates physiological endurance in red deer. The size of prey given as nuptial gifts by scorpionflies indicates foraging skill and strength. Territory quality in many birds indicates dominance and fighting ability. All these evolved under sexual selection, favored by mate choice.

In large-brained animals, there are good reasons to suspect that complex psychological adaptations could function particularly well as sexually selected indicators. Brains are complex, hard to grow, and expensive to maintain. Higher cortical functions can be easily disrupted by poor nutrition, disease, injury, and low status (leading to depression). Moreover, in primates, probably half of all genes are involved in brain growth, and perhaps a third specifically expressed in brain growth. This means that for humans, with about 100,000 genes, brain indicators could reveal the state of up to 50,000 genes in prospective mates. Thus, brain functioning provides a clear window onto the quality of a large proportion of an animal's heritable genome. Behaviors that large brains generate can function as a particularly sensitive indicator, and mate choice would be unlikely to ignore such a mine of useful information. Any behavioral signal that is difficult to produce if one is sick, injured, starving, old, depressed, or brain damaged can function as a reliable indicator, so can become amplified by sexual selection into a courtship display.

This theory has an almost inescapable corollary: the more important brains became in human survival and reproduction, the more incentive mate choice would have had to focus on brain-specific indicators. Even if one supposed that hominid brains originally started to expand through natural selection for better tool making or higher social intelligence rather than directly under sexual selection, sexual selection would tend to hijack brain evolution. If natural selection favored tool-making ability, sexual selection would quickly come to favor exaggerated displays of the mental and physical skills relevant in tool making. Similarly, for almost any naturally selected mental capacity, if individuals vary in the capacity in ways that can be perceived in mate choice, incentives exist for mate choice to preempt natural selection and filter out individuals with lower capacities.

Music, considered as a concrete behavior rather than an abstract facet of culture, shows many features that may function as indicators. Dancing reveals aerobic fitness, coordination, strength, and health. Because nervousness interferes with fine motor control, including voice control, singing in key may reveal self-confidence, status, and extroversion. Rhythm may reveal the brain's capacity for sequencing complex movements reliably, and the efficiency and flexibility of its central pattern generators. Virtuosic performance of instrumental music may reveal motor coordination, capacity for automating complex learned behaviors, and having the time to practice (which in turn indicates not having heavy parental responsibilities, and hence sexual availability). Melodic creativity may reveal learning ability to master existing musical styles and social intelligence to go beyond them in producing optimally exciting novelty.

These indicator functions for music are all speculative, but well-established empirical methods are available in biology for testing indicator hypotheses. First, one can look for a population-level correlation between an indicator's value (e.g., dancing ability) and the putative underlying trait that it is supposed to indicate (e.g., aerobic capacity and motor coordination). Second, one can look for individual-level effects by experimentally manipulating the underlying trait and measuring its effect on the indicator (e.g., improve aerobic capacity through three months of exercise) and seeing if it improves the indicator value (e.g., dancing ability). Third, one can do experiments on mate preferences to see whether people are more sexually attracted by individuals with higher rather than lower indicator values, and whether they attribute higher underlying trait values to those with high indicator values. None of these empirical studies has yet been done, to my knowledge, to analyze human music as a set of sexually selected indicators. Many such studies would have such obvious outcomes that doing them hardly seems necessary. But even obvious studies such as those showing that healthier peacocks have larger tails (Petrie, Halliday, and Sanders 1991; Petrie 1992) were critical in demonstrating the importance of indicators in other species.

Music as a Set of Sexually Selected Aesthetic Displays

Whereas indicators reveal useful information, aesthetic displays play on psychological foibles. The basic idea of aesthetic displays is that mate choice works through animal sensation, perception, and cognition, and these psychological processes sometimes have biased sensitivities that other animals can exploit with their courtship displays. For example, a certain species of bird may eat red berries a lot, so evolves eyes with high sensitivity to red and brains that are attracted by the color. This perceptual bias may affect mate choice, predisposing the birds to mate with others who have red rather than blue or yellow plumage. The result would be that the red-biased eyes result in red-biased evolution of courtship plumage (Endler 1992, 1993). Thus many sexually selected aesthetic displays may originate as side effects of perceptual adaptations evolved for other functions.

Several examples show these perceptual biases affecting mate choice. Burley (1988) found that female zebra finches have latent aesthetic preferences for the red and black plastic leg bands that she used to tag certain males, and not for the yellow or blue bands she put on other males. Of course, male zebra finches of the future will not evolve plastic bands on their legs, but they may very well evolve red coloration if the right mutations pop up (consider the blue-footed booby of the Galapagos). According to Basolo (1990), female platyfish have latent aesthetic preferences for long plastic "swords" that he glued onto male platyfish tails; in the platyfish's close relatives, the swordtails, those latent preferences seem to have resulted in males evolving the display. Ridley (1981) noted that the popularity of eye spots in courtship displays in peacocks and argus pheasants results from the birds' general sensitivity to eyelike stimuli. Thus, almost any perceptual bias that animals have can shape how sexual selection plays out, and which courtship displays evolve in a species.

Biologists have documented the importance of perceptual biases in sexual selection for many species (Ryan 1990; Guilford and Dawkins 1991; Endler 1992). Ryan and Keddy-Hector (1992) and found that these biases are not randomly distributed, but are typically pointed in one direction. With respect to visual traits, for example, all species they investigated preferred bright colors over duller colors, larger displays over smaller ones, and higher contrast over lower contrast. With respect to acoustic traits, all species they investigated preferred calls that were louder rather than softer, more frequent rather than less frequent, longer in duration rather than shorter, lower in pitch rather than higher, higher in complexity rather than lower, and with larger repertoire sizes over smaller repertoires. The relevance to sexual selection for music is obvious: any acoustic preferences that our ancestors had could have been exploited, attracted, and entertained by production of the appropriate musical display.

Aesthetic traits tend to be hard to distinguish from indicators, because in almost all cases, perceptual biases push sexual selection in the same direction that mate choice for reliable indicators would. Lower-pitched calls, for example, are reliable indicators of body size, because very small animals cannot physically produce very low pitches. Often, traits may function as both aesthetic displays and as indicators (Miller 1997a, 1998; Miller and Todd 1998). The power and focus of the two explanations is rather different, however. The advantage of the aesthetic display theory is that it makes us recognize that any aspect of music that we find appealing could also have been appealing to our ancestors, and if it was, that appeal would have set up sexual selection pressures in favor of musical productions that fulfilled those preferences.

An important twist on the aesthetic display theory is Fisher's (1930) theory of runaway sexual selection. Fisher considered situations in which both mate preferences and courtship traits are heritable and asked what would happen to both over evolutionary time. He observed that if peahens varied in the length of tail they preferred, and if peacocks varied in their tail lengths, they would end up mating assortatively, with length-obsessed females mating most often with the longest-tailed males. Their offspring would tend to inherit genes for both long-tail preference and for long tails at above-average frequencies. If the population had an initial bias, with more females preferring long tails than short, and with more females wanting long tails than long tails were available, this assortative mating effect would set up a positive-feedback loop between mate preference and courtship trait, leading to ever more extreme preferences and ever more exaggerated traits. Only when the courtship trait's survival costs became very high might the runaway effect reach an asymptote. Although Fisher's startling idea was rejected for fifty years, it has been vindicated by mathematical models (Kirkpatrick 1982; Pomiankowski, Iwasa, and Nee 1991).

The power of the runaway theory is that it can explain the extremity of sexual selection's outcomes: how species are caught up in an endless arms race between unfulfillable sexual demands and irresistible sexual displays. Most relevant for us, the preferences involved need not be cold-blooded assessments of a mate's virtues, but can be deep emotions or lofty cognitions. Any psychological mechanism used in mate choice is vulnerable to this runaway effect, which not only makes the displays that it favors more extreme, but makes the emotions and cognitions themselves more compelling. Against the claim that evolution could never explain music's power to move emotionally and inspire spiritually, the runaway theory says that any emotional or spiritual preferences that influence mate choice, no matter how extreme or subjectively overwhelming, are possible outcomes of sexual selection (cf. Dissanayake 1992). If music that moves emotionally or inspires spiritually tended to attract sexually as well over ancestral time, sexual selection can explain its appeal at every level.

Indeed, sexual selection during human evolution seems to have led to a division of labor between two major courtship displays, with language displays playing on receivers' conceptual systems and music playing on their emotional systems. As a tool for activating specific conceptual thoughts in other people's heads, music is very bad and language is very good. As a tool for activating certain emotional states, however, music is much better than language. Combining the two in lyrical music such as love songs is best of all as a courtship display.

Music has many features that can be interpreted as aesthetic displays that fulfill preexisting perceptual and cognitive preferences. Rhythmic signals are known to be capable of optimally exciting certain kinds of recurrent neural networks as found in mammalian brains. Tonal systems, pitch transitions, and chords probably play on the physical responsiveness of auditory systems to certain frequency relationships. Musical novelty attracts attention by violating expectations, overcoming habituation and boredom, and increasing memorability. Music with lyrics reaches deep into cognition through the media of language and imagination.

As with indicators, biology has developed empirical methods for demonstrating aesthetic displays that could be extended to human music. The first step is to perform perceptual experiments to explore the preferences of receivers for various types of stimuli, charting out which ones are optimally exciting and attractive. For example, vary the beats per minute of a musical stimulus and see which rhythmic speeds best excite various feelings in people. The second step is to measure stimuli actually produced by conspecifics to see how close they come to being optimally exciting given these preferences. For example, measure the beats per minute in a large sample of commercially produced song and see whether the speeds match the optimal responsiveness curves of human receivers. Many such experiments are pretty obvious, but they become more interesting if they are extended across closely related species to see whether the preference is phylogenetically ancient, or whether it evolved to an extreme form through runaway selection in one species but not in others. For example, if humans respond best to dance music played at 120 beats per minute, but chimpanzees and gorillas do not respond differently to different rhythmic speeds, we would have some evidence for runaway selection affecting rhythmic preferences in the human lineage.

Computer simulations of evolution under sexual selection may also prove useful in showing how aesthetic displays evolve (e.g., Enquist and Arak 1993). My colleagues Peter Todd and Greg Werner extended our previous sexual selection simulations (Miller and Todd 1995; Todd and Miller 1993, 1997; Todd, this volume) to model the evolution of musical complexity and variety under mate choice (Werner and Todd 1997). In these simulations, a population of males produces acoustic sequences that are received by females. Both males and females are represented as recurrent neural networks with network architectures, connections, weights, and biases determined by heritable genes. Each simulation run is started with randomly generated male and female genotypes, and all evolution is simply the outcome of the female networks imposing mate choice on male networks based on the sequences they produce. The runaway effect is possible because male and female networks can become genetically correlated through assortative mating. We found that, under such conditions, pure sexual selection can favor ever more complex acoustic sequences and can maintain considerable diversity in such sequences between individuals and across generations (Werner and Todd 1997).

Order and Chaos: The Interplay between Ritualization and Creativity in Human Music

Human music shows an unusual combination of order and chaos, with some elements highly ritualized and stereotyped, such as tonality, rhythm, pitch transitions, song structure, and musical styles, and others highly variable and innovative, such as specific melodies, improvisation, and lyrical content. Hartshorne (1973:56) commented, "Songs illustrate the aesthetic mean between chaotic irregularity and monotonous regularity." How could sexual selection favor both in a single display medium? With a better understanding of indicators and aesthetic displays, we are in a position to answer.

Ritualization means evolutionary modification of movements and structures to improve their function as signals. Ritualization is a typical outcome of signals and displays being under selection to excite optimally the perceptual systems of receivers. Examples of ritualized animal signals are most courtship displays, food-begging displays, warning signals, threat displays, territorial defense displays, play behavior signals, and social grooming behavior. Ritualization results in four typical features: redundancy (repetition over time and over multiple channels), conspicuousness (high intensity, strong contrast), stereotypy (standardized components and units), and alerting components (loud, highly standardized warnings that a more complex signal will follow). Julian Huxley (1966:259–260) observed:

The arts involve ritualization or adaptive canalization of the creative imagination . . . Creative works of art and literature show ritualization in this extended sense, in being "adaptively" (functionally) organized so as to enhance their aesthetic stimulatory effect and their communicatory function. They differ from all other products of ritualization in each being a unique creation (though they may share a common style, which of course is itself a ritualizing agency).

Huxley introduced the apparent problem: why do human displays such as music contain so much novelty and creativity if adaptive signals tend to be ritualized? The problem with completely ritualized signals is that they are boring. Brains are prediction machines, built to track what is happening in the environment by constructing an internal model of it. If the senses indicate that the internal model matched external reality, sensory information hardly even registers on consciousness. Highly repetitive stimuli are not even noticed after a while. But if the senses detect a mismatch between expectation and reality, attention is activated and consciousness struggles to make sense of the novelty. Although ritualization makes signals recognizable and comprehensible, novelty and unpredictability make them interesting. Adding some unpredictability is the only way to move a signal past the filters of expectation and into a smart animals' conscious attention.

Thus, sexual selection can often favor novelty in courtship displays. Darwin (1871) observed that novel songs sometimes attract female birds, just as novel fashions attract humans. Large song repertoires, as seen in some species such as sedge warblers and nightingales, allow birds to produce the appearance of continuous musical novelty (Catchpole 1987; Podos et al. 1992; Catchpole and Slater 1995). Small (1993) emphasized the importance of neophilia in primate sexual selection: "The only constant interest seen among the general primate population is an interest in novelty and variety. Although the possibility of choosing for good genes, good fathers, or good friends remains an option open to female primates, they seem to prefer the unexpected." In humans of course, neophilia is so intense that it drives a substantial proportion of the global economy, particularly the television, film, publishing, news, fashion, travel, pornography, scientific research, psychoactive drug, and music industries. It seems likely that our hominid ancestors were highly appreciative of novelty, and that this spilled over into mate choice, where it favored not so much diversity of sexual partners but selection of highly creative partners capable of generating continuous behavioral novelty throughout the long years necessary to collaborate on raising children (Miller 1997b, 1998).

The challenge became to convince sexual prospects that one could keep them entertained over long-term relationships, so they did not become bored and incur the maladaptive costs of separation and searching again. The main way hominids evolved to do this was through language, using linguistic courtship displays to entertain each other and to indicate their intelligence and creativity. But music could have functioned as another creativity indicator, and seems to have been sexually selected as such. As with other indicator hypotheses, this one could be tested by seeing whether the capacity for musical improvisation and innovation correlates significantly with intelligence and creativity (according to standard psychological measures).

Music in the Pleistocene

Contemporary readers tend to think of music as something made by a tiny group of professionals after years of intensive practice, using expensive instruments, recorded on digital media, and broadcast by radio, television, or live amplification. And so it is for most of us, most of the time. These technologies permit the production of musical signals far beyond the reach of our Pleistocene ancestors. Even a modest techno dance group such as The Prodigy, with just a single principal musician-composer, tours with many truckloads of sound and video equipment, many kilowatts of amplification, and an armory of keyboards, samplers, and sequencers that contain vast computational power. The mockingbird's ability to mimic songs of other species is risible compared with the power of modern digital sampling and sequencing equipment. The result is that modern musicians can produce sound sequences that use any possible timbre, at any possible pitch, and at any possible speed, and volumes capable of causing permanent deafness.

Music production during human evolution must have been quite different. We know our ancestors lived primarily as highly mobile hunter-gatherers in Africa, and hunter-gatherers cannot carry much stuff around. Still, we should not underestimate the complexity and diversity of music that could have been created in premodern conditions. The human voice is an astoundingly flexible instrument in its own right. Our vocal cords cannot produce two distinct notes at once like the syrinxes of songbirds, but we can produce a great variety of pitches, volumes, and timbres. In fact, almost any musical sequence that can be perceived by humans can be recreated in recognizable form by the human voice. The singing group The Bobs, for example, recorded a reasonably arousing version of Led Zeppelin's heavy metal classic "Whole Lotta Love." Unaccompanied human voice is sufficient to produce a vast spectrum of musical styles, such as Gregorian chant, Italian opera, Chinese opera, Tibetan throat singing, Meredith Monk's minimalism, Weimar-era Berlin cabaret songs, Baptist gospel singing, Bulgarian women's chants, Irish folk songs, Islamic calls to prayer, Alpine yodeling, and MTV's "Unplugged" concert series. Recall that the haunting yodels of American country singer Slim Whitman were sufficient, in Tim Burton's film *Mars Attacks*, to melt the brains of invading aliens if played at even moderate volume. I leave it as an exercise for the reader to imagine whether it could have melted the heart of an ovulating ancestor.

The addition of percussive instruments to the human voice could have come relatively early in the evolution of musical capacities. We do not know when the first proper drum, with a stretched skin over a resonating chamber, was invented. But, as any parent of an acoustically extroverted toddler knows, it is not difficult for a determined percussionist to improvise given ordinary objects. Strike two rocks together once, and you have noise. Strike them together twice, and you have rhythm. Rocks are not the best natural material though; wood, bamboo, and bone are better. Bones are especially convenient, because they are natural by-products of hunting and are often hollow. Human skulls, for example, are often used to make the Tibetan ritual drum called a *damaru*. Many other materials make simple rattles, stampers, clappers, and scrapers. The San people of southern Africa make ankle rattles out of springbok ears sewn together and filled with pebbles. Clamshells can be clapped together with two hands. A scraper can be made be rasping the jawbone of a bison with its femur. The top of a gourd can be broken off and the open end pounded against the ground, as in western Africa, or in and out of water, as in the Solomon Islands, or beaten with sticks. More complex are the slit gongs of Africa, where a log is hollowed out, carved with slits, and beaten to produce up to seven different tones.

In terms developed by musicologist Curt Sachs in the 1930s, these are all idiophones that make sounds from their own material, as opposed to membranophones (with a stretched skin, such as a drum), aerophones (with a tube to blow through, like a trumpet), or chordophones (with a stretched string, like a violin). Idiophones may well have been used hundreds of thousands of years ago, whereas the other types were probably invented more recently, in the last 100,000 years. All cultures have idiophones, but not all have the other types. Australian aborigines, for example, do not have drums (membranophones), only clapsticks (idiophones) and drone pipes (aerophones). Even if restricted to idiophones, a wide range of rhythmic patterns is possible, especially in groups with different people playing different rhythm lines (see Arom 1991).

The recent discovery of a Neanderthal bone flute of 40,000 years (see Kunej and Turk, this volume) suggests not only that aerophones are reasonably ancient but that Neanderthals made music. Many Upper Paleolithic cave paintings of the same era portray dancing and the use of idiophones. Together with the universality of singing, rhythmic drumming, and dancing across all human cultures (some of which, like the Australian aborigines, have been genetically distinct for at least 40,000 years), this evidence suggests that human music was both common and sophisticated by 40,000 years ago. The ease of making idiophones out of readily available Pleistocene materials would also give scope for percussion instruments to be something on the order of 1 million years old. Despite the lack of Zildjian cymbals, Stratocaster guitars, and Fairlight synthesizers, our ancestors would have had plenty of opportunity to make decent music a very long time ago.

Nor should we confuse the production of musical signals permitted only by modern technology with the production of musical experiences. Contemporary rock concerts are much louder and use a wider variety of timbres than ancestral music could have, but an evening of rhythmic dance in tribal societies seems to produce effects at least as intense. Traditional music in tribal societies has a few key features that distinguish it from music we tend to enjoy in modern society, and that are much more likely to represent the music made by our ancestors. First, music is almost always a group affair, with everyone actively participating and no one simply sitting and listening contemplatively. Competence at music and dance was probably expected of every sexually mature adult, instead of being the specialty of a few schooled professionals. Second, music is almost always accompanied by dancing, such that to enjoy music and to dance to it are virtually synonymous. There were probably no Pleistocene "concerts" with hundreds of hominids sitting in rows for hours, meditatively listening without moving a muscle like bourgeois symphony goers. The young Londoner dancing all night at a rave makes a more accurate model for how our ancestors appreciated their music. Third, ancestral groups were small, egalitarian, and informal, so none of music's functions in military marches, state coronations, national anthems, or other rituals of our vast hierarchical societies would have been relevant to music's evolutionary origins.

Why Is Human Music so Different from Acoustic Courtship in Other Species?

This question is a special case of the general quandary: why are humans so unique, with extralarge brains, intelligence, culture, and creativity? Three basic answers are available from evolutionary theory. Humans had different phylogenetic origins from other species, arising from anthropoid apes. Human ancestors faced different selection pressures in their ancestral environment, reflecting the demands of the African savanna habitat, the hunter-gatherer econiche, group living, and the like. The random effects of mutation and genetic drift interacted with positive-feedback processes that amplify these stochastic effects. All of these are important, but I think the interaction of group living and runaway sexual selection provide the key. Music is what happens when a smart, group-living, anthropoid ape stumbles into the evolutionary wonderland of runaway sexual selection for complex acoustic displays.

Ideally, we need more specific hypotheses linking specific features of the ancestral environment to specific features of music. One feature of music is that its attractions work indirectly rather than immediately. This is a luxury allowed by living in stable social groups. Primates are highly social, and anthropoid apes have particularly high social intelligence and complex social strategies (Whiten and Byrne 1997). Our hominid ancestors almost certainly lived in large groups where they developed complex, long-term relationships with many relatives and nonrelatives. They would have had lots of time to develop in-depth assessments of which nonrelatives might make good mates. Rather than relying on short-term courtship displays as so many nonsocial species do, hominid courtship could have been a subtle, low-key, long-term affair. Courtship displays did not have to provoke immediate copulation; they only had to insinuate themselves into the memory of a sexual prospect, influencing mating decisions in the months and years to come.

Another feature of music is how exhausting its performance tends to be in hunter-gatherer tribal societies. People dance a long time and get really tired doing so. Many anthropologists have observed that human hunting strategies are rather different from those of other carnivorous animals, relying on projectile weapons to injure prey, which are then chased for hours until they drop from injury and exhaustion. This type of persistence hunting, which relies on long-range running, high aerobic capacity, and sweating ability of humans, creates incentives for mate choice to focus on indicators of ability to maintain good motor control under conditions of high aerobic effort over long periods. Because most courtship happens in the evening when the sexes are in the same place, and because it would be impractical for females and males to run around after each other in the dark to see how far they could go, our hominid ancestors evolved the convention of dancing around in place, with everyone in the group using the same rhythm. Most tribal and folk dancing includes repeated high stepping, stamping, and jumping, using the largest, most energy-hungry muscles in the human body. One could not ask for a better test of aerobic endurance (before modern sports medicine treadmills) than the coordinated group dancing of human tribal societies. Many anthropologists tend to report that tribal dancing involves all members of the group, but I can scarcely believe that the very young, the old, the sick, and the injured would dance quite as long or as hard as the young, healthy, and single. We desperately need more quantitative data from cultural anthropologists on such questions.

If Sexual Selection Shaped Music, Why Is Music Made in Groups?

Many theories about the evolution of music suggest that, since traditional tribal music is almost always made in groups where everyone participates and dances, music must have some kind of group-level function rather than an individual-level function such as sexual selection would suggest. Indeed, this is a quandary, but it is not a serious one.

Some male birds display their charms in large congregations known as leks, strutting, displaying, and sometimes singing by the dozens or hundreds (Balmford 1991). Such congregations make it efficient for females to wander around the lek, searching for good males. The apparent group display in such species apparently results from natural selection to minimize search costs for females, pushing males to congregate and compete in local clusters. Similarly, many male frogs and insects produce their songs in the same area, resulting in large choruses. Sometimes, these males take turns singing so females have some hope of locating at least one of them. Thus, apparently coordinated group displays can sometimes arise through the interaction of selfishly displaying males without group selection.

It is crucial to distinguish between behaviors done *in* groups and those done *for* groups. Primates are highly social, often group-living animals. Although almost all of their daily behavior is groupish, with intense, intricate, dynamic social interactions, primatologists have never found it necessary to invoke group selection to explain these behaviors. Quite the opposite: progress in primatological studies of social behavior boomed after the selfish gene revolution in biological theory, which showed why group selection almost never works (Williams 1966; Wilson 1975; Dawkins 1976). Unfortunately, this sort of methodological individualism, which views group-level effects as emergent phenomena arising from selfish interactions among individuals, has never become very popular in cultural anthropology or musicology. This has created a persistent problem: the fact that music is made in groups is almost always interpreted as meaning that it is made for groups, and that this putative group-level function is most important both biologically and culturally.

The trouble with evolution theories that invoke group-level functions is that they usually end up explaining music through group selection, explicitly or implicitly. For example, group production of music is said to result in a "group-bonding" effect, which supposedly facilitates cooperation and mutual understanding (Richman 1987; Freeman 1995), which in turn supposedly confers an advantage over other groups with less effective group musical behavior. Other theorists view music as a means for a group to remember and perpetuate its shared values and knowledge (e.g., Farnsworth 1969; Nettl 1983; Sloboda 1985), or for it to coordinate rhythmic work (which, unfortunately for the theory, is almost absent among hunter-gatherers). Even the sociobiologist E. O. Wilson (1975) fell into positing a group function for music.

Group selection models are not illogical or impossible as theoretical possibilities (see Boyd and Richerson 1990; Miller 1994; Wilson and Sober 1994; Wilson 1997). However, theorists commonly make two errors when invoking group selection in specific situations. The first error is ideological: group selection is often favored because it is thought to be a kinder, gentler, more cooperative, more humane form of evolution than individual level selection, more suited to the production of positive, enjoyable adaptations such as language, art, and music. But like all selection, it depends on competition, with some groups winning and some losing. Biologist George Williams observed that group competition replaces the logic of murder with the logic of genocide. Not a great moral improvement. Group selection models of music evolution are not just stories of warm, cuddly bonding within a group; they must also be stories of those warm, cuddly groups out-competing and exterminating other groups that do not spend so much time dancing around their campfires.

The second common error about group selection is failing to consider free riding: ways that individuals could enjoy group benefits without paying individual costs. If this is possible, selfish mutants can invade cooperating groups, eroding the power of group selection and the utility of group-selected adaptation. Suppose an ancestral group evolves a "rave" gene that makes them dance every night, doing their group-bonding thing, enjoying their group-competitive advantages over other less musical groups. Perhaps a "wallflower" mutation emerges among these people of the rave that predisposes its possessors to rest while their comrades dance. Because the wallflower mutant does not pay the enormous time and energy costs of dancing all night, but still enjoys the advantages its group has over other groups, it inevitably spreads through the people of the rave. Within a few generations, music would go away, and we would back to a population of well-rested wallflowers. If musical behavior has no individual-level advantage but does have individual costs, it would be difficult for group selection to have an effect on the evolution of music. The same holds true for any other "altruistic" trait that has individual costs and only group benefits. No biologist ever made a good case for such an altruistic trait evolving in any vertebrate species, so it is not the kind of explanation one would wish to invoke for human music. (It should go without saying that anthropological claims that some tribes have "no concept of the separate individual" have no bearing whatsoever on the scientific status of group selection versus selfish gene theory in human evolution. Animals do not have to know they are individuals for selection to act on them as such.)

On the other hand, we must not be dogmatic about group selection always being an unworkable or outdated idea. If music did have individual-level benefits, such as courtship benefits under sexual selection, it may be possible for group selection to reinforce them with group benefits. Under this model of group selection, no tension would be necessary between individual and group levels of selection: music would not be altruistic, with individual costs and only group benefits. If none of the ravers was willing to mate with a wallflower, the wallflower gene could never invade the group. This type of group selection model has been very poorly studied in theoretical biology, but it is not implausible (see Boyd and Richerson 1990). I think this sort of interplay between sexual selection and group selection may be the only sensible way to introduce group selection into models of music evolution.

Another overlooked factor is kin selection, which is easy to mistake for group selection when groups are composed largely of genetic relatives. However, to posit that music evolved under kin selection, for some kind of kin-bonding function, seems implausible, because no other species with cooperation between kin requires a special bonding ritual. Nor do music and dance seem to play the major role in family groups that they play when nonkin come together.

The main appeal of the group-bonding theory is, I think, our subjective experience that music feels better when others are around enjoying it too. The production of this warm groupish glow, delight, or euphoria should not be mistaken for music's adaptive function, however. If music evolved principally under sexual selection, it would make sense for its enjoyment to be greater when one is surrounded by a large number of others, especially young, attractive, single others. Rock concerts make teenagers feel giddy with excitement not because they will feel an oceanic oneness with their peers in any behaviorally significant way—there are too many fights after concerts for that theory to work—but because concerts afford an excellent opportunity for meeting partners. It is not necessary for us to be aware of this adaptive logic for it to have worked over many millennia in shaping the group production and enjoyment of music. Apart from mating, the experience of producing music in a large group may feel good simply for mood-calibration purposes (see Tooby and Cosmides 1990). Singing lyrical music together, for example, would have given powerful evidence under ancestral conditions that one was part of a successful band: a large group of healthy, energetic people with few social tensions who share a common language.

Many ethnomusicologists (e.g., Nettl 1983) take a different view on music's group-bonding functions, and seem at certain points to view music as a means for collective access to the supernatural. This merits a brief evolutionary critique: accessing the supernatural can be the adaptive function of a biological trait such as music only if the supernatural actually exists, and if accessing it gives concrete fitness benefits. Evolution would not be impressed by animals that merely think they attain godlike powers through music; they would really have to do it for selection to favor this function. Of course, convincing others that a supernatural exists and that one has special powers to access it might function as a perfectly good courtship display. Composers who view music as an intermediary between humans and gods (e.g., Stravinsky 1947) are, of course, setting themselves up for worship as high priests without taking vows of celibacy.

A Plea for More Quantitative Behavioral Data on Music Production and Reception

As we have seen, evolutionary biology has a rich set of theories concerning sexual selection and animal signal systems, and an ever more sophisticated set of behavioral research methods for testing hypotheses about the functions of animal signal systems such as human music. However, these methods demand much more detailed quantitative data about music production and reception than are typically available from ethnomusicology, psychomusicology, or cultural anthropology. In terms of quantitative data relevant to sexual selection hypotheses, we know more about the calls of the small, drab, neotropical Tungara frog *Physalaemus pustulosus* (Ryan 1985) than we do about human music.

Some key questions require further research. To test the hypothesis that music production functions in part as a set of sexually selected indicators, we need to know much more about the genetic heritability of musical capacities in modern human populations; the genetic heritability of relevant fitness components such displays might indicate, such as intelligence, creativity, aerobic capacity, and motor control; phenotypic correlations between musical capacities and underlying traits they represent; mate preferences people have concerning musical displays, and inferences they make from manifest musical ability to underlying traits; and sexual payoffs for different degrees of musicality in tribal and modern populations. To test the hypothesis that music production functions in part as a set of aesthetic displays, we need to know much more about perceptual and cognitive preferences people (and other apes) have with respect to many dimensions of musical stimuli; the frequency distribution of actual musical productions with respect to those dimensions; whether there is strong assortative mating for musical traits; and whether genetic correlations are present between musical tastes and music-production tendencies in modern populations, which might indicate a runaway effect in progress.

To test the more general hypothesis that sexual selection through mate choice was a major factor in the evolution of human music, we have to see whether music production behavior matches what we would expect for a courtship display. Some suggestive evidence in this direction is available. I took random samples of over 1,800 jazz albums from Carr, Fairweather, and Priestley (1988), over 1,500 rock albums from Strong (1993), and over 3,800 classical music works from Sadie (1991), and analyzed the age and sex of the principal music-producer for each. The resulting plots indicated that, for each genre, males produced about ten times as much music as females, and their musical output peaked in young adulthood, around age thirty, near the time of peak mating effort and peak mating activity. This is almost identical to the age and sex profiles discovered by Daly and Wilson (1988) for homicides, which they took as evidence for sexual selection shaping propensities for violent sexual competitiveness. Here, the same profiles suggest that music evolved and continues to function as a courtship display, mostly broadcast by young males to attract females. Of course, my samples may be biased, because only the best musicians have opportunities to record albums or have their works documented in classical music encyclopedias. However, Simonton's (1993) studies of creativity suggest that the demographics of extremely creative cultural production are not significantly different from those of ordinary cultural production, so the former can usually be taken as a proxy for the latter. If so, it seems likely that most music at all levels, from local pub bands to internationally televised concerts, is produced by young men. And that is exactly the pattern sexual selection would produce (see Buss and Schmitt 1993; Daly and Wilson 1994).

In any case, for evolutionary studies of human music to flourish, we must adopt the same quantitative methods that have worked so well for studies of signaling systems in other species (Martindale 1990; Simonton 1991, 1993; Hauser 1996). Music must be viewed as a behavior generated by signalers and sent to receivers, rather than as an abstract system of communication, emotion, and cultural meaning. Behavioral details of music production and reception are much more informative about music's evolutionary origins and adaptive functions than details of it as a disembodied formal system. Studies of language evolution provide a cautionary tale in this respect: 200 years of speculation about the origins of human language have shed virtually no light on language's survival and reproductive payoffs, because language has usually been treated as an abstract system of syntax, morphology, and vocabulary (e.g., Pinker 1994; Bickerton 1995), rather than as a concrete behavior with some people talking to others in ways that affect their fitness.

Conclusion

Although ornithologists and acousticians agree about the musicality of the sounds uttered by birds, the gratuitous and unverifiable hypothesis of the existence of a genetic relation between birdsong and music is hardly worth discussing (Levi-Strauss 1970:19).

Cultural theorists such as Levi-Strauss have been too quick to dismiss evolutionary analogs of human music. Birdsong and human music do not share a common phylogenetic origin, but they may very well share a common adaptive function. This chapter holds that the functional analogs between human music and animal acoustic courtship have been dismissed too readily, too contemptuously, and with too little appreciation of sexual selection theory.

Sexual selection through mate choice is almost unfairly powerful as an evolutionary explanation for things like music that seem impressive and attractive to us, but that seem useless for survival under ancestral conditions. The reason is that any feature one is even capable of noticing about somebody else (including the most subtle details of their musical genius) could have been sexually selected by our ancestors. If one can perceive the quality, creativity, virtuosity, emotional depth, and spiritual vision of somebody's music, sexual selection through mate choice can notice it too, because the perceptions of ancestors with minds like ours were literally agents through which sexual selection operated. If both musical tastes and musical capacities were genetically heritable (as practically all behavioral traits are; see Plomin et al. 1997), runaway sexual selection would have had no trouble seizing on early, primitive, acoustic displays and turning them over thousands of generations into a specieswide adaptation known as music.

This chapter has advanced just a few rather obvious ideas about the evolution of music, first articulated by Darwin, but worth reiterating in the light of contemporary biology. Music is a biological adaptation, universal within our species, distinct from other adaptations, and too complex to have arisen except through direct selection for some survival or reproductive benefit. Since music production has no plausible survival benefits, reproductive benefits seem worth a look. As Darwin emphasized, most complex, creative acoustic displays in nature are outcomes of sexual selection and function as courtship displays to attract sexual partners. The behavioral demographics of music production are just what we would expect for a sexually selected trait, with young males greatly overrepresented in music making. Music shows several features that could function as reliable indicators of fitness, health, and intelligence, and as aesthetic displays that excite our perceptual, cognitive, and emotional sensitivities. Opportunities for both music production and selective mate choice would have been plentiful under ancestral hunter-gatherer conditions. In short, the evolutionary analogy between birdsong and human music may be much closer than previously believed: both are sexually selected courtship displays first, and fulfill other functions less directly.

We have plenty left to do. We need much more quantitative behavioral data on music production and reception, of many different types, ranging from genetic heritability studies, to physiological studies on the costs of music-playing and dancing, to perceptual experiments on music preferences. The quandary remains of why individual courtship displays would be produced in groups, and whether group selection may have interacted with sexual selection in music evolution. There is scope for more computer simulations of how musical complexity and novelty might evolve under sexual selection. More centrally, the design features of human music must be related much more securely and less speculatively to specific functions under ancestral conditions.

Progress concerning music evolution seems most likely by adopting the same adaptationist approach that has proven so fruitful in understanding birdsong and other complex signal systems. Modern biology provides a great wealth of evolutionary theory and empirical methods, many of which can be applied with little modification to analyzing human music. To many musicologists, this may seem like a radical approach, threatening to impose a psychologically and genetically reductionist view on music. To students of sexual selection, however, saying that a human adaptation has been shaped by mate choice is to grant it the least reductionistic, most humane origin as a part of the mind selected by minds like ours for its ability to provide mental and emotional enjoyment. Music arose as a natural outcome of psychology mixing with sexuality in the genetic stream that became humanity.

References

Andersson, M. (1994). *Sexual Selection*. Princeton, NJ: Princeton University Press.

Arom, S. (1991). *African Polyphony and Polyrhythm*. Cambridge, UK: Cambridge University Press.

Balmford, A. (1991). Mate choice on leks. *Trends in Ecology and Evolution* 6:87–92.

Basolo, A. L. (1990). Female preference predates the evolution of the sword in swordfish. *Science* 250:808–810.

Bickerton, D. (1995). *Language and Human Behavior*. Seattle: University of Washington Press.

Blacking, J. (1976). *How Musical Is Man?* London: Faber and Faber.

Blacking, J. (1987). *A Commonsense View of all Music*. Cambridge, UK: Cambridge University Press.

Boyd, R. and Richerson, P. J. (1990). Group selection among alternative evolutionarily stable strategies. *Journal of Theoretical Biology* 145:331–342.

Burley, N. (1988). Wild zebra finches have band-color preferences. *Animal Behavior* 36:1235–1237.

Buss, D. M. and Schmitt, P. (1993). Sexual strategies theory: An evolutionary perspective on human mating. *Psychological Review* 100:204–232.

Carr, I., Fairweather, D., and Priestley, B. (1988). *Jazz: The Essential Companion*. London: Paladin.

Catchpole, C. K. (1987). Birdsong, sexual selection and female choice. *Trends in Evolution and Ecology* 2:94–97.

Catchpole, C. K. and Slater, P. J. B. (1995). *Bird Song: Biological Themes and Variations*. Cambridge, UK: Cambridge University Press.

Cronin, H. (1991). *The Ant and the Peacock: Altruism and Sexual Selection from Darwin to Today*. Cambridge, UK: Cambridge University Press.

Daly, M. and Wilson, M. (1988). *Homicide*. New York: Aldine.

Daly, M. and Wilson, M. (1994). Evolutionary psychology of male violence. In J. Archer (Ed.) *Male Violence* (pp. 253–288). London: Routledge.

Darwin, C. (1862). *On the Various Contrivances by which Orchids Are Fertilized by Insects*. London: Murray.

Darwin, C. (1871). *The Descent of Man, and Selection in Relation to Sex* (2 vols.). London: Murray.

Dawkins, R. (1976). *The Selfish Gene*. Oxford: Oxford University Press.

Dawkins, R. (1996). *Climbing Mount Improbable*. London: Penguin Books.

Dawkins, R. and Krebs, J. R. (1978). Animal signals: Information or manipulation? In J. R. Krebs and N. B. Davies (Eds.) *Behavioral Ecology: An Evolutionary Approach* (pp. 282–309). Oxford: Blackwell Scientific.

Dissanayake, E. (1988). *What Is Art for?* Seattle: University of Washington Press.

Dissanayake, E. (1992). Homo aestheticus: *Where Art Comes from and Why*. New York: Free Press.

Endler, J. A. (1992). Signals, signal conditions, and the direction of evolution. *American Naturalist* 139:S125–S153.

Endler, J. A. (1993). Some general comments on the evolution and design of animal communication systems. *Philosophical Transactions of the Royal Society of London B* 340:215–225.

Enquist, M. and Arak, A. (1993). Selection of exaggerated male traits by female aesthetic senses. *Nature* 361:446–448.

Farnsworth, P. (1969). *The Social Psychology of Music.* Iowa City: Iowa State University Press.

Fisher, R. A. (1930). *The Genetical Theory of Natural Selection.* Oxford: Clarendon Press.

Freeman, W. (1995). *Societies of Brains: A Study in the Neuroscience of Love and Hate.* Hillsdale, NJ: Erlbaum.

Grafen, A. (1990). Biological signals as handicaps. *Journal of Theoretical Biology* 144:517–546.

Guilford, T. and Dawkins, M. S. (1991). Receiver psychology and the evolution of animal signals. *Animal Behavior* 42:1–14.

Hartshorne, C. (1973). *Born to Sing.* Bloomington: Indiana University Press.

Hauser, M. (1996). *The Evolution of Communication.* Cambridge: MIT Press.

Huxley, J. (1966). A discussion of ritualization of behaviour in animals and man: Introduction. *Philosophical Transactions of the Royal Society of London B* 251:247–271.

Kirkpatrick, M. (1982). Sexual selection and the evolution of female choice. *Evolution* 36:1–12.

Kirkpatrick, M., Price, T., and Arnold, S. J. (1990). The Darwin-Fisher theory of sexual selection in monogamous birds. *Evolution* 44:180–193.

Knight, C. (1991). *Blood Relations: Menstruation and the Origins of Culture.* New Haven, CT: Yale University Press.

Krebs, J. R. and Dawkins, R. (1984). Animal signals: Mindreading and manipulation. In J. R. Krebs and N. B. Davies (Eds.) *Behavioral Ecology: An Evolutionary Approach,* 2nd ed. (pp. 380–402). Oxford: Blackwell.

Levi-Strauss, C. (1970). *The Raw and the Cooked.* London: Cape.

Martindale, C. (1990). *The Clockwork Muse: The Predictability of Artistic Change.* New York: Basic Books.

Miller, G. F. (1994). Beyond shared fate: Group-selected mechanisms for cooperation and competition in fuzzy, fluid vehicles. *Behavioral and Brain Sciences* 17:630–631.

Miller, G. F. (1997a). Mate choice: From sexual cues to cognitive adaptations. In G. Cardew (Ed.) *Characterizing Human Psychological Adaptations.* Ciba Foundation Symposium 208 (pp. 71–87). London: John Wiley.

Miller, G. F. (1997b) Protean primates: The evolution of adaptive unpredictability in competition and courtship. In A. Whiten and R. W. Byrne (Eds.) *Machiavellian Intelligence,* Vol. II: *Extensions and Evaluations.* Cambridge, UK: Cambridge University Press.

Miller, G. F. (1998). How mate choice shaped human nature: A review of sexual selection and human evolution. In C. Crawford and D. Krebs (Eds.) *Handbook of Evolutionary Psychology: Ideas, Issues, and Applications* (pp. 87–129). Hillsdale, NJ: Lawrence Erlbaum.

Miller, G. F. and Todd, P. M. (1995). The role of mate choice in biocomputation: Sexual selection as a process of search, optimization, and diversification. In W. Banzaf and F. Eeckman (Eds.) *Evolution and Biocomputation: Computational Models of Evolution. Lecture Notes in Computer Science* 899 (pp. 169–204). Berlin: Springer-Verlag.

Miller, G. F. and Todd, P. M. (1998). Mate choice turns cognitive. *Trends in the Cognitive Sciences* 2:190–198.

Nettl, B. (1983). *The Study of Ethnomusicology: Twenty-Nine Issues and Concepts.* Chicago: University of Illinois Press.

Petrie, M. (1992). Peacocks with low mating success are more likely to suffer predation. *Animal Behavior* 44:585–586.

Petrie, M., Halliday, T., and Sanders, C. (1991). Peahens prefer peacocks with elaborate trains. *Animal Behavior* 41:323–331.

Pinker, S. (1994). *The Language Instinct*. London: Lane.

Plomin, R., DeFries, J. C., McClearn, G. E., and Rutter, M. (1997). *Behavioral Genetics*, 3rd ed. New York: Freeman.

Podos, J., Peters, S., Rudnicky, T., Marler, P., and Nowicki, S. (1992). The organization of song repertoires in song sparrows: Themes and variations. *Ethology* 90:89–106.

Pole, W. (1924). *The Philosophy of Music*, 6th ed. London: Kegan Paul, Trench, Trubner.

Pomiankowski, A., Iwasa, Y., and Nee, S. (1991). The evolution of costly mate preferences. I. Fisher and biased mutation. *Evolution* 45:1422–1430.

Richman, B. (1987). Rhythm and melody in gelada vocal exchanges. *Primates* 28:199–223.

Ridley, M. (1981). How the peacock got his tail. *New Scientist* 91:398–401.

Ridley, M. (1993). *The Red Queen: Sex and the Evolution of Human Nature*. New York: Viking.

Rousseau, J. J. (1761/1986). Essay on the origin of languages which treats of melody and musical imitation. In J. H. Moran and A. Gode (Eds.) *On the Origins of Language* (pp. 5–74). Chicago: University of Chicago Press.

Ryan, M. J. (1985). *The Tungara Frog: A Study in Sexual Selection and Communication*. Chicago: University of Chicago Press.

Ryan, M. J. (1990). Sexual selection, sensory systems, and sensory exploitation. *Oxford Surveys of Evolutionary Biology* 7:156–195.

Ryan, M. J. and Keddy-Hector, A. (1992). Directional patterns of female mate choice and the role of sensory biases. *American Naturalist* 139:S4–S35.

Sadie, S. (Ed.). (1991). *The Grove Concise Dictionary of Music*. London: Macmillan.

Simonton, D. K. (1991). Emergence and realization of genius: The lives and works of 120 classical composers. *Journal of Personality and Social Psychology* 61:829–840.

Simonton, D. K. (1993). Genius and chance: A Darwinian perspective. In J. Brockman (Ed.) *Creativity* (pp. 176–201). New York: Simon and Schuster.

Sloboda, J. A. (1985). *The Musical Mind*. Oxford: Clarendon Press.

Small, M. (1993). *Female Choices: Sexual Behavior of Female Primates*. Ithaca, NY: Cornell University Press.

Stravinsky, I. (1947). *Poetics of Music*. New York: Vintage Books.

Storr, A. (1992). *Music and the Mind*. New York: Harper Collins.

Strong, M. C. (1993). *The Great Rock Discography*. Edinburgh: Canongate Press.

Tiger, L. (1992). *The Pursuit of Pleasure*. London: Little, Brown.

Todd, P. M. and Miller, G. F. (1993). Parental guidance suggested: How parental imprinting evolves through sexual selection as an adaptive learning mechanism. *Adaptive Behavior* 2:5–47.

Todd, P. M. and Miller, G. F. (1997). Biodiversity through sexual selection. In C. G. Langton and K. Shimohara (Eds.) *Artificial Life*, Vol. V, *Proceedings of the Fifth International Workshop on the Synthesis and Simulation of Living Systems* (pp. 289–299). Cambridge: MIT Press/Bradford Books.

Tooby, J. and Cosmides, L. (1990). The past explains the present: Emotional adaptations and the structure of ancestral environments. *Ethology and Sociobiology* 11:375–424.

Tooby, J. and Cosmides, L. (1992). The psychological foundations of culture. In J. H. Barkow, L. Cosmides, and J. Tooby (Eds.) *The Adapted Mind: Evolutionary Psychology and the Generation of Culture* (pp. 19–136). Oxford: Oxford University Press.

Wallace, A. R. (1889). *Darwinism: An Exposition of the Theory of Natural Selection, with Some of Its Applications*. London: Macmillan.

Werner, G. M. and Todd, P. M. (1997). Too many love songs: Sexual selection and the evolution of communication. In P. Husbands and I. Harvey (Eds.) *Fourth European Conference on Artificial Life* (pp. 434–443). Cambridge: MIT Press/Bradford Books.

Whiten, A. and Byrne, R. W. (Eds.) (1997). *Machiavellian Intelligence*, Vol. II: *Extensions and Evaluations*. Cambridge, UK: Cambridge University Press.

Williams, G. C. (1966). *Adaptation and Natural Selection*. Princeton, NJ: Princeton University Press.

Wilson, D. S. (1997). Introduction: Multilevel selection comes of age. *American Naturalist* 150:S1–S4.

Wilson, D. S. and Sober, E. (1994). Re-introducing group selection to the human behavioral sciences. *Behavioral and Brain Sciences* 17:585–654.

Wilson, E. O. (1975). *Sociobiology: The New Synthesis*. Cambridge: Harvard University Press.

Zahavi, A. (1975). Mate selection: A selection of handicap. *Journal of Theoretical Biology* 53:205–214.

Zahavi, A. (1997). *The Handicap Principle*. Oxford: Oxford University Press.

Peter Todd

Abstract

Prehistoric musical behavior did not fossilize very well, and relatively few species are alive today with which we can take a comparative approach to the origins of human musical ability. Evolutionary computer simulations provide another means of exploring this question: by constructing a population of artificial music producers whose behavior can be selected by various fitness-determining critics, we can study hypothetical scenarios for the evolution of musical behavior. To date, most simulations of this type were constructed to create new forms of computerized music composition systems, rather than to answer scientific questions. But we can survey these systems and the simulation techniques they use to learn about the effects of different types of knowledge representations in music creators and critics on the evolutionary process. In addition, a simulation was explicitly designed to explore the question of the evolutionary impact of various forms of selection, focusing on sexual selection by coevolving male song producers and female song critics. In this model, coevolving creators and critics can increase the diversity of musical behaviors seen both across generations and within any one population. This kind of simulation approach to the evolution of musical behavior can answer other questions as well.

Our ancestors did not leave us much to go on for piecing together the evolution of our musical abilities. A disputed bear-bone fragment that may or may not have been a Neanderthal flute some 40,000 years ago (see Kunej and Turk, this volume) is one of the few clues we have to our musical heritage; most of this ephemeral behavior did not leave a fossil trace. A few species are around today whose quasi-musical behavior we can compare, as other chapters in this volume attest. But environmental pressures acting on this aspect of the evolution of songbirds, whales, gibbons, and humans may have been rather different, and we are still left with little evidence of past behavioral changes. We would like to be able to replay the evolutionary tape from the beginning to hear the whole piece, but all we have available are a few scattered snippets along with bits from the end of some individual species' records.

If we cannot replay the original tape, perhaps we can make a new one. To gain insights into the origins of music in another way, we can turn to a method of exploration that was technologically unfeasible even a couple of decades ago: evolutionary computer simulations. Using this approach we can construct artificial "worlds" within the computer in which populations of simulated creatures create and possibly perceive musical signals (typically just represented as sequences of numbers, rather than as actual physical vibrations). Loosely speaking, if we allow these creatures to reproduce differentially in response to their musical behaviors (e.g., those that create a certain kind of song might have more offspring), successive generations of creatures will evolve different musical production or perception abilities. By tailoring the selective forces of the artificial environment and behavioral endowments of the artificial creatures, we can set up evolutionary simulations to answer a variety of questions about the evolution of musical behavior. Furthermore, we can listen in on the process of artificial evolution in a way that we could never do in nature. This is akin to using a cheap electronic synthesizer to replay an orchestral symphony, perhaps, but it can still give us an evocative impression of the piece's outline, and may be one of the only options available if the natural orchestra can no longer be assembled.

The kinds of questions that evolutionary computer simulations can address fall into two main categories. First, simulation models can act as proofs of concept, demonstrating that a certain behavior could evolve from some initial state through a series of cumulative stages. For instance, they could help us explore whether and how a particular kind of proposed mental mechanism, say, a neural network with certain learning capacities, could evolve into a system capable of learning and producing hierarchically structured musical sequences. Second, simulations are one of the best tools for elucidating the dynamics of an evolutionary process, showing what the course of evolution of a certain behavior could have looked like over time. For instance, one could show how a population of singing creatures with some memory ability may build up a shared culture of songs over time. More generally, one could test hypotheses as "runnable models," instantiated, dynamic thought experiments that can be put in motion within the computer. This provides a means of discovering the implications of ideas that may be too complex to explore purely verbally. Simulations also can be used to generate hypotheses about the evolution of real behaviors or about reasons that certain behaviors might not have evolved.

Evolutionary simulations have several advantages for exploring behavioral questions (Todd 1996). Perhaps the most obvious and important is that they can proceed much more rapidly than natural evolution. This allows observation of many generations of behavioral adaptation, and, combined with precise parametric control of simulations, makes it possible to replay the evolutionary movie under different experimental conditions. To make simulations run quickly, the evolutionary models they instantiate must be relatively simple and clear, and to run at all, they must be coherent and complete (as in any computer program). This is also an advantage, since it requires that models be carefully thought out by the researcher and understandable by others. Simulations can also include a degree of complexity much greater than that allowed, for instance, by mathematical modeling. Numerous levels of adaptive processes, including information processing, learning, development, culture, and evolution, can all be incorporated into the models, adding greatly to their realism and predictive power. But we must be careful to avoid the attraction of building complex models for their own inherent interesting behavior, and instead construct specific models to address specific questions in an accurate and analyzable fashion. Finally, simulated creatures can be dissected, probed, and prodded in ways that normal animals would not withstand, and a battery of psychological and "neurological" tests can be performed to assess their behavior for comparison with living experimental subjects.

In this chapter we consider ways in which evolutionary computer simulations can be built to help investigate questions regarding the evolution of musical behavior. In the next section we describe the main approaches currently used to make computer models of individual musical behavior: rule-based and learning systems. These are the behavioral mechanisms that an evolutionary simulation will modify over time, through selective forces acting on their musical output. In the third section we explore tools available for simulating the evolutionary process itself. This process requires the ability to generate new musically behaving individuals and assess their fitness before reproducing the most-fit individuals in the next generation. We list four main ways of evaluating individual fitness: human critics, automated rule-based critics, learning critics, and coevolving critics. The latter form of fitness evaluator is used in the fourth section in a system designed to explore the generation of musical diversity through the coevolution of music creators and critics, akin to male songbird singers and female listeners choosing mates from among those singers. Finally, we conclude with further questions on the origins of music that can be pursued with evolutionary simulations.

What Should We Evolve in a Music System?

To investigate the evolution of musical behavior and cognition in a computational system, we must first determine what exactly we want to evolve. We are not in general interested in the evolution of specific instances of music per se, but rather in how music-generating or -processing mechanisms change over time. We therefore need computational models of music composition and comprehension. Two main types of models have been developed for these tasks over the past few decades: rule-based and learning mechanisms (see Loy 1989, for more details). Generally, the former are given their rules by the designer, but it is possible to create a system that learns rules as well, combining the two approaches. Both kinds of systems can be used for either musical production or perception; here I describe their use in a compositional role, which has been more common in recent evolutionary music simulations, but the reader should keep in mind that they can typically be inverted into an analysis or perceptual role as well. The choice of which mechanism to use in a particular simulation is determined by the research question the simulation is designed to answer.

Probably the most intuitive means of creating an artificial system for music composition or analysis, particularly one to be implemented on a computer, is to come up with a set of compositional rules for the computer to follow either in producing or assessing music. The rules in a musical algorithm can be very simple, as for example, in musical dice games developed by Mozart and others in which precomposed phrases were merely combined in new random orders (Loy 1991). They can also embody complex knowledge about specific musical styles, as in Ebcioglu's (1984) collection of rules for chorale harmonization. Because the computer is constrained to follow the rules it is given, its compositions will generally be well formed according to those rules, and thus will attain at least some minimal level of musicality. (Indeed, Mozart's dice compositions cannot help but sound reasonable.) On the other hand, we pay the price for this rule-following lawfulness: compositions from rule-based systems are unlikely to be surprising. One could hardly be shocked by the combinations produced by Mozart's dice music.

Perhaps more discouraging, coming up with rules to put into the algorithm in the first place is no simple matter. For centuries, scholars have tried to specify fully the rules involved in particular musical styles, such as counterpoint; but whenever a set of rules is nailed down, exceptions and extensions are always discovered that necessitate more rules (Loy 1991). This is the other price of a highly structured composition system— the cost of creating the *right* structure. This cost must be paid in any system that is evolving rule-based artificial composers as well. Most problematical, many artists question whether creativity can be captured by a set of rules at all. If not, we may well want to explore musical evolution using other computational models.

A second approach to construction of artificial musicians is to train a learning system to create new pieces of music. Rather than requiring the development of a set of musical rules, a learning composition system can simply be trained on a set of musical examples. These examples are chosen to represent the kind of music that the user would like the composition system to create new instances of (or at least mimic old instances of): for a waltz-composing system, train it on a corpus of waltzes; for a Bach-Hendrix amalgamator, train it on melodies from both composers. Thus, the big advantage of a learning composition system over a rule-based one is that, as the saying goes, the system builder does not have to know much about music, only what he or she likes. This means that the process of evolution does not have to shape a system made up of a set of musical rules, but rather must sculpt a music learner, and possibly a corpus of musical examples for each learner to be exposed to. (This corpus can also arise through interactions of each generation of artificial composers, for example, or could be evolved through a cultural process of learning and handing down musical examples across generations.)

Early instances of the learning approach to algorithmic composition analyzed a collected set of musical examples in terms of their overall pitch-ransition probabilities (Jones 1981; Loy 1991). Based on how often particular pitches followed each other in the examples, new compositions could be constructed with similar statistical structure. Such Markov-process music sounds good over the short term, reflecting the note-by-note structure in the original input. Novelty is also introduced through the probabilistic nature of the composition process. This matrix representation is also easy to represent and evolve computationally. But a difficulty arises when we listen to music generated in this way over the long term: it has no structure beyond the moment, and the novelty of randomness often accumulates and leads compositions to wander aimlessly.

The development of new neural network learning algorithms (Rumelhart and McClelland 1986) led to the possibility of connectionist music-composition systems (Todd 1988, 1989; Todd and Loy 1991; Griffith and Todd 1998). Feedforward and recurrent neural networks can be trained to produce successive notes or measures of melodies in a training set, given earlier notes or measures as input. Once they have learned to reproduce the training melodies, they can be induced to compose new melodies based on the patterns they have picked up. Neural networks can be made to learn more abstract and long-term patterns than typical Markov-process systems, allowing them to incorporate a greater amount of musical structure from the example set. In addition, they can have additional structure built into them, including psychologically motivated constraints on pitch and time representation (e.g., Mozer 1991, 1994) that help their output to be more musically appropriate. Furthermore, a reasonable amount of research has been conducted into the ways that neural networks can be represented and manipulated in evolutionary simulations (e.g., Miller, Todd, and Hegde 1989; see chapter 2 in Mitchell 1996, for a review).

Yet, despite the increasingly sophisticated neural network machinery being thrown at the problem of composition, results to date have been rather disappointing. As Mozer commented about his own CONCERT system, outputs are often "compositions that only their mother could love" (Mozer 1994:274). Much of the problem is that these networks are still learning and reproducing largely surface-level features of the example musical input; whereas they should in principle be able to pick up and use deeper temporal structure, "experiments . . . show no cause for optimism in practice" (Mozer 1994:274). In addition, by merely manipulating surface-level musical aspects of the training set, networks can come up with new compositions, but they will not be particularly novel in an interesting way. We do not currently have many good models of the generation of musical novelty at an individual level. But in an evolutionary computer simulation, we can at least explore the appearance of novelty in musical behavior at a population level, as we will see below. First, we must consider how evolutionary systems can act on the rule-following or learning behavior of simulated individuals and thereby create successive generations of new individuals.

Evolving Musical Systems

To simulate the evolution of musically behaving organisms (or anything else), we need only construct a rather simple loop: *generate, test, repeat.* Basically, we make a bunch of things, test them according to some criteria, and keep the ones that are best according to those criteria; then we repeat the process by generating a new bunch of things based on the old ones. This loop continues for possibly many generations until the things we are making are good enough according to the criteria being used, or when we have simulated enough of the evolutionary process to answer our particular research question. The complication comes when we have to specify what we mean by "generate" and "test." In natural evolution, what are being generated are individual organisms through a process of genetic modification (usually either sexual recombination or asexual cloning, both with some possible mutation), and the criteria of success are the forces of natural and sexual selection (i.e., ability to survive and reproduce). (Furthermore, in natural evolution there is no "stopping point" when some criteria have been met; the test keeps changing as a consequence of continuing evolution of other species as well.) What and how should we generate and test when dealing with artificial music-perceiving and -producing creatures?

On the generation side, our system should create artificial organisms endowed with either a set of musical rules to follow or a neural network or other learning mechanism, depending on the choice made according to considerations in the previous section. The means of testing also depend on the research question. Basically, we must first decide what we are on the lookout for: do we want to know when, for example, a certain kind of music-perceiving mechanism first appears in the neural network of a simulated creature? If so, we must devise an automated fitness-evaluation routine that can check for the presence of this mechanism and allot more offspring to those creatures that have something closer to this mechanism than others. Or do we want to see how a particular music-generating ability appears and spreads through the population? In this (more commonly explored) case, we could have one of several different types of critics evaluating individuals in the population and assigning them fitness values according to their musical ability. We can use humans directly as such critics, listening for certain behaviors, or we can again use automated critics that are themselves rule based, or learning, and possibly coevolving with the music-creating individuals themselves. Examples of each of these types of fitness-determining critics are given below.

Whatever type of generating process and fitness-testing function we use, the evolutionary process as a whole will embody several common features. These evolutionary systems are based on the general framework provided by Holland's original genetic algorithm (GA; Holland 1975; see also Goldberg 1989, and Mitchell 1996, for general introductions), either directly, or indirectly by way of the genetic programming paradigm of Koza (1993) in which chunks of computer program code are evolved. In nearly every case, new populations of potential solutions to some problem (here, one related to musical behavior) are created, generation after generation, through three main processes. First, to make sure that better solutions to the problem will increase over time, more copies of good solutions than of bad solutions from one generation are put into the next generation (this is fitness-proportionate reproduction, because fitter solutions have proportionally more offspring). Second, to introduce new solutions into the population, a low level of mutation operates on all acts of reproduction, so that some offspring will have randomly changed characteristics. Third, to combine good components between solutions, sexual crossover is often employed, in which the "genes" of two parents are mixed to form offspring with aspects of both.

Evolutionary simulations, like evolving populations in nature, are good at exploring the space of possible solutions to the posed problem, because they can consider several such solutions in parallel and combine aspects of the best. However, evolution is not often described as being fast, although it can be in some cases (see e.g., Weiner 1994), and patience is commonly called for in artificial evolutionary systems. It can take many generations of artificial creatures, each of which must be evaluated in a time-consuming fashion (by whatever type of critic we are using, especially those that must "listen" to lengthy musical output, leading to what Biles [1994] and others identify as the "fitness bottleneck"), before any interesting behavior comes along. The main reason for this sometimes glacial pace is that evolution builds systems through gradual accrual of beneficial bits and pieces, rather than through systematic design or rapid learning from the environment.

As a consequence of this piecemeal tinkering approach, what Wimsatt (in press) terms "evolution as a backwoods mechanic," designs that evolution ultimately comes up with are not intended to be clean, or simple, or easy to understand—they are just whatever worked in the particular situations encountered. The implication for artificially evolved music-composition systems is that, even once they do fulfill the preset fitness criteria to a certain extent, they will likely be unfathomable in their workings. However, this need not be a problem if one is interested in the evolutionary dynamics or mere appearance of particular types of musical behavior without understanding the internal mechanisms generating that behavior. So far, most research on evolving musical systems has been done by musicians interested in building interesting artificial compositional tools, rather than answering scientific questions, and so they have taken this pragmatic approach (see Todd and Werner 1999, for a detailed review of evolutionary music composition systems). We can still look at a few examples of this work, though, and get a feeling for the way in which different types of fitness evaluators can lead to different musical results. Appreciation for these more artistically inclined efforts can help us make better choices of tools to use in exploring scientific ideas.

Humans as Critics

Part of the reason that evolution in nature is often slow is that forces of selection can be very noisy and temporarily ineffectual. Weak, sickly, or just plain ugly individual organisms may still succeed in finding mates, having offspring, and thus passing on their genes, whereas organisms with a new advantageous trait may not manage to live long enough to find a mate and influence the next generation. One way to speed up evolution is thus to implement a more ruthless, strict, and observant selective pressure on a population. This is the principle behind artificial selection, in which humans play the major selective role, letting only those organisms, be they pet animal breeds or garden flower varieties, that meet certain phenotypic criteria produce offspring for the next generation. With such careful supervision, large changes in traits can be achieved in a few generations. Darwin, for instance, discussed how breeders have effected more or less rapid accumulation of human-desired traits in pigeons, dogs, and cabbages, noting that such artificially selected domestic races "often have a somewhat monstrous character" (1859:16). This is due in part to breeders' ability to rescue interesting new "hopeful monsters" (even those only slightly monstrous) from a childless fate and ensure that their desired traits are kept in the gene pool of successive generations.

This teratogenic power was harnessed more recently by musicians working with computer-based artificial selection systems to generate interesting musical structures. Putnam (1994) and Takala and colleagues (1993) explored the use of genetic algorithms to produce individual sounds or waveforms directly. Putnam evolved simple C program subroutines that generated waveform files that were then played for a human listener acting as critic. The listener's rating of the sound was used as the fitness for that particular routine, and new routines were bred according to methods of genetic programming (Koza 1993). However, the results were less than successful: ". . . many of the noises produced in the early generations are very irregular, noisy, and sometimes change loudness quite suddenly. In short, they are unpleasant and irritating and the process of listening to the noises and rating them is slow" (Putnam 1994:4). Reappearance of the fitness bottleneck mentioned earlier is here exacerbated by the painful nature of the sounds to be evaluated.

Less unpleasant results were obtained by incorporating more musical structure into the evolved entities, constraining them to be sequences of pitched notes rather than lower-level sound files. Biles (1994) used several techniques to build more musical structure into his GenJam system for evolving jazz solos. He employed a hierarchically structured musical form in which both measures of thirty-two eighth-notes and phrases of four of these measures evolve in two linked populations simultaneously. In fact, the populations themselves are another important hierarchical level, because GenJam's goal is not to evolve a single best measure or phrase but rather a set of such musical elements that can be drawn on to create pleasing solo sequences. Measures and phrases are put together into solos that are played with a jazz accompaniment of piano, bass, and drum tracks all following a particular chord progression. The user listens to solos and reinforces those choices that are better or worse by entering "g" (good) or "b" (bad) keystrokes in real time as the measures are played. This reinforcement is acquired and summed for both measures and phrases simultaneously, and used to breed a new population of each structure. During the breeding phrase as well, Biles introduced more musical structure: he used "musically meaningful mutation" operators such as reverse, invert, transpose, and sort notes, rather than the usual blind random-replacement mutation of standard genetic algorithms.

Inclusion of all this musical structure pays off: results are typically quite pleasing to listen to (Biles 1995). As Biles himself put it: "After sufficient training, GenJam's playing can be characterized as competent with some nice moments" (1994:136). Sufficient training seems to be about ten generations, although the first few "are quite numbing for the mentor." But Biles acknowledged that all this extra musical structure has its downside as well: "A clever representation that efficiently represents alternative solutions, perhaps by excluding clearly unacceptable solutions, will lead to a more efficient search. However, if a representation 'cleverly' excludes the best solution, its efficiency is irrelevant. . . . GA designers walk a thin line between too large a search space on one side and inadequately sampled solutions on the other" (1994:132). This tradeoff between extra initial built-in musical knowledge, designed to give the population a head start and cut down on evolution time, and unwanted constraints on the search space of musical behaviors, must be considered as well in evolutionary simulations addressing specific research questions.

Rule-Based Critics

The fitness bottleneck encountered when humans are critics of evolutionary systems, listening to the musical output of each individual in the population, can be eliminated by creating automated fitness evaluators. Traditionally, computational evolutionary systems were designed with readily computable fitness functions in mind. This meant that genetic algorithms (see Goldberg 1989) and genetic programming methods (see Koza 1993) generally employed simple rules or more complex rule-based algorithms to compute the fitness of each member of the evolving population of problem solutions. It is not surprising, then, that the earliest applications of computational evolutionary methods to music also used rule-based fitness functions or critics. In what was probably the first musical genetic algorithm, Horner and Goldberg (1991a, b) used the GA to search for thematic bridges, sequences of simple operations that would transform an initial note set into a final desired note set within a certain number of steps. Both the nature of evolving individuals—sequences of operations that can be chopped up and mixed back together—and the specific goal of the fitness function made this musical application well suited for evolutionary search. As a consequence, the results were ". . . musically pleasing to the authors with the usual qualifications regarding personal taste" (1991b:5). But given its highly structured inputs, genetic operations, and goals, this compositional aid system could show little unexpected novelty in its output.

Spector and Alpern (1994) aimed at a more general goal: automatic construction of synthetic artists that could operate in any specified aesthetic tradition. They strove to accomplish this by segregating all aesthetic considerations into a distinct critic, and using a method that could create artists that met those critical criteria. The method they chose is genetic programming (Koza 1993), which in this application evolves programs that produce artistic output that is judged by the critic acting as a fitness function. Spector and Alpern further supplied much culture-specific knowledge that the artificial artist could draw on in a case base of prior works in the particular genre of interest. In the application they describe, the case base is a library of bebop jazz melodies. The evolved musician programs could take examples of melodies from the case base and alter them with a set of predetermined transformation functions, such as INVERT, AUGMENT, and COMPARE-TRANSPOSE, which are also largely culture specific.

The fitness function in this bebop case consisted of five critical criteria gleaned from jazz improvisation techniques, rules that looked for a balance of novel tonal material and material taken from the case base, or for rhythmic novelty balance, and so on. Musician programs that generated new bebop melodies meeting these criteria would have more offspring in the next generation (created by reproduction and crossover alone, to scramble existing combinations of transformation functions). Spector and Alpern ran their system with a case base of five Charlie Parker song fragments of four bars each. After 21 generations of populations with 250 evolving composers, individuals emerged that could produce four-bar "improvisations" that were found highly satisfying by the five-rule critic. The system's creators, however, were less impressed: "Although the response . . . pleases the critic, it does not please *us* [the authors] particularly well" (Spector and Alpern 1994:7). They do not see this as a failing of the evolutionary artist construction method in general. Instead, they believe that with proper choice of critical rules, the approach can be made to succeed, and "nobody said it would be easy to raise an artist" (p. 8).

But a deeper problem remains with rule-based critic approaches in general, as people found earlier with rule-based composers. Artificial critics who go strictly by their given rules, as opposed to more forgiving (or sloppier) human critics, are generally very brittle. They may rave about the technically correct but rather trite melody, while panning the inspired but slightly off passage created by just flipping two notes. In fact, for good composers it is critical to know when to break the rules. As a consequence, for critics it is imperative to know when to *let* the composers break the rules. Rule-based systems, by definition, lack exactly this higher-level knowledge. Critics based on learning methods such as neural network models, on the other hand, can generalize judgments sufficiently to leave (artificial) composers much-needed rule-breaking "wiggle room," although this too can end in cacophony, as we will see.

Learning-Based Critics

To remove (or at least transform) the necessity of human interaction in the algorithmic composition process further, critics used in evolving artificial composers can be trained using easy-to-collect musical examples, rather than constructed using difficult-to-determine musical rules. Baluja, Pomerleau, and Jochem (1994), for instance, working in the visual domain, trained a neural network to replace the human critic in an interactive image-evolution system similar to that created by Sims (1991). The network "watches" the choices that a human user makes when selecting two-dimensional images from one generation to reproduce in the next generation, and over time learns to make the same kind of aesthetic evaluations as those made by the human. When the trained network is put in place of the human critic in the evolutionary loop, interesting images can be evolved automatically. With learning critics of this sort, whether applied to images or to music, even less structure ends up in the evolved artificial creators, because it must get there indirectly by way of the trained fitness-evaluating critic that learned its structural preferences from a user-selected training set. We can thus expect a great degree of novelty in compositions created by this approach, but how will they sound?

Spector and Alpern (1995) extended their earlier rule-based system to find out. They expected that a neural network trained to make aesthetic evaluations of a case base of melodies would be able to evaluate the musical output of evolving composers at a deeper structural level than their rule-based critics could. This time their composers were to create single-measure responses to single-measure calls in a collection of Charlie Parker melodies. The composers were again evolved in the genetic programming paradigm, but using more abstract (less musically specific) functions than before. The critic neural networks were trained to return a positive evaluation of one measure of original Charlie Parker followed by the correct next measure. They were also trained to return negative evaluations of one Charlie Parker measure followed by different kinds of bad continuations: silence, random melody, or chopped-up Charlie. To evaluate a given composer program, the program was given an original Charlie Parker measure as input, and both that input and the composer program's one-measure output were passed to the neural network critic. The critic then returned a fitness value indicating how well it thought the composed measure followed the original measure.

One advantage of such a system is that new critical constraints can be added simply by training the neural network critic on additional musical examples, rather than by constructing new rules. The problem, though, is that one can never be sure the network is learning the musical criteria one would like it to, as Spector and Alpern discovered. As in their earlier work, a composer program with very high fitness value was found quickly, in fact, after only a single generation of evolution. But as before, its performance did not meet the standards of its human overseers: in response to a simple measure of eight eighth-notes, it returned a monstrosity containing thirty-five notes of minuscule duration (mostly triplets) jumping over three octaves. The authors noted (1995:45): "In retrospect it is clear that the network had far too small a training set to learn about many of these kinds of errors. . . ."

The general problem here is that evolutionary search processes are highly adept at exploiting weaknesses and quirks of fitness functions: the evolving creators are constantly looking for the easy way to higher fitness, and jumping on it when they discover it. This means that in practice, a researcher may have to modify a particular fitness function a few times before it is specific enough to lead to the evolution of desired musical behaviors and to avoid being tricked by shortcut solutions. In nature, this kind of fitness-function evolution often happens automatically, for instance, when a species of predator discovers a new way of surprising its prey, and the prey must adapt a new defensive strategy in turn. This kind of back-and-forth reciprocal modification of selectee and selector can also be captured in evolutionary computer simulations, where it can be used to study another class of phenomena: coevolution of musical production behavior and perceptual preferences.

Evolution of Musical Diversity through Coevolving Creators and Critics

Evolutionary simulation tools developed by musicians looking for new ways to generate creative compositions can be adopted to explore specific scientific questions. We modified some of these tools, for instance, to investigate ways that musical diversity can be generated within and across generations, seeking to answer the question, "why are there so many love songs?" Some aspects of this project illustrate the way that evolutionary computer simulations can be put to scientific use (for more details, see Werner and Todd 1997).

Species with highly evolved, elaborate communication systems often have a great diversity of signals within a given population and between populations (including successive generations and recently diverged species) over time. Humans of course have an unmatched capacity to generate novel signals, both linguistic and musical. Many songbirds have repertoires of dozens of distinct song types, a few species can sing hundreds of different songs, and the brown thrasher checks in with a remarkable repertoire size of over 2,000 (Catchpole and Slater 1995). Moreover, any one male of a given songbird species typically sings a different repertoire from other conspecific males. Moving from air to ocean, humpback whales each sing a unique song (Payne and McVay 1971; Payne, this volume), and even cephalopods (particularly cuttlefish, octopuses, and squid) have a surprising variety of signal types, with some species using as many as thirty-five different displays in a wide range of combinations and sequences (Hanlon and Messenger 1996).

Traditional reasons given for the evolution of communication do not provide particularly compelling explanations for such between-individual signal diversity. If communication is viewed as a means of transferring veridical information from one organism to another (see Hauser 1996), we would expect repeated communications of the same information by one individual or within a population to be performed in a similar manner to avoid misinterpretation by the receiver. In the particular case of accurate species identification for mating purposes, there should also be little variation between signals of conspecifics. If communication is seen instead as a way to manipulate the behavior of another organism, which can include nonveridical deceit (see Krebs and Dawkins 1984), the signal used in any particular case should be the single one found to be most effective. And if communication is considered a means of altruistically benefiting one's genetic relatives (Ackley and Littman 1994), we would expect convergence onto stable but possibly family-specific ways to help one another.

What then can drive the evolution of a large variety of elaborate communication signals? Consider the evolutionary composition tools described in the previous section. A common problem with the automated (nonhuman) fitness functions was that they could be tricked by musically uninteresting solutions, on which the population would then converge because of their high fitness values. Human critics could avoid being so tricked by changing what they were listening for in the population, and reacting to any cheating musical behaviors. This type of responsive fitness evaluation can also keep the population from converging on a single sort of behavior and can thereby maintain a diversity of musical output. As a consequence, we decided to investigate the role that coevolution of critics and music creators could play in engendering musical diversity within a population and across several generations. In particular, we wanted to test the effects of different preference mechanisms on diversity to see if some mechanisms would lead to more diverse populations than others.

Coevolution, Sexual Selection, and Mate Choice

Coevolution can create a diversity of musical or other behavior in two ways. First, it can produce diversity within a population at any one time. This *synchronic diversity* can be generated, for example, through the process of sexual selection, when females choose mates based on particular traits the males bear. When both female preferences for particular traits and male traits themselves coevolve, new species can form, splitting up the original population into subpopulations of individuals with distinct traits and preferences (see Todd and Miller 1991a, for a simulation model of this speciation process). Coevolution's ability to generate synchronic diversity through speciation is a source of much of the variety and beauty of our natural world (Miller and Todd 1995; Skutch 1992).

Second, coevolution can generate diversity across time, *diachronic diversity* in which traits in a population continuously change, generation after generation. This pattern of constant change can be seen in arms races between different species, for instance, predators and prey, where adaptations in one species—ability to chase faster, say—are countered by new adaptations in the other species—ability to change direction quickly when fleeing (Futuyama and Slatkin 1983). In musical evolution systems, diachronic diversity is equivalent to generating a succession of new artificial composers and perceivers. As mentioned, this succession is something that human listeners can accomplish by changing their critical criteria over time; coevolving artificial critics allow us to take humans out of the evolutionary loop.

Thus, to generate musical diversity both across time and at any given instant, both diachronically and synchronically, we must build a system that can create a multitude of distinctly defined "species" within one population, and that can further induce those species to move around in musical space from one generation to the next. Sexual selection through mate choice allows the former, leading a population to cluster into subpopulations with specific (musical) traits and preferences. But we need some further force to push a population out of its attained stable pattern of speciation. Competing species, for instance, predators or parasites, can play this role (see Hillis' 1992 simulation of parasites driving a population out of suboptimal behaviors). Within the realm of sexual selection, this motive force can be achieved through directional mate preferences (Kirkpatrick 1987; Miller and Todd 1993, 1995) that, for example, cause females always to look for brighter or more colorful or more behaviorally complex males. These changing preferences can induce a population to continue evolving. For the evolution of musical creators, as we will see, this constant striving force can be effected through neophilia: females always looking for males who create musical patterns that are new and unexpected. Our coevolutionary model thus ends up looking like and being inspired by the evolution of birdsong through sexual selection of critical females choosing which singing males to mate with. But its application may be much wider: Miller (this volume) proposes that human musical behavior itself is the result of runaway coevolution between preferences and abilities.

Coevolving Hopeful Singers and Music Critics

To simulate the coevolution of music producers and critics who exert selective pressure on their songs, we created a population of male singers and female listeners who choose mates based on the songs they sing. Males and female individuals are all represented by a set of numeric genes on which the genetic algorithm can operate. Each simple male singer has genes that directly encode the notes of his song, which consists of thirty-two notes, each a single pitch selected from a two-octave (twenty-four pitch) range. Females' genes encode a transition matrix that is used to rate transitions from one note to another in male songs. This matrix is an N-by-N table, where N is the number of possible pitches males can produce (twenty-four in these experiments). Each entry in the table represents a female's expectation of the probability of one pitch following another. For instance, entry (four, eleven or C-G in our two-octave case) in a particular female's table captures how often she thinks pitch eleven will follow pitch four, on average. Given these expectations, a female can decide how well she likes a particular song in different ways, as we will see. Whatever method she uses, as she listens to a male she considers the transition from the previous note's pitch to the current note's pitch for each note in a song, gives each transition a score based on her transition table, and sums those scores to come up with her final evaluation of the male and his serenade.

Each female listens to the songs of a certain number of males who are randomly selected to be in her courting choir. All females hear the same number of males, and the size of the courting choir, that is, a female's sample size, is specified for each evolutionary run. After listening to all the males in her potential-mate choir, the female selects the one that she most prefers (i.e., the one with the highest score). This process ensures that all females have exactly one mate, but males can have a range of mates from zero (if his song is unpopular with everyone) to something close to the courting-choir size (if he has a platinum hit that is selected by all the females who listen to him). Each female has one child per generation created by crossover and mutation with her chosen mate. Thus this child will have a mix of musical traits and preferences genetically encoded in its mother and father. This temporarily puts the population at about 50% above a specified carrying capacity (target population size). We then kill off approximately a third of the individuals, bringing the population back to a predetermined carrying capacity. This process is repeated for a desired number of generations.

We studied three preference mechanisms for scoring male songs using these tables. In the first method, the female simply scores each transition as it occurs in the song by immediately looking up how much she expected that particular transition and adding it to the running total score for the song. Thus, songs that contain more of the individual transitions that the female expects (e.g., with many C-G transitions, if she expects Cs to be followed by Gs very often) will be scored higher, and she will prefer to mate with males who sing these songs. We call this the *local transition preference* scoring method.

In the second method, the female listens to a whole song first, counting the number each type of transition occurs (e.g., she might tally up Gs following Cs four times and other notes following Cs two times). Then from these counts she constructs a transition matrix for that particular song (e.g., with an entry of .66 for the C-G transition, because that is what occurred two-thirds of the time after a C). Finally, she compares that song's transition table with her expected (preferred) transition table, and the closer the tables match on an entry-by-entry basis, the higher score and preference she gives to that song.

Thus, this method means that a female will prefer songs that match the overall statistical pattern of transitions in her transition table. We call this the *global transition preference* scoring method. Continuing with our example, if the female has a value of .75 stored in her own transition table for the C-G transition, she will like songs most that have a C-G transition exactly three-fourths of the time (along with other C-x transitions, where x will be notes other than G, for the other quarter of the time that C appears). In contrast, with local transition scoring, she would prefer C-G transitions after every C, because they give a higher local score than any other transition from C.

The third scoring method produces females that enjoy being surprised. The female listens to each transition in the song individually as in the first method, looks up how much she expected that transition, and subtracts this probability value from the probability she attached to the transition she most expected to hear. Consider our female from the previous paragraph. Whenever she hears a C, she most expects a G to follow it (75% of the time). Imagine she instead hears a C-E transition. This is a surprise to her, because it violates the C-G transition expectation, and she likes this song more as a consequence.

But how much of a surprise was this note, and how much does it increase her preference for this song? To find out, the female critic first looks up the C-E transition in her table and finds she expected that transition 15% of the time (for example). Thus, this C-E transition was not a complete surprise, because she had some expectation for it, but it was a reasonably large one. We quantify the surprise level with a score of .75 − .15 = .6 for that transition (i.e., probability(C-G)—probability(C-E)). This expected-minus-actual transition probability score is summed for all transitions in the current song, and the final sum registers how much surprise the female experienced and therefore how much she preferred that song. No surprise, we call this the *surprise preference* scoring method. Note that it will not result in males singing random songs. To earn a high surprise score, a song must first build up expectations by making transitions to notes that have highly expected notes following them, and then violate those expectations by not using the highly expected note. Thus a constant tug-of-war exists between doing what is expected and what is unexpected in each song.

The first two scoring methods can be considered forms of non-directional mate preferences: evolved male songs that match evolved female expectations most precisely (either locally or globally) will receive the most mating interest. The surprise preference scoring method is a type of directional mate preference. Rather than rewarding male songs that match female expectations, surprising songs that are some ways off from the evolved female transition tables in song space will be sought after. Thus we expected to see less movement through song space for local and global transition preferences and more continual change—maintaining diversity over time—when surprise preferences were used.

We also expected that surprise scoring would create greater diversity within any given generation than would preferences based on matching local or global expectations, because there are more ways to violate expectations (causing surprise) than to meet them. Note that this is different from the kinds of directional preferences where only a single preferred direction was indicated (e.g., a greener versus a bluer patch of plumage). In those cases, the population could evolve to head all in one direction in phenotype space; here, the population will be more likely to scatter in many directions in phenotype space.

We also controlled the number of males a female listens to before selecting a mate; that is, the size of her courting choir (two or twenty). This parameter is essentially a "volume knob" on the overall impact of sexual selection in the simulation. If females can only sample one male, no sexual selection is taking place, whereas the greater the number of males she can listen to before choosing a mate, the stronger will be the selective force of her preferences. We expected that smaller samples would lead to greater diversity than larger ones, but that larger samples might support a number of distinct "species" of songs. Smaller samples should, on average, give males a better chance of reproducing even if their song is not close to what is desired by females, because each male in a female's small sample set faces less competition than if she sampled a large number of males. On the other hand, we believed that large samples would quickly draw males close to what was desired by females but that the preferences could aggregate in distinct clusters.

We further compared cases where female expectation-transition tables were fixed across time (i.e., female offspring contain exact copies of their mother's transition table) with runs where females were allowed to coevolve with male songs. In this way we tested our expectation that coevolving preferences would allow more change (or diversity) in songs over time because targets for males would themselves be moving. In a system without coevolution, male songs tend to converge on the female preferences and stay there, providing little evolutionary movement.

Resulting Song Change over Time

We ran populations of 1,000 individuals for 1,000 generations in six different conditions: all three preference scoring methods with fixed or coevolving preferences. We consider here cases in which the female's courting choir contained just two males (see Werner and Todd 1997, for other situations). In each case we initiated male songs randomly, and female transition tables were set in the first generation with probabilities calculated from a collection of simple folk-tune melodies. This way we could ensure that female preferences in our simulations at least started out with some resemblance to human melodic preferences; however, once evolution started moving preferences and songs around, any hope of the population's aesthetics matching human aesthetics would quickly be lost. Thus, we could not listen to the system and readily judge its progress; we had to resort to more objective measures, which is another reason for using the simplified form of song and preference representation.

To measure evolving song change over time—diachronic diversity— we used a progress chart technique modified from Cliff and Miller's (1995) work on tracking coevolutionary progress in pursuit-evasion games. This method allows us to compare and visualize the difference between the modal male song (i.e., the most common note at each of the thirty-two positions) at any generation G and that at any previous generation G', with difference measured as the number of positions where the two songs differ (from zero to thirty-two). More specifically, we plot generations G in time from left to right (from generation G = 0 to G = 1,000), and generations G' backward in time (relative to each generation G) from top to bottom (from generation G' = G-1 to generation G' = G-999). At each point (G, G') in the triangular region so formed, we plot the difference between the modal male song (i.e., the most common note at each of the thirty-two positions) at generation G and that at generation G', with difference measured as the number of positions where the two songs differ. This difference score, from zero to thirty-two, is indicated by the darkness of the plotted point, with greater differences mapping onto lighter points (figure 20.1).

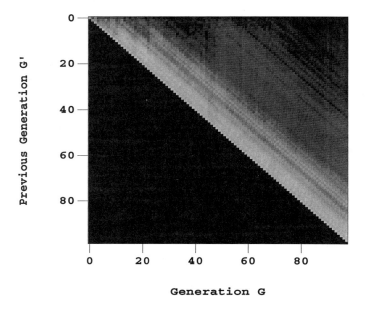

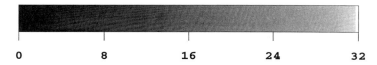

Figure 20.1
Change in modal song from current generation G (left to right) to all previous generations G′ (from G-1 at top to G-999 at bottom). Here a coevolving surprise-preference sample-size-two population shows continuous rapid change over time.

Using this technique, we compared the rate of change of population modal songs over time for our six conditions. Surprise scoring yielded greater change than either global or local transition scoring. Local scoring, in fact, made the population converge rather rapidly to locally preferred transitions so that male songs often degenerated to repetition of a single note or alternation between two notes. (This also gave these runs very low within-generation synchronic diversity scores, so we did not analyze this type of preference further.) Furthermore, coevolution led to faster change than fixed female preferences, primarily when surprise scoring was used. But the parameter with the biggest effect was choir size: listening to only two males yielded much faster evolutionary change than choosing from twenty. This effect could occur because with bigger samples, traits could match preferences much more closely, and so little movement of either would be necessitated over time.

We can easily visualize the difference between rate of change in the fastest case and its parametric "opposite" (i.e., changing all parameters),

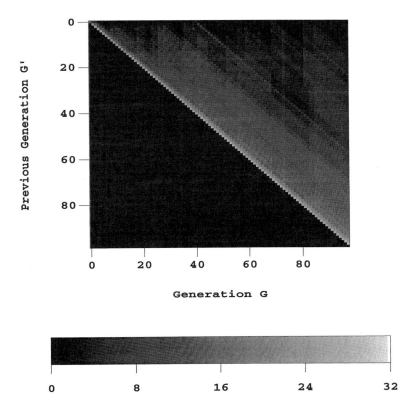

Figure 20.2
Change in modal song for a noncoevolving global-preference sample-size-twenty population, showing little change over time.

which is one of the slowest cases, by plotting their progress charts. Figure 20.1 shows modal song change for a coevolving surprise-scoring small (i.e., sample size two) population. The relatively small region of dark points, indicating small changes between past and present generations, is dominated by a large light region, indicating large changes over time. In figure 20.2, we plot the chart for a fixed-preference global-transition-scoring large (twenty) population. Here the differences between present and past modal songs are mostly small (dark points), meaning that little change occurred over time. The light band along the diagonal indicates a lot of change in the first few generations, as initially random male songs were most strongly winnowed down, but after that little more transpired.

Resulting Song Diversity within Populations

To measure the synchronic diversity of songs within a population at any particular generation, we computed the set of differences (again zero to thirty-two) between every pair of males' songs in the population. This set of differences can be plotted as a histogram for any given generation, with highly converged, low-diversity populations having histograms skewed toward low values, and unconverged, high-diversity populations having histograms skewed toward high values. Furthermore, populations with two or more distinct "species" of songs show up as multiple peaks in the histogram, representing distributions of between-species and within-species distances. To explore how this within-generation diversity changes across generations, we can simply line up several histograms next to each other. This gives us a plot with generation G along one dimension and distance between each male song and the modal song along the other dimension, with the darkness of each point indicating the number of males who are that different from the population's current modal song.

We used this visualization method to compare the evolving synchronic diversity of songs in populations in four conditions (leaving out degenerate hyperconverged local transition score populations). Again our expectations were mostly met: coevolution yielded greater synchronic diversity than fixed female preferences; that is, most songs in the population were about eighteen notes different from the modal song for the coevolving-female-preference surprise population versus about eleven notes different for the fixed-female-preference surprise population after 1,000 generations. The preference scoring method (surprise versus global transition) showed little consistent effect on within-generation diversity, however. Finally, sampling two males preserved diversity in the population to a much greater degree than sampling twenty males; in the former case, most males retained ten to twenty different notes from the modal song after 1,000 generations, whereas in the latter, most males had only one or two notes different.

We show the difference between the case with the greatest synchronic diversity and its parametric opposite with one of the lowest diversities in figures 20.3 and 20.4, respectively. Figure 20.3 displays the song diversity in a coevolving surprise-scoring sample-two population over time, starting at generation zero at the top of the graph and proceeding to generation 1,000 at the bottom. Diversity starts out maximal in the early generations when random initial male songs were all very far from the modal song, and declines somewhat over time. But even after 1,000 generations, most male songs have about twenty notes out of thirty-two that are different from their population's modal song. In contrast, the fixed global-transition scoring sample-twenty population in figure 20.4 converges from its initial diversity to population-wide homogeneity very rapidly. Within 150 generations, most males sing songs that are only slight (three position) variations on the population modal song, and this clustering even grows slightly tighter over time. However, tight clustering with a large choir size when combined with the directional

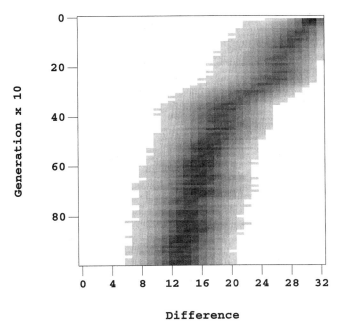

Figure 20.3
Diversity of songs in each generation G, from G = 1 at top to G = 1,000 at bottom. Each point shows the number of pairs of songs that have a certain number of notes different between them. Here, diversity is preserved in a coevolving surprise-preference sample-size-two population.

selection effects of surprise preferences can lead new song "species" to emerge and differentiate from each other over time. This effect is shown in figure 20.5. Thus, as choir size is increased, diversity across the whole population can be replaced by diversity between speciated subpopulations.

Implications and Conclusions

Our simulations lend support for the role of coevolving songs and directional (surprise-based) preferences in creating and maintaining musical diversity. Evolution is likely to stagnate unless females choose songs based not just on evolved preferences but also on a desire to be surprised by what they hear. Loosely speaking, when females are bored by the same old song, males must strive to provide them with something new to ensure their own mating success. As a consequence, a variety of male songs evolves, both within a single generation and across successive generations over time. With noncoevolving, nondirectional preferences, progress is slower and diversity collapses.

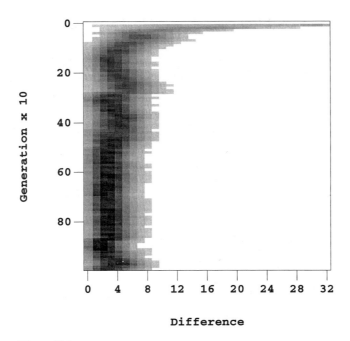

Figure 20.4
Diversity of songs in a noncoevolving global-preference sample-size-twenty population, showing loss of diversity over time.

This diversity could actually be increased if female song preferences could change faster, altering within any given female's lifetime rather than just between mother and daughter. This is exactly the role that learning can play, enabling adaptations faster than evolution can accomplish (Todd and Miller 1991b). By combining (co)evolution and learning, we may be able to explore further questions about musical diversity relating to culture and individual song complexity.

One obvious place we could add learning to our system is in the creation of female musical expectations: where should their transition tables come from? In our current setup, females inherit transition tables from their mother and father. Because of this, "surprising" note transitions can be surprising only relative to a particular female's inherited expectations. But certainly for humans, and for other animals as well, expectations are built up through experience and learning within one's lifetime (see Bharucha and Todd 1989). Instead we can let a female learn expectations about note transitions based on a set of songs from her current generation, or from the previous generation, as if she has heard those songs and picked up knowledge of her culture from them. Then she will be surprised when she hears something new that toys with these learned expectations, building them up, and violating them. We expect that using learning to

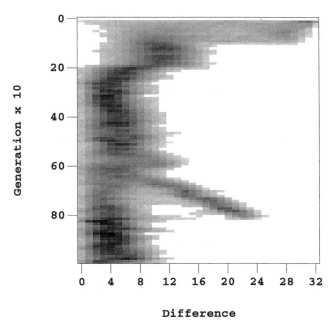

Figure 20.5
Diversity of songs in a coevolving surprise-preference sample-size-twenty population, showing evolution of two tightly clustered song species between generations 600 and 800.

create note transition expectations, rather than evolving them, will allow the population to change its tune even more rapidly than the cases described here, because expectations will be able to shift just as rapidly as the songs themselves—learning operates faster than selection.

Furthermore, we could allow learning in females to occur at an even faster time scale so that instead of habituating to songs heard too many times last week, for example, each female could habituate to notes and phrases heard too many times within the current male's song. In this case, females would seek novelty and expectation-violation within each song they hear. To sing preferred songs, males would have to balance the amount of repetition and novelty in their song. We expect that this type of real-time preference learning will lead to increased complexity of the internal structure of the songs themselves, not just of the population of songs.

Being able to witness and analyze interactions of musical behavior, learning, culture, and evolution in these new ways is the best argument for using evolutionary computer simulations to study the origins of music. By harnessing the power of computers to mimic these adaptive processes from nature, we gain a new way of listening in on the nascent songs of bygone worlds.

References

Ackley, D. H. and Littman, M. L. (1994). Altruism in the evolution of communication. In R. A. Brooks and P. Maes (Eds.) *Artificial Life V* (pp. 40–48). Cambridge: MIT Press.

Baluja, S., Pomerleau, D., and Jochem, T. (1994). Towards automated artificial evolution for computer-generated images. *Connection Science* 6:325–354.

Bharucha, J. J. and Todd, P. M. (1989). Modeling the perception of tonal structure with neural nets. *Computer Music Journal* 13:44–53. Also in P. M. Todd and D. G. Loy (Eds.) *Music and Connectionism* (pp. 128–137). Cambridge: MIT Press.

Biles, J. A. (1994). GenJam: A genetic algorithm for generating jazz solos. In *Proceedings of the 1994 International Computer Music Conference* (pp. 131–137). San Francisco: International Computer Music Association.

Biles, J. A. (1995). *The Al Biles Virtual Quintet: GenJam*. Compact disk DRK-CD-144. Rochester, NY: Dynamic Recording Studios.

Catchpole, C. K. and Slater, P. J. B. (1995). *Bird Song: Biological Themes and Variations*. Cambridge, UK: Cambridge University Press.

Cliff, D. and Miller, G. F. (1995). Tracking the Red Queen: Measurements of adaptive progress in co-evolutionary simulations. In F. Moran, A. Moreno, J. J. Merelo, and P. Cachon (Eds.) *Advances in Artificial Life: Proceedings of the Third European Conference on Artificial Life* (pp. 200–218). Berlin: Springer-Verlag.

Darwin, C. R. (1859). *On the Origin of Species*. London: Murray. (Reprinted in 1964 with an introduction by E. Mayr; Cambridge: Harvard University Press.)

Ebcioglu, K. (1984). An expert system for Schenkerian synthesis of chorales in the style of J. S. Bach. In *Proceedings of the 1984 International Computer Music Conference* (pp. 135–142). San Francisco: International Computer Music Association.

Futuyama, D. and Slatkin, M. (Eds.) (1983). *Coevolution*. Sunderland, MA: Sinauer.

Goldberg, D. E. (1989). *Genetic Algorithms in Search, Optimization, and Machine Learning*. Reading, MA: Addison-Wesley.

Griffith, N. and Todd, P. M. (Eds.) (1999). *Musical Networks: Parallel Distributed Perception and Performance*. Cambridge: MIT Press.

Hanlon, R. T. and Messenger, J. B. (1996). *Cephalopod Behavior*. Cambridge, UK: Cambridge University Press.

Hauser, M. (1996). *The Evolution of Communication*. Cambridge: MIT Press.

Hillis, W. D. (1992). Co-evolving parasites improve simulated evolution as an optimization procedure. In C. Langton, C. Taylor, J. D. Farmer, and S. Rasmussen (Eds.) *Artificial Life II* (pp. 313–324). Reading, MA: Addison-Wesley.

Holland, J. H. (1975). *Adaptation in Natural and Artificial Systems*. Ann Arbor: University of Michigan Press. (Second edition: MIT Press, 1992.)

Horner, A. and Goldberg, D. E. (1991a). Genetic algorithms and computer-assisted music composition. In *Proceedings of the 1991 International Computer Music Conference* (pp. 479–482). San Francisco: International Computer Music Association.

Horner, A. and Goldberg, D. E. (1991b). *Genetic Algorithms and Computer-Assisted Music Composition*. Urbana-Champaign: University of Illinois Center for Complex Systems Research, the Beckman Institute.

Jones, K. (1981). Compositional applications of stochastic processes. *Computer Music Journal* 5:45–61.

Kirkpatrick, M. (1987). The evolutionary forces acting on female preferences in polygynous animals. In J. W. Bradbury and M. B. Andersson (Eds.) *Sexual Selection: Testing the Alternatives* (pp. 67–82). New York: Wiley.

Koza, J. (1993). *Genetic Programming*. Cambridge: MIT Press.

Krebs, J. R. and Dawkins, R. (1984). Animal signals: Mind-reading and manipulation. In J. R. Krebs and N. B. Davies (Eds.) *Behavioral Ecology* (pp. 380–402). Sunderland, MA: Sinauer.

Loy, D. G. (1989). Composing with computers: A survey of some compositional formalisms and music programming languages. In M. V. Mathews and J. R. Pierce (Eds.) *Current Directions in Computer Music Research* (pp. 291–396). Cambridge: MIT Press.

Loy, D. G. (1991). Connectionism and musiconomy. In P. M. Todd and D. G. Loy (Eds.) *Music and Connectionism* (pp. 20–36). Cambridge: MIT Press.

Miller, G. F. and Todd, P. M. (1993). Evolutionary wanderlust: Sexual selection with directional mate preferences. In J.-A. Meyer, H. L. Roitblat, and S. W. Wilson (Eds.) *From Animals to Animats*, Vol. 2: *Proceedings of the Second International Conference on Simulation of Adaptive Behavior* (pp. 21–30). Cambridge: MIT Press.

Miller, G. F. and Todd, P. M. (1995). The role of mate choice in biocomputation: Sexual selection as a process of search, optimization, and diversification. In W. Banzhaf and F. H. Eeckman (Eds.) *Evolution and Biocomputation: Computational Models of Evolution* (pp. 169–204). Berlin: Springer-Verlag.

Miller, G. F., Todd, P. M., and Hegde, S. U. (1989). Designing neural networks using genetic algorithms. In J. D. Schaffer (Ed.) *Proceedings of the Third International Conference on Genetic Algorithms* (pp. 379–384). San Mateo, CA: Morgan Kaufmann.

Mitchell, M. (1996). *An Introduction to Genetic Algorithms*. Cambridge: MIT Press.

Mozer, M. C. (1991). Connectionist music composition based on melodic, stylistic, and psychophysical constraints. In P. M. Todd and D. G. Loy (Eds.) *Music and Connectionism* (pp. 195–211). Cambridge: MIT Press.

Mozer, M. C. (1994). Neural network music composition by prediction: Exploring the benefits of psychoacoustic constraints and multi-scale processing. *Connection Science* 6:247–280.

Payne, R. S. and McVay, S. (1971). Songs of humpback whales. *Science* 173:585–597.

Putnam, J. B. (1994). *Genetic Programming of Music*. Unpublished manuscript. Socorro: New Mexico Institute of Mining and Technology.

Rumelhart, D. E., McClelland, J. L., and The PDP Research Group. (1986). *Parallel Distributed Processing: Explorations in the Microstructure of Cognition*. Cambridge: MIT Press.

Sims, K. (1991). Artificial evolution for computer graphics. *Computer Graphics* 25: 319–328.

Skutch, A. F. (1992). *Origins of Nature's Beauty: Essays by Alexander F. Skutch*. Austin: University of Texas Press.

Spector, L. and Alpern, A. (1994). Criticism, culture, and the automatic generation of artworks. In *Proceedings of the Twelfth National Conference on Artificial Intelligence (AAAI94)* (pp. 3–8). Menlo Park, CA, and Cambridge: AAAI Press and MIT Press.

Spector, L. and Alpern, A. (1995). Induction and recapitulation of deep musical structure. In *Working Notes of the IJCAI-95 Workshop on Artificial Intelligence and Music* (pp. 41–48). Montreal, Canada: IJCAI Inc.

Takala, T., Hahn, J., Gritz, L., Geigel, J., and Lee, J. W. (1993). Using physically-based models and genetic algorithms for functional composition of sound signals, synchronized to animated motion. In *Proceedings of the 1993 International Computer Music Conference* (pp. 180–185). San Francisco: International Computer Music Association.

Todd, P. M. (1988). A sequential network design for musical applications. In D. Touretzky, G. Hinton, and T. Sejnowski (Eds.) *Proceedings of the 1988 Connectionist Models Summer School* (pp. 76–84). San Mateo, CA: Morgan Kaufmann.

Todd, P. M. (1989). A connectionist approach to algorithmic composition. *Computer Music Journal* 13:27–43.

Todd, P. M. (1996). The causes and effects of evolutionary simulation in the behavioral sciences. In R. Belew and M. Mitchell (Eds.) *Adaptive Individuals in Evolving Populations: Models and Algorithms* (pp. 211–224). Reading, MA: Addison-Wesley.

Todd, P. M. and Loy, D. G. (1991). *Music and Connectionism*. Cambridge: MIT Press.

Todd, P. M. and Miller, G. F. (1991a). On the sympatric origin of species: Mercurial mating in the quicksilver model. In R. K. Belew and L. B. Booker (Eds.) *Proceedings of the Fourth International Conference on Genetic Algorithms* (pp. 547–554). San Mateo, CA: Morgan Kaufmann.

Todd, P. M. and Miller, G. F. (1991b). Exploring adaptive agency. II: Simulating the evolution of associative learning. In J.-A. Meyer and S. W. Wilson (Eds.) *From Animals to Animats: Proceedings of the First International Conference on Simulation of Adaptive Behavior* (pp. 306–315). Cambridge: MIT Press.

Todd, P. M. and Werner, G. M. (1999). Frankensteinian methods for evolutionary music composition. In N. Griffith and P. M. Todd (Eds.) *Musical Networks: Parallel Distributed Perception and Performance* (pp. 313–339). Cambridge: MIT Press.

Weiner, J. (1994). *The Beak of the Finch: A Story of Evolution in Our Time.* New York: Knopf.

Werner, G. M. and Todd, P. M. (1997). Too many love songs: Sexual selection and the evolution of communication. In P. Husbands and I. Harvey (Eds.) *Fourth European Conference on Artificial Life* (pp. 434–443). Cambridge: MIT Press.

Wimsatt, W. C. (In press). *Re-engineering Philosophy for Limited Beings: Piecewise Approximations to Reality.* Cambridge: Harvard University Press.

21 Antecedents of the Temporal Arts in Early Mother-Infant Interaction

Ellen Dissanayake

Abstract

Speculations about the biological origins of music, like other human social behaviors, typically assume that competition affecting reproductive success was and is the ultimate evolutionary driving force. A different approach maintains that human music originated in perceptual, behavioral, cognitive, and emotional competencies and sensitivities that developed from primate precursors in survival-enhancing affiliative interactions (using ritualized packages of sequential vocal, facial, and kinesic behaviors) between mothers and infants under six months of age. Thus music in its origins is viewed as a multimedially presented and multi-modally processed activity of temporally and spatially patterned—exaggerated and regularized—vocal, bodily, and even facial movements. It is held that because of increasing infant altriciality during hominization, the primate propensity for relationship or emotional communion, not simply sociability, became so crucial that special affiliative mechanisms evolved to enhance and ensure it. These mechanisms in turn could be further developed (as temporal arts, including music) to serve affiliative bonding among adults in a species where close cooperation also became unprecedentedly critical for individual survival. That musical ability (like any variable attribute) can be and is used competitively in particular instances is not denied. However, the hypothesis offered here is able to address and account for music's specific and widely attested power to coordinate and conjoin individuals, both physically and psychologically.

In *The Descent of Man, and Selection in Relation to Sex*, Charles Darwin (1885:566–573) speculated, as do we more than a century later, about the origins of human music. He identified analogues and possible precursors of music in the animal world, most of which evolved by sexual selection, and thereby set the course for subsequent evolutionary speculations about the arts. Darwin noted that male animals use their vocal organs in the excitement of love, rage, and jealousy (p. 566), and during the breeding season more than at any time (p. 567). Hence he inferred that the ancestors of humans probably also used musical tones and rhythm when excited by jealousy, rivalry, and triumph (p. 572), as well as for attracting and charming each other (p. 573). Still Darwin also observed that as "neither the enjoyment nor the capacity of producing musical notes are faculties of the least use to man in reference to his daily habits of life, they must be ranked amongst the most mysterious with which he is endowed" (pp. 569–570).

I suggest that the enjoyment and capacity of producing musical notes are faculties of indispensable use in the daily habits of life of countless women, specifically mothers, and their infants, and that it is in the evolution of affiliative interactions between mothers and infants—not male competition or adult courtship—that we can discover the origins of the competencies and sensitivities that gave rise to human music. Such a concept provides a new and promising approach to the longstanding mystery of music's origin and evolutionary purpose.

I do not refer to lullabies or to maternal singing but to early interactions, ritualized packages of sequential behaviors, vocal, facial, and kinesic, between mothers and infants under six months of age. I thus view music in its origins more broadly than as vocalizations, rather, as a multimodal or multimedia activity of temporally patterned movements. I also emphasize its capacity not only to attract and charm individuals, but to *coordinate the emotions of participants* and thus promote *conjoinment.*

My thesis begins with the physical helplessness of the human infant at birth. During hominization, as we know, increasing commitments to bipedal locomotion and to expanding brain size affected gestation length and compelled greater infant altriciality, since the narrow birth passage required by upright posture conflicted with continuing encephalization. The solution (or compromise) was that infants were born increasingly prematurely (Leakey 1994:45; Morgan 1995:59).

The trend toward increasingly helpless infants surely created intense selective pressure for proximate physiological and cognitive mechanisms to ensure longer and better maternal care.[1] I suggest that the solution to this problem was accomplished by coevolution in infants and mothers of rhythmic, temporally patterned, jointly maintained communicative interactions that produced and sustained positive affect—psychobiological brain states of interest and joy—by displaying and imitating emotions and motivations of affiliation, and thereby sharing, communicating, and reinforcing them.[2]

Typical Features of Mother-Infant Early Interaction

Early-interaction studies indicate that in the first half year of life infants possess quite remarkable unlearned abilities that predispose them for interaction and intimacy with a partner (e.g., Stern 1971, 1983; Trevarthen 1974, 1977, 1979a, b, 1993; Beebe 1982; Beebe and Gerstman 1984). Even neonates, for example, can perceive time and temporal sequence, estimate durations of intervals lasting seconds and fractions of seconds in their own and in others' behavior, detect contingencies between their behavior and environmental events, and develop expectancies of when events occur (Jaffe et al. submitted). Studies with neonates and six-week-old infants indicate that temporal organization composed of short cycles of attention and inattention underlies the earliest social interactions (Beebe, Stern, and Jaffe 1979; Trevarthen 1984; Jaffe et al. 1991; Feldstein et al. 1993; Jaffe et al. submitted). Infants can respond to variations in frequency, intensity, duration, and temporal or spatial patterning of sounds (Papoušek and Papoušek 1981:171); that is, to emotional-intonational aspects of the human voice (Locke 1993:369, 416; Schore 1994). By at least two months they respond to rhythmically presented facial and body movements as well (Beebe et al. 1982; Trevarthen 1984, 1995). The robustness of this evolved capacity is evident in the ability of even profoundly handicapped children or adults, totally physically dependent and incapable of learning language, to respond to vocal and facial expressions and body contact rhythms (action cycles) like those used by mothers with young infants (Burford 1988).

Using analyses of recorded vocal interactions and frame-by-frame (twenty-four/second) microanalyses of filmed face-to-face interactions with babies three and four months of age, psychologists reveal that mother and infant live in a split-second world where demonstrably significant signals (events) in kinesic, facial, and vocal modalities last approximately one-half second or less (Beebe, Stern, and Jaffe 1979:24; Beebe 1982:174; Beebe 1986:33, Feldstein et al. 1993; Jaffe et al. submitted).

By three to four months, levels of emotional engagement in both partners can be defined by particular coordinations of spatial orientation, visual attention, facial expressivity, and type of temporal reactivity (Beebe and Stern 1977; Beebe and Gerstman 1980). The mother's facial expressions are exaggerations of universal human adult expressions of affiliation and invitation to contact (e.g., look at, eyebrow flash, raise eyebrows, bob head backward, smile, nod) that have precursors in other primates (Schelde and Hertz 1994:386; Dissanayake 1996). Analyses of these interactions show that each partner is sensitive to the affective direction of the other's behavior. In their actions and reactions, each is able to enter the temporal world and feeling state of the other (Beebe et al. 1985; Beebe and Lachmann 1988a).

Together, mother and baby practice and perfect their attunement by engaging in mutually improvised (jointly constructed) dyadic interactions in which each partner tracks the durations of movements and holds in emotionally expressive behaviors of face and body, or vocal phrases and pauses (sounds and silences), of the other (Beebe, Jaffe, and Lachmann 1992:72). Some sequences are *coactive* (i.e., they occur almost simultaneously); others *overlap*; in still others there is a short lapse between the end of one partner's behavior and the beginning of the other's, so that *alternation* or turn taking occurs. Both coactive and alternating patterns occur in bouts or packages (Beebe and Gerstman 1984) that last one and a half to three seconds. The rapidity with which these sequences are performed suggests that they occur partly or fully out of conscious control.

Beebe and Gerstman (1984) chose as the unit of maternal behavior the one and a half to three-second repetitive run of kinesic patterns. This unit allows a looser temporal coupling or a higher order of synchronization between mother and infant, and does not require exact synchronization of onsets and offsets of behaviors (subsequently questioned on logical and methodological grounds by other researchers) claimed by Condon and Sander (1974). In their study, Beebe and Gerstman documented covariation between maternal "package" changes and infant facial-visual changes, and thereby retained Condon and Sander's concept of shared organizational forms. Feldstein et al. (1993) and Jaffe et al. (in preparation) studied coordinated interpersonal timing of vocalizations with comparable results.

Development of Early Interactions

From birth to age two and a half months, mothers touch and hold babies, cuddle, rock and pat them, look at their faces, and smile and speak softly to them in an undulant or melodic, high-pitched breathy voice called by researchers motherese (or parentese). Movements and utterances are simplified, repetitive, and regular. The general encounter is soothing, gently playful, and "protoconversational" (Bateson 1975), asking questions of or commenting on the infant's looks, digestion, and events in the vicinity.

For its part, a baby intently looks at its mother's face, whether or not she is regarding the child, and by six to eight weeks begins to produce a social smile, initially elicited most effectively by high-pitched vocalizations, nods with eye contact, touches, and smiles. Prolonged mutual gaze, which in humans as in other animals is usually avoided, is a notable component of early engagement in Western and many other cultures.

When the child is between two and a half and five and a half months the mother subtly adjusts her sounds and movements to the baby's changing needs and abilities, moving gradually from gentle cooing reassurance to animated play. Her utterances and facial expressions become more exaggerated, both in time and space. They are formed more slowly, held longer, given more dynamic intensity and variety, and punctuated with behavioral rests or silences. The baby responds to these positively with larger smiles, more active movements, and a range of sounds of delight, and the mother reacts in turn with greater exaggeration of mood, movement, and tempo.

Within a bout, the underlying temporal pattern, whose optimal beat is one fourth to one third of a second (Beebe 1986), may be varied with dynamic fasts and slows, louds and softs, and changes in vocal timbre. The baby may cut off arousal by looking away, thereby maintaining some control over the amount of information it takes in (Schore 1994:85). The mother may then modulate her behaviors to influence the infant's level of arousal according to her perception of its current state, altering her timing to incorporate the infant's responses into the stream of interaction (Mayer and Tronick 1985:212). Imitation and matching each other's vocalizations and facial expressions, both involuntary and deliberate, contribute to mutual enjoyment and attunement.

Benefits to Infants of Early Interactions

Early interactions provide a number of functional psychological and sociocultural benefits for infants that go far beyond the physical protection and care that are typically cited as the function of attachment behaviors in the second half-year of life.

1. They direct and modulate the infant's state or level of attention and arousal; for example, alert, soothe, praise, please (Fernald 1992:420).

2. They offer emotional regulation and support, thereby assisting the infant to achieve a coherent homeostatic equilibrium (Hofer 1990) and biobehavioral self-regulation (coping strategies) during mild stress (Beebe and Lachmann 1994; Spangler et al. 1994).

3. They provide acquaintance with the expressive (or prosodic) features of language by which even adults gain important information about others, such as sex, age, mood, and probable intentions (Fernald 1992; Locke 1996).

4. They give exposure to the prototypical and meaningful sounds and patterns of spoken language (Fernald 1992).

5. They develop cognitive abilities for recognizing agency, object, goal, and instrumentality, a narrative-like mode of thought and perception or "protonarrative envelope" (Stern 1995:92–93), and predispose the infant generally to intellectual and social competence, including intentionality, reciprocity, and expansion beyond the present situation (Hundeide 1991).

6. They reinforce neural structures predisposed for socioemotional functioning (Schore 1994; Trevarthen and Aitken 1995).

7. They introduce cultural norms of appropriate behavior.

8. They assist in establishing physiological and emotional dyadic attunement and reciprocity, enabling the pair to anticipate and adjust to each other's individual natures (Beebe, Jaffe, and Lachmann 1992), and laying the foundation for later Bowlbian attachment.

Quite clearly, early interactions with adults are adaptively beneficial for infants (Hundeide 1991). For example, vocal rhythmic matching ability at four months predicts attachment and cognition at one year (Beebe, Lachmann, and Jaffe 1997).

Musical Features of Mother-Infant Interactions

We can, I believe with good reason, claim that mother-infant interactions are composed of elements that are literally, not just metaphorically, musical.

It is, of course, immediately suggestive that the prosody of motherese, like music, is melodic, that it makes use of rhythmic regularity and variety (including pauses or rests), and dynamic variation in intensity (stress and accent), volume (crescendo and diminuendo), speed (accelerando and decelerando), and alterations of vocal timbre. Even though semantically meaningful words are used by the mother, they are presumably heard by the baby as combinations of sounds with particular features and relations, not as verbal messages, and these features and relations are musical (Dissanayake, 1999).

However, I would like to emphasize other compelling and less immediately evident similarities between music and mother-infant interaction, namely, their use of sequential structural features that rely on expectation to create emotional meaning; the importance in both of crossmodal neural processing, using kinesic and visual as well as vocal channels; the importance to both of physical movement; and the achievement in both of social regulation and emotional bonding.

Expectancy and Emotion

Because rhythms underlie all motor and vocal behavior (Lenneberg 1967, in Beebe, Lachmann, and Jaffe 1997:167), rhythmicity alone (which usually refers to rhythmic regularity) is not a sufficiently differentiated concept when considering either its role in infant affect or the relationship of mother-infant interaction to music. (The oft-heard assumption that the mother's heartbeat heard by the infant in utero is somehow relevant to music, either ontogenetically or phylogenetically, seems to me to be of limited interest.) The mother and infant do not synchronize their rhythms so much as coordinate and corespond to each other's alterations of these rhythms.[3]

Mother-infant engagement and music are temporal (or sequential) structures in which changes unfolding in the present create and are the experience (Stern 1995:34). Episodes are composed of smaller units that are often variations on a melodic, rhythmic, or narrative theme or themes. Anticipation is thereby created, manipulated, delayed, and ultimately, when all goes well, satisfied.

A mother's utterances also appear to be organized primarily into what can be transcribed as lines (or phrases), judged either by number of words, or by timed length, which is generally three to four seconds, as demonstrated by Turner (1985) and Pöppel (1985) to characterize universally lines of verse, and that Lynch et al. (1995) found to characterize phrases of prelinguistic vocalization, adult speech, oral poetry, and music (see also Krumhansl 1992; Beebe and Gerstman 1984). Indeed, segmented action units of one to four seconds generally characterize planning, preparatory behavior, perception, and speech, and segmentation may be a central feature of neuronal integration (Schleidt and Kien 1997).

It is well accepted among emotion theorists that affect in general is a response to some change—to novelty, strangeness, or uncertainty (Ellsworth 1994:151–152). It is also widely held that manipulation and delay of expectation, within acceptable parameters, is an important source of emotional meaning in music (Meyer 1956). Perhaps it is less well known that expectation and its manipulation within acceptable parameters plays a large part in the infant's reactivity to a partner. To capture and keep the three-month-old infant's attention, the mother's movements and vocalizations must take place within an optimal range of tempo, neither excessive nor insufficient, and degree of variability, not irregular or too slow (Beebe et al. 1982).

The infant's expectancies in dyadic interactions are organized according to three principles of salience (Beebe and Lachmann 1994):

1. Expectable continuing *regulation* (demonstrated across modalities of gaze, vocalization, facial expression, timing, and general affective involvement) refers to the characteristic and predictable ways in which an interaction unfolds.

2. Some interactions (*disruption and repair*) are organized by violations of expectancy, which may be mild or severe, and ensuing efforts to resolve these breaches. Experience is organized by contrast, disjunction, and difference; the gap between what is expected and what is happening may be repaired, leading to experiences of coping, effectance, and righting, or (in mismatchings) to frustration and distress.[4]

3. In *heightened affective moments*, infants may experience a powerful state transformation: one dramatic moment stands out in time.

I find these principles also relevant to an understanding of musical competence and sensitivity, which is exercised and experienced within a known and hence generally predictable tradition. Continuing regulation characterizes the sort of music that may be most common, comfortably constant, or regularly unfolding, such as (in the Western tradition) Gregorian chant, dance suites, much church and occasional music, Dixieland, and swing. Pygmy women's music, which may constitute the "world's oldest stock of sound" (Lomax, in Thompson 1995:206), superimposes rich polyphony upon a polyrhythmic continuum in an "infinite sound" of "chaotic unity" (Meurant 1995:180).

Disruption and repair characterize more exploratory, variable, and dramatic music (e.g., Indian ragas, late classical or romantic Western music, and jazz) that manipulates contrast and courts the unfamiliar, yet ultimately restores rightness. In some experiences of music, heightened affective moments and state transformations (boundary dissolutions) are paradigmatic, whether achieved through hypnotic continuation, manipulation of expectancy, or cathartic climactic release. Sometimes it happens that "one new fact" added to what has gone before will suddenly restructure aesthetic expectation and create an intensity of feeling that surpasses response to mere raw stimulus change or more conventional unfolding (Clore 1994:393).

Crossmodal and Supramodal Neural Processing

As described, mutual regulation of patterns of timing and general affective involvement can occur in various modalities (e.g., gaze, vocalization, facial expression), at numerous ages across the first year (Beebe, Jaffe, and Lachmann 1992). Evidence shows that for the infant, the modality of stimulation (acoustic, visual, tactual, kinesthetic) may be a less crucial feature of maternal behavior than the temporal patterning of that stimulation (Jaffe and Anderson 1979:18; Jaffe et al. submitted). Trevarthen (1986:154) found evidence for the existence of "a general expressive mechanism in the brain that links oral, auditory, manual, and visual sensory and motor channels in such a way that they are complementary and equivalent" for making ideas expressive in language, but he would probably agree for expressing emotions nonverbally as well.

Adult provision of a multimodal set of sensory stimuli selectively regulates an equally broad and multimodal physiological and behavioral homeostatic system in the infant (Kraemer 1992). Visual, somesthetic, auditory, and olfactory sensory input from the environment (i.e., mother) converges in the infant's orbitofrontal cortex, which is involved in the formation of cross-modal associations and projects extensive pathways to subcortical motivational-emotional integration centers (Tucker 1992; Schore 1994:35).

In addition to cross-modal association and processing of facial, vocal, and kinesic signals, Stern et al. (1985) showed that older infants can perceive such dynamic supramodal features of experience as intensity, contour, rhythm, and duration analogically (see also Eimas 1984; Marks, Hammeal, and Bornstein 1987). I suggest that younger infants may have similar supramodal abilities. Even one-month-old infants can recognize correspondences across perceptual modalities of vision and touch (Meltzoff 1985:18). The ability of neonates to imitate mouth and hand move-

ments of adults indicates an innate capacity for recognizing and acting
on certain isomorphisms (abstract, intermodal representations) between
themselves and other humans (Meltzoff 1985:3). Crown (1991) found
that mothers and six-week-old infants can engage in a cross-modal
(mother vocalize, infant gaze) interaction. At three to four months,
infants and mothers match each other's direction of affective change
cross-modally and supramodally, with mutually regulated faeial mirror-
ing, kinesic and vocal turn taking, and kinesic and vocal movements and
holds (Beebe and Lachmann 1988b:316–320).

The fundamental cross-modal and supramodal nature of infant neural
processing of the maternal package of varied sequential signals is consistent with a hypothesis that the temporal arts were ancestrally closely
associated. In addition, infant cross-modal processing and its emotional-
motivational concomitants suggest that similar nonverbal (hence inde-
scribable) associations may persist in adult experience, particularly in
responses to music and other arts.

The Importance of Movement

Of particular interest to appreciation of music's evolutionary origins
is the importance of bodily movement in mother-infant interaction,
whether in eliciting interactive behavior, sustaining intensity, coordinating synchrony, or recognizing each other's participation in the "beat" of
the encounter. I suggest that in their origins, movement and music were
inseparable, as they are today in premodern societies and in children.[5]

As theorists tended to neglect the importance of gesture to language
and thought (McNeill 1992) and the importance of prosody to spoken
language, so the integral importance of bodily movement in musical
behavior has been overlooked in the way we define music in Western
culture. Typically, hearers are also participants. What is atypical is silent
and motionless listening.

I consider it essential that we incorporate movement (or kinesics) with
song as integral to our thinking about the evolutionary origin of music.
For example, for Australian Aborigines, dance never occurs without
song and often accompanies singing (Clunies-Ross 1986:246). For the
Andamanese, singing and dancing are two aspects of one and the same
activity; the purpose of song is to accompany a dance (Radcliffe-Brown
1922/1948:334). Clapping, swaying, and head nodding are ways of participating without performing. A similar overemphasis on vocal behavior in mother-infant studies also distorted and confused theoretical
debate and conjecture, leading some researchers to question the universality of early interactive behaviors, since many cultures have little vocalizing and it is primarily Western, even middle-class, mothers who are
most highly vocal.

Fewer than a score of studies have looked specifically or closely at early interaction in other cultures, specifying sequences and relative amounts of smiling, vocalizing, head nodding, mutual gaze, and so forth (Leiderman, Tulkin, and Rosenfeld 1977; Field et al. 1981). It is not surprising that they showed many variations on a basic theme. Although the earliest behaviors of mothers to infants are most similar across cultures (Lewis and Ban 1977) and prosodic modifications of motherese are virtually universal (Fernald 1992:397), avoidance of face-to-face play, absence of direct talking to babies, and general disinclination to stimulate infants in some cultures led researchers to question the universality of attachment and, by extension, of early interactions. However, if one considers evidence of sensitivity to temporal organization, cross-modal and supramodal neural processing, and the importance of kinesics, the present cross-cultural literature holds promise for discerning common elements in early interactions.

Yet even in Western infants, matching of temporal patterns in kinesic interactions, movements that occur specifically to changes of orientation, gaze, and facial expression, is far more frequent than in vocal interactions (Beebe and Lachman 1988b:318). Despite the research emphasis on highly vocal, dramatic, American middle-class interactions of mothers and infants, kinesics is the dominant interactive modality at four months.

Although there are no studies outside America and Europe of "interactional synchrony," I suspect that in less vocal or dramatic cultures where stimulation and intensity are not developed, or in energetic but nonverbal interactions, investigation and analysis would reveal that mothers and infants nevertheless temporally and dynamically adjust their behavior to one another in ways that escape direct observation in real time, and thereby achieve individual and social adaptive benefits derived from largely Western models of early interactions (e.g., see Dixon et al. 1981; Martini and Kirkpatrick 1981).

Studies of infancy in contemporary hunter-gatherer societies such as the !Kung (Konner 1977), Arnhemland Aborigines (Hamilton 1981), Efe pygmies (Tronick et al. 1987), and Aka pygmies (Hewlett 1991) unanimously reported that caretaker-infant association is vocally, visually, and physically stimulating, giving plausibility to a hypothesis that such interaction may well be ancestral.

Social Regulation and Emotional Conjoinment

Both mother-infant engagement and music are social behaviors, a resemblance we might overlook without the ethnomusicological observation that people generally make music for and with other people (Feld 1974:207). Although our modern idea of musical experience tends to regard it as made by or happening to an individual, and contributing to individual well-being (or competitive selective advantage), musical aspects of mother-infant engagement suggest a different inference. In premodern societies all members of a social group generally participate in making music, thereby sharing the creation of its emotion and meaning. In almost every instance music is a means of group coordination and unification, recalling the emotional regulation and conjoinment in mother-infant engagement.

Affiliative Ritual and the Temporal Arts

I suggest that the interactive affiliative communicative mechanisms that evolved between human mothers and their altricial infants—based in sequentially organized, multimodally produced and processed signals that create sympathetic attunement and communion—developed sensitivities and competencies, incipient in other primates, that provided a foundation for and impetus to creating and responding to the temporal arts of music, dance, and mime. In combination, these arts compose what is termed ceremony, ritual, or ceremonial ritual. For example, in Oceania, preparations for war entail elaborate self-decoration and performance such as, music, oratory, dance, paintings, and carved artifacts as elements of larger sacred precincts, "not isolated art forms" (Thomas 1995:30). For the Australian Yolngu of Arnhemland, *mardayin* ("sacred law," the means of becoming directly involved with the ancestral past) consists of sets of songs, dances, paintings, sacred objects, and ritual incantations associated with ancestral beings (Morphy 1992:186).

Anthropologists customarily describe the material and behavioral components and belief systems coded in specific rituals, or discuss the general religious and social functions of ritual, but not the psychobehavioral means by which ritual beliefs and benefits are accomplished. Rarely is it emphasized that ritual achieves its enculturating and unifying effects by means of "producing changes in or structuring feelings" (Radcliffe-Brown 1922/1948:234).[6] I suggest that this happens, as in mother-infant interactions, through organized or patterned temporal sequences, both in unison and antiphonally, of exaggerated and regularized, graded, dynamic, multimodally presented, emotionally evocative kinesic, visual, and vocal behaviors that engender and sustain affiliative emotion and accord; that is, through the temporal arts of dance, mime, chant, and song.

Ritualization and Ritual

Tinbergen (1952) introduced the concept of "derived" activities that during evolution arise and become emancipated from earlier functional attributes, acquiring new communicative meaning as social signals. More recently, Eibl-Eibesfeldt (1989:439–440) outlined general changes that occur in this process that ethologists call ritualization. The ultimate result is to make the signal—the derived behavior in its new communicative context—prominent, unequivocal, and unmistakable to the perceiver. These changes include the following:

1. Movements (including vocalizations) are simplified, often repeated rhythmically, and their amplitude is exaggerated.

2. Variations in the intensity of the signal now convey information.

3. The releasing threshold is lowered, making elicitation more likely.

4. There is often a concomitant development of supporting organic structures (in animals, such things as manes, crests, tails; in humans, clothing, cosmetics, etc.).

5. The motivation for producing the original signal often changes as it acquires a new meaning.

Using these characteristics, I believe that it is warranted, despite cultural variations, to consider the general features of the dyadic behaviors of mothers and infants as a biologically endowed ritualized behavior, one that both partners are predisposed to engage in, that is, to elicit and respond to.

Similarly, in humans, unlike other animals, culturally created ritual ceremonies of varying degrees of complexity are also highly developed. They too manifest the regularization, exaggeration, formalization, and perceptual salience[7] of biologically evolved ritualized behaviors in animals, and are concerned with similar abiding concerns of social life—display of resources, threat, defense, and (conspicuously in humans) affirmations of affiliation.

It is well known that in many mammals, birds, and insects, elements of infant or caretaking behavior are the origin of biologically endowed ritualized expressive sounds or actions ("releasers") that promote social contact, appeasement, and affiliation in adults (Wickler 1972).[8] For example, in courtship, male sparrows shake their wings like a juvenile asking for food (Eibl-Eibesfeldt 1989:146) and male ravens make a silent coughing motion of the head that resembles parental feeding behavior (Morton and Page 1992:96). A courting male hamster utters contact calls like those of hamster babies (Eibl-Eibesfeldt 1989:146). Even in our own species' billing and cooing, fondling of the female breast, and kissing appear to derive from suckling and from parent-infant "kiss feeding" (Eibl-Eibesfeldt 1989:138).

Chimpanzees are especially likely to kiss—a signal that observably calms and reassures—during reconciliations (de Waal 1989). Mutual gaze is a feature of lovemaking in humans (Stern 1977), as it is in copulation in bonobos (de Waal 1989). In humans, love songs and courtship speech use childish words and refer to childish things to create and display intimacy, for example, the "tu" form of discourse, and popular songs that express sentiments such as "Cuddle up a little closer," or "Baby, I love you."

Smiling, which is first developed ontogenetically between infant and mother, becomes in adult social interactions a universally used means of appeasement and affiliation, along with other facial expressions and movements common in mother-infant interchange: looking at the other, eyebrow raising and flashing, and bobbing the head up and down (see also page 391 and the discussion in Schelde and Hertz 1994). Many adult mammals assume infantile postures and make infantile sounds to deflect aggression.

I suggest that the biologically endowed sensitivities and competencies of mother-infant interaction were found by evolving human groups to be emotionally affecting and functionally effective when used and when further shaped and elaborated in culturally created ceremonial rituals where they served a similar purpose—to attune or synchronize, emotionally conjoin, and enculturate the participants. These unifying and pleasurable features (maintained in children's play; see below) made up a sort of behavioral reservoir from which human cultures could appropriate appealing and compelling components for communal ceremonial rituals that similarly promoted affiliation and congruence in adult social life.[9] These features were then developed, culturally codified, and, in some societies, even emancipated, as music, as satisfactions in their own right, apart from ceremonial contexts.

Ceremonies, Temporal Arts, and Early Interactions

There are, of course, countless examples in premodern and modern societies of the use in ritual ceremonies of temporal sequences, usually integrating several simultaneous sensory modalities (i.e., temporal arts), whose structural and expressive elements resemble those of mother-infant engagement and that also acculturate and unify. As with interactions between mothers and infants, ceremonial rituals may use alternation and imitation as a way to create or express understanding and unity, or individuals may perform the same actions concurrently and also thereby create and confirm unity (e.g., Basso 1985).

Even societies that are poor in material culture or the visual arts engage in the temporal arts. For example, the Tikopia in the South Seas have relatively undeveloped plastic arts, but their music, poetry, and dance display a range of variation and elaborate articulation with many nuances of form and expression (Firth 1973). The people of Alor pay little attention to material objects but have dances with versification; older men play gongs of different sizes in an "orchestra" where new rhythms or set patterns may be experimented with (Dubois 1944). Hunter-gatherer groups such as Australian Aborigines, Kalahari Bushmen, and Ba-Benjellé pygmies have highly developed musical traditions; song, dance, and poetry are integral parts of their lives (Anderson 1990; Sarno 1993). The Aborigines, of course, have a rich tradition of visually elaborating artifacts as well.

As well as using musical elements, some human rituals of appeasement or social solidarity come directly from infantlike behavior. The Bedouin *ghinnawa* ("little song") is an improvised sung poem that employs metaphorical terms evocative of childhood to reveal, in a socially acceptable way, sentiments such as personal emotional weakness and desire for sympathy that are otherwise prohibited (Abu-Lughod 1986). The song voice heard in the *gisalo* ceremony of the Kaluli uses sounds associated with a child whining for food to make listeners feel sorrow and pity, and thereby reinforces cultural themes of reciprocity and obligation (Feld 1982).

The many structural and functional resemblances to be seen in mother-infant interaction, ceremonial ritual, and the arts of time are, I believe, neither accidental nor spurious. They suggest not only an evolutionary relationship, as I have outlined, but argue for the existence of an underlying intermodal neural propensity in the human species to respond, cognitively and emotionally, to certain kinds of dynamic temporal patterns produced by other humans in contexts of affiliation (see Addendum, below). An evolved propensity for relationship[10] is thus at least as robust as the self-interest that has to date been the primary focus of sociobiological concern. Because of human infant altriciality, the primate propensity for relationships or emotional communion—not just sociability—became so crucial that special affiliative mechanisms evolved to enhance and ensure it. These mechanisms in turn could be further developed (as temporal arts) to serve affiliative bonding among adults in a species where close cooperation also became unprecedentedly critical for individual survival.

Vocal Play and Imitation

Convincing evidence in studies of infant and child development indicates that the motivation to appropriate and elaborate prosodic (as well as lexical) features of language exists universally in humans, in children's vocal play. The earliest vocal play, after eight weeks when infants have some control of respiration and the vocal tract, consists of prolonging sounds (Papoušek, Papoušek, and Harris 1987); between four and six months they produce more substantial vowellike sounds, bilabial trills, squealing, and growling (Locke 1993:176). True babbling begins between six and ten months of age (Oller and Eilers 1988) and occurs more when alone than with others.

Children spontaneously initiate speech activities—sound play, word play, distorted speech, and monologues—that are unlike any shown to them by their elders. In the southern Highlands of Papua New Guinea, Kaluli parents consider such antics to interfere with proper development of language and specifically terminate them whenever they hear them. Nevertheless, Kaluli children, like all children, continue to manipulate pitch, prosody, and timing in their sound play, and invite turn taking (Schieffelin 1990:99). The same applies to patterning and elaborating movements in games and dance, which children everywhere invent and enjoy.

Such sound play is surely musical. Indeed, one could maintain that the differences between song and speech prosody are only in degree of elaboration, including sustaining, repeating, and patterning tones such as exaggeration and regularization reminiscent of the ritualization process. Kartomi (1991) studied the spontaneous improvised musical phrases uttered by children while they concentrated on their play, and claimed that "play song" is distinct from the lullabies and nursery rhymes or songs created by adults for children. Rather, it is created by children for use in their own adultless play world (p. 53). Such "musical doodling" is ephemeral. The few improvised songs that are remembered and adapted into the corpus of established children's songs tend to be those whose texts express a memorable experience of pleasure, pain, fear, solidarity, or derision, and these songs are normally sung when playing games, eating together, and teasing each other, and on occasions demanding solidarity with each other (p. 62). Even these more stable songs include an element of improvisation. Whereas rhythm and meter are usually primary and fixed, melody and form are secondary and variable. Such a propensity in children suggests that ancestral adults could well have followed a similar course in ritualizing natural vocalizations at times of strong emotions and when solidarity was displayed or required.

As children naturally draw, sing, dance, and play with words, they spontaneously like to make believe, dress up in costumes, and adorn their possessions and surroundings. Although these characteristic and universal activities can be called play, it seems clear that they predispose humans to ceremonial participation. They may easily be channeled into appropriate ritual and artistic elaborations, just as children's play with objects and wish to imitate adults' practical activities develop into ordinary subsistence activity.

The readiness of children to imitate adults and each other is of course well known as an attribute of sociability and, ultimately, educability (Bruner 1972). Imitation in adults also has a bonding effect (Bavelas et al. 1987); inviting a partner to imitative behavior by starting some action oneself or using imitation to express accord and thus readiness for group play is a principle of many bonding rituals. Doing things together confirms a sense of unity (Eibl-Eibesfeldt 1989:510).

Addendum: A "Grammar" of the Emotions?   [SUMMARY]

OWR SeNTeNce

The arts of humans, like language and thought, are based on presymbolic and prelinguistic dynamic states and analogically perceived and processed communicative signals that are suffused with emotional salience derived from their primitive origin in infancy when they were, through sympathetic communion with others, one's principal means of connection with the world. In speech and symbolic thinking, these states and signals become overlaid with more or less precisely fixed terms or meanings assigned by cultures and used by them to encapsulate their communal truths.

Mother-infant dialogue seems to be the prototype for a kind of fundamental emotional narrative that adult music, dance movement, and poetic language can grow out of, build upon, exemplify, and sustain. In early interactions, sensitivities to rhythmic and dynamic change are manipulated to coordinate the pair emotionally and express their accord, thereby reinforcing it. By means of a kind of emotional (grammar) (to which adults remain sensitive) such as slight expansions and contractions of intensity in space and time (e.g., of speed, force, and duration of vocal and kinesic movement), mother and infant convey to each other and share the anticipation and fulfillment of beginnings and endings, implications and realizations, antecedents and consequents, qualifications and subordinations; of entailment, contrast, redirection, opposition, turntaking, pacing, and release. These grammatical abstractions can also describe affective (not only linguistic) responses to adults' verbal and nonverbal interactions with other people and to encounters with the various arts. Could we begin to describe their behavioral and neural manifestations and correlates?

BAD MeTAPh

Notes

1. Daly and Wilson (1995:1273) suggested that selection favors discriminative mechanisms of parental psychology that allocate "parental investment" in infants. They noted (p. 1282) that the newborn's precocious social response may be an adaptation for "advertising quality and eliciting maternal commitment." Their "three-stage theory of maternal bonding" does not, however, include or refer to cocreated mechanisms of communicative interaction and

attunement described in this chapter. Not only in the remote past, but even today in societies that experience scarcity, mothers may withdraw care and attention from (show benign neglect to) some infants to protect the survival of other family members who are vulnerable (Scheper-Hughes 1987:14). Infants differentially display traits (rhythmicity, adaptability, approach-withdrawal, threshold, intensity, mood, distractibility, persistence) that are associated with adult attribution of "easy" or "difficult" (Carey 1973). Such variability, assessed and reacted to by mothers in early interactions, could be acted on selectively.

2. According to Schore (1994) and Trevarthen and Aitken (1995:598), among others, infants are guided from birth by subcortical and limbic motive systems to seek the mutual coordination of dynamic mental states with caregivers.

3. The human ability to keep together in time, described by McNeill (1995) in his study of dance, drill, and "muscular bonding" in human history, is only one coordinative ability among several in the mother-infant repertoire (which McNeill does not include in his interesting and original study).

4. Cessation or loss of expected consequences results in discomfiture (Beebe and Lachmann 1988a). Even at two months of age, after two minutes of normal play infants will respond to their mother's unmoving, silent face with repeated efforts to reengage and eventual signs of distress (Tronick et al. 1978). At the same age they respond similarly to a delayed videotaped presentation of their mother's face as she interacted with them thirty seconds earlier (Murray and Trevarthen 1985), indicating that they expect a contingently responsive partner.

5. Until age four or five years children cannot distinguish the rhythm of a piece from accompanying movements, and find it difficult to sing without moving their hands and feet (Suliteanu 1979). Infants nine to thirteen months of age moved differently to a lively and to a slow recorded segment of music, indicating that they can respond appropriately to temporal patterning of complex auditory sequences (Trehub 1993).

6. Radcliffe-Brown (1922/1948:234) observed also that ceremonies are "intended to maintain and transmit from one generation to another the emotional dispositions [N.B. *not* "information" or "traditions"] on which the society depends for its existence." Darwin (1885:571) remarked that although music arouses various emotions, these do not include "terrible" ones like horror, fear, or rage. As it happens, the emotions he mentions are all affiliative (e.g., tenderness, love), even "triumph and ardor for war," which also reinforce community and are communally aroused and expressed.

7. In traditional societies, visual forms are rarely created without the intention to use them in structured ceremonies, hence one might even propose that visual arts were initially developed to accent and make more salient the temporal arts in a multimodal event.

8. Darwin (1885, chapter IV) suggested that human social affections are probably an extension of parental or filial sentiments. Eibl-Eibesfeldt (1989:144) pointed out that wherever brood care exists, there is also affective behavior between adults; where it does not, even where the creature is gregarious (e.g., iguanas), adults have no affiliative or contact behavior, and communication is restricted to display. The role of oxytocin, a neuropeptide that induces labor and milk secretion, in mammalian prosocial behaviors, including adult contact with young pups' response to social separation, maternal caretaking, grooming, sexual behavior in males and females, and adult pair bonding, suggests a neurochemical basis for adult affiliative behaviors (Insel 1992; Freeman, this volume) deriving phylogenetically from maternal-infant behavior.

9. Aiello and Dunbar (1993) suggested that human language developed as a bonding mechanism, driven by increasing group size and the need to supplement existing mechanisms (e.g., grooming) of social cohesion. A concomitant or prior development of the temporal arts (as rituals) would seem to be additionally plausible in archaic *sapiens* or late *erectus*, providing neural and anatomical bases for (and development alongside) spoken language. Similar suggestions were made by others (e.g., Donald 1991), but, like Aiello and Dunbar, without reference to the role of mother-infant interactions. Jaffe and Anderson (1979) suggested that human communication, including chant, song, poetry, pantomime, kinesic cueing, sign language, and speaking, is based on an evolved capacity for the acquisition, use, and elaboration of rhythmically structured gestural systems, including the articulatory apparatus.

10. What are simulated and exchanged in early interactions are emotional states: interest, pleasure, desire to establish relationship with, intention to please, and intention to communicate with the other (Trevarthen 1984, 1990).

References

Abu-Lughod, L. (1986). *Veiled Sentiments: Honor and Poetry in a Bedouin Society*. Berkeley: University of California Press.

Aiello, L. C. and Dunbar, R. I. M. (1993). Neocortex size, group size, and the evolution of language. *Current Anthropology* 34:184–193.

Anderson, R. (1990). *Calliope's Sisters: A Comparative Study of Philosophies of Art*. Englewood Cliffs, NJ: Prentice-Hall.

Basso, E. (1985). *A Musical View of the Universe: Kalapalo Rhythmic and Ritual Performance*. Philadelphia: University of Pennsylvania Press.

Bateson, M. C. (1975). Mother-infant exchanges: The epigenesis of conversational interaction. In D. Aaronson and R. Rieber (Eds.) *Developmental Psycholinguistics and Communication Disorders* (pp. 101–113). New York: New York Academy of Sciences.

Bavelas, J. B., Black, A., Lemery, C. R., and Mullett, J. (1987). Motor mimicry as primitive empathy. In N. Eisenberg and J. Strayer (Eds.) *Empathy and Its Development* (pp. 317–338). Cambridge, UK: Cambridge University Press.

Beebe, B. (1982). Micro-timing in mother-infant communication. In M. R. Key (Ed.) *Nonverbal Communication Today* (pp. 169–195). The Hague: Mouton.

Beebe, B. (1986). Mother-infant mutual influence and precursors of self- and object-representations. In J. Masling (Ed.) *Empirical Studies of Psychoanalytic Theories*, Vol. 2 (pp. 27–48). Hillsdale, NJ: Erlbaum.

Beebe, B. and Gerstman, L. (1980). The "packaging" of maternal stimulation in relation to infant facial-visual engagement: A case study at four months. *Merrill-Palmer Quarterly* 26:321–339.

Beebe, B. and Gerstman, L. (1984). A method of defining "packages" of maternal stimulation and their functional significance for the infant with mother and stranger. *International Journal of Behavioral Development* 7:423–440.

Beebe, B., Gerstman, L., Carson, B., Dolins, M., Zigman, A., Rosensweig, H., Faughey, K., and Korman, M. (1982). Rhythmic communication in the mother-infant dyad. In M. Davis (Ed.) *Interaction Rhythms* (pp. 79–100). New York: Human Sciences Press.

Beebe, B., Jaffe, J., Feldstein, S., Mays, K., and Alson, D. (1985). Interpersonal timing: The application of an adult dialogue model to mother-infant vocal and kinesic interactions. In T. Field and N. Fox (Eds.) *Social Perception in Infants* (pp. 217–247). Norwood, NJ: Ablex.

Beebe, B., Jaffe, J., and Lachmann, F. (1992). A dyadic systems view of communication. In N. Skolnick and S. Warshaw (Eds.) *Relational Perspectives in Psychoanalysis* (pp. 61–81). Hillsdale, NJ: Analytic Press.

Beebe, B. and Lachmann, F. (1988a). Mother-infant mutual influence and precursors of psychic structure. In A. Goldberg (Ed.) *Frontiers in Self Psychology: Progress in Self Psychology*, Vol. 3 (pp. 3–26). Hillsdale, NJ: Analytic Press.

Beebe, B. and Lachmann, F. (1988b). The contribution of mother-infant mutual influence to the origins of self- and object-representations. *Psychoanalytic Psychology* 5:305–337.

Beebe, B. and Lachmann, F. (1994). Representation and internalization in infancy: Three principles of salience. *Psychoanalytic Psychology* 11:127–165.

Beebe, B., Lachmann, F., and Jaffe, J. (1997). Mother-infant interaction structures and presymbolic self and object representations. *Psychoanalytic Dialogues* 7:133–182.

Beebe, B. and Stern, D. (1977). Engagement-disengagement and early object experiences. In N. Freedman and S. Grand (Eds.) *Communicative Structures and Psychic Structures* (pp. 35–55). New York: Plenum Press.

Beebe, B, Stern, D., and Jaffe, J. (1979). The kinesic rhythm of mother-infant interactions. In A. W. Siegman and S. Feldstein (Eds.) *Of Speech and Time: Temporal Speech Patterns in Interpersonal Contexts* (pp. 23–34). Hillsdale, NJ: Erlbaum.

Bruner, J. (1972). Nature and uses of immaturity. *American Psychologist* 27:687–708.

Burford, B. (1988). Action cycles: Rhythmic actions for engagement with children and young adults with profound mental handicap. *European Journal of Special Needs Education* 3:189–208.

Carey, W. B. (1973). Measurement of infant temperament in pediatric practice. In J. C. Westman (Ed.) *Individual Differences in Children* (pp. 293–306). New York: Wiley.

Clore, G. L. (1994). Why emotions vary in intensity. In P. Ekman and R. J. Davidson (Eds.) *The Nature of Emotion: Fundamental Questions* (pp. 386–393). New York: Oxford University Press.

Clunies-Ross, M. (1986). Australian aborigine oral traditions. *Oral Tradition* 1:231–271.

Condon, W. S. and Sander, L. (1974). Neonate movement is synchronized with adult speech: Interactional participation and language acquisition. *Science* 183:99–101.

Crown, C. L. (1991). Coordinated interpersonal timing of vision and voice as a function of interpersonal attraction. *Journal of Language and Social Psychology* 10:29–46.

Daly, M. and Wilson, M. (1995). Discriminative parental solicitude and the relevance of evolutionary models to the analysis of motivational systems. In M. S. Gazzaniga (Ed.) *The Cognitive Neurosciences* (pp. 1269–1286). Cambridge: MIT Press.

Darwin, C. (1885). *The Descent of Man, and Selection in Relation to Sex*, 2nd ed. London: Murray.

Dissanayake, E. (1996). Protocultural aptitudes in early mother-infant interaction. Presented at the annual conference of the Human Behavior and Evolution Society, Evanston, IL, June 26–30.

Dissanayake, E. (1999). Antecedents of musical meaning in the mother-infant dyad. In L. B. Cooke and F. Turner (Eds.) *Biopoetics: Evolutionary Explorations in the Arts* (pp. 367–397). New York: Paragon House.

Dixon, S., Tronick, E., Keefer, C., and Brazelton, T. B. (1981). Mother-infant interaction among the Gusii of Kenya. In T. M. Field, A. M. Sostek, P. Vietze, and P. H. Leiderman (Eds.) *Culture and Early Interactions* (pp. 149–168). Hillsdale, NJ: Erlbaum.

Donald, M. (1991). *Origins of the Modern Mind: Three Stages in the Evolution of Culture and Cognition*. Cambridge: Harvard University Press.

Dubois, C. (1944). *The People of Alor*. Minneapolis: University of Minnesota Press.

Eibl-Eibesfeldt, I. (1989). *Human Ethology*. New York: Aldine de Gruyter.

Eimas, P. D. (1984). Infant competence and the acquisition of language. In D. Caplan, A. Roch Lecours, and A. Smith (Eds.) *Biological Perspectives on Language* (pp. 109–129). Cambridge: MIT Press.

Ellsworth, P. (1994). Some reasons to expect universal antecedents of emotion. In P. Ekman and R. J. Davidson (Eds.) *The Nature of Emotion: Fundamental Questions* (pp. 150–154). New York: Oxford University Press.

Feld, S. (1974). Linguistic models in ethnomusicology. *Ethnomusicology* 18:197–218.

Feld, S. (1982). *Sound and Sentiment: Birds, Weeping, Poetics and Song in Kaluli Expression*. Philadelphia: University of Pennsylvania Press.

Feldstein, S., Jaffe, J., Beebe, B., Crown, C. L., Jasnow, M., Fox, H., and Gordon, S. (1993). Coordinated interpersonal timing in adult-infant vocal interactions: A cross-site replication. *Infant Behavior and Development* 16:455–470.

Fernald, A. (1992). Human maternal vocalizations to infants as biologically relevant signals: An evolutionary perspective. In J. H. Barkow, L. Cosmides, and J. Tooby (Eds.) *The Adapted Mind: Evolutionary Psychology and the Generation of Culture* (pp. 391–428). New York: Oxford University Press.

Field, T. M., Sostek, A. M., Vietze, P., and Leiderman, P. H. (Eds.) (1981). *Culture and Early Interactions*. Hillsdale, NJ: Erlbaum.

Firth, R. (1973). Tikopia art and society. In A. Forge (Ed.) *Primitive Art and Society* (pp. 25–48). London: Oxford University Press.

Hamilton, A. (1981). *Nature and Nurture: Aboriginal Child-Rearing in North-Central Arnhem Land*. Canberra: Australian Institute of Aboriginal Studies.

Hewlett, B. S. (1991). *Intimate Fathers: The Nature and Context of Aka Pygmy Paternal Infant Care*. Ann Arbor: University of Michigan Press.

Hofer, M. A. (1990). Early symbiotic processes: Hard evidence from a soft place. In R. A. Glick and S. Bones (Eds.) *Pleasure Beyond the Pleasure Principle* (pp. 55–78). New Haven, CT: Yale University Press.

Hundeide, K. (1991). *Helping Disadvantaged Children: Psycho-Social Intervention and Aid to Disadvantaged Children in Third World Countries*. London: Kingsley.

Insel, T. R. (1992). Oxytocin and the neurobiology of attachment. *Behavioral and Brain Sciences* 15:515–516.

Jaffe, J. and Anderson, S. (1979). Communication rhythms and the evolution of language. In A. W. Siegman and S. Feldstein (Eds.) *Of Speech and Time* (pp. 17–22). Hillsdale, NJ: Erlbaum.

Jaffe, J., Beebe, B., Feldstein, S., Crown, C., and Jasnow, M. (submitted). Rhythms of dialogue in infancy: Coordinated timing and social development. New York: New York State Psychiatric Institute.

Jaffe, J., Feldstein, S., Beebe, B., Crown, C. L., Jasnow, M. D., Fox, H., Anderson, S., and Gordon, S. (1991). Interpersonal timing and infant social development. New York: New York State Psychiatric Institute, Department of Communication Sciences.

Kartomi, M. J. (1991). Musical improvisations of children at play. *The World of Music* 33:53–65.

Konner, M. (1977). Infancy among the Kalahari Desert San. In P. H. Leiderman, S. R. Tulkin, and A. Rosenfeld (Eds.) *Culture and Infancy* (pp. 287–328). New York: Academic Press.

Kraemer, G. W. (1992). A psychobiological theory of attachment. *Behavioral and Brain Sciences* 15:493–541.

Krumhansl, C. L. (1992). Grouping processes in infants' music perception. In J. Sundberg, L. Nord, and R. Carl (Eds.) *Gluing Tones: Grouping in Music Composition, Performance, and Listening* (pp. 53–76). Stockholm: Royal Swedish Academy of Music.

Leakey, R. (1994). *The Origin of Humankind*. New York: Basic Books.

Leiderman, P. H., Tulkin, S. R., and Rosenfeld, A. (Eds.) (1977). *Culture and Infancy*. New York: Academic Press.

Lewis, M. and Ban, P. (1977). Variance and invariance in the mother-infant interaction: A cross-cultural study. In P. H. Leiderman, S. R. Tulkin, and A. Rosenfeld (Eds.) *Culture and Infancy* (pp. 329–355). New York: Academic Press.

Locke, J. L. (1993). *The Child's Path to Spoken Language*. Cambridge: Harvard University Press.

Locke, J. L. (1996). Why do infants begin to talk? Language as an unintended consequence. *Journal of Child Language* 23:251–268.

Lynch, M. P., Kimbrough-Oller, D., Steffens, M. L., and Buder, E. H. (1995). Phrasing in prelinguistic vocalizations. *Developmental Psychobiology* 28:3–25.

Marks, L. E., Hammeal, R. J., and Bornstein, M. (1987). Perceiving similarity and comprehending metaphor. *Monographs of the Society for Research in Child Development* 52:1–92.

Martini, M. and Kirkpatrick, J. (1981). Early interactions in the Marquesa Islands. In T. M. Field, A. M. Sostek, P. Vietze, and P. H. Leiderman (Eds.) *Culture and Early Interactions* (pp. 189–213). Hillsdale, NJ: Erlbaum.

Mayer, N. M. and Tronick, E. Z. (1985). Mother's turn-giving signals and infant turn-taking in mother-infant interaction. In T. M. Field (Ed.) *Social Perception in Infants* (pp. 199–21). Norwood, NJ: Ablex.

McNeill, D. (1992). *Hand and Mind: What Gestures Reveal About the Brain*. Chicago: University of Chicago Press.

McNeill, W. H. (1995). *Keeping Together in Time: Dance and Drill in Human History*. Cambridge: Harvard University Press.

Meltzoff, A. N. (1985). The roots of social and cognitive development: Models of man's original nature. In T. M. Field (Ed.) *Social Perception in Infants* (pp. 1–30). Norwood, NJ: Ablex.

Meurant, G., (Ed.) (1995). *Mbuti Design: Paintings by Pygmy Women of the Ituri Forest* (C. Rees, Trans.). London: Thames and Hudson.

Meyer, L. B. (1956). *Emotion and Meaning in Music*. Chicago: Phoenix.

Morgan, E. (1995). *The Descent of the Child: Human Evolution from a New Perspective*. New York: Oxford University Press.

Morphy, H. (1992). From dull to brilliant: The aesthetics of spiritual power among the Yolngu. In J. Coote and A. Shelton (Eds.) *Anthropology, Art, and Aesthetics* (pp. 181–208). Oxford: Clarendon.

Morton, E. S. and Page, J. (1992). *Animal Talk: Science and the Voices of Nature*. New York: Random House.

Murray, L. and Trevarthen, C. (1985). Emotional regulation of interactions between two-month-olds and their mothers. In T. M. Field and N. A. Fox (Eds.) *Social Perception in Infants* (pp. 177–198). Norwood, NJ: Ablex.

Oller, D. K. and Eilers, R. E. (1988). The role of audition in infant babbling. *Child Development* 59:441–449.

Papoušek, H. and Papoušek, M. (1981). Musical elements in the infant's vocalization: Their significance for communication, cognition, and creativity. In L. P. Lipsitt and C. K. Rovee-Collier (Eds.) *Advances in Infancy Research*, Vol. I (pp. 163–224). Norwood, NJ: Ablex.

Papoušek, M., Papoušek, H., and Harris, B. J. (1987). The emergence of play in parent-infant interactions. In D. Gorlitz and J. F. Wohlwill (Eds.) *Curiosity, Imagination, and Play: On the Development of Spontaneous Cognitive and Motivational Processes* (pp. 214–246). Hillsdale, NJ: Erlbaum.

Pöppel, E. (1985). *Mindworks: Time and Conscious Experience*. Boston: Harcourt Brace Jovanovich.

Radcliffe-Brown, A. R. (1922/1948). *The Andaman Islanders*. Glencoe, IL: Free Press.

Sarno, L. (1993). *Song from the Forest: My Life Among the Ba-Benjellé Pygmies*. Boston: Houghton Mifflin.

Schelde, T. and Hertz, M. (1994). Ethology and psychotherapy. *Ethology and Sociobiology* 15:383–392.

Scheper-Hughes, N. (1987). The cultural politics of child survival. In N. Scheper-Hughes (Ed.) *Child Survival: Anthropological Perspectives on the Treatment and Maltreatment of Children* (pp. 1–29). Boston: Reidel.

Schieffelin, B. (1990). *The Give and Take of Everyday Life*. New York: Cambridge University Press.

Schleidt, M. and Kien, J. (1997). Segmentation in behavior and what it can tell us about brain function. *Human Nature* 8:77–111.

Schore, A. N. (1994). *Affect Regulation and the Origin of the Self: The Neurobiology of Emotional Development*. Hillsdale, NJ: Erlbaum.

Spangler, G., Schieche, M., Ilg, U., Maier, U., and Ackermann, C. (1994). Maternal sensitivity as an external organizer for biobehavioral regulation in infancy. *Developmental Psychobiology* 27:425–437.

Stern, D. (1971). A microanalysis of mother-infant interaction. *Journal of the American Academy of Child Psychiatry* 10:501–517.

Stern, D. (1977). *The First Relationship*. Cambridge: Harvard University Press.

Stern, D. (1983). The early development of schemas of self, of other, and of "self with other." In J. Lichtenberg and S. Kaplan (Eds.) *Reflections on Self Psychology* (pp. 49–84). Hillsdale, NJ: The Analytic Press.

Stern, D. (1995). *The Motherhood Constellation: A Unified View of Parent-Infant Psychotherapy*. New York: Basic Books.

Stern, D., Hofer, L., Haft, W., and Dore, J. (1985). Affect attunement: The sharing of feeling states between mother and infant by means of intermodal fluency. In T. M. Field (Ed.) *Social Perception in Infants* (pp. 249–268). Norwood, NJ: Ablex.

Suliteanu, G. (1979). The role of songs for children in the formation of musical perception. In J. Blacking and J. W. Kealiinohomoku (Eds.) *The Performing Arts: Music and Dance* (pp. 205–219). The Hague: Mouton.

Thomas, N. (1995). *Oceanic Art*. London: Thames and Hudson.

Thompson, R. F. (1995). Impulse and repose: The art of Ituri women. In G. Meurant (Ed.) *Mbuti Design: Paintings by Pygmy Women of the Ituri Forest* (pp. 185–214). London: Thames and Hudson.

Tinbergen, N. (1952). Derived activities: Their causation, biological significance, origin, and emancipation during evolution. *Quarterly Review of Biology* 27:1–32.

Trehub, S. E. (1993). Temporal auditory processing in infancy. In P. Tallal, A. M. Galaburda, R. R. Llinás, and C. von Euler (Eds.) *Temporal Information Processing in the Nervous System*. Annals of the New York Academy of Sciences, Vol. 682 (pp. 137–149). New York: New York Academy of Sciences.

Trevarthen, C. (1974). Conversations with a two-month-old. *New Scientist* 2 May, 230–235.

Trevarthen, C. (1977). Descriptive analyses of infant communication behavior. In H. R. Schaffer (Ed.) *Studies in Mother-Infant Interaction: The Loch Lomond Symposium* (pp. 227–270). London: Academic Press.

Trevarthen, C. (1979a). Communication and cooperation in early infancy: A description of primary intersubjectivity. In M. Bullowa (Ed.) *Before Speech: The Beginning of Human Communication* (pp. 321–347). London: Cambridge University Press.

Trevarthen, C. (1979b). Instincts for human understanding and for cultural cooperation: Their development in infancy. In M. von Cranach, K. Foppa, W. Lepenies, and D. Ploog (Eds.) *Human Ethology: Claims and Limits of a New Discipline* (pp. 530–571). Cambridge, UK: Cambridge University Press.

Trevarthen, C. (1984). Emotions in infancy: Regulators of contact and relationships with persons. In K. Scherer and P. Ekman (Eds.) *Approaches to Emotion* (pp. 129–157). Hillsdale, NJ: Erlbaum.

Trevarthen, C. (1986). Form, significance and psychological potential of hand gestures of infants. In J.-L. Nespoulous, P. Perron, and A. Roch Lecours (Eds.) *The Biological Foundations of Gestures: Motor and Semiotic Aspects* (pp. 149–20). Hillsdale, NJ: Erlbaum.

Trevarthen, C. (1990). Growth and education in the hemispheres. In C. Trevarthen (Ed.) *Brain Circuits and Functions of the Mind* (pp. 334–363). Cambridge, UK: Cambridge University Press.

Trevarthen, C. (1993). The self born in intersubjectivity: The psychology of an infant communicating. In U. Neisser (Ed.) *The Perceived Self: Ecological and Interpersonal Sources of Self-Knowledge* (pp. 121–173). New York: Cambridge University Press.

Trevarthen, C. (1995). Contracts of mutual understanding: Negotiating meanings and moral sentiments with infants. *Journal of Contemporary Legal Issues* 6:373–407.

Trevarthen, C. and Aitken, K. J. (1995). Brain development, infant communication and empathy disorders: Intrinsic factors in child mental health. *Development and Psychopathology* 6:597–633.

Tronick, E. Z. (1989). Infant-mother face-to-face interaction: Age and gender differences in coordination and miscoordination. *Child Development* 59:85–92.

Tronick, E. Z., Als, H., Adamson, L., Wise, S., and Brazelton, T. B. (1978). The infant's response to entrapment between contradictory messages in face-to-face interaction. *American Academy of Child Psychiatry* 17:1–13.

Tronick, E. Z., Morelli, G. A., and Winn, S. (1987). Multiple caretaking of Efe (pygmy) infants. *American Anthropologist* 89:96–106.

Tucker, D. M. (1992). Developing emotions and cortical networks. In M. R. Gunnar and C. A. Nelson (Eds.) *Minnesota Symposium on Child Psychology*, Vol. 24, *Development, Behavior, Neuroscience* (pp. 75–128). Hillsdale, NJ: Erlbaum.

Turner, F. (1985). The neural lyre: Poetic meter, the brain, and time. In F. Turner (Ed.) *Natural Classicism* (pp. 61–108). Charlottesville: University Press of Virginia.

de Waal, F. (1989). *Peacemaking Among Primates*. Cambridge: Harvard University Press.

Wickler, W. (1972). *The Sexual Code: The Social Behavior of Animals and Man*. Garden City, NY: Doubleday.

22

A Neurobiological Role of Music in Social Bonding

Walter Freeman

Abstract

Music is regarded in biological terms as originating in the brain, so that most explanations concentrate on the ways in which brains process information. Studies of the nonlinear dynamics of the primary sensory cortices show that patterns that are constructed by chaotic nonlinear dynamics in cortical neuropil replace stimulus-driven activity. This finding supports the concept that knowledge in brains is entirely constructed within them without direct transfer of information from outside. As knowledge increases by learning, brains of individuals grow progressively apart because of the uniqueness of the knowledge that is constructed within each one. The resulting condition of isolation is known among philosophers as epistemological solipsism. This view is reinforced by the tenets of aesthetics, which emphasize the deeply personal experiences of individuals, not as active listeners but as passive recipients of beauty in music and other arts. Neither conventional neuroscience nor aesthetics can explain the deep emotional power of music to move humans to action. In an alternative view, human brains are seen to have evolved primarily in response to environmental pressures to bridge the solipsistic gulf between individuals and form integrated societies. An evolutionary origin is found in neurohumoral mechanisms of parental bonding to altricial infants. A case is made that music together with dance co-evolved biologically and culturally to serve as a technology of social bonding. Findings of anthropologists and psychiatrists show how rhythmic behavioral activities that are induced by drum beats and music can lead to altered states of consciousness, through which mutual trust among members of societies is engendered.

In seeing or writing the phrase "the biology of music" one is struck by the seeming intractability of the problem of understanding emotions in the contrasting contexts of aesthetics and neuroscience. On one hand, the scientific study of brains must emphasize features that are regular, reproducible, and common to all participants in making and listening to music. The description is commonly made in terms of information processing by sensory pathways up to the auditory cortex, with only cursory reference to the meaning and emotion attached to perceptions of music. The emergence of skills in performing and listening to music are described and explained in terms of Darwinian determinism: how and in response to what environmental circumstances have these capabilities evolved?

On the other hand, appreciation of music is a deeply personal activity accompanied by individual feelings that are notoriously difficult to express in words or nonverbal ways. The creativity that is required for active listening as well as singing or playing an instrument for oneself and others seems antithetical to scientific determinism. The difficulty of devising a biological connection is compounded by the fact that no other species of animals displays either the capacity for shared rhythms or the semantics of music as it appears in humans. Birds, whales, and cicadas "sing" and "signal," but they do not manifest the richness of compassion and understanding that we experience in speaking and singing with one another. Humans in all societies have these capabilities in varying individual degrees, but we cannot make an evolutionary tree to describe their origin from neurohumoral mechanisms of mammalian behavioral controls.

We must go past the cognitive and aesthetic aspects of music to seek understanding of the biology of music. Neural mechanisms of sensory and motor processing are necessary for complex patterns to be produced and apprehended. The contribution of aesthetics is required to enlarge the scope of inquiry to include emotional textures. But the role of music as an instrument of communication beyond words strikes to the heart of the ways in which we humans come to trust one another. Trust is the basis of all human social endeavors, and a case is made that it is created through the practice of music. How and why, in biological terms, can music and dance bring humans together with a depth of bonding that cannot be achieved with words alone?

The Biological Dynamics of Perception

The mechanisms of the ear that transform sounds to neural messages and the pathways that carry messages to the auditory cortex are well understood (Clynes 1982; Pribram 1982; Wallin 1991). The inner ear has been likened to a harp, the strings of which resonate to a range of frequencies and excite sensory neurons selectively in accordance with their tuning. The process expresses complex sounds as spatiotemporal patterns of neural activity that are shaped by filters when they pass through relays to the primary auditory cortex. What happens thereafter is a matter of conjecture, as the information is processed through neighboring cortical areas concerned with speech and music. This is revealed by older observations on deficits produced by brain trauma and by newer techniques of brain imaging to study patterns of augmented cortical blood flow during speaking, listening, and singing. It is thought that exchanges between association cortices in the newer brain and older parts of the forebrain, which comprise the deep-lying limbic lobe, generate memories evoked by listening to music and arouse emotional states that have become associated with now familiar songs through previous experiences.

Music involves not just the auditory system but the somatosensory and motor systems as well, reflecting its strong associations with dance, the rhythmic tapping, stepping, clapping, and chanting that accompany and indeed produce music. It is inevitable that musical experience involves the motor cortex, basal ganglia, and cerebellum in producing song and dance, based in the genesis and maintenance of rhythmic spatiotemporal patterns of neural activity in widely distributed areas of the brain. How these patterns arise and where the pacemakers may be located is unknown. At best, neurophysiological information can explain some of the physical constraints on the production and apprehension of music, such as the range of auditory frequencies in instruments and the human voice, rates at which repetitive movements can be made and sustained in playing and dancing, and their limitations owing to inertia of parts of the body.

My own view of the functions of the auditory and somatosensory pathways was shaped by my experimental observations of their electrical activity patterns during learned behavior elicited by simple conditioned stimuli. These patterns do not have the periodic oscillations that are characteristic of music and dance. They are remarkably aperiodic waves that reflect shared oscillations of millions of neurons in cortical areas that are about the size of one's fingernail. Oscillations form patterns that last only a tenth of a second, but they form and collapse at unpredictable time intervals several times each second. The content related to the auditory, somatic, visual, or olfactory stimuli is found in the spatial pattern of amplitude modulation (AM) of the common chaotic waveform that serves as a carrier (Freeman and Barrie 1994; Barrie, Freeman, and Lenhart 1996). An analogy is the sequence of spatial patterns in the frames of a black and white movie, in which the carrier is white light. The AM patterns are elicited by stimuli in each of the primary sensory cortices, and they all converge and are combined in the limbic system, deep within the forebrain (Freeman 1998). Particulars of the patterns that relate to structures of the eye, ear, nose, and skin are deleted in the formation of multisensory percepts known as gestalts. These integrated patterns are the basis for awareness of musical sounds and the somatosensory (both exteroceptive and proprioceptive) and visual contexts in which they are perceived.

In tracing the path in brains of rabbits taken by neural activity that accompanied and followed transformation of an odor stimulus by sensory receptors and its transmission to the cerebral cortex, I found that stimulus-dependent activity vanished. What appeared in place of this activity was a new pattern of cortical activity. My students and I first noticed this anomaly in the olfactory system (Freeman and Schneider 1982), and looking elsewhere we found it in visual, auditory, and somatic cortices, too (Freeman and Barrie 1994; Barrie, Freeman and Lenhart 1996). In all systems, traces of the stimuli were replaced by novel patterns of neural activity, which were created by the chaotic dynamics of the cortices. These individualized patterns lacked invariance with respect to the stimuli that triggered them (Freeman 1992). They were not eidetic or derived images. Instead, they reflected the experiences, contexts, and significances of stimuli, in a word, the *meanings* of the stimuli for individuals. Our evidence from other sensory cortices indicated that this principle holds for all senses in all animals, including humans. The conclusion is that the only knowledge that animals and humans can have of the world outside themselves is what they construct within their own brains.

This finding could not have been obtained by introspection, because the process of observation contains within it some well-known operations that compensate for accidental changes in appearances of objects owing to variations in perspective, context, and so forth (Smythies 1994). We are drenched in perceptual constancies as a necessary condition for daily living. No one can tell from one's own experience or from the constant response R of someone else to a repeated stimulus S that an apparently invariant S-R relation is mediated by inconstant patterns of brain activity. I explain the lack of invariance as owing to the unity of individual experience (Freeman 1995), because every perception is influenced by all past experience. Each exposure to a stimulus changes the brain's synaptic structure so that it cannot respond identically over time, although it may appear subjectively to be so. As Heraclitus remarked, one cannot step twice in the same river.

Biological Isolation of Brains from Each Other

These findings can be summarized by saying that a form of solipsism isolates each brain from all others. The word as it is commonly used is applied to an individual who is so self-centered that he or she believes that all others are mere projections of their own imaginations. That is metaphysical solipsism, by which everything that exists is the projection of a brain. That would lead to the absurd conclusion that all of us are the fantasy of a dreaming rabbit. I am proposing a less common use of the word to mean epistemological solipsism, which holds that all knowledge is created within the brains of individuals. Each mind constructs its world view under the realization that other minds must exist. Knowledge is not instilled by indoctrination, as held by programmers who feed information into their computers. It is encouraged to grow by exhortation and example, as held by educators and insightful parents.

Solipsistic views have been held in some degree by many philosophers since Descartes, but they pose difficulties. It is impossible for minds to disprove metaphysical solipsism by logic alone, so how can a mind really be sure that any other mind exists, or, for that matter, the world? How can knowledge be based on the experience of each individual separately through sensory systems that form the windows of minds onto the world? How can knowledge of natural laws and mathematics emerge? If knowledge is expressed in a private language within each mind, how can it be shared and verified as being the same in different minds?

These formidable difficulties are not found in views that knowledge is universal and is there to be taken in like water, or that it is built into minds as categorical structures in order for minds to exist at all. Neural mechanisms by which solipsistic knowledge can be created, made public, and validated between individuals become clear only in the context of intentional action. Repeated attempts to answer these questions by logic and computation have not succeeded. Hence, biological data that emerged from animal brain studies and that support the solipsistic view offer new and interesting questions. Why do brains work this way, seeming to throw away the great bulk of their sensory input? what part do they keep? where and how do they keep it? how do they express what they know in themselves? how do they acquire it? how do they mobilize the past to embed it in the future? above all, how do they communicate with other brains? This problem lies not in translating or mapping knowledge from one brain onto another but rather in establishing mutual understanding and trust through shared actions during which brains create the channels, codes, agreements, and protocols that precede that reciprocal mappings of information in dialogues. It takes more than a telephone line and a dictionary to make a call to a foreign country.

Therefore, to say that a brain is solipsistic is to say that it grows like a neuron within itself, and that it has a boundary around itself in much the way that a neuron has a bounding membrane entirely around itself, preserving its unity and integrity. The barrier is not merely the skin and bone around each brain. It is the private language in each brain, in some respects like the labeling of the self by the immune system. Yet brains arise and are shaped in evolution not as isolated entities but as units in societies ranging upward from pairs to empires. Rainer Maria Rilke described the way in which individuals resonate together in his poem *Liebeslied* ("Love Song"), first published in *Neue Gedichte* (1907):

Doch alles, was uns anrührt, dich und mich,
nimmt uns zusammen wie ein Bogenstrich,
der aus zwei Saiten eine Stimme zieht.
Auf welches Instrument sind wir gespannt?
Und welcher Geiger hat uns in der Hand?
O süsses Lied. (pp. 239–240)

Yet all that touches us, you and me,
takes us together like a violin bow,

that draws one voice from two strings.
On what instrument are we strung?
And which violinist has us in hand?
O sweet song. [My translation]

For biologists, the instrument is brain chemistry and the player is evolution. Growth from within each individual is necessary so that each brain may cope with the infinite complexity of the world, but cooperation with other brains is also a social imperative, because the gulf must be bridged. Rilke saw the isolation as having beneficial aspects by providing ultimate privacy for everyone.

Aesthetics Supports the Solipsistic View

Something of the solipsistic aspect of music appreciation is conveyed in the term "aesthetics," which is commonly considered to be a branch of philosophy that analyzes beauty in the fine arts as distinct from that which is pleasant, moral, or useful. The essential character of beauty and tests by which it may be recognized are deeply individual. Ability to appreciate it is attributed to individuals who have engaged in years of study of the arts as to refine their capacities for appreciation and judgment. In this view, sensations and emotions that have the fine arts for their stimulus are based on the impact of a stimulus coming from a work of art or a piece of music, to which the observer or listener responds in an educated but still passive manner, as by sitting in a concert hall and letting the sound waves pour through.

The word aesthetic, from the Greek *aistetikos* and the Latin form *aesthetica*, was first used about 1750 by Alexander Gottlieb Baumgarten to designate a cognitive science of sensuous knowledge whose goal is beauty, in contrast to logic whose goal is truth. Kant used transcendental aesthetics to denote a priori principles of sensory experience couched in categories of time and space. Hegel (1830) broke from cognitive, rational science to a phenomenology of the fine arts appealing to the senses, which he called *Aesthetik*. This was so in accord with nineteenth-century Romanticism that since then the word is widely used in his sense.

The social dimension of aesthetics is largely reduced to relations between artists and critics. According to Giddings (1932): "All arts, we must remember, are phases of the social mind. We are so much in the habit of thinking of them in terms of art products that we forget that the arts themselves are groups of ideas and acquisitions of skill that exist only in the minds, muscles, and nerves of living men" (p. 7). Whereas art and aesthetics are both creative processes, they differ in their directions of change in complexity. The artist begins with a high degree of complexity steeped in chaos, but is constrained by the physical medium in which the work is done and by the discipline of the Academy. The critic begins in a rigid academic milieu and has his or her mind opened by a work of art into a higher degree of complexity over the edge of order into chaos, which is not otherwise accessible. Artist and critic interact reciprocally to construct the dynamics through which art and aesthetics come into being. For both, the experience of beauty is achieved through a sense of closure within their fields of intentionality, which are developed, maintained, and evolved by the neurodynamics within their brains.

These fields of intentional neural activity reveal neurodynamic operations that construct the psychological space-time arena in which logic is performed. They may provide the raw materials from which a new biological science of beauty in music might be constructed, which might explain the forms of brain activity that underlie our attainment of harmony, balance, congruity, proportion, and symmetry, and neural operations that support critical judgment, taste, discernment, and critical responsiveness. However, these aspects contribute little to understanding raw emotions induced by music in circumstances where beauty is not at issue, but power is.

Selected Neuropeptides Dissolve the Solipsistic Barrier

Even though the neural mechanisms are unclear, there is no doubt that music has the power to induce and modulate different emotional states, and that these states are accompanied by release of neurohormones in affected brains. Under the theory founded by Walter Cannon (1939), each state of emotion is mediated by a neurohormone acting on the hypothalamus as well as other parts of the brain. It supplanted the James-Lange theory of emotion, according to which emotional states are felt and identified by sensory systems, including those of the viscera. Neither of these is wrong nor entirely satisfactory, and in interesting respects they were both anticipated in practice by the ancient Greeks, who formulated three main classes of music relating to emotional states. Phrygian music was martial and served with trumpets to incite action in battle. Emotions of fear and rage are associated with intracerebral release of norepinephrine. Similar forms of aggressive or terrified behavior in modern times are induced by cocaine and amphetamine, which mimic some of the central effects of norepinephrine. Lydian music was solemn, slow, plaintive, and religious, with reliance on flutes instead of trumpets. Contemplative and relaxed moods induced by this Muzak-like music are associated with release of serotonin in the brain. Similar effects were induced by ingestion of mushroom hallucinogens, which preceded LSD, and are now gained by Prozac, which blocks endogenous serotonin reuptake and prolongs its action. Ionian music was convivial, joyful, and, according to Plato effeminate, relying heavily on drums to induce dancing. Pleasurable states are now associated with intracranial release of dopamine and endorphins. Then as now they were induced by alcohol and tetrahydrocannabinol, which serve as adjuvants to facilitate the passive onset of such states at modern rock concerts and rave dances.

These partial explanations still fall short of explaining the deep roots of the appeal of music in human affairs, particularly with respect to the call for communal action and understanding. The use of language is an evolutionary triumph that has made civilization possible, but its use for communication by representations, both oral and written, requires preparation and shaping of brains to create trust. Trust is an implicit expectation and faith in the predictability of the behavior of those to whom one has committed oneself by a transformation of the self. It transcends the solipsistic barrier.

Such a commitment is seen at the most primitive level in mammals in the transformation that takes place in a mother at the time of giving birth and committing herself to the care of her newborn infant. In many species, including humans, the transformation occurs in the father as well, by which a child's behavior is transformed into that of a parent. Studies of brain function during copulation to orgasm in both males and females and in females during lactation show that the neuropeptide oxytocin is released into the basal forebrain (Pedersen et al. 1992). It appears to act by dissolving preexisting learning by loosening the synaptic connections in which prior knowledge is held. This opens an opportunity for learning new knowledge. The meltdown does not instill knowledge. It clears the path for the acquisition of new understanding through behavioral actions that are shared with others, including cooperative caring for the infant and the other parent.

A well-documented example of this process of transformation in adults comes from the biology of brain-washing. Well known techniques of sensory isolation, overload, stress, and chemical manipulation can lead to a crisis in brain function that Pavlov called "transmarginal inhibition" and is followed by a remarkable state of malleability and opportunity for reeducation. This condition has also been characterized as an altered state and as a trance. The transformation goes beyond acceptance of what cannot be changed, and it is not a loss of recollection of the past. It constitutes a wholesale change in beliefs and attitudes by which a new person emerges with new social commitments. Sargant (1957) documented striking similarities between these techniques and those used to arouse the fervor of dancers in preliterate tribes and parishioners of evangelistic churches in congregations from the seventeenth century to the present, in which the avowed goal was religious conversion to save souls. Features characterizing the process were the presence of strong emotional arousal, such as by fear of devils or of pain; severe physical exercise, such as by prolonged dancing; sensory overload as by continual loud singing, chanting, and stomping in time to loud drums and horns; and lack of sleep by all-night revelry.

Music and Dance as the Biotechnology of Group Formation

Anthropologists and ethnopsychiatrists documented the prevalence in preliterate tribes of singing and dancing to the point of physical and psychological collapse during religious and social ceremonies. Typically, members of a community gather at a central place surrounded by musicians and their instruments, priests and shamans as masters of ceremony (Price 1982), a central altar, and icons that symbolize tribal totems and deities. Rhythmic drumming, chanting, clapping, marching in step, and pirouetting around bonfires last for hours, through the night into dawn, as one by one the participants drop from exhaustion. They are then succored by other, older members of the tribe, and brought into rituals to symbolize their admission to new adult status. This is the moment of change.

Emile Durkheim (1915) described the socializing process as the use of "... totemic emblems by clans to express and communicate collective representations," which begins where the individual feels he *is* the totem and evolves beliefs that he will become the totem or that his ancestors are in the totem. Religious rites and ceremonies lead to "collective mental states of extreme emotional intensity, in which representation is still undifferentiated from the movements and actions which make the communion towards which it tends a reality to the group. Their participation in it is *so effectively lived* that it is not yet properly imagined" (pp. 465–472).

Verger (1954) recorded in photographs the ceremony of ritual death and rebirth in which participants who collapsed into the deep unawareness of transmarginal inhibition were sewn into shrouds, carried by tribesmen to the local cemetery, and returned thereafter to tribeswomen for rebirth by unsewing, revival, and succor as new persons. The choice of fertility symbols and behaviors of the participants indicate the powerful basis in sexuality of the ceremonies, which commonly become orgiastic.

There is no reason to doubt that these activities give great pleasure and catharsis to those caught up in the communal spirit of the events, and that immersion in dance is followed by a refreshed sense of belonging to the tribe. What is at issue is the extent to which feelings of bonding and formation of a neural basis for social cooperation might be engendered by the same neurochemical mechanisms that evolved to support sexual reproduction in altricial species like ourselves, and that might mediate religious, political, and social conversions, involving commitment of the self to a person as in transference, fraternity, military group, sports team, corporation, nation, or new deity. The common feature is formation of allegiance and trust.

Music as sound appeals to the ear, but making and appreciating it involve the entire body through the somatosensory and motor systems of the performer and the active audience (Clynes 1982). Dance on a stage appeals to the eye, but its real charm is found by participants who shape their movements into a living and evolving unity. The strongest basis for cooperation lies in rhythmically repeated motions, because they are predictable by others, and others can thereby anticipate and move in accord with their expectations. Music gives the background beat.

Biocultural Evolution of Music in Socialization

Here in its purest form is a human technology for crossing the solipsistic gulf. It is wordless, illogical, deeply emotional, and selfless in its actualization of transient and then lasting harmony between individuals (Wilson 1992), and perhaps even among higher apes despite their lack of a sense of rhythm (Williams 1967). It constructs the sense of trust and predictability in each member of the community on which social interactions are based. Dance alone does not suffice, but it is exemplary of the nature of wordless give-and-take cooperation by which are constructed channels for verbal communication. A significant discovery by our remote ancestors may have been the use of music and dance for bonding in groups larger than nuclear families. According to Roederer (1984), who also proposed the utility of music for training in language skills, for understanding musical aspects of speech, and for signaling emotional states, ". . . the role of music in superstitious or sexual rites, religion, ideological proselytism, and military arousal clearly demonstrates the value of music as a means of establishing behavioral coherency in masses of people. In the distant past this would indeed have had an important survival value, as an increasingly complex human environment demanded coherent, collective actions on the part of groups of human society" (p. 356). That accomplishment may have accompanied or even preceded the invention of fire, tools and shelter, because the maintenance, development, and transmission across generations of information about techniques for working matter into useful forms must have required existence of channels to support social interactions. These channels form through emotional attachments, not logical debate.

Formation of a social group, such as a tribe, has its dark sides, one of which is formation of a boundary, with exclusion of nonself from the self that constitutes the unity. Individuals who do not "belong" become enemies who are to be walled off, expelled, and possibly destroyed, if they are perceived as menacing the welfare of the group. The process is similar to sexual jealousy, which manifests the exclusionary nature of the pair bond. Internecine tribal warfare that is fueled by the unknown chemistry of hatred is just as illogical and selfless as bonding within a community. Outsiders are seen as objects or animals that are treated as tools or slaves. Biologists refer to the phenomenon in terms of nearest neighbor competitive inhibition, winner-take-all networks, and survival of the fittest. It may well be that wholesale extermination was the necessary price for the exceedingly rapid pace of human evolution over the past half-million years. Fortunately, our more recent ancestors discovered civilized alternatives to death-dealing, unrestricted warfare. Music and dance have close relatives in team sports, which are forms of ritualized combat, actions and reactions that are carefully choreographed toward symbolic goals, and which instill powerful feelings of identity not only in players as "team spirit" but in spectators who root for the teams.

Another dark side is the use of drugs (Fort 1969) such as wine, opium, and hallucinogenic mushrooms to induce the pleasurable subjective correlates of neurochemical bonding. Repeated dissolutive trances can result in derelicts like hermits, alcoholics, addicts, dropouts, zombies, and other marginalia of society. Prehistorical records compiled by Frazer (1890) in *The Golden Bough* and Graves (1948) in *The White Goddess* show how religious rites of the ancient world were imbued with neuroactive substances that may have facilitated destructive practices such as self-castration and suicide, particularly quintessence that was embodied in alcohol. (The four essences of which the earth was made were air, earth, water, and fire. The heavens were made of ether, the fifth essence. Agents that altered the states of consciousness were interpreted as touching participants with the spiritual liquor.) The persistence of savage and asocial behavior appears to have led to the development of larger social structures, governments, academies, and universities through which to channel and control destructive side effects of orgiastic bonding. Shamans, priests, and church bureaucracies regulated the time, place, and manner of ceremonies with respect to stars and seasons. Chiefs, kings, and armies imposed constraints on tribes for the sake of peace and general welfare.

With the emergence of city states run by bureaucrats and academic intelligentsia, the Greeks relegated the Dionysian orgies to the lower classes (James 1993). Plato banned all music except the Lydian from his Academy in recognition of music's power to degrade rational minds and subvert social order. The Catholic Church in the Middle Ages labeled the Dionysian rituals as pagan and suppressed them to maintain political control, opening the way for Apollonian music (Nietzsche 1872) such as Gregorian chants. Close harmony provided for bonding of a different kind among intellectuals, stripped of its sexual overtones. Syncopation was forbidden. The "Devil's interval" was allegedly called that because God and the world could not exist between the beats. Physicians also used the medical term syncope to signify cessation of function in a transient loss of consciousness. The dialectic between Apollo and Dionysus reemerged in the Baroque, and it continues to infuse fresh energy into music through syncopation and atonality in jazz, blues, and rock-and-roll, which, through radio and television, are bonding young people in nations everywhere. They stand opposed to older generations; intentional bonding is always exclusionary.

Conclusion

I conclude that music and dance originated through biological evolution of brain chemistry, which interacted with the cultural evolution of behavior. This led to the development of chemical and behavioral technology for inducing altered states of consciousness. The role of trance states was particularly important for breaking down preexisting habits and beliefs. That meltdown appears to be necessary for personality changes leading to the formation of social groups by cooperative action leading to trust. Bonding is not simply a release of a neurochemical in an altered state. It is the social action of dancing and singing together that induces new forms of behavior, owing to the malleability that can come through the altered state. It is reasonable to suppose that musical skills played a major role early in the evolution of human intellect, because they made possible formation of human societies as a prerequisite for the transmission of acquired knowledge across generations.

Acknowledgment

Parts of this chapter were adapted from my 1995 book *Societies of Brains* with permission of the publisher. Research support of the National Institute of Mental health is gratefully acknowledged.

References

Baumgarten, A. G. (ca. 1750/1961). *Aesthetica*. Hildesheim, Germany: G. Olms.

Barrie, J. M., Freeman, W. J., and Lenhart, M. D. (1996). Spatiotemporal analysis of prepyriform, visual, auditory and somesthetic surface EEGs in trained rabbits. *Journal of Neurophysiology* 76:520–539.

Cannon, W. B. (1939). *The Wisdom of the Body*. New York: Norton.

Clynes, M. (Ed.) (1982). *Music, Mind and Brain: The Neuropsychology of Music*. New York: Plenum Press.

Durkheim, E. (1915/1926). *The Elementary Forms of the Religious Life: A Study in Religious Sociology* (J. W. Swain, Trans.). New York: Macmillan.

Fort, J. (1969). *The Pleasure Seekers: The Drug Crisis, Youth and Society*. New York: Grove Press.

Frazer, J. G. (1890/1949). *The Golden Bough: A Study in Magic and Religion*. New York: Macmillan.

Freeman, W. J. (1992). Tutorial in neurobiology. *International Journal of Bifurcation and Chaos* 2:451–482.

Freeman, W. J. (1995). *Societies of Brains. A Study in the Neurobiology of Love and Hate*. Mahwah, NJ: Erlbaum.

Freeman, W. J. (1998). The neurobiology of multimodal sensory integration. *Integrative Physiological and Behavioral Science* 33:12–17.

Freeman, W. J. and Barrie, J. M. (1994). Chaotic oscillations and the genesis of meaning in cerebral cortex. In G. Buzsaki, R. Llinás, W. Singer, A. Berthoz, and Y. Christen (Eds.) *Temporal Coding in the Brain* (pp. 13–37). Berlin: Springer-Verlag.

Freeman, W. J. and Schneider, W. (1982). Changes in spatial patterns of rabbit olfactory EEG with conditioning to odors. *Psychophysiology* 19:44–56.

Giddings, F. H. (1932). *Civilization and Society: An Account of the Development and Behavior of Human Society*. New York: Holt.

Graves, R. (1948). *White Goddess*. New York: Vintage.

Hegel, G. W. F. (1830/1975). *Aesthetics: Lectures on Fine Art* (T. M. Knox, Trans.). Oxford: Clarendon Press.

James, J. (1993). *The Music of the Spheres: Music, Science and the Natural Order of the Universe*. Berlin: Copernicus, Springer-Verlag.

Nietzsche, F. (1872/1993). *The Birth of Tragedy* (S. Whiteside, Trans.; M. Tanner, Ed.). New York: Penguin Books.

Pedersen, C. A., Caldwell, J. D., Jirikowski, G. F., and Insel, T. R. (Eds.) (1992). *Oxytocin in Maternal, Sexual, and Social Behaviors. Annals of the New York Academy of Sciences*, Vol. 652. New York: New York Academy of Sciences.

Pribram, K. (1982). Brain mechanisms in music: Prolegomena for a theory of the meaning of meaning. In M. Clynes (Ed.) *Music, Mind and Brain: The Neuropsychology of Music* (pp. 21–36). New York: Plenum Press.

Price, R. (Ed.) (1982). *Shamans and Endorphins*. Washington, DC: Society for Psychological Anthropology.

Rilke, R. M. (1907/1982). Liebeslied. In H. Wagener (Ed.) *Deutsche Liebeslyrik*. Stuttgart: Philipp Reclam.

Roederer, J. G. (1984). The search for a survival value of music. *Music Perception* 1:350–356.

Sargant, W. W. (1957). *Battle for the Mind*. Westport, CT: Greenwood.

Smythies, J. R. (1994). *The Walls of Plato's Cave: The Science and Philosophy of Brain, Consciousness and Perception*. Aldershot, UK: Avebury.

Verger, P. (1954). *Dieux d'Afrique*. Paris: Hartmann.

Wallin, N. L. (1991). *Biomusicology: Neurophysiological, Neuropsychological, and Evolutionary Perspectives on the Origins and Purposes of Music.* Stuyvesant, NY: Pendragon.

Williams, L. (1967). *The Dancing Chimpanzee: A Study of Primitive Music in Relation to the Vocalizing and Rhythmic Action of Apes.* New York: Norton.

Wilson, S. G. (1992). *The Drummer's Path: Moving the Spirit With Ritual and Traditional Drumming.* New York: Destiny Books.

V UNIVERSALS IN MUSIC

23 Human Processing Predispositions and Musical Universals

Sandra Trehub

Abstract

The chapter considers the possibility of human predispositions for processing music, and speculates about the broader question of musical universals. A number of similarities in musical pattern perception between adults with extensive exposure to music and infants with minimal exposure suggest a biological basis for several aspects of music processing. For example, infants and adults focus largely on the pitch contour and rhythm of novel melodies, reflecting a disposition to attend to relational pitch and timing cues rather than to specific pitches and durations. Moreover, infants and adults retain more information from sequences whose component tones are related by small-integer ratios (2:1, 3:2) than by large-integer ratios (45:32). Infants remember the component tones of scales more readily when the scale steps are of unequal size (e.g., tones and semitones), as in the major scale, rather than of equal size. Furthermore, they encode more details of a melody when its rhythmic arrangement is conventional rather than unconventional. Although music may seem irrelevant to the lives of infants, it is not. Caregivers throughout the world sing to infants, using distinctive musical materials and expressive variations that are finely tuned to infants' ability and mood. Indeed, these informal musical performances have important attentional and affective consequences for the infant audience. Finally, universals of musical pattern processing have provocative parallels in universals or near-universals of musical structure. Musics of the world reveal greater emphasis on global structure than on local details and on small-integer frequency ratios than on large ratios. Other cross-cultural similarities include the ubiquity of unequal steps in scales, preferred rhythms, and a special genre of music for infants.

The prevailing wisdom is that long-term exposure to the music of a particular culture is largely responsible for adults' implicit knowledge of music (Jones 1982; Bharucha 1987; Krumhansl 1990). Several lines of evidence are consistent with this view. First, children exhibit better perception and retention of music with increasing age (e.g., Krumhansl and Keil 1982; Trainor and Trehub 1994). Second, adults and children show superior memory for melodies that are structured in conventional rather than unconventional ways (Cuddy, Cohen, and Mewhort 1981; Trehub et al. 1986). Third, formal musical training is associated with enhanced perception and retention of music by children as well as by adults (Krumhansl and Kessler 1982; Oura and Hatano 1988; Morrongiello and Roes 1990; Lynch and Eilers 1991; Lynch et al. 1991). Nevertheless, basic principles of auditory pattern perception may still lie at the heart of mature music processing (Handel 1989), which would explain why the skills of trained and untrained listeners are more similar than different (Bharucha and Stoeckig 1986, 1987; Cuddy and Badertscher 1987). What is unclear, however, is whether the similarities stem from processing dispositions that are common to all members of the species or from long-term exposure to similar kinds of music.

Studying human infants provides an opportunity to explore the possibility of such processing predispositions. If substantial adult-infant similarities were evident in the perception of music, one could argue that at least some aspects of music processing have a biological basis. That is not to deny an important role for experience but rather to hold that perception of music is inherently biased rather than unbiased. One could go even further, proposing that the musics of the world have capitalized on these biases or universals of auditory pattern processing. If that were the case, music from different cultures could be expected to share some fundamental properties that make it discernible and memorable, perhaps even appealing.

With these goals in mind, my colleagues and I studied infants' perception of music or musiclike patterns (for reviews, see Trehub and Trainor 1993; Trehub, Schellenberg, and Hill 1997). For the most part, melodies consisted of sequences of pure tones (sine waves) rather than rich, complex tones, which allowed us to maximize control over cues available to listeners. Naturally, we were unable to obtain verbal responses from infants, but we still used rigorous means of estimating their ability to detect specific changes in a repeating melody. In this manner, we ascertained which features of a melody are salient and memorable for such naive listeners. Specifically, we presented six- to nine-month-olds with repetitions of a melody emanating from a loudspeaker at one side, and rewarded them with an interesting visual display for responding (by turning to the loudspeaker) to specified changes in the melody (figure 23.1). Melody repetitions were generally presented at different pitch levels or tempos, forcing infants to solve the detection task on the basis of relational cues (e.g., pitch or temporal patterning) rather than absolute cues such as specific pitches or durations (figure 23.2). Comparisons of responses in the presence of a change (i.e., "hits") and in the absence of a change (i.e., "false alarms") indicated whether infants detected the change in question (for methodological details, see Trehub, Thorpe, and Morrongiello 1987). These procedures revealed that infants' perception of musiclike patterns is remarkably similar to that of adults (see Trehub and Trainor 1993; Trehub, Schellenberg, and Hill 1997).

Relational Processing of Auditory Patterns

After listening to a brief, unfamiliar melody, adults generally remember little more than its melodic contour (pattern of pitch directional changes, or ups and downs) and rhythm (Bartlett and Dowling 1980; Dowling 1994). Similarly, if infants hear a melody which is subsequently transposed, with all pitches changed but the exact pitch relations (i.e.,

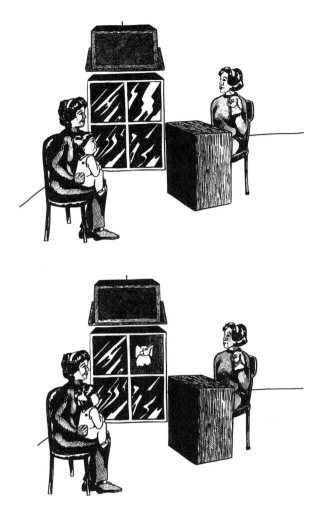

Figure 23.1
Depiction of the test. The infant sits on a parent's lap facing the experimenter (upper panel). Patterns are presented on a loudspeaker to the infant's left. Turns to the loudspeaker in response to the target change lead to the illumination and activation of animated toys (lower panel).

intervals) maintained, they treat the transposition as equivalent to the original melody (Chang and Trehub 1977; Trehub, Bull, and Thorpe 1984). Even if exact pitch relations are altered but contour is preserved, infants treat the altered melody as familiar rather than new (Trehub, Bull, and Thorpe 1984). In contrast, a change in contour resulting from the substitution of a single tone (Trehub, Thorpe, and Morrongiello 1985) or the reordering of tones (Trehub, Bull, and Thorpe 1984) leads infants to consider the altered melody as unfamiliar, much like adults. As a

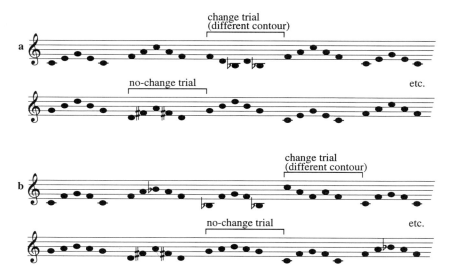

Figure 23.2
Sample stimuli from Trehub, Thorpe, and Morrongiello (1987). Note that successive patterns are presented at different pitch levels. Repetitions in example (a) are exact transpositions; those in example (b) alter the component intervals but maintain the contour. (From Trehub et al. 1997.)

result, infants can detect contour changes even when comparison patterns are presented at different pitch levels than the original (Trehub, Thorpe, and Morrongiello 1987), as shown in figure 23.2. In other words, the pitch contour of a melody seems to be central to its identity. Rhythm also makes important contributions to the identity of a pattern. For example, infants consider faster or slower versions of a tone sequence as functionally equivalent, provided the rhythm or temporal pattern remains unchanged (Trehub and Thorpe 1989). Comparable perceptual compensations for differences in pitch level (Kuhl 1979) and speaking rate (Eimas and Miller 1980; Miller and Eimas 1983) are evident in infants' and adults' perception of speech.

It is also clear that infants group or chunk components of tone sequences on the basis of similar pitch, timbre, or loudness (Demany 1982; Thorpe et al. 1988; Thorpe and Trehub 1989; Trehub, Endman, and Thorpe 1990) in much the same way as adults (see Bregman 1990). For example, they detect a pause inserted *within* a group of similar tones (e.g., XXXO OO) more readily than a comparable pause inserted *between* groups of tones (e.g., XXX OOO; Thorpe et al. 1988; Thorpe and Trehub 1989). Within-group pauses disrupt the perceptual organization of the pattern, but between-group pauses do not. Similarly, pauses inserted within musical phrases disrupt infants' attention whereas comparable pauses between phrases do not (Krumhansl and Jusczyk 1990;

Jusczyk and Krumhansl 1993). On the basis of these findings, one can tentatively propose three processing universals: the priority of contour over interval processing; the priority of temporal patterning over specific timing cues; and the relevance of gestalt principles of grouping. All of these principles involve a priority for global, relational cues over precise, absolute cues. Of interest, this contrasts markedly with the predilection of nonhuman species to focus on absolute pitch details in auditory sequences (D'Amato 1988; Hulse and Page 1988).

Interval Processing: Frequency Ratios

Infants' ability to perceive invariant contour and rhythm across changes in individual pitches and durations, although important, is not confined to music. After all, contour, rhythm, and perceptual grouping principles are important for perceiving and remembering spoken as well as musical patterns (Handel 1989; Trehub 1990; Trehub, Trainor, and Unyk 1993; Rubin 1995). For example, sentencelike prosody enhances prelinguistic infants' memory for phonetic information (Mandel, Jusczyk, and Kemler Nelson 1994), as it does for adults.

Other adult-infant similarities, such as sensitivity to small-integer frequency ratios, are more specifically linked to music. Ancient and medieval scholars claimed that tones related by small-integer ratios are pleasant, or consonant, and that those related by large-integer ratios are unpleasant, or dissonant (see Plomp and Levelt 1965; Schellenberg and Trehub 1994b). Galileo, for example, speculated that intervals with small-integer ratios produce regular or pleasing neural patterns. Although this notion and comparable neurophysiological proposals (Boomsliter and Creel 1961; Roederer 1979; Patterson 1986) remain unsubstantiated, it is clear that small-integer ratios play a critical role not only in Western music but in musical systems across cultures (Sachs 1943; Meyer 1956; Trehub, Schellenberg, and Hill 1997). Note that tones an octave (twelve semitones) apart are related by an approximate frequency ratio of $2:1$; tones seven semitones apart (perfect fifth) exemplify a $3:2$ ratio, and tones five semitones apart (perfect fourth) a $4:3$ ratio. By contrast, tones six semitones apart, the tritone interval, exemplify the large-integer ratio of $45:32$. Of interest, use of the tritone was prohibited in medieval times, when it was considered *diabolus in musica* (Piston 1969:27) or "the devil in music" (Kennedy 1994:901).

In a number of studies, infants, children, and adults were found to retain more information from sequences whose component tones were related by small-integer ratios than by large-integer ratios (Trehub et al. 1986; Cohen, Thorpe, and Trehub 1987; Trehub, Thorpe, and Trainor 1990;

Schellenberg and Trehub 1994a, 1996a, b). Thus, for example, infants show better retention of melodic (sequential) intervals of perfect fifths and fourths (consonant intervals) compared with tritones (dissonant intervals; Schellenberg and Trehub 1996b), as can be seen in figure 23.3. They also show superior retention of harmonic (simultaneous) intervals exemplifying small-integer rather than large-integer ratios (Schellenberg and Trehub 1996b; Trainor 1997). Moreover, infants and adults tend to categorize intervals on the basis of consonance or dissonance rather than size (Schellenberg and Trainor 1996). Accordingly, they more readily detect a change from a consonant harmonic interval (seven semitones, or perfect fifth) to a dissonant interval (six semitones, or tritone) than to another consonant interval (five semitones, or perfect fourth) despite the greater pitch difference in the latter change (two semitones rather than one). Even European starlings (*Sturnus vulgaris*) that are trained to produce distinctive responses to a specific consonant and dissonant chord generalize their responses to another consonant and dissonant chord (Hulse, Bernard, and Braaten 1995). Findings such as these suggest physiological concomitants of consonance and dissonance.

Infants also exhibit affective and attentional preferences for consonant over dissonant chords and harmonizations of melodies (Crowder, Reznick, and Rosenkrantz 1991; Zentner and Kagan 1996; Trainor and Heinmiller 1998), which implies that rudimentary aesthetic judgments may be partly independent of musical exposure. Overall, data on infants' processing of simultaneous and sequential tones are in line with the claims of ancient and medieval scholars and are readily interpretable in terms of a processing bias for tones related by small-integer ratios. This

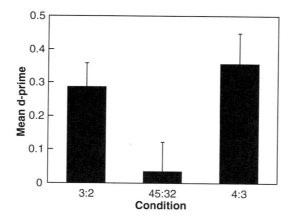

Figure 23.3
Infants' discrimination (d′) scores as a function of the frequency ratio of tones in melodic (sequential) intervals. (From Schellenberg and Trehub 1996b.)

inherent bias for consonant intervals may well be linked to the pervasiveness of octaves (2:1 ratio), perfect fifths (3:2 ratio), and perfect fourths (4:3 ratio), all of which are perfect consonances in musical systems the world over (Sachs 1943; Kolinski 1967). In contrast, this bias is inconsistent with claims that musical consonance is primarily a matter of convention (Serafine 1983; Blacking 1992). Indeed, the near absence of small-integer ratios or "natural" melodic and harmonic intervals in contemporary atonal music may contribute to its inaccessibility for most untrained listeners and, therefore, its relegation to elite milieus (Meyer 1994; Schellenberg and Trehub 1996b). Small-integer ratios may function as perceptual anchors, facilitating the encoding and retention of melodies and, consequently, detection of subtle variations (Schellenberg and Trehub 1996a, b). In short, the priority of small-integer over large-integer frequency ratios can be considered another processing universal.

Scale Structure

Another domain that is related only to music is the set of pitches in musical scales. Scales, as formalizations of the pitches that occur in melodies of a particular style, indicate the conventional means of filling an octave interval with intermediate pitches. Despite considerable variability in scale structure across cultures, a number of similarities are evident. For example, the typical division of the octave into five to seven different pitches likely originates in cognitive constraints (Dowling and Harwood 1986). Specific intervals tend to predominate, notably those with small-integer ratios. Moreover, non-Western as well as Western scales incorporate variations in step size as a general rule (Sloboda 1985). The Western major scale consists of seven steps that are either two semitones in size, as in *doh-re*, or one semitone, as in *ti-doh* (figure 23.4); the harmonic minor scale has a contrasting sequence of unequal steps. Pentatonic scales (five tones per octave) date from at least 2000 B.C. (Kennedy 1994) and feature unequal step sizes. Although the music of Thailand is thought to be based on an equal-step scale (Meyers-Moro 1993), Morton's (1976) comprehensive analysis of the traditional Thai repertoire yielded a pentatonic scale. (Some challenges of scale specification in different cultures are described in Arom, Léothaud, and Voisin 1997.)

Unequal-step scales are thought to confer processing advantages, such as allowing different tones to assume distinctive functions (Balzano 1980), facilitating the perception of tension and resolution (Shepard 1982), and providing the listener with a sense of location within a melody (Brown 1988; Butler 1989). If unequal-step scales are inherently easier

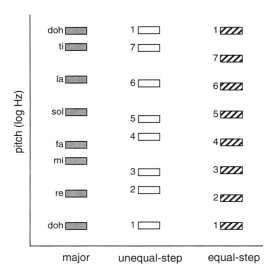

Figure 23.4
Schematic illustration of major, unequal-step, and equal-step scales. Note that successive tones in the major scale are separated by one or two semitones. Some steps in the unequal-step scale are twice as large as other steps; step size in the equal-step scale (larger than one semitone but smaller than two semitones) does not vary. (From Trehub, Schellenberg, and Kamenetsky, in press.)

to encode and retain than equal-step scales, such advantages might be apparent with infant listeners.

We presented infants and adults with transposed repetitions of three ascending-descending scales: an equal-step scale that was used in previous research with adults (Shepard and Jordan 1984; Jordan and Shepard 1987), the major (unequal-step) scale, and a novel, unequal-step scale (Trehub, Schellenberg, and Kamenetsky, in press), all of which are shown in figure 23.4. The equal-step scale consisted of dividing the octave into seven equal steps. In the novel, unequal-step scale, the octave was arbitrarily partitioned into eleven subdivisions, and a scale was constructed with steps separated by one or two subdivisions. For each ascending-descending scale, infants were required to detect a three/four-semitone change in one tone; adults were required to detect a one/two-semitone change. It was no surprise that adults performed better on the familiar major scale than on either unfamiliar scale, but they performed no better on the unfamiliar, unequal-step scale than on the unfamiliar, equal-step scale. For Western adults with long-term exposure to music based on the major scale, the ascending major scale is probably as familiar as most tunes. Infants, for whom all scales were presumably unfamiliar, performed significantly better on both unequal-step scales than on the equal-step scale (figure 23.5). Moreover, the major scale had no

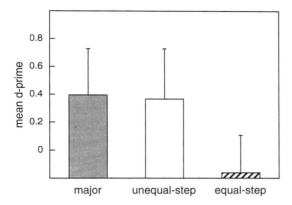

Figure 23.5
Infant performance on the ascending-descending major, unequal, and equal-step scales.
(From Trehub, Schellenberg, and Kamenetsky, in press.)

advantage over the novel, unequal-interval scale, which rules out exposure as a factor contributing to performance differences. Not only was
infants' performance poorer for the equal-step scale, infants were simply
unable to detect the pitch change within that context. These findings are
consistent with the view that unequal-step scales have their origin in perceptual processing predispositions, but they also indicate the potency
of culture-specific exposure. In any case, priority for unequal over equal
steps in scales qualifies as another processing universal.

Rhythmic Structure

The diversity of rhythmic structures across cultures makes it easy to
imagine that musical rhythms have their foundation in culture rather
than in nature. To explore this issue, we generated "good" and "bad"
rhythmic organizations of a ten-note melody (Trehub, Hill, and
Kamenetsky 1997a). To identify the best of several "good" rhythms, the
patterns were presented in pairs to musically untrained adults, who were
required to choose the better rhythm. A comparable procedure was used
to ascertain the worst of the "bad" rhythms. The most preferred and least
preferred versions served as "good" and "bad" rhythms for six-month-
old infants (figure 23.6). Half of the infants were required to detect a
pitch change in one tone of the melody with "good" or "bad" rhythm;
the other half had to detect a rhythmic change. Infants performed better
for the pitch and rhythmic changes in the context of adults' preferred
rhythm, which suggests a natural bias for certain rhythmic forms. Of
interest, the "good" rhythm exemplified gestalt grouping principles and
tone durations related by small-integer ratios; the "bad" rhythm did not.

Figure 23.6
The upper panel depicts the "good" rhythmic arrangement; the lower panel depicts the "bad" rhythmic arrangement of the same tune.

Lateral Asymmetries in Processing

Asymmetries in brain structure and function are evident from the earliest days of life (e.g., Witelson and Pallie 1973; Molfese and Molfese 1979; Previc 1991). In dichotic listening tasks, infants generally exhibit the characteristic right-ear (left hemisphere) advantage for speech and left-ear (right hemisphere) advantage for music (Best, Hoffman, and Glanville 1982; Bertoncini et al. 1989). The global approach to music processing has been superseded by a componential approach, which revealed a left-ear advantage for contour processing in adults and a right-ear advantage for interval processing (Peretz and Morais 1980; Peretz 1987; Peretz and Babaï 1992). Comparable lateral asymmetries have been documented for infants age eight and a half months, with left-ear superiority for the perception of contour and right-ear superiority for the perception of intervals (Balaban, Anderson, and Wisniewski 1998).

Implications of Adult-Infant Similarities

Any one of these adult-infant similarities in itself could be considered a mere coincidence. Taken together, however, these striking similarities between infant listeners with minimal exposure to music and adult listeners with extensive exposure make a compelling case for inherent perceptual biases in relation to music, or "innate learning preferences" (Marler 1990). These information-processing constraints are unlikely to be limited to perceptual aspects of music but may also have implications for the design of musical systems across cultures. As Nettl (1983) noted, musical systems across cultures are considerably "more restricted than the boundaries of the imaginable" (p. 43). Undoubtedly, diversity exists, but it is not unlimited. One consequence of musical cultures building on perceptual processing predispositions is that exposure and training often lead to progressive improvement in the skills that are favored by nature.

As a result, distinctions between processing biases and familiarity effects may be obscured.

Speech and Sign for Infants

Do music-processing skills of infants have relevance or consequences beyond the laboratory? They do, indeed. Caregivers the world over enhance their vocal messages to prelinguistic infants by making them more musical than usual. They use simple but distinctive pitch contours but articulate words poorly; they raise their pitch level, slow their tempo, and make their utterances more rhythmic and repetitive compared with their conventional speech patterns (Papoušek, Papoušek, and Bornstein 1985; Grieser and Kuhl 1988; Fernald et al. 1989; Fernald 1991; Papoušek, Papoušek, and Symmes 1991; Cooper 1993). In general, playful speech to infants embodies high pitch and expanded pitch contours that are rising or rise-fall in shape; soothing speech involves low pitch, a reduced pitch range, and pitch contours that are level or falling (Fernald 1989; Papoušek, Papoušek, and Symmes 1991).

The pervasiveness of musical features in infant-directed utterances led several investigators to characterize these utterances as melodies (Fernald 1989; Papoušek et al. 1990; Papoušek, Papoušek, and Symmes 1991). Such primitive messages have attentional and affective consequences for the noncomprehending infant audience. For example, infants show more positive affect to approving than to disapproving utterances (Papoušek et al. 1990; Fernald 1993) and to infant-directed speech than to adult-directed speech (Werker and McLeod 1989). Beginning in the newborn period and continuing thereafter, infant-directed speech effectively recruits and maintains infant attention (Fernald 1985; Cooper and Aslin 1990; Pegg, Werker and McLeod 1992; Werker, Pegg, and McLeod 1994). According to Fernald (1992), infants' biological makeup predisposes them to attend selectively to distinctive pitch contours of infant-directed speech, whose primitive emotional meanings can be decoded in the absence of language. Cross-cultural similarities in some emotion-bearing aspects of adult speech (Krauss, Curran, and Ferleger 1983; Frick 1985) are consistent with Fernald's (1992) claim of the transparency of infant-directed messages.

Natural attention-getting properties of infant-directed speech may include highly contrastive fundamental frequencies (Fernald 1989; Cooper 1997). Of interest, highly contrastive visual movements in infant-directed sign language (Erting, Prezioso, and O'Grandy Hynes 1990; Masataka 1992) result in greater attentional and affective responsiveness relative to adult-directed signing, not only by deaf infants (Masataka 1996) but also by hearing infants with no previous exposure to sign (Masataka 1998).

Music for Infants

Caregivers in every culture not only speak to their infant charges, they sing to them (Trehub and Schellenberg 1995; Trehub and Trainor 1998). The most ubiquitous song, the lullaby, is perceptually distinct from other song genres. Thus, naive adult listeners can distinguish foreign lullabies from nonlullabies with comparably slow tempo, even when the musical culture is entirely unfamiliar (Trehub, Unyk, and Trainor 1993a). Structural simplicity or repetitiveness is one factor that prompts adults to label a song as a lullaby; a preponderance of falling pitch contours is another (Unyk et al. 1992). Although reduplicated syllables such as *loo-loo*, *lo-lo*, *la-la*, *na-na*, *ne-ne*, and *do-do* are common in lullabies across cultures (Brakeley 1950; Cass-Beggs and Cass-Beggs 1969; Brown 1980), lullabies are identifiable even when such verbal cues are obscured (Trehub, Unyk, and Trainor 1993a).

Beyond a distinct repertoire of music for infants, which includes lullabies and play songs (analogous to soothing and playful speech), is a distinct style of performance for infant audiences. When mothers sing the same song in two contexts, once directly to their infant and once in the infant's absence, naive adult listeners can identify with near-perfect accuracy the version sung to an infant (Trehub, Unyk, and Trainor 1993b). Even when parents (fathers as well as mothers) attempt to reproduce or simulate their usual performance to infants, but with no infant present, listeners can still distinguish the genuine or contextually appropriate version from the simulation (Trehub et al. 1997). It is likely that the infant's presence alters the caregiver's emotional state, which, in turn, affects the vocal musculature (Scherer 1986) and resulting voice quality (Laver 1980; Fonagy 1981; Sundberg 1991; Tartter and Braun 1994).

In general, sung performances for infants involve higher pitch, slower tempo, distinctive timbre, and perturbations in fundamental frequency (jitter) and intensity (shimmer; Trainor, Schellenberg, and Hill 1997; Trehub et al. 1997; Trehub and Trainor 1998), all of which may reflect heightened emotional expressiveness. High pitch has been associated with happiness, affection, tenderness, and increased arousal (Fonagy and Magdics 1963; Ekman, Friesen, and Scherer 1976; Ohala 1984), slow tempo with tenderness and affection (Magdics 1963; Davitz 1964; Juslin 1997), and frequency and intensity perturbations with greater emotionality (Bachorowski and Owren 1995). Vocal adjustments such as these do not depend on the singer's parental status but are evident as well in songs sung by young children to their infant siblings (Trehub, Unyk, and Henderson 1994). Although mothers generally produce more expressive renditions of melody and lyrics than do fathers, parents, especially fathers, are more expressive with their infant sons than with their infant daughters (Trehub, Hill, and Kamenetsky 1997b), which is consistent with claims of greater attachment to same-sex infants (Fagot and Leinbach 1987; Morgan, Lyle, and Condran 1988). In short, the infant audience contributes to the nature of the performance, much like the adult audience of an oral performance (Rubin 1995).

Mothers' performances exhibit some fine-tuning to the mood and abilities of their young listeners. For example, the same song (e.g., "Twinkle, Twinkle Little Star") may be sung in a soothing manner on one occasion and in a playful manner on another (Trainor and Rock 1997; Trehub et al. 1997b). Moreover, mothers subtly alter their performances of the same song for infant or preschool children (Bergeson and Trehub 1998). Typically, they sing at a slightly higher pitch level for infants and enunciate the lyrics more clearly for preschoolers. Of interest, their emotive quality is relatively similar in both contexts, which may reflect comparable affect and nurturant feelings. Vocal differences that are evident may constitute age-appropriate means of recruiting and maintaining attention. Despite the subtlety of these performance differences, naive adult listeners successfully identify infant-directed versions.

Infants' Responsiveness to Infant-Directed Music

Do particular song types and styles of performance make any difference to the infant audience? On the basis of our pattern perception research over the past several years, we know that infants can perceive the relevant acoustic distinctions. Thus they are capable, in principle at least, of exhibiting attentional and affective preferences for different musical materials, as they do for contrastive speech registers (Werker and McLeod 1989; Cooper and Aslin 1990; Papoušek et al. 1990; Fernald 1991, 1993; Papoušek, Papoušek, and Symmes 1991; Pegg, Werker, and McLeod 1992; Werker, Pegg, and McLeod 1994). As noted, infants "prefer" consonant harmonizations of melodies to dissonant harmonizations (Zentner and Kagan 1996; Trainor and Heinmiller 1998). Moreover, they show enhanced attention to recordings of a woman singing to her infant relative to a comparable performance (same song and singer) with no infant audience (Trainor 1996). Men's infant-present and infant-absent songs do not generate different responsiveness except when the pitch of both versions is artificially raised to the characteristic pitch range of women (O'Neill 1997).

Different responsiveness was assessed by videotaping infants as they listened to two contrastive recordings. Adults judged for each infant which of two soundless video segments suggested greater infant enjoyment (Trehub and Kamenetsky, in preparation). Such judgments revealed that infants "enjoy" lullabies more than adult songs or even play songs. Adults also had some success in judging whether infants were listening to soothing or playful renditions of the same song (Trainor and Rock 1997). Moreover, infants showed greater enjoyment for women's singing than for men's (Trehub and Kamenetsky, in preparation).

Although it is tempting to attribute the apparent preference for women's singing over men's to women's higher-pitched voices, this interpretation may be premature. Because mothers are the predominant singers in the household (Trehub et al. 1997), familiarity with their voices could be responsible for such preferences. A preference for women's singing over higher-pitched children's singing would implicate familiarity; the reverse would implicate pitch level. In general, however, infants prefer women's singing over children's singing (Trehub and Fellegi 1997). For infants with siblings, children's singing is preferred despite the greater familiarity of women's voices. Perhaps pitch level is an important determinant of infant preferences as long as other features of the singing voice are not entirely unfamiliar.

To summarize what we know about infant song preferences, infants prefer the most ubiquitous song form, the lullaby, the typical performer, a woman, and the infant-directed performing style. If out-of-context audio recordings such as these have measurable attentional and affective consequences, and visual-gestural recordings have comparable consequences (Masataka 1996, 1998), one would expect the typical multimodal performances of caregivers to have especially pronounced effects.

Despite the fact that mothers and other caregivers have no way of knowing about the music perception skills of infants, it is remarkable that they provide musical experiences for infants that are both accessible and enjoyable. This musical agenda seems to be intuitively driven, as is the expressive agenda in infant-directed speech (Papoušek, Papoušek, and Bornstein 1985; Fernald 1992) and sign (Masataka 1992, 1996, 1998). Aside from primary benefits for infants, such musical performances may offer secondary benefits for singers. Music making in general and singing in particular generate feelings of well-being (Merriam 1964; Keil 1979) and foster identification between singer and audience (Booth 1981; Pantaleoni 1985). Moreover, the relative privacy of the caregiving context provides a safe outlet for negative or ambivalent feelings, making it possible to say what might otherwise be unsayable (Bascom 1954; Finnegan 1977; Masuyama 1989; Trehub and Trainor 1998), such as the following sung threats for noncompliant infants:

Now the owls are looking at you, looking at you;
Saying, "Any crying child, Yellow-Eyes will eat him up"
(Curtis 1921:557)

Come, wolf, bite this baby
He won't sleep
(Colombo 1983:60)

Dissanayake (1992) proposed a universal, biologically based disposition to "make things special," a "drive" to embellish valued objects, events, and states of being to set them apart from ordinary objects, events, and states. From this perspective, songs could be considered embellishments of human vocal communication or ritualized expressions of love, hope, or complaint. In all likelihood, this type of behavior, by ministering to the emotional needs of mother and infant, promotes reciprocal affectional ties (Trehub and Trainor 1998).

Consequences for Musical Structure

The proposed processing universals that were derived from infants' perceptual abilities have their counterparts in universals or near-universals of musical structure. Indeed, examination of music from different regions and historical periods reveals greater relative emphasis on global features (e.g., contour, rhythm) than on local details (e.g., specific pitch levels and durations); the prevalence of small-integer frequency ratios (2:1, 3:2, 4:3), unequal scale steps, and preferred rhythms; and existence of a special genre of music for infants (e.g., lullabies). These parallels between perceptual processing predispositions and musical features across cultures lend credence to Terhardt's (1987) contention that composers intuitively create patterns that build on universal principles of pattern perception. In their own informal way, mothers intuitively create performances that are remarkably well suited to the needs and abilities of their immature audience, who reciprocate with age-appropriate gratitude.

Archeological evidence is responsible for raising further intriguing questions about musical universals. One such example concerns an ancient Sumerian love song from approximately 1400 B.C. that was decoded from clay tablets found in the Middle East (Kilmer, Crocker, and Brown 1976). Listeners at the song's North American premiere did not hear the exotic melody that they had anticipated; what they heard, instead, sounded like an ordinary lullaby, hymn, or folk song (Forsburgh 1974; Schonberg 1974). This feeling of familiarity may have originated in the apparent diatonicity of the underlying scale. Kilmer, Crocker, and Brown (1976) remained confident about the precise pitch relations between notes of the song, if not about its pitch level. Their claim of small-integer frequency ratios in music from 1400 B.C. is consistent with a biological basis for such ratios.

Another piece of archeological evidence concerns Ivan Turk's discovery of a Neanderthal "flute" (approximately 44,000 years old), whose holes were reportedly chipped from the femur of a bear cub (Kunej and Turk, this volume). According to Fink (1997), the distance between the second and third of four visible holes (two complete holes and two partial holes) is twice that between the third and fourth holes, which would be consistent with whole steps and half steps in a diatonic scale (but see Kunej and Turk, this volume, for an alternative view). Finally, one historical tidbit that links music to infants portrays Babylonian and Assyrian lullabies from the first millennium B.C. as incantations or magical formulas for soothing babies (Farber 1990). In sum, the convergence of empirical findings from our laboratory with cross-cultural evidence and with the admittedly speculative historical record makes an intriguing case for the biological basis of at least some musical principles. Such converging perspectives offer encouragement for further empirical study of infants in the search for universals, or bottom-up principles, of musical processing and form.

Acknowledgments

Research reported in this chapter was funded by grants from the Natural Sciences and Engineering Research Council and the Social Sciences and Humanities Research Council of Canada.

References

Arom, S., Léothaud, G., and Voisin, G. (1997). Experimental ethnomusicology: An interactive approach to the study of musical scales. In I. Deliège and J. Sloboda (Eds.) *Perception and Cognition of Music* (pp. 3–30). East Sussex, UK: Psychology Press.

Bachorowski, J. A. and Owren, M. J. (1995). Vocal expression of emotion: Acoustical properties of speech are associated with emotional intensity and context. *Psychological Science* 6:219–224.

Balaban, M. T., Anderson, L. M., and Wisniewski, A. B. (1998). Lateral asymmetries in infant melody perception. *Developmental Psychology* 34:39–48.

Balzano, G. J. (1980). The group-theoretic description of 12-fold and microtonal pitch systems. *Computer Music Journal* 4:66–84.

Bartlett, J. C. and Dowling, W. J. (1980). Recognition of transposed melodies: A key-distance effect in developmental perspective. *Journal of Experimental Psychology: Human Perception and Performance* 6:501–515.

Bascom, W. R. (1954). Four functions of folklore. *Journal of American Folklore* 67:333–349.

Bergeson, T. and Trehub, S. E. (1998). Mothers' singing to infants and preschool children. Presented at the International Conference on Infant Studies, Atlanta, GA.

Bertoncini, J., Morais, J., Bijeljac-Babic, R., McAdams, S., Peretz, I., and Mehler, J. (1989). Dichotic perception and laterality in neonates. *Brain and Language* 37:591–605.

Best, C. T., Hoffman, H., and Glanville, B. B. (1982). Development of infant ear asymmetries in speech and music. *Perception and Psychophysics* 31:75–85.

Bharucha, J. J. (1987). Music cognition and perceptual facilitation: A connectionist framework. *Music Perception* 5:1–30.

Bharucha, J. J. and Stoeckig, K. (1986). Reaction time and musical expectancy: Priming of chords. *Journal of Experimental Psychology: Human Perception and Performance* 12:403–410.

Bharucha, J. J. and Stoeckig, K. (1987). Priming of chords: Spreading activation or overlapping frequency spectra? *Perception and Psychophysics* 41:519–524.

Blacking, J. (1992). The biology of music-making. In H. Myers (Ed.) *Ethnomusicology: An Introduction* (pp. 301–314). New York: Norton.

Boomsliter, P. and Creel, W. (1961). The long pattern hypothesis in harmony and hearing. *Journal of Music Theory* 5:2–31.

Booth, M. W. (1981). *The Experience of Songs*. New Haven, CT: Yale University Press.

Brakeley, T. C. (1950). Lullaby. In M. Leach and J. Fried (Eds.) *Standard Dictionary of Folklore, Mythology, and Legend* (pp. 653–654). New York: Funk and Wagnalls.

Bregman, A. S. (1990). *Auditory Scene Analysis*. Cambridge: MIT Press.

Brown, M. J. E. (1980). Lullaby. In S. Sadie (Ed.) *The New Grove Dictionary of Music and Musicians* (pp. 313–314). London: Macmillan.

Brown, H. (1988). The interplay of set content and temporal context in a functional theory of tonality perception. *Music Perception* 5:219–250.

Butler, D. (1989). Describing the perception of tonality in music: A critique of the tonal hierarchy theory and proposal for a theory of intervallic rivalry. *Music Perception* 6:219–242.

Cass-Beggs, B. and Cass-Beggs, M. (1969). *Folk Lullabies*. New York: Oak Publications.

Chang, H. W. and Trehub, S. E. (1977). Auditory processing of relational information by young infants. *Journal of Experimental Child Psychology* 24:324–331.

Cohen, A. J., Thorpe, L. A., and Trehub, S. E. (1987). Infants' perception of musical relations in short transposed tone sequences. *Canadian Journal of Psychology* 41:33–47.

Colombo, J. R. (1983). *Songs of the Indians*, Vol. 2. Ottawa: Oberon Press.

Cooper, R. P. (1993). The effect of prosody on young infants' speech perception. In C. Rovee-Collier and L. P. Lipsitt (Eds.) *Advances in Infancy Research*, Vol. 8 (pp. 137–167). Norwood, NJ: Ablex.

Cooper, R. P. (1997). An ecological approach to infants' perception of intonation contours as meaningful aspects of speech. In C. Dent-Read and P. Zukow-Goldring (Eds.) *Evolving Explanations of Development: Ecological Approaches to Organism-Environment Systems* (pp. 55–85). Washington, DC: American Psychological Association.

Cooper, R. P. and Aslin, R. N. (1990). Preference for infant-directed speech in the first month after birth. *Child Development* 61:1584–1595.

Crowder, R. G., Reznick, J. S., and Rosenkrantz, S. L. (1991). Perception of the major/minor distinction. V: Preferences among infants. *Bulletin of the Psychonomic Society* 29:187–188.

Cuddy, L. L. and Badertscher, B. (1987). Recovery of the tonal hierarchy: Some comparisons across age and levels of musical experience. *Perception and Psychophysics* 41:609–620.

Cuddy, L. L., Cohen, A. J., and Mewhort, D. J. K. (1981). Perception of structure in short melodic sequences. *Journal of Experimental Psychology: Human Perception and Performance* 7:869–883.

Curtis, N. (1921). American Indian cradle songs. *Musical Quarterly* 1:549–558.

D'Amato, M. R. (1988). A search for tonal pattern perception in cebus monkeys: Why monkeys can't hum a tune. *Music Perception* 5:453–480.

Davitz, J. R. (1964)..Personality, perception, and cognitive correlates of emotional sensitivity. In J. R. Davitz (Ed.) *The Communication of Emotional Meaning* (pp. 57–68). New York: McGraw-Hill.

Demany, L. (1982). Auditory stream segregation in infancy. *Infant Behavior and Development* 5:261–276.

Dissanayake, E. (1992). Homo aestheticus: *Where Art Comes from and Why*. New York: Free Press.

Dowling, W. J. (1994). Melodic contour in hearing and remembering melodies. In R. Aiello and J. A. Sloboda (Eds.) *Musical Perceptions* (pp. 173–190). New York: Oxford University press.

Dowling, W. J. and Harwood, D. L. (1986). *Music Cognition*. Orlando, FL: Academic Press.

Eimas, P. D. and Miller, J. L. (1980). Contextual effects in infant speech perception. *Science* 209:1140–1141.

Ekman, P., Friesen, N. V., and Scherer, K. R. (1976). Body movement and voice pitch in deceptive interaction. *Semiotica* 16:23–27.

Erting, C. J., Prezioso, C., and O'Grandy Hynes, M. (1990). The interactional context of deaf mother-infant communication. In V. Volterra and C. J. Erting (Eds.) *From Gesture to Language in Hearing and Deaf Children* (pp. 97–106). Berlin: Springer-Verlag.

Fagot, B. I. and Leinbach, M. D. (1987). Socialization of sex roles within the family. In D. B. Carter (Ed.) *Current Conceptions of Sex Roles and Sex Typing: Theory and Research* (pp. 89–100). New York: Praeger.

Farber, W. (1990). Magic at the cradle: Babylonian and Assyrian lullabies. *Anthropos* 85:139–148.

Fernald, A. (1985). Four-month-old infants prefer to listen to motherese. *Infant Behavior and Development* 8:181–195.

Fernald, A. (1989). Intonation and communicative intent in mothers' speech to infants: Is the melody the message? *Child Development* 60:1497–1510.

Fernald, A. (1991). Prosody in speech to children: Prelinguistic and linguistic functions. *Annals of Child Development* 8:43–80.

Fernald, A. (1992). Human maternal vocalizations to infants as biologically relevant signals: An evolutionary perspective. In J. H. Barkow, L. Cosmides, and J. Tooby (Eds.) *The Adapted Mind: Evolutionary Psychology and the Generation of Culture* (pp. 391–428). Oxford: Oxford University Press.

Fernald, A. (1993). Approval and disapproval: Infant responsiveness to vocal affect in familiar and unfamiliar languages. *Child Development* 64:657–674.

Fernald, A., Taeschner, T., Dunn, J., Papoušek, M., de Boysson-Bardies, B., and Fukui, I. (1989). A cross-language study of prosodic modifications in mothers' and fathers' speech to preverbal infants. *Journal of Child Language* 16:477–501.

Fink, B. (1997). Neanderthal flute. http://www.webster.sk.ca/greenwich/fl-compl.htm.

Finnegan, R. H. (1977). *Oral Poetry: Its Nature, Significance, and Social Context*. Cambridge, UK: Cambridge University Press.

Fonagy, I. (1981). Emotions, voice, and music. *Research Aspects on Singing* 33:51–79.

Fonagy, I. and Magdics, K. (1963). Emotional patterns in intonation and music. *Zeitschrift für Phonetik* 16:293–326.

Fosburgh, L. (1974, March 6). World's oldest song reported deciphered: Near-East origin. *New York Times*, pp. 1, 18.

Frick, R. W. (1985). Communicating emotion: The role of prosodic features. *Psychological Bulletin* 97:412–429.

Grieser, D. L. and Kuhl, P. K. (1988). Maternal speech to infants in a tonal language: Support for universal prosodic features in motherese. *Developmental Psychology* 24:14–20.

Handel, S. (1989). *Listening: An Introduction to the Perception of Auditory Events*. Cambridge: MIT Press.

Hulse, S. H., Bernard, D. J., and Braaten, R. F. (1995). Auditory discrimination of chord-based spectral structures by European starlings (*Sturnus vulgaris*). *Journal of Experimental Psychology: General* 124:409–423.

Hulse, S. H. and Page, S. C. (1988). Toward a comparative psychology of music perception. *Music Perception* 5:427–452.

Jones, M. R. (1982). Music as a stimulus for psychological motion. II: An expectancy model. *Psychomusicology* 2:1–13.

Jordan, D. S. and Shepard, R. N. (1987). Tonal schemas: Evidence obtained by probing distorted scales. *Perception and Psychophysics* 41:489–504.

Jusczyk, P. W. and Krumhansl, C. L. (1993). Pitch and rhythmic patterns affecting infants' sensitivity to musical phrase structure. *Journal of Experimental Psychology: Human Perception and Performance* 19:1–14.

Juslin, P. N. (1997). Perceived emotional expression in synthesized performances of a short melody: Capturing the listener's judgment policy. *Musicae Scientiae* 1:225–256.

Keil, C. (1979). *Tiv Song*. Chicago: University of Chicago Press.

Kennedy, M. (1994). *The Oxford Dictionary of Music*, 2nd ed. Oxford: Oxford University Press.

Kilmer, A. D., Crocker, R. L., and Brown, R. R. (1976). *Sounds from Silence: Recent Discoveries in Ancient Near Eastern Music*. Berkeley, CA: Bit Enki.

Kolinski, M. (1967). Recent trends in ethnomusicology. *Ethnomusicology* 11:1–24.

Krauss, R. M., Curran, N. M., and Ferleger, N. (1983). Expressive conventions and the cross-cultural expression of emotion. *Basic and Applied Social Psychology* 4:295–305.

Krumhansl, C. L. (1990). *Cognitive Foundations of Musical Pitch*. New York: Oxford University Press.

Krumhansl, C. L. and Jusczyk, P. W. (1990). Infants' perception of phrase structure in music. *Psychological Science* 1:70–73.

Krumhansl, C. L. and Keil, F. C. (1982). Acquisition of the hierarchy of tonal functions in music. *Memory and Cognition* 10:243–251.

Krumhansl, C. L. and Kessler, E. J. (1982). Tracing the dynamic changes in perceived tonal organization in a spatial representation of musical keys. *Psychological Review* 89:334–368.

Kuhl, P. K. (1979). Speech perception in early infancy: Perceptual constancy for spectrally dissimilar vowel categories. *Journal of the Acoustical Society of America* 66:1668–1679.

Laver, J. (1980). *The Phonetic Description of Voice Quality*. Cambridge, UK: Cambridge University Press.

Lynch, M. P. and Eilers, R. E. (1991). Children's perception of native and non-native musical scales. *Music Perception* 9:121–132.

Lynch, M. P., Eilers, R. E., Oller, D. K., Urbano, R. C., and Wilson, P. (1991). Influences of acculturation and musical sophistication on perception of musical interval patterns. *Journal of Experimental Psychology: Human Perception and Performance* 17:967–975.

Magdics, K. (1963). From the melody of speech to the melody of music. *Studia Musicologica* 4:325–346.

Mandel, D. R., Jusczyk, P. W., and Kemler Nelson, D. G. (1994). Does sentential prosody help infants organize and remember speech information? *Cognition* 53:155–180.

Marler, P. (1990). Innate learning preferences: Signals for communication. *Developmental Psychobiology* 23:557–568.

Masataka, N. (1992). Motherese in a signed language. *Infant Behavior and Development* 15:453–460.

Masataka, N. (1996). Perception of motherese in a signed language by 6-month-old deaf infants. *Developmental Psychology* 32:874–879.

Masataka, N. (1998). Perception of motherese in Japanese sign language by 6-month-old hearing infants. *Developmental Psychology* 34:241–246.

Masuyama, E. E. (1989). Desire and discontent in Japanese lullabies. *Western Folklore* 48:169–177.

Merriam, A. P. (1964). *The Anthropology of Music*. Evanston, IL: Northwestern University Press.

Meyer, L. B. (1956). *Emotion and Meaning in Music*. Chicago: University of Chicago Press.

Meyer, L. B. (1994). *Music, the Arts and Ideas: Patterns and Predictions in Twentieth-century Culture*. Chicago: University of Chicago Press.

Meyers-Moro, P. (1993). *The Music and Musicians in Contemporary Bangkok*. Berkeley, CA: Centers for South and Southeast Asia Studies.

Miller, J. L. and Eimas, P. D. (1983). Studies on the categorization of speech by infants. *Cognition* 13:135–165.

Molfese, D. L. and Molfese, V. J. (1979). Hemisphere and stimulus differences as reflected in the cortical responses of newborn infants to speech stimuli. *Developmental Psychology* 15:505–511.

Morgan, S. P., Lyle, D. N., and Condran, G. A. (1988). Sons, daughters, and the risk of marital disruption. *American Journal of Sociology* 94:110–129.

Morrongiello, B. A. and Roes, C. (1990). Developmental changes in children's perception of musical sequences: Effects of musical training. *Developmental Psychology* 26:814–820.

Morton, D. (1976). *The Traditional Music of Thailand*. Los Angeles: University of California Press.

Nettl, B. (1983). *The Study of Ethnomusicology: Twenty-Nine Issues and Concepts*. Urbana: University of Illinois Press.

Ohala, J. J. (1984). An ethological perspective on common cross-language utilization of F_0 of voice. *Phonetica* 41:1–16.

O'Neill, C. (1997). Fathers' infant-directed singing. Unpublished master's thesis. McMaster University, Hamilton, Canada.

Oura, Y. and Hatano, G. (1988). Memory of melodies among subjects differing in age and experience in music. *Psychology of Music* 16:91–109.

Pantaleoni, H. (1985). *On the Nature of Music*. Oneonta, NY: Welkin Books.

Papoušek, M., Bornstein, M. H., Nuzzo, C., Papoušek, H., and Symmes, D. (1990). Infant responses to prototypical melodic contours in parental speech. *Infant Behavior and Development* 13:539–545.

Papoušek, M., Papoušek, H., and Bornstein, M. H. (1985). The naturalistic vocal environment of young infants: On the significance of homogeneity and variability in parental speech. In T. M. Field and N. A. Fox (Eds.) *Social Perception in Infants* (pp. 269–297). Norwood, NJ: Ablex.

Papoušek, M., Papoušek, H., and Symmes, D. (1991). The meanings of melodies in motherese in tone and stress languages. *Infant Behavior and Development* 14:415–440.

Patterson, R. D. (1986). Spiral detection of periodicity and the spiral form of musical scales. *Psychology of Music* 14:44–61.

Pegg, J. E., Werker, J. F., and McLeod, P. J. (1992). Preference for infant-directed over adult-directed speech: Evidence from 7-week-old infants. *Infant Behavior and Development* 15:325–345.

Peretz, I. (1987). Shifting ear-asymmetry in melody comparison through transposition. *Cortex* 23:317–323.

Peretz, I. and Babaï, M. (1992). The role of contour and intervals in the recognition of melody parts: Evidence from cerebral asymmetries in musicians. *Neuropsychologia* 30:277–292.

Peretz, I. and Morais, J. (1980). Modes of processing melodies and ear-asymmetry in non-musicians. *Neuropsychologia* 30:277–292.

Piston, W. (1969). *Harmony*. New York: Norton.

Plomp, R. and Levelt, W. J. M. (1965). Tonal consonance and critical bandwidth. *Journal of the Acoustical Society of America* 38:548–560.

Previc, F. H. (1991). A general theory concerning the prenatal origins of cerebral lateralization in humans. *Psychological Review* 98:299–334.

Roederer, J. G. (1979). *Introduction to the Physics and Psychophysics of Music*, 2nd ed. New York: Springer-Verlag.

Rubin, D. C. (1995). *Memory in Oral Traditions: The Cognitive Psychology of Epic, Ballads, and Counting-Out Rhymes*. New York: Oxford University Press.

Sachs, C. (1943). *The Rise of Music in the Ancient World: East and West*. New York: Norton.

Schellenberg, E. G. and Trainor, L. J. (1996). Sensory consonance and the perceptual similarity of complex-tone harmonic intervals: Tests of adult and infant listeners. *Journal of the Acoustical Society of America* 100:3321–3328.

Schellenberg, E. G. and Trehub, S. E. (1994a). Frequency ratios and the discrimination of pure tone sequences. *Perception and Psychophysics* 56:472–478.

Schellenberg, E. G. and Trehub, S. E. (1994b). Frequency ratios and the perception of tone patterns. *Psychonomic Bulletin and Review* 1:191–201.

Schellenberg, E. G. and Trehub, S. E. (1996a). Children's discrimination of melodic intervals. *Developmental Psychology* 32:1039–1050.

Schellenberg, E. G. and Trehub, S. E. (1996b). Natural musical intervals: Evidence from infant listeners. *Psychological Science* 7:272–277.

Scherer, K. R. (1986). Vocal affect expression: A review and a model for future research. *Psychological Bulletin* 99:143–165.

Schonberg, H. C. (1974, March 6). World's oldest song reported deciphered: Out of prehistory. *New York Times*, pp. 1, 18.

Serafine, M. L. (1983). Cognition in music. *Cognition* 14:119–183.

Shepard, R. N. (1982). Structural representations of musical pitch. In D. Deutsch (Ed.) *The Psychology of Music* (pp. 343–390). New York: Academic Press.

Shepard, R. N. and Jordan, D. C. (1984). Auditory illusions demonstrating that tones are assimilated to an internalized scale. *Science* 226:1333–1334.

Sloboda, J. A. (1985). *The Musical Mind: The Cognitive Psychology of Music*. Oxford: Clarendon Press.

Sundberg, J. (1991). *The Science of Musical Sounds*. San Diego, CA: Academic Press.

Tartter, V. C. and Braun, D. (1994). Hearing smiles and frowns in normal and whisper registers. *Journal of the Acoustical Society of America* 96:2101–2107.

Terhardt, E. (1987). Gestalt principles and music perception. In W. A. Yost and C. S. Watson (Eds.) *Auditory Processing of Complex Sounds* (pp. 157–166). Hillsdale, NJ: Erlbaum.

Thorpe, L. A. and Trehub, S. E. (1989). Duration illusion and auditory grouping in infancy. *Developmental Psychology* 25:122–127.

Thorpe, L. A., Trehub, S. E., Morrongiello, B. A., and Bull, D. (1988). Perceptual grouping by infants and preschool children. *Developmental Psychology* 24:484–491.

Trainor, L. J. (1996). Infant preferences for infant-directed versus non-infant-directed play songs and lullabies. *Infant Behavior and Development* 19:83–92.

Trainor, L. J. (1997). The effect of frequency ratio on infants' and adults' discrimination of simultaneous intervals. *Journal of Experimental Psychology: Human Perception and Performance* 23:1427–1438.

Trainor, L. J., Clark, E. D., Huntley, A., and Adams, B. (1997). The acoustic basis for infant-directed singing. *Infant Behavior and Development* 20:383–396.

Trainor, L. J. and Heinmiller, B. M. (1998). The development of evaluative responses to music: Infants prefer to listen to consonance over dissonance. *Infant Behavior and Development* 21:77–88.

Trainor, L. J. and Rock, A. M. L. (1997). Distinctive messages in infant-directed lullabies and play songs. Presented at the biennial meeting of the Society for Research in Child Development, Washington, DC.

Trainor, L. J. and Trehub, S. E. (1994). Key membership and implied harmony in Western tonal music: Developmental perspectives. *Perception and Psychophysics* 56:125–132.

Trehub, S. E. (1990). The perception of musical patterns by human infants: The provision of similar patterns by their parents. In M. A. Berkley and W. C. Stebbins (Eds.) *Comparative Perception*, Vol. 1: *Basic Mechanisms* (pp. 429–459). New York: Wiley.

Trehub, S. E., Bull, D., and Thorpe, L. A. (1984). Infants' perception of melodies: The role of melodic contour. *Child Development* 55:821–830.

Trehub, S. E., Cohen, A. J., Thorpe, L. A., and Morrongiello, B. A. (1986). Development of the perception of musical relations: Semitone and diatonic structure. *Journal of Experimental Psychology: Human Perception and Performance* 12:295–301.

Trehub, S. E., Endman, M., and Thorpe, L. A. (1990). Infants' perception of timbre: Classification of complex tones by spectral structure. *Journal of Experimental Child Psychology* 49:300–313.

Trehub, S. E. and Fellegi, K. (1997). Infants' preferences for women's and children's songs. Presented at the biennial meeting of the Society for Research in Child Development, Washington, DC.

Trehub, S. E., Hill, D. S., and Kamenetsky, S. B. (1997a). Infants' perception of melodies with "good" or "bad" rhythms. Presented at the biennial meeting of the Society for Research in Child Development, Washington, DC.

Trehub, S. E., Hill, D. H., and Kamenetsky, S. B. (1997b). Parents' sung performances for infants. *Canadian Journal of Experimental Psychology* 51:36–47.

Trehub, S. E. and Kamenetsky, S. B. (In preparation). Infant musical preferences.

Trehub, S. E. and Schellenberg, E. G. (1995). Music: Its relevance to infants. In R. Vasta (Ed.) *Annals of Child Development*, Vol. 11 (pp. 1–24). New York: Kingsley.

Trehub, S., Schellenberg, E., and Hill, D. (1997). The origins of music perception and cognition: A developmental perspective. In I. Deliège and J. Sloboda (Eds.) *Perception and Cognition of Music* (pp. 103–128). East Sussex, UK: Psychology Press.

Trehub, S. E., Schellenberg, E. G., and Kamenetsky, S. B. (in press). Infants' and adults' perception of scale structure. *Journal of Experimental Psychology: Human Perception and Performance*.

Trehub, S. E. and Thorpe, L. A. (1989). Infants' perception of rhythm. Categorization of auditory sequences by temporal structure. *Canadian Journal of Psychology* 43:217–229.

Trehub, S. E., Thorpe, L. A., and Morrongiello, B. A. (1985). Infants' perception of melodies: Changes in a single tone. *Infant Behavior and Development* 8:213–223.

Trehub, S. E., Thorpe, L. A., and Morrongiello, B. A. (1987). Organizational processes in infants' perception of auditory patterns. *Child Development* 58:741–749.

Trehub, S. E., Thorpe, L. A., and Trainor, L. J. (1990). Infants' perception of *good* and *bad* melodies. *Psychomusicology* 9:5–15.

Trehub, S. E. and Trainor, L. J. (1993). Listening strategies in infancy: The roots of music and language development. In S. McAdams and E. Bigand (Eds.) *Thinking in Sound: The Cognitive Psychology of Human Audition* (pp. 278–327). London: Oxford University Press.

Trehub, S. E. and Trainor, L. J. (1998). Singing to infants: Lullabies and play songs. In C. Rovee-Collier and L. Lipsitt (Eds.) *Advances in Infancy Research* (pp. 43–77). Norwood, NJ: Ablex.

Trehub, S. E., Trainor, L. J., and Unyk, A. M. (1993). Music and speech processing in the first year of life. In H. W. Reese (Ed.) *Advances in Child Development and Behavior*, Vol. 24 (pp. 1–35). New York: Academic Press.

Trehub, S. E., Unyk, A. M., and Henderson, J. L. (1994). Children's songs to infant siblings: Parallels with speech. *Journal of Child Language* 21:735–744.

Trehub, S. E., Unyk, A. M., Kamenetsky, S. B., Hill, D. S., Trainor, L. J., Henderson, J. L., and Saraza M. (1997). Mothers' and fathers' singing to infants. *Developmental Psychology* 33:500–507.

Trehub, S. E., Unyk, A. M., and Trainor, L. J. (1993a). Adults identify infant-directed music across cultures. *Infant Behavior and Development* 16:193–211.

Trehub, S. E., Unyk, A. M., and Trainor, L. J. (1993b). Maternal singing in cross-cultural perspective. *Infant Behavior and Development* 16:285–295.

Unyk, A. M., Trehub, S. E., Trainor, L. J., and Schellenberg, E. G. (1992). Lullabies and simplicity: A cross-cultural perspective. *Psychology of Music* 20:15–28.

Werker, J. F. and McLeod, P. J. (1989). Infant preference for both male and female infant-directed talk: A developmental study of attentional and affective responsiveness. *Canadian Journal of Psychology* 43:230–246.

Werker, J. F., Pegg, J. E., and McLeod, P. J. (1994). A cross-language investigation of infant preference for infant-directed communication. *Infant Behavior and Development* 17:321–331.

Witelson, S. F. and Pallie, W. (1973). Left hemisphere specialization for language in the newborn: Neuroanatomical evidence of asymmetry. *Brain* 96:641–646.

Zentner, M. R. and Kagan, J. (1996). Perception of music by infants. *Nature* 383:29.

24 The Question of Innate Competencies in Musical Communication

Michel Imberty

Abstract

In this chapter I examine the implications of a certain number of theories in the domains of musical analysis and music cognition. The question of innate musical competencies is addressed both in gestalt hypotheses taken up in Lerdahl and Jackendoff's generative theory of tonal music and in a certain number of biological models. A dynamic theory of music perception has as its psychological basis the development of elementary processes of communication, such as those that appear in the infant in its social environment. Repetition, variation, and rhythm in both games and speech, and cognitive-affective exchange, are at the origin of temporal experiences that predispose human beings toward comprehension and creation of musical activities. These structures and elementary processes of communication can be said to be generated by competencies of the human species that prepare one as much for social life as for an artistic and musical life.

Since the early 1990s cognitivism has invaded the field of the humanities. Its objective is to present a coherent general theory of the totality of human activities through more or less domain-specific competence systems using a common set of functional rules. These competences, which are very specific in their content but together form a coherent set, are innate.

In this approach it is easy to recognize the basic ideas of Chomsky, who in 1957 proposed the first formulation of his famous generative grammar. Since then, the Chomskian approach has largely penetrated all domains of psychology, first the field of psycholinguistics, then the field of cognitive psychology, and today the field of music psychology. The most recent developments have implications for our concept of music as well as for our concept of the functioning of the human brain in general. A few consequences of the cognitivist approach might well lead to a dead end in our understanding of music.

Gestaltism

When we talk about the analogy between language and music, we think naturally of the magnificent work of Lerdahl and Jackendoff (1983) and their generative theory of tonal music (GTTM). This work has renewed our approach to musical analysis and has provided psychologists with many new hypotheses. In particular, it has contributed to a more general movement in psychology, namely, a return to the ideas and the experimental paradigms of gestalt theory. In fact, the first work on the properties of forms, in 1890, was written by a certain von Ehrenfels regarding melody ("the whole is greater than the sum of its parts," form is transposable, etc.).

Since Lerdahl and Jackendoff's work, many psychologists have tried experimentally to validate certain "rules" put forward in the GTTM, and in particular the famous rules of grouping structures. A pioneering effort in this regard is Irène Deliège's beautiful work (see below). The connection between the GTTM and gestalt theory is not without importance when one realizes that the perspective of the GTTM is based on at least three postulates that lie at the heart of the first major theory of scientific psychology, proposed by Köhler, Gottschaldt, Guillaume, and Lewin (see, for example, Köhler, 1929). These three postulates have important consequences for any psychology that is inspired by them and especially our conception of the human being.

1. Forms are innate and their rules function from birth.

2. Forms are universal, independent of culture and milieu.

3. Forms are subject to a general principle of isomorphism such that rules of physical form, rules of physiological form, rules of psychological form, and rules of sociological form correspond with each other.

However, as applied to cognitive theories of language and music, the postulates take the following form.

First, specific capacities, or competences, for language on the one hand and for music on the other are describable in terms of grammars; that is, systems capable of generating linguistic or musical sequences independent of learning. In terms of our concerns, musical competences constitute a set of aptitudes or innate capacities the proper functioning of which depends very little on particular conditions of concrete training during childhood and adulthood. Is this a return to the psychology of the musical gift?

Second, there are musical and linguistic universals that characterize human thought. They are expressed by basic rules that constitute a core grammar common to all languages and to all musical systems. These basic rules produce the sequence types or forms that we find everywhere in all cultures. Regarding music, analysis of diverse musical grammars should gradually allow better understanding of what these universal elementary forms are, whose structures are attributable to psychological systems that produce them, and that are presumably common to all human beings.

Finally, these grammatical systems, to the extent that they are formalizations of psychological competencies, should also have their equivalent in the internal functioning of the brain, which means that the competencies correspond to defined and independent neuronal systems. In music, diverse hypotheses have been developed, such as those concerning modular neural systems.

Universality and Innateness

One of the strongest hypotheses, and thus one of the most constraining for generative theories whether in linguistics or musicology, is that of innateness of competencies. This hypothesis may easily lose its meaning as a function of the way it is formulated. One argument in favor of innateness is that language, like music, is a specifically human activity that is not found in the animal world. Having said this we have said nothing about the degree of specification of the corresponding competencies. In other words, to what degree of generality can we describe universal competencies? In the field of language, it has been possible, to a certain extent, to show that, in almost all the studied cases, deep structures rely on identical production rules and functions. But until today, the only really serious attempt in music to define the general structures produced by innate capacities is the theory proposed by Lerdahl and Jackendoff (1983). As this attempt is presented as a theory of tonal music, it is scarcely possible to say with precision what its limitations are. It is quite probable that what is described in the GTTM as grouping structures can be generalized beyond Western tonal music. But we cannot say whether these phenomena, in their generality, refer to an innate cognitive competence since, contrary to the case of language, we cannot falsify the examples engendered by the model in the same consistent and reliable way we do for language. For example, how can we define a "good" melodic sequence, or more precisely, how can we falsify it? Surface modifications to a melody will not lead a subject to judge the new sequence melodic versus not melodic (in the way that a native speaker will judge a sentence in his language as being grammatical or not grammatical), but only more or less melodic, more or less surprising, more or less well organized. If we could define musical competence in the same way as linguistic competence, the subject would be able to say, when listening to an auditory sequence, it is music or it is not music. If such a judgment can be made, it is only with reference to a cultural and historically determined context, and not in reference to universally musical structures or to musical thought in general.

Here we touch on a profound difference between language and music: musical grammars, whether they be those of Lerdahl and Jackendoff or those of Schenker's (1935) theory of *Ursatz* that inspired them, proceed from the surface to a core through successive reductions that still conserve something like a skeleton of the sentence, its simplest tonal expression, that remains correct in the sense of its musical meaning. This reduced sequence only seems banal, not interesting aesthetically (see the numerous examples in Lerdahl and Jackendoff 1983). On the contrary, successive rewritings in Chomskian grammar reach basic structures that are not sentences and that imply sentence-production procedures on the surface.

Two difficulties appear to define the scope of innateness in the case of musical competence: musical competence seems to be reducible to the capacity to produce variations on prototypical schemas without possible limitations or recurrences; and the innateness of musical competence is knowable only through induction in terms of the universality of these prototypical schemas, thus suggesting that production processes are not as primary as they are in language where the sentence is generated according to syntagmatic functions. Here we find the third postulate of gestalt theory, the one that, under a different form, was expressed by Rameau: "Music is natural to us; we owe the sentiment that it makes us feel to pure instinct; this same instinct acts in us with many other objects which can very well be related to music" (1754:1). We thus see that the problems of innateness and universality are closely related in psychological theories of music more than in language theories, since the definition of musical competence is itself much more blurred.

Let us try to specify this point. One of the essential epistemological postulates of cognitive theory today is that we can study human behavior only by distinguishing carefully between subject variables and object variables, the first acting on the second, or actually, entirely determining the second. This position is contrary not only to classical behaviorism but to the whole idea of active interaction between subject and physical or social environment. In classical behaviorism, the subject's response to a stimulus is a reaction determined by the nature of stimulus; in post-Chomskian cognitivism, the response is not a reaction to the stimulus, but the triggering of an adapted program, a response to an internal perturbation of a competence system that is provoked by information in a format that does not conform to the system. The program's effect is to render the object consistent with its own characteristics and to modify atypical variables: thus, it is not the traits of the object that provoke the subject's response, but rather the mere fact that it is not consistent with the competence system. Creation of new adapted programs is one fundamental characteristic of human competence systems.

This theoretical necessity, formalized through artificial intelligence models, is assumed by the GTTM, even if the authors sometimes deny it. But it is so only because the GTTM models the Western classical tonal music system, perhaps the only system that allows definition of a grammar in terms of functions beyond grouping structures. This means that the GTTM gives the illusion that musical competence operates in the same way as all other human cognitive competencies; that is, it is of the same nature, being universal and biologically determined. The fact is

that today many specialists of cognitive science speak of tonal music—
but they never say "tonal"—as a privileged field for the study of the functions of the human brain. After mathematics and language, music
becomes the object of their preference.

Neurophysiological Cognitivism

All generative theories of human competence have an implicit reasoning that could become circular through a drift of psychologism or cognitivism. Concerning the GTTM, the virtual circle is as follows: the
existence of an innate musical competence is postulated that allows the
listener to understand an infinite number of musical sentences. This competence is construed in terms of a model based on the tonal system with
its hierarchical grouping structure. A listener's understanding of music is
interpreted in these terms, and corresponding mental operations are
attributed to the listener that are taken to be the product of the competence we started out with. Nothing is easier to prove than the psychological reality of this tonal grammar: it is enough to apply experimental
paradigms well established in psycholinguistics to tonal music, which is
what most research in vogue today does.

This vicious cognitive circle can be broken in only two ways: either
prove not only the psychological reality of the GTTM (i.e., its reduction
procedures) but the reality and the specificity of neural circuits corresponding to this competence; or validate certain properties in the comprehension of atonal music. In both cases, the task is difficult and the
approach is unclear.

The Question of Psychological Reality

The first alternative is in the logic of gestalt theory itself, since it consists
of looking for certain physiological isomorphisms, or rather certain
physiological equivalences, in psychological systems of specialized competencies. It helps to examine briefly one of these models, since it
demonstrates the epistemological risks involved.

According to the modularity model, the human cognitive system is
composed of physically separate subsystems, each one corresponding to
a specific body of knowledge or procedures. These subsystems are
autonomous and can be modified without important changes to the total
system. Such a modular system is more economical and efficient than
nonmodular, interdependent systems, and corresponds quite well to the
general hypothesis of cognitivism; that is, the existence of specific, biologically determined, relatively independent competencies. In domains
of both pathology and human cognition we find confirmation of the

modularity hypothesis. Fodor (1983) elaborated the diverse traits of such a system, of which the most important are that modules are specific to a field of activity and are related to specific, identifiable neuronal systems that can be affected in a specific manner by cerebral lesions; modules have their own processing capacity and their own memory resources, being independent of other modules and of more general processes; the action or operation of a module is rapid, automatic, and functional in accordance with a fixed neuronal architecture (circuit); and integration of fixed knowledge in the modules is ensured by central processes acting on the output of the modules, but not on the internal processes, which stay inaccessible.

The existence of modular systems for perception and music comprehension was also proposed by Gardner (1983) and Jackendoff (1987). But according to Fodor, distinct and specific modular mechanisms exist for processing pitch (melody) and rhythm (temporal organization). However, reality is much more complex. According to Peretz and Morais (1989), everything depends on the level of processing of musical information. At the earliest levels, pitch and duration are distinct; at later levels, they depend on central coordinating mechanisms. Doubt is thus cast on the relevance of the modular hypothesis once we reach higher levels of musical processing since in most musical systems pitch and duration are interdependent (unless we suppose that tonality in general, i.e., the existence of a determined scale of sounds and fixed intervals, can define itself as a modular system).

It is here that we enter the domain of conjectures and metaphorical analogies concerning language to which cognitivism can lead: this hypothesis of tonality as a modular system was strongly defended through work on what Francès (1958) called *l'intégration scalaire* of the perception of sound. This work tends to show that both nonmusicians and musicians perceive sounds in relation to an internal and implicit reference, which is none other than the scale of the musical system to which they belong. Apparently, such encoding has all the properties of a modular system: automatization of tonal processing independent of education or intervention; early appearance in child development; and dissociability of tonal perception from other types of perception in cases of cerebral damage (i.e., certain lesions touch only melodic perception, leaving verbal function intact, or vice versa).

In reality, modular function as described by Fodor pertains only to some aspects of music, and these are probably the least developed and the least musical, such as isolated sounds or sequences of a few sounds. Furthermore, hemispheric specialization, a concept through which modular models have been developed, is probably less evident for music than for speech. In 1974 Bever and Chiarello showed that musicians and nonmusicians process melodies in opposite hemispheres. The idea that perception and comprehension of music are based on general mechanisms and are not related to delimited neuronal circuits thus remains plausible as soon as we consider the level of the musical phrase, and even more, that of the whole musical piece. But this largely destroys the idea of musical competence in the sense of generative theories inspired by Chomsky, at least when construed as modular grammars. Actually, Lerdahl and Jackendoff presented their GTTM partly as a modular system, at least as a possible model of a system that could be implemented in neural terms. Nothing allows us to say so, not only because we lack knowledge of the existence of such circuits in the human brain, but also because the model is restricted to tonal music, and we are capable of understanding and appreciating other types of music.

The Question of Atonal Music

This brings us to the second direction in which we can try to break the epistemological circle that closes in on the cognitive psychology of music: to try to validate certain properties of the GTTM concerning atonal music. I am struck by the fact that young researchers in cognitive psychology of music still shy away from addressing problems related to atonal music. More specifically, I think a certain number of problems related to the perception and memory of music are formulated in a restrictive and exclusive manner, since the models used do not permit formalizations other than those that apply to tonal music. I will not develop here what I described elsewhere in detail (Imberty 1987, 1991a, b, 1993a, b). Lerdahl himself attempted this in 1989, showing the role that contextual salience could have in the organization of atonal music as a substitute for prolongation structures in tonal music. This can be presented in the following manner. The whole of the GTTM is based on the hypothesis of a certain equivalence between the musical piece's structure as it is described and the psychological need for hierarchical organization in perception and memory. This presents a problem for atonal music. More particularly, this difficulty concerns the structure of prolongational reductions.

In fact, these are clearly defined only because the GTTM is based on the definition of stability conditions of certain groups in relation to others, both melodically and harmonically. First, alternations between strong and weak tonal events are organized in a hierarchy that makes harmonically, melodically, or rhythmically strong events stable. These events determine the possibilities for prolongation by their functional predominance in the tonal system. But in fact this condition implies another condition: interaction of temporal webs (rhythmic-melodic organizations of reduction structures based on these alternations) and alternations of tensions and relaxations; that is, interaction of the cognitive organization of pitch and duration groupings on the one hand, and of phrases of stability and instability on the other, of which the succession and ordering are of both cognitive and affective nature. In fact, two essential notions define reductions of temporal webs in the GTTM: structural beginning and structural conclusion (or cadence) articulate the structure of groupings at the phrase level. Lerdahl and Jackendoff indicated that the movement of a phrase can be defined as a path between these two structural points, which themselves are stable events. Concerning these prolongational reductions, the experience of stability consists of a succession of tension and relaxation events that give the listener the feeling of a conclusion; that is, of a psychic release, a resolution of the tension that preceded it. Interaction between the two levels of organization in tonal music is thus psychologically clear, and structural stability coincides with dynamic and emotional stability.

A final condition, prior to the other two, is that auditory events that are perceptively salient are also stable. In the GTTM, rules concerning salience indicate that an event is salient not only when it is in a strong metric or tonal position (the preceding conditions), but also when it is in an extreme register, when it has a remarkable timbre or a color, or when it acquires a particular formal significance (e.g., a thematic one). We thus define here a correspondence between perceptual and structural stability that constitutes the fundamental hypothesis of the GTTM as a model of musical competence. Reductions are both a pertinent structural description of the underlying schema at any tonal musical surface and a model of the listener's mental operations for capturing the organic unity of the surface structure and storing its information in memory. The tonal system is thus based on a triple correspondence among music's emotional dynamics, its internal structure (grammar), and the mental operations that allow encoding and decoding of the perceptual surface in memory and the subject's perception through an interplay between complex intuitions and anticipations.

In atonal music, this triple correspondence does not exist, and the notion of functional hierarchy is in question, since the musical space is "flat" (functionally equivalent pitches, syntactically equivalent consonances and dissonances). From an analysis of Schoenberg's pieces, Lerdahl (1989) formulated a new proposal: in atonal music, prolongation structures are structures of the hierarchical organization of salience. On the surface, they are those of auditory events that immediately capture the listener's attention; on a more abstract level, they are those of motivic relations and of parallelisms in structure. In other words, to the extent that we cannot define stability conditions, conditions of contextual or relative salience are those that organize webs and prolongational structures for the listener. If we want briefly and intuitively to describe the analytic principle proposed by Lerdahl, salience most often consists of the obsessive and contextually dominant repetition of a sonority (chord). Dominance of the salient element plays a role in atonal music analogous to the role of the tonally stable element in tonal music and gives rise to what we may call prolongation by iteration.

This poses a major problem for the cognitive psychology of memory and perception, as Lerdahl noted himself: "The crux of the theory outlined above is the decision to regard contextual salience in atonal music as analogous to stability in tonal music. This step amounts to an acknowledgment that atonal music is not very grammatical. I think this is an accurate conclusion. Listeners to atonal music do not have at their disposal a consistent, psychologically relevant set of principles by which to organize pitches at the musical surface. As a result, they grab on to what they can: relative salience becomes structurally important, and within that framework the best linear connections are made. Schoenberg had reason to invent a new system" (1989:84). This is exactly the problem that concerns perception and interpretation of completely atonal pieces. Relative salience determines a temporary, always modifiable, hierarchy. One of the characteristics of atonal music, and serial music in particular, is that it is extremely fluent for the listener, that it does not have a definite structure, thus opening itself to the creative fantasy of the interpreter.

Dynamic Aspects of Salience Clues and the Concept of Macrostructure

In the case of atonal music, the question immediately arises of how relative salience can create, for listener and interpreter, the equivalent of alternations of tension and relaxation that underlie the emotional dynamism of tonal music. More exactly, does the relative contextual salience of an event also determine its degree of stability?

Until now, most theoretical and experimental studies responded in the affirmative, but dealt only with cognitive and structural aspects of salience clues, thus demonstrating stability only as abstract and conceptual. Deliège (1989, 1990, 1993) developed in detail concepts of clue extraction from the musical surface, and of imprint in memory. In a series of experiments on Berio's *Sequenza VI* and Boulez's *Eclat*, she showed that listeners, while listening repeatedly to pieces they do not know and for which there are no tonal reference points, create a simplified schema of what they hear in the form of an imprint stored in memory. Details of this imprint develop into a model-type in relation to numerous variations of successive listenings. This imprint, which is a sort of image the listener keeps of the musical piece, is progressively elaborated through clues taken from the musical surface. At first these clues are anything that can capture the listener's attention and make certain events salient in relation to others. As the piece unfolds, and over successive repetitions, certain clues are abandoned and others are reinforced that define groups of pitch and rhythm between which links are established. Here again, the most stable clues that are repeated between groups in an adjacent or distant manner allow a larger structure to be constructed that goes beyond grouping succession.

However, how can these clues, which in Deliège's work allow the constitution of the imprint in memory, give rise to a dynamic hierarchical organization? To what extent do they also reflect the organization of tensions and relaxations?

I have tried to provide an answer through the concepts of macrostructure and dynamic vectors. From the perceptual point of view, a tonal or atonal musical piece is a hierarchy of changes, contrasts, and ruptures perceived during listening. From the theoretical point of view this means, first, that perceptual organization is a hierarchy of saliences in the sense we have just defined, before being a syntactic functional hierarchy. Second, this means that this perceptual organization is founded first of all on temporal phenomena and not on phenomena having functional value, such as successions or repetitions, ruptures or continuities, that we would be tempted to designate by the concepts of strong prolongation, weak prolongation, or lack of prolongation (contrasted prolongation) of the GTTM. But the question arises of whether this perceptual hierarchy of changes can be considered a hierarchy of relative saliences. What I suggest is that the concept of salience is perhaps insufficient to explain the dynamism of phenomena of succession or prolongation. That is why I propose to define the macrostructure of a musical piece not from the syntactic point of view but from a psychological point of view, as a schema of the structuring of time; that is, as a reduction of temporal structures of tension and relaxation of the musical piece, or rather, a mental representation of the temporal progression of the musical piece. In other words, a musical piece is first of all an ordering of auditory events in time, and the macrostructure is a simplified type schema, a priori an ordering that is filled later by concrete auditory events of which the progression for the listener is thus more or less predictable. This progression can be defined as a structured and hierarchical succession of tensions and relaxations.

The Psychological Foundations of Macrostructure

The question now arises as to how the meaning of this progression might be founded, cognitively and emotionally. It so happens that in the past few years child psychologists have proposed relevant hypotheses.

Daniel Stern (1985) developed several interesting concepts that turn out to be related to music. The first is that of vitality affect: "many qualities of feeling that occur do not fit into our existing lexicon or taxonomy of affects. These elusive qualities are better captured by dynamic, kinetic terms, such as 'surging,' 'fading away,' 'fleeting,' 'explosive,' 'crescendo,' 'decrescendo,' 'bursting,' 'drawn out,' and so on. These qualities of experience are most certainly sensible to infants and of great daily, even momentary, importance" (1985:54). These vitality affects are thus characters related to emotions, to the ways of being, to the different ways of internally feeling emotions. They will be, for example, all that distinguishes explosive joy from fleeting joy, or the thousand ways of smiling, of getting up from one's chair, of taking a baby in one's arms, feelings that are not reducible to classic categorical affects but that color them in a sensitive way for the person.

If I were to translate Stern's idea differently, I would say that these feelings are first of all of a temporal and dynamic nature, and that is what makes for their originality. They give weight to the moment, to the present action, or to the emotion in progress, and this is undoubtedly what the baby first perceives in the acts, gestures, and attitudes of its mother or other people. These are ways of feeling—of being with—before being emotions or particular feelings. The comparison with music or dance seems evident, since the choreographer or composer translates a way of feeling rather than the feeling itself.

The notion corresponding to that of vitality affect in music is undoubtedly what, on the basis of experiments on the semantization of musical experience, I suggested characterizes the dynamic and temporal aspects of forms: it is the notion of a dynamic vector. Dynamic vectors are musical elements that transport temporal significations of orientation, progression, diminution or growth, and repetition or return. Perceived and felt change is thus a dynamic vector that orients the listener's perception, anticipation, and internal representations. The quality of orientation depends on what the dynamic vector refers to, assimilated here to a set of vitality affects that the subject experiences or relives immediately in listening.

From all that precedes, the notion of temporal feeling-shape derives naturally. It is defined by Stern (1995) as a form of representation of affective experience. It is thus a contour of affectivity, the temporal form of a set of profiles of intensity, rhythm, and duration of vitality affects, of which it ensures, for the subject, the coherence in a present that lasts. Its emergence for the subject is an event that is produced in real time, on the inside of experience. But to understand the range of this notion, we have to ask, what is being linked? what is being woven, like a plot is woven, what is it that is waiting to be given meaning?

In the language of Stern (1995:86–87) it is the "protonarrative enve-lope." In effect the narrative form is what, in the universe of language and of signs to which the baby will have access later, constructs the unity of time, clarifies the reality of human becoming. The temporal "after the fact" is thus a semiotization of activation profiles of vitality affects; more exactly, it is what allows the semiotization to develop in duration, what gives their form to the temporal feeling-shapes. In short, it is what makes something weave itself and assume meaning in time. The protonarrative envelope is thus an affectivity contour distributed in time with the coher-ence of a quasi-plot, a line of intuitive dramatic tension. It is a proto-semiotic form of internal experience of time, a matrix of the story of tensions and relaxations related to the plot (or protoplot) in the search for satisfaction, it is what gives experience its global unity, whatever its degree of complexity.

These facts and reflections shed a new light on the concept of macrostructure. A musical piece is first of all an ordering of acoustic events in time. The macrostructure is a simplified schema type, an order-ing a priori that later will be filled by the concrete acoustic events of which the progression may be defined for the listener as a structured and hierarchical succession of tensions and relaxations. In consequence it is simultaneously defined at the level of musical grammar, cognitive oper-ations active in composition and comprehension of the piece, but also at the level of expressivity and feelings of the listener. The temporal pro-gression through tensions and relaxations, and through formal patterns that evoke what I can now call vitality affects, takes meaning in oriented continuity from the beginning to the end of the piece. It finds its coher-ence in this temporal web that links melodic, rhythmic, and harmonic gestures, telling protonarratives of a thousand nuances.

I tried to demonstrate this in an experimental manner several times (1981:132–138; 1987). I thus showed that listeners are sensitive to this story-without-words that music awakens in them. They feel the original-ity of the progression, its directionality, that translates the experiences of time, markedly different from one composer to another. For example, I observed that, in spite of their formal structural differences, two pieces by Debussy, such as *La Puerta del Vino* and *La Cathédrale Engloutie*, show profile similarities in comparison with the profile of pieces by Brahms: whereas the latter profile is in general symmetric, starting and ending in a somber and resigned mood, the former is strangely ascensional in spite of the important contrasts and the ruptures of tone and atmosphere. *La Cathédrale Engloutie* and *La Puerta* evolve for the listener from a somber and even violent mood to a calm, serene, luminous, and immobile ending that is blurred in a sort of complete atemporality and thus creates the illu-sion that time stops. This ascensional asymmetry of the temporal profile—

of its web—seems to characterize Debussy's universe and shows, as I demonstrated, a denial of time and death in the shape of a reflection of the tragic codas of musical romanticism.

Conclusion

Music, the art of time, works on time in its relation to the intentional conscious and to the unconscious. It plays on representations and fantasies that are created by experiences of temporal feelings in human life, between continuity and discontinuity, between fusional unity and fragmentation, and between mobility and immobility. The history of musical creation is the history of our relation with time on both the individual and collective levels. But the remarkable works of Stern suggest a new depth: the constant reference to the fact that the individual psychology of time is built on interactions with others. The major assertion that the feeling of duration is created in the game of interactive communication makes us understand that music touches us only through the other. I agree with J. J. Nattiez (1987) when he says that musical communication (in the banal sense) is but an illusion. But I think that the problem of musical expression lies elsewhere: music takes its power in its profoundly social nature, like language, as a vehicle of interiorized representations. All its temporal substance is nourished by our way of being in the world; that is, in our time, our culture, our perceptions, our bodies, our emotions, and our sentiments. It is not communication but a representation of our ability to communicate, it is a stylized game for our opening to the world, it is communication without an object to communicate. In this sense, music is indeed the symbol of our fundamental relation to time, life, and death. To what extent the capacity for musical communication depends on innate competencies, related not only to gestalt properties of musical processing but to the dynamic and affective aspects of music perception, will be a subject of intense interest in the coming years.

References

Bever, T. and Chiarello, R. (1974). Cerebral dominance in musicians and nonmusicians. *Science* 185:537–539.

Deliège, I. (1989). A perceptual approach to contemporary musical forms. *Contemporary Music Review* 4:213–220.

Deliège, I. (1990). Mechanisms of cue extraction in musical grouping: Study of *Sequenza 6* by L. Berio. *Psychology of Music* 18:18–44.

Deliège, I. (1993). Mechanisms of cue extraction in memory for musical time. *Contemporary Music Review* 9:191–205.

von Ehrenfels, C. (1890). Über Gestaltqualitäten. *Viertel Jahrsschriften für Wissenschaften und Philosophie* 3:249–299.

Fodor, J. (1983). *The Modularity of Mind*. Cambridge: MIT Press.

Francès, R. (1958). *La Perception de la Musique*. Paris: Vrin.

Gardner, H. (1983). *Frames of Mind: The Theory of Multiple Intelligences*. New York: Basic Books.

Imberty, M. (1981). *Les Ecritures du Temps*. Paris: Dunod.

Imberty, M. (1987). L'occhio e l'orecchio: "Sequenza III" di Berio. In L. Marconi and G. Stefani (Eds.) *Il Senso in Musica* (pp. 163–186). Bologna: Clueb.

Imberty, M. (1991a). Le concept de hiérarchie perceptive face à la musique atonale. *Communicazioni Scientifiche de Psicologia Generale* 5:119–133.

Imberty, M. (1991b). Stabilité et instabilité: Comment l'interprète et l'auditeur organisent-ils la progression temporelle d'un oeuvre musicale? (Analyse, mèmorisation et interprètation). *Psychologica Belgica* 31:173–195.

Imberty, M. (1993a). Le style musical et le temps: Aspects esthésiques et aspects poïètiques. *Analyse Musicale* 32:14–19.

Imberty, M. (1993b). L'utopie de combelment: A propos de l'*Adieu* du *Chant de la Terre* de Gustav Mahler. *Cahiers de l'IRCAM* 4:53–62.

Jackendoff, R. (1987). *Consciousness and the Computational Mind*. Cambridge: MIT Press.

Köhler, W. (1929). *Gestalt Psychology*. New York: Liveright.

Lerdahl, F. and Jackendoff, R. (1983). *A Generative Theory of Tonal Music*. Cambridge: MIT Press.

Lerdahl, F. (1989). Atonal prolongational structure. *Contemporary Music Review* 4:65–87.

Nattiez, J.-J. (1987). *Musicologie Générale et Sémiologie*. Paris: Chirstian Bourgois.

Peretz, I. and Morais, J. (1989). Music and modularity. *Contemporary Music Review* 4:279–293.

Rameau, J.-P. (1754). *Observations sur Notre Instinct pour la Musique*. Paris: Prault.

Schenker, H. (1935). *Neue Musikalische Theorien und Phantasien III: Der Freie Satz*. Vienna: Universal Edition.

Stern, D. N. (1985). *The Interpersonal World of the Infant: A View from Psychoanalysis and Developmental Psychology*. New York: Basic Books.

Stern, D. N. (1995). *The Motherhood Constellation: A Unified View of Parent-Infant Psychotherapy*. New York: Basic Books.

25 An Ethnomusicologist Contemplates Universals in Musical Sound and Musical Culture

Bruno Nettl

Abstract

The existence and identification of universals in music have long been a matter of concern to ethnomusicologists who considered them helpful in theorizing about the origins of music. Identification of universals depends on definitions of music, of musical units analogous to culture units, and on an interculturally valid concept of music, all problematic issues. It may be helpful to consider various levels of universals—those extant in music at all times, those present in each musical utterance, others present in some sense in each musical system or musical culture, and yet others found in most but not all cultures. A group of simple styles with limited scalar structure, and forms consisting of one or two repeated phrases, and found in virtually all known musics, may be the contemporary phenomena closest to the earliest human music. However, musical universals can provide only the most tentative guide to the origins of music.

Ethnomusicology, Universals, and the Origins of Music

When I meet with colleagues at my university who are in other departments and explain to them that I work in a field known as ethnomusicology, they usually ask me about what they call "ancient" music and are surprised when I tell them that this is not a primary focus of my discipline. On the other hand, during the last conference of the Society for Ethnomusicology, while some 600 people devoted to that field had gathered in Toronto, the *New York Times* and the Toronto papers published an article about what is supposed to be the oldest known musical instrument, a bone "flute" with at least two finger holes, coming from a Neanderthal archeological site in Slovenia (see Kunej and Turk, this volume). I found it interesting that no one at this meeting, to my knowledge, noted or mentioned the discovery. The point is that ethnomusicologists today have no special claim to be concerned with or to know something about the origins of music. They are really more concerned with beliefs or myths of the world's societies about the origins of music, and with what these myths may tell us about the way each of the world's peoples conceives of music and its role in culture. It is this discontinuity of attitudes that makes universals as guides to the origins of music an issue wrapped in ambiguity.

The origins of music were once a hot topic in ethnomusicology, as suggested by the title of one of the earliest classics of the field by Carl Stumpf, *The Beginnings of Music* (1911), but it has cooled off considerably. In contrast, universals were once a matter of little concern but they have come closer to being a hot topic. When I was a student I was taught that any attempt to generalize about the music of the world should be countered by an example falsifying that generalization. I was taught to reject the notion that all of the world's musics had anything in common. But by the 1970s all this had changed. A new student arrived in my department and declared that she understood that the purpose of studying ethnomusicology was to study universals. And two journals, at least, undertook special issues on the subject: *Ethnomusicology* in 1971 (vol. 15, no. 3), with contributions by some of the most venerable figures in North America— David McAllester, Klaus Wachsmann, Charles Seeger, and George List—and in 1977, *The World of Music* (vol. 19, no. 1/2) in a special issue with contributions by John Blacking, Frank Harrison, Gertrude Kurath, Mantle Hood, Tran Van Khe, Jean-Jacques Nattiez, Alan Lomax, and myself. It may be no surprise that virtually all of these authors looked with considerable skepticism at the possibility that universals can be defined, identified, and described. Modern classic books about ethnomusicology, by Merriam (1964) and Hood (1971), for example, do not deal with the subject. More recently again, following, I think, trends in linguistics and social anthropology, the interest among ethnomusicologists has warmed.

If ethnomusicological involvement has some justification, it concerns the interface among three areas of concern: cultural universals, musical universals specifically, and the origins of music. I think that if we are to discover the origins of music, with all the problems of definition that this entails, some understanding of universals may be helpful. But also I need to be the devil's advocate or dog in the manger and suggest why universals should be drawn in as a guide only with the greatest care.

Universals of Music and Universals among Musics

A brief definition of what I mean by universals is in order. This depends in turn, of course, on the definition of music, something I ought not to attempt, but also on a general conceptualization of the world's music. We might consider music as a single vast body of sound and thought, a kind of universal language of humankind, and accepting this would lead us to a particular way of constructing universals. This would not be my choice, nor would it seem to have been, may I say, the choice of my teacher, George Herzog (1939), one of whose little-known but insightful articles was entitled "Music's Dialects: a Non-Universal Language." A more typically ethnomusicological view would provide for a world of music that consists of a large group of discrete musics, somewhat analogous to languages, with stylistic, geographical, and social boundaries. We used to think that the boundaries were clear and that each music had a style or grammar, a repertory or vocabulary, logic, and consistency. Where these boundaries lay would differ depending on analytical approach and historical depth.

Thus, there might be Blackfoot music, South Indian music, and Western music; or Czech folk music, Carnatic Indian classical music, and

European common-practice music; or, continuing my interest in Native Americans as a basis, all music known to the Arapaho no matter what its origin; or all of the intertribally used repertory of Peyote music, no matter that in each tribe it is exceptional; or the body of Native American popular music, despite its clear similarity to mainstream popular music. Not as easy, I think, as dividing the world of language into languages, although I know that's not so simple either. Even so, we can look at the world of music in terms of musical languages.

The world of music also has social units. We may say that each social group has its music. In some cases, say, in isolated tribal societies before they had widespread contact with other cultures, this may have been thoroughly consistent or homogeneous. In others, such as twentieth-century Hungary, a great variety of musical styles and repertories makes up the music regarded in some sense as "Hungarian," or in which Hungarians have a stake. Then we also take into account bimusicality or multimusicality. The Blackfoot people today say that they have two kinds of music, Indian and white, and lay claim to both. My teachers in Persian classical music claimed only their own repertory, but maintained that they knew and understood other musics much as they spoke foreign languages competently while nevertheless regarding them as foreign.

There is, by the way, the question of association of music with ethnicity. I have asserted that each social group has one music—at least—that it regards as its own. Many social groups, in the United States they are particularly prominent, use music and dance as their principal markers of ethnicity, such as Polish-Americans and Italian-Americans celebrating their heritage and exhibiting it to outsiders. This may be true of other social groups as well; age groups come to mind. Teenagers with hard rock, preteens with the bubble gum music of yore, old folks with organ concerts, all claim a musical language of their own.

If the world of music can be conceived as a single body of communication capable of being understood at some level by all humans, or as a group of discrete musics however designated, it can also be looked at as a network of ideas. It is too complicated to present in all its manifestations, but I can suggest a couple of relevant points.

Universality of the Music Concept

One problem with using universals as a guide to discovering the origins of music is the difficulty in defining music in a way that is equally valid for all cultures, and valid as well in the eyes of different societies of humans. The world's cultures vary (and varied in the past) in the degree to which they have the concept of music and in the value and function they assign to it. We say that music is a cultural universal, but do all peoples think they have music? Certainly not all have a term that translates as "music." Even European languages do not have all that much unanimity; look, for example, at the bifurcation of *Musik* and *Tonkunst* in German, or *Muzika* and *Hudba* in Czech. In Persian culture, much of what we conceive of as music is called *Musiqi*, a word derived from Greek by way of Arabic; but much that sounds to us Europeans as music would not be considered *Musiqi* but rather *Khandan*, a word that means reading, reciting, and singing; and some sounds or genres would be regarded as somehow between these two extremes. The Blackfoot language has as its principal gloss for music the word *saapup*, which means something like singing, dancing, and ceremony all rolled into one. Thus if we are to talk about music as a universal phenomenon, we cannot do it on the basis of a commonality of cultural conceptions.

As Klaus Wachsmann (1971) suggested, all cultures have something that sounds to us (he meant Europeans and Euro-Americans, I am sure) like music. I have heard music lovers and scholars assert that electronic music, rap, and Native American songs are not music. But can we say that all societies have a kind of sound communication that they distinguish from ordinary speech, and that this could be a kind of baseline for music? I like to think that we have here a solid universal. But wait: are the various things that are distinct from speech really at all the same kind of thing? The Shuar or Canelos Quichua in Ecuador have songs and speech, and some intermediate forms such as the *Auchmartin*, stylized speechlike or songlike sounds exchanged by men who do not know each other meeting on a jungle path, or the *Enermartin*, which is used by a group of men to raise their spirits and courage before a tribal or clan battle. Where do we draw the line? In any event, the typical anthropological approach to universals involves the concept of musics, societies, cultures, all definitely plural.

Types of Universals

Let me also suggest that we could look at the issue of universals as a set of concentric circles (for a more detailed discussion, see Nettl 1983:36–51). At the center is the definition of music—with all the problems this entails—and the universal in the extreme sense. A theoretical abstraction, to be sure. The central kind of universal is what is present in music at all times, in every moment of musical existence, if I may put it that way. There is little in a practical way that we can do with this kind of universal, but it ought be to mentioned. When we play a large group of musical examples for an unsophisticated listener and ask him or her what they have in common, we probably would not get a positive answer.

We might be told, "well, they are all music." They all have about them a certain "musicness"; and perhaps "musicness," which we cannot define further except to say that it is distinct from "speechness" and maybe from other sound phenomena, is a universal.

More concretely, can we say that something is present at some point in every musical utterance and is recognized as such? For example, does every bit of music, every piece or song, have a cadential element? Probably not, but possibly it does in enough cases to be tabled and discussed further a bit later. Or again, can it be true that every musical utterance has in it intervals approximating the major second or something of that general sort? Again, surely not *every* piece, but enough to postpone that discussion.

A related question concerns the nature of the musical utterance. It seems to me that in all societies of which I have heard, one is always singing or playing *something*, a particular song, composition, something that resulted from an act of creation, by human or supernatural forces, with a distinct identity. One does not ever just sing or play, as, for example, one may simply dance, without performing a particular dance composition.

Traits Found in Each Music?

Moving to the next circle, we ask whether certain features occur in every music or in the music of every society. It is easy to come up with concrete examples, but of course this issue is limited by the academic world's ignorance of many musics, present and, more important, past. As it is impossible to make concrete (in contrast to theoretical) statements, all we can do is rely on our admittedly fairly generous sampling of cultures that we know from twentieth-century study and perspective. In other words, we rely on samplings and so arrive at yet another of our concentric circles, things found virtually everywhere with the occasional exception, followed perhaps by what could best be labeled as statistical universals.

We are of course reduced to playing games. Accepting the idea of statistical universals means abandoning the principle that there is a significant difference between universality and popularity. Language is a true universal; there are no peoples that do not have it. The nature of languages varies incredibly, but the possession of language characterizes all human groups. The few humans unable for various reasons to acquire language are not regarded in their societies as being normal. For another example, some kind of regulation of sexual activity and relationship of generations; that is, social structure is something we find in every society. We have mentioned the existence of something that sounds like music to us, but what about features of culture that exist only in, say, 98% of the world's societies (as far as we can tell)? What usefulness would this have in establishing universals as guides to learning the origins of music?

Still, if we look at the musical cultures that we know, one thing that is bound to strike us is the presence of certain traits shared by a large, maybe overwhelming, proportion. As graduate students of ethnomusicology, we learn early, when faced with generalizations based essentially on Western music, to shout, "Hold on! there is nothing that is universal, and nothing that doesn't occur somewhere." Our profession began with a firm belief in the incredible variety of the world's musics. Universals, as a serious object of discussion, did not surface until the 1960s.

But we have had to admit that some things that are enormously widespread. It seems convenient though probably old-fashioned to separate sound from social context, but aside from having something that sounds to us like music, what are the style characteristics that one finds everywhere?

All societies have vocal music. Virtually all have instruments of some sort, although a few tribal societies may not, but even they have some kind of percussion. Vocal music is carried out by both men and women, although singing together in octaves is not a cultural universal, perhaps for social reasons. All societies have at least some music that conforms to a meter or contains a pulse. The intervallic structure of almost all musics involves, as the principal interval, something close to the major second but to be sure, not with precision; I am talking about anything, say, from a three-quarter tone to five quarters. All societies have some music that uses only three or four pitches, usually combining major seconds and minor thirds.

It is important to consider also certain universals that do not involve musical sound or style. I mentioned the importance of music in ritual, and, as it were, in addressing the supernatural. This seems to me to be truly a universal, shared by all known societies, however different the sound. Another universal is the use of music to provide some kind of fundamental change in an individual's consciousness or in the ambiance of a gathering. Music "transforms experience," in the words of David McAllester (1971). Also music is virtually universally used to mark the importance of an event—birthday party, political rally, appearance of the king, the coming-together of tribes. And it is virtually universally associated with dance; not all music is danced, but there is hardly any dance that is not in some sense accompanied by music.

The "World's Simplest Music" as a Universal

Most societies have in their music, either as the main style but more commonly as a special repertory, something I might label (cringing because musical complexity is not easily measured and subject to biases brought about by a culture that worships complexity) as "the world's simplest style." It consists of songs that have a short phrase repeated several or many times, with minor variations, using three or four pitches within a range of a fifth. This kind of music is interestingly widespread.

It appears to have been the only style, or the principal style, of some peoples living in widely separated isolated areas of the world. In addition, it is found in societies whose music is otherwise more complex, and here it is often relegated to the accompaniment of children's games, to games generally, and to obsolete rituals. We have reason to believe that it is old material, associated as it is with social contexts once central to the culture but overtaken by more complex music. Examples may be heard in recordings of songs of the Vedda of Sri Lanka recorded as early as 1910, songs of the "last wild Indian," Ishi, last surviving member of the Yahi tribe, music of certain Pacific islands such as Mangareva, in children's ditties of European and other societies, as well as certain pre-Christian ritual songs preserved in European folk cultures.

It is tempting to say this music is widespread, its geographic distribution in isolated areas suggests age, its association with social contexts no longer central makes it archaic, and so obviously this is what the earliest music of humans was like. Perhaps so. But there are also reasons to be skeptical.

Whereas these kinds of music, because of their similarity, their well-nigh universal distribution, and their simplicity, appear to provide the best guide available to the sounds of the earliest human music, let me mention some caveats. First, are they really so similar? For one thing, we who come from a conventional background in Western music tend to privilege melodic movement and to give particular emphasis to intervals. The pieces are quite different from each other in rhythm and also in other ways—singing style or timbre, dynamics, and perhaps much else. The point is that the similarity of these pieces, their unity of style, is based on one group of interrelated features involving intervals, range, and form: few intervals, small range, and short repeated lines or stanzas. Actually, music with few pitches but longer and more complex forms is found in folk music of Eastern Europe, in liturgical chants and some instrumental music. In other words, a number of the characteristic traits of the world's simplest music are also found in otherwise musically more complex environments. This is true of some of the Romanian Christmas carols recorded before World War II by Béla Bartòk.

The other thing that holds these simplest musical examples together is form, the sectioning and relationships between sections: a short line or stanza repeated and varied lightly. This kind of form is found in many other cultures and repertories, from complex African tribal music to south Slavic epics to modern urban minimalist music, from accompaniments of classical dance in India to rock music. Each feature by itself has a broad distribution in various contexts. Together they form a style but only if one ignores the ways they differ, rhythmically and by timbre, for example. So the idea of a world's simplest style may be flawed. I suggest this as a caveat, not as a devastating criticism.

Some simple musics do not quite conform to this model. This is true of a variety of styles of the Shuar or Canelos Quichua of eastern Ecuador that, while conforming to the model given above to some degree, really provide a different kind of flavor. Each song technically conforms to the simplest style definition, but as a group they provide a complex interweaving of musical patterns that suggests a substantial period of development. Does this contribute to the notion of universals, or is it part of a different historical strand?

Furthermore, how helpful to the discovery of the origins of music would be the kind of "statistical" universal with widespread distribution to which nevertheless significant exceptions exist? I mentioned some but others are significant although a bit less widespread: pentatonic scales, duple and quadruple meter, and certain instruments. We discover their distribution, but the question of age is vexing. Equating widespread distribution with antiquity, although sometimes credible, is hardly a dogma any more. After all, an archeologist in 4,000 A.D., finding the nearly universal distribution of pianos in the twentieth century might well believe that they are among the oldest musical artifacts.

All of these thoughts suggest that music does seem to have universals, belief in their existence is surrounded by problems. They are universals from the viewpoint of one culture that uses a select group of criteria. They might include musical features and artifacts that for a variety of reasons came to acquire widespread distribution in recent times and are thus perhaps universally present only in one culture and its tentacles. They are features that are widespread but exist in a variety of musical environments.

The relationship of universals to the origins of music is also fraught with possible doubts. The issue of identifying origins is complex and inevitably leads to questions. We can provide credible theories regarding evolutionary preparations for the introduction of music, and we can make guesses about the earliest human music, but the point at which nonmusic becomes music is obscure. Is music a characteristic of *Homo sapiens* alone? Most ethnomusicologists probably think so, I have to confess; but other chapters in this volume suggest that the taxonomy that we Western observers are hesitant to impose on non-Western cultures is possibly valid for other species. Once established, such a theory might require ethnomusicologists to change their definitions and approaches.

But what of the possibility that music actually came into being at different times in different places, and developed separately, and it is only we who think it all sounds the same, who think that it is one phenomenon? After all, it now seems possible that Neanderthal populations had flutes, despite the fact that their relationship to *Homo sapiens* has been moved into the more distant past. Did their music become the music of *Homo sapiens*, or are these two separate strands of origin and development? Indeed, in his last book, the venerable Curt Sachs (1962) suggested that music developed in two ways, from simple chants or from tumbling strains, echoing his earlier bifurcation of "logogenic" and "pathogenic" (Sachs 1943), and perhaps even further, of Apollonian and Dionysian motivations. We have ceased to take these distinctions very seriously. Still, was this a way for Sachs to tell us that music may have originated in more than one way?

So whereas we have some reason to look at universals as a guide, and to regard the world's simplest styles as a credible remnant of the world's earliest music, we also have reasons to be doubtful. Possibly we should throw off the virtually instinctive desire to accept a theoretical chronology in which music with few pitches precedes that with more numerous landing points, giving priority to the legendary Johnny-one-note song and the belief that monophony must have preceded multipart music. It might then make just as good sense to imagine an early human music that moves glissando-like through the voice's range like emotional speech as one coming from vocal expressions by groups, such as group singing of the Samaritans near Tel Aviv and Nablus, which has indistinct pitches and only very vaguely defined relationships among the voices.

Conclusion

I am not sure whether it is in fact helpful to try to deal with this question of universals, helpful in discovering the origins of music, helpful in the quest for a description of the totality of the world's musical cultures. Looking at the issues I raised and that others have raised may provoke a feeling of helplessness. One possible approach is to throw up one's hands and just admit that we will never know whether there are really universals, or whether we can ever learn about the earliest human music and the moment of invention, as it were. But that is not what this volume is about. The question is too interesting and in a sense too important to be left without at least a speculative conclusion. I suggest that it should continue to be of interest to ethnomusicologists, despite what appears to be their temporary abandonment of it. Indeed, I would welcome greater exchange of data and views between biomusicology and ethnomusicology.

Having been nothing if not equivocal in the presentation of certain approaches as well as caveats that must accompany them, let me nevertheless summarize. I think that universals do exist in musical sound and in musical conceptualization and behavior. Those that involve musical style are at best statistical, but they might tell us something about the earliest human music. Forced to guess at the musical style of early humankind, I would have to say that it was probably like that of some of my illustrations, but I do this with some reluctance. The relatively simple styles that nevertheless contradict the stylistic mainstream, differences in timbre and singing style, the possibility that even worldwide diffusion of components of culture and their clusters may have taken place aeons ago, all this makes me realize that even what appears to us to be the world's simplest music may or must have had a substantial history.

The group of ideas and forms of behavior includes, of importance, the prevailing ritual use of music and suggests that earliest human music was somehow associated with ritual. The use of music to mark significant events is related, and may also suggest its early use in aspects of social organization. The fact that agreement on definition and conceptualization of music itself does not even come close to being a cultural universal makes me wonder whether what we now call music came into existence only once or in one way. Although evidently not directly related to biology in the most specific sense, universals may, in the absence of other concrete data, help us discover the origins of music, or better said, perhaps, formulate a theory of the earliest human music on which we can agree. However, they provide at best only the most tentative of guides.

References

Herzog, G. (1939). Music's dialects: A non-universal language. *Independent Journal of Columbia University* 6:1–2.

Hood, M. (1971). *The Ethnomusicologist.* New York: McGraw-Hill.

McAllester, D. P. (1971). Some thoughts on universals in music. *Ethnomusicology* 15:379–380.

Merriam, A. P. (1964). *The Anthropology of Music.* Evanston, IL: Northwestern University Press.

Nettl, B. (1983). *The Study of Ethnomusicology: Twenty-Nine Issues and Concepts.* Urbana: University of Illinois Press.

Sachs, C. (1943). *The Rise of Music in the Ancient World, East and West.* New York: Norton.

Sachs, C. (1962). *The Wellsprings of Music.* The Hague: Nijhoff.

Stumpf, C. (1911). *Die Anfänge der Musik.* Berlin: Barth.

Wachsmann, K. (1971). Universal perspectives in music. *Ethnomusicology* 15:381–384.

The Necessity of and Problems with a Universal Musicology

François-Bernard Mâche

Abstract

The search for universals is no longer linked to the old belief that tonality is based on the laws of resonance and, as such, is more natural than any other system. Despite a period of excessive cultural relativism, the search for musical universals now seeks to understand on which bases different musical cultures can communicate and interact. Some universal features are restricted to human music: pentatonic polyphony on a drone, and isochronous ostinato, for example. For these, lack of evidence for historical diffusion leads us to suppose that they come from spontaneous universal genotypes. Furthermore, comparing music with animal sound organization gives still more convincing data to support the hypothesis of some basic innate schemes. In some animal species, rhythms and melodies exhibit several of the traits considered as typically musical. The existence of an aesthetic dimension in their use of sound signals might be referred to as a kind of hypertelia, the primary goals of nature (mating, defending a territory, etc.) being exceeded, so to speak. Artistic creation appears as invention with, and beyond, the commonplaces suggested by nature.

One could say that the purpose of this chapter is to analyze some consequences of a single machine in the field of music and musicology. From the middle of this century, the taperecorder has deeply modified the way that we think about music. Without the taperecorder, which allows us to hear and compare music from all over the world, we would perhaps have missed the fact that the tonal system can no longer be considered to be universal, since among so many different systems it proves to be completely irrelevant. We would also have much poorer knowledge of animal sound signals, since we would be forced to rely on our memory to compare them. The time of the emancipation of Asia, Africa, and so on has also been the time of the taperecorder. One century after Debussy, it helped a much wider audience to realize that we had no right to define their music as primitive just because most of them were lacking some dimensions or rules of ours. Eventually the taperecorder also had a tremendous impact on the musical industry, one of the most powerful—and problematic—phenomena of our time.

But the diversity among musical traditions is greater than the diversity of the basic schemes they use. If ethnomusicology has underlined, since 1950, the great amount of cultural diversity in musical traditions, it might now be useful to reconsider what all cultures have in common, and to understand why they are so easily and so widely prone to imitate each other and to yield to worldwide uniformity. Let us briefly look back at the first half of the twentieth century. When Curt Sachs published his *Geist und Werden der Musikinstrumente* (1929), very few people suspected that such basic notions as scales, key notes, bars, melody, and harmony, and tones as opposed to noises could sometimes prove irrelevant when applied to non-Western cultures. Bartók was among the first to realize how improper our notation was in some of those contexts, and Varèse met very little understanding when he tried to create his music on other, newer foundations.

It has been taught since Pythagoras, and it is still believed by some, that heptatonic scales express a natural law. In particular, theoreticians maintain that a perfect chord built upon them is given by nature, since the third and the fifth overtones of many musical sounds seem to sound like the fifth and third tones above the root. But the minor third, as frequent as the major one, can be identified only with the nineteenth overtone, and the fourth degree, one of the three pillars of the tonal temple, corresponds but vaguely to the eleventh overtone (minus a quarter-tone) or to the twenty-first overtone (minus twenty-nine cents). Anyhow, nobody has ever heard such high overtones, which represent sounds alien even to the chromatic scale, since starting from the seventh overtone many pitches do not coincide at all with it. In spite of all that, many theoreticians two centuries after Rameau keep teaching this acrobatic theory of natural resonance, ignoring the fact that a wide diversity of intervals and pitch steps are used in the different scales of different musical cultures.

Things changed after 1948 (the year of the taperecorder) and 1955 (the year of Bandung, when twenty-four former colonial countries defined a new international order). Ethnomusicology developed as a new approach to the music of the world, and pointed out that even the phenomenon of music itself could be properly understood only if considered from the inside; that is, from the point of view of the cultural system in which it appeared (in which even the concept of music might have a different definition than in Western societies, or not be defined at all). The result was that scholars tried to forget about any theory or category that might distort their appraisal of the music they tried to describe.

It would certainly be a caricature to characterize the comparative musicology of the 1920s and 1930s as a naive expression of cultural colonialism, and ethnomusicology as a point of the great illusion of a world revolution. But in some cases, such political considerations underlay the scientific approaches, at least until today, when it seems that everything has to be reconsidered. New ethnomusicologists born in Africa or Asia study their own culture from the inside, but they use a cosmopolitan technology to do it, and they are trained in no less cosmopolitan methods. Extreme cultural relativism, through its excessive focus on the specificity of every musical culture, tends to present the common aspects as pure misunderstanding. It claims that no culture has any right to superimpose its categories on any other. Doing so, it tends to favor a kind of reverse racism by isolating every culture from all others, while the ubiquitous blending of musical practice becomes unintelligible.

Another fact favoring the search for universals in music is the quick vanishing of traditional music, everywhere replaced by the professional model that the music industry has promoted and imposed: specialization of composers, interpreters, and listeners; musical works treated as commodities; and so on. Many practices testifying to the cultural diversity I referred to are no longer available outside the archives where our taperecorders have allowed us to freeze their images. We have to understand how and why cross-cultural features are met with everywhere in music, even if no universal definition of what music is has yet been agreed upon.

Instead of proposing my own theoretical definition, I submit a series of sampled universal features that, to my ears, oblige us to inquire into their real nature. The first one is limited to humans, but encompasses the whole world. It can be defined as pentatonic polyphony on a drone. Such polyphony can be found in such diverse musical sources as: the music of the Nùng An minority of Vietnam; the *Gerewol* song of the Peuls Bororo of Niger; music of the Paiwan aborigines of Taiwan; folk songs from Albania; Sena choir songs from Nagaland, India; and *Dondi'* (sitting funerary choir music) from Sulawesi, Indonesia.

Meeting such obvious similarities, an ethnomusicologist will often try to discover along which tracks they must have been circulating and trace them back to one common source. In my opinion it is quite unlikely that any relationship can be proved during historical times between Taiwan and Niger, or between Albania and Sulawesi. If we imagine that such likeness may refer not to historic relationships but to the supposedly common origins of humans, it seems that the two types of explanations differ little (through diffusion or through spontaneous similarities) between cultural history or natural innate schemes. Because if such close similarities, in music just as in mythology, are the only surviving tokens of an ancient diffusion, the question is, why have only these features seemed to survive? what was so important about them that they were not transformed after thousands of years? On the other hand, if they are not the result of forgotten migrations but of a natural scheme, problems related to geography and history no longer exist, and thousands of years count for nothing in evolutionary terms. The main problem is to understand how precise sound organizations can be inscribed in every brain, and how musical choices emerge from them or deal with them. I leave it to psychologists and neurophysiologists to explain the muscular and neural laws that help us understand the ubiquity of certain tempos and rhythms in animal vocalizations and human music.

To support my hypothesis of universals given by nature in music, I will illustrate several similarities between animal and human signals (see Mâche, F.-B. 1992, especially the chapter entitled "Zoomusicology"). I must first justify this approach. Culturalists claim that one may not apply the same categories to different cultures, and even that the definition of what is the same is always a matter of cultural relativity. In the same manner, some psychologists claim that it would be anthropocentric, and therefore wrong, to assimilate or even to compare animal and human sound features. In both cases a predefined category such as "music" or "culture" is raised against the observation of likeness. They are characterized as pure convergences. By using this term, one refers to likenesses that, strong as they may seem, have no explanatory value, because they refer to separate causal series. The thumb of the panda is no thumb; the whale's fins do not make it a fish. The question is, can acoustic features that are common to animals and humans be viewed as simple convergences, with no scientific value because they contradict many other differences? The question of universals in music is directly related to the question of its origins. Being a musician rather than a biologist, I tend to observe surface structures, musical features. I try to distinguish what is universally encountered among them. If they correspond to concepts provided by evolutionary theories, one can state that the universal and the biological coincide.

To propose an answer, I submit a number of examples taken from several animals, illustrating categories that are considered typically musical. I use the terms phenotypes and genotypes to designate, on the one hand, acoustic forms—surface structures—and, on the other hand, dynamic schemes that determine their appearance, at least partly. I borrow both terms from biologists, with a slightly different interpretation if musical genotypes should turn out to be less constraining than their counterparts in biology.

In my career as a composer I was interested in phenotypes long before I undertook to connect them with possible genotypes. It is only after long acquaintance with animal models, which I have used in many works since the beginning of my career in 1958, that I wondered why I could so willingly perceive some latent music in the sounds made by whales, frogs, crickets, and birds. Eventually I perceived the correctness of the mythic tradition that presents music as related to bird song. What is new about this antique intuition is the taperecorder, which allows us to compare and to verify.

The objection that bird song is only the expression of biological functions, like territorial defense or courting, and belongs to the semiotic sphere, not to the aesthetic, is not as weighty as it seems. I mention it now to indicate that it did not prevent me from looking for a natural justification for my use of natural models.

An important family of rhythms among the different musical systems is the *aksak*, which exist in a very large area corresponding to the empire of Alexander the Great, from the Balkans to the Pamirs. They oppose an irregular number of basic units, very often grouped by three and by two. This seems to exist also in some animal species. Examples are seen in the songs of *Tockus erythrorhynchus*, the red-billed hornbill, and *Alectoris rufa*, the red-legged partridge. Sometimes, a song is rhythmically organized as a whole. This means that the bird may have an overview of a very long duration. For example, in this song by *Turtur brehmeri*, a blue-headed dove, the first two notes of the accelerando are separated by 2.2 seconds, and one realizes only after having heard them that they are starting a long accelerando, whereas in the song of *Sarothrura lugens*, the chestnut-headed pygmy rail, the universal link among accelerando, crescendo, and rising in pitch, is clearly present.

What is most universally considered as musical is the occurrence of a set of discrete pitches. Speech or "noise" shows no fixed pitches, whereas music is claimed to begin with the invention of a scale (even if *Ionisation* by Varèse and rap music do not make use of it). Many mythic traditions, in Greece and China, for example, attribute this essential creation to a god or a cultural hero. In fact, many animals use precise and stable sets of pitches in their signals. *Halcyon badius,* the chocolate-backed kingfisher, moves up and down along his own scale, characterized by very small intervals. More subtly, *Cossypha cyanocampter*, the blue-shouldered robin-chat, is not satisfied with enumerating the tones of its scale, but operates on it by building melodic motives as elaborate as many human achievements, and even sounding so close to them that one might be mistaken. The same melodic use of a scale, but in this case a kind of chromatic scale, occurs in *Erythropygia leucosticta*, the northern bearded illadopsis. Sometimes, articulatory variations are added to the pitch variations. In the example of *Trichastoma albipectus*, the scaly-breasted illadopsis from Kenya, you get a legato instead of a previous staccato.

Still closer to human organization is the evidence for a hierarchy between the degrees of a scale. A note may assume a particular role according to its frequency and position in the melody. This is true for human systems, such as the tonic and dominant in tonal systems, or the *shâhed* or *forud* in Iranian *dastgâh*. It is also true for some animals. In the songs of *Erythropygia leucophrys,* the white-browed scrub robin, a kind of keynote appears at the end of each stanza. Even intervals as large as those found in Schoenberg's songs can be heard, as in the songs of *Cyphorhinus arada*, the musician wren.

The process of transposition is of particular relevance for a comparison between animals and humans. It implies memory for and consciousness of a given sound pattern treated as a whole. This can be shown in the song of *Hylobates lar*, the white-handed gibbon. Whenever a sound model is imitated by a bird whose range does not fit, it is transposed both in pitch and duration, as for example when *Lanius minor*, the lesser grey shrike, imitates a rooster.

Clearly, in many cases the syntax of animal signals has something in common with music. I think that nearly all processes involving repetition—an obvious universal in music—can be encountered among animals: refrains, rhymes, symmetry, reprises, *Liedform*, *Barform*, and so on. My view that we are dealing with a functional similarity in animal species and human often meets some objections, which can be summarized this way: animal sound signals belong to pure semiotics. There is nothing gratuitous about them. Every aspect must have an evolutionary utility.

My answer is first that the idea of a gratuitous aesthetic pleasure is but a very small part of musical behavior in humans. It took on special importance only one or two centuries ago, in European civilization. Many musical traditions have no idea of what a concert is. It is quite a naive idea to consider music only as the thing a young lady does when performing a piece on her piano, with friends and family attending. Many cultures make music only in ritual contexts. The Toradjas of Sulawesi never make music for the sole pleasure of singing or listening; they have no lullabies, no wedding songs, no dirges. They sing only in large polyphonic choirs during ceremonies. It would be bold to say that they have no music simply because this activity figures in social occasions where singing is just part of the whole.

Second, social singing between neighboring males of a given species, or even of different species, has been repeatedly reported; for example, *Acrocephalus palustris*, the marsh warbler, and *Trichastoma moloneyanum*, Moloney's illadopsis. No definitive biological advantage can explain this behavior. It is not proved that such singing neighbors avoid territorial conflicts more easily than those that sing alone or ignore each other. With regard to autumnal singing, its utility is not clear either.

I would rather suggest that the opinion maintained by several biologists such as Thorpe (1966) is right: there is also something like an intrinsic pleasure in singing. The luxurious display of some of the best singers suggests that they go far beyond the signals that would be necessary for keeping a territory or mating. Could we interpret birdsong, and consequently music, as a case of hypertelia? The views that the ethologist Sebeok (1975) expressed seem to support such a hypothesis, which I submit to more expert specialists. It implies that the whole elaboration of a culture, meaning a collective structure of symbolic imagination, might stem from this lavishness of nature exceeding its limited basic purposes. Diversity in song may at first have allowed an individual to prevail over a competitor, before gradually overshooting the mark. In that case the excess would have turned not into a disadvantage but an unexpected pleasure.

Of course viewing culture as something which originates in a natural function, and imagining that it turned out to bring a new end beyond pure survival, may look heretical both to a large majority of biologists and to many musicians as well. I leave my conclusion to the taperecorder. I can only say, as a composer, that *Craticus nigrogularis*, the pied butcher bird, is a kind of colleague.

References

Mâche, F.-B. (1992). *Music, Myth and Nature: Or the Dolphins of Orion*. Chur, Switzerland: Harwood Academic Publishers.

Sachs, C. (1929). *Geist und Werden der Musikinstrumente*. Berlin: Reimer.

Sebeok, T. A. (1975). *Zoosemiotics: At the Intersection of Nature and Culture*. Lisse, The Netherlands: de Ridder.

Thorpe, W. H. (1966). Ritualization in ontogeny. *Philosophical Transactions of the Royal Society of London, Series B* 251:311–319 and 351–358.

VI THE END OF THE BEGINNING

.Music   Music.

The book ends just as it began. With the sound of a voice. Perhaps it is a lone voice emanating from a weeping island or perhaps it is the chorus of all human beings reminding ourselves just how much we really do share. As many myths about the origins of music tell us, what is important about the sounds of these voices is that they move us: to elation, to pride, to calm, to action, to tears, to new understanding. What is important about these sounds is that they change us, that they tell us who we are and give our lives some purpose. In *Metamagical Themas*, Douglas Hofstader touches on this very point when, in paraphrasing the familiar refrain, "We can only imagine what incredible pieces Chopin would have composed had he lived longer" he says, "I cannot imagine who I would be if I knew those pieces." *Who I would be*. Music is very much about who we are, as individuals, as societies, and even as a species.

But as a species of musical and musically conscious animals, we wonder about all the other musical species that inhabit our world, and ask ourselves where our music comes from. Did it come from the music of the animals or did we just happen to have the same curious fate as those singing creatures? This is something we need to know if we are to understand why we are the way we are, and why music is the way it is. Some say that music came from the gods, but where did the gods get it? Did they simply imitate the sounds of animals? If that were the case, we certainly would not have needed the gods for that. So perhaps what the gods gave us was something more special, something more human, something that the animals could not have given us directly simply by filling our world with song.

However it was that we came to have music, we found incredible uses for it. In fact it became part of all our activities and helped define what those activities were. It is hard to imagine who we would be if we did not "know those pieces." Theories proposed to explain the origins of music differ not so much in the mechanisms they invoke as in the types of musical expressions that they choose to focus on, because there is so much to look at. Some talk about the tones of our voice when we talk to babies, others about the tones and rhythms of our utterances in general, others about wooing the girl or boy we desire, others about making the work group more workable, yet others about strengthening the bonds that hold people together. The real point is that music is so ubiquitous and so important that human culture just would not be human culture without it. This seems like a safe conclusion. And so we have no choice but to listen to music; not simply to listen to music but to *listen* to music, to what it is telling us about ourselves.

Whatever those functions are that made music into a human necessity, they are universal. They are felt and understood by all, even if the sounds that support them differ in superficial ways. It is a funny thing about the story of the Tower of Babel—two things are always left out. First, no one ever mentions anything about whether music suffered the same fate as language during the big scramble; the answer is almost certainly yes. Second, despite the terrible confusion that ensued after the actions of the great deity, people never stopped trying, even for a second, to communicate the same things they had tried to communicate before the big scramble. We are all, in fact, saying the same things to each other but using different sounds to say them. This is no less true of our musics. They all communicate the same basic things wherever we go, wherever we are; and if you don't believe that, you've probably never been to Babel.

But Babel's musical version will have to await a future telling, because the end of the beginning is here. And just like those fragile moments that follow the ending of a sheeringly beautiful piece of music, it is hoped that the melody and the rhythm of this book will linger for a while to come . . . and perhaps even fill your dreams.

Author Index

Subject Index